CLASSICAL CHINESE
A BASIC READER

TEXTS

袁乃瑛　　唐海濤　　蓋杰民
Naiying Yuan　Haitao Tang　James Geiss

PRINCETON UNIVERSITY PRESS

PRINCETON, NEW JERSEY

Copyright © 2004 by Princeton University Press
Published by Princeton University Press, 41 William Street,
Princeton, New Jersey 08540
In the United Kingdom: Princeton University Press, 6 Oxford Street,
Woodstock, Oxfordshire OX 20 1TR

Library of Congress Control Number: 2004100562

Volume 1 (Texts) ISBN: 0-691-12089-7
Volume 2 (Glossaries) ISBN: 0-691-12090-0
Volume 3 (Analyses) ISBN: 0-691-12091-9
3-Volume Set Paperback ISBN: 978-0-691-11831-4

First one volume printing, 2017
Paperback ISBN: 978-0-691-17457-0

British Library Cataloging-in-Publication Data is available

This publication has been made possible by generous grants from
The Mercer Trust and The Consortium for Language Teaching and Learning

The publisher would like to acknowledge the authors of this volume for
providing the camera-ready copy from which this book was printed

Printed on acid-free paper

press.princeton.edu

Printed in the United States of America

10 9 8 7 6 5 4 3 2 1

Contents

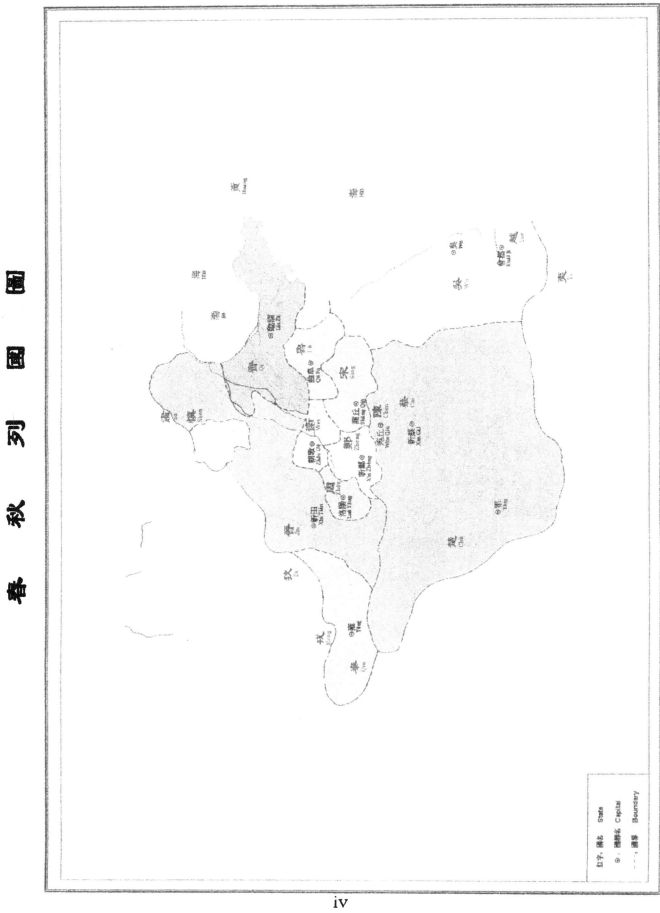

戦 国 七 雄 圖

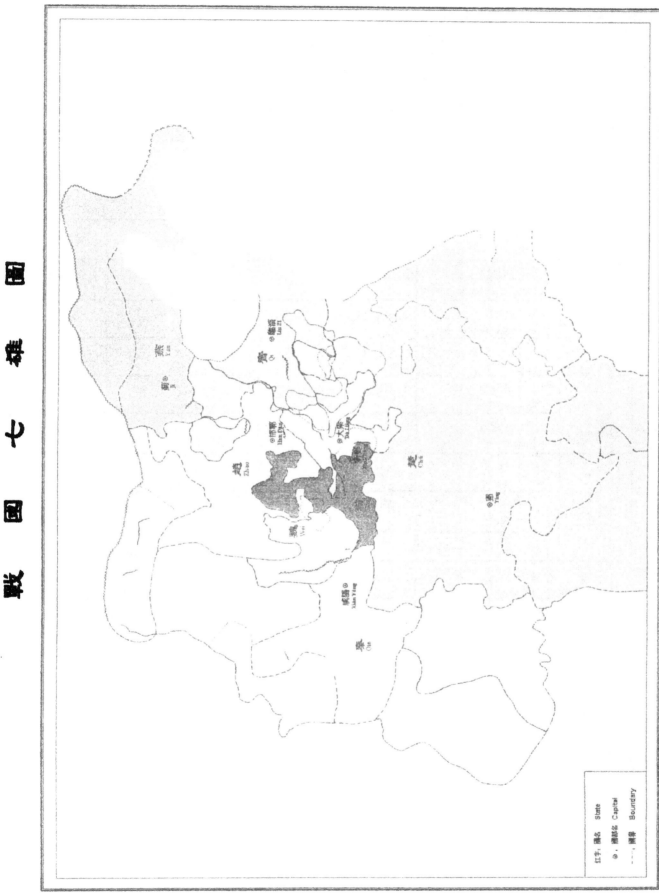

中國歷史年代簡表
A Brief Chinese Chronology

夏 Xia Dynasty		約前21世紀- 約前16世紀		北齊 Northern Qi	550-577
商 Shang Dynasty		約前16世紀- 約前11世紀		西魏 Western Wei	535-556
周 Zhou Dynasy	西周 Western Zhou Dynasty	約前11世紀- 前771		北周 Northern Zhou	557-581
	東周 Eastern Zhou Dynasty	前770-前256		隋 Sui Dynasty	581-618
	春秋 Spring and Autumn Period	前770-前476		唐 Tang Dynasty	618-907
	戰國 Warring States Period	前770-前221	五代 Five Synasties	後梁 Later Liang	907-923
秦 Qin Dynasty		前221-前207		後唐 Later Tang	923-936
漢 Han Dynasty	西漢 Western Han	前206-公元24		後晉 Later Jin	936-946
	東漢 Eastern Han	25-220		後漢 Later Han	947-950
三國 Three Kingdoms	魏 Wei	220-265		後周 Later Zhou	951-960
	蜀 Shu	221-263	宋 Song Dynasty	北宋 Northern Song Dynasty	960-1127
	吳 Wu	222-280		南宋 Southern Song Dynasty	1127-1279
西晉 Western Jin Dynasty		265-316		遼 Liao Dynasty	916-1125
東晉 Eastern Jin Dynasty		317-420		金 Jin Dynasty	1115-1234
宋 Song		420-479		元 Yuan Dynasty	1271-1368
南朝 齊 Southern Qi		479-502		明 Ming Dynasty	1368-1644
南北朝 Dynasties 梁 Southern Liang and Northern Dynasties	陳 Chen	502-557 557-589		清 Qing Dynasty	1644-1911
				中華民國 Republic of China	1912-
北朝 北魏 Northern Northern Wei Dynastties 東魏 Eastern Wei		368-534 534-550		中華人民共和國 People's Republic of China	1949-

Foreword

Classical, or literary, Chinese is a written language that matured long before the Qín era. It developed and was used in China's governing and elite culture for nearly three millenia. Though it has undergone changes and developments, its syntactical structures in general have remained intact. Its importance lies in part because the great legacies of Chinese culture down to the twentieth century were recorded and preserved in this medium. Classical Chinese is thus the language in which much of Chinese culture has long been transmitted. In consequence, it is only through this medium that one can most fully and accurately understand Chinese cultural traditions. In addition, many idioms, set phrases, allusions, and sentence patterns in modern Chinese are inherited from classical Chinese. Even when reading academic writings in modern Chinese, one benefits greatly from having an adequate proficiency in classical Chinese, because in discussing specific topics or making their own points, Chinese scholars tend to cite or quote relevant supporting material from classical Chinese texts. For this reason, a good command of classical Chinese is indispensable for the study of Chinese literature, thought, history, political and social institutions, etc.

Confucius said: "If an artisan wishes to do his work well, he must first sharpen his tools." With this textbook we therefore seek to introduce the major grammatical structures of classical Chinese using an analytical and comparative approach, so as to provide students the 'sharpened tools' with which they can explore classical Chinese texts, or, to put it in another way, this textbook seeks to provide students the key that unlocks the door to the bright and fertile field of Chinese studies.

To accomplish this, the textbook is set up in three volumes. Volume one contains the main texts by which the student is introduced to the various lingual and syntactic aspects of classical Chinese. Volume two contains the glossaries to these texts, and volume three, the detailed grammatical analyses of the texts.

The forty textual selections in volume one have been chosen from fourteen Chinese classics written between the fifth century B.C. and the first century A. D. They have been taken directly from authoritative editions such as SBBY (SPPY) and SBCK (SPTK), with no words or structure altered for pedagogical reasons. Thus, the student, from the very beginning of his or her study, deals directly with authentic classical texts. These texts have been carefully selected on the basis of their merits both in terms of their form--because they illustrate important grammatical patterns--and in terms of their content--because they represent important salient features of Chinese culture, such as the wit, humor, wisdom, moral conviction, and political ideals it exhibits. The classical Chinese texts and their modern Chinese translations occupy opposite pages in the book, so that they can be consulted and compared readily. Both the classical and the modern texts are provided with pinyin phonetics for pronunciation, so that students can vocalize them correctly. The English translation of the text facilitates for the students a quick and thorough understanding of the classical passage as a whole. These reading texts are pedagogically arranged so that they proceed from short texts to longer ones, and from the grammatically simple and easy to the more complicated and difficult. The appended exercises that are provided in a variety of formats are meant to help students review and reinforce their classroom learning.

Volume two contains all the glossaries to the texts in Volume one. Each glossary entry is phonetically spelled out, grammatically classified, and its meaning within the context in which it is used, fully explained. Within the explanation, should there be unfamiliar yet important terms, these terms are further explained, so that students can understand fully both the original classical texts and the explanatory modern ones. The annotations are given in both modern Chinese and in English. Also should there exist a proverb or a set phrase that has been derived from a text, this has been duly noted.

Volume three provides both grammatical analyses as well as literal translations of the texts in Volume one. Every sentence that appears in a text in Volume one is fully diagrammed to show the grammatical relations between its various parts. In the diagrams it has often been necessary to insert items of context that classical Chinese texts may omit, such as subjects and/or objects, or items that are customarily omitted in classical Chinese, such as prepositions, in order to show the entire grammatical structure of the sentence in terms of modern Chinese or English. Such added elements have been put in **brackets** in the translations. When there is a major grammatical point that deserves special attention, it has been fully explained with an **asterisk** preceding it. After this diagrammatic analysis, each sentence is translated into both modern Chinese and English. This translation generally is provided in three clear steps: first, the sentence is translated verbatim; second, the differences between classical and modern Chinese, and between Chinese and English are highlighted; and third, the entire sentence is rendered into smooth modern Chinese and natural English respectively. Of these steps, the second is the most important. In this step, all the contemporary lingual components classical Chinese omits are reflected in **brackets** in the modern Chinese translation, any words added to make the meaning of a sentence clear and its flow natural in modern translation are marked by a **smaller font type**, with those changes made for rhetorical reasons given in **boldface**. In the English version, all the counterparts of the aforementioned changes and additions shown in the modern Chinese translation appear in the English translation as well, in **brackets**, in **smaller font type**, and in **boldface**, while words in *italics* in the English translation represent the elements that have no counterpart in the original Chinese texts but that are obligatory to make sense in English. Furthermore, these words in *italics* pinpoint the grammatical differences between Chinese and English. Students interested in comparing the two languages will find this most helpful.

In order to anticipate the sorts of questions that might be raised in a classroom, we have tried our best to provide clear and detailed explanations. In addition, this textbook has been designed so as to be useful whether a teacher conducts the course in Chinese or in English. We do wish to point out that this textbook represents a bold attempt to experiment with a new, though not untried, approach to the teaching of classical Chinese, and, as such, will inevitably yet have some shortcomings. We hope that they are few, and hope, furthermore, that the users of this textbook would provide us comments on their experiences with it as well as offering us any constructive suggestions they might have for its improvement.

The Authors

Acknowledgments

First and foremost, we want to express our heartfelt gratitude to Professor Frederick Wade Mote, the founder of the East Asian Studies Department at Princeton Uiversity, and to the late Professor Ta-Tuan Ch'en, the Director of the Chinese Language Program in the EAS Department at Princeton University for nearly three decades. Had it not been for their great insight, recognizing classical Chinese as an important link in the teaching of Chinese culture, and their strong support, encouraging the constant improvement of teaching materials and methods, this textbook project would not have been undertaken, much less completed. Next, we are much indebted to Ms. Deborah Herndon, the former secretary of the Chinese Linguistics Project at Princeton University, who designed the format for this textbook; to our former students of classical Chinese, Michael Chang, Ryan O'Connor, and the many others who helped at various times in its development with inputting texts; to Ms. Zhāng Yào, our computer specialist, who drew the two historical maps of the Spring and Autumn Period and of the Warring States Period. Our earnest thanks then go to Mr. Ralph L. Meyer, Editor in the Cambridge History of China Project, Professor Andrew H. Plaks of Princeton University, and Professor Thomas Nimick of The United States Military Academy at West Point. All three of them have rendered significant assistance in producing the final form of the manuscript. And last, but not least, this textbook, at its inception, was sponsored by the Consortium for Language Teaching and Learning, and, upon its publication, has been granted a generous subsidy by the Mercer Trust Fund, to both of which institutions we are immensely grateful.

The Authors

課 文 目 錄

課文目錄

課文目錄

課文目錄

List of Errata to the Texts

page	line	was	should be
vi	6	770	476
17	11	cì.bú chuän	cì.bù chuän
55	11	bäo.zhe	bào.zhe
149	8	lììng	lìng
183	20	to hit against	(shift right)
187	24	the words	the word
188	9	to herd ship; to tend ship	a man from the State of Chû
191	4	of he words	of the words
191	18	to vover	to cover
193	31	trong	strong
199	7	second	(delete)
199	8	the predicate	the second predicate
200	12	surnamedWèi	surnamed Wèi
203	31	「名詞」	「動詞」
203	39	「動語」	「動詞」
207	21	「名詞語」	「名詞」
207	33	「名詞語」	「名詞」
209	13	torepay	to repay
211	8	to hjave	to have
222	15	Sün Shüaó	Sünshü Áo
226	14	worries	worried
229	8	verb	word
232	3	動	(delete)
234	16	to make of	to make fun of
234	18	shèng rén	suô yû xï
235	28	understanding the Way	(shift right)
239	25	stratagist	strategist
240	9	preferrable	preferable
240	11	as Adj,as B	as Adj. as B
241	6	a husband	wise; intelligent
241	11	the Heir Apparent …	(delete)
244	13	cóng zhèng	dïng zhuàng
259	2	he following	Punctuate the following
259	9	named Nígn	named Níng
265	3	Xú Jùbó	Xún Jùbó
268	21	; lantzuu	(delete)
274	30	(the whole line)	(delete)
278	23	; to	; to butcher
279	6	to learn' to study	to learn; to study
281	8	a wqork of	a work of

合抱之木生於毫末
九層之臺起於壘土
千里之行始於足下
　　　　　老子・六十四章

A tree as big as a man's embrace grows from a tiny shoot.
A tower of nine stories begins with a heap of earth.
The journey of a thousand li starts from where one stands.

Translated by Wing-Tsit Chan

第一課

鄭相卻魚

新序 節士

昔者有餽魚於鄭相者，鄭相不受。或謂鄭相曰："子嗜魚，何故不受？"對曰："吾以嗜魚，故不受。受魚失祿，無以食魚。不受得祿，終身食魚。"

Zhèng Xiàng Què Yú

Xīnxù Jiéshì

Xī zhě yǒu kuì yú yú Zhèng xiàng zhě, Zhèng xiàng bú shòu. Huò wèi Zhèng xiàng yuē: "Zǐ shì yú, hé gù bú shòu?" Duì yuē: "Wú yǐ shì yú, gù bú shòu. Shòu yú shī lù, wú yǐ shí yú. Bú shòu dé lù, zhōng shēn shí yú."

Jenq Shianq Chiueh Yu

Shinshiuh Jyeshyh

Shi jee yeou kuey yu yu Jenq shianq jee, Jenq shianq bu show. Huoh wey Jenq shianq iue: "Tzyy shyh yu, her guh bu show?" Duey iue: "Wu yii shyh yu, guh bu show. Show yu shy luh, wu yii shyr yu. Bu show der luh, jong shen shyr yu."

白話翻譯

鄭 相 卻 魚

　　從前有個贈送魚給鄭國宰相的人，鄭國宰相不接受。有人對鄭國宰相說：“您既然非常喜歡吃魚，那麼因爲什麼緣故不接受呢？”他回答說：“我因爲非常喜歡吃魚，所以才不接受。我假若接受了魚，就會失掉薪俸，那麼就沒有法子吃魚了。我不接受魚呐，就能得到薪俸，那麼就一輩子都吃得到魚。”

Zhèng Xiàng Què Yú

　　Cóngqián yǒu.gè zèngsòng yú gěi Zhèngguó zǎixiàng .de rén, Zhèngguó zǎixiàng bù jiēshòu. Yǒu rén duì Zhèngguó zǎixiàng shuō: "Nín jìrán fēicháng xǐ.huān chī yú, nà.me yīn.wèi shén.me yuán.gù bù jiēshòu .ne?" Tā huídá shuō: "Wǒ yīn.wèi fēicháng xǐ.huān chī yú, suǒ.yǐ cái bù jiēshòu. Wǒ jiǎruò jiēshòu.le yú, jiù huì shīdiào xīnfèng, nà.me jiù méi.yǒu fá.zǐ chī yú .le. Wǒ bù jiēshòu yú .na, jiù néng dédào xīnfèng, nà.me jiù yībèi.zǐ dōu chī.dé dào yú."

THE PRIME MINISTER OF ZHENG REFUSES A GIFT OF FISH

　　Once there was a person who presented a gift of fish to the prime minister of the state of Zhèng; the prime minister of the state of Zhèng did not accept it. Someone addressed the prime minister of the state of Zhèng saying: "Since you relish eating fish, why then did you not accept?" He replied, saying: "Because I relish eating fish, I thus did not accept. If I were to accept the fish, I might lose my official salary; then I would have no way at all to eat fish. If I do not accept, I can get my official salary and so can eat fish until the end of my life."

第二課

宋有富人

韓非子　說難

　　宋有富人，天雨牆壞。其子曰："不築，必將有盜。"其鄰人之父亦云。暮而果大亡其財。其家甚智其子，而疑鄰人之父。

Sòng Yǒu Fù Rén

Hánfēizǐ　Shuìnán

Sòng yǒu fù rén, tiān yǔ qiáng huài. Qí zǐ yuē: "Bú zhù, bì jiāng yǒu dào." Qí lín rén zhī fù yì yún. Mù ér guǒ dà wáng qí cái. Qí jiā shèn zhì qí zǐ, ér yí lín rén zhī fù.

Song Yeou Fuh Ren

Harnfeitzyy　Shueynan

Sonq yeou fuh ren, tian yeu chyang huay. Chyi tzyy iue: "Bu juh, bih jiang yeou daw." Chyi lin ren jy fuu yih yun. Muh erl guoo dah wang chyi tsair. Chyi jia shenn jyh chyi tzyy, erl yi lin ren jy fuu.

白話翻譯

宋有富人

宋國有個很有錢的人，天下雨，他家的牆壞了。他的兒子說："您要是不修理牆，那麼一定會有賊。"他的鄰居的老頭儿也這麼說。到了天黑了的時候，有錢的人果然丟了很多他的錢。那家人覺得他們的孩子很聰明，可是都懷疑鄰居的老頭儿。

Sòng Yǒu Fù Rén

Sòngguó yǒu.ge hén yǒuqián .de rén, tiān xià yǔ, tā jiā.de qiáng huài.le. Tā.de ér.zǐ shuō: " Nín yào.shi bù xiūlǐ qiáng, nà.me yídìng huì yǒu zéi." Tā.de línjū .de lǎotóur yě zèn.me shuō. Dào.le tiān hēi.le .de shí.hòu, yǒuqián.de rén guǒrán diū.le hěn duō tā.de qián. Nà jiā rén jué.dé tā.mén.de hái.zǐ hěn cōng.míng, kěshì dōu huáiyí línjū .de lǎotóur.

THERE WAS A WEALTHY MAN OF SÒNG

In the state of Sòng there was a wealthy man. It rained, and the wall around his house was damaged. His son said: "If you do not repair the wall, we will definitely be robbed." The old man next door said so too. When it got dark, the wealthy man, as expected, lost a great amount of his money. That family considered their child very bright, but suspected the old man next door.

第三課

守株待兔

韓非子 五蠹

宋人有耕者。田中有株，兔走觸株，折頸而死。因釋其耒而守株，冀復得兔。兔不可復得，而身為宋國笑。

Shǒu Zhū Dài Tù

Hánfēizǐ Wǔdù

Sòng rén yǒu gēng zhě. Tián zhōng yǒu zhū, tù zǒu chù zhū, zhé jǐng ér sǐ. Yīn shì qí lěi ér shǒu zhū, jì fù dé tù. Tù bù kě fù dé, ér shēn wéi Sòng guó xiào.

Shoou Ju Day Tuh

Harnfeitzyy Wuuduh

Sonq ren yeou geng jee. Tyan jong yeou ju, tuh tzoou chuh ju, jer jiing erl syy. In shyh chyi leei erl shoou ju, jih fuh der tuh. Tuh bu kee fuh der, erl shen wei Sonq gwo shiaw.

6

白話翻譯

守 株 待 兔

　有個耕田的宋國人。在田裡有截樹樁子，一隻兔子跑過來，碰到樹樁子上，碰斷了脖子就死了。耕田的人於是放下他的犁去看守樹樁子，希望再得到兔子。兔子他再也得不到，他自己反倒被宋國人嘲笑了。

Shǒu Zhū Dài Tù

　Yǒu.ge gēng tián.de Sòngguó rēn. Zài tián.lǐ yǒu jié shù zhuāng.zǐ, yì zhī tù.zǐ pǎo guò.lái, pèng dào shù zhuāng.zǐ shàng, pèngduàn.le bó.zǐ jiù sǐ.le. Gēng tián.de rén yúshì fàng.xià tā.de lí qù kānshǒu shù zhuāng.zǐ, xīwàng zài dédào tù.zǐ. Tù.zǐ tā zài yě dé.búdào, tā zìjǐ fǎndào bèi Sòngguó rén cháoxiào .le.

WAITING FOR A HARE AT THE TREE STUMP

　There was a person in the state of Sòng who was tilling his field. In the field there was a tree stump. A hare ran by, dashed into the tree stump, broke its neck, and then died. The person tilling the field then put down his plough to watch the tree stump, hoping to get a hare again. A hare he could not get again; instead, he was derided by the people of the state of Sòng.

第四課

逐臭

呂氏春秋 遇合

人有大臭者，其親戚、兄弟、妻妾、知識無能與居
者。自苦而居海上。海上人有說其臭者，晝夜隨之而弗
能去。

Zhú Xiù

Lǔshìchūnqiū Yùhé

Rén yǒu dà chòu zhě, qí qīn qī, xiōng dì, qī qiè, zhī shì wú néng yǔ jū zhě. Zì kǔ ér jū hǎi shàng. Hǎi shàng rén yǒu yuè qí xiù zhě, zhòu yè suí zhī ér fú néng qù.

Jwu Shiow

Leushyhchuenchiou Yuhher

Ren yeou dah chow jee, chyi chin chi, shiong dih, chi chieh, jy shyh wu neng yeu jiu jee. Tzyh kuu erl jiu hae shanq. Hae shanq ren yeou yueh chyi shiow jee, jow yeh swei jy erl fwu neng chiuh.

白話翻譯

逐臭

　　有個非常臭的人，他的親戚、哥哥、弟弟、太太、姨太太和朋友沒有能跟他一塊兒居住的。他自己感到很苦惱就到海邊上去住。海邊上的人有喜歡他的臭味的，他們白天夜裡都跟隨著他，不能離開他。

Zhú Xiù

　　Yǒu.ge fēicháng chòu.de rén, tā.de qīnqī, gē.gē, dì.dì, tài.tài, yítài.tài hé péng.yǒu méi.yǒu néng gēn tā yíkuàir jūzhù .de. Tā zìjǐ gǎn.dào hěn kǔnǎo jiù dào hǎibiān.shàng qù zhù. Hǎibiān.shàng.de rén yǒu xǐ.hūan tā.de chòuwèi.de, tāmén bái.tiān yè.lǐ dōu gēnsuí.zhe tā, bù néng lí.kāi tā.

CHASING AFTER THE SMELL

There was a very stinky person. None of his relatives by blood and by marriage, his elder and younger brothers, his principal wife, concubines, and friends could stand to live with him. He himself felt very embittered and so went to live by the seashore. There were people at the seashore who liked his stink. They followed him day and night, unable to leave.

第五課

先王之義勝

韓非子 喻老

子夏見曾子。曾子曰："何肥也?" 對曰："戰勝，故肥也。" 曾子曰："何謂也?" 子夏曰："吾入見先王之義則榮之，

Xiān Wáng Zhī Yì Shèng

Hánfēizǐ Yùlǎo

Zǐxià jiàn Zēngzǐ. Zēngzǐ yuē: "Hé féi yě?" Duì yuē: "Zhàn shèng, gù féi yě." Zēngzǐ yuē: "Hé wèi yě?" Zǐxià yuē: "Wú rù jiàn xiān wáng zhī yì zé róng zhī,

---

Shian Wang Jy Yih Shenq

Harnfeitzyy Yuhlao

Tzyyshiah jiann Tzengtzyy. Tzengtzyy iue: "Her feir yee?" Duey iue: "Jann shenq, guh feir yee." Tzengtzyy iue: "Her wey yee?" Tzyyshiah iue: "Wu ruh jiann shian wang jy yih tzer rong jy,

10

白話翻譯

先王之義勝

　　子夏去拜訪曾子。曾子說："您怎麼胖了呢？"子夏回答說："我因為打仗打勝了，所以胖啦。"曾子說："這句話是什麼意思呢？"子夏說："我從外面回到家裡，在書上看到古代聖王的正道，就覺得那些正道很崇高；

Xiān Wáng Zhī Yì Shèng

　　Zǐxià qù bàifǎng Zēngzǐ. Zēngzǐ shuō: "Nín zěn.me pàng.le.ne?" Zǐxià huídá shuō: "Wǒ yīn.wèi dǎzhàng dǎshèng .le, suǒ.yǐ pàng .la." Zēngzǐ shuō: "Zhè jù huà shì shén.me yì.si .ne?" Zǐxià shuō: "Wǒ cóng wài.miàn huí dào jiā.lǐ, zài shū.shàng kàn.dào gǔdài shèng wáng.de zhèngdào, jiù jué.dé nèi.xiē zhèngdào hěn chónggāo;

THE RIGHTEOUS WAYS OF ANCIENT KINGS TRIUMPH

　　Zǐxià paid a visit to Zēngzǐ. Zēngzǐ said: "How did you get so fat?" Zǐxià replied saying: "I have won a battle; as a result, I have gotten fat." Zēngzǐ said: "What do you mean by that?" Zǐxià said: "When I returned home, I saw written in books the righteous ways of the sage kings of antiquity and thought them magnificent.

出見富貴之樂又榮之。兩者戰于胸中，未知勝負，故臞。今先王之義勝，故肥。"

chū jiàn fù guì zhī lè yòu róng zhī. Liǎng zhě zhàn yú xiōng zhōng, wèi zhī shèng fù, gù qú. Jīn xiān wáng zhī yì shèng, gù féi."

chu jiann fuh guey jy leh yow rong jy. Leang jee jann yu shiong jong, wey jy shenq fuh, guh chyu. Jin shian wang jy yih shenq, guh feir."

我從家裡出去，在路上看到有錢有地位的快樂，又覺得那種
快樂很榮耀。兩種感覺在我心裡打仗，因為我還不知道哪個
勝哪個敗，所以我很瘦。現在因為古代聖王的正道在我心裡
打勝了，所以我就胖啦。"

Wǒ cóng jiā.lǐ chū.qù, zài lù.shàng kàn.dào yǒu qián yǒu dìwèi .de kuàilè, yòu jué.dé nèizhǒng kuàilè hěn róngyào. Liǎng zhǒng gǎnjué zài wǒ xīn.lǐ dǎzhàng, yīn.wèi wǒ hái bù zhī.dào něi.gè shèng něi.gè bài, suǒ.yǐ wǒ hěn shòu. Xiànzài yīn.wèi gǔdài shèng wáng.de zhèngdào zài wǒ xīn.lǐ dǎ shèng .le, suǒ.yǐ wǒ jiù pàng .la."

When I left home, I saw in the streets the pleasures of wealth and rank and thought them splendid as well. These two feelings fought with each other in my mind; because I still did not know which would triumph and which would be defeated; as a result, I got skinny. Now the righteous ways of the sage kings of antiquity have triumphed in my mind, and as a result I have gotten fat."

第六課

梟逢鳩

說苑 談叢

梟逢鳩。鳩曰：“子將安之？”梟曰：“我將東徙。”鳩曰：“何故？”梟曰：“鄉人皆惡我鳴，以故東徙。”鳩曰：“子能更鳴，可矣；不能更鳴，東徙，猶惡子之聲。”

Xiāo Féng Jiū

Shuōyuàn Táncóng

Xiāo féng jiū. Jiū yuē: "Zǐ jiāng ān zhī?" Xiāo yuē: "Wǒ jiāng dōng xǐ." Jiū yuē: "Hé gù?" Xiaō yuē: "Xiāng rén jiē wù wǒ míng, yǐ gù dōng xǐ." Jiū yuē: "Zǐ néng gēng míng, kě yǐ; bù néng gēng míng, dōng xǐ, yóu wù zǐ zhī shēng."

Shiau Ferng Jiou

Shuoyuann Tarntsorng

Shiau ferng jiou. Jiou iue: "Tzyy jiang an jy?" Shiau iue: "Woo jiang dong shii." Jiou iue: "Her guh?" Shiau iue: "Shiang ren jie wuh woo ming, yii guh dong shii." Jiou iue: "Tzyy neng geng ming, kee yii; bu neng geng ming, dong shii, you wuh tzyy jy sheng."

白話翻譯

梟 逢 鳩

　　貓頭鷹遇見斑鳩。斑鳩説：“您打算到哪儿去？”貓頭鷹説：“我打算搬到東邊去。”斑鳩説：“因爲什麼緣故呢？”貓頭鷹説：“鄉村裡的人都討厭我叫，因爲這個緣故我才搬到東邊去。”斑鳩説：“要是您能改變叫的聲音，那就行了；要是您不能改變叫的聲音，那麼就是您搬到東邊去，那儿的人還是會討厭您的叫聲。”

Xiāo Féng Jiū

　　Māotóuyīng yù.jiàn bānjiū.　Bānjiū shuō: "Nín dǎ.suàn dào nǎr qù ?"　Māotóuyīng shuō: "Wǒ dǎ.suàn bān dào dōng.biān qù."　Bānjiū shuō: "yīn.wèi shén.me yuángù`.ne?"　Māotóuyīng shuō: "Xiāngcūn.lǐ de rén dōu tǎoyàn wǒ jiào,　yīn.wèi zhèi.gè yuángù wǒ cái bān dào dōng.biān qù."　Bānjiū shuō: "Yào.shì nín néng gǎibiàn jiào.de shēngyīn, nà jiù xíng.le; yào.shì nín bùnéng gǎibiàn jiào.de shēngyīn, nà.me jiù.shi nín bān dào dōng.biān qù, nàr.de rén hái.shì huì tǎoyàn nín .de jiàoshēng."

THE OWL MEETS THE RINGDOVE

　　An owl met a ringdove. The ringdove said: "Where do you intend to go?" The owl said: "I am going to move to the east." The ringdove said: "For what reason?" The owl said: "The villagers all detest that I screech; for this reason, I am moving to the east." The ringdove said: "If you can change the sound of your cry, then it will be all right; if you cannot change the sound of your cry, then even if you move to the east, the people there will still detest your cry."

第七課

矛盾

韓非子 難一

楚人有鬻盾與矛者，譽之曰：“吾盾之堅，物莫能陷也。”又譽其矛曰：“吾矛之利，於物無不陷也。”或曰：“以子之矛陷子之盾，何如？”其人弗能應也。夫不可陷之盾與無不陷之矛不可同世而立。

Máo Dùn

Hánfēizǐ Nànyī

Chǔ rén yǒu yù dùn yǔ máo zhě, yù zhī yuē: "Wú dùn zhī jiān, wù mò néng xiàn yě." Yòu yù qí máo yuē: "Wú máo zhī lì, yú wù wú bú xiàn yě." Huò yuē: "Yǐ zǐ zhī máo xiàn zǐ zhī dùn, hé rú?" Qí rén fú néng yìng yě. Fú bù kě xiàn zhī dùn yǔ wú bú xiàn zhī máo bù kě tóng shì ér lì.

Mau Duenn

Harnfeitzyy Nann'i

Chuu ren yeou yuh duenn yeu mau jee, yuh jy iue: "Wu duenn jy jian, wuh moh neng shiann yee." Yow yuh chyi mau iue: "Wu mau jy lih, yu wuh wu bu shiann yee." Huoh iue: "Yii tzyy jy mau shiann tzyy jy duenn, her ru?" Chyi ren fwu neng yinq yee. Fwu bu kee shiann jy duenn yeu wu bu shiann jy mau bu kee torng shyh erl lih.

白話翻譯

矛 盾

有個賣盾和矛的楚國人，誇他的盾説："我的盾堅固得沒有一個東西刺得穿啊。"又誇他的矛説："我的矛鋒利得沒有一個東西刺不穿啊。"有人説："要是有人用您的矛來刺您的盾，那麼會怎麼樣？"那個人可就回答不出來啦。刺不穿的盾和什麼東西都刺得穿的矛不可能同時存在。

Máo Dùn

Yǒu.ge mài dùn hé máo .de Chǔguó rén, kuā tā.de dùn shuō: "Wǒ.de dùn jiāngù dé méi.yǒu yí.gè dōng.xī cì.dé chuān .a" Yòu kuā tā.de máo shuō: "Wǒ.de máo fēnglì dé méi.yǒu yí.gè dōng.xī cì.bú chuān .a." Yǒu rén shuō: "Yào.shì yǒu rén yòng nín.de máo lái cì nín.de dùn, nà.me huì zěn.me yàng?" Nèi.gè rén kě jiù huídá bù chū lái .la. Cì.bù chuān .de dùn hé shén.me dōng.xī dōu cì.dé chuān .de máo bù kěnéng tóngshí cúnzài.

SPEARS AND SHIELDS

There was a man of the state of Chǔ who sold shields and spears. He bragged about his shields saying: "My shields are so hard that nothing can pierce through them." He bragged about his spears as well, saying: "My spears are so sharp that there is nothing they can not pierce through." Someone said: "What would happen if one were to use your spears to pierce your shields?" That person could not answer! Now, shields that cannot be pierced through and spears that can pierce through anything cannot exist at once.

第八課

逆旅二妾

莊子　山木

陽子之宋，宿於逆旅。逆旅人有妾二人，其一人美，其一人惡。惡者貴而美者賤。

Nì Lǚ Èr Qiè

Zhuāngzǐ Shānmù

Yángzǐ zhī Sòng, sù yú nì lǚ. Nì lǚ rén yǒu qiè èr rén, qí yì rén měi, qí yì rén è. È zhě guì ér měi zhě jiàn.

Nih Leu Ell Chieh

Juangtzyy Shanmuh

Yangtzyy jy Sonq, suh yu nih leu. Nih leu ren yeou chieh ell ren, chyi i ren meei, chyi i ren eh. Eh jee guey erl meei jee jiann.

白話翻譯

逆旅二妾

陽子到宋國去，住宿在旅館裡。旅館的主人有兩個姨太太，其中的一個很美麗，其中的一個很醜陋。醜的受寵，美的反倒不受寵。

Nì Lǚ Er Qiè

Yángzǐ dào Sòngguó qù, zhù sù zài lǚguǎn.lǐ. Lǚguǎn.de zhǔrén yǒu liǎng.gè yítài.tài, qízhōng.de yí .gè hěn měilì, qízhōng.de yí.gè hěn chǒulòu. Chǒu.de shòu chǒng, měi.de fǎndào bú shòu chǒng.

THE INNKEEPER'S TWO CONCUBINES

Yángzǐ went to the state of Sòng and spent the night in an inn. The innkeeper had two concubines. One of them was very beautiful; one of them was very ugly. The ugly one was favored; the beautiful one, on the contrary, was not favored.

陽子問其故，逆旅小子對曰：“其美者自美，吾不知其
美也；其惡者自惡，吾不知其惡也。”陽子曰：“弟子
記之，行賢而去自賢之心，安往而不愛哉？”

Yángzǐ wèn qí gù, nì lǚ xiǎo zǐ duì yuē: "Qí měi zhě zì měi, wú bù zhī qí měi yě; qí è zhě zì è, wú bù zhī qí è yě." Yángzǐ yuē: "Dì zǐ jì zhī, xíng xián ér qù zì xián zhī xīn, ān wǎng ér bú ài zāi ?"

Yangtzyy wenn chyi guh, nih leu sheau tzyy duey iue: "Chyi meei jee tzyh meei, wu bu jy chyi meei yee; chyi eh jee tzyh eh, wu bu jy chyi eh yee." Yangtzyy iue: "Dih tzyy jih jy, shyng shyan erl chiuh tzyh shyan jy shin, an woang erl bu ay tzai?"

陽子問爲什麼這樣，旅館的小伙子回答說："那個美的覺得她自己很美，可是我並不感到她美；那個醜的覺得她自己很醜，可是我並不感到她醜。"陽子說："徒弟們記住這句話，要是一個人做高尚的事，卻去掉覺得自己很高尚的心理，那麼他到哪裡去不受歡迎呢？"

Yángzǐ wèn wèi shén.me zhèiyàng, lǚguǎn .de xiǎohuǒ.zǐ huídá shuō: "Nèi.gè měi.de jué.dé tā zìjǐ hěn měi, kě.shì wǒ bìng bù gǎndào tā měi; nèi.gè chǒu.de jué.dé tā zìjǐ hěn chǒu, kě.shì wǒ bìng bù gǎndào tā chǒu." Yángzǐ shuō: "Túdì.mén jì .zhù zhè jù huà, yào.shì yí.gè rén zuò gāoshàng .de shì, què qùdiào jué.dé zìjǐ hěn gāoshàng .de xīnlǐ, nà.me tā dào nǎ.lǐ qù bú shòu huānyíng .ne?"

Yángzǐ asked why this was. The young man who kept the inn replied, saying: "The beautiful concubine considers herself very beautiful, but I definitely do not feel that she is beautiful. The ugly concubine considers herself very ugly, but I definitely do not feel that she is ugly." Yángzǐ said: "Disciples, remember these words, if a person does good deeds without being smug about it, then where could he go and not be welcomed?"

第九課

盜錘 (鐘)

淮南子　說山

范氏之敗，有竊其錘負而走者。鎗然有聲，懼人聞之，遽掩其耳。憎人聞之，可也；自掩其耳，悖矣。

Dào Zhōng

Huáinánzǐ　Shuōshān

Fàn shì zhī bài, yǒu qiè qí zhōng fù ér zǒu zhě. Qiāng rán yǒu shēng, jù rén wén zhī, jù yǎn qí ěr. Zēng rén wén zhī, kě yě; zì yǎn qí ěr, bèi yǐ.

Daw Jong

Hwainantzyy　Shuoshan

Fann shyh jy bay, yeou chieh chyi jong fuh erl tzoou jee. Chiang ran yeou sheng, jiuh ren wen jy, jiuh yean chyi eel. Tzeng ren wen jy, kee yee; tzyh yean chyi eel, bey yii.

白話翻譯

盜 鍾 (鐘)

　　當范吉射被打敗了的時候，有個偷了他的鐘背著它逃
跑的人。鐘玎玎鐺鐺地發出聲音來，偷鐘的人害怕別人聽見
鐘聲，趕緊捂住他自己的耳朵。厭惡別人聽見鐘聲，還算說
得過去；自己捂住自己的耳朵，太荒唐啦！

Dào Zhōng

　　Dāng Fàn Jíshè bèi dǎbài.le.de shí.hòu, yǒu.gè tōu.le tā.de zhōng bēi.zhe tā táopǎo.de rén. Zhōng dīngdīng dāngdāng.de fā.chū shēngyīn.lái, tōu zhōng.de rén hàipà biérén tīng.jiàn zhōngshēng, gǎnjǐn wǔ.zhù tā zìjǐ.de ěr.duǒ. Yànwù biérén tīng.jiàn zhōngshēng, hái suàn shuō.dé guò.qù; zìjǐ wǔ.zhù zìjǐ .de ěr.duǒ, tài huāng.táng .lā!

STEALING THE BELL

　　When Fàn Jíshè was defeated, there was a person who stole his bell and fled carrying it on his back. The bell was clanging. Fearing that other people would hear it, he covered his own ears quickly. To hate other people hearing the sound of the bell is reasonable, but it is extremely absurd of him to cover up his own ears!

第十課

鄭人買履

韓非子 外儲說

　　鄭人有且買履者，先自度其足，而置之其座。至之市而忘操之。已得履，乃曰：“吾忘持度。”

Zhèng Rén Mǎi Lǚ

Hánfēizǐ Wàichǔshuō

　　Zhèng rén yǒu qiě mǎi lǚ zhě, xiān zì duò qí zú, ér zhì zhī qí zuò. Zhì zhī shì ér wàng cāo zhī. Yǐ dé lǚ, nǎi yuē: "Wú wàng chí dù."

Jenq Ren Mae Leu

Harnfeitzyy Waychuushuo

　　Jenq ren yeou chiee mae leu jee, shian tzyh duoh chyi tzwu, erl jyh jy chyi tzuoh. Jyh jy shyh erl wanq tsau jy. Yii der leu, nae iue: "Wu wanq chyr duh."

白話翻譯

鄭 人 買 履

　　有個將要買鞋的鄭國人，先自己量一量他的腳，然後就把量好的尺碼放在他的座位上。等到他到市場去的時候兒忘了帶尺碼。他已經拿到鞋了，才想起來說：“我忘了把尺碼帶來。”

Zhèng Rén Mǎi Lǚ

　　Yǒu.gè dǎ.suàn mǎi xié .de Zhèngguó rén, xiān zìjǐ liángyìliáng tā.de jiǎo, ránhòu jiù bǎ liáng hǎo .de chǐmǎ fàng zài tā.de zuòwèi.shàng. Děng.dào tā dào shìchǎng qù .de shí.hoùr wàng.le dài chǐmǎ. Tā yǐ.jīng nádào xiéʹ.le, cái xiǎng.qǐ.lái shūo: "Wǒ wàng.le bǎ chǐmǎ dài.lái."

A MAN OF ZHÈNG BUYS SHOES

There was a man from the state of Zhèng who was going to buy a pair of shoes. First he measured his feet; then he put the measurement on his seat. When it was time to go to the marketplace, he forgot to take it along. Only when he had already gotten his shoes did he think of it and say: "I forgot to bring along the measurement."

反歸而取之。及反，市罷，遂不得履。人曰：“何不試之以足？”曰：“寧信其度，無自信也。”

Fǎn guī ér qǔ zhī. Jí fǎn, shì bà, suì bù dé lǚ. Rén yuē: "Hé bú shì zhī yǐ zú?" Yuē: "Nìng xìn qí dù, wú zì xìn yě."

Faan guei erl cheu jy. Jyi faan, shyh bah, suey bu der leu. Ren iue: "Her bu shyh jy yii tzwu?" Iue: "Ninq shinn chyi duh, wu tzyh shinn yee."

他轉身回家去拿尺碼。等到他回來的時候儿，市己經收了，他就沒買到鞋。有人説："您爲什麼不用腳來試一試鞋呢？"買鞋的人説："我寧可相信那個尺碼，也不相信我自己啊。"

Tā zhuǎnshēn huíjiā qù ná chǐmǎ. Děng.dào tā huílái .de shí.hoùr, shì yǐ.jīng shōu .le, tā jiù méi mǎi.dào xié. Yǒu rén shuō: "Nín wèi shén.me bú yòng jiǎo lái shì.yíshì xié .ne?" Mǎi xié .de rén shuō: "Wǒ nìng kě xiāngxìn nèi.gè chǐmǎ, yě bù xiāngxìn wǒ zìjǐ .a."

He turned around and went back home to get it. By the time he had returned, the market was closed, so he didn't get any shoes. Someone said: "Why didn't you use your feet to try them on?" The person buying shoes said: "I would rather trust in that measurement than trust in myself!"

第十一課

仁義

列子　說符

　　昔有昆弟三人，游齊魯之間，同師而學，進仁義之
道而歸。其父曰：“仁義之道若何？”伯曰：“仁義使我
愛身而後名。”

Rén Yì

Lièzǐ　Shuōfú

　　Xī yǒu kūn dì sān rén, yóu Qí Lǔ zhī jiān, tóng shī ér xué, jìn rén yì zhī dào ér guī.
Qí fù yuē: "Rén yì zhī dào rùo hé?" Bó yuē: "Rén yì shǐ wǒ ài shēn ér hòu míng."

Ren Yih

Liehtzyy　Shuofwu

　　Shi yeou kun dih san ren, you Chyi Luu jy jian, torng shy erl shyue, jinn ren yih jy
daw erl guei.　Chyi fuh iue: "Ren yih jy daw ruoh her?" Bor iue: "Ren yih shyy woo ay
shen erl how ming."

白話翻釋

仁義

　從前有三兄弟，離家到齊魯一帶去求學，跟隨著同一位老師讀書，把仁義的道理學得很透徹就回家了。他們的父親說：「仁義的道理怎麼樣？」大兒子說：「仁義使我看重自己的生命看輕名聲。」

Rén Yì

　　Cóngqián yǒu sān xiōngdì, lí jiā dào Qí Lǔ yí dài qù qiúxué, gēnsuí .zhē tóng yíwèi lǎoshī dúshū, bǎ rényì .de dàolǐ xué.dé hěn tòuchè jiù huíjiā .le. Tā.mén.de fùqīn shuō: "Rényì.de dàolǐ zěn.me yàng?" Dà ér.zǐ shuō: "Rényì shǐ wǒ kànzhòng zìjǐ.de shēngmìng kànqīng míngshēng."

BENEVOLENCE AND RIGHTEOUSNESS

　　Once upon a time, there were three brothers; they left home and travelled in the region of the states of Qí and Lǔ to seek learning, and studied with the same teacher. They exhaustively studied the doctrine of benevolence and righteousness, and then returned home. Their father said: "What is the doctrine of benevolence and righteousness like?" The eldest son said: "Benevolence and righteousness would make me value my life and put my reputation second."

仲曰：“仁義使我殺身以成名。”叔曰：“仁義使我身名並全。”彼三術相反，而同出於儒，孰是孰非耶？

Zhòng yuē: "Rén yì shǐ wǒ shā shēn yǐ chéng míng." Shū yuē: "Rén yì shǐ wǒ shēn míng bìng quán." Bǐ sān shù xiāng fǎn, ér tóng chū yú Rú, shú shì shú fēi yé?

Jonq iue: "Ren yih shyy woo sha shen yii cherng ming." Shu iue: "Ren yih shyy woo shen ming binq chyuan." Bii san shuh shiang faan, erl torng chu yu Ru, shwu shyh shwu fei ye?

二兒子說：「仁義使我犧牲自己的生命來建立名聲。」三兒子說：「仁義使我把生命和名聲都保全住。」那三種道理互相衝突，可是都從儒家發展出來，哪個對哪個錯呢？

Èr ér.zǐ shuō: "Rényì shǐ wǒ xīshēng zìjǐ.de shēngmìng lái jiànlì míngshēng." Sān ér.zǐ shuō: "Rényì shǐ wǒ bǎ shēngmìng hé míngshēng dōu bǎoquán zhù." Nà sān.zhǒng dàolǐ hùxiāng chōngtū, kě.shì dōu cóng Rújiā fāzhǎn chū.lái, něi.gè duì něi.gè cuò .ne?

The second son said: "Benevolence and righteousness would make me sacrifice my life in order to establish my reputation." The third son said: "Benevolence and righteousness would make me preserve both my life and my reputation intact." These three doctrines are mutually contradictory, yet they all come from the teachings of the Confucian school. Which of them is right, which wrong?

第十二課

蘇代諫趙王

戰國策 燕策

趙且伐燕，蘇代為燕謂惠王曰：“今者臣來，過易水，蚌方出曝，而鷸啄其肉。蚌合而箝其喙。鷸曰：‘今日不雨，明日不雨，即有死蚌。’蚌亦謂鷸曰：

Sū Dài Jiàn Zhào Wáng

Zhànguócè Yāncè

Zhào qiě fá Yān, Sū Dài wèi Yān wèi Huì Wáng yuē: " Jīn zhě chén lái, guò Yì Shuǐ, bàng fāng chū pù, ér yù zhuó qí ròu. Bàng hé ér qián qí huì. Yù yuē: ' Jīn rì bù yǔ, míng rì bù yǔ, jí yǒu sǐ bàng.' Bàng yì wèi yù yuē:

Su Day Jiann Jaw Wang

Janngwotseh Iantseh

Jaw chiee far Ian, Su Day wey Ian wey Huey Wang iue: "Jin jee chern lai, guoh Yih Shoei, banq fang chu puh, erl yuh jwo chyi row. Banq her erl chyan chyi huey. Yuh iue: 'Jin ryh bu yeu, ming ryh bu yeu, jyi yeou syy banq.' Banq yih wey yuh iue:

白話翻譯

蘇代諫趙王

趙國將要攻打燕國，蘇代爲燕國對趙惠王説："這次我來，渡過易水時，一個蚌正出來曬太陽，一隻鷸啄住牠的肉，蚌合攏起來夾住牠的嘴。鷸説：'今天老天不下雨，明天老天也不下雨，就會有曬死了的蚌。'蚌也對鷸説：

Sū Dài Jiàn Zhào Wáng

Zhàoguó jiāng.yào gōngdǎ Yānguó, Sū Dài wèi Yānguó duì Zhào Huìwáng shuō: "Zhèi cì wǒ lái, dùguò Yìshuǐ shí, yí.gè bàng zhèng chūlái shài tài.yáng, yì zhī yù zhuó.zhù tā.de ròu, bàng hé.lǒng.qǐ.lái jiā.zhù tā.de zuǐ. Yù shuō: 'Jīntiān lǎotiān bú xiàyǔ, míngtiān lǎotiān yě bú xiàyǔ, jiù huì yǒu shàisǐ.le .de bàng.' Bàng yě duì yù shuō:

SU DAI ADMONISHES THE KING OF ZHAO

When the state of Zhào was on the brink of attacking the state of Yān, Sū Dài spoke to King Huì of Zhào on behalf of the state of Yān, saying: "This time when I came to the state of Zhào and was crossing the Yì River, a clam had just come out to sun itself, when a snipe pecked at its flesh. The clam closed up and clamped down on its beak. The snipe said: 'If today it does not rain, and if tomorrow it also does not rain, then there will be a dead clam.' The clam also said to the snipe:

'今日不出，明日不出，即有死鷸。'兩者不肯相舍，漁父得而并擒之。今趙且伐燕，燕趙久相支以敝大眾，臣恐強秦之為漁父也，故願王熟計之也。"惠王曰："善。"乃止。

'Jīn rì bù chū, míng rì bù chū, jí yǒu sǐ yù.' Liǎng zhě bù kěn xiāng shě, yú fǔ dé ér bìng qín zhī. Jīn Zhào qiě fá Yān, Yān Zhào jiǔ xiāng zhī yǐ bì dà zhòng, chén kǒng qiáng Qín zhī wéi yú fǔ yě, gù yuàn wáng shú jì zhī yě." Huì wáng yuē: "Shàn." Nǎi zhǐ.

'Jin ryh bu chu, ming ryh bu chu, jyi yeou syy yuh.' Leang jee bu keen shiang shee, yu fuu der erl binq chyn jy. Jin Jaw chiee far Ian, Ian Jaw jeou shiang jy yii bih dah jonq, chern koong chyang Chyn jy wei yu fuu yee, guh yuann wang shwu jih jy yee." Huey Wang iue: "Shann." Nae jyy.

'今天你的嘴拔不出去，明天你的嘴也拔不出去，就會有夾死了的鷸。' 雙方誰也不願意放開誰，捕魚的老頭兒發現了牠們就把牠們倆一齊捉住了。現在趙國將要攻打燕國，燕國趙國長久地互相撐拒結果使老百姓疲乏，我擔心強大的秦國會成爲捕魚的老頭兒啊，所以希望大王周密地考慮一下這件事啊。" 趙惠王説："好。" 趙國就不去攻打燕國了。

'Jīn tiān nǐ.de zuǐ bá bù chū qù, míngtiān nǐ.de zuǐ yě bá bù chū qù, jiù huì yōu jiāsǐ.le de yù.' Shuāngfāng shéi yě bú yuàn.yì fàngkāi shéi, bǔyú .de lǎo.tóur fāxiàn .le tā.mén, jiù bǎ tā.mén liǎ yìqí zhuō.zhù .le. Xiànzài Zhàoguó jiāngyào gōngdǎ Yānguó, Yānguó Zhàoguó chángjiǔ.de hùxiāng chēngjù jiéguǒ shǐ lǎobǎixìng pífá, wǒ dānxīn qiángdà .de Qínguó huì chéngwéi bǔyú .de lǎo.tóur .a, suǒyǐ xīwàng dàwáng zhōumì.de kǎolǜ yíxià zhèjiàn shì .a." Zhào Huìwáng shuō: "Hǎo." Zhàoguó Jiù bú qù gōngdǎ Yānguó .le.

'If today your beak cannot be pulled out, and if tomorrow your beak also cannot be pulled out, then there will be a dead snipe.' Neither was willing to let the other go; an old fisherman found them and caught them both at once. Now the state of Zhào is on the verge of attacking the state of Yān. If the states of Yān and Zhào are at a standoff for a long time, fighting to the point where the common people become worn out, I fear that the powerful state of Qín will become the old fisherman; therefore, I would like your majesty to consider this carefully." King Huì of Zhào said: "Agreed." Whereupon Zhào stopped the attack on Yān.

第十三課

郢書燕說

韓非子 外儲說

郢人有遺燕相國書者，夜書，火不明，因謂持燭者曰：“舉燭。”云而過書“舉燭。”“舉燭”非書意也。

Yǐng Shū Yān Shuō

Hánfēizǐ Wàichǔshuō

Yǐng rén yǒu wèi Yān xiàng guó shū zhě, yè shū, huǒ bù míng, yīn wèi chí zhú zhě yuē: "Jǔ zhú." Yún ér guò shū "jǔ zhú." "Jǔ zhú" fēi shū yì yě.

Yiing Shu Ian Shuo

Harnfeitzyy Waychuushuo

Yiing ren yeou wey Ian shianq gwo shu jee, yeh shu, huoo bu ming, in wey chyr jwu jee iue: "Jeu jwu." Yun erl guoh shu "jeu jwu." "Jeu jwu" fei shu yih yee.

白話翻譯

郢書燕說

　　有個送給燕國的宰相一封信的郢都人，在晚上寫信，燭光不夠亮，他就告訴拿蠟燭的人說：「把蠟燭舉高一點兒。」郢都人因說這句話結果就錯誤地寫上了「舉燭」這兩個字。「舉燭」並不是信裡的意思啊。

Yǐng Shū Yān Shuō

　　Yǒu .gè sòng.gěi Yānguó .de zǎixiàng yì fēng xìn .de Yǐngdū rén, zài wǎn.shàng xiě xìn, zhúguāng bú gòu liàng, tā jiù gào.sù ná là.zhú .de rén shuō: "Bǎ là.zhú jǔ gāo yì.diǎnr." Yǐngdū rén yīn shuō zhèi jù huà, jiéguǒ jiù cuòwù.de xiě .shàng .le "jǔ zhú" zhè liǎng .gè zì. "Jǔ zhú" bìng búshì xìn.lǐ .de yì.sī .a.

THE LETTER FROM YING EXPLAINED IN YAN

　　There was a man from the capital city of Yǐng who sent a letter to the prime minister of the state of Yān. He wrote the letter in the evening; the candlelight was not bright enough, so he said to the person holding the candle: "Raise up the candle a bit." As a result of saying these words he mistakenly wrote in the two characters: "Raise candle." "Raise up the candle" was not meant to be in the letter.

燕相受書而說之，曰：“‘舉燭’者，尚明也。‘尚明’
也者，舉賢而任之。”燕相白王，大說，國以治。治則
治矣，非書意也。今世學者多似此類。

Yān xiàng shòu shū ér shuō zhī, yuē: " 'Jǔ zhú' zhě, shàng míng yě. 'Shàng míng' yě zhě,
jǔ xián ér rèn zhī." Yān Xiàng bái Wáng, dà yuè, guó yǐ zhì. Zhì zé zhì yǐ, fēi shū yì yě.
Jīn shì xué zhě duō sì cǐ lèi.

Ian shianq show shu erl shuo jy, iue: " 'Jeu jwu' jee, shanq ming yee. 'Shanq ming' yee
jee, jeu shyan erl renn jy." Ian Shianq bair Wang, dah yueh, gwo yii jyh. Jyh tzer jyh yii, fei
shu yih yee. Jin shyh shyue jee duo syh tsyy ley.

燕國宰相接到了這封信就解釋這兩個字，說：「『舉燭』是崇尚明智的意思；『崇尚明智』啊，是推舉有道德、有才能的人來任用他們的意思。」燕國宰相把他的想法稟告給燕王，燕王非常高興，燕國因為舉用賢人就變得很太平。燕國太平倒是太平了，可是燕國宰相的解釋並不是信裡的意思啊。在現代的學者中，多數像燕國宰相這類的人。

Yānguó zǎixiàng jiēdào .le zhè fēng xìn jiù jiěshì zhè liǎng.gè zì, shuō: " 'Jǔ zhú' shì chóngshàng míngzhì .de yì.sī, 'chóngshàng míngzhì' .a, shì tuījǔ yǒu dàodé yǒu cáinéng .de rén lái rènyòng tā.mén .de yì.sī." Yānguó zǎixiàng bǎ tā.de xiǎngfǎ bǐnggào gěi Yān Wáng, Yān Wáng fēi.cháng gāo.xìng, Yānguó yīn.wèi jǔ yòng xiánrén jiù biàn.dé hěn tài.píng. Yān.guó tài.píng dào.shì tài.píng .le, kě.shì Yānguó zǎixiàng.de jiě.shì bìng bú.shì xìn.lǐ .de yì.sī .a. Zài xiàndài .de xuézhě zhōng, duōshù xiàng Yānguó zǎixiàng zhè lèi .de rén.

When the prime minister of the state of Yān received the letter, he expounded on these two characters and said: "'Raise up the candle' means to esteem wisdom; 'to esteem wisdom' means to select people of virtue and talent and to employ them." The prime minister of the state of Yān reported his interpretation of this phrase to the king of Yān, who was greatly pleased by it; the king of Yān then used this policy of selecting virtuous and talented people to govern the state well and the state was consequently well-governed. Now for the state of Yān to achieve orderly government is one thing, but the prime minister of Yān's interpretation of the phrase was not what the letter meant. Among contemporary scholars, the majority are like the sort of this prime minister of Yān.

第十四課

狐假虎威

戰國策　楚策

虎求百獸而食之，得狐。狐曰：“子無敢食我也，天帝使我長百獸，今子食我，是逆天帝命也。

Hú Jiǎ Hǔ Wēi

Zhànguócè　Chǔcè

Hǔ qiú bǎi shòu ér shí zhī, dé hú. Hú yuē: "Zǐ wú gǎn shí wǒ yě, tiān dì shǐ wǒ zhǎng baǐ shòu, jīn zǐ shí wǒ, shì nì tiān dì mìng yě.

Hwu Jea Huu Uei

Janngwotseh　Chuutseh

Huu chyou bae show erl shyr jy, der hwu. Hwu iue: "Tzyy wu gaan shyr woo yee, tian dih shyy woo jaang bae show, jin tzyy shyr woo, shyh nih tian dih minq yee.

白話翻譯

狐 假 虎 威

老虎尋找各種動物來吃牠們，得到了一隻狐狸。狐狸說：「您絕不敢吃我，老天爺使我做各種動物的領袖，現在您要是吃我，這是違背老天爺命令的行為啊。

Hú Jiǎ Hǔ Wēi

Laǒhǔ xúnzhǎo gè zhǒng dòngwù lái chī tā.mén, dé dào.le yìzhī huʹlí. Huʹlí shuō: "Nín jué bù gǎn chī wǒ, lǎotiānyé shǐ wǒ zuò gèzhǒng dòng.wù .de lǐngxiù, xiànzài nín yào.shì chī wǒ, zhè .shì wéibèi lǎotiānyé mìnglìng de xíngwéi .a.

THE FOX BORROWS THE TIGER'S PRESTIGE

A tiger was looking for all sorts of wild animals to eat; he got a fox. The fox said: "You certainly dare not eat me: Heaven has made me the leader of all the wild animals; now, if you eat me, it goes against the command of Heaven.

子以我為不信，吾為子先行，子隨我後，觀百獸之見我
而敢不走乎？"虎以為然，故遂與之行，獸見之皆走。
虎不知獸畏己而走也，以為畏狐也。

Zǐ yǐ wǒ wéi bú xìn, wú wèi zǐ xiān xíng, zǐ suí wǒ hòu, guān baǐ shòu zhī jiàn wǒ ér gǎn bù zǒu hū?" Hǔ yǐ wéi rán, gù suì yǔ zhī xíng, shòu jiàn zhī jiē zǒu. Hǔ bù zhī shòu wèi jǐ ér zǒu yě, yǐ wéi wèi hú yě.

Tzyy yii woo wei bu shinn, wu wey tzyy shian shyng, tzyy swei woo how, guan bae show jy jiann woo erl gaan bu tzoou hu?" Huu yii wei ran, guh suey yeu jy shyng, show jiann jy jie tzoou. Huu bu jy show wey jii erl tzoou yee, yii wei wey hwu yee.

要是您認爲我不誠實，我爲您在前頭走，您跟隨在我後頭，
您看看各種動物看見我卻還敢不逃跑嗎？"老虎覺得狐狸的
話很有道理，所以就跟牠一塊兒走，動物看見牠們倆都逃跑
了。老虎不知道動物因爲怕自己才逃跑啊，還以爲牠們怕狐
狸吶。

Yàoshì nín rènwéi wǒ bù chéngshí, wǒ wèi nín zài qián.tóu zǒu, nín gēnsuí .zài wǒ hòu.tóu, nín kàn.kàn gèzhǒng dòng.wù kàn.jiàn wǒ què hái gǎn bù táopǎo .ma?" Lǎohǔ jué.dé hú.lí .de huà hěn yǒu daòlǐ, suǒ.yǐ jiù gēn tā yíkuàir zǒu, dòng.wù kàn.jiàn tā.mén liǎ dōu táopaǒ .le. Laǒhǔ bù zhī.dào dòng.wù yīn.wèi pà zìjǐ cái táopaǒ .a, hái yǐwéi tā.mén pà hú.lí .ne.

If you think me untrustworthy, I will walk ahead of you; you follow behind me, and observe whether any wild animals see me and dare not flee." The tiger thought the fox's words reasonable, so he just went along with him. When the animals saw these two, they all fled. The tiger, thinking they feared the fox, did not know that only because the wild animals feared him did they run away.

第十五課

攫金

列子　說符

　　昔齊人有欲金者。清旦，衣冠而之市，適鬻金者之所，因攫其金而去。吏捕得之，問曰："人皆在焉，子攫人之金何？"對曰："取金之時，不見人，徒見金。"

Jué Jīn

Lièzǐ　Shuōfú

Xī Qí rén yǒu yù jīn zhě. Qīng dàn, yì guàn ér zhī shì, shì yù jīn zhě zhī suǒ, yīn jué qí jīn ér qù. Lì bǔ dé zhī, wèn yuē: "Rén jiē zài yān, zǐ jué rén zhī jīn hé?" Duì yuē: "Qǔ jīn zhī shí, bú jiàn rén, tú jiàn jīn."

Jyue Jin

Liehtzyy　Shuofwu

Shi Chyi ren yeou yuh jin jee. Ching dann, yih guann erl jy shyh, shyh yuh jin jee jy suoo, in jyue chyi jin erl chiuh. Lih buu der jy, wenn iue: "Ren jie tzay ian, tzyy jyue ren jy jin her?" Duey iue: "Cheu jin jy shyr, bu jiann ren, twu jiann jin."

白話翻譯

攫 金

從前有個想要金子的齊國人。在大清早他穿上衣服，戴上帽子就到市場去了，到了賣金子的人的鋪子，即刻搶了他的金子就跑了。警官逮著了他，問他說："別人都在那裡，您搶人家的金子，爲什麼？"他回答說："在拿金子的時候，我沒看見什麼人，只看見了金子。"

Jué Jīn

Cóngqián yǒu.gè xiǎng yào jīn.zǐ .de Qíguó rén. Zài dàqīngzǎo tā chuān.shàng yī.fú, dài.shàng māo.zǐ jiù dào shìchǎng qù .le, dào .le mài jīn.zǐ .de rén .de pù.zǐ, jíkè qiǎng.le tā.de jīn.zǐ jiù pǎo .le. Jǐgguān dǎizháo .le tā, wèn tā shuō: "Bié rén dōu zài nà.lǐ, nín qiǎng rénjiā.de jīn.zǐ, wèi shén.me?" Tā huídá shuō: "Zài ná jīn.zǐ .de shí.hòu, wǒ méi kàn.jiàn shén.me rén, zhǐ kàn.jiàn .le jīn.zǐ."

GRABBING THE GOLD

There once was a man from the state of Qí who lusted after gold. Bright and early one morning, he donned his cap and gown and went to the marketplace; upon arriving at a goldsmith's shop, he straightaway snatched up the man's gold and fled. After the constable had caught him, he asked him: "There were other people there, yet you grabbed the man's gold--why?" He answered saying: "When I took the gold, I didn't see any people, I saw only gold."

第十六課

君子慎所藏

說苑 雜言

　　孔子曰：“不知其子，視其所友；不知其君，視其所使。”又曰：“與善人居，如入蘭芝之室，久而不聞其香，則與之化矣；

Jūn Zǐ Shèn Suǒ Cáng

Shuōyuàn Záyán

Kǒngzǐ yuē: "Bù zhī qí zǐ, shì qí suǒ yǒu; bù zhī qí jūn, shì qí suǒ shǐ." Yòu yuē: "yǔ shàn rén jū, rú rù lán zhī zhī shì, jiǔ ér bù wén qí xiāng, zé yǔ zhī huà yǐ;

Jiun Tzyy Shenn Suoo Tsarng

Shuoyuann Tzaryan

Koongtzyy iue: "Bu jy chyi tzyy, shyh chyi suoo yeou; bu jy chyi jiun, shyh chyi suoo shyy." Yow iue: " Yeu shann ren jiu, ru ruh lan jy jy shyh, jeou erl buh wen chyi shiang, tzer yeu jy huah yii;

白話翻譯

君子慎所藏

孔子說：“一個人要是不了解他自己的孩子，那就看看他孩子結交的朋友；一個人要是不了解他自己的君主，那就看看他的君主派遣的人。”又說：“一個人跟善良的人在一塊兒住，好像是進入了養蘭芝的屋子一樣，待久了就聞不見蘭芝的香氣了，這就是人受到薰染變得跟蘭芝一樣香了；

Jūn Zǐ Shèn Suǒ Cáng

Kǒngzǐ shuō: "Yí.gè rén yào.shì bù liǎojiě tā zì.jǐ .de hái.zǐ, nà jiù kàn.kàn tā.de hái.zǐ jiéjiāo .de péng.yǒu; yí.gè rén yàw.shì bù liǎojiě tā zì.jǐ.de jūnzhǔ, nà jiù kàn.kàn tā.de jūnzhǔ pàiqiǎn .de rén." Yòu shuō: "Yí.ge rén gēn shàn.liáng.de rén zài yí.kuàir zhù, hǎoxiàng shì jìnrù .le yǎng lánzhī .de wū.zǐ yí.yàng, dāi jiǔ .le jiù wén.bú.jiàn lánzhī.de xiāngqì .le. Zhè jiù shì rén shòu dào xūnrǎn biàn.dé gēn lánzhī yí.yàng xiāng .le;

A PERSON OF HIGH MORAL CHARACTER IS EXCEEDINGLY CIRCUMSPECT IN SELECTING HIS LIVING CONDITIONS

Confucius said : "If one does not understand one's own child, one need only observe whom one's child befriends. If one does not understand one's ruler, one need only observe whom one's ruler dispatches." Confucius also said: "Living together with a person of good character is like going into a room where sweet-scented plants are being raised: after having stayed a long while, one cannot smell the fragrance of the sweet-scented plants anymore; this is because the person has been changed by the influence of the environment and has become as fragrant as the sweet-scented plants.

與惡人居，如入鮑魚之肆，久而不聞其臭，亦與之化矣。”故曰：“丹之所藏者赤；烏之所藏者黑。”君子慎所藏。

---

yǔ è rén jū, rú rù baò yú zhī sì, jiǔ ér bù wén qí chòu, yì yǔ zhī huà yǐ.” Gù yuē: “Dān zhī suǒ cáng zhě chì; wū zhī suǒ cáng zhě hè.” Jūn zǐ shèn suǒ cáng.

---

yeu eh ren jiu, ru ruh baw yu jy syh, jeou erl buh wen chyi chow, yih yeu jy huah yii.” Guh iue: “Dan jy suoo tsarng jee chyh; u jy suoo tsarng jee heh.” Jiun tzyy shenn suoo tsarng.

一個人跟邪惡的人在一塊兒住，好像是進入了賣鹹魚的鋪子一樣，待久了就聞不見鹹魚的臭味了，這就是人受到薰染也變得跟鹹魚一樣臭了。"所以有人説："朱紅色中儲藏的那個東西會變紅；烏黑色中儲藏的那個東西會變黑。"品德高尚的人對於選擇自己生活的環境採取非常慎重的態度。

Yí.gè rén gēn xié è .de rén zài yí.kuàir zhù, hǎoxiàng shì jìnrù .le mài xiányú.de pù.zǐ yíyàng, dāi jiǔ .le jiù wén.bù.jiàn xiányú.de chòu.wèir .le, zhè jiù shì rén shòudào xūnrǎn yě biàn.dé gēn xiányú yíyàng chòu .le." Suǒ.yǐ yǒu rén shuō: "Zhūhóng sè zhōng chǔcáng.de nèi.ge dōng.xī huì biàn hóng; wūhēi sè zhōng chǔcáng.de nèi.ge dōng.xī huì biàn hēi." Pǐndé gāoshàng.de rén duìyú xuǎnzé zì.jǐ shēng.huó.de huánjìng cǎiqǔ fēi.cháng shènzhòng .de tài.dù.

Living with a malevolent person is like going into a store that sells salted fish: after having stayed a long while, one cannot smell the stench of the salted fish anymore; this too is because the person has been changed by the influence of the environment and has become as malodorous as the salted fish." So it has been said: "That which is kept in cinnabar red reddens; that which is kept in raven black blackens." A person of high moral character is exceedingly circumspect about selecting his living conditions.

第十七課

刻舟求劍

呂氏春秋 察今

楚人有涉江者，其劍自舟中墜於水。遽契其舟曰：
"是吾劍之所從墜。" 舟止，從其所契者入水求之。舟
已行矣，而劍不行。求劍若此，不亦惑乎？

Kè Zhōu Qiú Jiàn

Lǔshìchūnqiū　Chájīn

Chǔ rén yǒu shè jiāng zhě, qí jiàn zì zhōu zhōng zhuì yú shuǐ. Jù qì qí zhōu yuē: "Shì wú jiàn zhī suǒ cóng zhuì." Zhōu zhǐ, cóng qí suǒ qì zhě rù shuǐ qiú zhī. Zhōu yǐ xíng yǐ, ér jiàn bù xíng. Qiú jiàn ruò cǐ, bú yì huò hū?

Keh Jou Chyou Jiann

Leushyhchuenchiou　Charjin

Chuu ren yeou sheh jiang jee, chyi jiann tzyh jou jong juey yu shoei. Jiuh chih chyi jou iue: "Shyh wu jiann jy suoo tsorng juey." Jou jyy, tsorng chyi suoo chih jee ruh shoei chyou jy. Jou yii shyng yii, erl jiann buh shyng. Chyou jiann ruoh tsyy, bu yih huoh hu?

白話翻譯

刻舟求劍

　　有個渡河的楚國人，他的劍從船上掉到水裡去了。渡河的人趕緊在那條船邊上刻了個記號說：“這裡是我的劍從船上掉下去的地方。”船停了，他從他刻記號的那個地方跳進水裡去找劍。船已經往前走了，可是劍並沒移動。他這樣地找劍，不也很糊塗嗎？

Kè Zhōu Qiú Jiàn

　　Yǒu .gè dù hé .de Chǔguó rén, tā.de jiàn cóng chuán.shàng diào.dào shuǐ.lǐ .qù .le. Dù hé .de rén gǎnjǐn zài nèi tiáo chuán biān.shàng kè .le yí.gè jì.hào shuō: "Zhè.lǐ shì wǒ.de jiàn cóng chuán.shàng diào .xià.qù .de dì.fāng." Chuán tíng .le, tā cóng tá kè jì.hào .de nèi.gè di.fāng tiào.jìn shuǐ.lǐ qù zhǎo jiàn. Chuán yǐ.jīng wǎng qián zǒu .lē, kě.shì jiàn bìng méi yídòng. Tā zhèiyàng.zǐ .de zhǎo jiàn, bú yě hěn hú.tú .ma?

CARVING THE BOAT AND SEEKING THE SWORD

There was a man from the state of Chǔ who was crossing a river; his sword dropped from the boat into the water. He immediately cut a notch on the side of the boat, saying: "This is the place where my sword dropped from the boat." When the boat had stopped, he jumped into the water to look for it from the place where he had cut the notch. The boat had moved ahead but the sword had not. Looking for the sword like this is very dim-witted, is it not?

第十八課

和氏之璧

韓非子　和氏

楚人和氏得玉璞楚山中，奉而獻之厲王。厲王使玉人相之，玉人曰："石也。"王以和為誑，而刖其左足。

Hé Shì Zhī Bì

Hánfēizǐ　Héshì

Chǔ rén Hé shì dé yù pú Chǔ shān zhōng, fèng ér xiàn zhī Lì Wáng. Lì Wáng shǐ yù rén xiàng zhī. Yù rén yuē: "Shí yě." Wáng yǐ Hé wéi kuáng, ér yuè qí zuǒ zú.

Her Shyh Jy Bih

Harnfeitzyy　Hershyh

Chuu ren Her shyh der yuh pwu Chuu shan jong, fenq erl shiann jy Lih Wang. Lih Wang shyy yuh ren shianq jy. Yuh ren iue: "Shyr yee." Wang yii Her wei kwang, erl yueh chyi tzuoo tzwu.

白話翻譯

和氏之璧

　　楚國人和氏從楚國的山裡得到了一塊含著玉的石頭，就捧著去把它獻給厲王。厲王命令玉匠鑑定那塊玉石。玉匠說：“這是普通的石頭。”厲王認爲和氏是個騙子，就砍掉了他的左腳。

Hé Shì Zhī Bì

　　Chǔguó rén Héshì cóng Chǔguó.de shān.lǐ dédào .le yí-kuài hán.zhē yù .de shí.tóu, jiù pěng.zhē qù bǎ tā xiàn gěi Lì Wáng. Lì Wáng mìng.lìng yùjiàng jiàndìng nèi kuài yùshí. Yùjiàng shuō: "Zhè shì pǔtōng.de shí.tóu." Lì Wáng rènwéi Héshì shì.gè piàn.zǐ, jiù kǎndiào .le tā.de zuǒ jiǎo.

THE PIERCED JADE DISK OF A MAN SURNAMED HE

　　A man of the state of Chǔ surnamed Hé got a stone containing jade from the mountains of Chǔ; he respectfully presented it to King Lì of Chǔ. King Lì orderd a jade worker to appraise it; the jade worker said: "This is ordinary stone." The king thought Hé a liar and so cut off his left foot.

及厲王薨，武王即位，和又奉其璞而獻之武王。武王使
玉人相之，又曰：“石也。”王又以和為誑，而刖其右
足。武王薨，文王即位，和乃抱其璞，而哭於楚山之下
，三日三夜，淚盡而繼以血。

Jí Lì Wáng hōng, Wǔ Wáng jí wèi, Hé yòu fèng qí pú ér xiàn zhī Wǔ Wáng. Wǔ Wáng shǐ
yù rén xiàng zhī, yòu yuē: "Shí yě." Wáng yòu yǐ Hé wéi kuáng, ér yuè qí yòu zú. Wǔ
Wáng hōng, Wén Wáng jí wèi, Hé nǎi bào qí pú, ér kū yú Chǔ shān zhī xià, sān rì sān yè,
lèi jìn ér jì yǐ xuè.

Jyi Lih Wang hong, Wuu Wang jyi wey, Her yow fenq chyi pwu erl shiann jy Wuu Wang.
Wuu Wang shyy yuh ren shianq jy, yow iue: "Shyr yee." Wang yow yii Her wei kwang,
erl yueh chyi yow tzwu. Wuu Wang hong, Wen Wang jyi wey, Her nae baw chyi pwu, erl
ku yu Chuu shan jy shiah, san ryh san yeh, ley jinn erl jih yii shiueh.

等到厲王死了，武王登上了王位，和氏又捧著那塊玉石去把它獻給武王。武王命令玉匠鑑定那塊玉石，玉匠又說："這是普通的石頭。"武王也認爲和氏是個騙子，就砍掉了他的右腳。武王死了，文王登上了王位。和氏就抱著那塊玉石，在楚國的山下哭，哭了三天三夜，眼淚都哭光了，接著哭出血來。

Děngdào Lì Wáng sǐ .le, Wǔ Wáng dēng.shàng .le wángwèi, Héshì yòu pěng.zhe nà.kuài yùshí qù bǎ tā xiàn.gěi Wǔ Wáng. Wǔ Wáng mìng.lìng yùjiàng jiàndìng nàkuài yùshí, yùjiàng yòu shuō: "Shì pǔtōng.de shí.tóu." Wǔ Wáng yě rènwéi Héshì shì .gè piàn.zǐ, jiù kǎndiào .le tā.de yòu jiǎo. Wǔ Wáng sǐ .le, Wén Wáng dēng.shàng .le wángwèi. Héshì jiù bāo.zhe nàkuài yùshí, zài Chǔguó.de shān.xià kū, kū.le sāntiān sānyè, yǎnlèi dōu kū guāng.le, jiē.zhē kǔ.chū xuè lái.

When King Lì died, King Wǔ acceded to the throne; Hé again respectfully presented the stone containing jade to King Wǔ. King Wǔ ordered a jade worker to appraise it; again he said: "It is ordinary stone." The king too thought Hé a liar and so cut off his right foot. When King Wǔ died, King Wén acceded to the throne. The man surnamed Hé then cradled the stone containing jade in his arms and cried at the foot of the mountains of Chǔ. He cried for three days and three nights; when he had cried out all his tears, he kept on crying with tears of blood.

王聞之，使人問其故，曰：“天下之刖者多矣，子奚哭
之悲也？”和曰：“吾非悲刖也。悲夫！寶玉而題之以
石，貞士而名之以誑，此吾所以悲也。”王乃使玉人理
其璞，而得寶焉，遂命曰：“和氏之璧。”

Wáng wén zhī, shǐ rén wèn qí gù, yuē: "Tiān xià zhī yuè zhě duō yǐ, zǐ xī kū zhī bēi yě?"
Hé yuē: "Wú fēi bēi yuè ye. Bēi fú! Bǎo yù ér tí zhī yǐ shí, zhēn shì ér míng zhī yǐ kuáng,
cǐ wú suǒ yǐ bēi yě." Wáng nǎi shǐ yù rén lǐ qí pú, ér dé bǎo yān, suì mìng yuē: "Hé Shì zhī
Bì."

Wang wen jy, shyy ren wenn chyi guh, iue: "Tian shiah jy yueh jee duo yii, tzyy shi ku jy
bei yee ?" Her iue: "Wu fei bei yueh yee. Bei fwu! Bao yuh erl tyi jy yii shyr, jen shyh erl
ming jy yii kwang, tsyy wu suoo yii bei yee." Wang nae shyy yuh ren lii chyi pwu, erl der
bao ian, suey minq iue: "Her Shyh jy Bih."

文王聽到這件事，派人去問他痛哭的緣故，説："天下被砍掉腳的人多啦，您爲什麼哭得那麼悲痛呢？"和氏説："我並不是因爲被砍掉了腳而悲痛。我悲痛啊！玉石是塊寶貴的玉，可是玉匠叫它作石頭，我是個忠誠正直的人，可是王叫我作騙子，這才是我悲痛的緣故啊！"文王就命令玉匠切開那塊玉石，結果從石中得到一塊寶玉，王於是就給它取名叫作"和氏之璧"。

Wén Wáng tīngdào zhèjiàn shì, pài rén qù wèn tā tòngkū.de yuángù, shuō: "Tiān.xià bèi kǎndiào jiǎo .de rén duō .la, nín wèi shén.me kū.dé nà.me bēitòng .ne?" Héshì shuō: "Wǒ bìng bú.shì yīn.wèi bèi kǎndiào .le jiǎo ér bēitòng. Wǒ bēitòng.a! Yùshí shì kuài bǎoguì .de yù, kě.shì yùjiàng jiào tā zuò shí.tóu. Wǒ shì .gè zhōngchéng zhèngzhí .de rén, kě.shì wáng jiào wǒ zuò piàn.zǐ, zhè cái shì wǒ bēitòng.de yuán.gù .a!" Wénwáng jiù mìng.lìng yùjiàng qiē kāi nèikuài yùshí, jiéguǒ cóng shí zhōng dé.dào yíkuài bǎoyù, wáng yúshì jiù gěi tā qǔ míng jiàozuò "Héshì zhī bì".

Upon hearing of this, the king sent a person to ask about the reason for his great wailing, who said: "In this world there are many who have had a foot cut off; why do you cry so grievously?" Hé said: "I do not grieve because my feet were cut off. Oh, I grieve because this is a piece of precious jade, yet the jade worker calls it ordinary stone. I am an upright man, but am called a liar by the king: this is why I grieve." The king then ordered a jade worker to cut open this piece of stone containing jade and got from it a piece of precious jade. Thereupon the king named it "The pierced jade disk of the man surnamed Hé."

第十九課

東周欲為稻

戰國策　東周策

東周欲為稻，西周不下水，東周患之。蘇子謂東周君曰：“臣請使西周下水，可乎？”乃往見西周之君，曰：“君之謀過矣。今不下水，所以富東周也。

Dōng Zhōu Yù Wéi Dào

Zhànguócè　Dōngzhōucè

Dōng Zhōu yù wéi dào, Xī Zhōu bú xià shuǐ, Dōng Zhōu huàn zhī. Sūzǐ wèi Dōng Zhōu jūn yuē: "Chén qǐng shǐ Xī Zhōu xià shuǐ, kě hū?" Nǎi wǎng jiàn Xī Zhōu zhī jūn, yuē: "Jūn zhī móu guò yǐ. Jīn bú xià shuǐ, suǒ yǐ fù Dōng Zhōu yě.

Dong Jou Yuh Wei Daw

Janngwotseh　Dongjoutseh

Dong Jou yuh wei daw, Shi Jou bu shiah shoei, Dong Jou huann jy. Sutzyy wey Dong Jou jiun iue: "Chern chiing shyy Shi Jou shiah shoei, kee hu?" Nae woang jiann Shi Jou jy jiun, iue: "Jiun jy mou guoh yii. Jin bu shiah shoei, suoo yii fuh Dong Jou yee.

白話翻譯

東周欲爲稻

　東周想要種稻子，西周不放下水來，東周擔心這個情形。蘇子對東周君説：“請讓我使西周放下水來，可以嗎？”蘇子就去見西周的君主説：“您的計劃錯啦。現在您不放下水去，這是您用來使東周富足的辦法啊。

Dōng Zhōu Yù Wéi Dào

Dōng Zhōu xiǎng.yào zhòng dào.zǐ, Xī Zhōu bú fàng.xià shuǐ .lái, Dōng Zhōu dānxīn zhèi.gè qíng.xíng. Sūzǐ duì Dōng Zhōu jūn shuō: "Qǐng ràng wǒ shǐ Xī Zhōu fàng.xià shuǐ .lái, kě.yǐ .ma?" Sūzǐ jiù qù jiàn Xī Zhōu .de jūnzhǔ shuō: "Nín.de jì.huà cuò .la. Xiàn.zài nín bú fàng.xià shuǐ .qù, zhè shì nín yònglái shǐ Dōng Zhōu fùzú .de bàn.fǎ .ā.

EASTERN ZHOU PLANTS RICE

The Eastern Zhōu kingdom wanted to plant rice; the Western Zhōu kingdom would not let the river water flow downstream, and the Eastern Zhōu ruler was worried about the situation. Sūzǐ spoke to the Eastern Zhōu ruler saying: "I ask that you allow me to make the Western Zhōu let the river water flow downstream; may I?" Sūzǐ then went to see the ruler of the Western Zhōu and said: "Your plan is wrong. If you now do not let the water flow downstream, that will be your way to enrich the Eastern Zhōu kingdom.

今其民皆種麥，無他種矣。君若欲害之，不若一為下水，以病其所種。下水，則東周必復種稻；種稻，而復奪之。若是，則東周之民可令一仰西周，而受命於君矣。"西周君曰："善。"蘇子亦得兩國之金也。

Jīn qí mín jiē zhòng mài, wú tuō zhòng yǐ. Jūn ruò yù hài zhī, bú ruò yí wèi xià shuǐ, yǐ bìng qí suǒ zhòng. Xià shuǐ, zé Dōng Zhōu bì fù zhòng dào; zhòng dào, ér fù duó zhī. Ruò shì, zé Dōng Zhōu zhī mín kě lìng yī yǎng Xī Zhōu, ér shòu mìng yú jūn yǐ." Xī Zhōu jūn yuē: "Shàn." Sūzǐ yì dé liǎng guó zhī jīn yě.

Jin chyi min jie jonq may, wu tuo jonq yii. Jiun ruoh yuh hay jy, bu ruoh i wey shiah shoei, yii binq chyi suoo jonq. Shiah shoei, tzer Dong Jou bih fuh jonq daw; jonq daw, erl fuh dwo jy. Ruoh shyh, tzer Dong Jou jy min kee linq i yeang Shi Jou, erl show minq yu jiun yii." Shi Jou jiun iue: "Shann." Sutzyy yih der leang gwo jy jin yee.

現在東周的百姓都種麥子，不種別的糧食了。您假若想要
害東周，不如給他們放一次水來損害他們種的麥子。您要是
放下水去，那麼東周一定會再種稻子；東周種稻子，您就再
停止放水。如果像這樣，那麼您就能使東周的百姓完全依賴
西周，結果就接受您的命令了。"西周君說："好。"蘇
子也得到兩國的酬金啊。

Xiàn.zài Dōng Zhōu .de bǎixìng dōu zhòng mài.zǐ, bú zhòng bié.de liáng.shí .le. Nín jiǎruò
xiǎngyào hài Dōng Zhōu, bù rú gěi tā.mén fàng yícì shuǐ lái sǔnhài tā.mén zhòng.de mài.zǐ.
Nín yào.shì fàng.xià shuǐ .qù, nà.me Dōng Zhōu yí dìng huì zài zhòng dào.zǐ; Dōng Zhōu
zhòng dào.zǐ, nín jiù zài tíngzhǐ fàng shuǐ. Rúguǒ xiàng zhèi.yàng, nà.me nín jiù néng shǐ
Dōng Zhōu .de bǎixìng wánquán yīlài Xī Zhōu, jiéguǒ jiù jiēshòu nín.de mìnglìng .le." Xī
Zhōu jūn shuō: "Hǎo." Sūzǐ yě dé.dào liǎng guó .de chóujīn .ā.

Now the Eastern Zhōu people all are planting wheat and nothing else. If you wish to harm
them, it would be better to let the water flow downstream once to spoil the wheat that they
have planted. If you let the water flow downstream, the Eastern Zhōu will certainly plant rice
again; when they have planted rice, then you stop it again. If you do it this way, you can
make the people of the Eastern Zhōu depend completely on the Western Zhōu and as a result
accept orders from you." The Western Zhōu ruler said: "Excellent!" Sūzǐ also received
compensation for his services from both kingdoms.

第二十課

結草報恩

左傳　宣公十五年

　　初，魏武子有嬖妾，無子。武子疾，命顆曰："必嫁是。"疾病則曰："必以為殉。"及卒，顆嫁之，曰："疾病則亂，吾從其治也。"

Jié Cǎo Bào Ēn

Zuǒzhuàn　Xuāngōng shíwǔnián

Chū, Wèi Wǔzǐ yǒu bì qiè, wú zǐ. Wǔzǐ jí, mìng Kē yuē: "Bì jià shì." Jí bìng zé yuē: "Bì yǐ wéi xùn." Jí zú, Kē jià zhī, yuē: "Jí bìng zé luàn, wú cóng qí zhì yě."

Jye Tsao Baw En

Tzuoojuann　Shiuangong shyrwuunian

Chu, Wey Wuutzyy yeou bih chieh, wu tzyy. Wuutzyy jyi, minq Ke iue: "Bih jiah shyh." Jyi binq tzer iue: "Bih yii wei shiunn." Jyi tzwu, Ke jiah jy, iue: "Jyi binq tzer luann, wu tsorng chyi jyh yee."

白話翻譯

結 草 報 恩

　　起初，魏武子有個寵愛的姨太太，她沒有孩子。武子病了，命令他的兒子魏顆說：「你一定要把這個妾嫁出去。」武子病重了卻說：「你一定要用她來給我陪葬。」等到武子死了，魏顆把那個姨太太嫁了出去，他說：「人病重了就神志不清了，我聽從他神志清醒時的命令啊。」

Jié Cǎo Bào Ēn

　　Qǐ chū, Wèi wǔzǐ yǒu .gè chǒngài .de yí tài.tài, tā méi.yǒu hái.zǐ. Wǔzǐ bìng .le, mìnglìng tā.de ér.zǐ Wèi Kē shuō: "Nǐ yídìng yào bǎ zhèi.gè qiè jià chū.qù." Wǔzǐ bìng zhòng .le què shuō: "Nǐ yídìng yào yòng tā lái gěi wǒ péi zàng." Děngdào Wǔzǐ sǐ .le, Wèi Kē bǎ nèi.gè yí tài.tài jià .le chū.qù, tā shuō: "Rén bìng zhòng .le jiù shénzhì bùqīng .le, wǒ tīngcóng tā shénzhì qīngxǐng shí .de mìng.lìng .a."

KNOTTING GRASS TO REPAY A KINDNESS

　　Originally, Wèi Wǔzǐ had a favorite concubine; she had no children. When Wǔzǐ fell ill, he ordered his son, Wèi Kē, saying: "You must marry her off." When Wǔzǐ became severely ill, he said instead: "You must have her buried with me as a sacrificial offering." When Wūzǐ died, Wèi Kē married her off. He said: "When a person is so severely ill, his senses are disordered, I obeyed the charge he gave when his mind was right."

及輔氏之役，顆見老人結草以亢杜回。杜回躓而顛，故獲之。夜夢之曰："余，而所嫁婦人之父也。爾用先人之治命，余是以報。"

Jí 'Fǔshì zhī yì', Kē jiàn lǎo rén jié cǎo yǐ kàng Dù Huí. Dù Huí zhì ér diān, gù huò zhī. Yè mèng zhī yuē: "Yú, ěr suǒ jià fù rén zhī fù yě. Ěr yòng xiān rén zhī zhì mìng, yú shì yǐ baò."

Jyi 'Fuu shyh jy yih', Ke jiann lao ren jye tsao yii kanq Duh Hwei. Duh Hwei jyh erl dian, guh huoh jy. Yeh menq jy iue: "Yu, eel suoo jiah fuh ren jy fuh yee. Eel yonq shian ren jy jyh minq, yu shyh yii baw."

等到‘輔氏之役’的時候，魏顆看見一個老人把草打成結來攔阻杜回。杜回絆了一下就跌倒了，所以魏顆俘獲了他。夜裡魏顆夢見那個老人說："我就是你嫁出去的那個女人的父親啊。你用你父親生前神志清醒時的命令，我因此報答你。"

Děngdào 'Fǔshì zhī yì'.de shí.hòu , Wèi kē kàn.jiàn yí.gè lǎorén bǎ cǎo dǎchéng jié lái lánzǔ Dù Huí. Dù Huí bàn .le yí.xià jiù diēdǎo .le, suǒ.yǐ Wèi kē fúhuò .le tā. Yè.lǐ Wèi kē mèngjiàn nèi.gè lǎorén shuō: "Wǒ jiù.shì nǐ jiàchū.qù .de nèi.ge nǚ.rén .de fù.qīn .a. Nǐ yòng nǐ fù.qīn shēngqián shénzhì qīngxǐng shí .de mìnglìng, wǒ yīncǐ bàodá nǐ."

At the time of 'The battle of Fǔshì', Wèi Kē saw an old man knotting up grass to impede Dù Huí. Dù Huí stumbled and fell down; therefore Wèi Kē captured him. At night, Wèi Kē dreamt he saw this old man, who said: "I am the father of that woman whom you married off. You followed the order that your deceased father gave when he was in his right mind; for this I am repaying you."

第二十一課

歧路亡羊

列子　說符

　　楊子之鄰人亡羊，既率其黨，又請楊子之豎追之。楊子曰：“嘻！亡一羊，何追者之眾？”鄰人曰：“多歧路。”

Qí Lù Wáng Yáng

Lièzǐ　Shuōfú

　　Yángzǐ zhī lín rén wáng yáng, jì shuài qí dǎng, yòu qǐng Yángzǐ zhī shù zhuī zhī. Yángzǐ yuē: "Xī! Wáng yì yáng, hé zhuī zhě zhī zhòng?" Lín rén yuē: "Duō qí lù."

Chyi Luh Wang Yang

Liehtzyy　Shuofwu

　　Yangtzyy jy lin ren wang yang, jih shuay chyi daang, yow chiing Yangtzyy jy shuh juei jy. Yangtzyy iue: "Shi! Wang i yang, her juei jee jy jonq?" Lin ren iue: "Duo chyi luh."

白話翻譯

歧 路 亡 羊

楊子的鄰居丟了羊，鄰居既率領著他的親屬，又請求楊子的小廝一塊兒去追趕跑掉的羊。楊子說："咦！丟了一隻羊，為什麼追牠的人那麼多?" 鄰居說："因為有很多岔路。"

Qí Lù Wáng Yáng

Yángzǐ .de línjū diū .le yáng, línjū jì shuàilǐng .zhe tā.de qīnshǔ, yòu qǐngqiú Yángzǐ .de xiǎosī yíkuàir qù zhuīgǎn pǎodiào .de yáng. Yángzǐ shuō: "Yí! diū.le yìzhī yáng, wèi shén.me zhuī tā .de rén nà.me duō?" Línjū shuō: "Yīn.wèi yǒu hěn duō chàlù."

A SHEEP IS LOST AT THE FORKED ROAD

Yángzǐ's neighbor lost a sheep; the neighbor not only led his relatives, but also asked Yángzǐ's young servant boys to go together with them to chase after the lost sheep. Yángzǐ said: "Hey! You've lost one sheep, why are so many people chasing after it?" The neighbor said: "Because there are many forked paths."

既反，問：“獲羊乎？”曰：“亡之矣。”曰：“奚亡之？”曰：“歧路之中又有歧焉，吾不知所之，所以反也。”楊子戚然變容，不言者移時，不笑者竟日。

Jì fǎn, wèn: "Huò yáng hū?" Yuē: "Wáng zhī yǐ." Yuē: "Xī wáng zhī?" Yuē: "Qí lù zhī zhōng yòu yǒu qí yān, wú bù zhī suǒ zhī, suǒ yǐ fǎn yě." Yángzǐ qī rán biàn róng, bù yán zhě yí shí, bú xiào zhě jìng rì.

Jih faan, wenn: "Huoh yang hu?" Iue: "Wang jy yii." Iue: "Shi wang jy?" Iue: "Chyi luh jy jong yow yeou chyi ian, wu bu jy suoo jy, suoo yii faan yee." Yangtzyy chi ran biann rong, bu yan jee yi shyr, bu shiaw jee jinq ryh.

鄰居回來了以後，楊子問：“找到羊了嗎？”鄰居説：“把羊給丟了。”楊子説：“爲什麽把羊給丟了呢？”鄰居説：“岔路裡又有岔路，我不知道牠跑到哪條岔路上去了，所以就回來啦。”楊子很憂傷地改變了臉上的神情，沈默了很久，一整天都不笑。

Línjū huílái .le yǐhòu, Yángzǐ wèn: "Zhǎodào yáng .le .mā?" Línjū shuō: "Bǎ yáng .gěi diū .le." Yángzǐ shuō: "Wèi shén.me bǎ yáng .gěi diū .le .ne?" Línjū shuō: "Chàlù .lǐ yòu yǒu chàlù, wǒ bù zhīdào tā pǎo.dào nǎ tiáo chàlù shàng .qù.le, suǒ.yǐ jiù huílái .la." Yángzǐ hěn yōushāng .de gǎibiàn .le liǎnshàng .de shénqíng, chénmò .le hěn jiǔ, yì zhěngtiān dōu bú xiào.

After the neighbor had returned, Yángzǐ asked: "Did you find the sheep?" The neighbor said: "I have lost it." Yángzǐ said: "Why did you lose it?" The neighbor said: "There are even more forked paths in the forked paths; I do not know down which path it ran; therefore, I returned." Yángzǐ's expression became very morose; he was silent then for a long time and did not laugh even once the whole day.

第二十二課

揠苗

孟子　公孫丑上

　宋人有閔其苗之不長而揠之者。芒芒然歸，謂其人曰：「今日病矣！予助苗長矣！」其子趨而往視之，苗則槁矣。

Yà Miáo

Mèngzǐ　Gōngsūnchǒushàng

Sòng rén yǒu mǐn qí miáo zhī bù zhǎng ér yà zhī zhě.　Máng máng rán guī, weì qí rén yuē: "Jīn rì bìng yǐ!　Yú zhù miáo zhǎng yǐ!"　Qí zǐ qiū ér wǎng shì zhī, miáo zé gaǒ yǐ.

Yah Miau

Menqtzyy　Gongsuenchooushanq

Sonq ren yeou miin chyi miau jy bu jaang erl yah jy jee.　Mang mang ran guei, wey chyi ren iue: "Jin ryh binq yii!　Yu juh miau jaang yii!"　Chyi tzyy chiu erl woang shyh jy, miau tzer gao yii.

白話翻譯

揠 苗

　　有個擔心他的苗長不大就去把苗拔高一點兒的宋國人，他很累地回家，告訴他家裡的人説：「今天我可累壞啦！我剛才幫助苗長高了！」他的兒子跑著到田裡去看苗，苗原來都已經枯啦。

Yà Miáo

　　Yǒu.gè dānxīn tā.de miáo zhǎng .bú dà jiù qù bǎ miáo bá gāo yī.diǎnr .de Sòng.guó rén, tā hěn lèi .de huí jiā, gào.sù tā jiā.lǐ .de rén shuō: "Jīn.tiān wǒ kě lèi huài .lā! wǒ gāngcái bāngzhù miáo zhǎng gāo .le!" Tā.de ér.zǐ pǎo.zhe dào tián.lǐ qù kàn miáo, miáo yuán.lái dōu yǐ.jīng kū .lā.

PULLING UP THE SPROUTS

There was a person from the state of Sòng who was concerned that his sprouts would not grow tall and so pulled them up a bit. He returned home exhausted and spoke to the people in his family saying: "Today I am tired out! I have just helped the sprouts grow taller!" His son ran to the fields to look at the sprouts, but it turned out that the sprouts had all withered.

天下之不助苗長者寡矣。以為無益而舍之者，不耘苗者也；助之長者，揠苗者也。非徒無益，而又害之。

Tiān xià zhī bú zhù miáo zhǎng zhě guǎ yǐ. Yǐ weí wú yì ér shě zhī zhě, bù yún miáo zhě yě; zhù zhī zhǎng zhě, yà miáo zhě yě. Fēi tú wú yì, ér yòu hài zhī.

Tian shiah jy bu juh miau jaang jee goa yii. Yii wei wu yih erl shee jy jee, bu yun miau jee yee; juh jy jaang jee, yah miau jee yee. Fei twu wu yih, erl yow hay jy.

天下不幫助苗長的人太少啦。認爲培養它沒有好處就放棄
它的人是不替苗除掉野草的人；幫助它長的人是把苗拔高一
點儿的人。揠苗這種做法不僅沒有好處，反而還害了它。

Tiān.xià bù bāng.zhù miáo zhǎng .de rén tài shǎo .la. Rènwèi péiyǎng tā méi.yǒu hǎo.chù jiù
fàngqì tā .de rén shì bú tì miáo chúdiào yěcǎo .de rén; bāngzhù tā zhǎng .de rén shì bǎ miáo
bá gāo yì.diǎnr .de rén. Yàmiáo zhèi zhǒng zuòfǎ bùjǐn méi.yǒu hǎo.chù, fǎn.ér hái hài .le tā.

The people in the world who do not help their sprouts grow are few indeed! The people who
think there is no advantage in nurturing something and thus abandon it are the people who do
not weed their sprouts. The people who want to help something grow are the people who
pull their sprouts up a bit. This method of pulling the sprouts up a bit not only has no
benefit, but on the contrary also harms them.

第二十三課

燕人

列子　周穆王

　　燕人生於燕，長於楚，及老而還本國。過晉國，同行者誑之，指城曰：“此燕國之城。”其人愀然變容。

Yān Rén

Lièzǐ　Zhōumùwáng

Yān rén shēng yú Yān, zhǎng yú Chǔ, jí laǒ ér húan běn guó.　Guò Jìn guó, tóng xíng zhě kuáng zhī, zhǐ chéng yuē: "Cǐ Yān guó zhī chéng." Qí rén qiǎo rán biàn róng.

Ian Ren

Liehtzyy Joumuhwang

Ian ren sheng yu Ian, jaang yu Chuu, jyi lao erl hwan been gwo.　Guoh Jinn gwo, torng shyng jee kwang jy, jyy cherng iue: "Tsyy Ian gwo jy cherng." Chyi ren cheau ran biann rong.

白話翻譯

燕人

　　有一個燕國人在燕國出生，在楚國長大，等到老了的時候回他自己的老家去。在他經過晉國的時候，跟他一起走的人騙他，指著城牆說：「這是燕國的城牆。」那個燕國人很難過地改變了臉上的神情。

Yān Rén

　　Yǒu yí.gè Yānguó rén, zài Yānguó chūshēng, zài Chǔguó zhǎngdà, děng dào lǎo .le .de shí.hòu huí tā zì.jǐ .de lǎo.jiā .qù. Zài tā jīng.guò Jìnguó .de shí.hòu, gēn tā yìqǐ zǒu.de rén piàn tā, zhǐ.zhē chéngqiáng shuō: "Zhè shì Yānguó .de chéngqiáng." Nèi.gè Yānguó rén hěn nánguò.de gǎibiàn .le liǎn.shàng.de shénqíng.

THE MAN FROM YAN

There was a man of the state of Yān who was born in Yān, grew up in the state of Chǔ, and when he grew old, returned to his native land. While he was passing through the state of Jìn, the person travelling together with him tricked him; pointing at the city wall, he said: "This is the city wall of the state of Yān." This man from Yān glumly changed his expression.

指社曰：“此若里之社。”乃嘳然而歎。指舍曰：“此若先人之廬。”乃涓然而泣。指壟曰：“此若先人之塚。”其人哭不自禁。

Zhǐ shè yuē: "Cǐ ruò lǐ zhī shè." Nǎi kuì rán ér tàn. Zhǐ shè yuē: "Cǐ ruò xiān rén zhī lú." Nǎi juàn rán ér qì. Zhǐ lǒng yuē: "Cǐ ruò xiān rén zhī zhǒng." Qí rén kū bú zì jìn.

Jyy sheh iue: "Tsyy ruoh lii jy sheh." Nae kuey ran erl tann. Jyy sheh iue: "Tsyy ruoh shian ren jy lu." Nae jiuann ran erl chih. Jyy loong iue: "Tsyy ruoh shian ren jy joong." Chyi ren ku bu tzyh jinn.

一起走的人指著土地廟說：“這是你村子裡的土地廟。”那個燕國人就很悲哀地歎氣。一起走的人指著房子說：“這是你祖先的茅舍。”那個燕國人就眼淚紛紛落下地哭了。一起走的人指著一片墳堆說：“這是你祖先的墳墓。”那個燕國人哭得止不住自己。

Yìqǐ zǒu.de rén zhǐ.zhe tǔdìmiào shuō: "Zhè shì nǐ cūn.zǐ.lǐ.de tǔdìmiào." Nèi.gè Yānguó rén jiù hěn bēiāi .dē tàn qì. Yìqǐ zǒu.de rén zhǐ.zhē fáng.zǐ shuō: "Zhè.shì nǐ zǔxiān.de máoshè." Nèi.gè Yānguó rén jiù yǎnlèi fēnfēnluòxià.de kū .le. Yìqǐ zǒu.de rén zhǐ .zhē yípiàn féndūi shuō: "Zhè shì nǐ zǔxiān .de fénmù." Nèi.gè Yānguó rén kū .dé zhǐ .bú zhù zì.jǐ.

The person travelling with him pointed at an altar to the local god of the soil and said: "This is your village's altar to the local god of the soil." The man from Yān then sighed heavy-heartedly. The person travelling with him pointed at a cottage and said: "This is your ancestors' thatched cottage." The man from Yān then cried, the tears streaming in rivulets down his face. The person travelling with him pointed at some tumuli and said: "These are your ancestors' grave mounds." This person from Yān could not stop himself from crying.

同行者啞然大笑曰：「予昔紿若，此晉國耳。」其人大慚。及至燕，真見燕國之城社，真見先人之廬塚，悲心更微。

Tóng xíng zhě è rán dà xiào yuē: "Yú xī dài ruò, cǐ Jìn guó ěr." Qí rén dà cán. Jí zhì Yān, zhēn jiàn Yān guó zhī chéng shè, zhēn jiàn xiān rén zhī lú zhǒng, bēi xīn gèng wēi.

Torng shyng jee eh ran dah shiaw iue: "Yu shi day ruoh, tsyy Jinn gwo eel." Chyi ren dah tsarn. Jyi jyh Ian, jen jiann Ian gwo jy cherng sheh, jen jiann shian ren jy lu joong, bei shin genq uei.

跟他一起走的人哈哈大笑説：“我剛才騙你，這裡只不過是晉國罷了。”那個燕國人非常慚愧。等到他到了燕國的時候，真看見了燕國的城牆跟土地廟，真看見了祖先的茅廬跟墳墓，他的悲傷的心情反倒輕微多了。

Gēn tā yìqǐ zǒu .de rén hāhā dà xiào shuō: "Wǒ gāngcái piàn nǐ, zhè.li zhǐ búguò shì Jìnguó bà.le." Nèi.ge Yānguó rén fēicháng cánkuì. Děngdào tā dào .le Yānguó .de shíhòu, zhēn kànjiàn .le Yānguó .de chéngqiáng gēn tǔdìmiào, zhēn kànjiàn .le zǔxiān .de máolú gēn fénmù, tā .de bēishāng .de xīnqíng fǎndào qīngwēi duō .le.

The person travelling with him spoke with a gaffaw, said: "Just now I tricked you; this is only the state of Jìn." This man from Yān was mortified. When he arrived in the state of Yān and truly saw the state of Yān's city wall and altar to the local god of the soil and truly saw his ancestors' thatched cottage and grave mounds, his feelings of grief were instead even less intense than before.

第二十四課

畫蛇添足

戰國策 齊策

楚有祠者，賜其舍人卮酒。舍人相謂曰："數人飲之，不足；一人飲之，有餘。請畫地為蛇，先成者飲酒。"一人蛇先成。

Huà Shé Tiān Zú

Zhànguócè Qícè

Chǔ yǒu cí zhě, cì qí shèrén zhī jiǔ. Shèrén xiāng wèi yuē: "Shù rén yǐn zhī, bù zú; yì rén yǐn zhī, yǒu yú. Qǐng huà dì wéi shé, xiān chéng zhě yǐn jiǔ." Yì rén shé xiān chéng.

Huah Sher Tian Tzwu

Janngwotseh Chyitseh

Chuu yeou tsyr jee, tsyh chyi shehren jy jeou. Shehren shiang wey iue: "Shuh ren yiin jy, buh tzwu; yih ren yiin jy, yeou yu. Chiing huah dih wei sher, shian cherng jee yiin jeou." Yih ren sher shian cherng.

白話翻譯

畫 蛇 添 足

　　楚國有個祭祀的人，賜給他的門客一杯酒。門客們一塊儿商量説："幾個人喝這杯酒，酒不夠；一個人喝它，卻又太多。讓咱們在地面上畫作一條蛇，先畫完的人喝酒。"一個人蛇先畫成了。

Huà Shé Tiān Zú

　　Chǔguó yǒu .gè jìsì .dē rén, cì.gěi tā .de ménkè yì bēi jiǔ. Ménkè.mén yíkuàir shāng.liáng shuō: "Jǐ.gè rén hē zhèi bēi jiǔ, jiǔ búgòu; yí.gè rén hē tā, què yòu tài duō. Ràng zá.mén zài dìmiàn .shàng huà zuò yìtíao shé, xiān huà wán .de rén hē jiǔ." Yí.gè rén shé xiān huà chéng .le.

DRAWING A SNAKE AND ADDING FEET

　　In the state of Chǔ there was a person performing a sacrifice; he offered his retainers a goblet of liquor. The retainers discussed this among themselves saying: "With several people drinking this goblet, the liquor will not suffice; with one person drinking it, there will be more than enough. Let us each draw a picture of snake on the ground; the one who finishes first drinks the liquor." One person finished drawing a snake first.

引酒且飲，乃左手持卮，右手畫蛇曰：＂吾能為之足。＂未成，一人之蛇成。奪其卮曰：＂蛇固無足，子安能為之足？＂遂飲其酒。為蛇足者終亡其酒。

Yǐn jiǔ qiě yǐn, nǎi zuǒ shǒu chí zhī, yoù shǒu huà shé yuē: "Wú néng wèi zhī zú." Wèi chéng, yì rén zhī shé chéng. Duó qí zhī yuē: "Shé gù wú zú, zǐ ān néng wèi zhī zú ?" Suì yǐn qí jiǔ. Wèi shé zú zhě zhōng wáng qí jiǔ.

Yiin jeou chiee yiin, nae tzuoo shoou chyr jy, yow shoou huah sher iue: "Wu neng wey jy tzwu." Wey cherng, yih ren jy sher cherng. Dwo chyi jy iue: "Sher guh wu tzwu, tzyy an neng wey jy tzwu ?" Suey yiin chyi jeou. Wey sher tzwu jee jong wang chyi jeou.

他拿過酒來將要喝，卻用左手端著酒杯，用右手畫著蛇說：
"我能給它添上腳。"他的蛇腳還沒有畫完，另一個人的蛇
畫成了。那個人搶過那隻酒杯說："蛇本來沒有腳，您怎麼
能給它添上腳呢？"就把那杯酒喝掉了。給蛇添腳的人終於
失掉了他的酒。

Tā ná .guò jiǔ lái jiāng.yào hē, què yòng zuǒshǒu duān .zhe jiǔbēi , yòng yòushǒu huà .zhe
shé shuō: " Wǒ néng gěi tā tiān .shàng jiǎo." Tā .de shéjiǎo hái méi.yǒu huà wán, lìng yí.gè
rén .de shé huà chéng .le. Nèi.gè rén qiǎng .guò nèi zhī jiǔbēi shuō : "Shé běnlái méi.yǒu
jiǎo, nín zěn.me néng gěi tā tiān .shàng jiǎo .ne?" jiù bǎ nèi bēi jiǔ hē diào .le. Gěi shé tiān
jiǎo .de rén zhōngyú shīdiào .le tā .de jiǔ.

He took up the liquor and was about to drink, but using his left hand to hold the goblet while
drawing the snake with his right, he said: "I can add feet to it." His snake's feet were not
yet completed, when another person's snake was completed. That person grabbed away the
goblet and said: "A snake by nature has no feet; how can you add feet to it?" Thereupon, he
drank the liquor. In the end, the one who added feet to his snake lost his liquor.

第二十五課

濠梁之遊

莊子　秋水

　　莊子與惠子遊於濠梁之上。莊子曰："鯈魚出游從容，是魚之樂也。"惠子曰："子非魚，安知魚之樂？"莊子曰："子非我，安知我之不知魚之樂？"

Háo Liáng Zhī Yóu

Zhuāngzǐ　Qiūshuǐ

Zhuāngzǐ yǔ Huìzǐ yóu yú Háo liáng zhī shàng. Zhuāngzǐ yuē: "Tiáo yú chū yóu cōng róng, shì yú zhī lè yě." Huìzǐ yuē: "Zǐ fēi yú, ān zhī yú zhī lè?" Zhuāngzǐ yuē: "Zǐ fēi wǒ, ān zhī wǒ zhī bù zhī yú zhī lè?"

Haur Liang Jy You

Juangtzyy　Chioushoei

Juangtzyy yeu Hueytzyy you yu Haur liang jy shanq. Juangtzyy iue: "Tyau yu chu you tsong rong, shyh yu jy leh yee." Hueytzyy iue: "Tzyy fei yu, an jy yu jy leh?" Juangtzyy iue: "Tzyy fei woo, an jy woo jy bu jy yu jy leh?"

白話翻譯

濠梁之遊

莊子跟惠子在濠水的橋上閒遊。莊子說：“儵魚浮出水面或在水中游動得很自在，這是魚快樂啊。”惠子說：“您不是魚，您怎麼知道魚快樂呢？”莊子說：“您不是我，您怎麼知道我不知道魚快樂呢？”

Háo Liáng Zhī Yóu

Zhuāngzǐ gēn Huìzǐ zài Háoshuǐ .de qiáo shàng xiányóu. Zhuāngzǐ shuō: "Tiáo yú fúchū shuǐmiàn huò zài shuǐzhōng yóudòng .dé hěn zì.zài, zhè shì yú kuàilè .a!" Huìzǐ shuō: "Nín bú.shì yú, nín zěn.me zhī.dào yú kuàilè .ne?" Zhuāngzǐ shuō: "Nín bú.shì wǒ, nín zěn.me zhī.dào wǒ bù zhī.dào yú kuàilè .ne?"

A STROLL ON THE BRIDGE OVER THE HAO RIVER

Zhuāngzǐ and Huìzǐ were strolling on the Háo River bridge. Zhuāngzǐ said: "The minnows dart in and out of the water, leisurely and contendedly swimming -- this is fish being happy." Huìzǐ said: "You are not a fish; how do you know that the fish are happy?" Zhuāngzǐ said: "You are not I; so how do you know that I do not know the fish are happy?"

惠子曰：“我非子，固不知子矣；子固非魚也，子之不知魚之樂，全矣。”莊子曰：“請循其本。子曰‘汝安知魚樂’云者，既已知吾知之而問我，我知之濠上也。”

Huìzǐ yuē: "Wǒ fēi zǐ, gù bù zhī zǐ yǐ; zǐ gù fēi yú yě, zǐ zhī bù zhī yú zhī lè, quán yǐ." Zhuāngzǐ yuē: "Qǐng xún qí běn. Zǐ yuē 'Rǔ ān zhī yú lè' yún zhě, jì yǐ zhī wú zhī zhī ér wèn wǒ, wǒ zhī zhī háo shàng yě."

Hueytzyy iue: "Woo fei tzyy, guh bu jy tzyy yii; tzyy guh fei yu yee, tzyy jy bu jy yu jy leh, chyuan yii." Juangtzyy iue: "Chiing shyun chyi been. Tzyy iue 'Ruu an jy yu leh' yun jee, jih yii jy wu jy jy erl wenn woo, woo jy jy Haur shanq yee."

惠子說："我不是您，我固然不知道您了；您本來不是魚啊，您不知道魚快樂是毫無疑問的啦。"莊子說："讓咱們回到辯論的起點。您說'您怎麼知道魚快樂啊，'您已經知道我知道魚快樂了才問我從哪儿知道魚快樂的。我在濠水的橋上知道魚快樂的啊。"

Huìzǐ shuō: "Wǒ bú.shì nín, wǒ gùrán bù zhī.dào nín .lā; nín běnlái yě bú.shì yú .a, nín bù zhī.dào yú kuàilè shì háowúyíwèn .de .lā." Zhuāngzǐ shuō: "Ràng zá.mén huí.dào biànlùn .de qǐdiǎn. Nín shuō 'nín zěn.me zhī.dào yú kuàilè .a,' nín yǐjīng zhī.dào wǒ zhī.dào yú kuàilè .le cái wèn wǒ cóng nǎr zhī.dào yú kuàilè .dē. Wǒ zài Háoshuǐ .de qiáo.shàng zhī.dào yú kuàilè .de .a."

Huìzǐ said: "I am not you; indeed, I don't know you; you by nature are not a fish: there is absolutely no question that you don't know that the fish are happy." Zhuāngzǐ said: "Let's go back to the starting point of our argument. When you said, 'How did you come to know this,' you already had to have known that I knew the fish are happy, only then could you have asked me where I knew it from. I came to know it from being on the bridge over the Háo River."

第二十六課

齊桓公使管仲治國

說苑 尊賢

　　齊桓公使管仲治國，管仲對曰：“賤不能臨貴。”桓公以為上卿，而國不治。桓公曰：“何故？”管仲對曰：“貧不能使富。”桓公賜之齊國市租一年，而國不治。

Qí Huángōng Shǐ Guǎn Zhòng Zhì Guó

Shuōyuàn Zūnxián

　　Qí Huángōng shǐ Guǎn Zhòng zhì guó, Guǎn Zhòng duì yuē: "Jiàn bù néng lín guì." Huángōng yǐ wéi shàng qīng, ér guó bú zhì. Huángōng yuē: "Hé gù?" Guǎn Zhòng duì yuē: "Pín bù néng shǐ fù." Huángōng cì zhī Qí guó shì zū yì nián, ér guó bú zhì.

Chyi Hwangong Shyy Goan Jonq Jyh Gwo

Shuoyuann Tzuenshyan

　　Chyi Hwangong shyy Goan Jonq jyh gwo, Goan Jonq duey iue: "Jiann bu neng lin guey." Hwangong yii wei shanq ching, erl gwo bu jyh. Hwangong iue: "Her guh?" Goan Jonq duey iue: "Pyn bu neng shyy fuh." Hwangong tsyh jy Chyi gwo shyh tzu i nian, erl gwo bu jyh.

白話翻譯

齊桓公使管仲治國

　　齊桓公命令管仲管理國政，管仲回答説："地位低的人不能統治地位高的人。"桓公任命管仲作上卿，可是國家還不太平。桓公説："國家因爲什麼緣故還不太平呢？"管仲回答説："貧窮的人不能差遣富有的人。"桓公賜給他齊國一年的貨物税，可是國家還不太平。

Qí Huángōng Shǐ Guǎn Zhòng Zhì Guó

　　Qí Huángōng mìng.lìng Guǎn Zhòng guǎnlǐ guózhèng, Guǎn Zhòng huídá shuō: "Dì.wèi dī .de rén bùnéng tǒngzhì dì.wèi gāo .de rén." Huángōng rènmìng Guǎn Zhòng zuò shàngqīng, kěshì guójiā hái bú tài.píng. Huángōng shuō: "Guójiā yīn.wèi shén.me yuán.gù hái bú tài.píng .ne?" Guǎn Zhòng huídá shuō: "Pínqióng .de rén bùnéng chāiqiǎn fùyǒu .de rén." Huángōng cì.gěi tā Qíguó yì nián .de huòwù shuì, kě.shǐ guójiā hái bú tài.píng.

DUKE HUAN OF QI ORDERS GUAN ZHONG TO ADMINSTER THE AFFAIRS OF STATE

　　Duke Huán of Qí ordered Guǎn Zhòng to administer the affairs of state. Guǎn Zhòng responded, saying: "Those of low rank cannot rule over those of high rank." Duke Huán appointed Guǎn Zhòng the chief minister, yet still the state of Qí was not peaceful and orderly. Duke Huán said: "Why is the state not yet peaceful and orderly?" Guǎn Zhòng responded, saying: "Those who are poor cannot order about those who are rich." Duke Huán bestowed on him the proceeds from the commodity taxes of Qí for one year, yet the state was still not peaceful and orderly.

桓公曰：“何故？”對曰：“疏不能制親。”桓公立以
為仲父，齊國大安，而遂霸天下。孔子曰：“管仲之賢
，不得此三權者，亦不能使其君南面而霸矣。”

Huángōng yuē: "Hé gù?" Duì yuē : "Shū bù néng zhì qīn." Huángōng lì yǐ wéi jòngfù, Qí guó dà ān, ér suì bà tiān xià. Kǒngzǐ yuē: "Guǎn Zhòng zhī xián, bù dé cǐ sān quán zhě, yì bù néng shǐ qí jūn nán miàn ér bà yǐ."

Hwangong iue: "Her guh?" Duey iue: "Shu bu neng jyh chin." Hwangong lih yii wei Jonqfuh, Chyi gwo dah an, erl suey bah tian shiah. Koongtzyy iue: "Goan Jonq jy shyan, bu der tsyy san chyuan jee, yih bu neng shyy chyi jiun nan miann erl bah yii."

桓公説：“國家因爲什麼緣故還不太平呢？”管仲回答説：
“跟君主關係遠的人不能控制跟君主關係近的人。”桓公把
他升到極高的地位，尊稱他爲仲父，齊國就變得非常太平，
終於成爲全天下諸侯的領袖。孔子説：“憑管仲那麼有才幹
，要是他得不到這三種權勢啊，那麼也就不能使他的君主
面對著南方成爲諸侯的領袖了。”

Huángōng shuō: "Guójiā yīn.wèi shén.me yuán.gù hái bú tài.píng .ne?" Guǎn Zhòng huídá
shuō: "Gēn jūnzhǔ guān.xì yuǎn .de rén bùnéng kòng.zhì gēn jūnzhǔ guān.xì jìn .de rén."
Huángōng bǎ tā shēng dào jí gāo .de dì.wèi, zūnchēng tā wéi Zhòngfù, Qíguó jiù biàn .dé
fēicháng tàipíng, zhōngyú chéng.wéi quán tiānxià zhūhóu .de lǐngxiù. Kǒngzǐ shuō: "Píng
Guǎn Zhòng nà.me yǒu cáigàn, yào.shì tā débúdào zhè sānzhǒng quánshì .a, nà.me yě jiù
bùnéng shǐ tā .de jūnzhǔ miànduì .zhe nánfāng chéngwéi zhūhóu .de lǐngxiù .le!"

Duke Huán said: "Why is the state still not peaceful and orderly?" Guǎn Zhòng responded,
saying: "Those distant from the ruler cannot control those close to the ruler." Duke Huán
raised him up to the highest position, and with all due respect called him Uncle Zhòng. Then
the state of Qí became very peaceful and in the end gained control over all the feudal lords on
earth. Confucius said: "Even someone with Guǎn Zhòng's capability, had he been unable to
get these three kinds of power, would, indeed, not have been able to have caused his ruler to
be facing south, acknowledged as the leader of the feudal princes."

第二十七課

知音

說苑 尊賢

伯牙子鼓琴，鍾子期聽之。方鼓而志在太山。鍾子期曰：「善哉乎，鼓琴。巍巍乎若太山。」少選之間，而志在流水。

Zhī Yīn

Shuōyuàn Zūnxián

Bó Yá zǐ gǔ qín, Zhōng Zǐqī tīng zhī. Fāng gǔ ér zhì zài Tài shān. Zhōng Zǐqī yuē: "Shàn zāi hū, gǔ qín. Wēi wēi hū ruò Tài shān." Shǎo xuǎn zhī jiān, ér zhì zài liú shuǐ.

Jy In

Shuoyuann Tzuenshyan

Bor Ya tzyy guu chyn, Jong Tzyychi ting jy. Fang guu erl jyh tzay Tay shan. Jong Tzyychi iue: "Shann zai hu, guu chyn. Uei uei hu ruoh Tay shan." Shao sheuan jy jian, erl jyh tzay liou shoei.

白話翻譯

知音

伯牙先生彈琴，鍾子期聽他彈奏出來的曲子。伯牙先生在彈著琴的時候，心裡想著泰山。鍾子期說："您彈琴彈得真美妙啊！琴聲雄壯肅穆得像泰山一樣。"過了一會儿，伯牙的心思轉到流水那儿去了。

Zhī Yīn

Bó Yá xiānshēng tán qín, Zhōng Zǐqī tīng tā tánzòu chūlái .de qǔ.zi. Bó Yá xiānshēng zài tán .zhe qín .de shíhòu, xīn.lǐ xiǎng .zhe Tàishān. Zhōng Zǐqī shuō: "Nín tánqín tán .dé zhēn měimiào .a! Qínshēng xióngzhuàng sùmù dé xiàng Tàishān yíyàng." Guò .le yìhuǐr, Bó Yá .de xīnsī zhuǎn .dào liúshuǐ nàr .qù .le.

UNDERSTANDING THE MUSIC

Master Bó Yá was playing the lute; Zhōng Zǐqī was listening to the tune he was playing. While playing, Bó Yá's thoughts dwelt on Mount Tai. Zhōng Zǐqī said: " Oh! How superb your lute playing is! The sound of the lute is majestic and solemn like Mount Tài." A moment later, Bó Yá's thoughts turned to flowing waters.

鍾子期復曰：“善哉乎，鼓琴。湯湯乎若流水。”鍾子期死，伯牙破琴，絕絃，終身不復鼓琴，以為世無足為鼓琴者。

Zhōng Zǐqī fù yuē: " Shàn zāi hū, gǔ qín. Shāng shāng hū ruò liú shuǐ." Zhōng Zǐqī sǐ, Bó Yá pò qín, jué xián, zhōng shēn bú fù gǔ qín, yǐ wéi shì wú zú wèi gǔ qín zhě.

Jong Tzyychi fuh iue: " Shann tzai hu, guu chyn. Shang shang hu ruoh liou shoei." Jong Tzyychi syy, Bor Ya poh chyn, jyue shyan, jong shen bu fuh guu chyn, yii wei shyh wu tzwu wey guu chyn jee.

鍾子期又説："您彈琴彈得真美妙啊！琴聲洶湧澎湃得像流水一樣。"鍾子期死了，伯牙把琴摔破，把弦折斷，一輩子再也不彈琴了，他認爲世上再也沒有值得爲他彈琴的人了。

Zhōng Zǐqī yòu shuō: " Nín tánqín tán .dé zhēn měimiào a! Qínshēng xiōngyǒng pēngpài .dé xiàng liúshuǐ yíyàng." Zhōng Zǐqī sǐ .le, Bó Yá bǎ qín shuāi pò, bǎ xián zhé duàn, yíbèi.zi zài .yě bù tánqín .le, tā rèn.wéi shì.shàng zài yě méi.yǒu zhí.dé wèi tā tán qín .de rén .le.

Again Zhōng Zǐqī said: "Oh! How superb your lute playing is! The sound of the lute is surging and crashing like a torrent." After Zhōng Zǐqī died, Bó Yá smashed his lute, snapped the strings, and to the day of his death never again played the lute, for he felt that there was no longer any one in the world worth playing for.

第 二 十 八 課

曾子辭邑

孔子家語 在厄

曾子弊衣而耕於魯，魯君聞之而致邑焉。曾子固辭
不受。或曰：“非子之求，君自致之，奚固辭也？”

Zēng Zǐ Cí Yì

Kǒngzǐjiāyǔ Zàiè

Zēngzǐ bì yī ér gēng yú Lǔ, Lǔ jūn wén zhī ér zhì yì yān. Zēngzǐ gù cí bú shòu. Huò yuē: "Fēi zǐ zhī qiú, jūn zì zhì zhī, xī gù cí yě?"

Tzeng Tzyy Tsyr Yih

Koongtzyyjiayeu Tzayeh

Tzengtzyy bih i erl geng yu Luu, Luu jiun wen jy erl jyh yih ian. Tzengtzyy guh tsyr bu show. Huoh iue: "Fei tzyy jy chyou, jiun tzyh jyh jy, shi guh tsyr yee?"

白話翻譯

曾子辭邑

　　曾子穿著破舊的衣服在魯國耕田，魯國的君主聽到這件事就送給他一塊封地。曾子堅決地推辭不接受。有人說："這不是您乞求的，是國君自動把封地送給您的，您爲什麼要堅決地推辭呢？"

Zēngzǐ Cí Yì

　　Zēngzǐ chuān .zhe pòjiù .de yī.fú zài Lǔ guó gēngtián, Lǔ guó .de jūnzhǔ tīng .dào zhè jiàn shì jiù sòng .gěi tā yíkuài fēngdì.　Zēngzǐ jiānjué .de tuīcí bù jiēshòu.　Yǒu rén shuō: "Zhè bú.shì nín qǐqiú .de, shì guójūn zìdòng bǎ fēngdì sòng .gěi nín .de, nín wèi shén.me yào jiānjué .de tuīcí .ne?"

ZENGZI REFUSES A GRANT OF LAND

　　Zēngzǐ was wearing old, threadbare clothes and tilling his fields in the state of Lǔ. The ruler of the state of Lǔ heard about this matter and bestowed a benefice on him.　Zēngzǐ firmly declined to accept it.　Someone said: "It is not that you sought it; the ruler bestowed it on you of his own volition; why do you so steadfastly decline it?"

曾子曰：“吾聞‘受人施者常畏人，與人者常驕人。
’縱君有賜，不我驕也，吾豈能勿畏乎？”孔子聞之曰
：“參之言足以全其節也。”

Zēngzǐ yuē: "Wú wén 'Shòu rén shī zhě cháng wèi rén, yǔ rén zhě cháng jiāo rén.' Zòng jūn yǒu cì, bù wǒ jiāo yě, wú qǐ néng wù wèi hū?" Kǒngzǐ wén zhī yuē: "Shēn zhī yán zú yǐ quán qí jié yě."

Tzenqtzyy iue: "Wu wen 'Show ren shy jee charng wey ren, yeu ren jee charng jiau ren.' Tzonq jiun yeou tsyh, bu woo jiau yee, wu chii neng wuh wey hu?" Koongtzyy wen jy iue: "Shen jy yan tzwu yii chyuan chyi jye yee."

曾子說：“我聽說：‘接受別人施捨的人常常懼怕施捨的人；送給別人東西的人常常對接受東西的人表現出驕傲的態度。’即使國君有賞賜給我，不對我表現出驕傲的態度；我難道能不怕他嗎？”孔子聽到這件事說：“曾參的話足夠用來保全他的節操啊！”

Zēngzǐ shuō: " Wo tīngshuō: 'Jiēshòu bié.rén shīshě .de rén chángcháng jùpà shīshě .de rén; sòng.gěi bié.rén dōng.xī .de rén chángcháng duì jiēshòu dōng.xī .de rén biǎoxiàn chū jiāoào .de tài.dù.' Jíshǐ guójūn yǒu shǎngcì gěi wǒ, bú duì wǒ biǎoxiàn .chū jiāoào .de tài.dù; wǒ nán.dào néng bú pà tā .ma?" Kǒngzǐ tīng .dào zhè jiàn shì shuō: " Zēng Shēn .de huà zúgòu yòng .lái bǎoquán tā .de jiécāo .a!"

Zēngzǐ said: "I have heard: 'Those who receive a benefaction often fear the benefactor; those who give things to others often treat the recipient with arrogant disdain.' Even if the ruler were to bestow a benefice on me without displaying a haughty attitude, how could I not fear him?" When Confucius heard this, he said: "What Zēng Shēn has said will suffice to preserve his integrity."

第二十九課

孔子猶江海

說苑　善說

　　趙簡子問子貢曰："孔子為人何如？"子貢對曰："賜不能識也。"簡子不說，曰：

Kǒngzǐ Yóu Jiāng Hǎi

Shuōyuàn　Shànshuō

　　Zhào Jiǎnzǐ wèn Zǐgòng yuē : " Kǒngzǐ wéi rén hé rú ?" Zǐgòng duì yuē: " Cì bù néng shì yě." Jiǎnzǐ bú yuè, yuē :

Koongtzyy You Jiang Hae

Shuoyuann　Shannshuo

　　Jaw Jeantzyy wenn Tzyygonq iue : " Koongtzyy wei ren her ru?" Tzyygonq duey iue : " Tsyh bu neng shyh yee." Jeantzyy bu yueh, iue:

白話翻譯

孔子猶江海

　　趙簡子問子貢説：「孔子做人的態度怎麼樣？」子貢回答説：「我不能了解孔子啊。」簡子很不高興，説：

Kǒngzǐ Yóu Jiāng Hǎi

Zhào Jiǎnzǐ wèn Zǐgòng shuō: " Kǒngzǐ zuòrén de tài.dù zěn.méyàng?" Zǐgòng huídá shuō: " Wǒ bùnéng liǎojiě Kǒngzǐ .a." Jiǎnzǐ hěn bù gāoxìng, shuō:

CONFUCIUS IS LIKE A RIVER, LIKE A SEA

Zhào Jiǎnzǐ questioned Zǐgòng, saying: " How does Confucius conduct himself?" Zǐgòng responded, saying: "I cannot fathom Confucius." Jiǎnzǐ, not at all pleased, said:

101

"夫子事孔子數十年，終業而去之；寡人問子，子曰不能識，何也？"子貢曰："賜譬渴者之飲江海，知足而已。孔子猶江海也，賜則奚足以識之？"簡子曰："善哉！子貢之言也。"

"Fūzǐ shì Kǒngzǐ shù shí nián, zhōng yè ér qù zhī; guǎrén wèn zǐ, zǐ yuē bù néng shì, hé yě?" Zǐgòng yuē : "Cì pì kě zhě zhī yǐn jiāng hǎi, zhī zú ér yǐ. Kǒngzǐ yóu jiāng hǎi yě, Cì zé xī zú yǐ shì zhī?" Jiǎnzǐ yuē : " Shàn zāi! Zǐgòng zhī yán yě."

"Futzyy shyh Koongtzyy shuh shyr nian, jong yeh erl chiuh jy; goaren wenn tzyy, tzyy iue bu neng shyh, her yee?" Tzyygonq iue: "Tsyh pih kee jee jy yiin jiang hae, jy tzwu erl yii. Koongtzyy you jiang hae yee, Tsyh tzer shi tzwu yii shyh jy?" Jeantzyy iue: "Shann tzai! Tzyygonq jy yan yee."

"您追隨孔子追隨了幾十年，完成了學業才離開他；我向您問孔子，您說您不能了解他，這是什麼緣故呢？"子貢說："我追隨孔子好比口渴的人在江海邊喝水，覺得夠了就停了。孔子像是江海一樣深廣啊，我卻怎麼夠得上了解他呢？"簡子說："子貢的話，真有道理啊！"

"Nín zhuīsuí Kǒngzǐ zhuīsuí .le jǐ shí nián , wánchéng .le xuéyè cái lí.kāi tā; wǒ xiàng nín wèn Kǒngzǐ, nín shuō nín bùnéng liǎojiě tā, zhè.shì shén.me yuán.gù .ne?" Zǐgòng shuō: "Wǒ zhuīsuí Kǒngzǐ hǎobǐ kǒukě.de rén zài jiāng hǎi biān hē shuǐ, jué.dé gòu .le jiù tíng .le. Kǒngzǐ xiàng.shì jiāng hǎi yíyàng shēnguǎng .a, wǒ què zěn.me gòu.déshàng liǎojiě tā .ne?" Jiǎnzǐ shuō: "Zǐgòng .de huà, zhēn yǒu dào.lǐ .a!"

"You accompanied Confucius for several decades; only when you had completed your studies did you leave him. I asked you about Confucius; you said that you could not fathom him. Why?" Zǐgòng said: "My accompanying Confucius can be likened to a thirsty man drinking at the bank of a river or the shore of a sea: when he has had enough, he stops. Confucius is deep and vast like a river or a sea. However, how could I ever be up to fathoming him?" Jiǎnzǐ said: "What you have said is indeed true!"

第三十課

苛政猛於虎

禮記 檀弓

孔子過泰山側，有婦人哭於墓者而哀。夫子式而聽之。使子路問之曰：“子之哭也，壹似重有憂者。”

Kē Zhèng Měng Yú Hǔ

Lǐjì Tángōng

Kǒngzǐ guò Tài shān cè, yǒu fù rén kū yú mù zhě ér āi. Fū zǐ shì ér tīng zhī. Shǐ Zǐlù wèn zhī yuē: "Zǐ zhī kū yě, yí sì chóng yǒu yōu zhě."

Ke Jenq Meeng Yu Huu

Liijih Tarngong

Koongtzyy guoh Tay shan tseh, yeou fuh ren ku yu muh jee erl ai. Fu tzyy shyh erl ting jy. Shyy Tzyyluh wenn jy iue: "Tzyy jy ku yee, yi syh chorng yeou iou jee."

白語翻譯

苛政猛於虎

　　有一次孔子乘車經過泰山旁邊的時候，遇見一個在墳前哭的婦人而且她哭得很悲痛。孔子扶著軾聽她哭，派子路去問她說：「您那麼痛哭啊，實在像是遭遇過好幾次傷心事的樣子。」

Kē Zhèng Méng Yú Hǔ

Yǒu yí cì Kǒngzǐ chéng chē jīng.guò Tàishān páng.biān .de shíhòu, yù.jiàn yí.gè zài fén qián kū .de fùrén érqiě tā kū .dé hěn bēitòng. Kǒngzǐ fú .zhe shì tīng tā kū, pài Zǐlù qù wèn tā, shuō: "Nín nà.mé tòngkū .a, shí.zài xiàng .shì zāoyù .guò hǎo.jǐ cì shāngxīn shì .de yàng.zǐ."

OPPRESSIVE GOVERNMENT IS MORE FEARSOME THAN A TIGER

Once when Confucius was passing along side Mount Tài in a carriage, he came upon a married woman weeping at a grave mound, and weeping dolorously. Confucius rested his hands on the front rail of the carriage and listened to her weeping, and then he sent Zǐlù to question her by saying: "From the way you are crying, it truly seems as though you have repeatedly encountered misfortune."

而曰：“然。昔者吾舅死於虎，吾夫又死焉，今吾子又死焉。”夫子曰：“何為不去也？”曰：“無苛政。”夫子曰：“小子識之，苛政猛於虎也。”

Eŕ yuē: "Rán. Xī zhě wú jiù sǐ yú hǔ, wú fū yòu sǐ yān, jīn wú zǐ yòu sǐ yān." Fū zǐ yuē: "Hé wèi bú qù yě?" Yuē: "Wú kē zhèng." Fū zǐ yuē: "Xiǎo zǐ zhì zhī, kē zhèng měng yú hǔ yě."

Erl iue: "Ran. Shi jee wu jiow syy yu huu, wu fu yow syy ian, jin wu tzyy yow syy ian." Fu tzyy iue: "Her wey bu chiuh yee?" Iue: "Wu ke jenq." Fu tzyy iue: "Sheau tzyy jyh jy, ke jenq meeng yu huu yee."

那個婦人聽了就說："您說的很對。從前我的公公被老虎咬死了，後來我的丈夫又被老虎咬死了，現在我的兒子又被老虎咬死了。"孔子說："你為什麼不離開這兒呢？"婦人說："這兒沒有暴虐的政治。"孔子說："弟子們記住這句話，暴虐的政治比老虎更凶猛可怕啊。"

Nèi.gè fùrén tīng .le jiù shuō: "Nín shuō .de hěn duì. Cóngqián wǒ .de gōng.gōng bèi lǎo.hǔ yǎo sǐ .le, hòu.lái wǒ .de zhàng.fū yòu bèi lǎo.hǔ yǎo sǐ .le, xiàn.zài wǒ .de ér.zǐ yòu bèi lǎo.hǔ yǎo sǐ .le." Kǒngzǐ shuō: "Nǐ wèi shén.me bù líkāi zhèr .ne?" Fùrén shuō: "Zhèr méi.yǒu bàonüè .de zhèngzhì." Kǒngzǐ shuō: "Dìzǐ.mén jìzhù zhèi jù huà, bàonüè .de zhèngzhì bǐ lǎo.hǔ gèng xiōngměng kěpà .a."

The woman then said: "You are right. Before this, my father-in-law was bitten to death by a tiger; later, my husband was also bitten to death by a tiger; now, my son has also been bitten to death by a tiger." The master said, "Why do you not leave?" The woman said: "There is no tyrannical government here." The master said, "Young men, take note of this: tyrannical government is more ferocious and fearsome than even a tiger."

第三十一課

曳尾於塗中

莊子 秋水

莊子釣於濮水，楚王使大夫二人往先焉，曰：“願以竟內累矣。”莊子持竿不顧，曰：

Yè Wěi Yú Tú Zhōng

Zhuāngzǐ Qiūshuǐ

Zhuāngzǐ diào yú Pú shǔi, Chǔwáng shǐ dài fū èr rén wǎng xiān yān, yuē: "Yuàn yǐ jìng nèi lèi yǐ." Zhuāngzǐ chí gān bú gù, yuē:

Yeh Woei Yu Twu Jong

Juangtzyy Chioushoei

Juangtzyy diaw yu Pwu shoei, Chuuwang shyy day fu ell ren woang shian ian, iue: "Yuann yii jinq ney ley yii." Juangtzyy chyr gan bu guh, iue:

白話翻譯

曳尾於塗中

　　莊子在濮水邊釣魚，楚王派遣兩位大夫到濮水那儿去先去見莊子說明他的願望，兩位大夫說：“楚王希望請您到楚國來做宰相，管理全國的政事。”莊子拿著釣魚竿不回頭看，說：

Yè Wěi Yú Tú Zhōng

　　Zhuāngzǐ zài Púshuǐ biān diào yú, Chǔwáng pàiqiǎn liǎngwèi dàifū dào Púshuǐ nàr qù xiān qù jiàn Zhuāngzǐ shuōmíng tā .de yuànwàng, liǎngwèi dàifū shuō: "Chǔwáng xīwàng qǐng nín dào Chǔguó lái zuò zǎixiàng, guǎnlǐ quán guó .de zhèngshì." Zhuāngzǐ ná .zhe diàoyúgān bù huítóu kàn, shuō:

DRAGGING HIS TAIL THROUGH THE MUD

Zhuāngzǐ was fishing by the Pú River. The king of Chǔ sent two high officials to go there first to see Zhuāngzǐ and to make the king's wishes known. The two high officials said: "The king of Chǔ has now expressed a desire to invite you to Chǔ as prime minister to supervise the administration of the whole kingdom." Zhuāngzǐ, holding his fishing pole and not turning round to look at them, said:

"吾聞楚有神龜，死已三千歲矣，王巾笥而藏之廟堂之上。此龜者寧其死為留骨而貴乎，寧其生而曳尾於塗中乎？"二大夫曰："寧生而曳尾塗中。"莊子曰："往矣，吾將曳尾於塗中。"

"Wú wén Chǔ yǒu shén guī, sǐ yǐ sān qiān suì yǐ, wáng jīn sì ér cáng zhī miào táng zhī shàng. Cǐ guī zhě nìng qí sǐ wèi liú gǔ ér guì hū, nìng qí shēng ér yè wěi yú tú zhōng hū?" Èr dài fū yuē: "Nìng shēng ér yè wěi tú zhōng." Zhuāngzǐ yuē: "Wǎng yǐ, wú jiāng yè wěi yú tú zhōng."

"Wu wen Chuu yeou shern guei, syy yii san chian suey yii, wang jin syh erl tsarng jy miaw tarng jy shanq. Tsyy guei jee ninq chyi syy wey liou guu erl guey hu, ninq chyi sheng erl yeh woei yu twu jong hu?" Ell day fu iue: "Ninq sheng erl yeh woei twu jong." Juangtzyy iue: "Woang yii, wu jiang yeh woei yu twu jong."

"我聽說楚國有隻靈驗的烏龜，死了巳經三千年了，楚王用手巾包著放在竹簍裡地把牠珍藏在宗廟大堂的裡面。這隻烏龜啊，寧願牠自己爲了留下背骨受重視死掉呢，還是寧願牠自己活著在泥裡拖著尾巴爬呢？"兩位大夫説："牠寧願活著在泥裡拖著尾巴爬。"莊子説："你們走吧，我要在泥裡拖著尾巴爬。"

"Wǒ tīngshuō Chǔguó yǒu zhī língyàn .de wūguī, sǐ .le yǐ.jīng sān qiān nián .le, Chǔwáng yòng shǒujīn bāo .zhe fàng zài zhúlǒu.lǐ de bǎ tā zhēn cáng zài zōngmiào dàtáng .de lǐ.miàn. Zhèi zhī wūguī .a, nìngyuàn tā zìjǐ wèi .le liú.xià bèigǔ shòu zhòngshì sǐdiào .ne, hái.shì nìngyuàn tā zìjǐ huó.zhe zài ní.lǐ tuō .zhe wěibā pá .ne?" Liǎng wèi dàifū shuō: "Tā nìngyuàn huó .zhe zài nì.lǐ tuō .zhe wěi.bā pá." Zhuāngzǐ shuō: "Nǐmén zǒu .ba, wǒ yào zài ní.lǐ tuō .zhe wěi.bā pá."

"I have heard that the state of Chǔ has a divine tortoise that must have died more than three millenia ago; the king wrapped it in a piece of cloth, put it in a rectangular bamboo basket, and treasured it in the hall of the ancestral temple. Now this tortoise, would it rather die in order to be an honored empty shell, or would it rather be alive and crawling, dragging its tail through the mud?" The two high officials said: "The tortoise would rather be alive and crawling, dragging its tail through the mud." Zhuāngzǐ said: "Leave! I am going to drag my tail through the mud."

111

第三十二課

塞翁失馬

淮南子 人間

　　近塞上之人有善術者，馬無故亡而入胡，人皆弔之。其父曰：“此何遽不能為福乎？”居數月，其馬將胡駿馬而歸，人皆賀之。

Sài Wēng Shī Mǎ

Huáinánzǐ Rénjiān

　　Jìn sài shàng zhī rén yǒu shàn shù zhě, mǎ wú gù wáng ér rù hú, rén jiē diào zhī. Qí fù yuē: "Cǐ hé jù bù néng wéi fú hū?" Jū shù yuè, qí mǎ jiāng hú jùn mǎ ér guī, rén jiē hè zhī.

Say Ueng Shy Maa

Hwainantzyy Renjian

　　Jinn say shanq jy ren yeou shann shuh jee, maa wu guh wang erl ruh hwu, ren jie diaw jy. Chyi fuh iue: "Tsyy her jiuh bu neng wei fwu hu?" Jiu shuh yueh, chyi maa jiang hwu jiunn maa erl guei, ren jie heh jy.

白話翻譯

塞翁失馬

　　靠近邊界上的人裡有個很會占卜的人，他的馬無緣無故地逃跑進胡人的領土去了，別人都來慰問他。他的父親說：「這件事怎麼就不能變成福呢？」過了幾個月，他的馬帶著胡人的好馬回來了，別人都來向他道賀。

Sài Wēng Shī Mǎ

　　Kàojìn biānjiè .shàng .de rén.lǐ yǒu .gè hěn huì zhānbǔ .de rén, tā .de mǎ wúyuán wúgù .de táopǎo jìn húrén .de lǐngtǔ qù .le, bié rén dōu lái wèiwèn tā. Tā .de fù.qīn shuō: "Zhèi jiàn shì zěn.me jiù bùnéng biànchéng fú .ne?" Guò .le jǐ .gè yuè, tā .de mǎ dài .zhe húrén .de hǎo mǎ huí.lái .le, bié rén dōu lái xiàng tā dàohè.

THE OLD MAN AT THE FRONTIER LOSES HIS HORSE

Among the people near the frontier, there was one skilled at prognostication. For no reason, his horse ran off into the territory of the northern barbarians; the other people all consoled him. His father said: "As for this, why then can't it become good fortune?" After several months had passed, his horse returned leading some fine barbarian horses; the other people all congratulated him.

其父曰：「此何遽不能為禍乎？」家富良馬，其子好騎，墮而折其髀，人皆弔之。其父曰：「此何遽不能為福乎？」居一年，胡人大舉入塞，丁壯者引弦而戰。

Qí fù yuē: "Cǐ hé jù bù néng wéi huò hū?" Jiā fù liáng mǎ, qí zǐ hào qí, duò ér zhé qí bì, rén jiē diào zhī. Qí fù yuē: "Cǐ hé jù bù néng wéi fú hū?" Jū yì nián, hú rén dà jǔ rù sài, dīng zhuàng zhě yǐn xián ér zhàn.

Chyi fuh iue: "Tsyy her jiuh bu neng wei huoh hu?" Jia fuh liang maa, chyi tzyy haw chyi, duoh erl jer chyi bih, ren jie diaw jy. Chyi fuh iue: "Tsyy her jiuh buh neng wei fwu hu?" Jiu i nian, hwu ren dah jeu ruh say, ding juanq jee yiin shyan erl jann.

他的父親說：＂這件事怎麼就不能變成災禍呢？＂家裡有
很多好馬，他的兒子喜歡騎馬，從馬上摔下來，摔斷了他的
胯骨，別人都來慰問他。他的父親說：＂這件事怎麼就不能
變成福呢？＂過了一年，胡人大規模地發動軍隊侵入邊界，
成年的男人都拿起弓去打仗。

Tā .de fù.qīn shuō: "Zhèi jiàn shì zěn.me jiù bùnéng biànchéng zāihuò .ne?" Jiā.lǐ yǒu hěn
duō hǎo mǎ, tā .de ér.zǐ xǐ.huān qí mǎ, cóng mǎ.shàng shuāi .xiàlái, shuāiduàn .le tā .de
kuàgǔ, bié rén dōu lái wèiwèn tā. Tā .de fù.qīn shuō: "Zhèi .jiàn shì zěn.me jiù bùnéng
biànchéng fú .ne?" Guò .le yì nián, húrén dà guīmó .de fādòng jūnduì qīn rù biānjiè,
chéngnián .de nánrén dōu ná .qǐ gōng qù dǎzhàng.

His father said: "As for this, why can't it become misfortune?" There were many good
horses in the household: his son liked to ride, fell off a horse, and broke his thighbone; the
other people all consoled him. His father said: "As for this, why can't it become good
fortune?" After a year, the barbarians mobilized on a large scale and entered the frontier; all
the adult males took up their bows to do battle.

近塞之人，死者十九，此獨以跛之故，父子相保。故福
之為禍，禍之為福，化不可極，深不可測也。

Jìn sài zhī rén, sǐ zhě shí jiǔ, cǐ dú yǐ bǒ zhī gù, fù zǐ xiāng bǎo. Gù fú zhī wéi huò, huò zhī wéi fū, huà bù kě jí, shēn bù kě cè yě.

Jinn say jy ren, syy jee shyr jeou, tsyy dwu yii boo jy guh, fuh tzyy shiang bao. Guh fwu jy wei huoh, huoh jy wei fwu, huah bu kee jyi, shen bu kee tseh yee.

靠近邊界的人，死掉的有十分之九，只有這家人因為兒子瘸了的緣故，父子還能平安地活在一塊儿。所以福變成禍，禍變成福，變化得不能推究到盡頭，深得不能測量啊。

Kàojìn biānjie .de rén sǐdiào .de yǒu shífēn zhī jiǔ, zhǐ yǒu zhèi jiā rén yīn.wèi ér.zǐ qué.le .de yuángù, fù zǐ hái néng píngān .de huó zài yíkuàir. Suǒ.yǐ fú biàn .chéng huò, huò biàn .chéng fú, biànhuà .dé bùnéng tuījiù dào jìntóu, shēn .dé bùnéng cèliáng .a.

Of the people near the frontier, nine out of ten died. Because of the son's being lame, in this family alone were father and son still together safe and sound. Thus, as to how fortune becomes misfortune and how misfortune becomes fortune, the ultimate ending of this transformation is unascertainable; it is of unfathomable depth.

第三十三課

齒亡舌存

說苑 敬慎

常摐有疾，老子往問焉，曰："先生疾甚矣，無遺教可以語諸弟子者乎？"常摐曰："子雖不問，吾將語子。"常摐曰："過故鄉而下車，子知之乎？"

Chǐ Wáng Shé Cún

Shuōyuàn Jìngshèn

Cháng Chuāng yǒu jí, Lǎozǐ wǎng wèn yān, yuē: "Xiān shēng jí shèn yǐ, wú yí jiào kě yǐ yù zhū dì zǐ zhě hū?" Cháng Chuāng yuē: "Zǐ suí bú wèn, wú jiāng yù zǐ." Cháng Chuāng yuē: "Guò gù xiāng ér xià chē (jū), zǐ zhī zhī hū?"

Chyy Wang Sher Tswen

Shuoyuann Jinqshenn

Charng Chuang yeou jyi, Laotzyy woang wenn ian, iue: "Shian sheng jyi shenn yii, wu yi jiaw kee yii yuh ju dih tzyy jee hu?" Charng Chuang iue: "Tzyy swei bu wenn, wu jiang yuh tzyy." Charng Chuang iue: "Guoh guh shiang erl shiah che (jiu), tzyy jy jy hu?"

白話翻譯

齒亡舌存

　　常摐生病了，老子到他那儿去問候他，說："先生病得很重了，您沒有什麼可以告訴給弟子的遺教嗎？"常摐說："即使你不問，我也打算告訴你。"常摐說："人經過故鄉就下車，你知道這樣做的緣故嗎？"

Chǐ Wáng Shē Cún

　　Cháng Chuāng shēng bìng .le, Lǎozǐ dào tā nàr qù wènhòu tā, shuō: "Xiānshēng bìng .dé hěn zhòng .le, nín méi.yǒu shén.me kě.yǐ gào.sù gěi dìzǐ de yíjiào ma?" Cháng Chuāng shuō: "Jíshǐ nǐ bú wèn, wǒ yě dǎ.suàn gào.sù nǐ." Cháng Chuāng shuō: "Rén jīngguò gùxiāng jiù xiàchē, nǐ zhī.dào zhè.yàng zuò .de yuán.gù ma?"

SOFT AND WEAK OVERCOMES HARD AND STRONG

　　Cháng Chuāng fell ill. Lǎozǐ went to him to inquire after him. He said: "Master, you must be very sick now. Do you not have some teaching to pass on that can be told to your disciple?" Cháng Chuāng said: "Even if you did not ask, I was going to tell you." Cháng Chuāng said: "When people pass their ancestral village, they dismount from their chariots; do you know the reason for it?"

老子曰：“過故鄉而下車，非謂其不忘故耶？”常摐曰：“嘻！是已。”常摐曰：“過喬木而趨，子知之乎？”老子曰：“過喬木而趨，非謂敬老耶？”常摐曰：“嘻！是已。”

Lǎozǐ yuē: "Guò gù xiāng ér xià chē (jū), fēi wèi qí bú wàng gù yé?" Cháng Chuāng yuē: "Xī! shì yǐ." Cháng Chuāng yuē: "Guò qiáo mù ér qū, zǐ zhī zhī hū?" Lāozǐ yuē: "Guò qiáo mù ér qū, fēi wèi jìng lǎo yé?" Cháng Chuāng yuē: "Xī! shì yǐ."

Laotzyy iue: "Guoh guh shiang erl shiah che (jiu), fei wey chyi bu wanq guh ye?" Charng Chuang iue: "Shi! shyh yii." Charng Chuang iue: "Guoh chyau muh erl chiu, tzyy jy jy hu?" Laotzyy iue: "Guoh chyau muh erl chiu, fei wey jinq lao ye?" Charng Chuang iue: "Shi! shyh yii."

老子説：“過故鄉就下車，不是説一個人不忘故舊嗎？”
常摐説：“啊！對啦。”常摐説：“人經過大樹就邁著小步
快快地走過去，你知道這樣做的緣故嗎？”老子説：“經過
大樹就邁著小步快快地走過去，不是説敬老嗎？”常摐説：
“啊！對啦。”

Lǎozǐ shuō: "Guò gùxiāng jiù xiàchē, búshì shuō yí.gè rén búwàng gùjiù .ma?" Cháng Chuāng shuō: "Á! duì.la." Cháng Chuāng shuō: "Rén Jīng.guò dàshù jiù mài.zhē xiǎobù kuàikuài .de zǒu guò .qù, nǐ zhī.dào zhè.yàng zuò .de yuán.gù .ma?" Lǎozǐ shuō: "Jīng.guò dàshù jiù mài.zhē xiǎobù kuàikuài .de zǒu guò .qù, búshì shuō jìng lǎo .ma?" Cháng Chuāng shuō: "Á! duì .la."

Lǎozǐ said: "To dismount from the chariot when passing by one's ancestral village, is this not to say one does not forget one's origins?" Cháng Chuāng said, "Yes it is, indeed!" Cháng Chuāng said, "When passing a mighty tree, one walks by hurriedly with small steps; do you know the reason why?" Lǎozǐ said: "To pass by a mighty old tree one walks by hurriedly with small steps, is that not to say one pays respect to what is aged?" Cháng Chuāng said, "Yes it is, indeed!"

張其口而示老子曰：“吾舌存乎？”老子曰：“然。”
“吾齒存乎？”老子曰：“亡。”常摐曰：“子知之乎
？”老子曰：“夫舌之存也，豈非以其柔耶？齒之亡也
，豈非以其剛耶？”常摐曰：“嘻！是已。天下之事已
盡矣，無以復語子哉！”

Zhāng qí kǒu ér shì Lǎozǐ yuē: "Wú shé cún hū?" Lǎozǐ yuē: "Rán." "Wú chǐ cún hū?"
Lǎozǐ yuē: "Wáng." Cháng Chuāng yuē: "Zǐ zhī zhī hū?" Lǎozǐ yuē: "Fú shé zhī cún yě, qǐ
fēi yǐ qí róu yé? Chǐ zhī wáng yě, qǐ fēi yǐ qí gāng yé?" Cháng Chuāng yuē: "Xī! Shì yǐ.
Tiān xià zhī shì yǐ jìn yǐ, wú yǐ fù yù zǐ zāi!"

Jang chyi koou erl shyh Laotzyy iue: "Wu sher tswen hu?" Laotzyy iue: "Ran." "Wu chyy
tswen hu?" Laotzyy iue: "Wang." Charng Chuang iue: "Tzyy jy jy hu?" Laotzyy iue:
"Fwu sher jy tswen yee, chii fei yii chyi rou ye? Chyy jy wang yee, chii fei yii chyi gang
ye?" Charng Chuang iue: "Shi! Shyh yii. Tian shiah jy shyh yii jinn yii, wu yii fuh yuh
tzyy tzai!"

常摐張開他的嘴來給老子看，説："我的舌頭還在嗎？"老子説："在。" "我的牙齒還在嗎？"老子説："沒有了。" 常摐説："你知道這樣子的緣故嗎？"老子説："舌頭還在，難道不是因爲它柔軟嗎？牙齒沒有了，難道不是因爲它堅硬嗎？"常摐説："啊！對啦。天下的事理人情已經全都包含在內了，我沒有甚麼拿來再告訴你的話啦！"

Cháng Chuāng zhāng .kāi tā .dē zuǐ lái gěi Lǎozǐ kàn, shuō: "Wǒ .de shé.tóu hái zài .ma?" Lǎozǐ shuō: "Zài." "Wǒ .de yá.chǐ hái zài .ma?" Lǎozǐ shuō: "Méi yǒu le." Cháng Chuāng shuō: "Nǐ zhī.dào zhè yàng.zǐ .de yuán.gù .ma?" Lǎozǐ shuō: "Shé.tóu hái zài, nán.dào búshì yīnwèi tā róuruǎn .ma? Yá.chǐ méi yǒu le, nán.dào búshì yīn.wèi tā jiānyìng .ma?" Cháng Chuāng shuō: "Á! Duì la. Tiānxià .de shìlǐ rénqíng yǐjīng quándōu bāohán zài nèi .le, wǒ méi.yǒu shén.me kě.yì ná .lái zài gào.sù nǐ .de huà .lā!"

Cháng Chuāng opened his mouth and showed the inside to Lǎozǐ, saying: "Does my tongue still exist?" Lǎozǐ said: "Yes, it does." Cháng Chuāng said: "Do my teeth still exist?" Lǎozǐ said: "They don't exist any more." Cháng Chuāng said: "Do you know why this is?" Lǎozǐ said: "Now, the tongue's still existing, is it not because it is soft? As for not having the teeth, is it not because they are hard?" Cháng Chuāng said: "Yes it is, indeed! All the principles of human relations in the world have already been encapsulated in this understanding; I have nothing more to say to you!"

第三十四課

晏子與楚王論盜

晏子春秋 內篇 雜下

晏子將使楚。楚王聞之，謂左右曰："晏嬰齊之習
辭者也。今方來，吾欲辱之，何以也？"

Yànzǐ Yǔ Chǔ Wáng Lùn Dào

Yànzǐ-Chūnqiū Nèipiān Záxià

Yànzǐ jiāng shì Chǔ, Chǔwáng wén zhī, wèi zuǒ yòu yuē: "Yàn Yīng Qí zhī xí cí zhě yě. Jīn fāng lái, wú yù rù (rǔ) zhī, hé yǐ yě?"

Yanntzyy Yeu Chuu Wang Luenn Daw

Yanntzyy-Chuenchiou Neypian Tzarshiah

Yanntzyy jiang shyh Chuu, Chuuwang wen jy, wey tzuoo yow iue: "Yann Ing Chyi jy shyi tsyr jee yee. Jin fang lai, wu yuh ruh (ruu) jy, her yii yee?"

白話翻譯

晏子與楚王論盜

晏子將要出使到楚國去。楚王聽到這個消息，對侍從們說：“晏嬰是齊國嫻習辭令的人。現在他快要來了，我想要羞辱他，我應該用什麼法子呢？”

Yànzǐ Yǔ Chǔ Wáng Lùn Dào

Yànzǐ jiāngyào chūshǐ dào Chǔguó qù. Chǔwáng tīngdào zhèi.gè xiāo.xí, duì shìcóng.mén shuō: "Yàn Yīng shì Qíguó xiánxí cílìng .de rén. Xiàn.zài tā kuàiyào lái .le, wǒ xiǎng yào xiūrù tā, wǒ yīnggāi yòng shén.me fá.zǐ .ne?"

YANZI AND THE KING OF CHU DISCUSS ROBBING

Yànzǐ was about to go to the state of Chǔ as an envoy. When the king of Chǔ heard this news, he spoke to his retainers saying: "Yàn Yīng is a man of the state of Qí accomplished in rhetoric. Now he is about to come; I want to humiliate him: what means should I employ to do this?"

左右對曰：“為其來也，臣請縛一人，過王而行。王曰：‘何為者也？’對曰：‘齊人也。’王曰：‘何坐？’曰：‘坐盜。’”晏子至，楚王賜晏子酒。酒酣，吏二人縛一人詣王。

Zuǒ yòu duì yuē: "Wèi qí lái yě, chén qǐng fù yì rén, guō wáng ér xíng. Wáng yuē: 'Hé wéi zhě yě?' Duì yuē: 'Qí rén yě.' Wáng yuē: 'Hé zuò?' Yuē: 'Zuò dào.'" Yànzǐ zhì, Chǔwáng cì Yànzǐ jiǔ. Jiǔ hān, lì èr rén fù yì rén yì wáng.

Tzuoo yow duey iue: "Wey chyi lai yee, chern chiing fuh yih ren, guo wang erl shyng. Wang iue: 'Her wei jee yee?' Duey iue: 'Chyi ren yee.' Wang iue: 'Her tzuoh?' Iue: 'Tzuoh daw.'" Yanntzyy jyh, Chuuwang tsyh Yanntzyy jeou. Jeou han, lih ell ren fuh yih ren yih wang.

一個侍從回答説："當他來的時候啊，請大王讓我捆綁一個人，從您面前走過。您説："這個人是幹什麼的啊？'我就回答您説："這個人是齊國人。'您説："他犯了什麼罪？'我説"他犯了偷東西的罪。'"晏子到了，楚王擺酒招待晏子。在他們喝酒喝到很暢快的時候，兩個小官儿捆著一個人到楚王面前來了。

---

yígè shìcóng huídá shuō: "Dāng tā lāi .de shí.hòu .a, qǐng dàwáng ràng wǒ kǔnbǎng yí.gè rén, cóng nín miàn .qián zǒu guò. Nín shuō: 'Zhèi.gè rén shì gàn shén.me .de .a?' Wǒ jiù huídá nín shuō: 'Zhèi.gè rén shì Qí guó rén.' Nín shuō: 'Tā fàn .le shén.me zuì?' Wǒ shuō: 'Tā fàn .le tōu dōng.xī .de zuì.'" Yànzǐ dào .le, Chǔwáng bǎi jiǔ zhāodài Yànzǐ. Zài tā.mén hē jiǔ hē dào hěn chàngkuài .de shí.hòu, liǎng.gè xiǎo guānr kǔn .zhe yí.gè rén dào Chǔwáng miàn .qián lái .le.

One of his attendants responded saying: "When he comes, please let me have a man tied up and have him walk past you. You will say: 'What is this person doing?' I will respond saying: 'This is a person from the state of of Qí.' You will say: 'What is he charged with?' I will say: 'He is charged with robbery.'" Yànzǐ arrived. The king of Chǔ laid out a banquet to entertain him. When they had drunk to their hearts' content, two minor officials tied up a man and brought him before the king of Chǔ.

王曰：“縛者曷為者也？”對曰：“齊人也，坐盜。”
王視晏子曰：“齊人固善盜乎？”晏子避席對曰：“嬰
聞之，橘生於淮南則為橘；生於淮北則為枳。

Wáng yuē: "Fù zhě hé wéi zhě yě ?" Duì yuē: "Qí rén yě, zuò dào." Wáng shì Yànzǐ yuē: "Qí rēn gù shàn dào hū ?" Yànzǐ bì xí duì yuē: "Yīng wén zhī, jú shēng yú Huái nán zé wéi jú; shēng yú Huái běi zé wéi zhǐ.

Wang iue: "Fuh jee her wei jee yee?" Duey iue: "Chyi ren yee, tzuoh daw." Wang shyh Yanntzyy iue: "Chyi ren guh shann daw hu?" Yanntzyy bih shyi duey iue: "Ing wen jy, jyu sheng yu Hwai nan tzer wei jyu; sheng yu Hwai beei tzer wei jyy.

楚王説：“捆著的人是幹什麼的啊？”兩個小官兒回答説：“這個人是齊國人，犯了偷東西的罪。”楚王看著晏子説：“齊國人本來就很善於偷東西嗎？”晏子離開了座位回答説：“我聽説，橘樹如果生長在淮河以南，就是橘樹；如果生長在淮河以北，就變成枳樹了。”

Chǔwáng shuō: "Kǔn .zhe .de rén shì gàn shén.me .de .a?" Liǎng .gè xiǎoguānr huídá shuō: "Zhèi.gè rén shì Qí guó rén, fàn .le tōu dōng.xī .de zuì." Chǔwáng kàn .zhe Yànzǐ shuō: "Qí guó rén běnlái jiù hěn shàn yú tōu dōng.xī .ma?" Yànzǐ líkāi .le zuòwèi huídá shuō: "Wǒ tīngshuō, júshù rúguǒ shēngzhǎng zài Huáihé yǐ nán, jiù shì júshù; rúguǒ shēngzhǎng zài Huáihé yǐ běi, jiù biàn chéng zhǐshù .le."

The king said: "What is the bound man doing?" The two minor officials responded, saying: "This is a man from the state of Qí who is charged with robbery." The king of Chǔ, looking at Yànzǐ, said: "Are the people of the state of Qí innately skilled at robbing?" Yànzǐ left his seat and responded saying: "I have heard that if the mandarin orange tree grows south of the Huái River, then it becomes a mandarin orange tree; if it grows north of the Huái River, then it becomes a citron tree.

葉徒相似，其實味不同。所以然者何？水土異也。今民生長於齊不盜，入楚則盜，得無楚之水土使民善盜耶？"

Yè tú xiāng sì, qí shí wèi bù tóng. Suǒ yǐ rán zhě hé? Shuǐ tǔ yì yě. Jīn mín shēng zhǎng yú Qí bù dào, rù Chǔ zé dào, dé wú Chǔ zhī shuǐ tǔ shǐ mín shàn dào yé?"

Yeh twu shiang syh, chyi shyr wey bu torng. Suoo yii ran jee her? Shoei tuu yih yee. Jin min sheng jaang yu Chyi bu daw, ruh Chuu tzer daw, der wu Chuu jy shoei tuu shyy min shann daw ye?"

兩種樹的葉子白白相像，它們的果實味道不同。橘子變成枳
子的緣故是什麼？這是因爲淮南淮北的水土不同啊。現在人
民生長在齊國不偷東西，到了楚國卻偷東西了，大概是楚國
的環境使人民特別會偷東西吧？"

Liǎng zhǒng shù .de yè.zǐ báibái xiāngxiàng, tāmén .de guǒshí wèidào bùtóng. Jú.zǐ biàn chéng zhǐ.zǐ .de yuán.gù shì shén.me? Zhè shì yīnwèi Huái nán Huái běi .de shuǐ tǔ bùtóng .a. Xiànzài rénmín shēngzhǎng zài Qíguó bù tōu dōng.xī, dào .le Chǔguó què tōu dōng.xī .le, dàgài shì Chǔguó .de huán.jìng shǐ rénmín tèbié huì tōu dōng.xī .ba?"

Their leaves uselessly resemble each other, for their fruits do not taste the same. Why do mandarin oranges become citrons? Because in south of the Huái River and north of the Huái the water and soil are different. At present, people who grow up in the state of Qí do not rob; after they have entered the state of Chǔ though, then they begin to rob. Probably it is the environment of the state of Chǔ that causes people to be particularly skilled at robbing, isn't it?"

第三十五課

彌子瑕

韓非子 說難

　　昔者彌子瑕有寵於衛君。衛國之法：竊駕君車者，罪刖。彌子瑕母病，人聞，有夜告彌子。彌子矯駕君車以出。

Mí Zǐxiá

Hánfēizǐ Shuìnán

Xī zhě Mí Zǐxiá yǒu chǒng yú Wèi jūn. Wèi guó zhī fǎ: qiè jià jūn chē (jū) zhě, zuì yuè. Mí Zǐxiá mǔ bìng, rén wén, yǒu yè gào Mízǐ. Mízǐ jiǎo jià jūn chē (jū) yǐ chū.

Mi Tzyyshya

Harnfeitzyy Shueynan

Shi jee Mi Tzyyshya yeou choong yu Wey jiun. Wey gwo jy faa: chieh jiah jiun che (jiu) jee, tzuey yueh. Mi Tzyyshya muu binq, ren wen, yeou yeh gaw Mitzyy. Mitzyy jeau jiah jiun che (jiu) yii chu.

白話翻譯

彌子瑕

　　從前彌子瑕很受衛國君主的寵愛。衛國的法律是：偷著駕駛君主車子的人，他的刑罰是砍斷腳。彌子瑕母親病了，別人聽到了這個消息，有人在夜裡告訴彌子。彌子騙人說是君主命令地駕著君主的車子從宮裡出去了。

Mí Zǐxiá

Cóngqián Mí Zǐxiá hěn shòu Wèi guó jūnzhǔ .de chǒngài.　Wèi guó .de fǎlǜ shì: tōu.zhe jiàshǐ jūnzhǔ chē.zǐ .de rén, tā .de xíngfá shì kǎnduàn jiǎo. Mí Zǐxiá mǔqīn bìng .le, biérén tīng.dào .le zhèi.gè xiāoxí, yǒurén zài yè.lǐ gào.sù Mízǐ. Mízǐ piànrén shuō shì jūnzhǔ mìng.lìng .de jià .zhe jūnzhǔ .de chē.zǐ cóng gōng.lǐ chū.qù .le.

Mi Zixia

Once, Mí Zǐxiá was well-loved by the ruler of the state of Wèi. According to the laws of Wèi, whosoever drives the ruler's carriage illicitly shall be punished by having one foot cut off. Mí Zǐxiá's mother became ill; someone who had heard the news told Mí Zǐxiá during the night. Having feigned permission to drive the ruler's carriage, Mí Zǐxiá left the palace.

君聞而賢之曰：「孝哉！為母之故，忘其犯刖罪。」
　異日與君遊於果園。食桃而甘，不盡，以半啗君。
君曰：「愛我哉！忘其口味，以啗寡人。」及彌子瑕色衰
，愛弛，得罪於君。

Jūn wén ér xián zhī yuē: "Xiào zāi! Wèi mǔ zhī gù, wàng qí fàn yuè zuì."
　Yì rì yǔ jūn yóu yú guǒ yuán. Shí táo ér gān, bú jìn, yǐ bàn dàn jūn. Jūn yuē: "Ài wǒ zāi! Wàng qí kǒu wèi, yǐ dàn guǎ rén." Jí Mí Zǐxiá sè shuāi, ài chí, dé zuì yú jūn.

Jiun wen erl shyan jy iue: "Shiaw tzai! Wey muu jy guh, wanq chyi fann yueh tzuey."
　Yih ryh yeu jiun you yu guoo yuan. Shyr taur erl gan, bu jinn, yii bann dann jiun. Jiun iue: "Ay woo tzai! Wanq chyi koou wei, yii dann goa ren." Jyi Mi Tzyyshya seh shuai, ay chyr, der tzuey yu jiun.

君主聽到這件事就誇獎彌子說：“彌子瑕真孝順啊！他爲了母親的緣故，忘記自己犯了砍斷腳的罪。”

另一天，彌子瑕跟君主一塊兒在果園裡閒遊。他吃桃子，覺得桃子很甜，不把它吃完，拿半個給君主吃。君主說：“彌子瑕真愛我啊！他忘了他嘴裡的甜味兒拿桃子來給我吃。”等到彌子瑕美麗的容顏變老變醜的時候，君主愛情減弱消失了，他受到君主的責怪。

Jūnzhǔ tīng.dào zhè jiàn shì jiù kuājiǎng Mízǐ shuō: " Mí Zǐxiá Zhēn xiào.shùn a! Tā wèi .le mǔqīn .de yuán.gù, wàng.jì zìjǐ fàn .le kǎn duàn jiǎo .de zuì."

Lìng yì tiān, Mí Zǐxiá gēn jūnzhǔ yíkuàir zài guǒyuán .lǐ xiányóu. Tā chī táo.zǐ, jué.dé táo.zǐ hěn tián, bù bǎ tā chī wán, ná bàn.gè gěi jūnzhǔ chī. Jūnzhǔ shuō: "Mí Zǐxiá zhēn ài wǒ .a! Tā wàng .le tā zuǐ.lǐ .de tiánwèir ná táo.zǐ lái gěi wǒ chī." Děng.dào Mí Zǐxiá měilì .dē róngyán biànlǎo biànchǒu .de shí.hòu, jūnzhǔ àiqíng jiǎnruò xiāoshī .le, tā shòu .dào jūnzhǔ .de zéguài.

The ruler heard of this and found him praiseworthy, saying: "How filial he is! On account of his mother, he forgot that he was committing an offense punishable by having one foot cut off."

One day, Mí Zǐxiá was strolling through an orchard with the ruler. He was eating a peach which he thought tasted quite sweet; not finishing it, he fed the other half to the ruler. The ruler said: "Truly, he loves me! Forgetting the sweet taste in his own mouth, he fed me with it." When Mí Zǐxiá's good looks faded, the ruler's ardor cooled, and he was reproached by the ruler.

135

君曰：“是固嘗矯駕吾車，又嘗啗我以餘桃。”故彌子之行未變於初也，而以前之所以見賢，而後獲罪者，愛憎之變也。

Jūn yuē: "Shì gù cháng jiǎo jià wú chē (jū), yòu cháng dàn wǒ yǐ yú táo." Gù Mízǐ zhī xíng wèi biàn yú chū yě, ér yǐ qián zhī suǒ yǐ jiàn xián, ér hòu huò zuì zhě, ài zēng zhī biàn yě.

Jiun iue: "Shyh guh charng jeau jiah wu che (jiu), yow charng dann woo yii yu taur." Guh Mi Tzyy jy shyng wey biann yu chu yee, erl yii chyan jy suoo yii jiann shyan, erl how huoh tzuey jee, ay tzeng jy biann yee.

君主説：“這個人本來曾經騙別人説是我的命令地駕駛過我的車子，又曾經把吃剩的桃子給我吃過。”本來彌子的行為跟當初比並沒有什麼改變啊，以前彌子受到誇獎、可是後來得到責怪的緣故，是因為君主寵愛跟憎惡的感情改變了啊。

Jūnzhǔ shuō: "Zhèi.gè rén běnlái céngjīng piàn bié .rén shuō shì wǒ .de mìng.lìng .de jiàshǐ.guò wǒ .de chē.zǐ, yòu céngjīng bǎ chī shèng .de táo.zǐ gěiwǒ chī .guò." Běnlái Mízǐ .de xíngwéi gēn dāngchū bǐ bìng méi.yǒu shé.me gǎibiàn .a, yǐqián Mízǐ shòu.dào kuājiǎng, kě.shì hòu.lái dé.dào zéguài .de yuán.gù, shì yīn.wèi jūnzhǔ chǒngài gēn zēngwù .de gǎnqíng gǎibiàn .le .a.

The ruler said: "This person actually once feigned permission to drive my carriage and also fed the remains of a peach that he had eaten from to me." Mízì's behavior never changed from what it had been all along since the beginning: the reason why he was praised for it at first and reproached for it later on is that the ruler's feelings for him changed from affection to revulsion.

第三十六課

楚莊王不殺絕纓者

說苑 復恩

　　楚莊王賜群臣酒。日暮，酒酣，燈燭滅，乃有人引美人之衣者。美人援絕其冠纓，告王曰：“今者燭滅，有引妾衣者，妾援得其冠纓持之。趣火來上，視絕纓者。”

Chǔ Zhuāng Wáng Bù Shā Jué Yīng Zhě

Shuōyuàn Fùēn

　　Chǔ Zhuāng Wáng cì qún chén jiǔ. Rì mù, jiǔ hān, dēng zhú miè, nǎi yǒu rén yǐn měi rén zhī yī zhě. Měi rén yuán jué qí guān yīng, gào wáng yuē: "Jīn zhě zhú miè, yǒu yǐn qiè yī zhě, qiè yuán dé qí guān yīng chí zhī. Cù huǒ lái shàng, shì jué yīng zhě. "

Chuu Juang Wang Bu Sha Jyue Ing Jee

Shuoyuann Fuhen

　　Chuu Juang Wang tsyh chyun chern jeou. Ryh muh, jeou han, deng jwu mieh, nae yeou ren yiin meei ren jy i jee. Meei ren yuan jyue chyi guan ing, gaw wang iue: "Jin jee jwu mieh, yeou yiin chieh i jee, chieh yuan der chyi guan ing chyr jy. Tsuh huoo lai shanq, shyh jyue ing jee."

白話翻譯

楚莊王不殺絕纓者

　　楚莊王賜給臣子們酒喝。天黑了，大家喝酒喝得很暢快，油燈、蠟燭滅了，竟有個拉美人的衣服的人。美人揪斷了他的帽帶子，告訴王說：「現在蠟燭滅了，席間有個拉我衣服的人，我揪到他的帽帶子拿在手裡，大王趕緊叫人拿火來點上燈，看看那個被揪斷了帽帶子的人。」

Chǔ Zhuāng Wáng Bù Shā Júe Ying Zhě

Chǔ Zhuāngwáng cì gěi chén.zǐ.mén jiǔ hē. Tiān hēi .le, dà jiā hē jiǔ hē .de hěn chàngkuài, yóu dēng, làzhú miè .le, jìng yǒu .gè lā měirén .de yī.fú .de rén. Měirén jiū duàn .le tā.de maòdaì.zǐ, gàosù wáng shuō: "Xiànzaì làzhú miè .le, xíjiān yǒu .gè lā wǒ yī.fú .de rén, wǒ jiū dào tā.de màodaì.zǐ ná .zaì shǒu .lǐ, dàwáng gǎnjǐn jiào rén ná huǒ laí diǎn .shàng dēng, kàn.kàn nèi.gè bèi jiū duàn .le màodaì.zǐ .de rén!"

KING ZHUANG OF CHU DOES NOT PUT TO DEATH
THE ONE WITH THE BROKEN CAPSTRING

King Zhuāng of Chǔ offered his officials wine. When it got dark and everyone was pleasantly inebriated, the lamps and candles went out; whereupon a person pulled at the clothing of one the king's concubines. The concubine grabbed and broke off his capstring and informed the king, saying: "Just now when the candles went out, one of the guests pulled at my clothing; I pulled at his capstring and held it in my hand. Quickly have fire brought in to light the lamps so that we can see the one with the broken capstring."

139

王曰：“賜人酒，使醉失禮，奈何欲顯婦人之節而辱士乎？”乃命左右曰：“今日與寡人飲，不絕冠纓者不歡。”群臣百有餘人皆絕其冠纓，而上火，卒盡歡而罷。

Wáng yuē: "Cì rén jiǔ, shǐ zuì shī lǐ, nài hé yù xiǎn fù rén zhī jié ér rǔ (rù) shì hū?" Nǎi mìng zuǒ yòu yuē: "Jīn rì yǔ guǎ rén yǐn, bù jué guān yīng zhě bù huān." Qún chén bó (bǎi) yòu yú rén jiē jué qí guān yīng, ér shàng huǒ, zú jìn huān ér bà.

Wang iue: "Tsyh ren jeou, shyy tzuey shy lii, nay her yuh shean fuh ren jy jye erl ruu (ruh) shyh hu?" Nae minq tzuoo yow iue: "Jin ryh yeu goa ren yiin, bu jyue guan ing jee bu huan." Chyun chern bor (bae) yow yu ren jie jyue chyi guan ing, erl shanq huoo, tzwu jinn huan erl bah.

王説：＂我賜給人酒喝，使人喝醉了做出不合禮貌的事來，怎麼可以爲了要顯示婦人的貞節去羞辱有學問有才幹的讀書人呢？＂就命令侍從們説：＂今天你們跟我一塊儿喝酒，要是你們不揪斷帽帶子的話我就不高興。＂臣子們有一百多個人都揪斷了他們的帽帶子，然後才點上燈，最後大家玩儿到最歡樂的程度才散。

Wáng shuō: "Wǒ cì gěi rén jiǔ hē, shǐ rén hē zùi .le zuò .chū bùhé lǐmào .de shì lái, zěn.me kě.yǐ wèi .le yào xiǎnshì fùrén .de zhēnjié qù xiūrù yǒu xuéwèn yǒu cáigàn .de dúshūrén .ne?" Jiù mìng.lìng shì.cóng .mén shuō: "Jīn tīan nǐ.mén gēn wǒ yí kuàir hē jiǔ, yào.shì nǐ.mén bù jiū duàn màodài.zǐ .de huà wǒ jiù bù gāoxìng." Chén.zǐ .mén yǒu yì baǐ duō .gè rén dōu jiū duàn .le tā.mén .de màodài.zǐ, ránhòu caí diǎn .shàng dēng, zuìhòu dàjiā wánr dào zuì huānlè .de chéngdù caí sàn.

The king said: "I offered wine to someone, made him drunk and made him commit a breach of etiquette; how could I disgrace a scholar just for the sake of making a display of your virtue?" The king then commanded his attendants, saying: "Today you are all drinking with me; if you don't break off your capstrings, I will not be happy." His officials, more than one hundred in all, all broke their capstrings; only afterwards were the lights lit: in the end they all enjoyed themselves to the utmost and only then dispersed.

居三年，晉與楚戰。有一臣常在前，五合五奮首卻
敵，卒得勝之。莊王怪而問曰：“寡人德薄，又未嘗異
子，子何故出死不疑如是？”

Jū sān nián, Jìn yǔ Chǔ zhàn. yǒu yì chén cháng zài qían, wǔ hé wǔ fèn shǒu què dí, zú dé shèng zhī. Zhuāng Wáng guài ér wèn yuē: "Guǎrén dé bó, yòu wèi cháng yì zǐ, zǐ hé gù chū sǐ bù yí rú shì ?"

Jiu san nian, Jinn yeu Chuu jann. yeou i chern charng tzay chyan, wuu her wuu fenn shoou chiueh dyi, tzwu der shenq jy. Juang Wang guay erl wenn iue: "Goa ren der bor, yow wey charng yih tzyy, tzyy her guh chu syy buh yi ru shyh ?"

過了三年，晉國跟楚國打仗。楚國有一個臣子常常在前面，晉楚五次會戰，那個臣子五次奮勇領先打退敵人，終於能夠戰勝了他們。莊王覺得很奇怪就問他說："我道德微少，又從來沒對待你特別好過，你因為什麼緣故這樣不遲疑地出去冒死的危險呢？"

Gùo .le sān nián, Jìnguó gēn Chǔguó dǎzhàng. Chǔguó yǒu yí.gè chén.zǐ cháng .cháng zaì qían.mìan, Jìn Chǔ wǔ cì huìzhàn, nèi.gè chén.zǐ wǔ cì fènyǒng lǐngxiān dǎ tuì dírén, zhōngyú néng.gòu zhàn shèng .le tā.mén. Zhuāngwáng júe.dé hěn qíguaì jiù wèn tā shūo: "Wǒ daòdé wēishǎo, yòu cónglaí méi duìdài nǐ tèbié hǎo .guò, nǐ yīn.wèi shén.me yuán.gù zhè.yàng bù chíyí .de chū.qù maò sǐ .de wéixiǎn .ne?"

Three years passed; then the states of Jìn and Chǔ went to war. There was one official of Chǔ who was always at the front of the ranks. In five engagements five times he mustered all his courage and led the army of Chǔ to repulse the enemy; in the end, he was able to vanquish them. King Zhuāng thought it extraordinary and so questioned him, saying: "My virtue as a ruler is meagre; moreover, I have never treated you especially well. Why did you resolutely go out and risk death like this?"

對曰：「臣當死。往者醉失禮，王隱忍不加誅也；臣終不敢以蔭蔽之德而不顯報王也。常願肝腦塗地，用頸血濺敵久矣。臣乃夜絕纓者也。」遂敗晉軍，楚得以強。

Duì yuē: "Chén dāng sǐ. Wǎng zhě zuì shī lǐ, wáng yǐn rěn bù jiā zhū yě; chén zhōng bù gǎn yǐ yìn bì zhī dé ér bù xiǎn bào wáng yě. Cháng yuàn gān nǎo tú dì, yòng jǐng xuè jiàn dí jiǔ yǐ. Chén nǎi yè jué yīng zhě yě." Suì bài Jìn jūn, Chǔ dé yǐ qiáng.

Duey iue: "Chern dang syy. Woang jee tzuey shy lii, wang yiin reen bu jia ju yee; chern jong bu gaan yii yinn bih jy der erl bu shean baw wang yee. Charng yuann gan nao twu dih, yonq jiing shiueh jiann dyi jeou yii. Chern nae yeh jyue ing jee yee." Suey bay Jinn jiun, Chuu der yii chyang.

那個臣子回答說：＂臣應當死。從前臣喝醉了做出不合禮貌
的事來，王忍耐著不動聲色，沒懲罰臣；臣到底不敢因為受
了王暗中庇護的恩惠就不公開地報答王啊。臣一直希望把
肝和腦塗抹在地上，用脖子裡的血噴濺敵人已經很久啦。臣
就是那天晚上被揪斷了帽帶子的人啊。＂終於打敗了晉國的
軍隊，楚國能夠因這次戰爭變得很強大。

Nèi.ge chén.zǐ huídá shuō: "Chén yīngdāng sǐ. Cóngqián chén hēzuì .le zuòchū bùhé lǐmào
.de shì lái, wáng rěnnài .zhe búdòng shēngsè, méi chéngfá chén; chén dàodǐ bùgǎn yīn.wèi
shòu.le wáng ànzhōng bìhù .de ēnhuì jiù bù gōngkāi.de bàodá wáng a. Chén yìzhí xīwàng bǎ
gān hé nǎo túmǒ .zài dì.shàng, yòng bó.zǐ lǐ .de xuè pēnjiàn dírén yǐjīng hěnjiǔ .la. Chén
jiù.shì nèitiān wǎn.shàng bèi jiū duàn .le màodài.zǐ .de rén .a." Zhōngyú dǎ baì .le Jìnguó .de
jūnduì, Chǔguó néng.gòu yīn zhèi cì zhànzhēng biàn.dé hěn qiángdà.

The official responded saying: "Your servant deserves to die. Once I got drunk and
committed a breach of etiquette; your majesty bore it without any show of displeasure and
did not punish me; having received the favor of your majesty's covert protection, your
servant ultimately dared not not openly repay your majesty. For such a long time, I have
constantly wished to splatter my brains and liver on the ground and to let my blood spurt out
from my neck onto the enemy to repay you. Your servant is the one whose capstring was
broken that night." Eventually, he defeated the armies of the state of Jìn, and the state of Chǔ
was able to grow strong as a result of this battle.

第三十七課

子羔為衛政

說苑 至公

子羔為衛政，刖人之足。衛之君臣亂，子羔走郭門，郭門閉。刖者守門，曰：“於彼有缺。”子羔曰：“君子不踰。”曰：“於彼有竇。”子羔曰：“君子不隧。”

Zǐ Gāo Wéi Wèi Zhèng

Shuōyuàn Zhìgōng

Zǐgāo wéi Wèi Zhèng, yuè rén zhī zú. Wèi zhī jūn chén luàn, Zǐgāo zǒu guō mén, guō mén bì. Yuè zhě shǒu mén, yuē: "Yú bǐ yǒu quē." Zǐgāo yuē: "Jūn zǐ bù yú." Yuē: "Yú bǐ yǒu dòu." Zǐgāo yuē: "Jūn zǐ bú suì."

Tzyy Gau Wei Wey Jenq

Shuoyuann Jyhgong

Tzyygau wei Wey jenq, yueh ren jy tzwu. Wey jy jiun chern luann, Tzyygau tzoou guo men, guo men bih. Yueh jee shoou men, iue: "Yu bii yeou chiue." Tzyygau iue: "Jiun tzyy bu yu." Iue: "Yu bii yeou dow." Tzyygau iue: "Jiun tzyy bu suey."

白話翻譯

子羔爲衞政

　　子羔治理衞國的政事，砍斷了一個犯人的腳。衞國的政府發生了政變，子羔逃到外城的城門，外城的城門已經關上了。那個被砍斷腳的人正把守著外城的城門，對子羔說："在那邊有個缺口。"子羔說："君子不跳牆。"被砍斷腳的人說："在那邊有個洞。"子羔說："君子不鑽洞。"

　　Zǐgāo zhìlǐ Wèiguó .de zhèngshì, kǎnduàn .le yí.gè fànrén .de jiǎo. Wèiguó .de zhèngfǔ fāshēng .le zhèngbiàn, Zǐgāo táo .dào wàichéng .de chéngmén, wāichéng .de chéngmén yǐjīng guān.shàng .le. Nèi.gè bèi kǎnduàn jiǎo .de rén zhèng bǎshǒu .zhe wàichéng .de chéngmén, duì Zǐgāo shuō: "Zài nèibiān yǒu .gè quēkǒu." Zǐgāo shuō: "Jūnzǐ bú tiào qiáng." Bèi kǎnduàn jiǎo .de rén shuō: "Zài nèibiān yǒu .gè dòng." Zǐgāo shuō: "Jūnzǐ bù zuān dòng."

ZIGAO ADMINISTERS THE GOVERNMENT OF THE STATE OF WEI

　　When Zǐgāo was administering the government of the state of Wèi, he had a person's foot cut off as punishment for a crime. During the political crisis in the state of Wèi, Zǐgāo fled to the outer city wall gate; the outer city wall gate was already closed. The person whose foot had been cut off was guarding the gate of the outer city wall; he said: "Over there is a breach in the wall." Zǐgāo said: "A man of noble character does not climb over the wall to escape." The person whose foot had been cut off said: "Over there is a hole beneath the wall." Zǐgāo said: "A man of noble character does not go through a hole under the wall to escape."

曰：「於此有室。」子羔入，追者罷。子羔將去，謂刖
者曰：「吾不能虧損主之法令，而親刖子之足。吾在難
中，此乃子之報怨時也。何故逃我？」

Yuē: "Yú cǐ yǒu shì." Zǐgāo rù, zhuī zhě bà. Zǐgāo jiāng qù, wèi yuè zhě yuē: "Wú bù néng kuī sǔn zhǔ zhī fǎ lìng, ér qīn yuè zǐ zhī zú. Wú zài nàn zhōng, cǐ nǎi zǐ zhī bào yuàn shí yě. Hé gù táo wǒ ?"

Iue: "Yu tsyy yeou shyh." Tzyygau ruh, juei jee bah. Tzyygau jiang chiuh, wey yueh jee iue: "Wu bu neng kuei soen juu jy faa linq, erl chin yueh tzyy jyu tzwu. Wu tzay nann jong, tsyy nae tzyy jy baw yuann shyr yee. Her guh taur woo ?"

被砍斷腳的人說：＂在這裡有間屋子。＂子羔進屋子去了
，追趕的人回去了。子羔將要離開的時候，對被砍斷腳的
人說：＂我不能不遵守君主的法令，才親自下令把你的腳砍
斷了。我在災難裡，這正是你的報仇時機啊。你為甚麼讓我
逃走呢？＂

Bèi kǎnduàn jiǎo .de rén shuō: "Zài zhè.lǐ yǒu jiān wū.zǐ." Zǐgāo jìn wū.zǐ qù .le, zhuīgǎn .de rén huí.qù .le. Zǐgāo jiāngyào líkāi .de shí.hòu, duì bèi kǎn duàn jiǎo .de rén shuō: "Wǒ bùnéng bù zūnshǒu jūnzhǔ .de fǎlìng, cái qīnzì xià liìng bǎ nǐ.de jiǎo kǎn duàn .le. Wǒ zài zāinàn lǐ, zhè zhèng shì nǐ .de bào chóu shíjī .a. Nǐ wèi shén.me ràng wǒ táo zǒu .ne?"

The man whose foot had been cut off said: "Over here there is a room." Zǐgāo entered the room; his pursuers left. When Zǐgāo was about to leave, he spoke to the person whose foot had been cut off, saying: "I can not disobey the laws and orders of the ruler, so I had to have your foot cut off. Now I am in distress; this then is your chance for revenge. Why did you let me escape?"

刖者曰："斷足固我罪也，無可奈何。君之治臣也，傾
側法令，先後臣以法，欲臣之免於法也，臣知之。獄決
罪定，臨當論刑，君愀然不樂，見於顏色，臣又知之。
君豈私臣哉！天生仁人之心，其固然也。此臣之所以脫
君也。"

Yuè zhě yuē: "Duàn zú gù wǒ zuì yě, wú kě nài hé. Jūn zhī zhì chén yě, qīng cè fǎ lìng, xiān hòu chén yǐ fǎ, yù chén zhī miǎn yú fǎ yě, chén zhī zhī. Yù jué zuì dìng, lín dāng lùn xíng, jūn qiǎo rán bú lè, xiàn yú yán sè, chén yòu zhī zhī. Jūn qǐ sī chén zāi! Tiān shēng rén rén zhī xīn, qí gù rán yě. Cǐ chén zhī suǒ yǐ tuō jūn yě."

Yueh jee iue: "Duann tzwu guh woo tzuey yee, wu kee nay her. Jiun jy jyh chern yee, ching tseh faa linq, shian how chern yii faa, yuh chern jy mean yu faa yee, chern jy jy. Yuh jyue tzuey dinq, lin dang luenn shyng, jiun cheau ran bu leh, shiann yu yan seh, chern yow jy jy. Jiun chii sy chern tzai! Tian sheng ren ren jy shin, chyi guh ran yee. Tsyy chern jy suoo yii tuo jiun yee."

被砍斷腳的人說：“砍斷腳本來是我的罪，您沒有法子能對它做什麼。當您懲治我的時候啊，您從各種角度來研究法令，根據法律來慎重衡量我的罪，想要我免受刑罰，這我知道。案子判決了，罪名確定了，快到該依法決定刑罰的時候，您憂傷不樂，在神色中流露出來，這我也知道。您那裡是偏袒我呢？這是天生來仁人的心腸本來如此啊。這就是我放您逃走的緣故啊。”

Bèi kǎn duàn jiǎo .de rén shuō: "Kǎn duàn jiǎo běnlái shì wǒ .de zuì, nín méiyǒu fá.zǐ néng duì .tā zuò shén.me. Dāng nín chéngzhì wǒ .de shíhòu .a, nín cóng gèzhǒng jiǎodù lái yánjiù fǎlìng, gēnjù fǎlù lái shènzhòng héngliáng wǒ.de zuì, xiǎngyào wǒ miǎn shòu xíngfá, zhè wǒ zhīdào. Ǎnzǐ pànjué .le, zuìmíng quèdìng .le, kuài dào gāi yī fǎ juédìng xíngfá .de shí.hòu, nín yōushāng búlè, zài shénsè zhōng liúlù chū.lái, zhè wǒ yě zhīdào. Nín nǎ.lǐ shì piāntǎn wǒ .ne? Zhè .shì tiānshēnglái rénrén .de xīncháng běnlái rúcǐ .a. Zhè jiù shì wǒ fàng nín táozǒu .de yuán.gù .a."

The person whose foot had been cut off said: "The cutting off of my foot was all along for my offense; you could do nothing about it. As for your punishing me, you considered the laws from every angle, prudently deliberated my case against the law, and wanted me exempted from punishment; I know this. The facts of the case had been ascertained; the category of the offense had been determined: when the time to pass sentence drew near, you were pained and unhappy; this was revealed in your demeanor, and I also know this. How was this showing favor toward me? The heaven sent heart of a humane person, it is ever so! That is why I enabled you to escape."

第三十八課

鄒忌諷齊王納諫

戰國策 齊策

　　鄒忌修八尺有餘，而形貌昳麗。朝服衣冠窺鏡，謂其妻曰：「我孰與城北徐公美？」其妻曰：「君美甚，徐公何能及君也？」城北徐公，齊國之美麗者也。

Zōu Jì Fěng Qí Wáng Nà Jiàn

Zhànguócè Qícè

Zōu Jì xiū bā chǐ yòu yú, ér xíng mào yì lì. Zhāo fú yī guān kuī jìng, wèi qí qī yuē: "Wǒ shú yǔ chéng běi Xú gōng měi?" Qí qī yuē: "Jūn měi shèn, Xú gōng hé néng jí jūn yě?" Chéng běi Xú gōng, Qí guó zhī měi lì zhě yě.

Tzou Jih Feng Chyi Wang Nah Jiann

Janngwotseh Chyitseh

Tzou Jih shiou ba chyy yow yu, erl shyng maw yih lih. Jau fwu i guan kuei jinq, wey chyi chi iue: "Woo shwu yeu cherng beei Shyu gong meei?" Chyi chi iue: "Jiun meei shenn, Shyu gong her neng jyi jiun yee?" Cherng beei Shyu gong, Chyi gwo jy meei lih jee yee.

152

白話翻譯

鄒忌諷齊王納諫

　　鄒忌身高八尺多，而且相貌非常英俊。他在早上穿上衣服戴好帽子照照鏡子，對他的妻子説：“我跟城北的徐先生比哪一個更好看？”他的妻子説：“您好看極了，徐先生哪兒能比得上您呢？”城北的徐先生是齊國的美男子。

Zōu Jì Fěng Qí Wáng Nà Jiàn

　　Zōu Jì shēn gāo bā chǐ duō, érqiě xiàngmào fēicháng yīngjùn. Tā zài zǎo.shàng chuān .shàng yī.fú dài hǎo mào.zǐ zhào.zhào jìng.zǐ, duì tā.de qīzǐ shuō: "Wǒ gēn chéng běi .de Xú xiān.shēng bǐ nǎ yí .gè gèng haǒkàn?" Tā.de qīzǐ shuō: "Nín hǎokàn .jí .lē, Xú xiān.shēng nǎr néng bǐ .dé shàng nín .ne?" Chéngběi .de Xú xiān.shēng shì Qíguó .de měi nánzǐ.

ZOU JI SUBTLY ADMONISHES THE KING OF QI TO ACCEPT CRITICISM

　　Zōu Jì was over six feet tall and of radiant and beauteous countenance. One morning when he put on his cap and gown, he looked into the mirror and spoke to his wife saying: "Between myself and Master Xú in the north of the city, who is the better looking?" His wife said, "You are exceedingly good-looking; how could Master Xú be as good-looking as you?" Master Xú in the north of the city was a good-looking man of the state of Qí.

忌不自信，而復問其妾曰：“我孰與徐公美？”妾曰：“徐公何能及君也？”旦日，客從外來，與坐談，問之：“吾與徐公孰美？”客曰：“徐公不若君之美也。”

Jì bú zì xǐn, ér fù wèn qí qiè yuē: “Wǒ shú yǔ Xú gōng měi?” Qiè yue: “Xú gōng hé néng jí jūn ye?” Dàn rì, kè cóng wài lái, yǔ zuò tán, wèn zhī: “Wú yǔ Xú gōng shú měi?” Kè yuē: “Xú gōng bú ruò jūn zhī měi yě.”

Jih bu tzyh shinn, erl fuh wenn chyi chieh iue: “Woo shwu yeu Shyu gong meei?” Chieh iue: “Shyu gong her neng jyi jiun yee?” Dann ryh, keh tsorng way lai, yeu tzuoh tarn, wenn jy: “Wu yeu Shyu gong shwu meei?” Keh iue: “Shyu gong bu ruoh jiun jy meei yee.”

鄒忌不相信自己比徐先生美，就又問他的妾說：“我跟徐先生比哪一個更美？”妾說：“徐先生哪兒能比得上您呢？”到了第二天，一位客人從外邊來了，鄒忌跟他坐下談話，問他：“我跟徐先生比哪一個更美？”客人說：“徐先生不如您美啊。”

Zōu Jì bù xiāngxìn zì.jǐ bǐ Xú xiān.shēng měi, jiù yòu wèn tā.de qiè shuō: "Wǒ gēn Xú xiān.shēng bǐ nǎ yí.gè gèng měi?" Qiè shuō: "Xú xiān.shēng nǎr néng bǐ .dé shàng nín .ne?" Dào .le dì èr tiān, yíwèi kè.rén cóng wài.biān lái .le, Zōu Jì gēn tā zuò .xià tán huà, wèn tā: "Wǒ gēn Xú xiān.shēng bǐ nǎ yí .gè gèng měi?" Kèrén shuō: "Xú xiān.shēng bùrú nín měi .a."

Zōu Jì did not believe himself to be better looking than Master Xú and so next asked his concubine saying: "Between myself and Master Xú, who is the better looking?" The concubine said: "How could Master Xú be as good-looking as you?" The following day a guest arrived from outside the area; Zōu Jì sat talking with him and asked him: "Between Master Xú and myself, who is the better looking?" The guest said: "Master Xú is not as good-looking as you are."

明日，徐公來，熟視之，自以為不如；窺鏡而自視，又
弗如遠甚。暮寢而思之，曰："吾妻之美我者，私我也
；妾之美我者，畏我也；客之美我者，欲有求於我也。
"於是入朝見威王曰：

Míng rì, Xú gōng lái, shú shì zhī, zì yǐ wéi bù rú; kuī jìng ér zì shì, yòu fú rú yuǎn shèn. Mù qǐn ér sī zhī, yuē: "Wú qī zhī měi wǒ zhě, sī wǒ yě; qiè zhī měi wǒ zhě, wèi wǒ yě; kè zhī měi wǒ zhě, yù yǒu qiú yú wǒ yě." Yú shì rù cháo jiàn Wēi wáng yuē:

Ming ryh, Shyu gong lai, shwu shyh jy, tzyh yii wei bu ru; kuei jinq erl tzyh shyh, yow fwu ru yeuan shenn. Muh chiin erl si jy, iue: "Wu chi jy meei woo jee, sy woo yee; chieh jy meei woo jee, wey woo yee; keh jy meei woo jee, yuh yeou chyou yu woo yee." Yu shyh ruh chaur jiann Uei wang iue:

到了第二天，徐先生來了，鄒忌仔細地看他，覺得自己不如他。照鏡子來看看自己，又覺得自己遠遠比不上他。晚上睡覺的時候思考這件事，對自己說：「我的妻子認爲我美的緣故，是她偏愛我啊；我的妾認爲我美的緣故，是她畏懼我啊；客人認爲我美的緣故，是他有事要求我啊。」在這種想通了的情況之下，他就進朝廷去見齊威王，說：

Dào .le dì èr tiān, Xú xiān.shēng lái .le, Zōu Jì zǐxì.de kàn tā, jué.dé zì.jǐ bùrú tā. Zhào jìng.zǐ lái kàn.kàn zì.jǐ, yòu juédé zìjǐ yuǎnyuǎn bǐ.bú shàng ta. Wǎn.shàng shuìjiào .de shí.hòu sīkǎo zhèi jiàn shì, duì zìjǐ shuō: "Wǒ.de qīzǐ rènwéi wǒ měi .de yuángù, shì tā piānài wǒ .a; wǒ.de qiè rènwéi wǒ měi .de yuángù, shì tā wèijù wǒ .a; kèrén rènwéi wǒ měi .de yuángù, shì tā yǒu shì yào qiú wǒ .a." Zài zhèzhǒng xiǎng tōng .le .de qíngkuàng zhī xià, tā jiù jìn cháotíng qù jiàn Qí Wēiwáng, shuō:

On the next day, Master Xú came. Zōu Jì looked at him closely and felt he himself was not as good-looking as Master Xú. Looking at himself in the mirror, again he felt that he was far inferior to Master Xú. In the evening when he went to bed, he thought this over and said to himself: "The reason my wife thinks I am good-looking is that she is partial to me; the reason my concubine thinks I am good-looking is that she fears me; the reason the guest thinks I am good-looking is that he wants to ask me for something." Having had this insight, he entered the court, saw King Wēi of Qí and said:

"臣誠知不如徐公美。臣之妻私臣，臣之妾畏臣，臣之客欲有求於臣，皆以臣美於徐公。今齊地方千里，百二十城。宮婦左右，莫不私王；朝廷之臣，莫不畏王；四境之內，莫不有求於王。由此觀之，王之蔽甚矣！"

"Chén chéng zhī bù rú Xú gōng měi. Chén zhī qī sī chén, chén zhī qiè wèi chén, chén zhī kè yù yǒu qiú yú chén, jiē yǐ chén měi yú Xú gōng. Jīn Qí dì fāng qiān lǐ, bǎi èr shí chéng. Gōng fù zuǒ yòu, mò bù sī wáng; cháo tíng zhī chén, mò bú wèi wáng; sì jìng zhī nèi, mò bù yǒu qiú yú wáng. Yóu cǐ guān zhī, wáng zhī bì shèn yǐ!"

"Chern cherng jy bu ru Shyu gong meei. Chern jy chi sy chern, chern jy chieh wey chern, chern jy keh yuh yeou chyou yu chern, jie yii chern meei yu Shyu gong. Jin Chyi dih fang chian lii, bae ell shyr cherng. Gong fuh tzuoo yow, moh bu sy wang; chaur tyng jy chern, moh bu wey wang; syh jinq jy ney, moh bu yeou chyou yu wang. You tsyy guan jy, wang jy bih shenn yii!"

158

"我確實知道自己不如徐先生美。我的妻子偏愛我，我的妾畏懼我，我的客人有事要求我，他們都說我比徐先生美。現在齊國有國土一百萬平方里，全國有一百二十座城。在宮廷美女及侍從中沒有一個人不偏袒大王；在朝廷的臣子中沒有一個人不畏懼大王；在四面國境之內，沒有一個人不有求於大王。從這情形來看，大王受蒙蔽得太厲害啦！"

"Wǒ quèshí zhī.dào zì.jǐ bùrú Xú xiān.shēng měi. Wǒ.de qīzǐ piānài wǒ; wǒ.de qiè wèijù wǒ; wǒ.de kèrén yǒu shì yào qiú wǒ, tā.mén dōu shuō wǒ bǐ Xú xiān.shēng měi. Xiànzài Qíguó yǒu guótǔ yì bǎiwàn píng fāng lǐ, quánguó yǒu yìbǎi èrshí .zuò chéng. Zài gōngtíng měinǚ jí shìcóng zhòng méi.yǒu yí.gè rén bù piāntǎn dàwáng; zài cháotíng .de chén.zǐ zhōng méi.yǒu yí.gè rén bú wèijù dàwáng; zài sìmiàn guójìng zhī nèi, méiyǒu yí.gè rén bù yǒu qiú yú dàwáng. Cóng zhè qíng.xíng lái kàn, dàwáng shòu méngbì dé tài lì.hài .la!"

"I really do know that I am not as good-looking as Master Xú. My wife is partial to me; my concubine fears me; my guest wanted to ask something of me: so they all say that I am better looking than Master Xú. At present, the state of Qí has territory encompassing one million square *lǐ*, and the whole state has one hundred and twenty walled cities. Among the palace ladies and personal attendants, there is not one who is not partial to you; among the officials of the royal court, there is not one who does not fear you; within the four borders of the realm, there is not one who does not have something to ask of you. Looking at your situation in this light, your have been severely deluded indeed!"

王曰：“善！”乃下令：“群臣吏民能面刺寡人之過者，
受上賞；上書諫寡人者，受中賞；能謗議於朝市聞寡人
之耳者，受下賞。”

Wáng yuē: "Shàn!" Nǎi xià lìng: "Qún chén lì mín néng miàn cì guǎ rén zhī guò zhě, shòu shàng shǎng; shàng shū jiàn guǎ rén zhě, shòu zhōng shǎng; néng bàng yì yú cháo shì wén guǎ rén zhī ěr zhě, shòu xià shǎng."

Wang iue: "Shann!" Nae shiah linq: "Chyun chern lih min neng miann tsyh goa ren jy guoh jee, show shanq shaang; shanq shu jiann goa ren jee, show jong shaang; neng banq yih yu chaur shyh wen goa ren jy eel jee, show shiah shaang."

威王説：“有道理！”就下命令：“眾大臣、官吏、民眾能當面指出我的過失的，會受到上等的獎賞；上奏章來諫正我的，會受到中等的獎賞；能在朝廷或市場公開地批評議論讓我聽到耳中的，會受到下等的獎賞。”

Wēi Wáng shuō: "Yǒu dào.lǐ!" Jiù xià mìnglìng: "Zhòng dàchén, guānlì, mínzhòng néng dāng miàn zhǐ.chū wǒ.de guòshī .de, huì shòu.dào shàng děng .de jiǎngshǎng; shàng zòu zhāng lái jiànzhèng wǒ .de, huì shòu.dào zhōng děng .de jiǎngshǎng; néng zài cháotíng huò shìchǎng gōngkāi .de pīpíng yìlùn ràng wǒ tīng .dào ěr zhōng .de, huì shòu.dào xià děng .de jiǎngshǎng."

The king said, "Agreed!" Whereupon he issued an order: "Those court officials, functionaries and common people who can criticize my faults to my face shall receive the highest reward; those who present a memorial to admonish me shall receive the middle reward; those who can publicly criticize and discuss my faults in the court and the marketplace and are heard about by me shall receive the lowest reward."

令初下，群臣進諫，門庭若市。數月之後，時時而間進
。期年之後，雖欲言，無可進者。燕、趙、韓、魏聞之
，皆朝於齊。此所謂戰勝於朝廷。

Lìng chū xià, qún chén jìn jiàn, mén tíng ruò shì. Shù yuè zhī hòu, shí shí ér jiàn jìn. Jī nián zhī hòu, suí yù yán, wú kě jìn zhě. Yān, Zhào, Hán, Wèi wén zhī, jiē cháo yú Qí. Cǐ suǒ wèi zhàn shèng yú cháo tíng.

Linq chu shiah, chyun chern jinn jiann, men tyng ruoh shyh. Shuh yueh jy how, shyr shyr erl jiann jinn. Ji nian jy how, swei yuh yan, wu kee jinn jee. Ian, Jaw, Harn, Wey wen jy, jie chaur yu Chyi. Tsyy suoo wey jann shenq yu chaur tyng.

命令剛下來的時候，眾大臣來進獻諫言，王宮的門前跟院中擠得像市場一樣。幾個月以後，有時偶然有人進獻諫言。一週年以後，眾大臣、官吏及民眾就是想說也沒有甚麼可以進獻的了。燕國、趙國、韓國、魏國聽到這件事，都到齊國來朝見。這就是一般人說的“在朝廷中獲得勝利”的情形。

Mìnglìng gāng xià.lái .de shíhòu, zhòng dàchén lái jìnxiàn jiànyán, wánggōng .de mén.qián gēn yuàn.zhōng jǐdé xiàng shìchǎng yíyàng. Jǐ.gè yuè yǐ.hòu, yǒushí ǒurán yǒu rén jìnxiàn jiànyán. Yì zhōu nián yǐ.hòu, zhòng dàchén, guānlì jí mínzhòng jiù.shì xiǎng shuō yě méi.yǒu shén.me kě.yǐ jìnxiàn .de .le. Yān guó, Zhào guó, Hán guó, Wèi guó tīngdào zhèijiàn shì, dōu dào Qí guó lái cháo jiàn. Zhèi jiù.shì yìbānrén shuō .de "Zài cháotíng zhōng huò.dé shènglì" .de qíng.xíng.

When the order was first issued, all the officials came to present remonstrances; in front of the palace gates and in the courtyard it was as crowded as a marketplace. After several months had passed, people occasionally presented remonstrances from time to time. After a full year had passed, even if someone wanted to speak out, there was nothing to present. The states of Yān, Zhào, Hán, and Wèi heard of this and all came to pay court to the king of Qí. This is what is called "gaining the victory at court."

第三十九課

魏節乳母

列女傳 節義

魏節乳母者，魏公子之乳母也。秦攻魏，破之，殺魏王瑕，誅諸公子，而一公子不得。令魏國曰：「得公子者，賜金千鎰；匿之者罪至夷。」節乳母與公子俱逃。

Wèi Jié Rǔ Mǔ

Liènǚzhuàn Jiéyì

Wèi jié rǔmǔ zhě, Wèi gōngzǐ zhī rǔmǔ yě. Qín gōng Wèi, pò zhī, shā Wèi wáng Xiá, zhū zhū gōngzǐ, ér yì gōngzǐ bù dé. Lìng Wèi guó yuē: "Dé gōngzǐ zhě, cì jīn qiān yì; nì zhī zhě zuì zhì yí." Jié rǔmǔ yǔ gōngzǐ jù táo.

Wey Jye Ruu Muu

Liehneujuann Jyeyih

Wey jye ruumuu jee, Wey gongtzyy jy ruumuu yee. Chyn gong Wey, poh jy, sha Wey wang Shya, ju ju gongtzyy, erl yih gongtzyy bu der. Linq Wey gwo iue: "Der gong tzyy jee, tsyh jin chian yih; nih jy jee tzuey jyh yi." Jye ruumuu yeu gongtzyy jiuh taur.

164

白話翻譯

魏節乳母

　　魏國節烈的乳母，是魏國公子的奶媽。秦國攻打魏國，把魏國打敗了，殺了魏王瑕，也殺死了眾多公子，可是還有一位公子捉不到。秦王在魏國下了一道命令，說："捉到公子的人，我賞賜他一千鎰黃金；藏匿公子的人，他的刑罰重到全家被殺死的地步。" 節乳母跟公子一起逃亡。

Wèi Jié Rǔ Mǔ

　　Wèi guó jiéliè .de rǔmǔ, shì Wèi guó gōngzǐ .de nǎemā. Qín guó gōngdǎ Wèi guó, bǎ Wèi guó dǎ bài .le, shā .le Wèi wáng Xiā, yě shā sǐ .le zhòng duō gōngzǐ, kě.shì hái yǒu yíwèi gōngzǐ zhuō .bú.dào. Qín wáng zài Wèi guó xià .le yídào mìnglìng, shuō: "Zhuō dào gōngzǐ .de rén, wǒ shǎngcì tā yì qiān yì huángjīn; cángnì gōngzǐ .de rén, tā.de xíngfá zhòng dào quánjiā bèi shāsǐ .de dìbù." Jié rǔmǔ gēn gōngzì yíqǐ táo wáng.

THE UPRIGHT WET NURSE OF WEI

　　The upright wet nurse of Wèi was the wet nurse of a prince of Wèi. The state of Qín attacked the state of Wèi and defeated it; the army of Qín killed the king of Wèi, Xiá, and executed the princes of Wèi, but one prince was not captured. The king of Qín issued an order to the people of the state of Wèi, which said: "Whosoever captures the prince shall be awarded one thousand ingots of gold; whosoever hides him shall suffer severe punishment to the extent of the extermination of his entire clan." The upright wet nurse fled together with the prince.

魏之故臣見乳母而識之，曰：“乳母無恙乎？”乳母曰
：“嗟乎！吾奈公子何？”故臣曰：“今公子安在？吾
聞秦令曰：‘有能得公子者，賜金千鎰；匿之者罪至夷
。’

Wèi zhī gù chén jiàn rǔmǔ ér shì zhī, yuē: "Rǔmǔ wú yàng hū?" Rǔmǔ yuē: "Jiē hū! wú nài gōngzǐ hé?" Gù chén yuē: "Jīn gōngzǐ ān zài? Wú wén Qín lìng yuē: 'Yǒu néng dé gōngzǐ zhě, cì jīn qiān yì; nì zhī zhě zuì zhì yí.'

Wey jy guh chern jiann ruumuu erl shyh jy, iue: "Ruumuu wu yanq hu?" Ruumuu iue: "Jie hu! wu nay gongtzyy her?" Guh chern iue: "Jin gongtzyy an tzay? Wu wen Chyn linq iue: 'Yeou neng der gongtzyy jee, tsyh jin chian yih; nih jy jee tzuey jyh yi.'

魏國的一個舊臣看見乳母就認出她來了，說："乳母平安無事嗎？"乳母說："唉！我把公子怎麼辦呢？"那個舊臣說："現在公子在哪兒啊？我聽到秦國下命令說：'要是有能捉到公子的人，秦王賜給他一千鎰黃金；藏匿公子的人，他的刑罰重到全家被殺死的地步。'

Wèi guó .de yí.gè jiù chén kànjiàn rǔmǔ jiù rèn .chū tā .lái .le, shuō: "Rǔmǔ píngān wúshì .ma?" Rǔmǔ shuō: "Āi! Wǒ bǎ gōngzǐ zěn.me bàn .ne?" Nàgè jiù chén shuō: "Xiàn.zài gōngzǐ zài nǎr .a? Wǒ tīng.dào Qín guó xià mìnglìng shuō: 'Yào.shì yǒu néng zhuōdào gōngzǐ .de rén, Qínwáng cìgěi tā yì qiān yì huángjīn; cángnì gōngzǐ .de rén, tā.dē xíngfá zhòng dào quánjiā bèi shāsǐ .de dìbù.'

A former minister of the state of Wèi saw the wet nurse and recognized her, said: "Are you safe and sound?" The wet nurse said: "Alas! What shall I do about the prince?" The former minister said: "Where is the prince now? I have heard that the state of Qín issued an order saying: 'Whosoever is able to capture the prince shall be awarded one thousand ingots of gold; whosoever hides him shall be severely punished to the extent of exterminating the entire clan.'

乳母倘言之，則可以得千金；知而不言，則昆弟無類矣
。”乳母曰：“吁！吾不知公子之處。”故臣曰：“我聞
公子與乳母俱逃。”母曰：“吾雖知之，亦終不可以言
。”

Rǔmǔ tǎng yán zhī, zé kě yǐ dé qiān jīn; zhī ér bù yán, zé kūn dì wú lèi yǐ." Rǔmǔ yuē: "Xū!
Wú bù zhī gōngzǐ zhī chù." Gù chén yuē: "Wǒ wén gōngzǐ yǔ rǔmǔ jù táo." Mǔ yuē: "Wú
suí zhī zhī, yì zhōng bù kě yǐ yán."

Ruumuu taang yan jy, tzer kee yii der chian jin; jy erl bu yan, tzer kuen dih wu ley yii."
Ruumuu iue: "Shiu! Wu bu jy gongtzyy jy chuh." Guh chern iue: "Woo wen gongtzyy yeu
ruumuu jiuh taur." Muu iue: "Wu swei jy jy, yih jong bu kee yii yan."

乳母倘若把公子藏匿的地方説出來，就可以得到一千鎰黃金
；你知道卻不説出來，那麼你的兄弟就會都被殺光了。”乳
母説：“唉！我不知道公子藏匿的地方。”舊臣説：“我聽
説公子跟您一起逃亡的。”乳母説：“我就是知道公子藏在
哪儿，也到底不可以説出來。”

Rǔmǔ tǎngruò bǎ gōngzǐ cángnì .de dìfàng shuō.chū.lái, jiù kě.yǐ dédào yì qiān yì huángjīn;
nǐ zhīdào què bù shuō.chū.lái, nà.me nǐ.dē xiōngdì jiù huì dōu bèi shā guāng .le.” Rǔmǔ
shuō: “Aī! wǒ bù zhī.dào gōngzǐ cángnì .de dìfāng.” Jiù chén shuō: “Wǒ tīngshuō gōngzǐ
gēn nín yìqǐ táowáng .de.” Rǔmǔ shuō: “Wǒ jiù.shì zhī.dào gōngzǐ cáng .zài nǎr, yě dàodǐ
bù kě.yǐ shuō .chū .lái.”

If you reveal the whereabouts of the prince, then you can get one thousand ingots of gold; if
you know yet do not say, then your elder and younger brothers will most certainly be
slaughtered.” The wet nurse said: “Alas! I do not know where the prince is hiding.” The
former minister said: “I have heard that the prince fled together with you.” The wet nurse
said: “Even if I did know, I still could never speak of it.”

故臣曰：〝今魏國已破亡，族已滅，子匿之尚誰為乎？〞母吁而言曰：〝夫見利而反上者，逆也；畏死而棄義者，亂也。今持逆亂而以求利，吾不為也。

Gù chén yuē: "Jīn Wèi guó yǐ pò wáng, zú yǐ miè, zǐ nì zhī shàng shuí wèi hū?" Mǔ xū ér yán yuē: "Fú jiàn lì ér fǎn shàng zhě, nì yě; wèi sǐ ér qì yì zhě, luàn yě. Jīn chí nì luàn ér yǐ qiú lì, wú bù wéi yě.

Guh chern iue: "Jin Wey gwo yii poh wang, tzwu yii mieh, tzyy nih jy shanq shwei wey hu?" Muu shiu erl yan iue: "Fwu jiann lih erl faan shanq jee, nih yee; wey syy erl chih yih jee, luann yee. Jin chyr nih luann erl yii chyou lih, wu bu wei yee.

舊臣説：“現在魏國已經被打破滅亡了，魏王的家族已經被
消滅了，你藏匿公子，還爲了誰呢？”乳母嘆著氣説：“看
見利益就背叛主上，是叛逆的行爲；畏懼死亡就廢棄正義，
是昏亂的行爲。現在要憑藉逆亂的行爲來謀求利益，這我絶
對不幹。

Jiù chén shuō: "Xiànzài Wèi guó yǐjīng bèi dǎ pò mièwáng .le, Wèi wáng .de jiā zú yǐjīng bèi
xiāomiè .le, nǐ cángnì gōngzǐ, hái wèi.le shéi ne?" Rǔmǔ tàn.zhē qì shuō: "Kànjiàn lìyì jiù
bèi pàn zhǔ.shàng, shì pànnì dē xíngwéi; wèijù sǐwáng jiù fèiqì zhèngyì, shì hūnluàn. dē
xíngwéi. Xiànzài yào píngjiè nì luàn .de xíngwéi lái móuqiú lìyì, zhè wǒ juéduì bú gàn.

The former minister said: "Now the state of Wèi has already been destroyed, and the royal
clan has already been exterminated; for whom are you still hiding the prince?" The wet nurse
said with a sigh, "To see some advantage and turn against one's ruler is to commit treason; to
abandon what is right and proper for fear of death is folly. To commit treason and folly now
and to seek profit thereby -- that I absolutely will not do.

且夫為人養子者，務生之，非為殺之也，豈可以利賞而畏誅之故，廢正義而行逆節哉！妾不能生而令公子擒也。”遂抱公子逃於深澤之中。故臣以告秦軍。

Qiě fú wèi rén yǎng zǐ zhě, wù shēng zhī, fēi wèi shā zhī yě, qǐ kě yǐ lì shǎng ér wèi zhū zhī gù, fèi zhèng yì ér xíng nì jié zāi! Qiè bù néng shēng ér lìng gōngzǐ qín yě." Suì bào gōngzǐ táo yú shēn zé zhī zhōng. Gù chén yǐ gào Qín jūn.

Chiee fwu wey ren yeang tzyy jee, wuh sheng jy, fei wey sha jy yee, chii kee yii lih shaang erl wey ju jy guh, fey jenq yih erl shyng nih jye tzai! Chieh bu neng sheng erl linq gong tzyy chyn yee." Suey baw gong tzyy taur yu shen tzer jy jong. Guh chern yii gaw Chyn jiun.

而且那些爲別人照顧孩子的人，盡力使孩子活著，並不是爲了把他殺死啊，怎麼可以因爲貪圖賞賜跟怕被誅殺的緣故，廢棄正義去做違背節操的事呢？我決不能自己活著讓公子被人捉去啊。"於是她就抱著公子逃到一片窪地的深處去。舊臣把這件事報告給秦國的軍隊。

Érqiě nàxiē wèi bié rén zhàogù hái.zǐ .de rén, jìnlì shǐ hái.zǐ huó.zhe, bìng bú.shì wèi.le bǎ tā shāsǐ .a, zěn.me kěyǐ yīn.wèi tāntú shǎngcì gēn pà bèi zhūshā .de yuángù, fèiqì zhèngyì qù zuò wéibèi jiécāo .de shì .ne?" Wǒ jué bùnéng zìjǐ huó.zhe ràng gōngzǐ bèi rén zhuōqù .a." Yú.shì tā jiù bào.zhe gōngzǐ táo dào yí piàn wādì .de shēnchù qù. Jiù chén bǎ zhèijiàn shì bàogào gěi Qínguó .de jūnduì.

Moreover, those who raise another's child do their utmost to keep the child alive, not to kill it. How can one abandon what is fitting and proper to act against what is righteous because one covets rewards and fears death? I certainly cannot let the prince be captured while I still live." Whereupon, cradling the little prince in her arms, she fled deep into the fens. The former official reported this matter to the Qín army.

秦軍追見，爭射之。乳母以身為公子蔽，矢著身者數十
，與公子俱死。秦王聞之，貴其守忠死義，乃以卿禮葬
之，祠以太牢。寵其兄為五大夫，賜金百鎰。

Qín jūn zhuī jiàn, zhēng shè zhī. Rǔmǔ yǐ shēn wèi gōngzǐ bì, shǐ zhuó shēn zhě shù shí, yǔ gōngzǐ jù sǐ. Qín wáng wén zhī, guì qí shǒu zhōng sǐ yì, nǎi yǐ qīng lǐ zàng zhī, cí yǐ tài láo. Chǒng qí xiōng wéi wǔ dàifū, cì jīn bǎi yì.

Chyn jiun juei jiann, jeng sheh jy. Ruumuu yii shen wey gongtzyy bih, shyy jwo shen jee shuh shyr, yeu gongtzyy jiuh syy. Chyn wang wen jy, guey chyi shoou jong syy yih, nae yii ching lii tzanq jy, tsyr yii tay lau. Choong chyi shiong wei wuu dayfu, tsyh jin bae yih.

秦國的軍隊追上去看見他們，爭著用箭射他們。乳母用自己的身體替公子遮擋著，射在她身上的箭有好幾十枝，她跟公子一起死了。秦王聽到這件事，敬重乳母保持忠心為道義而犧牲，就用埋葬卿的禮儀來埋葬她，用豬牛羊三牲來祭祀她。秦王還封她的哥哥作五大夫，賜給他一百鎰黃金。

Qín guó .de jūnduì zhuī.shàng.qù kànjiàn tā.mén, zhēng.zhē yòng jiàn shè tā.mén Rǔmǔ yòng zìjǐ .de shēn.tǐ tì gōngzǐ zhēdǎng.zhe, shè zài tā shēn.shàng .de jiàn yǒu hǎo jǐ shí zhī, tā gēn gōngzǐ yíqǐ sǐ .le. Qín wáng tīng.dào zhèi jiàn shì, jìngzhòng rǔmǔ bǎochí zhōngxīn wèi dàoyì ér xīshēng, jiù yòng máizàng qīng .de lǐyí lái máizàng tā, yòng zhū niú yáng sān shēng lái jìsì tā. Qín wáng hái fēng tā.de gē.gē zuò wǔ dàifǔ, cìgěi tā yì-bǎi yì huángjīn.

The Qín army pursued them and upon seeing them, the soldiers competed to loose the first arrow. The wet nurse, covering the little prince with her own body, was pierced by scores of arrows and died together with him. When the king of Qín heard of this, he esteemed the wet nurse for preserving her loyalty by dying for a righteous cause and so had her interred with the ceremonial appropriate for a great minister of state and sacrificed to her spirit with the Great Offering. He favored her elder brother, appointing him a Grandee of the Fifth Order, and bestowed on him one hundred ingots of gold.

第四十課

子産不毀鄉校

左傳　襄公三十一年

　　鄭人游于鄉校，以論執政。然明謂子産曰：“毀鄉校，何如？”子産曰：“何為？夫人朝夕退而游焉，以議執政之善否。

Zǐ Chǎn Bù Huǐ Xiāng Xiào

Zuǒzhuàn　Xiānggōngsānshíyīnián

Zhèng rén yóu yú xiāng xiào, yǐ lùn zhí zhèng. Ránmíng wèi Zǐchǎn yuē: "Huǐ xiāng xiào, hé rú?" Zǐchǎn yuē: "Hé wèi? Fú rén zhāo xī tuì ér yóu yān, yǐ yì zhí zhèng zhī shàn fǒu.

Tzyy Chaan Bu Hoei Shiang Shiaw

Tzuoojuann　Shianggongsanshyrinian

Jenq ren you yu shiang shiaw, yii luenn jyr jenq. Ranming wey Tzyychaan iue: "Hoei shiang shiaw, her ru?" Tzyychaan iue: "Her wey? Fwu ren jau shi tuey erl you ian, yii yih jyr jenq jy shann foou.

白話翻譯

子產不毀鄉校

　　鄭國人到鄉校去遊玩，來評論執掌政權的人。鄭國的大夫然明對子產說：「把鄉校毀掉，怎麼樣？」子產說：「為什麼把鄉校毀掉呢？人民時常工作完了回來到鄉校那兒去遊玩，來議論執掌政權的人實行的政策妥不妥善。

Zǐchǎn Bù Huǐ Xiāng Xiào

Zhèng guó rén dào xiāng xiào qù yóuwán, lái pínglùn zhízhǎng zhèng quán .de rén. Zhèng guó .de dàifū Ránmíng duì Zǐchǎn shuō: "Bǎ xiāng xiào huǐ diào, zěn.mé yàng?" Zǐchǎn shuō: "Wèi shé.me bǎ xiāng xiào huǐ.diào .ne? Rénmín shícháng gōng.zuò wán .le huí.lái, dào xiāng xiào nàr qù yóuwán, lái yìlùn zhízhǎng zhèngquán .de rén shíxíng .de zhèng cè tuǒ .bù tuǒ shàn.

Zichan Does not Destroy the Local School

The people of the state of Zhèng sauntered into the local schools to comment on the conduct of government officials. Ránmíng, a grand master of the state of Zhèng, said to Zǐchǎn: "How about destroying the local schools?" Zǐchǎn said: "Why do that? Now, upon returning from work, people frequently saunter to the local schools to discuss whether the policies of those governing are appropriate or not.

其所善者，吾則行之；其所惡者，吾則改之。是吾師也
，若之何毀之？我聞忠善以損怨，不聞作威以防怨。豈
不遽止？然猶防川：大決所犯，傷人必多，吾不克救也
；

Qí suǒ shàn zhě, wú zé xíng zhī; qí suǒ è zhě, wú zé gǎi zhī. Shì wú shī yě, ruò zhī hé huǐ zhī? Wǒ wén zhōng shàn yǐ sǔn yuàn, bù wén zuò wēi yǐ fáng yuàn. Qǐ bú jù zhǐ? Rán yóu fáng chuān: dà jué suǒ fàn, shāng rén bì duō, wú bú kè jiù yě;

Chyi suoo shann jee, wu tzer shyng jy; chyi suoo eh jee, wu tzer gae jy. Shyh wu shy yee, ruoh jy her hoei jy? Woo wen jong shann yii soen yuann, bu wen tzuoh uei yii farng yuann. Chii bu jiuh jyy? Ran you farng chuan: dah jyue suoo fann, shang ren bih duo, wu bu keh jiow yee;

他們認為妥善的那些政令，我就實行；他們認為不妥善的那些政令，我就更改。鄉校中人民的議論是我的老師，怎麼可以把鄉校毀掉呢？我聽說盡心竭力實行妥善的政策來減少人民的怨恨，卻沒聽說採取嚴厲的措施來防堵人民的怨恨。毀掉鄉校難道不能很快地把人民的議論制止住？然而這好像是防堵河流一樣：河水在大規模衝破堤防時淹沒的地方，傷害人一定傷害得很多，我不能拯救；

Tāmén rènwéi tuǒshàn .de nàxiē zhènglìng, wǒ jiù shíxíng; tāmén rènwéi bù tuǒshàn .de nàxiē zhènglìng, wǒ jiù gēnggǎi. Xiāng xiào zhōng rénmín .de yìlùn shì wǒ .de lǎoshī, zěn.me kě.yǐ bǎ xiāng xiào huǐ.diào .ne? Wǒ tīngshuō jìnxīnjiélì shíxíng tuǒshàn .de zhèngcè lái jiǎnshǎo rénmín .de yuànhèn, què méi tīngshuō cǎiqǔ yánlì .de cuòshī lái fángdǔ rénmín .de yuànhèn. Huǐ .diào xiāng xiào nán.dào bùnéng hěnkuài.de bǎ rénmín .de yìlùn zhìzhǐ .zhù? Ránér zhè hǎoxiàng shì fángdǔ héliú yíyàng: héshuǐ zài dàguīmó chōngpò dīfáng shí yānmò .de dìfāng, shānghài rén yídìng shānghài .dé hěnduō, wǒ bùnéng zhěngjiù;

Those policies they deem appropriate I will carry out, and those policies they deem inappropriate I will alter. They are my teachers: how can the local schools be destroyed? I have heard that one should be utterly dedicated to implementing good policies in order to lessen the people's ill-will, yet I have not heard that an administration should take harsh measures to stop up their ill-will. Wouldn't the destruction of the local schools quickly stop the people's discussion? Even so, it is like damming up running water: in the area inundated when the river water breaches the dikes on a large scale, surely many people will be injured, I can not save them;

不如小決使道，不如吾聞而藥之也。"然明曰："蔑也
今而後知吾子之信可事也，小人實不才。若果行此，其
鄭國實賴之，豈唯二三臣？"仲尼聞是語也，曰："以
是觀之，人謂子產不仁，吾不信也。"

bù rú xiǎo jué shǐ dǎo, bù rú wú wén ér yào zhī yě." Ránmíng yuē: "Miè yě jīn ér hòu zhī wú zǐ zhī xìn kě shì yě, xiǎo rén shí bù cái. Ruò guǒ xíng cǐ, qí Zhèng guó shí lài zhī, qǐ wéi èr sān chén?" Zhòngní wén shì yǔ yě, yuē: "Yǐ shì guān zhī, rén wèi Zǐchǎn bù rén, wú bú xìn yě."

bu ru sheau jyue shyy dao, bu ru wu wen erl yaw jy yee." Ranming iue: "Mieh yee jin erl how jy wu tzyy jy shinn kee shyh yee, sheau ren shyr bu tsair. Ruoh guoo shyng tsyy, chyi Jenq gwo shyr lay jy, chii wei ell san chern?" Jonqni wen shyh yeu yee, iue: "Yii shyh guan jy, ren wey Tzyychaan bu ren, wu bu shinn yee."

不如在堤防那儿開個小口使河水流出去，不如我聽取他們的議論然後把它當作良藥來改善政策啊。"然明説："我從今以後才知道您確實值得人敬佩追隨啊。我的確看事看得不透徹。假若您果真實行這種政策，我們鄭國實在依靠它，哪裡只是我們幾個臣子呢？"仲尼聽到這些話，説："根據這件事情來看，人説子產不愛人民，我絕對不相信。"

Bùrú zài dīfáng nàr kāi .gè xiǎo kǒu shǐ héshuǐ liú .chū.qù , bùrú wǒ tīngqǔ tāmén .de yìlùn ránhòu bǎ tā dàng zuò liángyào lái gǎishàn zhèngcè .a." Ránmíng shuō: "Wǒ cóngjīn yǐhòu cái zhī.dào nín quèshí zhídé rén jìngpèi zhuīsuí .a. Wǒ díquè kàn shì kàn .dé bú tòuchè. Jiǎruò nín guǒzhēn shíxíng zhèi.zhǒng zhèngcè, wǒ.mén Zhèng guó shízài yīkào tā, nǎ.lǐ zhǐ.shì wǒ.mén jǐ.gè chén.zǐ .ne?" Zhòngní tīng .dào zhèxiē huà, shuō: "Gēnjù zhèi .jiàn shì.qíng lái kàn, rén shuō Zǐchǎn bú ài rénmín, wǒ juéduì bù xiāngxìn."

---

it is preferable to open a small breach in the dike and channel the water out, and it is preferable to listen to their criticism and then use it as a remedy to improve the government." Ránmíng said: "From this day on, I now know you truly deserve people's respect and following your lead. I am really short-sighted. If in the end you implement this, actually our whole state of Zhèng will rely on it -- how could it be only a few of us court officials?" Zhòngní heard these words and said: "Considering him in light of this incident, when people say that Zǐchǎn did not love the people, I do not believe it at all."

List of Exercises

練習一

一　字彙復習　Vocabulary Review

1. 寫出左表各詞的讀音，再從右表找出相配的解釋來　In parentheses, give the pronunciation for each of the words in the left column, and then match each word in the left column with its definition in the right column:

2. 按照句意的需要從左表的詞中選出適當的來填入空內　Choose the appropriate words from the left column to fill in the blanks according to the contextual meaning of each sentence:

卻 (　　　) (　　　) 1. 聰明　wise
待 (　　　) (　　　) 2. 懷疑　to suspect
築 (　　　) (　　　) 3. 希望　to hope
嗜 (　　　) (　　　) 4. 放下　to put down
疑 (　　　) (　　　) 5. 傍晚　dusk
冀 (　　　) (　　　) 6. 不接受　to refuse to accept
受 (　　　) (　　　) 7. 贈送　to present as a gift
釋 (　　　) (　　　) 8. 下雨　to rain
餽 (　　　) (　　　) 9. 愛好　to relish
智 (　　　) (　　　) 10. 丟失　to lose
暮 (　　　) (　　　) 11. 修理　to build; to repair
雨 (　　　) (　　　) 12. 碰　to hit against
折 (　　　) (　　　) 13. 等待　to wait for
亡 (　　　) (　　　) 14. 折斷　to break
觸 (　　　) (　　　) 15. 接受　to accept

1. 鄭相＿＿＿＿魚，有＿＿＿＿＿魚於鄭相者，鄭相不＿＿＿＿＿。
2. 天＿＿＿＿＿，富人之牆壞，不＿＿＿＿，暮而大＿＿＿＿其財。
3. 富人甚＿＿＿＿其子，而＿＿＿＿鄰人之父。
4. 兔走＿＿＿＿株，＿＿＿＿＿頸而死。
5. 耕者＿＿＿＿其耒而守株，＿＿＿＿復得兔。

二　句子分析　Sentence Analysis

分析下列的句子，找出主語、動詞、賓語、介詞、副詞來，並把句子譯成白話或英文　Analyze the following sentences, identify the subjects, verbs, objects, prepositions, and adverbs, and then translate the sentences into modern Chinese or into English:

183

1. 宋有耕者。
2. 宋人有夜盜富人之財者。
3. 耕者得兔，餽之於富人。
4. 鄭相卻魚，鄭君聞而賢之。
5. 鄭相受魚失祿，為宋人笑。
6. 鄰人之父為富人疑，恥之，觸牆而死。

注解：

1. 夜 yè 【名詞】夜裡；〔在〕晚上 night; at night
2. 聞 wén 【動詞】聽到 to hear
3. 賢 xián 【形容詞】有道德；高尚 worthy
    賢之 【動詞語】以之為賢 to think him worthy
    xián zhī 　　　　　覺得他很高尚
4. 恥 chǐ 【形容詞】羞恥 to be shameful
    恥之 【動詞語】以之為羞恥 to think it shameful
    chǐ zhī 　　　　　覺得被懷疑很羞恥

三　"其"字的兩種主要用法　The Two Main Uses of "Qí"

A. 領屬性代詞：用在名詞或名詞語前作定語，可譯成"他
／她／它〔們〕的　Used as a possessive pronoun, meaning 'his,'
'her,' 'its,' or 'their,' preceding the noun or noun phrase it modifies.

如：其子曰：不築，必將有盜。

〔耕者〕因釋其耒而守株。

B. 指示形容詞：用在名詞或名詞語前作定語，可譯成"那
個"　Used as a demonstrative, meaning "that," preceding the noun or noun
phrase it modifies.

如：其家甚智其子。
君見其牧羊者乎？　　　　　（列子・楊朱）
（君：您 you　　　牧羊者：放羊的人 a shephard）

試辨別下列句中的「其」字各屬於哪種用法 (A or B)，並把句
子譯成白話或英文　Identify the two uses of the word 'qí' in the following
sentences as 'A' or 'B', and then translate the sentences into modern Chinese or
into English:

1. 北溟有魚，其名為鯤。　　　　（莊子・逍遙遊）

2. 今其人在是。　　　　　　　　（戰國策・趙策）

3. 爾愛其羊，我愛其禮。　　　　（論語・八佾）

4. 一尺之棰，日取其半，萬世不竭。（莊子・天下）

注解：

1. 溟 míng 　　【名詞】大海；海洋 a vast sea; an ocean

   北溟
   běi míng 　【名詞語】北方的大海 the northen sea; the northern ocean

2. 名 míng 　　【名詞】名字 name

3. 鯤 kūn 　　【名詞】鯤；魚名 name of a kind of fish

4. 是 shì 　　【代詞】此；這裡 here

5. 爾 ěr 　　【代詞】你 you

6. 愛 ài 　　【動詞】愛惜 to cherish

7. 禮 lǐ 　　【名詞】禮儀 the rite; the ritual

8. 棰 chuí 　　【名詞】短木棒 a short wooden club

9. 取 qǔ 　　【名詞】拿 to take

10. 半 bàn 　　【量詞】一半 one half

11. 萬 wàn 　　【數詞】一萬 ten thousand

12. 世 shì 　　【名詞】代；三十年為一世 generations; 30 years is a generation

    萬世
    wàn shì 　【名詞語】一萬代；三十萬年 ten thousand generations; 300 thousand years

13. 竭 jié 　　【形容詞】竭盡；完 to exhaust; to be exhausted

四　討論 Discussion

1. "鄭相卻魚" 的故事強調什麼？
   What is emphasized in the story of "the Prime Minister of Zhèng refuses a gift of fish"?

2. "宋有富人" 與 "守株待兔" 反映人性中哪些方面？
   Which aspects of human nature are reflected in the stories of "There was a Wealthy Man of Sòng" and "Waiting for a Hare at the Tree Stump"?

185

練習二

一　字彙復習　Vocabulary Review

1. 寫出左表各詞的讀音，再從右表找出相配的解釋來　In the parentheses, give the pronunciation for each of the words in the left column, and then match each word in the left column with its definition in the right column:

2. 按照句意的需要從左表的詞中選出適當的來填入空內　Choose the appropriate words from the left column to fill in the blanks according to the contextual meaning of each sentence:

A　　徙（　　）（　　）1. 氣味難聞 stinky
　　　更（　　）（　　）2. 跟在後面 to follow
　　　居（　　）（　　）3. 喜歡 to like
　　　鳴（　　）（　　）4. 都 all
　　　逢（　　）（　　）5. 搬 to move
　　　臭（　　）（　　）6. 苦惱 to be embittered
　　　逐（　　）（　　）7. 遇見 to meet with
　　　說（　　）（　　）8. 討厭 to detest
　　　皆（　　）（　　）9. 改變 to change
　　　隨（　　）（　　）10. 叫 to cry; to screech
　　　惡（　　）（　　）11. 追趕 to chase after
　　　苦（　　）（　　）12. 住 to live at/in

1. 梟＿＿＿鳩。鳩曰：“子將安之？”梟曰：“我將東＿＿＿。.”

2. 海上人有＿＿＿＿其臭者，晝夜＿＿＿＿之而弗能去。

B　　臞（　　）（　　）1. 白天 day time
　　　夜（　　）（　　）2. 回答 to respond
　　　義（　　）（　　）3. 有地位 to be highly placed
　　　勝（　　）（　　）4. 榮耀 glorious; splendid
　　　樂（　　）（　　）5. 快樂 happiness
　　　榮（　　）（　　）6. 正道 righteousness
　　　肥（　　）（　　）7. 勝利 to win a battle
　　　戰（　　）（　　）8. 瘦 to be lean or thin
　　　貴（　　）（　　）9. 打敗 to be defeated

186

畫 （　　　）（　　　） 10. 胖 to be fat

頁 （　　　）（　　　） 11. 夜裡 night time

對 （　　　）（　　　） 12. 打仗 to engage in a battle

吾入見先王之＿＿＿＿則榮之，出見富＿＿＿＿之樂又榮之。兩者＿＿＿＿於胸中，未知勝＿＿＿＿，故臞。今先王之義勝，故＿＿＿＿。

C　鄉人 （　　　）（　　　） 1. 心裡 in one's heart

　　先王 （　　　）（　　　） 2. 鄉村的人 villagers

　　親戚 （　　　）（　　　） 3. 朋友 acqaintances

　　兄弟 （　　　）（　　　） 4. 海邊上 at the sea shore

　　妻妾 （　　　）（　　　） 5. 哥哥弟弟 elder and younger brothers

　　知識 （　　　）（　　　） 6. 古代的聖王 the sage kings of antiquity

　　海上 （　　　）（　　　） 7. 太太跟姨太太 wife and concubines

　　胸中 （　　　）（　　　） 8. 內親外戚 relatives by blood or by marriage

1. 鳩曰："＿＿＿＿皆惡我鳴，以故東徙。"

2. 人有大臭者，其＿＿＿＿、兄弟、＿＿＿＿、知識無能與居者。自苦而居＿＿＿＿。

二　"者" 字 的 用 法 The Uses of "Zhǒ"

"者" 是被飾代詞，前面加上修飾語／定語，構成名詞語，用作句中的主語或賓語 As a modified pronoun, the wors 'zhě' combines with a preceding modifier to form a noun phrase that functions as the subject or object in a sentence.

如：耕者因釋其耒而守株。

　　人有大臭者⋯。

"者" 字前的定語可分三種形式： The three types of modifiers.

A. 動＋者　　如：耕者

B. 動＋賓＋者　如：鬻盾與矛者

C. 形＋者　　如：大臭者

187

試辨別下列句中用"者"字構成的名詞語的定語各屬於哪種形式？並把句子譯成白話或英文 Identify the different types of the modifiers of the pronoun 'zhe' in the following sentences as 'A,' 'B,' or 'C,' and then translate the sentences into modern Chinese or into English:

1. 楚人有涉江者。　　　（呂氏春秋・察今）　　（　　）
2. 智者不惑。　　　　　　（論語・子罕）　　　（　　）
3. 狂者東走，逐者亦東走。（韓非子・說林）　　（　　）

　　　注解：

　　1. 楚人　【名詞語】楚國人 to herd sheep; to tend sheep
　　　Chǔ rén

　　2. 涉 shè　【動詞】渡過 to cross

　　3. 江 jiāng【名詞】河　a river

　　4. 智 zhì　【形容詞】聰明 to be wise

　　5. 惑 huò　【形容詞】迷惑 comfused; deluded

　　6. 狂 kuáng【形容詞】瘋狂 to be mad; to be insane

　　7. 逐 zhú　【動詞】追趕 to chase; to pursue

　　8. 走 zǒu　【動詞】跑 to run

三　　語法復習　Review of Grammar

1. 在文言中，疑問代詞用作賓語時通常倒放在動詞或介詞之前
In classical Chinese, when an interrogative pronoun functions as an object, it is generally placed in front of the verb or preposition that governs it.

　　　如：　子將安之？

　　把下列的句子譯成白話或英文 Translate the following sentences into modern Chinese or into English:

　　1. 沛公安在？　　　　　　　　（史記・項羽本紀）
　　2. 孟嘗君曰："客何好？"　　　（戰國策・齊策）
　　3. 吾誰欺，欺天乎？　　　　　（論語・子罕）
　　4. 老母已死，雖欲報恩將安歸？（漢書・李陵傳）
　　5. 吾誰與為鄰？　　　　　　　（莊子・山木）

　　　注解：

　　1. 沛公　【名詞語】劉邦，即後來的漢高祖 Liú Bāng, Duke of
　　　Pèi Gōng　　　　　　Pèi at that time, and later became the founder of the
　　　　　　　　　　　　　Hàn dynasty

188

2. 孟嘗君【名詞語】田文，戰國時代四公子之一 Tian Wen,
   Mèngcháng Jūn   the Prince of Mèngcháng, one of four powerful
                               princes during the Warring States period

3. 客 kè　【名詞】客人 the guest

4. 好 hào　【動詞】愛好；特別喜歡 to like; to have a special liking of

5. 誰 shéi　【疑問代詞】誰 who? whom?

6. 欺 qī　【動詞】欺騙 to cheat

7. 報 bào　【動詞】報答 to repay; to pay back

8. 恩 ēn　【名詞】恩惠 a grace; a kindness

9. 歸 guī　【動詞】回去 to return; to go back to

10. 與 yǔ　【介詞】跟 with

11. 為鄰　【動詞語】做鄰居 to be neighbors
    wéi lín

2. 在文言中，方向詞通常倒放在動詞之前 In classical Chinese, a
directional word is generally placed in front of the verb of action.

如：我將東徙。

把下列的句子譯成白話或英文 Translate the following sentences
into modern Chinese or into English:

1. 孔子東遊。 　　　　　　　　　（列子・湯問）
2. 西風緊，北雁南飛。 　　　　　（王實甫・西廂記）
3. 夕陽西下幾時回？ 　　　　　　（晏殊・浣溪沙）
4. 操軍破，必北還。 　　　　　　（司馬光・資治通鑑）

注解：

1. 孔子　【名詞】孔子 Master; Confucius
   Kǒngzǐ

2. 遊 yóu　【名詞】旅遊；漫遊 to travel; to roam

3. 西 xī　【方向詞】西方；西邊 west; western; westerly

4. 風 fēng　【名詞】風 wind

   西風　【名詞語】來自西方的風 a westerly wind
   xī fēng

5. 緊 jǐn　【形容詞】急 tense; strong

6. 北 běi　【方向詞】北方；北邊 north; northern; northerly

7. 雁 yàn　【名詞】大雁 swan; goose

   北雁　【名詞語】北方的大雁 the northern swan
   běi yàn

8. 南 nán　【方向詞】南方；南邊 south; southern; southerly

189

9. 飛 fēi 　【動詞】飛 to fly

10. 夕陽 　【名詞語】傍晚的太陽 the setting sun
　　 xì yáng

11. 下 xià 　【動詞】落下 to set; to go down

12. 幾時 　【名詞語】什麼時候 what time; when
　　 jǐ shí

13. 操 Cāo 【名詞】曹操 Cáo Cāo, an important figure in the Three
　　　　　　 Kingdoms Period

14. 軍 jūn 　【名詞】軍隊 troops; army

15. 破 pò 　【動詞】打敗；被打敗 to defeat; to be defeated

16. 還 huán 【動詞】反回 to return

四 　翻譯 Translation

把下列句子譯成白話或英文　Translate the following sentences into
modern Chinese or into Engliah:

1. 大臭者不能去其臭，以故其兄弟妻妾皆不能與之居。

2. 先王之義與富貴之樂戰於子夏胸中，孰勝孰負？

3. 富貴之樂，人皆說（悅）之。

4. 東鄉之人皆嗜魚，以其地近海，易得之也。

5. 鳩謂梟曰："子若更鳴，則鄉人不復惡子之聲矣。何東徙也
　？"

6. 臞者逢肥者。臞者曰："子何肥也？"對曰："嗜兔，故肥
　。子何臞也？"對曰："嗜魚，故臞。"

　注解：

　　1. 去 qù 　【動詞】除去 to get rid of
　　2. 易 yì 　【副詞】容易 easily

五 　討論 Discussion

1. "逐臭"的故事要告訴人什麼？
　 What is the point of the story "Chasing the Smell"?

2. 談義利之戰。
　 Discuss the struggle between what is right and what is profitable.

3. "梟逢鳩"給人什麼啓發？
　 What does the story of "The Owl Meets the Ringdove" reveal?

190

練習三

一　字彙復習　Vocabulary Review

1. 寫出左表各詞的讀音，再從右表找出相配的解釋來　In the parentheses, give the pronunciation for each of he words in the left column, and then match each word in the left column with its definition in the right column:

2. 按照句意的需要從左表的詞中選出適當的來填入空內　Choose the appropriate words from the left column to fill in blanks according to the contextual meaning of each sentence:

賤 (	) (	)	1. 厭惡 to hate
懼 (	) (	)	2. 偷 to steal
堅 (	) (	)	3. 賣 to sell
掩 (	) (	)	4. 住宿 to stay overnight
利 (	) (	)	5. 醜陋 ugly
應 (	) (	)	6. 高尚 virtuous
宿 (	) (	)	7. 讚美；誇 to praise; to brag
頁 (	) (	)	8. 害怕 to fear
惡 (	) (	)	9. 背 to carry on the back
鬻 (	) (	)	10. 捂住 to vover {with one's hands]
貴 (	) (	)	11. 趕緊 hurriedly
敗 (	) (	)	12. 回答 to respond; to answer
憎 (	) (	)	13. 堅固 firm
悖 (	) (	)	14. 鋒利 sharp
陷 (	) (	)	15. 美麗 beautiful
鍾 (	) (	)	16. 地位低；不受寵 not favored
賢 (	) (	)	17. 荒唐 absurd
竊 (	) (	)	18. 刺穿 to pierce through
美 (	) (	)	19. 被打敗 to be defeated
罄 (	) (	)	20. 聽見 to hear
聞 (	) (	)	21. 鐘；樂器 a bell
遽 (	) (	)	22. 地位高；受寵 to be favored

1. 楚人有＿＿＿盾與矛者，＿＿＿之曰：「吾盾之＿＿＿＿＿，物莫能＿＿＿也。」又譽其矛曰。「吾矛之＿＿＿，於物無不陷也。」

191

2. 陽子之宋，＿＿＿於逆旅。逆旅人有妾二人，其一人美，
其一人＿＿＿。惡者貴而美者＿＿＿。

3. 〔竊鍾者〕＿＿＿人聞之，遽＿＿＿其耳。

4. ＿＿＿人聞之，可也；自掩其耳，＿＿＿矣。

二　　 “之”字的用法　The Uses of "Zhī"

“之”字的主要用法有三種：A.動詞 B.代詞賓語 C.結構助詞
The three major functions of 'zhi' are: 'A,' as a verb, 'B,' as a pronoun, and 'C,' as
a structual particle.

A. 動詞，到…去　As a verb meaning 'to go to...'
如：子將安之？

B. 代詞，用作賓語　As a pronoun in the objective case: 'him,' 'her,' 'it,' or
'them.'
如：海上人有說其臭者，晝夜隨之而弗能去。

C. 結構助詞　As a structural particle

1. 聯結定語跟名詞，構成一個名詞語，充當句子的主語或
賓語　It joins the adjectival modifier and the head noun it modifies to form a
noun phrase that serves as the subject or object in a sentence.

用作主語　Used as a subject
如："今先王之義勝，故肥。"

用作賓語　Used as an object
如："其家甚智其子，而疑鄰人之父。"

2. 用在主語和謂語之間，把句子轉化成主謂短語，作包孕
句中的主／賓和複句中的分句　It is used between the subject and
its predicate in a sentence to transform the sentence into a clausal phrase that
serves as the subject/object in an embedding sentence or a dependent clause in
a compound sentence.

如：吾矛之利，於物無不陷也。

范氏之敗，有竊其鍾負而走者。

試辨別下列句中的“之”字各屬於什麼用法 Identify the use of the
word 'zhī' in each of the following sentences as either 'A,' 'B,' or 'C':

192

1. 其人大臭，其妻不能與之居，請去。　　（　　）
2. 〔鬻盾與矛者〕譽之曰："吾盾之堅，物莫能陷也。"
　　　　　　　　　　　　　　　　　　　　　　（　　）
3. 以子之矛陷子之盾，何如？　　　　　　　（　　）
4. 不可陷之盾與無不陷之矛不可同世而立。（　　）
5. 吾出見富貴之樂又榮之。　　　　　　　　（　　）
6. 行賢而去自賢之心，安往而不愛哉？　　（　　）
7. 憎人聞之，可也；自掩其耳，悖矣。　　（　　）

三　語法復習　Review of Grammar

A. 在文言中，"自" 字用在動詞前時，是副詞用來修飾動詞，同時又是代詞用作動詞的賓語 In addition to its adverbial function, the word 'zì' has the characteristics of a pronoun, i.e., it is a reflexive pronominal object like 'himself.' For example:

　如：大臭者自苦而居海上

B. 用反問來表示肯定 In classical Chinese it is very common that a rhetorical quetion is used to express affirmation. For example:

　如：安往而不愛哉？

C. 用雙否定來表示肯定 A double negative construction can also be used to express affirmation. For example:

　如：吾矛之利，於物無不陷也。

把下列的句子譯成白話或英文 Translate the following sentences into modern Chinese or into English:

1. 勝人者有力，自勝者強。　　　　（老子・三十三章）

2. 見賢思齊焉，見不賢而內自省也。（論語・里仁）

3. 君子無入而不自得。　　　　　　（禮記・中庸）

4. 何求而不得？何為而不成？　　　（戰國策・魏策）

注解：

1. 勝 shèng【動詞】戰勝；克服　to win over; to conquer

2. 有力　【動詞語】有力量；強大　powerful
　yǒu lì

3. 強 qiáng【形容詞】堅強　steadfast; firm; trong

4. 思 sī　【動詞】想；思考　to think; to consider

5. 齊 qí　【形容詞】一樣；同等　to equal

193

6. 焉 yān 【合成詞】於之；跟他 with him

7. 內 nèi 【名詞】內心；心裡 inside; in the heart

8. 省 xǐng 【動詞】反省 to introspect

9. 君子 jūn zǐ 【名詞語】人格高尚的人 a man of virtue

10. 入 rù 【動詞】進入 to enter
   【名詞】進入的地方；置身的環境 where one finds oneself to be

11. 自得 zì dé 【動詞語】自己得到自己；感到自己很滿足 self content

12. 何 hé 【疑問代詞】什麼 what

13. 求 qiú 【動詞】追求；尋求 to pursue; to seek

14. 得 dé 【動詞】得到 to get; to obtain

15. 為 wéi 【動詞】做 to do

16. 成 chéng 【動詞】成功 to succeed

四 成語 Set Phrases

1. 選出適當的字來，填入下列成語的空內 Choose the appropriate words from the list provided below to fill in the blanks:

2. 寫出每個成語的讀音來 In the parentheses give the pronunciation for each of the above set phrases:

3. 用下列的成語各造一個句子，或選用三個成語來組成一段短文 Make sentences with each of the following set phrases, or choose three of them and use them to compose a short passage:

臭　賢　盜　廣　相　株

自以為 _____ (　　　　　　　　　　　　)

掩耳 _____ 鈴 (　　　　　　　　　　　　)

自 _____ 矛盾 (　　　　　　　　　　　　)

守 _____ 待兔 (　　　　　　　　　　　　)

逐 _____ 之夫 (　　　　　　　　　　　　)

心 _____ 體胖 (　　　　　　　　　　　　)

194

五　討論　Discussion

1. 談自相矛盾的普遍性。
   Comment on the univeral nature of self-contradiction as revealed in "Spears and Shields."

2. 討論自賢與自美之害。
   Discuss the harm brought about by thinking the self to be worthy or beautiful.

3. "盜鐘"（掩耳盜鈴）的故事說明什麼？
   What is the story of "Stealing the Bell" trying to illustrate?

練習四

一 **動詞複習** Review of Verbs

找出下列各句中的動詞，並寫出它們的讀音和意思來 Find the verbs in the following sentences, and give the pronunciation and meaning for each of them:

1. 鄭人有且買履者，先自度其足而置之其座。至之市而忘操之。

2. 昔有昆弟三人，游齊魯之間，同師而學，進仁義之道而歸。

3. 伯曰："仁義使我殺身以成名。"

4. 兩者不肯相舍，漁父得而并擒之。今趙且伐燕，燕趙久相支以敝大眾，臣恐強秦之為漁父也。

(   ) (   ) (   ) (   )

(   ) (   ) (   ) (   )

(   ) (   ) (   ) (   )

(   ) (   ) (   ) (   )

二 **副詞複習** Review of Adverbs

找出下列各句中的副詞，並寫出它們的讀音和意思來 Find the adverbs in the following sentences, and give the pronunciation and meaning for each of them:

1. 不築，必將有盜。 (   )

2. 〔富人〕暮果大亡其財。 (   )

3. 其家甚智其子，而疑鄰人之父。 (   )

4. 子何肥也？ (   )

5. 鄉人皆惡我鳴。 (   )

6. 不能更鳴，東徙，猶惡子之聲。 (   )

7. 其惡者自惡，吾不知其惡也。 (   )

8. 其人弗能應也。 (   )

9. 兩者不肯相舍，漁父得而并擒之。 (   )

10. 臣恐強秦之為漁父也，故願王熟計之也。 (   )

三 **反義字** Antonyms

1. **選出意思相反的字來，填入下列各字的旁邊** Choose words with the opposite meaning to fill in the blanks:

2. **寫出每對反義字的讀音來** In the parentheses give the pronunciation for each pair of antonyms:

196

	非	臞	惡	夜	失	疑
	憎	受	頁	樂	舍	昔

信＿＿（　　　　　）　　是＿＿（　　　　　　　　）

得＿＿（　　　　　）　　愛＿＿（　　　　　　　　）

勝＿＿（　　　　　）　　今＿＿（　　　　　　　　）

肥＿＿（　　　　　）　　取＿＿（　　　　　　　　）

美＿＿（　　　　　）　　卻＿＿（　　　　　　　　）

苦＿＿（　　　　　）　　畫＿＿（　　　　　　　　）

四　　翻譯　Translation

把下列句子譯成白話或英文　Translate the following sentences into modern Chinese or into English:

1. 子夏重仁義之道而輕富貴之樂。

2. 知人者智，自知者明。　　　　（老子・三十三章）

3. 寧為雞口，勿為牛後。　　（史記・蘇秦張儀列傳）

注解：

1. 重 zhòng	【形容詞】	重；重要	heavy; weighty; important
	【用作動詞】	以…為重；看重；重視	to think...important
2. 輕 qīng	【形容詞】	輕；不重要	light; unimportant
	【用作動詞】	以…為輕；看輕	to think...unimportant
3. 知 zhī	【動詞】	了解	to understand
4. 明 míng	【形容詞】	明察	perspicacious
5. 寧 nìng	【副詞】	寧願	would rather ...
6. 為 wéi	【動詞】	做	to be; to become
7. 雞 jī	【名詞】	雞	a chicken
8. 口 kǒu	【名詞】	嘴	mouth; beak
9. 勿 wù	【副詞】	不 not; 不要	do not
10. 牛 niú	【名詞】	牛	an ox; a cow
11. 後 hòu	【名詞】	屁股	end; buttocks

五　　點斷、分析、及翻譯　Puctuation, Analysis, and Translation

點斷下文、分析它的結構，找出主、動、賓、助動、介詞來，並譯成白話或英文　Punctuate the following passage, then analyze it by identifying the subjects, verbs, objects, auxiliary verbs, and prepositions in it, and finally, translate the passage into modern Chinese or into English:

197

蘇秦讀書欲睡引錐自刺其股血流至足
（戰國策‧秦策）

注解 ：

1. 欲 yù 　　【助動詞】想要 to want to
2. 睡 shuì 　　【動詞】睡覺 to sleep; to go to bed
3. 引 yǐn 　　【動詞】拿起 to take up
4. 錐 zhuī 　　【名詞】錐子 an awl
5. 刺 cì 　　【動詞】插(chā)入 to stab into
6. 股 gǔ 　　【名詞】大腿 leg; thigh
7. 血 xuě 　　【名詞】血 blood
8. 流 liú 　　【名詞】流；滴下來 to flow; to drip

六　　而字復習　Review of the Conjunction "而"

連詞 "而" 的主要用法有八種類型 The conjunction "而" has eight major types of the uses:

1. V-O 而 V-O　　表示時間先後的關係，"而" 字可譯成白話的 "就" 。 It links two predicates in a temporal sequence. The "而" in this usage can be rendered as "就" in spoken Chinese. (consult Analyses, L.10, 2, p.57)

　　先自度其足而置之其座。

2. V-O 而 V-O　　表示因果關係，"而" 字可譯成白話的 "就" 。 It links two predicates in a causal relation. The "而" in this usage can be rendered as "就" in spoken Chinese. (consult Analyses, L.3, 3, p.14)

　　兔走觸株，折頸而死。

3. V-O 而 V-O　　表示行動目的關係，"而" 字可譯成白話的 "來" 或 "去" 。 It links two predicates in sequence: the first predicate states an action, and the second predicate shows the purpose of that action. The "而" in this usage can be rendered as "來" or "去" in spoken Chinese. (consult Analyses, L.3, 4, p.15)

　　因釋其耒而守株，冀復得兔。

4. V-O 而 V-O　　表示相逆的關係，"而" 字可譯成白話的 "卻" 或 "可是" 。 It connects two predicates that are

198

mutually contrary. The "而" in this usage can be rendered as "卻" or "可是" in spoken Chinese.

(consult Analyses, L.2, 6, p.11)

其家甚智其子，而疑鄰人之父兔。

5. V-O 而 V-O
adv

前一動詞／動詞語 (V/V-O) 用如副詞，"而"字不必翻譯，但須加上白話的"地"或"著"來顯示副詞性。 The first predicate functions as an second adverbial modifier of the predicate. The "而" in this usage does not have a counterpart in spoken Chinese. The first predicate can be translated into English as verbals, such as an adjectival participle. (consult Analyses, L.9, 1, p.53)

竊其鐘，頁之而走。

6. Prep-O 而 V-O
adv

"而"字前的介詞語用如副詞，通常指出主要謂語表示的事件或行動發生的時間或地點。"而"字不必譯出。 It links a prepositional phrase to the main predicate. The prepositional phrase functions as an adverbial modifier that indicates a time or place. The "而" in this usage need not be translated.(consult Analyses, L.10, 3, p.59)

至之市而忘操之。

7. V-O 而 V-O

"而"字配合音節，不必翻譯。 The "而" serves only to make the sentence more euphonic, and it does not have a grammatical function. It need not be translated.

(consult Analyses, L.4, 5, p. 20)

晝夜隨之而弗能去。

8. V-O 而 V-O

"而"字前後的謂語一意相因，"而"字不必譯出。 The "而" connects two predicates that express a single interconnected thought; it need not be translated into spoken Chinese. (consult Analyses, L.11, 4, p.66)

仁義使我愛身而後名。

試辨別下列各句中而字的用法屬於八類中的哪一類 Identify the uses of "而" in the following sentences as which of the eight types:

1. 夫不可陷之盾與無不陷之矛不可同世而立。　　　(　　)
2. 行賢而去自賢之心，安往而不愛哉？　　　(　　)
3. 楚人和氏得玉璞楚山中，奉而獻之厲王。　　　(　　)
4. 已得履，乃曰："吾忘持度。"反歸而取之。　　　(　　)

199

5. 彼三術相反，<u>而</u>同出於儒，孰是孰非耶？   (   )

6. 燕相受書<u>而</u>說之。   (   )

7. 尚明也者，舉賢<u>而</u>用之。   (   )

8. 大臭者自苦<u>而</u>居海上。   (   )

9. 孫叔敖為嬰兒之時，出遊，見兩頭蛇，殺<u>而</u>   (   )
　　埋之，歸<u>而</u>泣。　　　　（新序‧雜事）   (   )

10. 其母問其故。叔敖對曰：“聞見兩頭之蛇者死，
　　嚮者吾見之，恐去母<u>而</u>死也。”   (   )
　　　　　　　　　　　　　（新序‧雜事）

注 解 ：

1. 孫叔敖【名詞】人名；姓蔿名敖字孫叔，楚莊王相 personal
Sūnshú Áo name; surnamed Wěi, named Áo, courtesy named Sūnshú, he was the prime minister of Chǔ during the reign of King Zhuāng

2. 嬰兒 【名詞語】小孩子 a child
yīng ér

3. 兩頭蛇【名詞語】長了兩個頭的蛇 a snake with two heads
liǎng tóu shé

4. 殺 shā 【動詞】殺死 to kill

5. 埋 mái 【動詞】埋葬 to bury

6. 泣 qì 【動詞】哭泣 to weep; to sob

7. 嚮者 【時間詞】剛才 just now; a while ago
xiàng zhě

8. 恐 kǒng 【動詞】恐怕 to fear; to be afraid that

七　討論　Discussion

1. 從 “蘇代諫趙王” 看諫的技巧。
Comment on the skill of remonstrance in light of "Sū Dài Admonishes the King of Zhào".

2. “鄭人買履” 批評什麼？
What is criticized in the story "A Man of Zhèng Buys Shoes"?

3. “仁義之道” 是儒家思想的中心，學習者卻有不同的領會，為什麼？
"Benevolence and Righteousness" are the core of Confucian teachings, yet scholars have different understanding of them. Why?

練習五

一　辨別詞意　Distinguish the Meaning of Words

請辨別下列短文中各畫線詞的意思是 "A" 還是 "B" Identify the meaning of the underlined words in the following passage as "A," or "B":

　　　書（A. 信　　　B. 寫）
　　　舉（A. 舉高　　B. 推舉）
　　　說（A. 解說　　B. 高興）

郢人有遺燕相國書者，夜書，火不明，因謂持燭者曰："舉燭

。"云而過書舉燭。舉燭，非書意也。燕相得書而說之曰：

"舉燭者，尚明也。尚明也者，舉賢而任之。"燕相白王，大

說，國以治。

二　名詞語的三種類型　Three Types of Noun Phrases

　A. 定語＋之＋名詞　　　　　郢人之父
　B. 定語＋被飾代詞 "者"　　　鬻金者
　C. 代詞 "其" ＋名詞　　　　　其子

請分辨下列四個名詞語的結構各屬 A, B, C 中哪一類　Identify the structural type of the following noun phrases as 'A,' 'B,' or 'C':

　　1. 欲金者　　　　（　　　　　　　　　）
　　2. 欲金者之所　　（　　　　　　　　　）
　　3. 其金　　　　　（　　　　　　　　　）
　　4. 人之金　　　　（　　　　　　　　　）

三　填空　Fill in Blanks

選擇適當的介詞填入各句的空中　Fill in the following blanks with the appropriate prepositions:

爲　　於　　以　　與

　　1. 蘇代＿＿＿＿燕謂惠王曰：
　　2. 鄭人餽魚＿＿＿＿鄭相。
　　3. 鄉人皆惡我鳴，＿＿＿＿＿＿故東徙。
　　4. 子何不試之＿＿＿＿＿足？

201

5. 其親戚、兄弟、妻妾、知識無能_____居者。

6. _____子之矛陷子之盾，何如？

7. 陽子之宋，宿_____逆旅。

8. 彼三術相反而同出_____儒，孰是孰非耶？

9. 虎以為然，故遂_____之行。

10. 子以我為不信，吾_____子先行，觀百獸之見我而敢不走乎？

四　翻譯　Translation

把下列句子翻譯成白話或英文　Translate the following sentences into modern Chinese or into English:

1. 趙王以蘇代之言為然。

2. 趙且伐燕，蘇代甚不以為然。

3. 燕王使燕相舉賢而任之。

4. 今欲以先王之政（政策；治國方法）治當世之民，皆守株之類也。　　　　（韓非子·五蠹）

五　簡句的三種類型　Three Types of Simple Sentences

A. 敘述句	Declarative (Narrative) Sentences	S	P(V/V-O)
B. 描寫句	Descriptive Sentences	S	P(Adj.)
C. 判斷句	Determinative Sentences	S	P(L.V.- N)
			P(S.L.V.- N)

1. 分辨下列的句子各是什麼簡句　Identify the following simple sentences as 'A' narrative, 'B' descriptive, or 'C' determinative:

1. 蘇代諫趙王。　　（　　　）　（戰國策·燕策）

2. 鄭人買履。　　　（　　　）　（韓非子·外儲說）

3. 簡子不說／悅。　（　　　）　（說苑·善說）

4. 君美甚。　　　　（　　　）　（戰國策·齊策）

5. 此若先人之廬。　（　　　）　（列子·周穆王）

6. 孔子賢人也。　　（　　　）　（戰國策·趙策）

7. 智者不惑。　　　（　　　）　（論語·子罕）

8. 仁者愛人。　　　（　　　）　（孟子·離婁）

9. 江山如畫。　　　（　　　）　（宋·蘇軾·念奴嬌）

10. 夜半鐘聲到客船。（　　　）　（張繼·楓橋夜泊）

11. 其人大慚。　　　（　　　）（列子・周穆王）

12. 烏鵲南飛。　　　（　　　）（曹操・短歌行）

13. 霜葉紅於二月花。（　　　）（杜牧・山行）

14. 老子莊周，吾之師也。（　　　）

（嵇康・與山巨源絕交書）

15. 夫天地者，萬物之逆旅。（　　　）

（李白・春夜宴桃李園序）

注解：

1. 簡子 Jiǎnzǐ 【名詞】人名；姓趙(Zhào)、名鞅(Yǎng)，是晉國的權臣 the name of a powerful high minister in the state of Jìn

2. 說 yuè 【形容詞】高興 pleased

3. 此 cǐ 【代名詞】這個 this

4. 先人 xiān rén 【名詞語】祖先 ancestors

5. 廬 lú 【名詞】茅廬；茅草頂的房子 thatched huts

6. 孔子 Kǒngzǐ 【名詞】孔丘 (Qiū)，儒家的創立者 Confucius; founder of the Confucian School

7. 賢人 xián rén 【名詞語】有道德、有才能的人 men of moral integrity and ability

8. 智者 zhì zhě 【名詞語】有智慧的人 those who are wise

9. 仁者 rén zhě 【名詞語】有仁德（愛心）的人 those who are benevolent

10. 江山 jiāng shān 【名詞語】江跟山 rivers and mountains; the scenery

11. 畫 huà 【名詞】圖畫 a painting; a picture

12. 夜半 yè bàn 【時間詞】夜到一半的時候 half way into the night 半夜 midnight

13. 鐘聲 zhōng shēng 【名詞語】敲鐘的聲音 sound of a bell

14. 到 dào 【名詞】到達；傳到 to reach; to spread to

15. 客船 kè chuán 【名詞語】旅客的船 a boat that carries guests

16. 其人 qí rén 【名詞語】那個人 that person

17. 慚 cán 【形容詞】慚愧 embarrassed; mortified

18. 烏鵲 wū què 【名詞語】烏鴉和喜鵲 crows and magpies

19. 飛 fēi 【動語】飛 to fly

203

20. 霜 shuāng【名語】霜 frost

21. 葉 yè 【名語】樹葉 leaves

霜葉 【名詞語】經霜的葉子；被霜打過的葉子 leaves colored
shuāng yè by the frost

22. 紅 hóng【形容詞】紅 red

23. 於 yú 【介詞】用在形容詞後，表示比較的意思 When used after
an adjective, it indicates comparison of the noun before it
with the noun after it, meaning: "A is more adj. than B."

N1	Adj.	於	N2
N1		比	N2 Adj.

24. 花 huā 【名詞】花 flowers

25. 二月花【名詞語】二月間盛開的花 flowers blooming in March
èr yuè huā (approximately equivalent to the second lunar month)

26. 老子 【名詞語】人名；姓李、名耳，是道家的創始人
Lǎozǐ Lǐ Ěr, the founder of the Taoist (Daoist) School

27. 莊周 【名詞】人名；即莊子，是道家的第二位大師
Zhuāng Zhōu Zhuāng Zhōu, the second great master of the Taoist School

28. 夫 fú 【助語】用在一句開始，表示議論 introductory particle,
now

29. 天地 【名詞語】天和地 Heaven and Earth
tiān dì

30. 萬物 【名詞語】世上所有的東西 everything in the world
wàn wù

2. 把五到十五句譯成白話或英文 Translate sentences 5 to 15 above into
modern Chinese or into English:

六 討論 Discussion

"郢書燕說"、"狐假虎威"、與"攫金"三個故事中，你覺
得最有意思的是哪個？為什麼？

Among the stories "The Letter from Yǐng Explained in Yān," "The Fox Borrows the
Tiger's Prestige," and "Grabbing the Gold," which one do you think is the most
interesting? Why do you think so?

練習六

一 重要生詞復習 Vocabulary Review

1. 寫出每個字的讀音和意思來 On the line and in the parentheses give the pronunciation and meaning for each of the words:

2. 根據句子的意思選出適當的字來填入空內 Fill in the following blanks with the the appropriate words according to the contextual meaning of each sentence:

墜____ (	)	惑____ (	)
慎____ (	)	自____ (	)
契____ (	)	此____ (	)
涉____ (	)	赤____ (	)

1. 君子 _____所藏。
2. 丹之所藏者 _____，烏之所藏者黑。
3. 楚人有 _____江者，其劍 _____舟中 _____於水。
4. 遽_____其舟。
5. 求劍若 _____，不亦_____乎？

二 同義字 Synonyms

1. 選出意思相同或相近的字來填入下列各字的旁邊 On the line fill in the word from the list with the same or similar meaning:

2. 寫出每對同義字的讀音來 In the parentheses give the pronunciation for each pair of synonyms:

斷　捕　盜　得　獻　逐　惡　取　懼　刺

畏____ (	)	憎____ (	)
折____ (	)	攫____ (	)
追____ (	)	獲____ (	)
契____ (	)	擒____ (	)
竊____ (	)	奉____ (	)

三 成語 Set Phrases

1. 選出適當的字來，填入下列成語的空內 Choose the appropriate words from the list proveded below to fill in the blanks:

2. 寫出每個成語的讀音來 Give the pronunciation for each of the set phrases above :

3. 用每個成語造一個句子，或選用四個成語來組成一段短文
Make sentences with each of the set phrases, or choose six of them and use them to compose a short passage:

義　劍　説　墨　昏　翁　戚　守　爭　赤

郢書燕_____（　　　　　　　　）
狐假虎_____（　　　　　　　　）
利令智_____（　　　　　　　　）
舍生取_____（　　　　　　　　）
刻舟求_____（　　　　　　　　）
墨_____成規（　　　　　　　　）
鷸蚌相____，漁____得利（　　　　　　　　　　　　）
近朱者____，近____者黑（　　　　　　　　　　　　）

四　　所字的用法　The Uses of "Suǒ"

一　用敘述句中動詞的賓語當作主語造一個包括所字的判斷句並把判斷句譯成白話或英文

Make the object of the verb in the narrative sentence the subject of a determinative sentence containing the particle "suo"; then translate the determinative sentence into modern Chinese or into English:

例：鄭相卻魚
　　魚乃鄭相〔之〕所卻

1. 楚人刻舟

2. 燕攻齊（攻：攻打 attack）

3. 齊人攫金

4. 富人疑鄰人之父

二　用敘述句中介詞的賓語當作主語造一個包括所字的判斷句並把判斷句譯成白話或英文

Make the object of the preposition in the narrative sentence the subject of a determinative sentence containing the particle "suo"; then translate the determinative sentence into modern Chinese or into English:

例：鄭相以嗜魚卻魚
　　嗜魚乃鄭相〔之〕所以卻魚

1. 楚人以刀刻舟（以：用）

2. 燕以火攻齊

3. 齊人以欲金攫金（以：因）

4. 富人以亡財疑鄰人之父
　　　　　　（以：因）

206

5. 燕王舉用賢才　　　　　　5. 燕王以尚明舉用賢才
　　　　　　　　　　　　　　　　　　（以：因）

6. 蘇代諫趙王　　　　　　　6. 蘇代以鷸蚌相爭漁翁得利諫趙
　　　　　　　　　　　　　王　　　　　　（以：用）

五　　翻譯　Translation

把下列的句子譯成白話或英文　Translate the following sentences into
modern Chinese or into English:

1. 玉人以璞為石，而楚王信之，不亦惑乎？
2. 和氏貞士也，而楚王名之以誑，此其（和氏之）所以悲也。
3. 蘭芝之室乃君子之所居。
4. 大臭者與逐臭者相逢於鮑魚之肆，俱說（悅）其臭，久而猶
　　不欲去。
5. 和氏璧天下所共傳寶也。　　　（史記・廉頗藺相如列傳）
6. 此韓非之所著書也。　　　　　（史記・老莊申韓列傳）
7. 君子以文會友，以友輔仁。　　（論語・顏淵）
8. 甘羅曰："君侯何不快之甚也？"（史記・甘茂傳）

注解：

1. 共 gòng	【副詞】共同	jointly; commonly
2. 傳 chuán	【動詞】傳說	to talk about
3. 寶 bǎo	【名詞】寶物；珍貴的東西	treasure
4. 韓非 Hán Fēi	【名詞語】人名，法家的重要人物	name of a famous Legalist
5. 著 zhù	【動詞】作；寫	to write
6. 書 shū	【名詞】書	a book
7. 君子 jūnzǐ	【名詞語】道德高尚的人	a man of great virtue; a superior man
8. 以 yǐ	【介詞】用；憑藉	with; by means of
9. 文 wén	【名詞】文章學問	literature and learning; culture
10. 會 huì	【動詞】聚會	to get together; to draw together
11. 友 yǒu	【名詞】朋友	friends
12. 輔 fǔ	【動詞】輔助；幫助培養	to assist; to help cultivate
13. 仁 rén	【名詞】仁德	virtue; morality
14. 甘羅 Gān Luó	【名詞語】人名；姓甘名羅，戰國時人	the name of a man in the Warring States Period

207

15. 君侯　　【名詞語】古代對諸侯的敬稱；您　a polite way
　　jūn hóu　　　　　　　　　　　addressing a feudal lord; Your Lordship

16. 快　kuài　　【形容詞】快樂；高興　happy; cheerful

17. 甚　shèn　　【副詞】厲害　muchly; seriously

六　　討論　　Discussion

1. 人爲什麼得慎所藏？除了慎所藏之外，還應慎什麼？
Why should one be exceedingly circumspect in selecting ones living conditions?
Besides living conditions, what other aspects of life requires circumspection?

2. "刻舟求劍"中介紹了幾個很有代表性的句構，請選出三個
你認爲最好的來，並説明爲什麼？
In the story "Carving the Boat and Seeking the Sword" there are many typical
sentence patterns; choose three that you think are the best and explain why.

3. 討論"和氏之璧"這個故事並評論主要人物和氏。
Discuss the story "The Pierced Jade Disk of a Man Surnamed Hé" and comment
on the main character Mr. Hé.

208

練習七

一　字彙復習　Vocabulary Review

寫出左表各字的讀音，再從右表找出相配的解釋來　In parentheses, give the pronunciation for each of the words in the left column, and then match each word in the left column with its definition in the right column:

患 (	) (	)	1. 依賴 to depend on
謀 (	) (	)	2. 多 many
奪 (	) (	)	3. 一整天 for a whole day
仰 (	) (	)	4. 親屬 relatives
疾 (	) (	)	5. 很久 after a long while
殉 (	) (	)	6. 擔心 to be worried
亂 (	) (	)	7. 生病 to be ill
治 (	) (	)	8. 報答 torepay
報 (	) (	)	9. 計劃 plan
歧 (	) (	)	10. 神志清醒 in right mind
率 (	) (	)	11. 搶奪 to take by force
黨 (	) (	)	12. 率領 to lead
豎 (	) (	)	13. 陪葬 funeral offerings
眾 (	) (	)	14. 憂傷地 morosely
竟日 (	) (	)	15. 小厮 young servants
戚然 (	) (	)	16. 岔路 forked paths
變容 (	) (	)	17. 神志不清 confused
移時 (	) (	)	18. 改變臉色 to change one's facial expression

二　填空　Fill in Blanks

根據每句的上下文及文法選出適當的虛字來填入空內　Fill in the following blanks with the appropriate particles according to the contextual meaning and grammatical pattern of each sentence:

之	結構助詞	a strusctural particle
之、其、爲	代詞	pronouns
於、以、爲	介詞	prepositions
而、則	連詞	conjunctions
矣、也	直述語氣詞	final particles (narrative)
乎	疑問語氣詞	a final particle (interrogative)

209

1. 楊子曰："嘻，亡一羊，何追者＿＿＿＿眾？"鄰人曰：
　"多歧路。"既反，問："獲羊＿＿＿＿＿？"曰："亡之
　＿＿＿＿。"曰："奚亡＿＿＿？"曰："歧路之中又有歧
　＿＿＿＿，吾不知所之，所以反＿＿＿。"

2. 魏顆夜夢＿＿＿曰："余，而所嫁婦人之父＿＿＿，爾用先
　人＿＿＿治命，余是＿＿＿報。"

3. "君＿＿＿謀過矣。今不下水，所＿＿＿富東周也。今＿＿＿＿
　民皆種麥，無他種＿＿＿。君若欲害＿＿＿，不若一＿＿＿＿
　下水以病＿＿＿＿＿所種。下水，則東周必復種稻；種稻，
　＿＿＿＿復奪之。若是，＿＿＿＿東周之民可令一仰西周而受
　命＿＿＿君矣。"

三　　句子分析及翻譯　Sentence Analysis and Translation

分析下列句子，找出主、動、賓、副、疑、助來，並把這些句
子譯成白話或英文　Analyze the following sentences; identify the subjects,
verbs, objects, adverbs, question words, and particles; then translate them into
modern Chinese or into English:

1. 何夫子之迂也？　　　　　　　　　《論語・子路》
2. 楊子見逵路而哭之，為其可以南，可以北。

　　　　　　　　　　　　　　　　　（淮南子・說林）

3. 夜聞漢軍四面皆楚歌，項王乃大驚曰："漢皆已得楚乎
　？是何楚人之多也？"　　　（史記・項羽本紀）

注　解：

1. 夫子　　【名詞語】老師　master
　　fū zǐ

2. 迂 yū　　【形容詞】迂闊；不實際　impractical

3. 逵路　　【名詞語】大路　a thoroughfare
　　kuí lù

4. 為 wèi　　【介詞】因為　because; for

5. 南 nán　　【方向詞】南；南向 v；向南行走　south; go southward

6. 北 běi　　【方向詞】北；北向 v；向北行走　north; go northward

7. 漢軍　　【名詞語】漢王劉邦的軍隊　the Hàn army
　　Hàn jūn

8. 四面　　【名詞語】東南西北四個方向　in four directions
　　sì miàn

9. 楚歌　　【動詞語】唱楚地的歌謠　to sing folksongs of Chǔ
　　Chǔ gē

10. 項王　　【名詞】項羽，又稱西楚霸王　Xiàng Yǔ, also know as the
　　Xiàng Wáng　　　　　　　　　　　　Hegemon of Western Chǔ

11. 乃 nǎi　【副詞】就；於是　thereupon

12. 驚 jīng　【動詞】吃驚　surprised; alarmed

13. 已 yǐ　　【副詞】已經　already

14. 得楚　　【動詞語】占領楚地　to hjave occupied the Chǔ territory
　　dé Chǔ

15. 是 shì　【代名詞】這裡　here; this place

四　翻譯　Translation

把下面的一段短文譯成白話或英文　Translate the following passage into
modern Chinese or into English:

臧與穀二人相與牧羊而俱亡其羊。問臧奚事？則挾策讀書；問
穀奚事？則博塞以遊。二人者，事業不同，其於亡羊均也。

（莊子・駢拇）

注解：

1. 臧 zāng　【名詞】男僕　a male servant

2. 穀 gǔ　　【名詞】童僕　a servant boy

3. 相與　　【副詞】在一塊兒　together
　　xiāng yǔ

4. 牧羊　　【動詞語】放羊　to tend sheep; to herd sheep
　　mù yáng

5. 俱 jù　　【副詞】都　all; both

6. 奚 xī　　【疑問代詞】什麼　what

7. 事 shì　【動詞】幹；做　to do

　　奚事　【動詞語】幹〔了〕什麼　what did he do?
　　xī shì

8. 則 zé　　【連詞】"則"所連的下一事與人所預期的情況相反
　　　　　　　　　　，白話可譯成"卻"　yet; unexpectedly

9. 挾 xiá　【動詞】持；拿　to carry

10. 策 cè　【名詞】竹簡；古人用來寫書，長二尺四寸
　　　　　　　　bamboo slips used for wrting on in ancient times

11. 博塞　　【動詞語】擲骰子下棋　to throw dice and play chess
　　bó sài

12. 遊 yóu　【副詞】遊玩　to play; to have fun

211

13. 者 zhě 【助詞】表停頓，可譯成"啊" a particle indicating a pause

14. 事 shì 【動詞】從事；做；幹 to do

15. 業 yè 【名詞】事情 things; endeavor

16. 均 jūn 【形容詞】均等；一樣 equal; same

五　包孕句　Embedding Sentences

包孕句含有兩個小句，其中一個是主要小句，其餘的是不獨立
的小句。不獨立小句只作主要小句的文法成分，有三種主要類
型：小句；主謂短語；動賓結構。

An embedding sentence contains two clauses: the main clause, and the subordinate clause that functions as a grammatical element of the main clause. The three major types of dependent clauses are: 'A' SP, 'B' S之P/ 其 P, and 'C' V-O.

例如 For example:

A. 竊鐘者懼<u>人聞之</u>。	SP
B. 臣恐<u>強秦之為漁父</u>也。	S之P
B. 吾不知<u>其美</u>也。	其P
C. 耕者冀<u>復得兔</u>。	V-O

1. 辨別下列各句中的不獨立小句分別屬於哪一種　Identify the structural type of the following underlined dependent clauses as either 'A,' 'B,' or 'C':

1. 鄉人皆惡<u>我鳴</u>。	L.6
2. 其惡者自惡，吾不知<u>其惡</u>也。	L.8
3. 已得履，乃曰："吾忘<u>持度</u>。"	L.10
4. 臣恐<u>強秦之為漁父</u>也，故願<u>王熟計之</u>也。	L.12
5. 觀<u>百獸之見我而敢不走</u>乎？	L.14
6. <u>子攫人之金</u>何？	L.15
7. 顆見<u>老人結草以亢杜回</u>。	L.20
8. 子非魚，安知<u>魚之樂</u>？	L.25
9. 彌子瑕為母之故忘<u>其犯刖罪</u>。	L.35
10.鳥，吾知<u>其能飛</u>；魚，吾知<u>其能游</u>；獸，吾知<u>其能走</u>。	
	（史記‧老莊申韓列傳）

2. 把八到十句譯成白話或英文　Translate sentences 8-10 into modern Chinese or into English:

注 解 ：

1. 非 fēi　　　　【繫詞】不是　not to be; are not

2. 安 ān　　　　【疑問副詞】怎麼；哪裡　how? whencefrom?

3. 樂 lè　　　　【形容詞】快樂　happy

4. 彌子瑕　　　　【名詞語】人名；春秋時衛國的臣子　Mí Zǐxiá, an official
　　Mí Zǐxiá　　　　　　　　　in the state of Wèi during the Spring and Autumn period

5. 母 mǔ　　　　【名詞】母親　mother

6. 故 gù　　　　【名詞】緣故　cause; reason, the sake of

　　為⋯之故　　【介詞語】為了⋯的緣故　for the sake of ...
　　wèi...zhī gù

7. 忘 wàng　　　【動詞】忘記　to forget

8. 犯 fàn　　　　【動詞】犯　to commit [a crime]

9. 刖 yuè　　　　【動詞】砍斷腳　to cut off one foot [as a punishment]

　　刖罪　　　　【名詞語】砍斷腳的罪　a crime punishable by cutting off a foot
　　yuè zuì

10. 鳥 niǎo　　　【名詞】鳥　birds

11. 飛 fēi　　　　【動詞】飛　to fly

12. 游 yóu　　　【動詞】游水　to swim

13. 獸 shòu　　　【名詞】動物　animals

14. 走 zǒu　　　【動詞】跑　to run

六　討論　Discussion

1. 根據 "東周欲為稻"，談諫的技巧。
Talk about the skills of remonstrance in light of the story "Eastern Zhōu Wants to Plant Rice."

2. 談 "報恩" 的觀念。
Comment on the concept of "Repaying a Kindness."

3. 鄰人丟了一隻羊，楊子為什麼那麼不快樂？
When his neighbor lost a sheep, Yangzi became extremely unhappy. Why?

練習八

一 字彙復習 Vocabulary Review

1. 寫出左表各詞的讀音，再從右表找出相配的解釋來 In parentheses, give the pronunciation for each of the words in the left column, and then match each word in the left column with its definition in the right column:

2. 按照句意的需要從左表的詞中選出適當的來填入空內 Choose the appropriate words from the left column to fill in the blanks according to the contextual meaning of each sentence:

閔 （ ） （ ）			1. 很快地走 to hurry; to go quickly
視 （ ） （ ）			2. 枯 withered
槁 （ ） （ ）			3. 回家 to return home
趨 （ ） （ ）			4. 幫助 to help
舍 （ ） （ ）			5. 看 to look at
歸 （ ） （ ）			6. 擔心 to worry about
揠 （ ） （ ）			7. 放棄 to give up
助 （ ） （ ）			8. 拔起 to pull upward

宋人有＿＿＿＿其苗之不長而＿＿＿＿＿＿之者，茫茫然＿＿＿＿＿＿＿＿，謂其人曰："今日病矣，予＿＿＿＿＿＿苗長矣。"其子＿＿＿＿＿而往視之，苗則＿＿＿＿＿＿矣。

廬 （ ） （ ）			1. 克制；停止 to restrain; to stop
慚 （ ） （ ）			2. 嘆氣 to sigh
塚 （ ） （ ）			3. 哭泣 to sob; to weep
嘆 （ ） （ ）			4. 茅舍 a thatched hut
誑 （ ） （ ）			5. 慚愧 mortified
泣 （ ） （ ）			6. 騙 to deceive
容 （ ） （ ）			7. 墳墓 grave mounds
禁 （ ） （ ）			8. 臉色 facial expression

過晉國，同行者＿＿＿＿＿之，指城曰："此燕國之城。"其人愀然變＿＿＿＿。指社曰："此若里之社。"乃喟然而＿＿＿＿＿＿＿。指舍曰："此若先人之＿＿＿＿＿。"乃涓然而＿＿＿＿＿＿。指壟曰："此若先人之＿＿＿＿＿。"其人哭不自＿＿＿＿＿＿。同行者啞然大笑曰："予昔紿若，此晉國耳。"其人大＿＿＿＿＿＿。

214

添	（	）	（	）	1. 搶奪 to take by force
畫	（	）	（	）	2. 剩餘 leftover
賜	（	）	（	）	3. 添上；加上 to add
奪	（	）	（	）	4. 畫 to draw
餘	（	）	（	）	5. 夠 enough; sufficient
飲	（	）	（	）	6. 門客 retainers
足	（	）	（	）	7. 喝 to drink
足	（	）	（	）	8. 加上腳 to add feet
足	（	）	（	）	9. 賜給 to give; to bestow
舍人	（	）	（	）	10. 腳 foot; feet

1. ＿＿＿＿＿蛇＿＿＿＿＿足。

2. 楚有祠者，＿＿＿＿＿其舍人卮酒。＿＿＿＿＿相謂曰：“數人
＿＿＿＿之，不＿＿＿＿；一人飲之，有＿＿＿＿。”

3. 〔蛇足〕未成，一人之蛇成。＿＿＿＿其卮曰：“蛇固無＿＿＿＿
，子安能為之＿＿＿＿？”

二　翻譯 Translation

把下列句子譯成白話或英文　Translate the following sentences into
modern Chinese or into Engliah:

1. 燕人自楚反國，見先人之廬冢，愀然變容，哭不自禁。
2. 何揠苗者之多也？
3. 燕人何慚之甚也？
4. 蛇本無足而子為之足，何子之悖也？
5. 欲速則不達。　　　（論語・子路）
6. 過猶不及。　　　　（論語・先進）

注解：

1. 速 sù	【形容詞】	迅速；快 quick；做得快 to do ...quickly
2. 達 dá	【動詞】	到達 to reach; to attain
3. 過 guò	【動詞】	超過；做得太多 beyond; to overdo; doing too much
4. 猶 yóu	【準繫詞】	如同 is just like
5. 及 jí	【動詞】	達到 to reach [the goal]; up to [the standard]
不及 bù jí	【動詞語】	沒到；做得不夠；沒達到應有的標準 to fall short; doing not enough; not up to the standard

三　翻譯　Translation

把下面的詩譯成白話或英文　Translate the following poem into modern Chinese or into English:

少小離家老大回，鄉音未改鬢毛催。

兒童相見不相識，笑問客從何處來？

（賀知章・回鄉偶書）

注解：

1.	少小 shào xiǎo	【形容詞】年輕	young; when one is young
2.	離家 lí jiā	【動詞語】離開家	to leave home
3.	老大 lǎo dà	【形容詞】年老	old; when one gets old
4.	鄉音 xiāng yīn	【名詞語】家鄉的口音	the native accent
5.	鬢毛 bìn máo	【名詞語】兩鬢的頭髮	hair on the temples
6.	摧 cuī	【形容詞】摧損；變白	demaged; turned white
7.	兒童 ér tóng	【名詞】小孩子	children
8.	相 xiāng	【副詞】互相 mutually; here it has the characteristics of a pronoun. 此處"相"字兼有代詞"我"的作用	
	相見 xiāng jiàn	【動詞語】見我；看見我	to see me
	相識 xiāng shì	【動詞語】識我；認識我	to recognize me
9.	笑 xiào	【動詞】笑	to smile
	笑問 xiào wèn	【動詞語】笑著問	to ask smilingly
10.	客 kè	【名詞】客人	guest; stranger
12.	何處 hé chù	【名詞語】什麼地方；哪裡	what place; where

四　兼語句、雙賓句、包孕句　Pivotal Sentences, Double-Objects Sentences, Embedding Sentences

A. 兼語句：句中有個兼詞同時作第一小句的賓語及第二小句的主語　Pivotal Sentence: A sentence in which the Pivotal Element simoutaneously serves as the object of the first clause and the subject of the second clause.

B. 雙賓句：句中的動詞必須有直接賓語及間接賓語才能使意思完整 Double-Objects Sentence: A sentence in which the verb must take both a direct object and an indirect object to complete the meaning of the sentence.

C. 包孕句：句中包含另一個不獨立的小句－－敘述句中動詞的主語或賓語，判斷句中繫詞的主語或表語是一個主謂短語、句子形式、或動賓結構 Embedding Sentence: A sentence that contains a dependent clause (including clausal phrase and V-O construction) that serves as the subject/object in a narrative sentence, or the subject/determinator in a determinative sentence.

辨別下列的句子各屬於上面A, B, C三類中的哪一類 Identify the type of each of the following sentences as A, B, or C:

1. 王以和為誑而刖其左足。 （　）
2. 其惡者自惡，吾不知其惡也。 （　）
3. 楚有祠者，賜其舍人卮酒。 （　）
4. 仁義使我身名並全。 （　）
5. 郢人遺燕相國書。 （　）
6. 舉燭，非書意也。 （　）
7. 因釋其耒而守株，冀復得兔。 （　）
8. 〔買履者〕已得履，乃曰："吾忘持度。" （　）
9. 虎以〔狐之言〕為然，故遂與之行。 （　）
10. 臣恐強秦之為漁父也。 （　）

五　討論　Discussion

1. 談 "揠苗助長" 與 "畫蛇添足" 的異同。
Comment on the differences and similarities between the two stories "Pulling up the Sprouts," and "Drawing a Snake and Adding Feet."

2. "燕人" 年老歸國的故事透露出人性的哪些方面？
"The Man from Yān" went back to his native land when he got old. What does the story reveal about human nature?

217

練習九

一 字彙復習 Vocabulary Review

1. 寫出左表各詞的讀音，再從右表找出相配的解釋來 In
parentheses, give the pronunciation for each of the words in the left column, and
then match each word in the left column with its definition in the right column:

2. 按照句意的需要從左表的詞中選出適當的來填入空內 Choose
the appropriate words from the left column to fill in the blanks according to the
contextual meaning of each sentence:

治 （　　　） （　　　） 1. 貧窮 poor
賤 （　　　） （　　　） 2. 權力 power
貧 （　　　） （　　　） 3. 有才幹 endowed with great capability
君 （　　　） （　　　） 4. 疏遠 distant
霸 （　　　） （　　　） 5. 君主 a ruler
賢 （　　　） （　　　） 6. 管理 to administer
權 （　　　） （　　　） 7. 地位低 of low status
疏 （　　　） （　　　） 8. 稱霸 to be acknowledged as a hegemon

1. 齊桓公使管仲＿＿＿＿國，管仲對曰：“＿＿＿＿＿不能
臨貴，＿＿＿＿不能使富，＿＿＿＿不能制親。”

2. 孔子曰：“管仲之＿＿＿＿，不得此三＿＿＿＿者，亦不能
使其＿＿＿＿南面而＿＿＿＿矣。”

絕 （　　　） （　　　） 1. 心思 thoughts
鼓 （　　　） （　　　） 2. 摔破 to smash
遊 （　　　） （　　　） 3. 閒遊 to stroll
破 （　　　） （　　　） 4. 彈奏 to play
志 （　　　） （　　　） 5. 雄壯肅穆 majestic and solumn
從容 （　　　） （　　　） 6. 折斷 to snap
巍巍 （　　　） （　　　） 7. 洶湧澎湃 surging and crushing
湯湯 （　　　） （　　　） 8. 自由自在地 leisurely and
　　　　　　　　　　　　　　contendedly

1. 莊子與惠子＿＿＿＿於濠梁之上。莊子曰：“鯈魚出游
＿＿＿＿，是魚之樂也。”

218

2. 伯牙子＿＿＿＿＿琴，鍾子期聽之。方鼓而＿＿＿＿＿在太山。鍾子期曰：“善哉乎鼓琴，＿＿＿＿＿乎若太山。”少選之間，而志在流水。鍾子期又曰：“善哉乎鼓琴，＿＿＿＿＿＿乎若流水。”

3. 鍾子期死，伯牙＿＿＿＿＿＿琴，＿＿＿＿＿絃，終身不復鼓琴。

二 句子分析及翻譯 Sentence Analysis and Translation

分析以下的句子，找出主、動、助動、繫、賓、副、介、疑、助、定、及主謂短語來，並譯成白話或英文 Analyze the following sentences; identify the subjects, verbs, auxiliary verbs, linking verbs, objects, adverbs, prepositions, question words, particles, adjectival modifiers, and clausal phrases; then translate the sentences into modern Chinese or into English:

1. 人非生而知之者，孰能無惑？ （韓愈·師說）
2. 智者樂水。 （論語·雍也）
3. 夫智者何以樂水也？ （說苑·雜言）
4. 士為知己者用，女為悅己者容。 （司馬遷·報任少卿書）
5. 哀樂之來，吾不能禦；其去弗能止。 （莊子·知北遊）
6. 管仲賢，能使其君南面而霸。
7. 鍾子期死，伯牙以為世無知音，終身不復鼓琴。

注解：

1. 生 shēng	【動詞】	出生 to be born
2. 知之 zhī zhī	【動詞語】	知道它；了解道理 to understand the 'Way'
3. 孰 shú	【代名詞】	誰 who?
4. 惑 huò	【名詞】	疑惑 doubts
5. 智 zhì	【形容詞】	聰明；有智慧 wise
智者 zhì zhě	【名詞語】	聰明人；有智慧的人 a wise man
6. 何以 hé yǐ	【介詞語】	以何；因為什麼 for what? why
7. 樂 yào	【動詞】	喜愛；愛好 to like; to be fond of; to delight in
8. 士 shì	【名詞】	有學識才幹的讀書人 a learned and able scholar
9. 知己者 zhī jǐ zhě	【名詞語】	了解並欣賞自己的人 one who understands and appreciates him
10. 用 yòng	【動詞】	效力 to serve

11. 悅己者　【名詞語】喜歡自己的人　one who loves her
　　 yuè jǐ zhě

12. 容 róng　【動詞】化妝；打扮　to dress up; to make up

13. 哀 āi　【名詞】悲哀　sadness

14. 樂 lè　【名詞】快樂　happiness

15. 禦 yù　【動詞】抵禦；阻擋　to block; to prevent [from approaching]

16. 弗 fú　【副詞】不　not

17. 止 zhǐ　【動詞】阻止　to stop; to prevent [from leaving]

18. 賢 xián　【形容詞】有才幹　endowed with great capability

三　翻譯 Translation

把下面的詩譯成白話或英文 Translate the following poem into modern Chinese or into English:

兩人對酌山花開，一杯一杯復一杯。

我醉欲眠卿且去，明朝有意抱琴來。

（李白・山中與幽人對酌）

注解：

1. 對酌　【動詞語】相對飲酒；面對面地喝酒　to drink facing each
　　 duì zhuó　　　　　　　　　other

2. 山花　【名詞語】山上的花　flowers on the mountain
　　 shān huā

3. 開 kāi　【動詞】開放　to bloom

4. 杯 bēi　【名詞】酒杯　wine cup

5. 復 fù　【副詞】又　again

6. 醉 zuì　【形容詞】喝醉了　to be drunk

7. 欲 yù　【助動詞】想要　would like to

8. 眠 mián　【動詞】睡覺　to sleep; to go to bed

9. 卿 qīng　【名詞】好朋友可以互相稱卿，意思是"您"　you

10. 且 qiě　【副詞】姑且；暫時　for the time being

11. 有意　【動詞語】有心意；有興趣　to be interested
　　 yǒu yì

12. 抱 bào　【動語】抱著；帶著　to carry; to bring along

四　等立複句 Coordinate Compound Sentences

220

1. 連動式 Sequential Constructions: (consult the Analyses, p.14)
   兔走觸株，折頸而死。

2. 平行式 Parallel Constructions: (consult the Analyses, p.106)
   丹之所藏者赤，烏之所藏者黑。

3. 加合式 Additive Constructions: (consult the Analyses, p.142)
   楊子之鄰人既率其黨，又請楊子之豎追之。

4. 補充式 Complementary Constructions: (consult the Analyses, p.166)
   數人飲之不足，一人飲之有餘。

5. 對待式 Antithetical Constructions: (consult the Analyses, p.97)
   取金之時，不見人，徒見金。

6. 轉折式 Contradictive Constructions: (consult the Analyses, p.12)
   其家甚智其子，而疑鄰人之父。

7. 比較式 Comparative Constructions: (consult the Analyses, p.131)
   不下水不若一爲下水。

8. 取捨式 Preferential Constructions: (consult the Analyses, p.62)
   吾寧信其度，無自信也。

辨別下列的句子各屬於哪種句式 Identify the different type of each of the following sentences:

1. 孫叔敖見兩頭蛇，殺而埋之，歸而泣。   (   )
   （新序・雜事）

2. 寶玉而題之以石，貞士而名之以誑。   (   )
   （韓非子・和氏）

3. 既不能令，又不受命，是絕物也。   (   )
   （孟子・離婁上）

4. 滿招損，謙受益。   (   )
   （尚書・大禹謨）

5. 君子成人之美，不成人之惡。   (   )
   （論語・顏淵）

6. 舟已行矣，而劍不行。   (   )

221

（呂氏春秋・察今）

7. 百聞不如一見。　　　　　　　　　　　　（　　）

（漢書・趙充國傳）

8. 寧我負人，勿人負我。　　　　　　　　　（　　）

（三國志・魏志）

注　解　：

1. 成 chéng【動詞】成全；促成；幫助人做成 to facilitate; to help ...bring out

2. 美 měi 【名詞】美事；好事 good things

3. 惡 è 【名詞】惡事；壞事 bad things

4. 令 lìng 【動詞】命令 to order; to give orders

5. 命 mìng 【名詞】命令 orders

6. 絕物 jué wù 【動詞語】斷絕人事來往 to cut off social intercourse with others

7. 孫叔敖 Sūn Shúaó 【名詞】人名；姓蔿、名敖、字孫叔，春秋時楚國的令尹（宰相）personal name; Surnamed Wěi, named Aó, and courtesy named Sūnshú; he was a prime minister in the state of Chǔ during the Spring and Autumn Period

8. 頭 tóu 【名詞】頭 head

9. 殺 shā 【動詞】殺死 to kill

10. 埋 mái 【動詞】埋葬 to bury

11. 歸 guī 【動詞】回家 to return home

12. 泣 qì 【動詞】哭泣 to weep; to sob

13. 滿 mǎn 【名詞】自滿 haughtiness

14. 招 zhāo 【動詞】招致 to invite

15. 損 sǔn 【名詞】損害 loss; harm

16. 謙 qiān 【名詞】謙虛 modesty

17. 益 yì 【名詞】利益 benefit; profit

18. 百聞 bǎi wén 【動詞語】聽見一百次 to hear a hundred times

19. 一見 yí jiàn 【動詞語】看見一次 to see once

20. 負 fù 【動詞】辜負；對不起 to let down; to betray

222

五　　討論　　Discussion

1. 對莊子與惠子人知不知魚樂的辯論，你贊成誰的説法？爲什麼？

   Zhuāngzǐ and Huìzǐ debated about whether or how one can know that a fish is happy. Which side do you take? Why?

2. 政治家得憑藉哪些條件才能實行他的政策？

   What are the prerequisites for a statesman to carry out his policies?

3. 俞伯牙失掉了知音一輩子再也不彈琴了，你同意他的作法嗎？爲什麼？

   After Zhōng Zǐqī died, Yú Bóyá never played the lute again. Do you approve of what he did? Why or why not?

練習十

一 字彙復習 Vocabulary Review

1. 寫出左表各詞的讀音，再從右表找出相配的解釋來 In
   parentheses, give the pronunciation for each of the words in the left column, and
   then match each word in the left column with its definition in the right column:

2. 按照句意的需要從左表的詞中選出適當的來填入空內 Choose
   the appropriate words from the left column to fill in the blanks according to the
   contextual meaning of each sentence:

固 （　　）（　　） 1. 施捨 to bestow
施 （　　）（　　） 2. 破舊的 threadbare
求 （　　）（　　） 3. 魯國 the state of Lǔ
魯 （　　）（　　） 4. 推辭 to decline
弊 （　　）（　　） 5. 驕傲 arrogant
致 （　　）（　　） 6. 堅決地 steadfastly;firmly
驕 （　　）（　　） 7. 送給 to give
辭 （　　）（　　） 8. 乞求 to seek; to entreat

曾子_____衣而耕於_____。魯君聞而_____邑焉。曾
子_____辭不受。或曰："非子之_____，君自致之
。奚固_____也。"曾子曰："吾聞：'受人_____者常
畏人，與人者常_____人。'"

奚 （　　）（　　） 1. 如同 to be like
已 （　　）（　　） 2. 學業 one's study
識 （　　）（　　） 3. 好比 can be likened to
事 （　　）（　　） 4. 停止 to stop
飲 （　　）（　　） 5. 事奉；追隨 to wait on; to follow
業 （　　）（　　） 6. 喝 to drink
譬 （　　）（　　） 7. 了解 to understand; to fathom
猶 （　　）（　　） 8. 何 how

簡子不說，曰："夫子_____孔子數十年，終_____而去
之；寡人問子，子曰不能_____，何也？"子貢曰："賜
_____渴者之_____江海，知足而_____。孔子_____江海也，
賜則_____足以識之？"

224

二 結構復習　Review of a Few Constructions

1. 辨認下列句中 "足以"、"不足以"、"何足以"、"豈足以" 的用法，並把這些句子譯成白話或英文　Distinguish the uses of "suffice to ...", "not suffice to ...", "would it suffice to ...?", and "how could it suffice to...?" Then translate these sentences into modern Chinese or into English:

例如：

參之言足以全其節也。	（肯定）affirmative
參之言不足以全其節也。	（否定）negative
參之言足以全其節乎？	（詢問）interrogative
參之言奚／何足以全其節乎？	（反問）rhetorical
參之言豈足以全其節哉？	（反問）rhetorical

2. 於字用在形容詞後，表示比較　When the preposition "yú" is used after an adjective, it indicates comparison of the noun before it with the noun after it:

N1 Adj.於 N2 = N1 比 N2 Adj.

例如：苛政猛於虎。　　　　　　　　　　**(L. 30)**

3. 在否定句中，代詞賓語須置於動詞之前　In a negative sentence, the pronominal object should be placed before the verb that governs it:

例如：今其民皆種麥，無他種矣。　　　**(L. 19)**

把下面的句子翻譯成白話或英文　Translate the following sentences into modern Chinese or into English:

1. 畏人與驕人，豈賢者所為哉？
2. 曾子重節輕邑，此乃孔子之所以譽之也。
3. 賜不足以識孔子也。
4. 賜豈足以識孔子哉？
5. 仁義足以使人身名並全。
6. 子貢賢於仲尼。　　　　　　　　（論語・子張）
7. 天下之水莫大於海。　　　　　　（莊子・秋水）
8. 不患人之不己知，患不知人也。　（論語・學而）
9. 青，取之於藍而青於藍；冰，水為之而寒於水。

《荀子・勸學》

注解：

　1. 為 wéi　　【動詞】做 to do

225

	所為 suǒ wéi	【名詞語】做的事 things that one does
2.	重 zhòng	【形容詞】重；重要 heavy; important
		【意動用法】以…為重；看重 to regard as important
3.	節 jié	【名詞】節操 moral integrity
4.	輕 qīng	【形容詞】輕；不重要 light; unimportant
		【意動用法】以…為輕；看輕 to regard as unimportant
5.	邑 yì	【名詞】封邑；封地 a fief; a benefice
6.	以 yǐ	【介詞】因 because; for
7.	譽 yù	【動詞】讚美 to praise
8.	仲尼 Zhòngní	【名詞】孔子的字 the coutesy name of Confucius
9.	莫 mò	【無指代詞】沒有一個 no one
10.	患 huàn	【動詞】擔心 to worry; to be worries
11.	己 jǐ	【代詞】自己 self
12.	青 qīng	【名詞】藍色 blue; blue pigment
		【形容詞】藍 blue
13.	取 qǔ	【動詞】萃取 to extract
14.	藍 lán	【名詞】藍草 an indigo plant
15.	冰 bīng	【名詞】冰 ice
16.	為 wéi	【動詞】做；製造 to make
17.	寒 hán	【形容詞】冷 cold

二　成語　Set Phrases

1. 選出適當的字來，填入下列成語的空內 Choose the appropriate words from the list provided below to fill in the blanks:

2. 寫出每個成語的讀音來 In the parentheses give the pronunciation for each of the following set phrases:

3. 用每個成語各造一個句子，或選五個成語組成一段短文
Make sentences with each of the set phrases, or choose five of them and use them to compose a short passage:

測　禁　添　嘆　嬰　歧　苗　翁　恩　福　猛

結草報_____（　　　　　　　　　）
哭不自_____（　　　　　　　　　）
嗒然而_____（　　　　　　　　　）

畫蛇_____足　（　　　　　　　　　　　）
誤入_____途　（　　　　　　　　　　　）
揠_____助長　（　　　　　　　　　　　）
愀然_____容　（　　　　　　　　　　　）
深不可_____　（　　　　　　　　　　　）
苛政____於虎　（　　　　　　　　　　　）
塞____失馬，焉知非____　（　　　　　　　　　　　）

三　討論　Discussion

1. 談畏人與驕人。
   Comment on "fearing others" and "being arrogant toward others."

2. 從 "孔子猶江海"、"苛政猛於虎" 談比喻的重要。
   Discuss the importance of analogy or metaphor in light of "Confucius Is Like a River, Like a Sea," and "Oppressive Government Is More Fearsome Than a Tiger."

3. 在莊子、惠子、子貢、曾子四人中，你最想跟誰做朋友？最不要跟誰做朋友？為什麼？
   In the group of Zhuāngzǐ, Huìzǐ, Zǐgòng and Zēngzǐ, with whom would you most like to be friends, and with whom you least like to associate? Why?

227

練習十一

一　**動詞復習**　Review of Verbs

寫出左表各動詞的讀音，再從右表找出相配的解釋來　In the parentheses, give the pronunciation for each of the words in the left column, and then match each word in the left column with its definition in the right column:

聞 （　　　） （　　　）	1. 珍藏 to treasure; to store
釣 （　　　） （　　　）	2. 派遣 to dispatch
顧 （　　　） （　　　）	3. 受重視 to be highly thought of
藏 （　　　） （　　　）	4. 回頭看 to turn around and look at
曳 （　　　） （　　　）	5. 釣魚 to fish [with line and hook]
使 （　　　） （　　　）	6. 煩勞 to burden...with
累 （　　　） （　　　）	7. 拖 to drag
貴 （　　　） （　　　）	8. 聽說 to hear; to have heard

根據句意選出適當的動詞來填入空內　According to the contextual meaning of the following passage, choose the appropriate verb to fill in each of the blanks below:

莊子＿＿＿＿於濮水。楚王＿＿＿＿＿＿大夫二人往先焉，曰："願以境內＿＿＿矣。"莊子持竿不＿＿，曰："吾＿＿＿楚有神龜，死已三千歲矣。王巾笥而＿＿＿＿＿之廟堂之上。此龜者寧其死為留骨而＿＿＿乎？寧其生而＿＿＿尾於塗中乎？"

二　**字彙復習**　Vocabulary Review

寫出左表各詞的讀音，再從右表找出相配的解釋來　In the parentheses, give the pronunciation for each of the words in the left column, and then match each word in the left column with its definition in the right column:

術 （　　　） （　　　）	1. 強壯 strong; adult
福 （　　　） （　　　）	2. 騎馬 to ride
騎 （　　　） （　　　）	3. 占卜 prognostication
塞 （　　　） （　　　）	4. 慶賀 to congratulate
壯 （　　　） （　　　）	5. 好馬 a fine horse; a thoroughbred
弔 （　　　） （　　　）	6. 福氣 good fortune
賀 （　　　） （　　　）	7. 瘸 lamed

禍　　（　　　）（　　　）　　8. 掉下來 to fall down/off

墮　　（　　　）（　　　）　　9. 災禍 a disaster

跛　　（　　　）（　　　）　　10. 弓 bows

弦　　（　　　）（　　　）　　11. 邊界上險要地方 strategic locations along the frontier

駿馬　（　　　）（　　　）　　12. 慰問 to console

根據句意選出適當的詞來填入空內 According to the contextual meaning of the following passage, choose the appropriate verb to fill in each of the blanks below:

1. 近＿＿＿＿上之人有善＿＿＿＿者，馬無故亡而入胡，人皆＿＿＿＿之。其父曰：“此何遽不能為＿＿＿＿乎？”居數月，其馬將胡＿＿＿＿而歸，人皆＿＿＿＿之。其父曰：“此何遽不能為＿＿＿＿乎？”

2. 家富良馬，其子好＿＿＿＿，＿＿＿＿而折其髀，人皆＿＿＿＿之。其父曰：“此何遽不能為＿＿＿＿乎？”

3. 居一年，胡人大舉入塞，丁＿＿＿＿者引＿＿＿＿而戰。近塞之人，死者十九。此獨以＿＿＿＿之故，父子相保。

寫出左表各詞的讀音，再從右表找出相配的解釋來 In the parentheses, give the pronunciation for each of the words in the left column, and then match each word in the left column with its definition in the right column:

齒　（　　　）（　　　）　　1. 高大的樹 lofty, mighty trees

語　（　　　）（　　　）　　2. 舌頭 the tongue

舌　（　　　）（　　　）　　3. 柔軟 soft

柔　（　　　）（　　　）　　4. 家鄉 hometown; native place

剛　（　　　）（　　　）　　5. 告訴 to tell

遺教　（　　）（　　　）　　6. 堅硬 hard

故鄉　（　　）（　　　）　　7. 牙齒 teeth

喬木　（　　）（　　　）　　8. 留下來的教誨 teachings to pass on

根據句意選出適當的詞來填入空內 According to the contextual meaning of the following passage, choose the appropriate verb to fill in each of the blanks below:

1. 常摐有疾，老子往問焉，曰：“先生疾甚矣。無＿＿＿＿可以

_____諸弟子者乎？"

2. 常摐曰："過_____而下車，過_____而趨，子知之乎？"

3. 老子曰："夫_____之存也，豈非以其_____耶？_____之亡也，豈非以其_____耶？"

三　句子分析及翻譯　Sentence Analysis and Translation

分析下列句子的結構，找出主、動、賓、繫、副、補來，並譯成白話或英文　Analyze the structure of the following sentences, identify the subject, verb, object, linking verb, adverb, and complement, and then translate them into modern Chinese or into Engliah:

1. 福兮乃禍所倚，禍兮乃福所藏，孰知其極。（老子‧五十章）

2. 巧者勞而智者憂，無能者無所求。〔無能者〕飽食而遨遊，汎若不繫之舟。　　　　　　　　（莊子‧列禦寇）

注　解：

1.	兮	xī	【助詞】表停頓，可譯成"啊"	a particle indicating a pause
2.	所＋V		【名詞語】V的地方	the place where V
3.	倚	yǐ	【動詞】倚靠	to lean on
4.	藏	cáng	【動詞】隱藏	to hide in
5.	極	jí	【名詞】盡頭	the end; the extremity
6.	巧	qiǎo	【形容詞】靈巧	skillful
7.	勞	láo	【形容詞】辛勞	toilsome
8.	憂	yōu	【形容詞】憂慮	worried
9.	求	qiú	【動詞】追求	to pursue
10.	遨遊	aó	【動詞】隨意遊玩	to ramble; to roam freely
11.	汎	fàn	【動詞】漂浮	to float; drifting
12.	若	ruò	【準繫詞】像；好像是	to be like
13.	繫	xì	【動詞】拴住	to be tied-up; fastened

四　主從複句　Subordinate Compound Sentences (i.e., Complex Sentences)

1. 時間式　Temporal Constructions:　　　　　(consult the Analyses, p.52)

范氏之敗，有竊其鐘負而走者。

2. 因果式　Causal Constructions:　　　　　(consult the Analyses, p.5)

吾以嗜魚，故不受。

EXERCISES

3. 假設式 Hypothetical Constructions: (consult the Analyses, p.5)
　　不築，必將有盜。

4. 推論式 Inferential Constructions: (consult the Analyses, p.3)
　　子嗜魚，何故不受？

5. 目的式 Purposive Constructions: (consult the Analyses, p.15)
　　耕者因釋其耒而守株，冀復得兔。

6. 容認式 Concessive Constructions: (consult the Analyses, p.33)
　　縱君有賜，不我驕也，吾豈能勿畏乎？

辨別下列的句子各屬於哪種句式 Identify the construction type of each of the the following sentences:

1. 虎求百獸而食之。　　　　　　　　　　（　　）
2. 子雖不問，吾將語子。　　　　　　　　（　　）
3. 鄉人皆惡我鳴，以故東徙。　　　　　　（　　）
4. 子非魚，安知魚之樂？　　　　　　　　（　　）
5. 受魚失祿，無以食魚。　　　　　　　　（　　）
6. 今者臣來，過易水，蚌方出曝，而鷸啄其肉。（　　）

五　討論 Discussion

1. 從“曳尾塗中”的故事看莊子的人生觀。
What is Zhūangzǐ's "outlook on life" as represented in the story "Dragging Its Tail Through the Mud"?

2. "塞翁失馬"的故事給人的啓發。
What does the story of "The Old Man at the Frontier Loses His Horse" reveal?

3. 常摐認為「念舊」、「敬老」、「守柔」三個觀念對人生存於世很重要，你同意嗎？爲什麼？
Cháng Chūang thinks that "remembering one's origin," "respecting what is aged," and "being soft" are the three basic principles of human life. Do you agree with him? Why or why not?

231

練習十二

一　動詞復習　Review of Verbs

寫出左表各動詞的讀音，再從右表找出相配的解釋來　In the parentheses, give the pronunciation for each of the words in the left column, and then match each word in the left column with its definition in the right column:

罷 （　　　　　） （　　　　　） 1. 貞節 chastity; virtue

縛 （　　　　　） （　　　　　） 2. 半醉 pleasantly inebriated

詣 （　　　　　） （　　　　　） 3. 遲疑 to hesitate

節 （　　　　　） （　　　　　） 4. 停止 to stop

滅 （　　　　　） （　　　　　） 5. 顯示 to make a display of

顯 （　　　　　） （　　　　　） 6. 犯了竊盜罪 charged with robbery

孝 （　　　　　） （　　　　　） 7. 善於辭令 accomplished in rhetoric

士 （　　　　　） （　　　　　） 8. 奮勇 to muster one's courage

辱 （　　　　　） （　　　　　） 9. 捆綁 to tie up

奮 （　　　　　） （　　　　　） 10. 侮辱 to insult

疑 （　　　　　） （　　　　　） 11. 孝順 filial

酣 （　　　　　） （　　　　　） 12. 到…去 to go to

坐盜 （　　　　） （　　　　　） 13. 熄滅 extinguished

習辭 （　　　　） （　　　　　） 14. 有學問才幹的讀書人 learned and talented scholar

二　字彙復習及填空　Vocabulary Review and Fill in Blanks

寫出各詞的讀音和意思來，再根據句意選出適當的詞來填入空內　In the parentheses give the pronunciation and meaning for each of the words, and then fill the words in the blanks according to the contextual meaning of the passage:

a. 徒 （　　　） （　　　　　）　　b. 然 （　　　） （　　　　　）

c. 異 （　　　） （　　　　　）　　d. 味 （　　　） （　　　　　）

e. 避席 （　　　　　　） （　　　　　　　　　）

晏子＿＿＿＿＿對曰："嬰聞之，橘生於淮南則為橘，生於淮北

則為枳。葉＿＿＿＿＿相似，其實＿＿＿＿不同。所以＿＿＿＿＿

者何？水土＿＿＿＿也。"

a. 矯 （　　　） （　　　　　）　　b. 衰 （　　　） （　　　　　）

c. 唱 （　　　） （　　　　　）　　d. 罪 （　　　） （　　　　　）

232

及彌子瑕色_____愛弛，得_____於君。君曰："是固嘗
_____駕吾車，又嘗_____我以餘桃。"

a. 塗（　　）（　　　　）　　b. 禮（　　）（　　　　）
c. 顥（　　）（　　　　）　　d. 瀎（　　）（　　　　）
e. 陰蔽（　　　　　　）　　　（　　　　　　）
f. 隱忍（　　　　　　）　　　（　　　　　　）

臣當死，往者醉失_____，王_____不加誅也。臣終不敢
以_____之德，而不_____報王也。常願肝腦_____地，
以頸血_____敵久矣。

三　填虛字　Fill in Grammatical Particles

選出適當的虛字來，填入下列句子的空內　Fill in the following
blanks with the appropriate particles according to the contextual meaning and
grammatical pattern of each sentence:

則　而　以　與　於　之　其　者　耶　哉

1. 今民生長_____齊不盜，入楚_____盜，得無楚之水
   土使民善盜_____？

2. 異日_____君遊於果園，食桃_____甘，不盡，_____
   半啗君。君曰："愛我_____，忘其口味，以啗寡人。"

3. 今者燭滅，有引妾衣_____，妾援得_____冠纓，持_____
   。

四　翻譯　Translation

把下列句子譯成白話或英文　Translate the following sentences into
modern Chinese or into Engliah:

1. 人生如朝露，何久自苦如此？　　　（漢書・李陵傳）
2. 民不畏死，奈何以死懼之？　　　　（老子・七十四章）
3. 子夏避席問曰："夫子何歎焉？"　　（孔子家語・六本）
4. 欲加之罪，其無辭乎？　　　　　　（左傳・僖公十年）
5. 聖人非〔人之〕所與熙也，寡人反取病焉。

　　　　　　　　　　　　　　　　　（晏子春秋・内雜下）

6. 婦人所以有師〔者〕〔為〕何？〔婦人之所以有師〕學事人之道
也。 （白虎通・嫁娶）

注解 ：

1. 朝露 zhāo lù	【名詞語】	早上的露水　morning dew
2. 自苦 zì kǔ	【動詞語】	自己使自己苦　to make oneself suffer
3. 加 xī	【動詞】	加給；強加　to impose on
4. 罪 zuì	【名詞】	罪名　a charge; an accusation
5. 其 qí; qǐ	【副詞】	同 "豈"；難道　could it?
6. 辭 cí	【名詞】	藉口　a pretext; an excuse
其 … 乎？ qǐ wú cí hū?	【反問句】	難道…嗎？　could it...?
7. 聖人 shèng rén	【名詞語】	聖人　a sage; a morally superior person
8. 熙 xī	【動詞】	同 "嬉"，戲；開玩笑　to make of; to jock [with]
所與熙 shèng rén	【名詞語】	所＋介＋V＝N　跟他V的人 跟他V的人　one to joke with
9. 反 fǎn	【副詞】	反倒　instead; on the contrary
10. 病 bìng	【名詞】	此處意為 "辱"；羞辱　an insult; a humiliation
取病 qǔ bìng	【動詞語】	取辱；招來侮辱　to ask for an insult
11. 事 shì	【動詞】	侍奉　to serve; to look after; to attend on
12. 道 dào	【名詞】	道理；正道　the proper way; the right way

五　被動句的句式　Sentence patterns of passive constructions

1. 在動詞前用介詞 "為" 引出主動者　Consult Analyses, p. 17
N1 為 N2　V
身為宋國笑。

2. 在動詞前用被動記號 "見"　Consult Analyses, p. 278
N1　　　見 V
彌子以前見賢

3. 在動詞後用介詞 "於" 引出主動者　Concult Analyses, p. 224
N1　V 於 N2
昔者吾舅死於虎。

4. 在動詞前後合用 "見" 跟 "於"　　　Consult Analyses, p. 279

    N1　見 V 於 N2

昔者彌子瑕見愛於衛君。　（史記・老莊申韓列傳）

5. 合用介詞 "爲" 跟被動助詞 "所"　　This is a variation of pattern 1.

    N1　爲 N2　所 V

楚遂削弱，<u>爲</u>秦<u>所</u>輕。　　（戰國策・秦策）

注解 ：

   1. 遂 suì　　　【副詞】就；於是就　then; thereupon

   2. 削 xuē; xiāo　【動詞】削割　to pare; to whittle; to be pared down

   3. 弱 ruò　　　【形容詞】弱　weak

             【動詞】使…變弱　to weaken; to be weakened

    削弱　　　【形容詞】地削兵弱；土地減少兵力變弱　the territory
    xuē ruò　　　　　　　　　was pared down and the troops were weakened

   4. 輕 qīng　　　【動詞】輕視；看不起　to despise; to look down upon

辨別下列的句子各屬於哪種句式　Identify the construction type of each of the the following sentences:

1. 吾長見笑於大方之家。　　（莊子・秋水）　　　　　（　　　）

2. 人皆以見侮為辱。　　　　（荀子・正論）　　　　　（　　　）

3. 有間，晏子見疑於景公。（晏子春秋・內雜）　　　　（　　　）

4. 〔晉國〕東敗於齊，南辱於楚。　　　　　　　　　　（　　　）

                         （孟子・梁惠王上）

5. 直議者，不為人所容。（韓非子・外儲說左下）　　（　　　）

6. 不為酒困。　　　　　　　（論語・鄉黨）　　　　　（　　　）

7. 有備則制人，無備則制於人。（鹽鐵論・險固）　（　　　）

注解 ：

   1. 長 cháng　　【副詞】長久地　for a long time

   2. 大方之家　【名詞語】懂得大道理的人　those who have great
    dà fāng zhī jiā　　　　understanding of the Way

   3. 侮 wǔ　　　【動詞】侮辱　to insult

   4. 辱 rù　　　【名詞】羞辱　a shame; a humiliation

   5. 間 jiàn　　　【名詞】很短的時間　a short time

    有間　　　【動詞語】在很短時間內；不久　before long
    yǒu jiàn

   6. 疑 yí　　　【動詞】懷疑　to suspect

7. 景公 Jǐnggōng	【名詞語】	齊景公，齊國的君主 Duke Jǐng pf Qí
8. 敗 bài	【動詞】	戰敗 to be defeated
9. 辱 rù	【動詞】	羞辱 to be humiliated
10. 直 zhí	【副詞】	率直 frankly; strtaightforwardly
11. 議 yì	【動詞】	議論 to discuss
直議 yǒu jiàn	【動詞語】	率直地議論；率直地發表意見 to discuss or express opinion frankly
12. 容 róng	【動詞】	容忍；寬容 to tolerate
13. 困 kùn	【動詞】	困擾；傷害 to bother; to impair
14. 備 shēn	【名詞】	準備 preparation
15. 制 zhí	【動詞】	控制 to control

六　討論　Discussion

1. 從 “晏子與楚王論盜” 看出色的外交家應具備哪些條件？
Having read the story "Yànzǐ and the King of Chǔ Discuss Robbing," what do you find to be the essential qualifications of a great diplomat?

2. 「色衰愛弛」是古今中外都存在的現象，對人性的弱點，它説明什麼？
"Looks decline, love slackens" is a universal phenomenon. What does it say about the weakness of human nature?

3. 選擇一個角度來評論 “楚莊王不殺絕纓者” 這個故事。
Choose an appropriate angle to interpret the story of "King Zhuāng of Chǔ Does Not Put to Death the One with Broken Capstring".

練習十三

一　字彙復習　Vocabulary Review

　　1. 寫出左表各詞的讀音，再從右表找出相配的解釋來　In parentheses, give the pronunciation for each of the words in the left column, and then match each word in the left column with its definition in the right column:

　　2. 根據句意的需要從左表選出適當的詞來填入空內　Choose the appropriate words from the left column to fill in the blanks according to the contextual meaning of each sentence:

刖 (	) (	)	1. 難道 could it be ...
逃 (	) (	)	2. 砍斷腳 to cut off a foot
獄 (	) (	)	3. 缺口 a breach; a gap
踰 (	) (	)	4. 臉色 one's facial expression
難 (	) (	)	5. 罪案 a criminal case
樂 (	) (	)	6. 免除 to exempt from
免 (	) (	)	7. 災難 disaster; distress
缺 (	) (	)	8. 報仇 to avenge a grievance
閉 (	) (	)	9. 逃走 to escape
豈 (	) (	)	10. 跳過 to jump over
郭門 (	) (	)	11. 損害 to impair
虧損 (	) (	)	12. 快樂 happy
固然 (	) (	)	13. 關閉 to close
報怨 (	) (	)	14. 本來如此 naturally ever so
顏色 (	) (	)	15. 外城的城門 the gate of the outer city wall

　　1. 子羔為衛政，＿＿＿＿人之足。衛之君臣亂，子羔走郭門，郭門＿＿＿＿＿＿。刖者守門，曰：“於彼有＿＿＿＿。” 子羔曰：“君子不＿＿＿＿＿。”

　　2. 子羔將去，謂刖者曰：“吾不能＿＿＿＿＿＿主之法令而親刖子之足。吾在＿＿＿＿中，此乃子之＿＿＿＿＿時也，何故＿＿＿＿我？”

　　3. 臨當論刑，君愀然不＿＿＿＿＿，現於＿＿＿＿＿，臣又知之。君＿＿＿＿＿＿私臣哉？天生仁人之心，其＿＿＿＿＿也。

237

市 （　　　　　）（　　　　　）　　1. 偏愛 to be partial to
書 （　　　　　）（　　　　　）　　2. 觀察 to view
賞 （　　　　　）（　　　　　）　　3. 獎賞 rewards
諷 （　　　　　）（　　　　　）　　4. 奏章 disaster; distress
觀 （　　　　　）（　　　　　）　　5. 睡覺 to go to bed
諫 （　　　　　）（　　　　　）　　6. 市場 a marketplace
視 （　　　　　）（　　　　　）　　7. 蒙蔽 to delude
朝 （　　　　　）（　　　　　）　　8. 規勸 to admonish; remonstrance
朝 （　　　　　）（　　　　　）　　9. 朝見 to pay a court
寢 （　　　　　）（　　　　　）　　10. 接受 to accept
蔽 （　　　　　）（　　　　　）　　11. 身高 height
納 （　　　　　）（　　　　　）　　12. 畏懼 to fear
脩 （　　　　　）（　　　　　）　　13. 早上 in the morning
求 （　　　　　）（　　　　　）　　14. 看 to look at
畏 （　　　　　）（　　　　　）　　15. 相貌 countenance
私 （　　　　　）（　　　　　）　　16. 照鏡 to look into a mirror
謗議 （　　　　　）（　　　　　）　17. 要求 request
形貌 （　　　　　）（　　　　　）　18. 批評議論 to criticize and discuss
朝庭 （　　　　　）（　　　　　）　19. 君主視朝聽政的地方 a royal or imperial court
窺鏡 （　　　　　）（　　　　　）　20. 用委婉的話勸告 to criticize in a roundabout way

1. 鄒忌＿＿＿＿齊王＿＿＿＿＿諫。

2. 鄒忌＿＿＿＿八尺有餘，而＿＿＿＿昳麗。＿＿＿＿＿服衣冠窺鏡，謂其妻曰：“我孰與城北徐公美？”

3. 明日，徐公來，〔忌〕熟＿＿＿＿＿之，自以為不如。＿＿＿＿＿而自視，又弗如遠甚。暮＿＿＿＿＿而思之，曰：“吾妻之美我者，＿＿＿＿＿我也。”

4 今齊地方千里，百二十城，宮婦左右，莫不私王，朝廷之臣，莫不＿＿＿＿＿王，四境之內，莫不有＿＿＿＿＿於王。由此＿＿＿＿之，王之＿＿＿＿甚矣。

238

5. 群臣吏民能面刺寡人之過者，受上 ＿＿＿＿；上＿＿＿＿諫寡人者，受中賞；能＿＿＿＿於朝市聞寡人之耳者，受下賞。

6. 令初下，群臣進＿＿＿＿，門庭若＿＿＿＿。燕、趙、韓、魏聞之，皆＿＿＿＿＿於齊。此所謂戰勝於＿＿＿＿＿。

二　翻譯　Translation

把下列句子譯成白話或英文　Translate the following sentences into modern Chinese or into Engliah:

1. 甚矣，汝之不惠也。 　　　　　　　　（列子・湯問）

2. 齊威王用孫子、田忌之徒，而諸侯東面朝齊。
　　　　　　　　　　　　　　　　　　（史記・孫吳列傳）

3. 夫刑者，所以禁邪也，而賞者，所以助禁也。
　　　　　　　　　　　　　　　　　　（商君書・算地）

4. 此孫子之所謂不戰而屈人之兵。

5. 齊王以重賞求諫，群臣吏民或面刺其過，或上書進諫，或謗議於朝市，齊王俱說（悅）而納之，更民之所惡，行民之所欲，三年而齊國大治。

6. 昔子羔治守門之刖者也，傾側法令，先後之以法，欲其免於法也，刖者固知之，此其所以脫子羔於難也。

注解：

1. 汝 rǔ	【代詞】	你 you
2. 惠 huì	【形容詞】	同 "慧"，聰明 wise
3. 威王 Wēi wáng	【名詞語】	姓田，名因齊，在位三十九年 King Wēi of Qí (r. 358- 319 B.C.)
4. 孫子 Sūnzǐ	【名詞】	孫臏；戰國時著名軍事家 Sūn Bìn, a famous military stratagist
5. 田忌 Tián Jì	【名詞】	人名，齊威王時大將 Tián Jì, commander of the Qí army
6. 禁 jìn	【動詞】	禁止 to prohibit; to prevent
7. 邪 xié	【名詞】	邪惡 evil
8. 助 zhù	【動詞】	幫助 to assist
9. 屈 qū	【動詞】	屈服；此處：使…屈服 to submit; here: to subdue

10. 兵 bīng 　　【名詞】軍隊 troops
11. 或 huò 　　【或指代詞】有的，分指前面已經說過的人中的一部分 some, separately referring to a part of the fore-mentioned noun phrase (群臣吏民)

12. 固 gù 　　【副詞】很久 for a long time

三　　比較句的句式　　Sentence patterns of comparative constructions

1. A 如／若 B 　　　　A is like B; A and B are equal or similar.
　　孔子如江海。

2. A 不如／若 B 　　　A is not as good as B; B is preferrable than A.
　　〔不下水〕不若一爲下水。

3 A 不如／若 B Adj 　　A is not as Adj.as B; B is more Adj. than A.
　　徐公不若君之美也。

4. A 何能及 B (A 不能及 B; A 不如 B) How could A be as good as B?
　　徐公何能及君也？

5. A 弗如 [B] 遠甚 　　A is far inferior to B.
　　〔鄒忌〕窺鏡而自視，又〔自以爲〕弗如遠甚。

6. A 與 B 孰 Adj. 　　Between A and B, which is more Adj.
　　吾與徐公孰美？

7. A 孰與 B Adj. 　　Between A and B, which is more Adj.
　　吾孰與徐公美？

8. A Adj. 於 B 　　　A is more Adj. than B.
　　〔臣之妻、妾、客〕皆以臣美於徐公。

辨別以下的句子各屬於哪種句式　Identify the comparison type of each of the following sentences:

1. 衛君不若楚莊王之明也。　　　　　　（　　　　　）
2. 子貢自以爲不如子夏遠甚。　　　　　（　　　　　）
3 父與夫孰親？ （左傳・桓公十五年）　（　　　　　）
4. 聲如宏鐘。 （蘇軾・石鐘山記）　　　（　　　　　）
5. 知之者不如好之者，好之者不如樂之者。（　　　　　）
　　　　　（論語・雍也）

240

6. 王如知此，則無望民之多於鄰國也。 　　　　（ 　　　 ）

　　　　（孟子·梁惠王上）

7. 〔龐涓〕自以為能不及孫臏。 　　　　　　（ 　　　 ）

　　　　（史記·孫吳列傳）

注 解 ：

1. 明 míng	【形容詞】英明 a husband
2. 夫 fū	【名詞】丈夫 a husband
3. 親 qīn	【形容詞】親密；關係密切 close in relation
4. 宏 hóng	【形容詞】大 big; huge
5. 知之 zhī zhī	【動詞語】知道它 to know it; to have knowledge of something the Heir Apparent for treason
6. 好之 hào zhī	【動詞語】愛好它 to like it; to have a liking of it
7. 樂之 lè zhī	【動詞語】以之為樂 to take it as a pleasure; to enjoy it
8. 望 wàng	【動詞】希望 to hope
9. 龐涓 Páng Juān	【名詞】人名，魏國的大將 name of a famous general of the state of Wèi
10. 能 néng	【名詞】才能 talents and ability
11. 孫臏 Sūn Bìn	【名詞】人名，齊國的軍師 name of a famous military strategist of the state of Qí

四　討論 Discussion

1. 子羔刖人之足而不為刖足者怨，為什麼？
Zǐgāo had someone's foot cut off, yet he was not resented by that person. Why?

2. "戰勝於朝廷" 是什麼意思？怎樣才能戰勝於朝廷？
What does the phrase "winning the battle at court" mean? How can one achieve that?

241

練習十四

一 字彙復習 Vocabulary Review

1. 寫出各詞的讀音和意思來 In parentheses, give the pronunciation and
meaning for each word:

2. 根據句意的需要選出適當的來填入下列各句的空內 Choose
the appropriate words to fill in the blanks according to the contextual meaning of
each sentence:

a. 誅 (　　) (　　　)　　f. 滅 (　　) (　　　)
b. 亡 (　　) (　　　)　　g. 破 (　　) (　　　)
c. 逆 (　　) (　　　)　　h. 持 (　　) (　　　)
d. 反 (　　) (　　　)　　i. 攻 (　　) (　　　)
e. 棄 (　　) (　　　)　　j. 匿 (　　) (　　　)

1. 秦＿＿＿＿魏，＿＿＿＿之，殺魏王瑕，＿＿＿＿諸公子，而一公
子不得。

2. 故臣曰：“今魏國已破＿＿＿，族已＿＿＿，子＿＿＿之尚誰為
乎？”

3. 母吁而言曰：“夫見利而＿＿＿＿上者，＿＿＿＿也。畏死而
＿＿＿＿義者，亂也。”

4. 今＿＿＿＿逆亂而以求利，吾不為也。

a. 澤 (　　) (　　　)　　f. 節 (　　) (　　　)
b. 忠 (　　) (　　　)　　g. 蔽 (　　) (　　　)
c. 廢 (　　) (　　　)　　h. 祠 (　　) (　　　)
d. 擒 (　　) (　　　)　　i. 葬 (　　) (　　　)
e. 賞 (　　) (　　　)　　j. 務 (　　) (　　　)

“且夫為人養子者，＿＿＿＿＿＿生之，非為殺之也。豈可以利

＿＿＿＿＿＿而畏誅之故，＿＿＿＿＿＿正義而行逆＿＿＿哉？妾不

能生而令公子＿＿＿＿也。”遂抱公子逃於深＿＿＿＿＿＿之中。

故臣以告秦軍。秦軍追見，爭射之。乳母以身為公子＿＿＿

，矢著身者數十，與公子俱死。秦王聞之，貴其守＿＿＿＿＿＿

死義，乃以卿禮＿＿＿＿之，＿＿＿＿以太牢。

a.防（　　　）（　　　　）　　b.犯（　　　）（　　　　　）
c.克（　　　）（　　　　）　　d.損（　　　）（　　　　　）
e.傷（　　　）（　　　　）　　f.藥（　　　）（　　　　　）
g.逮（　　　）（　　　　）　　h.怨（　　　）（　　　　　）
i.道（　　　）（　　　　）　　j.威（　　　）（　　　　　）

我聞忠善以＿＿＿＿＿＿怨，不聞作＿＿＿＿＿以防＿＿＿＿＿。〔毀鄉校〕

豈不＿＿＿＿＿＿止〔民之議〕？然〔防議〕猶＿＿＿＿＿川，〔川於〕

大決所＿＿＿＿＿，＿＿＿＿＿＿人必多，吾不＿＿＿＿＿救也。〔防川〕不如

小決使＿＿＿＿＿，〔防議〕不如吾聞而＿＿＿＿＿＿之也。

二　成語　Set phrases

1. 選出適當的字來，填入下列成語的空內 Chose the appropriate words to fill in the blanks of the following set phrases:

2. 寫出每個成語的讀音來 Give the pronunciation for the following set phrases:

3. 用每個成語造句，或選四個組成一段短文 Make sentences with each of the set phrases, or choose five and use them to compose a short passage:

衰　克　逆　歡　甚　逾　市　尾

1. 柔能 ＿＿＿＿＿＿ 剛。　　　　　（　　　　　　　　）
2. 色 ＿＿＿＿＿＿ 愛弛。　　　　　（　　　　　　　　）
3. 盡 ＿＿＿＿＿＿ 而散。　　　　　（　　　　　　　　）
4. 曳 ＿＿＿＿＿＿ 塗中。　　　　　（　　　　　　　　）
5. 忠言 ＿＿＿＿＿＿ 耳。　　　　　（　　　　　　　　）
6. 門庭若 ＿＿＿＿＿＿。　　　　　（　　　　　　　　）
7. 橘 ＿＿＿＿＿＿ 淮則為枳。　　　（　　　　　　　　）
8. 防民之口，＿＿＿＿＿＿於防川。（　　　　　　　　）

三　翻譯　Translation

把下列句子譯成白話或英文　Translate the following sentences into

243

modern Chinese or into Engliah:

1. 子產治鄭二十六年而死。丁壯號哭，老人兒啼，曰：“子
產去我而死乎？民將安居？” （史記‧循吏列傳）

2. 夫良藥苦於口，而智者勸而飲之，知其入而已己病也。忠言
拂於耳，而明主聽之，知其可以致功也。

（韓非子‧外儲說左上）

3. 防民之口，甚於防川。川壅而潰，傷人必多。民亦如之。是
故為川者，決之使導；治民者，宣之使言。 （國語‧周語上）

4. 玉不琢，不成器；人不學，不知道；是故古之王者，建國君
民，教學為先。 （禮記‧學記）

注 解 ：

1.	丁壯 cóng zhèng	【名詞語】	壯年人 people in their prime age
2.	啼 tí	【動詞】	哭 to wail; to cry
	兒啼 ér tí	【動詞語】	像小孩一樣地哭 to cry like a child
3.	去 qù	【動詞】	離開 to depart; to leave
4.	安居 ān jū	【動詞語】	居住何處？ where to live?
5.	智者 zhì zhě	【名詞語】	聰明的人 wise men
6.	勸 quàn	【動詞】	勸勉；勉力；努力 to force oneself to...
7.	已 yǐ	【動詞】	停止 to stop；此處：治好 to cure
8.	己病 jǐ bìng	【名詞語】	自己的病 one's own illness
9.	忠言 zhōng yán	【名詞語】	好的勸告 good advice
10.	拂 fú	【動詞】	拂逆 to go against
11.	耳 ěr	【名詞】	耳朵 ears
	拂耳 fú ěr	【動詞語】	逆耳 to be unpleasant to the ear
12.	明主 míng zhǔ	【名詞語】	英明的君主 an enlightened ruler
13.	致 zhì	【動詞】	招致；獲致；獲得 to bring about; to obtain
14.	功 gōng	【名詞】	功效 effect; results

15. 防 fáng 【動詞】防堵 to prevent; to block

16. 甚 shèn 【形容詞】厲害；嚴重 more serious

16. 壅 yōng 【動詞】堵塞 to clog up

17. 潰 kuì 【動詞】潰決；水衝破堤防 to break the dike

18. 亦 yì 【副詞】也 also

19. 為川 wéi chuān 【動詞語】治理河水 to regulate rivers and watercourses

20. 治民 zhì mín 【動詞語】治理人民 to rule the people

21. 宣 xuān 【動詞】宣洩；抒發 to let out; to vent

22. 琢 zhuó 【動詞】雕琢 to carve and polish

23. 器 qì 【名詞】器皿；有用的東西 utensils; useful things

24. 道 dào 【名詞】道理 the proper way; the right way

25. 建國 jiàn guó 【動詞語】建立國家 to found a nation

26. 君民 jūn mín 【動詞語】做人民的君主 to be a ruler of the people

27. 教學 jiāo xué 【動詞語】教誨、學習；教育 teaching and learning; education

28. 先 xiān 【名詞】首要的事 the most important thing; priority

四 使動式與意動式 The Causative Constructions and the Putative Constructions

使動常式 Typical causative constructions:

齊桓公使管仲治國

使動變式 Atypical causative constructions:

A 為人養子者，務生之，非為殺之也。 （動詞使動）

B 工欲善其事，必先利其器。 （形容詞使動）

意動常式 Typical putative constructions:

王以和為誑而刖其左足。 （以為分用）

虎以為〔狐之言〕然，故遂與之行。 （以為合用）

意動變式 Atypical putative constructions:

C 其家甚智其子。 （形容詞意動）

D 不如吾聞而藥之也。 （名詞意動）

試辨別下列句子各屬 (A, B, C, or D) 中哪種用法 Identify the construction type of each of the the following sentences as 'A,' 'B,' 'C,' or 'D':

1. 吾妻之<u>美我</u>者，私我也。 (　　　)
2. 是固嘗矯駕吾車，又嘗<u>啗我</u>以餘桃。 (　　　)
3. 吾在難中，此乃子之報怨時也，何故<u>逃我</u>？ (　　　)
4. 豈可以<u>利賞</u>而畏誅之故，廢正義而行逆節哉？ (　　　)
5. 漁人甚<u>異之</u>。 （陶潛‧桃花源記） (　　　)
6. 能<u>富貴將軍</u>者上也。 （史記‧魏其武安侯列傳） (　　　)
7. <u>飲馬</u>長城窟，水寒傷馬骨。 (　　　)
   （陳琳‧飲馬長城窟）
8. 人主自智而<u>愚人</u>，自巧而<u>拙人</u>。 (　　　)
   （呂氏春秋‧知度）
9. 儒者在本朝則<u>美政</u>，在下位則<u>美俗</u>。 (　　　)
   （荀子‧儒效）

注解：

1. 異 yì 　【形容詞】奇怪　strange
2. 將軍 jiāngjūn 　【名詞】將軍；此處稱對方，您 a general; here refers to the addressee, you sir
3. 長城 cháng chéng 　【名詞】長城　the Great Wall
4. 窟 kū 　【名詞】洞　a cave; a hole
5. 骨 gǔ 　【名詞】骨　the bones
6. 上 shàng 　【名詞】皇上　the Emperor; His Majesty
7. 愚 yú 　【形容詞】愚笨　foolish; stupid
8. 巧 qiǎo 　【形容詞】靈巧　skillful; ingenious
9. 拙 zhuó 　【形容詞】笨拙　awkward; clumsy
10. 儒者 rú zhě 　【名詞語】讀儒家書的人 Confucian scholars
11. 本朝 běn cháo 　【名詞語】朝廷；指在朝為官 the court; meaning as an official
12. 下位 xià wèi 　【名詞語】民間；指在野為民 among the people; as a commoner
13. 俗 sú 　【名詞】風俗　the social custom

把上面五到九句譯成白話或英文 Translate sentences 5-9 above into modern Chinese or into English:

246

五　　"奈何" 的兩種用法　The Two Uses of ' 奈何 '

A. 奈何…乎？　　　　　(used adverbially meaning: "why" or "how could")

如之何…〔乎〕？

奈何欲顯婦人之節而辱士乎？

〔鄉校之民議〕是吾師也，如之何毀之？

B. N1 奈 N2 何？　(used verbally, meaning "what/how to do/deal with"

N1 無可奈 N2 何。

嗟乎，吾奈公子何？

斷足固我罪也，無可奈何。

辨別下面各句中的「奈何」各屬於A或B類並譯成白話或英文
Identify each of the following sentences as belong to A or B, and then translate them
into modern Chinese or English:

1. 少壯幾時兮，奈老何？　　（漢武帝‧秋風辭）　　（　　）

2. 晉公子賢，又同姓，窮而過我，奈何不禮？　　（　　）
　　　　　　　　　　　　　　（史記‧晉世家）

3. 太史伯陽曰："禍成矣。無可奈何。"　　　　（　　）
　　　　　　　　　　　　　　（史記‧周本紀）

4. 奈何使人之君七年不飲酒、不食肉？　　　　（　　）
　　　　　　　　　　　　　　（公羊傳‧成公八年）

注解：

1. 少壯　　　【形容詞】年輕健壯　young and strong; youthhood
shào zhuàng

2. 幾時　　　【名詞語】多久　how long; 有 多久 for how long
jǐ shí

3. 兮 xī　　　【助詞】啊　a particle

4. 同姓　　　【名詞語】同樣的姓　of the same family name/surname
tóng xìng

5. 窮 qióng　【形容詞】窮困　in distress

6. 過 guō　　【動詞】拜訪　to visit

7. 禮 lǐ　　　【動詞】禮待　to treat with courtesy

8. 伯陽　　　【名詞語】即老子，作太史官　Laozi, once served as
Bóyáng　　　　　　　　　the Grand Historian

247

9. 禍 huò 【名詞】災禍 disaster

10. 成 chéng 【動詞】造成；釀成 to be created; brought about

11. 人之君 【名詞語】別人的君主 a ruler of other people
    rén zhī jūn

12. 飲 yǐn 【動詞】喝 to drink

13. 肉 ròu 【名詞】肉 meat; meat dish

六　討論 Discussion

1. 魏節乳母如何體現儒家的仁義之道？
   How did the upright wet nurse of Wèi embody the Confucian doctrine of "benevolence and righteousness"?

2. 子產的政治理念是什麼？
   What is Zǐchǎn's political ideal?

總 復 習

一　破音字復習　Review of Homonyms

Review the following pairs of homonyms that have the same graph with different pronunciations and meaning.

1. a.	相 xiàng	宰相	8. a.	遺 wèi	送給
b.	相 xiāng	互相	b.	遺 yí	遺留
2. a.	惡 wù	憎惡	9. a.	說 shuō	解釋
b.	惡 è	醜惡	b.	說 yuè	悅；高興
3. a.	臭 chòu	臭；難聞	10. a.	衣 yī	衣服
b.	臭 xiù	氣味	b.	衣 yì	穿衣服
4. a.	見 jiàn	看見；拜訪	11. a.	冠 guān	帽子
b.	見 xiàn	表現	b.	冠 guàn	戴帽子
5. a	更 gēng	改變	12. a.	使 shǐ	派遣；命令
b.	更 gèng	更加	b.	使 shì	出使
6. a.	度 duò	量	13. a.	識 shì	了解
b.	度 dù	尺碼	b.	識 zhì	記住
7. a.	為 wèi	替；給	14. a.	朝 zhāo	早上
b.	為 wéi	成為；是	b.	朝 cháo	朝廷

請辨別下列各句中畫線的詞是a還是b　Using the list provided, identify the proper reading and meaning of the underlined words in each sentence as 'A,' or 'B':

1. 有餽魚於鄭相者，鄭相不受。　(　　　　　)
2. 人有大臭者。　(　　　　　)
3. 海上人有說其臭者。　(　　　　　)
4. 子夏見曾子。　(　　　　　)
5. 鄉人皆惡我鳴，以故東徙。　(　　　　　)
6. 子能更鳴，可矣。　(　　　　　)
7. 惡者貴而美者賤。　(　　　　　)
8. 先自度其足而置之其座。　(　　　　　)
9. 已得履，乃曰，吾忘持度。　(　　　　　)
10. 蘇代為燕謂趙惠王曰：　(　　　　　)
11. 兩者不肯相舍，漁父得而并擒之。　(　　　　　)
12. 臣恐彊秦之為漁父也。　(　　　　　)
13. 鄚人有遺燕相國書者。　(　　　　　)

249

14. 燕相受書而說之。　　　　　　　　（　　　　　　　）
15. 燕相白王，〔王〕大說，國以治。　（　　　　　　　）
16. 天帝使我長百獸。　　　　　　　　（　　　　　　　）
17. 清旦，衣冠而之市。（　　　　　）（　　　　　　　）
18. 真見燕國之城社、真見先人之廬塚，悲心更微。（　　　　）
19. 曾子弊衣而耕於魯。　　　　　　　（　　　　　　　）
20. 賜不能識也。　　　　　　　　　　（　　　　　　　）
21. 小子識之，苛政猛於虎也。　　　　（　　　　　　　）
22. 先生疾甚矣。無遺教可以語諸弟子者乎？（　　　　　）
23. 晏子將使楚。　　　　　　　　　　（　　　　　　　）
24. 妾援得其冠纓，持之。　　　　　　（　　　　　　　）
25. 君愀然不樂，見於顏色。　　　　　（　　　　　　　）
26. 於是入朝見威王，曰：　　　　　　（　　　　　　　）
27. 夫人朝夕退而游焉，以議執政之善否。（　　　　　　）

二　　同義字復習　Review of Synonyms

1. 從表中選出意思相同或相近的字來，填入下列各字的旁邊
　Choose words with the same or similar meaning to fill in the blanks:

2. 寫出各對同義字的讀音來 In the parentheses give the pronunciation for
　each pair of synonyms:

逆　持　逐　適　良　多　將　長　奪　壯

生＿＿（　　　　　）　　　　且＿＿（　　　　　）
善＿＿（　　　　　）　　　　之＿＿（　　　　　）
強＿＿（　　　　　）　　　　操＿＿（　　　　　）
悖＿＿（　　　　　）　　　　追＿＿（　　　　　）
攫＿＿（　　　　　）　　　　眾＿＿（　　　　　）

引　樂　好　慕　刻　斷　旦　歸　獻　契

朝＿＿（　　　　　）　　　　反＿＿（　　　　　）
夕＿＿（　　　　　）　　　　何＿＿（　　　　　）
歡＿＿（　　　　　）　　　　援＿＿（　　　　　）
愛＿＿（　　　　　）　　　　折＿＿（　　　　　）
奉＿＿（　　　　　）　　　　契＿＿（　　　　　）

	盜	論	懼	卻	賴	示	絕	捕	墮	害

墜＿＿（　　　　　　）　　　擒＿＿（　　　　　　）
斷＿＿（　　　　　　）　　　辭＿＿（　　　　　　）
仰＿＿（　　　　　　）　　　畏＿＿（　　　　　　）
議＿＿（　　　　　　）　　　竊＿＿（　　　　　　）
顯＿＿（　　　　　　）　　　傷＿＿（　　　　　　）

	匿	哀	謀	亡	殺	賜	伐	盡	卒	患

誅＿＿（　　　　　　）　　　計＿＿（　　　　　　）
極＿＿（　　　　　　）　　　賞＿＿（　　　　　　）
藏＿＿（　　　　　　）　　　悲＿＿（　　　　　　）
逃＿＿（　　　　　　）　　　憂＿＿（　　　　　　）
攻＿＿（　　　　　　）　　　薨＿＿（　　　　　　）

三　　反義字復習　Review of Antonyms

1. 從表中選出意思相反的字來，填入下列各字的旁邊　Choose words with the opposite meaning to fill in the blanks:

2. 寫出各對反義字的讀音來　In the parentheses give the pronunciation for each pair of antonyms:

	異	亡	入	此	非	往	失	死	私	害

生＿＿（　　　　　　）　　　彼＿＿（　　　　　　）
存＿＿（　　　　　　）　　　是＿＿（　　　　　　）
出＿＿（　　　　　　）　　　得＿＿（　　　　　　）
來＿＿（　　　　　　）　　　同＿＿（　　　　　　）
公＿＿（　　　　　　）　　　利＿＿（　　　　　　）

	臭	受	近	福	富	醜	柔	苦	惡	贜

美＿＿（　　　　　　）　　　禍＿＿（　　　　　　）
甘＿＿（　　　　　　）　　　遠＿＿（　　　　　　）
肥＿＿（　　　　　　）　　　好＿＿（　　　　　　）
香＿＿（　　　　　　）　　　辭＿＿（　　　　　　）
剛＿＿（　　　　　　）　　　貧＿＿（　　　　　　）

疏　舍　慕　怨　負　亂　歡　樂　退　夕

悲＿＿（　　　　　　　　）　　苦＿＿（　　　　　　　　）
治＿＿（　　　　　　　　）　　恩＿＿（　　　　　　　　）
旦＿＿（　　　　　　　　）　　親＿＿（　　　　　　　　）
朝＿＿（　　　　　　　　）　　取＿＿（　　　　　　　　）
勝＿＿（　　　　　　　　）　　進＿＿（　　　　　　　　）

惡　辱　憎　否　寡　賤　賀　譽　益　夜

貴＿＿（　　　　　　　　）　　畫＿＿（　　　　　　　　）
謗＿＿（　　　　　　　　）　　弔＿＿（　　　　　　　　）
然＿＿（　　　　　　　　）　　眾＿＿（　　　　　　　　）
愛＿＿（　　　　　　　　）　　榮＿＿（　　　　　　　　）
善＿＿（　　　　　　　　）　　害＿＿（　　　　　　　　）

四　　重要虛字復習　Review of Important Grammatical Particles

根據句意和文法選出適當的虛字來填入空內 Fill in the following blanks with the appropriate particles according to the contextual meaning and grammatical pattern of each sentence:

之　乎　者　也　矣　焉　哉　其
所　而　則　以　於　與　為

1. 人有大臭者，其親戚、兄弟、妻妾、知識無能與居＿＿＿。
2. 或曰："＿＿＿子之矛陷子之盾，何如？"
3. 弟子記之：行賢而去自賢之心，安往而不愛＿＿＿＿！
4. 人皆在＿＿＿＿，子攫人之金何？
5. 舟已行矣，而劍不行。求劍若此，不亦惑＿＿＿？
6. 王乃使人理＿＿＿＿璞而得寶焉，遂命曰："和氏之璧。"
7. 歧路之中，又有歧焉，吾不知＿＿＿＿之，所以反也。
8. 〔蛇足〕未成，一人之蛇成。奪其卮曰："蛇固無足，子安能＿＿＿＿之足？"
9. 曾子衣弊衣而耕於野，魯君聞＿＿＿＿，使人致邑焉，曾子固辭不受。
10. 莊子釣＿＿＿＿濮水，楚王使大夫二人往先焉。
11. 楚有神龜，死已三千歲＿＿＿，王巾笥而藏之廟堂之上。

12. 異日彌子＿＿＿君遊於果園。

13. 魏節乳母者，魏公子之乳母＿＿＿＿＿。

14. 魏之故臣見乳母＿＿＿＿＿識之，曰：“乳母無恙乎？”

15. 故臣曰：“乳母倘言公子之處，＿＿＿＿可以得千金。”

五　句子結構複習　Review of Sentence Constructions

1.　敘述句　Narrative Sentences:

S　　　P (V -- O)

梟　　　逢　鳩。　　　　　　　　　　　　　　　(L.6)

2.　描寫句　Descriptive Sentences:

S　　　　P (Adj)

君　　　　美甚。　　　　　　　　　　　　　　(L. 38)

君　　　　美於徐公。　　　　　　　　　　　　(L. 38)

3.　判斷句　Detarminative Sentences:

　　　S　　　　　　　　　P (N)

魏節乳母者，魏公子之乳母也。　　　　　　　　(L.39)

　　　S　　　P.L.V.　　　　P (N)

孔子　　　猶　　　江海也。　　　　　　　　　(L.29)

子　　　非　　　魚。　　　　　　　　　　　　(L.25)

4.　敘述句帶介賓或副詞　Narrative Sentences with PP or Adverb:

A.　　S　　Prep -- O　　V　Prep -- O

劍　　自　舟中　墜　於　　水。　(L.17)

B.　S　　　　Adv　　V　　Prep -- O

乳母與故臣　相　　遇　於　　塗。　(L.39)

253

C.　S　　V -- O　　Prep -- O
　龜　曳　尾　於　塗中。　　　　　(L.31)

5.　疑問句　Interrogative Sentences:

A. S　　Adv　Adv　　V -- O　　　　Prep -- O ?
　子　何　不　試之（履）以　足？ (L.10)

B. S　　O-Prep　Adv　V　也 ?
　子　何為　不　去　也？　　　　(L.30)

C. S　Adv　Adv　　V -- O　　乎 ?
　君　何　不　毀　鄉校　乎？　　(L.40)

6.　反問句　Rhetorical Interrogative Sentences:

A.　[S]　　V - O　comp. Adv　Adv　Adj　乎 ?
　〔涉江者〕求劍　若此　不　亦　惑　乎？ (L.17)

B. S　　Adv　Aux.V　Adv　V --　[O]　　乎 ?
　吾　豈　能　勿　畏　〔之〕　乎？　(L.28)

C.　"奈何　　　V　O　而 V -- O　乎" ?
　奈何　　欲顯婦人之節而辱　士　乎？ (L.36)

D.　S　　Adv　Aux.V　V -- O　哉 !　　(L.39)
　忠臣　豈　可　作　亂　哉！

7.　疑問感嘆句　Exclamatory Interrogative Sentences:

A.　　　　　　　　S Adv V 之 comp 也 ?

254

天下之跀者多矣，子奚 哭之悲 也？ (L.18)

B.　　　　P(Adj.)　S (S 之　P(Adj.))？
亡一羊，何　　迫者之 眾？ (L.21)

8.　雙賓語句 Double Objects Sentences:

S　　V　Oi　Od
郢人　遺 燕相國 書。 (L.13)

楚莊王 賜 群臣　酒。 (L.36)

9.　兼語句 Pivotal Sentences:

A. 使動句 Causative Sentences:

　　N1　使　　N2　P (V - O)
1. S　　使　　O/S　V - O
仁義 使　我　愛身而後名。 (L.11)

桓公 使 管仲 治 國。 (L.26)

2. S　以→使　O/S　L.V. - Pn
桓公 以　　管仲 為　上卿。 (L.26)

B. 意動句 Putative Sentences:

　　N1　以　　N2　為　Adj
1. S　以　O/S　為　Adj
虎　以 狐之言 為　然。 (L.14)

　　N1　以為　N2　　Adj
2. S　以為　O/S　Adj
虎　以為 狐之言　然。 (L.14)

255

```
                 N          Adj ->V    N
```
3.   S   以 為   O   Adj
     其 家   甚 智   其 子。   (L.2)


```
                 N    自    Adj ->V
```
4.   S   以 為自己   Adj
     其美者   自   美。   (L.8)

10.   包孕句 Embedding Sentences:

1.   S   Adv   V   O (S___P)
     鄉人   皆   惡   我   鳴。   (L.6)

2.   S Adv. V   S之P   也
     〔其美者自美，〕吾 不 知   其美   也。   (L.8)

11.   複句 Compound Sentences:

等立複句 Coordinate Compound Sentences:

例如：取捨式 For example: The Preferential Construction

〔吾〕寧信其度，無自信也。）   (L.10)
For other constructions, see Exercise 9, p. 220

主從複句 Subordinate Compound Sentences (Complex Sentences):

例如：容認式 For example: The Concessive Construction

縱君有賜，不我驕也，吾豈能勿畏乎？   (L.28)
For other constructions, see Exercise 11, p. 230

12.   所字句 Sentences with the Particle 'suo':

A. 所 + V = N

1.〔人〕不知其子，視其（其子之）<u>所友</u>。　　(L.16)

2.君若欲害之，不若一為下水以病其<u>所種</u>。　(L.19)

3.余〔乃〕<u>爾所嫁</u>婦人之父也。　　　　　(L.20)

4. 此<u>所謂</u>戰勝於朝廷。　　　　　　　　(L.38)

5.其（民之）<u>所善</u>者，吾則行之。　　　(L.40)

B. <u>所</u> + Prep + V= **N**

　　　N1　乃　N2　　之所以　　V　　也。
1.　　此　乃　和氏　之<u>所以</u>　悲　也。　(L.18)
　　　　　　　　　（以：因為）

2.　不下水　乃　君　　之<u>所以</u>　富東周　也。　(L.19)
　　　　　　　　　（以：用）

3.　　是　乃　吾劍　之<u>所從</u>　墜。　　(L.17)

4.　　聖人　非　　　　<u>所與</u>　熙也。
　　　　　　　　　　　（晏子春秋 · 內雜下）

13.　**足以句** Sentences Using 'zuyi':

　　　N　　足以　　　V - O　　　也。
A.　參之言　<u>足以</u>　　全　其節　也。　　(L.28)

B.　　賜　<u>不足以</u>　　識　孔子。　　　(L.29)

C.　　賜　<u>奚足以</u>　　識　孔子？　　　(L.29)

257

14.　　**被動句**　Passive Sentences:

N1　為　N2　　　V（為＝被）

A. 兔不可復得，而身　為　宋人　　笑。　(L.3)

N1　為　N2　所　V（為…所＝被）

B.　　　　　楚　為　秦　所輕。

(戰國策・秦策)

N1　　見　V

C. 彌子　見賢。　　　　　　　(L.35)

　愛人者 必見 愛也。　(墨子・兼愛下)

N1　　見　V　於　　N2

D.　彌子瑕　見愛　於　衛君。

(史記・老莊申韓列傳)

N1　V　於　　N2

E.　謗議　聞〔於〕寡人之耳。　　(L.38)

翻譯練習一

一　點斷下文，並把它翻譯？ he following passage and then translate it into modern Chinese or into
English:

管寧華歆嘗同席讀書有乘軒冕過門者寧讀如故歆廢
書出看寧割席分坐曰子非吾友也世因謂絕交曰割席

《世說新語‧德行》

注解：

1. 管寧　　【名詞】人名；姓管，名寧，字幼安 personal name;
Guǎn Níng　　　surnamed Guǎn, named Nígn, and courtesy named Yòu-ān

2. 華歆　　【名詞】人名；性華，名歆，字子魚 personal name;
Huà Xīn　　　surnamed Huà, named Xīn, and courtesy named Zǐ-yú

3. 嘗 cháng　【副詞】曾經 once

4. 席 xí　　【名詞】坐席 a mat

5. 乘 chéng　【動詞】坐〔車〕to ride [on a carriage]

6. 軒 xuān　【名詞】軒車；古代大夫以上的官員坐的車子；
高大的車子 a carriage

7. 冕 miǎn　【名詞】古代大夫以上的官員戴的禮冠。此處用作動詞，
戴著大夫的帽子 a ceremonial cap; here, wearing an official cap

8. 廢 fèi　　【動詞】拋棄；丟開 to cast aside; 放下 to put aside

廢書　　【動詞語】放下書 to put aside the book
fèi shū

9. 割 gē　　【動詞】割開；切開 to cut apart

10 謂 wèi　　【動詞】稱；叫 to call

11.絕交　　【動詞語】斷絕交往；不再來往；不再作朋友
jué jiāo　　　to break off relations [between friends]

謂A曰B　【句型】稱A作B；叫A作B；把A叫做B
wèi...yuē　　to call A B; to speak of A as B.

12.世說新語【名詞】書名，宋(420-479 A.D.)劉義慶(403 - 444 A.D.)著。書中
Shìshuō Xīnyǔ　　記載東漢(25 - 220 A.D.)魏(220-265 A.D.)晉(265 - 419 A.D.)
間政治界人物及名士的故事。文字簡潔，是一本
極有趣的文學作品，也是一部研究一世紀到五世
紀社會的珍貴史料。

259

title of a book; A New Account of the Tales of the World, authored by the retainers of Prince of Linchuan, Liu Yiqing (403-444), and published under Liu's name. As a lively record of words and deeds of scholar-officials from Eastern Han down to the end of the Jin dynasty, it is a valuable source for the study of Chinese society and intellectual life. The book has been translated into English by Richard Mather.

13. 德行 　　【名詞】《世說新語》書中篇名之一，專門記載品德高尚

　　Déxìng 　　的人的言語及行為

　　Moral Conduct--a chapter heading in *Shìshuō Xīnyǔ*

二　　問答 Answer the following questions in either Chinese or English:

1. 你認為管寧和華歆絕交的理由夠不夠充分？
Do you think that Guǎn Níng's breaking off with Huà Xīn is fully justified?

2. 如果你是管寧，你要怎麼做？
What would you do if you were in the position of Guǎn Níng?

翻譯練習二

一　請參看注解將下面的短文譯成白話或英文
Consult the glossaries given below and then translate the following passage into
modern Chinese or into English:

蜀之鄙有二僧，其一人貧，其一人富。貧者語於富者曰："吾
欲之南海，何如？"富者曰："子何恃而往？"曰："吾一瓶一缽
足矣。"富者曰："吾數年來欲買舟而下，猶未能也；子何恃而往
？"越明年，貧者自南海還，以告富者。富者有慚色。

清 彭端淑 (Péng Duānshú)《為學一首示子姪》

注 解 ：

1. 蜀 shǔ　　【名詞】四川　Sìchuān, name of a province

2. 鄙 bǐ　　【名詞】邊鄙；邊遠的地方　border area; a remote place

3. 僧 sēng　　【名詞】和尚　a monk

4. 貧 pín　　【形容詞】窮；沒有錢　poor

5. 語 yù　　【動詞】告訴　to tell

6. 欲 yù　　【動詞】想要　to intend to

7. 南海 Nánhǎi　　【名詞】指浙江省的普陀 (tuó)山 Mt. Pǔtuó in Zhèjiāng province; a sacred place for Buddhism

8. 恃 shì　　【動詞】靠　to rely on

　 何恃 hé shì　　【動詞語】靠〔著〕甚麼 what to rely on?

9. 往 wǎng　　【動】到…去　to go there

10. 瓶 píng　　【名詞】瓶子　a bottle

11. 缽 bō　　【名詞】和尚盛飯的東西，像碗 an alms bowl [of a Buddhist monk/nun]（和尚，尼姑可以拿著缽向人化緣）

　　 ◆ 尼姑 (nígū)　a nun

　　 ◆ 化緣 (huà yuán)　to solicite alms (as a means for favorable karma)

12. 足 zú　　【形容詞】足夠；夠　enough

13. 來 lái　　【助詞】以來　ever since

14. 數年來 shù nián lái　　【時間詞】好幾年以來；從幾年前到現在 for the past several years; since several years ago

261

15. 買舟　　　【動詞語】僱(gù)一條船；賃(lìn)一條船 to rent/hire a boat
　　mǎi zhōu

16. 下 xià　　【動詞】到南方／邊去 to go to the south

17. 猶 yóu　　【副詞】還 still

18. 越明年　　【動詞語】越過明年；過了明年 past the second year
　　yuè míng nián　　　　　　　→ 到了第三年 on the third year

19. 告 gào　　【動詞】告訴 to tell; to inform

　　以告富者【動詞語】以〔之〕告富者 to tell the wealthy monk of it
　　yǐ gào fù zhě

20. 慚 cán　　【形容詞】慚愧 to be ashamed

　　慚色　　　【名詞語】慚愧的臉色；慚愧的神色 a shamefaced look
　　cán sè

二　　問答 Answer the following questions:

1. 這個小故事要告訴讀者什麼？
　　What do you think the story is trying to say?

2. 評富僧。
　　Comment on the wealthy monk.

翻譯練習三

一　把下面的短文翻譯成白話或英文
Translate the following passage into modern Chinese or into English:

荀巨伯遠看友人疾，值胡賊攻郡。友人語巨伯曰：“吾今死矣，子可去。”巨伯曰：“遠來相視，子令吾去。敗義以求生，豈巨伯所為邪？”賊既至，謂巨伯曰：“大軍至，一郡盡空。汝何男子而敢獨止？”巨伯曰：“友人有疾，不忍委之；寧以我身代友人命。”賊相謂曰：“我輩無義之人，而入有義之國。”遂班師而還，一郡並獲全。　　　　　　　　　　　　　　　《世說新語 · 德行》

注解：

1. 荀巨伯 Xún Jùbó	【名詞】	人名，漢朝人
2. 遠 yuǎn	【副詞】	遠遠地──→到很遠的地方去 to travel far
3. 疾 jí	【名詞】	病 illness
4. 值 zhí	【動詞】	遇到 it happens that
5. 胡賊 hú zéi	【名詞語】	胡人；中國北方文化落後的人 the nomads
6. 攻 gōng	【動詞】	攻打 to attack
7. 郡 jùn	【名詞】	中國古代的行政區域，比縣略大 a political division in ancient China; a prefecture
8. 語 yù	【動詞】	告訴 to tell
9. 相 xiāng	【副詞】	互相 mutually；如 “相” 字後是及物動詞但無賓語，“相” 字便用如代名詞 “我” 、 “你” 、 或 “他” ，作賓語。 When the word 'xiang' is followed by a transitive which does not have an object, the word 'xiang' then functions as the pronominal object meaning 'me', 'you' or 'him/her' 此處 “相” 用如代名詞 “你” here it means 'you'
10. 相視 xiāng shì	【動詞語】	看你 to visit you
11. 敗 bài	【動詞】	敗壞 to corrupt; to ruin
12. 義 yì	【名詞】	道義 a sense of righteousness
13. 敗義 bài yì	【動詞語】	敗壞[朋友間的]道義 to spoil our friendship

263

14. 豈…邪　【句型】哪裡[是]...呢？ can this be...?
　　qǐ　yé　　　　怎麼[是]...呢？ how can this be...?

15. 既 jì　【副詞】已經 already

16. 軍 jūn　【名詞】軍隊 army; troop

17. 大軍　【名詞語】強大的軍隊──→我們的軍隊 our troops
　　dà jūn

18. 一郡　【名詞語】全郡；整個郡 the entire prefecture
　　yí jùn

19. 盡 jìn　【副詞】完全；全部 totally; completely

20. 空 kōng　【形容詞】空 empty
　　　　　　【動詞】變空了 to be evacuated

21. 汝 rǔ　【代名詞】你 you

　　汝何男子　【疑問判斷句】汝〔為〕何男子？ What a man are you?
　　rǔ hé nán zǐ

22. 獨 dú　【副詞】獨自 alone; singly

23. 止 zhǐ　【動詞】停留──→留下 to stay; to remain

24. 不忍　【動詞語】不忍心；心裡忍受不了
　　bù rěn　　　　　 disturbed (characterized by pity); cannot stand the sight of
　　　　　　　　　　 [something]; cannot bear to [do something]

25. 委 wěi　【動詞】委棄；丟下 to abandon; to desert

26. 寧 nìng　【助動詞】寧願 would rather

27. 以 yǐ　【動詞】用──→拿 to use; to take

28. 身 shēn　【名詞】身體──→生命 life

29. 代 dài　【動詞】代替 to take the place of; to substitute for

　　以我身代友人命：拿我的生命代替友人的生命
　　　　　　　　　──→代替朋友死 to die instead of my friend

30. 我輩　【名詞語】我們 we; we folks
　　wǒ bèi

31. 班師　【動詞語】調回軍隊 to recall the troop; to withdraw the troop
　　bān shī

32. 還 huán　【動詞】回去(回國去) to return

33. 全 quán　【動詞】保全；沒受到傷害 to preserve

　　並獲全　【動詞語】都得到保全；都沒受到傷害
　　bìng huò quán　　　　　 all be preserved without harm

二　　問答 Answer the following questions in either Chinese or English:

1. 你讀了這個故事以後對荀巨伯有什麼評論？

   Having read this story, what do you think of Xú Jùbó?

2. 在 "敗義以求生" 和 "捨生取義" 之間是否能取得一個平衡點？請解釋。

   Is it possible to find a point of equilibrium between "corrupting righteousness to preserve one's own life" and "sacrificing one's own life to uphold righteousness"? Expound.

翻譯練習四

一　點斷下文並把它譯成白話或英文 Puctuate the following passage and then translate it into modern Chinese or into English:

西 施 病 心 而 矉 其 里 其 里 之 醜 人 見 而 美 之 歸 亦 捧 心 而 矉 其 里 其 里 之 富 人 見 之 堅 閉 門 而 不 出 貧 人 見 之 挈 妻 子 而 去 之 走 彼 知 矉 美 而 不 知 矉 之 所 以 美

《莊子・天運》

注解：

1. 西施　【名詞】人名；古代著名的美女。
   Xīshī　　　　　　　name of a famous beauty

2. 病心　【動詞語】病於心；有心痛的病
   bìng xīn　　　　　to suffer a heart ailment

3. 矉 pín　【動詞】皺眉 to frown; to knit the eyebrows

4. 里 lǐ　【名詞】古代二十五家為一里；鄰里　a local area of 25 households; neighborhood

5. 醜 chǒu　【形容詞】美的反面；醜；難看 ugly

6. 美之　【動詞語】以之為美；以為西施皺眉很美；覺得西施皺眉很好
   měi zhī　　　　　看 to take it (the frowning of Xīshī) as beautiful

7. 捧心　【動詞語】用手捂著心口
   pěng xīn　　　　to put one's hand over the chest cavity

8. 富人　【名詞語】富有的人；有錢的人 the rich persons
   fù rén

9. 堅 jiān　【副詞】堅固地；緊緊地 firmly; tightly

10. 閉門　【動詞語】關上大門 to shut the gates up
    bì mén

11. 出 chū　【動詞】出門；走出去 to go out

12. 貧人　【名詞語】貧窮的人；沒有錢的人 the poor persons
    pín fén

13. 挈 qiè　【動詞】牽著；帶著 to take in hands; to lead

14. 妻子　【名詞語】太太跟孩子 wife and children
    qī zǐ

15. 去之　【動詞語】離開她；躲開她 to get away from her
    qù zhī

16. 走 zǒu　【動詞】逃走 to run away; to flee

17. 彼 bǐ　　【代詞】她　she

18. 所以美【名詞語】因之而美的緣故；為什麼美；為什麼好看
　　suǒ yǐ měi　　　　the reason why it (i.e., the frowning) is beautiful; that which makes it beautiful

二　　問答 Answer the following questions:

1. 作者要用這個故事說明什麼道理？
What message does the author try to convey with this story?

2. 故事中的哪一部分最生動有趣？
What is the most vivid and amusing part of this story?

翻譯練習五

一　點斷、翻譯、及分析

　　1. 點斷下文並把它譯成白話或英文 Punctuate the following
　　　passage and then translate it into modern Chinese or into English:

　　2. 分析句構：找出主、動、賓、狀、補、定來 Analyze the
　　　structure of each sentence and identify the subjects, verbs, objects, adverbial
　　　modifiers, complements, and adjectival modifiers.

薛譚學謳於秦青未窮青之技自謂盡之遂辭歸秦青弗止餞於郊
衢撫節悲歌聲振林木響遏行雲薛譚乃謝求反終身不敢言歸

《列子・湯問》

注解：

1.	薛譚 Xuē Tán	【名詞】	人名 name of a person
2.	謳 ōu	【動詞】	唱歌 to sing
3.	秦青 Qín Qīng	【名詞】	人名；聲樂家；唱歌的專家 a vocalist
4.	窮 qióng	【動詞】	窮盡；V 完 to exhaust
5.	技 jì	【名詞】	技巧 skill; ingenuity
6.	自謂 zì wèi	【動賓】	自己以為自己 one thinks of oneself ...
7.	辭 cí	【動詞】	告辭 to take leave; to say good-bye; to bid farewell
8.	止 zhǐ	【動詞】	阻止，攔阻 (lánzhǔ; lantzuu) to stop
9.	餞 jiàn	【動詞】	餞行；擺酒〔給 ...〕送行 to entertain a parting friend with a feast
10.	郊 jiāo	【名詞】	城外 suburb
11.	衢 qú	【名詞】	大路 a thoroughfare
12.	撫 fǔ	【動詞】	輕拍；輕輕地拍 to beat gently
13.	節 jie	【名詞】	節拍 beat, rhythm or time (of music)
	撫節 fǔ jié	【動賓】	輕輕地打拍子 to tap the beat gently
14.	悲 bēi	【形容詞】	悲哀 sad; grievous
15.	歌 gē	【動詞】	唱歌 to sing
	悲歌 bēi gē	【動詞語】	悲哀地唱歌 to sing sadly

268

16. 聲 shēng 　【動詞】聲音；歌聲 the sound [of her singing]

17. 振 zhèn 　【動詞】振動 to vibrate

18. 林木　　【動詞】林中的樹木 trees in the woods
　　lín mù

19. 響 xiǎng 　【名詞】回聲 an echo

20. 遏 è 　　【動詞】攔阻；擋住；使⋯不能過去 to block

21. 行雲　　【名詞語】浮動的雲 floating clouds
　　xíng yún

22. 謝 xiè 　　【動詞】謝罪；道歉 to apologize; to make an apology

23. 終身　　【動賓】一直到死 till the time of one's death
　　zhōng shēn
　　　　　　【副詞】一輩子 the whole life

二　　問答 Answer the following questions in either Chinese or English:

1. 這個故事的主旨是什麼？
　 What is the point of this story?

2. 評秦青。
　 Comment on Qín Qīng.

翻譯練習六

一　點斷下文並把它譯成白話或英文 Punctuate the following passage and then translate it into modern Chinese or into English:

孔子東游見兩小兒辯鬥問其故一兒曰我以日始出時去人近而日中時遠也一兒以日初出遠而日中時近也一兒曰日初出大如車蓋及日中則如盤盂此不為遠者小而近者大乎一兒曰日初出滄滄涼涼及其日中如探湯此不為近者熱而遠者涼乎孔子不能決也兩小兒笑曰孰為汝多知乎

《列子‧湯問》

注解：

1. 東游 dōng yóu	【動詞語】到東部去旅游	to take a tour to the east
2. 小兒 xiǎo ér	【名詞】小孩子；小孩兒	a child; children
3. 辯鬥 biàn dòu	【動詞】辯論鬥嘴；爭辯	to debate; to argue
4. 以 yǐ	【動詞】以為	to think; to believe
5. 始 shǐ	【動詞】開始	to start; to begin
6. 出 chū	【動詞】出來；升起	to come out; to rise
7. 去 qù	【動詞】距離	to be away from
8. 日中 rì zhōng	【時間詞】太陽升到天空的中間兒；中午	noontime; midday
9. 初 chū	【副詞】剛	just about [to do something]; to have just [done something]
10. 車蓋 chē gài	【名詞】古代車上的大傘	an umbrella-like carriage canopy
11. 盤盂 pán yú	【名詞】盤子或很淺(qiǎn)的大碗(wǎn)	a plate or a large shallow bowl
12. 為 wéi	【繫詞】是	to be
13. 滄涼 cāng liáng	【形容詞】寒涼	icy cold; frigid
14. 探湯 tàn tāng	【動詞語】伸手到熱水裡去	(lit.) to test boiling water with one's hand; here: to place one's hand into scalding hot water
如探湯 rú tàn tāng		像伸手到熱水裡去一樣 as if putting one's hand into scalding hot water

270

15. 熱 rè 　　【形容詞】熱 hot; warm

16. 涼 liáng 　　【形容詞】涼 cold; cool

17. 決 jué 　　【動詞】斷定[誰對誰錯] to decide [who is right and who is wrong]

18. 為 wèi 　　【動詞】通 "謂"，說 to say

19. 多知 　　【形容詞】知識豐富；有學問 knowledgeable; erudite; to have much
　　 dūo zhī 　　　　　　　　 learning

二　問答 Answer the following questions either in Chinese or in English:

1. 你認為這個故事提出了幾個問題？
   In your opinion, how many questions have been raised in this story?

2. 你能不能斷定哪個小孩兒的說法對？為什麼？要是你能斷定
   誰對誰錯，並且講出道理來，那你就賢於孔子啦！
   Can you decide which of the children is right? Why do you think so? If you can
   decide who is right and who is wrong, and explain the reason for your judgment,
   you are even wiser than Confucius.

271

翻譯練習七

一　把下列文言翻譯成白話或英文
　　Translate the following passage into modern Chinese or into English:

惠子相梁，莊子往見之。或謂惠子曰："莊子來，欲代子相。"於是惠子恐，搜於國中三日三夜。

莊子往見之，曰："南方有鳥，其名鵷鶵，子知之乎？夫鵷鶵發於南海而飛於北海。非梧桐不止；非練實不食；非醴泉不飲。於是鴟得腐鼠，鵷鶵過之。仰而視之，曰：'嚇！'今子欲以子之梁國而嚇我邪？"
　　　　　　　　　　　　　　　　　　　《莊子·秋水》

注解：

1. 鵷鶵 yuān chú	【名詞】	鵷雛；一種像鳳凰 (fènghuáng)的鳥　a bird that looks like a phoenix
2. 惠子 Huì zǐ	【名詞】	人名。姓惠，名施，戰國時代哲學家，也是莊子的好朋友 Huìzǐ, a famous dialectician
3. 相 xiàng	【動詞】	作宰相　to serve as the prime minister
4. 相梁 xiàng Liáng	【動詞語】	相〔於〕梁；在梁國作相 to serve as the prime minister in the state of Liáng
5. 莊子 Zhuāng zǐ	【名詞】	人名。姓莊，名周，戰國時代哲學家，是道家的重要人物 Zhuāngzǐ, a great Taoist master
6. 代 dài	【動詞】	代替 to replace
7. 恐 kǒng	【形容詞】	害怕 to be afraid; to be scared; to be alarmed
8. 搜 sōu	【動詞】	搜查 to search
9. 發 fā	【動詞】	出發 to set out
10. 南海 Nán hǎi	【名詞】	南海 the South China Sea
11. 飛 fēi	【動詞】	飛 to fly [to]
12. 北海 Běi hǎi	【名詞】	北海 the North China Sea
13. 梧桐 wú tóng	【名詞】	梧桐樹 firmiana; Chinese parasol [tree]
14. 止 zhǐ	【動詞】	棲息 to perch

15.非梧桐不止 【主從句】 〔若樹〕非梧桐〔則〕〔鵷雛〕不止
　fēi wú tóng bù zhǐ 　　〔要是樹〕不是梧桐〔那麼〕〔鵷雛〕〔就〕不

棲止 ...will not perch if it were not on a firmiana

非…不… 【主從句】 [若] [N1] 非 [N2], [則] [N3] 不 V
　fēi... bù... 　　　　[要是] [N1] 不是 [N2], [那麼] [N3] [就] 不 V

[N1] 必得是 [N2], [N3] 才 V

16. 練實　　　【名詞】竹子的果實 bamboo seeds
　liàn shí

17. 醴泉　　　【名詞】甜美的泉水 a sweet spring
　lǐ quán

18. 飲 yǐn　　【動詞】喝 to drink

19. 鴟 chī　　【名詞】梟；貓頭鷹 an owl

20. 腐 fǔ　　　【形容詞】腐爛的 rotten; decomposed

21. 腐鼠　　　【名詞】腐爛的死老鼠 a rotten rat
　fǔ shǔ

22. 仰 yǎng　　【動詞】抬頭 to raise one's head to look up

23. 嚇 hè　　　【動詞】發出嚇別人的聲音 Shoo! a sound made to frighten
　　　　　　　　others

二　　問答 Answer the following questions either in Chinese or in English:

1. 鵷雛、鴟、腐鼠各比喻 (bǐyù: to analogize) 什麼？
What analogy is drawn by the yuān chú, the owl, and the rotten rat?

2. 你欣賞 (xīnshǎng: to apprecaite) 這個故事嗎？為什麼？
Do you appreciate this story? Why or why not?

273

翻譯練習八

點斷下文並把它譯成白話 或英文 Punctuate the following passage and then translate it into modern Chinese or into English:

漢哀帝幸董賢與共臥起嘗晝寢偏藉上袖上欲起賢未覺不欲動賢乃斷袖而起　　　　《漢書‧董賢傳》

注解：

1. 漢哀帝 Hàn Āidì	【名詞】	漢哀帝劉欣，在位六年 Emperor Āi of Hàn, Liú Xīn (r. 6-1 B.C)
2. 幸 xìng	【動詞】	寵愛 to dote on; to favor
3. 董賢 Dǒng Xián	【名詞】	人名 personal name
4. 與 yǔ	【介詞】	跟〔他〕 with [him]
5. 共 gòng	【副詞】	同；一塊兒 together
6. 臥 wò	【動詞】	躺下；睡覺 to lie down; to sleep
7. 起 qǐ	【動詞】	起身 to get up; to rise
8. 嘗 cháng	【副詞】	曾經 once
9. 晝寢 zhòu qǐn	【動詞語】	白天睡覺；睡午覺 to have a nap
10. 偏 piān	【副詞】	偏側；一部分 sidewise; partly
11. 藉 jiè	【動詞】	壓住 to apply weight on; to pillow on; to lie on
12. 偏藉 piān jiè	【動詞語】	壓住一部分 to lie on part of ...
13. 上 shàng	【名詞】	皇上；皇帝；漢哀帝 the emperor
14. 袖 xiù	【名詞】	衣袖 sleeves
15. 欲 yù	【動詞】	想要 to intend to
16. 覺 jué	【動詞】	醒過來 to wake up
17. 動 dòng	【動詞】	驚動，打擾 to disturb; to awaken
18. 乃 nǎi	【副詞】	就 then; thereupon
19. 斷 duàn	【動詞】	弄斷 to break; to take apart
23. 此 cǐ	【代名詞】	這個；這個故事 this ; this story

二　問答 Answer the following questions either in Chinese or in English:

1. "分桃"、"斷袖" 這兩個詞語有什麼特別的含意？
   What is the connotation of the two terms 'fēn táo' and 'duàn xiù'?

2. 著名小說《儒林外史》中的人物杜慎卿說："千古只有一個漢哀帝獨得情之正。" 你認爲這種意見如何？
   Dù Shènqīng, a character in the famous novel *The Scholars*, said: "In all history, I consider that Emperor Ai of Hàn showed the truest understanding of love." What do you think of his opinion?

翻譯練習九

一　把下面的一段文言翻譯成白話或英文
Translate the following passage into modern Chinese or into English:

景公之時，雨雪三日而不霽。公被狐白之裘，坐堂側陛。晏子入見，立有間。公曰：“怪哉！雨雪三日而天不寒。”晏子對曰：“天不寒乎？”公笑。晏子曰：“嬰聞古之賢君，飽而知人之飢，溫而知人之寒，逸而知人之勞。今君不知也。”公曰：“善。寡人聞命矣。”乃令出裘發粟與飢寒。　《晏子春秋‧內篇諫上》

注解：

1. 雪 xuě	【名詞】	雪 snow	
2. 霽 jì	【動詞】	停止下雪；晴 to stop snowing; to clear up	
3. 被 pī	【動詞】	同披；披著 to throw on; to wear untidily	
4. 狐白 hú bái	【名詞語】	狐狸腋下的白皮 the fur underarms of a fox	
5. 裘 qiú	【名詞】	皮衣 furs; any garments, robes, etc. of fur	
狐白裘 hú bái qiu	【名詞語】	用狐狸腋下的白皮製成的衣服 fox-whiteskin robe ; a robe made of the white furs underarms of foxes; the warmest and most precious fur robe	
6. 堂 táng	【名詞】	大堂 the great hall	
7. 側 cè	【名詞】	旁邊 the side of ...	
8. 陛 bì	【名詞】	臺階 steps leading to a building	
9. 間 jiàn	【名詞】	一會兒 a short time; a while	
有間 yǒu jiàn	【動詞語】	有一會兒；過了一會兒 for a while; after a while	
10. 怪 guài	【形容詞】	奇怪 strange	
11. 飽 bǎo	【形容詞】	飽足；吃飽 to be full; well-fed	
12. 飢 jī	【形容詞】	飢餓 to be hungry	
13. 溫 wēn	【形容詞】	溫暖 to be warm	
14. 逸 yì	【形容詞】	安逸 to be at ease	
15. 勞 láo	【形容詞】	勞苦 to be toilsome	
16. 命 mìng	【名詞】	教命；教導 instruction; guidance	
聞命 wén mìng	【名詞語】	聽見教命 to have heard [your] instruction	

17. 令 lìng 　　【動詞】 下命令 to issue an order; to order

18. 出裘 chū qiú 　　【動詞語】拿出皮大衣 to take out fur coats

19. 發 fā 　　【動詞】 發放；散發 to distribute

20. 粟 sù 　　【名詞】 小米 millet ; 糧食 grain; cereal

　　 發粟 fā sù 　　【動詞語】 散發糧食 to distribute grain

21. 與 yǔ 　　【名詞】 給與 to give [to]

22. 飢寒 jī hán 　　【形容詞語】挨餓受凍 suffering from hunger and cold

　　【用如名詞語】挨餓受凍的人 people who suffer from hunger and cold

二　　問答 Answer these questions either in Chinese or in English:

1. 齊景公是一個什麼樣的國君？
   What kind of a 'ruler' is Duke Jǐng of Qí?

2. 晏子是一個什麼樣的臣子？
   What kind of a 'subject' is Yànzǐ?

277

翻譯練習十

一　把下面的一段文言翻譯成白話或英文
Translate the following passage into modern Chinese or into English:

子之武城，聞弦歌之聲。孔子莞爾而笑曰：“割雞焉用牛刀？”子游曰：“昔者偃聞諸夫子曰‘君子學道則愛人，小人學道則易使。’”孔子曰：“二三子，偃之言是也。前言戲之耳。”

《論語・陽貨》

注解：

1. 子 zǐ　　　【名詞】指孔子 master; here refers to Confucius

2. 之 zhī　　　【動詞】到…去 to go to

3. 武城　　　【名詞語】縣名，在今山東省　Wǔ chéng, name of a sub-prefecture,
   Wǔchéng　　　　　　　　in present day Shāndōng

4. 聞 wén　　　【動詞】聽到 to hear; to have heard

5. 弦 xián　　　【動詞】彈琴 lute playing; playing stringed instruments

6. 歌 gē　　　【動詞】唱歌 singing; singing songs

7. 聲 shēng　　【名詞】聲音 sound

   弦歌之聲　【名詞語】彈琴唱歌的聲音
   xián gē zhī shēng　　　　　sound of lute playing and singing

9. 孔子　　　【名詞語】孔夫子；姓孔、名丘、字仲尼，儒家的創立者
   Kǒngzǐ　　　　　　Master Kǒng; surnamed Kǒng, named Qiū, and courtesy named
   　　　　　　　　　Zhòngní, who was the founder of the Confucian School

10. 莞爾而笑　【動詞語】微微地笑一笑；微笑
    wǎn ěr ér xiào　　　　　to smile gently

11. 割 gē　　　【動詞】宰殺 to kill; to

12. 雞 jī　　　【名詞】雞 a chicken; a fowl

   割雞　　　【動詞語】殺雞 to kill a chicken; to kill a fowl
   gē jī

13. 焉 yān　　　【副詞】安；何；為什麼 how, why

14. 牛刀　　　【名詞語】宰殺牛的刀 an ox knife; a knife used to butcher oxen
    niú dāo

15. 昔者　　　【時間詞】從前 in the past
    xí zhě

16. 偃 Yǎn　　　【名詞】言偃，姓言名偃字子游，孔子弟子，當時正在做
    　　　　　　武城縣長 Yán Yǎn, with the courtesy name of Zǐ Yóu, was a
    　　　　　　disciple of Confucius and serving as the magistrate of Wǔ Chéng

17. 諸 zhū 　　【兼詞】 之於 it combines the meaning of 'it' and 'from'

　　聞諸夫子 【動詞語】 從老師那兒聽到它／這句話 to have heard this from
　　wén zhu fúzǐ 　　　　　　　the master/you

18. 君子 　　【名詞語】 做官的人 officials
　　jūn zǐ

19. 學 xué 　　【動詞】 學習 to learn' to study

20. 道 dào 　　【名詞】 道理 the Way; 此處指禮樂 here referring to protocal and music

21. 愛人 　　【動詞語】 關愛別人 to love people
　　ài rén

22. 小人 　　【名詞語】 一般人民；老百姓 the common people
　　xiǎo rén

23. 易 yì 　　【形容詞】 容易 to be easy

24. 使 shǐ 　　【動詞】 使喚 to order about

25. 二三子 　　【名詞語】 弟子們 disciples
　　èr sān zǐ

26. 是 shì 　　【形容詞】 對 to be right

27. 前言 　　【名詞語】 先前的話；剛才說的話 what I said a while ago
　　qián yán

28. 戲 xì 　　【動詞】 開玩笑 to joke with

　　戲之 　　【動詞語】 跟他開玩笑 to joke with him
　　xì zhī

29. 耳 ěr 　　【助詞】 罷了 merely; and that's all

二　　問答 Answer the following questions either in Chinese or in English:

1. "割雞"、"用牛刀" 各比喻什麼？
   What do "to kill a chicken" and "to use an ox-knife" stand for respectively?

2. 談 "弦歌之聲" 和 "道" 之間的關係。
   Discuss the relationship between "the sound of stringed instruments" and " the Way."

3. 你欣賞 (xīnshǎng: to apprecaite) 這個故事嗎？為什麼？
   Do you appreciate this story? Why or why not?

279

書目 (四部叢刊本)
Source of the Texts (SPTK edition)

左傳   *Zuŏ Commentary* is one of the earliest texts that records in detail historical events during the Spring and Autumn period. The authorship of this book is traditionally attributed to Zuŏ Qiū-míng, who was contemporary of Confucius (551-479 B.C.).
L.20, J.11, P.12B; L.40, J.19, PP.15B-16A

孟子   *The Work of Mencius*, written by Mèng Kē (c.372-289 B.C.), contains seven chapters and is perhaps the most widely read book along with the Confucian Analects. As one of the canonic books in the Confucian tradition, Mencius has been read by every educated men in China since the Hàn dynasty.
L. 22, J.3, PP.7B-8A

莊子   *Zhuāngzĭ*, written by Zhuāng Zhōu (c. 369-286 B.C.). He was a contemporary of Mencius, and is without a doubt the greatest philosopher in the Taoist school. His writing is so witty and inspirational that whether one agrees with the Taoist perspectives or not, one is bound to like his book. The seven inner chapters are probably genuine works by the master himself, while the other chapters may be later additions by followers of the Taoist school.
L.8, J.7, PP.28A-B; L.25, J.6, PP.28A-B; L.31, J.6, PP.27A-B

列子   Liè Yùkòu as a person lived earlier than Zhuāngzĭ, but the original writings of Lièzĭ are no longer extant. This current book entitled *Lièzĭ* was probably collected and compiled by a Jìn dynasty scholar named Zhāng Zhàn (4th Cent. A.D.). The texts in the *Lièzĭ* are, however, certainly Taoist in origin.
L.11, J.8, P.bB; L.15, J.8, P.8A; L.21, J.8, P.7A; L.23, J.3, P.5B

呂氏春秋 *Lŭshì Chūnqiū* is a book generally classified under Zájiā, meaning that it combines several schools of thought. It was written collectively by the retainers of Lŭ Bùwéi (d. 235 B.C.), who served as the Prime Minister of the state of Qín from 249 to 237 B.C., and was published under Lŭ's name.
L.4, J.14, P.20A; L.17, J.15, PP.21B-22A

晏子春秋 Yànzĭ or Yàn Yīng (c.589-500 B.C.) was contemporary with but senior to Confucius, and served in the state of Qí as Prime Minister for many years. Confucius praised him as one who commanded great respect. This current text of *Yànzĭ Chūnqiū* is a later collection of Yànzĭ's words and deeds; it was probably a book written by his disciples or followers.
L.34, J.6, PP.33A-B

韓非子　Hán Fēi (d. 233B.C.) was a disciple of the Confucian master Xúnzǐ, and later became the greatest master in the Legalist School. He was falsely charged by his classmate Lǐ Sī, the Prime Minister of Qín, and put to death by the First Emperor of Qín. *Hánfēizǐ*, nevertheless survived him and has had a great influence on Chinese rulers throughout history.
L.2, J.4, P. 6A; L.3, J.19, P.1A; L. 5, J.7, PP.4B-5A; L.7, J.15, P.2B; L.10, J.11, P.8A; L.13, J.11, P.8B; L.17, J.15, P.2B; L.18, J.4, P.6B; L.35, J.4, PP.6A-B

淮南子　*Huáinánzǐ*, like *Lǔshì Chūnqiū*, is a wqork of collective authorship. It was compiled by the retainers of Liú Ān (178-122 B.C.), the Prince of Huáinán, of the Hàn dynasty, and was published under Liú's name. This book incorporates many schools of thought, but its main ideas are closest to the Taoist School.
L.9, J.16, P.7A; L.32, J.18, P.6A

戰國策　*Strategies of the Warring States*, a collection of historical and anecdotal tales, was collected and compiled by the famous Hàn dynasty Librarian Liú Xiàng (77-6 B.C.).
L.12, J.9; P.33B; L.14, J.5, PP.2B-3A; L.19, J.2, PP.4B-5A; L.24, J.4, PP.17B-18A; L.38, J.4, PP.4B-5B

禮記　*TheBook of Rites*, one of the Thirteen Confucian Classics, was most likely a reconstruction by Hàn scholars of Confucian ideas about Ritual and Rites.
L.30, J.3, P.13B

孔子家語　All the stories and sayings mentioned in *Kǒngzǐ Jiāyǔ* are related to Confucius, but this is a book that made its first public appearance in the Wèi dynasty, and was annotated by Wáng Sù (195-256 A.D.).
L.28, J.5, P.13B

列女傳　*Biographies of Exemplary Women* has examples from Chinese history down to the Early Hàn dynasty. This book was compiled by the famous Hàn Librarian Liú Xiàng (77-6 B.C.)
L.39, J.5, PP.20B-21A

新序　*New Narratives* is a collection of stories from earlier works compiled by Liú Xiàng (77-6 B.C.)
L.1, J.20. P.8A

說苑　*Garden of Tales* is another collection of earlier stories compiled by Liú Xiàng (77-6 B.C.)
L.16, J.17, PP.21B-22A, L.26, J.8, PP.21A-B; L.27, J. 8, PP.9B-10A; L.29, J.11, PP.19B-20A; L.33, J.10, PP.4A-B; L.36, J.6, PP.8A-B, L.37, J.14, PP.15A-B

語法參考書簡目

A Short List of Grammatical References

劉淇　　　　助字辨略　　　　台北世界書局　　　1962
Liú Qí,　　Zhù zì biàn lüè,　　Taipei, Shìjiè Shūjú

馬建忠　　　馬氏文通　　　　北京中華書局　　　1961
Mǎ Jiànzhōng, Mǎ Shì Wén Tōng,　　Taipei, Zhōnghuá Shūjú

楊樹達　　　詞詮　　　　　北京中華書局　　　1965
Yáng Shùdá, Cí Quán　　　Beijing, Zhōnghuá Shūjú

呂叔湘　　　中國文法要略　　　上海商務印書館　　1954
Lǚ Shúxiāng, Zhōng Guó Wén Fǎ Yào Lüè, Shanghai, Shāngwù Yìnshūguǎn
　　　　　　文言虛字　　　　香港大光出版社　　1973
　　　　　　Wén Yán Xū Zì,　　Hong Kong, Dàguāng Chūbǎnshè

王力　　　　漢語史稿　　　　北京商務印書館　　1989
Wáng Lì　　Hàn Yǔ Shǐ Gǎo　　Beijing, Shāngwù Yìnshūguǎn
　　　　　　漢語語法史　　　　北京商務印書館　　1989
　　　　　　Hàn Yǔ Yǔ Fǎ Shǐ,　　Beijing, Shāngwù Yìnshūguǎn

楊伯峻　　　文言文法　　　　北京中華書局　　　1963
Yáng Bójùn, Wén Yán Wén Fǎ,　　Beijing, Zhōnghuá Shūjú

周法高　　　中國古代語法　　　中研院史語所專刊　1962
Zhōu Fǎgāo, Zhōng Guó Gǔ Dài Yǔ Fǎ, Zhōngyányuàn Shǐyǔsuǒ Zhuānkān

許世瑛　　　中國文法講話　　　台北開明書店　　　1967
Xǔ Shìyīng, Zhōng Guó Wén Fǎ Jiǎng Huà, Taipei, Kāimíng Shūdiàn
　　　　　　常用虛字用法淺釋　台北復興書局　　　1975
　　　　　　Cháng Yòng Xū Zì Yòng Fǎ Qiǎn Shì, Taipei, Fùxīng Shūjú

黃六平　　　漢語文言語法綱要　香港中華書局　　　1978
Huáng Liùpíng, Hàn Yǔ Wén Yán Yǔ Fǎ Gāng Yào, Hong Kong, Zhōnghuá Shūjú

易孟醇　　　先秦語法　　　　湖南教育出版社　　1989
Yì Mèngchún, Xiān Qín Yǔ Fǎ,　　Hunan, Jiàoyù Chūbǎnshè

王海茉　　　古漢語疑問詞語　　浙江教育出版社　　1987
Wáng Hǎifēn, Gǔ Hàn Yǔ Yí Wèn Cí Yǔ,　Zhèjiāng, Jiàoyù Chūbǎnshè

CLASSICAL CHINESE
A BASIC READER

GLOSSARIES

袁乃瑛　　唐海濤　　蓋杰民
Naiying Yuan　Haitao Tang　James Geiss

PRINCETON UNIVERSITY PRESS

PRINCETON, NEW JERSEY

字彙目錄

字彙目錄

字彙目錄

字彙目錄

List of Errata to the Glossaries

page	line	was	should be
2	8	"的時候	"的時候"
2	21	one another	(shift right)
4	7	honorific term	(shift right)
14	13	看到；	看到
36	numbers	14 - 23	13 - 22
37	numbers	24 - 32	23 - 31
40	4	zhïjián	zhïjiän
47	26	此處…	delete
61	5	to leave	to leave;
80	7	jiecíyu	jiècíyû
87	10	疲憊 (juàn)	疲倦 (juàn)
108	20	someone	(shift right)
108	24	thus	(shift right)
109	14	[chreished]	[cherished]
109	20	believe to	(shift right)
165	16	audience	(shift right)
189	numbers	43,42.43,44	42,43,44,45
190	numbers	45 - 51	46 – 52
191	numbers	52- 58, 58	53 – 60
192	numbers	59 - 61	61 - 63

第 一 課

鄭相卻魚

注解

1. 鄭 Zhèng 　【名詞】春秋時代國名（公元前806至375），在今河南省新鄭縣一帶及陝西省的一部分
A state that flourished from 806 to 375 B.C. and occupied parts of present-day Shǎnxī and Hénán provinces.

    ◆ 名詞 *míngcí*　　　　a noun

    ◆ 春秋時代 *Chūnqiūshídài*　　The Spring and Autumn period (722 - 481 B.C.)

    ◆ 省 *shěng*　　　　a province

    ◆ 縣 *xiàn*　　　　a county

2. 相 xiàng 　【名詞】相國，一個國家中地位最高的官員，幫助君主治理國家並管理各級官員。秦朝以後叫丞 (chéng) 相或宰 (zǎi) 相，現在叫總理 (prime minister)。本書中的白話翻譯依據口語的習慣都用"宰相"這個詞儿，以便聽起來比較自然。

Chief councilor. A title of distinction given to senior officials in a state's central administration who assisted the ruler in governing the state and overseeing the bureaucracy. After the Qín dynasty, such an official was known as 丞相 (lit: aide and minister) or 宰相 (lit: steward and minister). As the chief executive officers of the state, they were similar to present day prime ministers. In this book, these official titles are all translated into spoken Chinese as "宰相" and into English as "prime minister," so as to make it sound more natural.

    ◆ 官員 *guānyuán*　　an official

    ◆ 秦朝 *Qíncháo*　　the Qín dynasty (221 - 206 B.C.)

1

◆ 總理 *zǒnglǐ*　　　a Prime Minister

3. 卻 què　　【動詞】拒絶 to reject; 不接受 to refuse to accept

◆ 動詞 *dòngcí*　　　a verb

4. 魚 yú　　【名詞】魚 a fish

5. 昔 xī　　【時間詞】從前 formerly; in former times

◆ 時間詞　　　a time word
　shíjiāncí

6. 者 zhě　　【助詞】用在 "今" 、 "昔" 等時間詞的後面作
　　　為詞尾，表示 "…的時候。有的須選擇適當的時
　　　間詞譯成白話，例如 "從前"

When it follows such time words as "今" and "昔" ,the particle "者" has the sense of "[at] the ... time," as in "[at] the present time"; it nominalizes (i.e., makes into a noun or noun phrase) temporal adjectives "今" (present -- the present) "昔" (past -- the past). Such temporal phrases can be rendered in spoken Chinese by selecting an appropriate modern equivalent (e.g. "從前" for "昔者").

◆ 助詞 *zhùcí*　　　a particle (grammatical term)

昔者　　【時間詞】從前 formerly; in former times; once
xī zhě

7. 餽 kuì　　【動詞】通 "饋" 饋贈(zèng)；贈送
　　　to present as a gift

◆ 通 *tōng*　　　[of characters] to be interchangeable [with one another]

8. 於 yú　　【介詞】給，介紹動作的對象 a preposition used to introduce the target of an action; here: "to"

◆ 介詞 *jiècí*　　　a preposition

◆ 對象 *duìxiàng*　　　a target; an object

9. 者 zhě 【被飾代詞】之+名詞

此處(here)：…之人；…的人
the one who …

◆ 被飾代詞   a pronoun that must be preceded by a
bèishìdàicí   modifier

◆ 修飾 xiūshì   to modify

◆ 被飾 bèishì   to be modified

◆ 代詞 dàicí   a pronoun

10. 受 shòu 【動詞】接受   to accept

11. 或 huò 【虛指代詞】有人   someone

◆ 虛指代詞   an indefinite pronoun
xūzhǐdàicí

12. 謂 wèi 【動詞】對…說；告訴…說 to speak to [someone];
to address [someone]

※ 按：　"謂"，"曰"都是"說"的意思，後面都
有所說的話。但"謂"不與所說的話緊接，
而"曰"則與所說的話緊接。"謂"後可緊
接一間接賓語"某人"，然後再接上"曰"
，構成"謂…曰"句型

Note: 　"謂" and "曰" both mean "to say" and are both used to
introduce a direct quotation. However, whereas "曰"
always precedes the first word of the direct quotation, "謂"
does not necessarily have to; it can sometimes be followed by
an indirect object, and then followed by "曰" to form the
pattern "謂 [a person] 曰"(address [a person] saying).

13. 曰 yuē 【動詞】說   to say (always used to introduce direct
quotations)

14. 子 zǐ 【人稱代詞】對人的尊稱，多指男子；相當於
白話中的"您"

A personal pronoun used in polite discourse, generally referring to

3

males; it is equivalent to the polite second person personal pronoun "您" in spoken Chinese. There is no satisfactory equivalent in modern English.

◆ 人稱代詞   a personal pronoun
rénchēngdàicí

◆ 尊稱 *zūnchēng*   a polite way to address someone; an honorific term

15. 嗜 shì   【動詞】愛好；非常喜歡   to be fond of; to relish;

嗜魚   【動詞語】愛好魚；非常喜歡吃魚
zhōng shēn   to relish eating fish

◆ 動詞語   a verbal phrase
dòngcíyǔ

16. 何 hé   【疑問代詞】什麼，此處用作定語
an interrogative pronoun meaning "what"; here it functions as an adjectival modifier.

◆ 疑問代詞   an interrogative pronoun
yíwèndàicí

◆ 定語 *dìngyǔ*   an adjectival modifier

17. 故 gù   【名詞】緣故；原因   cause; reason

何故   【名詞語】甚麼緣故   what reason
hé gù

◆ 名詞語   a noun phrase
míngcíyǔ

18. 對 duì   【動詞】回答   to answer; to reply

19. 吾 wú   【代詞】我   I (first person pronoun)

20. 以 yǐ   【介詞】介紹出動作、行為形成的原因，多用在動詞前，可譯成"因為"

4

As a preposition that introduces the cause or reason leading to a certain course of action or behavior, "以" most often appears at the head of a phrase or clause that precedes the main verb of the sentence. It can be translated into spoken Chinese as "因為" and into English as "because".

21. 故 gù 　【連詞】所以　a conjunction meaning "therefore", "consequently", or "thus"

　　　◆ 連詞 liáncí　　　a conjunction

22. 失 shī 　【動詞】失掉；失去　to lose

23. 祿 lù 　【名詞】官吏的薪俸　official salary; emolument

　　　◆ 官吏 guānlì　　　government officials

　　　◆ 薪俸 xīnfèng　　　government emolument; official salary

24. 無以 wú yǐ 　【動詞語】沒有法子
　　　　　to have no means to; to have no way to

25. 食 shí 　【動詞】吃　to eat

26. 得 dé 　【動詞】得到　to get; to obtain

27. 終 zhōng 　【動詞】終竟；窮盡　to come to the end

　終身 zhōng shēn 　【動詞語】終竟一生；窮盡一生；過完一生
　　　　　to live to the end of one's life

　　　【副詞】一輩子　one's whole life; until the end of one's life

　　　◆ 副詞 fùcí　　　an adverb

第二課

宋有富人

注解

1. 宋 Sòng 【名詞】春秋戰國時代國名，在今河南省商邱(qiū)縣

A state that flourished from 858 to 286 B.C. and occupied part of present day Hénán province.

◆ 戰國時代
Zhànguóshídài

The period of the Warring States (403 - 221 B.C.) during which seven states --- 秦 (Qín) 楚 (Chǔ), 齊 (Qí), 燕 (Yān), 韓 (Hán), 趙 (Zhào) and 魏 (Wèi) -- contended for hegemony until Qín (秦) emerged victorious to become the unchallenged ruler of the empire under the First Emperor of Qín (秦始皇帝).

2. 富 fù 【形容詞】財產多；富裕(yù)；有錢 wealthy

◆ 形容詞
xíngróngcí

an adjective

富人
fùrén
【名詞語】有錢的人 a wealthy man

3. 雨 yǔ 【動詞】下雨 to rain

4. 牆 qiáng 【名詞】牆 wall

5. 壞 huài 【形容詞】壞 bad; damaged

【用作動詞】變壞；壞了
to become damaged; to be ruined

6. 其 qí 【人稱代詞】他的 his

6

7. 子 zǐ 　　【名詞】兒子；孩子　　son; child

8. 築 zhù zhú 　　【動詞】修；修理　　to build; to repair

9. 必 bì 　　【副詞】一定　　certainly

10. 將 jiāng 　　【助動詞】表示屬於人事自然的結果，不由意志決定的情況、事情等，白話可譯成＂會＂（參看楊樹達《詞詮》卷六，頁二九五）

Here the auxiliary verb "將" is used to indicate that an incident or situation *will simply occur* as part of the natural order of things rather than as the consequence of human volition. In this sense, it can be translated into spoken Chinese as "會" and into English with the simple future tense "will". (*See Yáng Shùdá, **Cíquán**, ch. 6, p. 295. Compare with L. 6, no. 4, p. 22*)

◆ 助動詞　　an auxiliary verb
　　zhùdòngcí

◆ 參看 cānkàn　　see ...

11. 盜 dào 　　【名詞】賊　　a thief; a robber

12. 鄰人 línrén 　　【名詞語】鄰居　　a neighbor

13. 之 zhī 　　【助詞】用在修飾語(定語)和被修飾語之間，表示前後兩項領屬性的關係，相當於白話中的＂的。＂

The word "之" is a particle that functions here as a possessive marker. Used between an adjectival modifier and the word being modified, it indicates that the word preceding it (the modifier) stands in a possessive relation to the word that follows it (the noun or noun phrase). It corresponds to the word "的" in spoken Chinese and is equivalent here to "of" in English. (Note: the construction "[modifier] 之 [noun]" in classical Chinese is equivalent to "[noun] of [modifier]" in English.)

◆ 修飾語　　an adjectival modifier
　　xiūshìyǔ
or 定語 dìngyǔ

7

◆ 被修飾語　　　a word being modified
　bèixiūshìyǔ

◆ 兩項 liǎngxiàng　　two items

◆ 相當於　　　corresponding to
　xiāngdāngyú

14. 父 fù　　【名詞】父親　father

　　　fǔ　　【名詞】對老年人的尊稱，老翁 (wēng)；老頭儿 an old man

15. 亦 yì　　【副詞】也　also; likewise

16. 云 yún　　【動詞】說　to say (sometimes also used to introduce a direct quotation)

17. 暮 mù　　【時間詞】傍晚；太陽落下去的時候；天黑了的時候　dusk; evening; the period when the sun is going down and it grows dark

18. 而 ér　　【連詞】連接介詞語與動詞語時，白話中不必翻譯。（參看第二課，句子分析五，第九頁）。

When it connects a prepositional phrase and a predicate, the particle "而" functions only as a linking word and need not be literally translated into spoken Chinese. *(See Lesson 2, sentence analysis 5, p.9.)*

19. 果 guǒ　　【副詞】果然　as expected; resulting in ...

20. 大 dà　　【副詞】大量地　in great quantity

21. 亡 wáng　　【動詞】失掉；丟 (diū) 失；丟　to lose

22. 財 cái　　【名詞】錢財　wealth; money

23. 其 qí　　【指示詞】那；那個　here: used as an adjective meaning "that"

8

◆ 指 示 詞   a demonstrative
zhǐshìcí

24. 家 jiā   【名 詞】 家庭；人家 family

其 家   【名 詞 語】 那個人家 that family
qí jiā   此處：那家人 members of that family

25. 甚 shèn   【副 詞】很；非常 very; extremely

26. 智 zhì   【形 容 詞】聰明 wise; bright

智 其 子   【動 詞 語】覺得他們的孩子聰明，（詳見句子分
zhì qí zǐ   析六，第十頁）。
"thought their son very bright." (*For more details, see sentence analysis 6, p.10*)

◆ 詳見 *xiángjiàn*   For more details, see ...

27. 而 ér   【連 詞】可是；卻
here: a conjunction meaning "but," "yet," "on the contrary"

28. 疑 yí   【動 詞】疑心；懷 (huái) 疑 to suspect

第三課

守株待兔

注解

1. 守 shǒu　【動詞】看守；守著　to watch

2. 株 zhū　【名詞】樹椿 (zhuāng) a stump; a tree stump

　◎ 截 jié　【量詞】樹椿等的量詞 a categorical measure word for tree stumps, etc.

　　　◆ **量詞** *liàngcí*　　a measure word

3. 待 dài　【動詞】等待　to wait for

4. 兔 tù　【名詞】兔子　a hare

5. 耕 gēng　【動詞】耕田；用犁把土翻鬆　to till; to plough; to use a plow to turn and loosen the soil

　　　◆ **犁** *lí*　　　a plough

　　　◆ **翻鬆** *fānsōng*　　to turn up and loosen [soil]

　耕者
　gēngzhě　【名詞語】耕田的人　"tilling one", one who tills [the land]; a farmer

6. 田 tián　【名詞】田地；農 (nóng)田
　　　field; farmland; agricultural land

7. 走 zǒu　【動詞】跑　to run

8. 觸 chù　【動詞】碰 (pèng)；撞 (zhuàng) to hit [against]; to dash into

9. 折 zhé　【動詞】折斷　to break

10

10. 頸 jǐng 【名詞】脖 (bó)子 neck

11. 而 ér 【連詞】就 here: a conjunction meaning "and then"

12. 死 sǐ 【動詞】死 to lose one's life; to die

13. 因 yīn 【副詞】在複句中通常用於第二小句，表示承接上文，後面的事是前述情況導致的結果，白話可譯成"於是"、"就"、或"於是就"
In a complex sentence, when the adverb "因" is used to introduce the second clause of the sentence, it indicates that what follows "因" is the direct consequence of the antecedent action described in the first clause of the sentence, which immediately precedes "因". In this usage, "因" can be translated into spoken Chinese as "於是"," 就", or "於是就" and into English as "whereupon", "thereupon", or "then".

◆ 承接 chéngjiē   to continue; to receive and carry on

◆ 導致 dǎozhì   to lead to; to bring about

14. 釋 shì 【動詞】放下 to let go; to put down

15. 耒 lěi 【名詞】犁 (lí)；古代耕地用的農具 a plough

◆ 農具 nóngjù   farm implements

16. 而 ér 【連詞】來；去
a conjunction meaning "in order to," "so as to"

17. 冀 jì 【動詞】希望 to hope

18. 復 fù 【副詞】再 again; a second time

19. 得 dé 【動詞】得到 to get

20. 可 kě 【助動詞】表示可以、能夠，白話可譯成"能"
can; may

11

21. 身 shēn 　　【代詞】自身　oneself

　　　　　　　　　　此處：[他]自己　[he] himself

22. 為 wéi 　　【介詞】，用在被動句中，介紹出主動者，可譯
　　　　　　　　　　為"被"。用"為"字構成的介詞語，表被動時
　　　　　　　　　　，必須放在動詞之前。

　　　　　　　　　　The preposion "為" introduces the agent in a passive sentence.
　　　　　　　　　　When it is thus used, the prepositional phrase must precede the
　　　　　　　　　　verb.

23. 笑 xiào 　　【動詞】笑話；嘲 (cháo)笑　to ridicule; to deride

成 語

守株待兔　　shǒuzhūdàitù

LITERALLY: "To watch a tree stump and wait for a hare."

比喻死守狹隘(xiáài)經驗，不知變通 (biàntōng)。

A metaphor for holding tenaciously to one's limited experience and for not
knowing how to adapt to changing circumstances.

比喻企圖 (qìtú)不經過主觀努力而僥幸 (jiǎoxìng)得到意外的收
穫 (shōuhuò)。

A metaphor for not taking the initiative and for relying instead on the
psychology of luck or chance, hoping to profit from some unexpected gain.

　　　　◆ 成語 chéngyǔ　　　a set phrase; a proverb; an idiom

　　　　◆ 比喻 bǐyù　　　　　to liken to; to be a metaphor for [something]

12

第四課

逐臭

注解

1. 逐 zhú 　　　【動詞】追逐；追趕 to chase after

2. 臭 xiù 　　　【名詞】氣味 a smell
　　　　　　　　此處指臭 (chòu)味 here it means a stinky smell

　　　　　　　　◆ 指 zhǐ 　　　　to refer to; to mean

　chòu 　　　【形容詞】氣味難聞，跟香相對
　　　　　　　　stinky; the opposite of "香"

　　　　　　　　◆ 香 xiāng 　　　　fragrant

　　　　　　　　◆ 相對 xiāngduì 　　　to be the opposite of [something]

3. 親戚 　　　【名詞】內親外戚 relatives by blood and by marriage
　qīn qī 　　古代指內親 (自己家庭裡的成員)外戚 (跟自己家庭有婚姻關係的家庭或它的成員。) 現代專指跟自己家庭有婚姻關係的家庭或它的成員。

　　　　　　In traditional China, the term "內親" (lit: inner relatives) referred to members of one's own household (i.e., relatives by blood), while the term "外戚" (lit: outer in-laws) referred to relatives by marriage or members of their families (i.e., in-laws or relatives by marriage). In contemporary usage, this distinction is no longer maintained, and the term now refers only to relatives by marriage or members of their families.

4. 兄弟 　　　【名詞】哥哥、弟弟 elder and younger brothers
　xiōng dì

5. 妻 qī 　　　【名詞】男子的配偶，跟 "夫" 相對；妻子；太太 a man's spouse; the opposite of "夫" (husband); principal or legal wife; wife

13

◆ 配偶 *pèiǒu*   a spouse

6. 妾 qiè   【名詞】男子在妻子之外另娶的女人；姨太太
a wife taken in addition to a man's principal or legal spouse;
a concubine

◆ 娶 *qǔ*   to get married; to take a wife [said of a man only]

7. 知識 zhī shì   【名詞】認識的人；朋友 acquaintances; friends

8. 能 néng   【助動詞】能夠 can; be able to

9. 居 jū   【動詞】居住；住 to live in/at [a place]

10. 苦 kǔ   【形容詞】苦惱；痛苦 embittered; pained

自苦 zìkǔ   【動詞語】自己感到很苦惱 himself felt very embittered

11. 海 hǎi   【名詞】海；大洋靠近陸地的部分 the sea; that part of the ocean near to the shore;

◆ 大洋 *dàyáng*   an ocean

◆ 陸地 *lùdì*   land; a landmass

海上 hǎishàng   【名詞語】海邊上 [at] the seashore

12. 說 yuè   【動詞】同"悅"，喜歡 Here "說" has the same meaning as the character "悅"; to take delight in; to like

13. 晝 zhòu   【時間詞】從天亮到天黑的一段時間；白天
the period from dawn to dusk; daylight hours; daytime

14. 夜 yè   【時間詞】從天黑到天亮的一段時間，跟"日"或"晝"相對；黑夜；夜裡 the period from dusk to dawn; the opposite of "日" (day) and "晝" (daytime); night; nightime

14

15. 隨 suí 　　【動詞】跟隨；跟在後面
　　　　　　　to follow [on]; to follow behind

16. 之 zhī 　　【代詞】相當於白話中的 "他"、"她"、
　　　　　　"牠"、"它"〔們〕。在本文內是 "他"，指
　　　　　　"大臭者。"

　　　　　　The word "之" functions as a singular and plural third person
　　　　　　pronoun: it is equivalent in meaning to "他" (him), "她" (her),
　　　　　　"它" (it) [們] (them). Here "it" refers to the "very stinky person."

17. 弗 fú 　　【副詞】不 not

18. 去 qù 　　【動詞】離開 to leave; to go [away]; to separate [from]

成 語

逐臭之夫 zhúxiùzhīfū

LITERALLY: "A man who chases after a stink"

比喻有奇特的癖好 (pǐhào) 的人

This expression is used to describe a person who behaves oddly or does
peculiar things; it is roughly equivalent to the expressions "an odd duck" or "a
queer bird" in English.

第五課

先王之義勝

注解

1. **先王**
xiān wáng
【名詞】古代的聖王，如堯、舜　the sage kings of antiquity (e.g., Yáo and Shùn)

   ◆ **聖王** *shèngwáng*　the most intelligent and virtuous rulers

   ◆ **堯** *Yáo*　a legendary ruler said to have reigned from 2357 to 2255 B.C.

   ◆ **舜** *Shùn*　a legendary ruler said to have reigned from 2255 to 2205 B.C.

2. **之** zhī
【助詞】用在修飾語 (定語) 和被修飾語之間，表示前後兩項領屬性的關係，相當於白話中的 "的。"

   The word "之" is a particle that functions here as a possessive marker. Used between an adjectival modifier and the word being modified, it indicates that the word preceding it (the modifier) stands in a possessive relation to the word that follows it (the noun or noun phrase). It corresponds to the word "的" in spoken Chinese and is equivalent here to "of" in English. (Note: the construction "[modifier] 之 [noun]" in classical Chinese is equivalent to "[noun] of [modifier]" in English.)

3. **義** yì
【名詞】正理；正道　what is right and proper; righteousness; righteous ways

4. **勝** shèng
【動詞】勝利　to win; to triumph

5. **子夏**
Zǐxià
【名詞】春秋時代衛國人。姓卜 (Bǔ)，名商 (Shāng)，子夏是他的字。他是孔子七十二大弟子之一，學問非常好。

   A person from the state of Wèi who lived during the Spring and Autumn period, he was one of Confucius' 72 disciples and was

16

renowned for his erudition. His surname was 卜 (Bǔ) and his given name 商 (Shāng).

◆ 衛國 *Wèiguó*		The name of an ancient state that flourished from 1112 - 209 B.C. and occupied parts of modern Héběi and Hénán provinces.
◆ 字 *zì*		In traditional China, boys formally entered adulthood through the ritual of the capping ceremony. After this, they wore their hair in a top knot under a cap. At the same time, they took a second or courtesy name. This was their "字". With the exception of the ruler, their elders, and their teachers, in polite discourse other people would address them by their "字" as a sign of courtesy. However, in formal documents and official works, the "名" continued to be used. When a man spoke of himself, he had to refer to himself by his "名" and could not refer to himself by his own "字".
◆ 孔子 *Kǒngzǐ*		Confucius
◆ 弟子 *dìzǐ*		disciples; pupils; students
◆ 學問 *xuéwèn*		learning; scholarship; erudition

6. 見 *jiàn*

【動詞】看見；看到； to see
此處：拜訪 to visit; to pay a visit to

7. 曾子 *Zēngzǐ*

【名詞】春秋時代魯國人。姓曾，名參 (Shēn)，字子輿 (yú)，也是孔子七十二大弟子之一。他不但學問好，道德也非常好。

A person from the state of Lǔ who lived during the Spring and Autumn period, he was also one of Confucius' 72 disciples and was renowned for his virtue as well as for his erudition. His surname was 曾 (Zēng), his given name 參 (Shēn), and his courtesy name 子輿 (Zǐyú).

◆ 魯國 *Lǔguó*		the name of an ancient state that flourished from 1108 - 249 B.C. and occupied part of modern Shāndōng province.
◆ 道德 *dàodé*		virtue

17

◆ 子 *zǐ* a polite form of address used in classical Chinese when speaking about or to a man; here it is roughly equivalent to "sir" in English.

8. 曰 yuē 【動詞】說 to say; always used to introduce a direct quotation

9. 何 hé 【疑問副詞】 為什麼；怎麼
Here the word "何" functions as an interrogative adverb meaning "why" or "how".

◆ 疑問副詞 an interrogative adverb
yíwènfùcí

10. 肥 féi 【形容詞】 a. 胖 (pàng) fat; robust
b. 胖 (pán) 安泰舒適 comfortable.

11. 也 yě 【助詞】用於句末與"何"相呼應，表示疑問的語氣，相當於白話中的"[為什麼]…呢？"
Here the final particle "也" is used in conjunction with "何" to indicate an interrogative mood, corresponding to "[為什麼]…呢？" in colloquial Chinese.

◆ 相呼應 to be used in conjunction with [something
xiānghūyìng else]

◆ 語氣 *yǔqì* tone; mood

12. 對 duì 【動詞】 回答 to respond

13. 戰 zhàn 【動詞】 打仗 to fight; to engage in a battle; to wage war

14. 也 yě 【助詞】用於句末表示解釋的語氣，相當於白話中的"啊"。
Here the final particle "也" expresses an explanatory tone; it corresponds to the word "啊" in spoken Chinese.

◆ 解釋 *jiěshì* to explain; explanatory

18

15. 何 hé 【疑問代詞】 什麼 what?
Here the word "何" functions as an interrogative pronoun meaning "what?"

16. 吾 wú 【人稱代詞】 我 I (first person pronoun)

17. 入 rù 【動詞】 進入 to enter；進入［家門］；與 "出" 相對 to enter [the gate of the house]; the opposite of "出" (chū) [to go out]
——→ 從外面回到家裡 to return home

18. 則 zé 【連詞】 相當於白話的 "就"、"便" then
The word "則" is a conjunction equivalent in meaning to "就" or "便" in spoken Chinese and to "then," "and thus," etc. in English.

19. 榮 róng 【形容詞】 盛大 grand
此處： a. 崇 (chóng)高 magnificent
b. 榮耀 (yào) splendid

20. 之 zhī 【代詞】 通常相當於白話中的 "他"、"她"、"牠"、"它"［們］。"它" 也可指上文提到的事、或指下文將要談到的事。在本文內是 "它"，指 "先王之義"，"富貴之樂。"
Usually the word "之" functions as a singular and plural third person pronoun: it is equivalent in meaning to "他" (him), "她" (her), "它" (it) ［們］ (them). "它" can also refer in general to something that has been mentioned in the foregoing text or that is about to be brought up in the text that follows. Here "it" refers to the phrases "先王之義" and "富貴之樂."

21. 出 chū 【動詞】 出去；出了［家門］ to go out; to leave home

22. 富 fù 【形容詞】 財產多；有錢 wealthy
◆財產 cáichǎn property

23. 貴 guì 【形容詞】 祿位高；有地位 highly ranked; highly placed

19

◆ 祿位 *lùwèi*   official salary and rank

24. 樂 lè   【名詞】快樂 happiness; pleasure

25. 又 yòu   【副詞】表示重複或繼續

The word "又" is an adverb used to express repetition or continuity; it can be translated into English as "again," "once more," etc.

◆ 重複 *chóngfù*   to repeat

◆ 繼續 *jìxù*   to continue

26. 者 zhě   【代詞】用在數詞後面構成名詞語，它所指代的對象一般見於上文。"者"不能譯成"…的"，而須在數詞與它指代的對象之間加進相應的量詞或名詞

When the word "者" immediately follows a number, it turns the number into a nominal construction (a noun or noun phrase): two ⟶ *the* two (*these* two, *those* two). What the number refers to generally has appeared in the foregoing text. In this usage, "者" cannot be translated into spoken Chinese as "的"; it is necessary to add an appropriate measure word and noun after the demonstrative pronoun and the number (這兩 + 種 + [想法]) in order to make clear what the number refers to. This reference must also be made clear in English by adding an appropriate noun or noun phrase after the number (these two [*ways of thinking*])

兩者
liǎng zhě   【名詞語】兩種[想法]；兩種[感覺] these two [ways of thinking]; these two [feelings]

27. 于 yú   【介詞】同"於"，在

The word "于" is a locative preposition equivalent to "於" (yú); it means "in," "at," "by," etc.

28. 胸 xiōng   【名詞】 a. 胸膛 (táng)   the chest; the breast
                      b. 胸懷 (huái)   one's heart; one's feelings

(Note: The sense of "胸" is close to the archaic meaning of "bosom" in English, i.e., the breast considered as the center of cherished and secret thoughts and the center of emotions.)

胸中　　　胸懷裡；心裡　in one's heart
xiōng zhōng

29. 未 wèi　【否定副詞】還沒有　not yet
The word "未" functions here as a negative adverb meaning "still not yet".

◆ 否定副詞　　　a negative adverb
　　fǒudìngfùcí

◎ 孰 shú　【疑問代詞】誰；哪個　who; which one
The word "孰" functions here as an interrogative pronoun meaning "which [one]."

30. 負 fù　【動詞】敗；失敗，與 "勝" 相對　to be defeated; to lose; to fail; the opposite of "勝"

31. 臞 qú　【形容詞】瘦 (shòu)　lean; emaciated

32. 今 jīn　【時間詞】現在　at present; now

相關的成語

心廣體胖　　　xīnguǎngtǐpán

心裡無憂無慮 (不發愁)，身體就會很安泰舒適
A clear conscience (or the absence of worries) contributes to physical well-being.

"心廣體胖 (pán)" 通俗的用法讀作 "心廣體胖 (pàng)," 意思是心裡無憂無慮，身體就會變胖。
The phrase "心廣體胖 (pán)" is commonly read as "心廣體胖 (pàng)"; it means that if one is carefree at heart and free from worries, one will become fat (i.e., healthy and robust).

第六課

梟逢鳩

注解

1. 梟 xiāo 　　【名詞】貓頭鷹 (yīng)　an owl

2. 逢 féng 　　【動詞】遇見　to meet

3. 鳩 jiū 　　【名詞】斑 (bān) 鳩　a ringdove; a cushat

4. 將 jiāng 　　【助動詞】將要；此處表示出於主觀意志的事，故白話可譯成 "打算"

   Here the auxiliary verb "將" is used to express future intention or volition -- it indicates that a future action will occur as the consequence of human volition. In this sense, it can be translated into spoken Chinese as "打算" and into English as "to intend to," "be going to," or "shall" (as opposed to "will"). (*See Yáng Shùdá, Cíquán, ch. 6, p. 295. Compare with L. 2, no. 10, p. 7.*)

5. 安 ān 　　【疑問代詞】何處；什麼地方；哪裡　where

6. 之 zhī 　　【動詞】到…去；去　to go to

7. 東 dōng 　　【方向詞】東邊　east; eastward

   ◆ 方向詞　　　a directional word
   　fāngxiàngcí

8. 徙 xǐ 　　【動詞】搬 (bān)　to move

9. 何 hé 　　【疑問形容詞】什麼　what

   ◆ 疑問形容詞　　　an interrogative adjective
   　yíwènxíngróngcí

22

10. 故 gù 　【名詞】緣故　a cause; a reason

11. 鄉 xiāng 　【名詞】鄉村 (cūn)　countryside; a village

12. 皆 jiē 　【副詞】都　all

13. 惡 wù 　【動詞】厭 (yàn) 惡；討厭　to detest; to abhor

14. 鳴 míng 　【動詞】叫　[of birds] to sing; to warble; to cry. Here: to screech ; [of owls] to hoot

　　　　　　【名詞】叫聲；叫的聲音　a bird's song or cry

15. 以 yǐ 　【介詞】因為　for; because

16. 能 néng 　【助動詞】能夠　to be able to

17. 更 gēng 　【動詞】更改；變改　to change

18. 可 kě 　【動詞】有"認可"的意思，可以翻譯成白話的 "可以" 或 "行"。

When it is used as a verb, the word "可" means "to sanction," or "to approve". It can be translated into spoken Chinese as "可以" or "行" and into English as "to be acceptable," "to be fine," "to be all right."

19. 矣 yǐ 　【助詞】表示一種新情況已經出現了，相當於白話中的 "了"

When it is used as a final or ending particle, the word "矣" indicates that a new situation or condition has come about; it corresponds to the word "了" in spoken Chinese and can be translated into English by using the past, present perfect, past perfect, or future perfect tenses, by adding such words as "now," "only then," etc., to the sentence, or by using a conditional sentence pattern.

20. 猶 yóu 　【副詞】仍然 (réngrán)；還　still

21. 聲 shēng 　【名詞】聲音　sound

23

第七課

矛盾

注解

1. 矛 máo
【名詞】矛；古代一種兵器，打仗時用來刺殺敵人 a spear; a weapon for thrusting, with a long shaft and a pointed tip

2. 盾 dùn
【名詞】盾牌 (pái)；古代打仗時用來護衛身體、擋住敵人刀箭等的兵器 a shield; a piece of armor used to protect the body from thrusts and arrows.

3. 楚 Chǔ
【名詞】古國名 (西周初至公元前223)。周成王封熊繹 (Xióng Yì)於楚，春秋時稱王，戰國時為七雄之一，領有今湖南、湖北、安徽、浙江及河南南部諸地，後為秦所滅。

The name of an ancient kingdom that flourished from c. 1115 to 223 B.C. King Chéng of the Zhōu dynasty enfeoffed Xióng Yì in the state of Chǔ. During the Spring and Autumn period the ruler of Chǔ declared himself king; during the Warring States period Chǔ was one of seven powerful states contending for hegemony. The kingdom of Chǔ occupied the area covered by present day Húnán, Húběi, Añhūi, Zhéjiāng and the southern part of Hénán provinces. It was subsequently vanquished by the state of Qín.

◆ 周成王
Zhōu Chéngwáng
the second king of the Zhōu dynasty (r. 1115 - 1079 B.C.)

◆ 封 fēng
to install as a feudal lord or noble; to enfeoff

◆ 熊繹 Xióng Yì
the first ruler of Chǔ

◆ 稱王 chēngwáng
to declare oneself a king

◆ 七雄 qīxióng
During the period of Warring States (403 - 222 B.C.), there were seven states 秦 (Qín), 楚 (Chǔ), 齊 (Qí), 韓 (Hán), 趙 (Zhào), 魏 (Wèi), 燕 (Yān)) that contended for hegemony

24

until Qín (秦) emerged victorious to become the unchallenged ruler of the empire under the First Emperor (始皇帝). The seven states were known as "the seven powers".

◆ 領有 *lǐngyǒu*　　to occupy

◆ 滅 *miè*　　to exterminate; to wipe out

4. 鬻 yù　　【動詞】賣　to sell

5. 與 yǔ　　【連詞】跟；和　and

6. 譽 yù　　【動詞】讚 (zàn) 美　to praise
　　　　　　　　此處：誇 (kuā) to brag [about]; to vaunt

7. 堅 jiān　　【形容詞】堅固　firm; hard

8. 物 wù　　【名詞】東西　things

9. 莫 mò　　【無指代詞】沒有一個人 (沒有誰)；沒有一個東西 (沒有什麼)。此處指沒有什麼
an indeterminate pronoun meaning "nobody" or "nothing"; here it means "nothing"

　　◆ 無指代詞　　an indeterminate pronoun
　　　 wúzhǐdàicí

10. 陷 xiàn　　【動詞】刺穿 to pierce through

11. 利 lì　　【形容詞】鋒 (fēng) 利　sharp

12. 何 hé　　【疑問代詞】什麼？ What

13. 如 rú　　【繫詞】像　to be like

何如
hé rú
【準繫詞語】像什麼？怎麼樣？ What would it be like? How would it be?

25

◆準繫詞語　　a pseudo linking-verbial phrase
zǔnxìcíyǔ

14. 弗 fú 　【副詞】不　not

15. 應 yìng 　【動詞】回答　to respond; to reply

16. 也 yě 　【助詞】表示堅決的語氣　an ending particle used to indicate a tone of resolution

17. 夫 fú 　【助詞】放在句首，表示將發議論
When it appears at the beginning of a sentence, the particle "夫" indicates that the writer or speaker is about to express an opinion or make a comment.

18. 可 kě 　【助動詞】能；可能　can; to be possible; to be likely

19. 世 shì 　【名詞】a. 時代　the times; the era
b. 世間　the world

同世：
tóngshì 　【名詞語】a. 同一個時代；同時
at the same time

b. 同一個世間；同一個世界上
in the same world

20. 立 lì 　【動詞】站立　to stand
此處：存在　to exist

26

成語

自相矛盾 zìxiāngmáodùn

LITERALLY: "To use your sword against your shield yourself"

比喻自己言語、行動前後抵觸 (dǐ chù)，不相應合
This proverb is used as a metaphor to describe a situation in which a person's words or deeds are self-contradictory.

第八課

逆旅二妾

注解

1. 逆 nì 　　【動詞】迎接　to receive

2. 旅 lǚ 　　【名詞】旅客　travelers

   逆旅 　　【名詞語】旅館；客舍　an inn
   nì lǚ

3. 妾 qiè 　　【名詞】姨太太　a concubine

4. 陽子 　　【名詞】陽子就是楊朱 (Yáng Zhū)。(按："陽"、
   Yáng zǐ 　　"楊"古代通用)。戰國時代衛國人。字子居，
   　　　　哲學家。他的書沒流傳下來，他的學說只能從
   　　　　《孟子》、《莊子》、《列子》中看到一部分。
   　　　　他主張"為我"、"拔一毛利天下而不為。"

   Yángzǐ is the philosopher Yáng Zhū (fl. 4th cent. B.C.), courtesy
   name Zǐjū. He lived in the state of Wèi during the era of the
   Warring States (403 - 221 B.C.). His works are no longer extant,
   and his philosophy can only be partially reconstructed on the basis
   of passages quoted in such pre-Qín (before 221 B.C.) texts as the
   Mencius, the *Zhuāngzǐ*, and the *Lièzǐ*. He held that self-interest
   (為我) governed human behavior and is famous for the remark:
   "Even if it were to benefit the whole world, I would not pluck out a
   single strand of my hair."

   (Note: In the pre-Qín period, the characters "陽" and "楊" were
   interchangeable.)

   ◆ 按 àn 　　　　　　note; author's/editor's comment

   ◆ 通用 tōngyòng 　　[of words or characters]
   　　　　　　　　　　interchangeable

   ◆ 衛國 Wèiguó 　　a state that flourished from the
   　　　　　　　　　　twelfth century to 209 B.C. and
   　　　　　　　　　　occupied parts of present day Héběi
   　　　　　　　　　　and Hénán provinces

28

◆ 流傳 *liúchuán* — to transmit, or to be transmitted, from person to person or from generation to generation

◆ 學説 *xuéshuō* — a theory

◆ 主張 *zhǔzhāng* — to hold a view; to advocate

◆ 爲我 *wèiwǒ* — [do something] for oneself

◆ 拔一毛利天下而不爲 *báyìmáolìtiānxià érbùwéi* — Even if it [would] benefit [all the people] under Heaven, [he] would not pluck out one strand of [his own] hair.

5. 之 zhī 【動詞】到…去；去 to go to

6. 宋 Sòng 【名詞】春秋戰國時代國名，在今河南省商邱 (qiū) 縣

A state that flourished from 858 to 286 B.C. and occupied part of present day Hénán province.

7. 宿 sù 【動詞】住宿；過夜 to lodge for the night; to stay overnight

8. 於 yú 【介詞】在 at; in

9. 逆旅人 nì lǚ rén 【名詞語】旅館的主人 the owner of the inn; the innkeeper

10. 美 měi 【形容詞】美麗 (lì) beautiful；好看 good-looking

11. 惡 è 【形容詞】醜陋 (chǒulòu)；醜；難看 ugly

12. 貴 guì 【形容詞】地位高；受重視 to be highly ranked; to be highly regarded

◎ 受寵 shòu chǒng 【動詞語】to be favored

13. 賤 jiàn 【形容詞】地位低；受輕視 to be of low status; to be held in contempt

29

◎不受寵　【動詞語】 to be out of favor
bú shòu chǒng

14. 小子　　【名詞】小伙 (huǒ) 子；年輕人　a young man
xiǎo zǐ　　　　(here it refers to the innkeeper)

15. 自美　　【動詞語】自以為美；覺得自己很美
zì měi　　　　　to think oneself very beautiful

16. 知 zhī　【動詞】覺察；感覺　to perceive

17. 也 yě　【助詞】此處表示堅決的語氣　a final particle used
here to indicate a tone of resolution

18. 自惡　　【動詞語】自以為醜；覺得自己很醜
zì è　　　　　　to think oneself very ugly

19. 弟子　　【名詞】學生們；徒 (tú) 弟們　pupils; disciples
dì zǐ

20. 記 jì　【動詞】記住　to remember; to bear in mind

21. 行 xíng　【動詞】實行；做　to put into practice; to do

22. 賢 xián　【形容詞】有德行；多才能 virtuous; talented
此處：有道德；高尚 virtuous; exalted

【名詞】有道德的事；高尚的事　[what is] virtuous;
[what is] worthy of esteem

23. 去 qù　【動詞】去掉；除去　to get rid of; to remove

24. 自賢　　【動詞語】自以為賢；覺得自己很高尚
zì xián　　　to be self-righteous; to vaunt oneself

25. 心 xīn　【名詞】心理；感覺　mentality; sensibility; feelings

26. 愛 ài　【動詞】對人或事物有深摯 (zhì) 的感情 to have strong
or intense feelings toward someone or something

此處：受歡迎 to be loved; to be welcome

27. 哉 zāi 【感嘆詞】表感嘆，可譯成"啊"。與疑問詞
"何"同用於句中，構成疑問句或反問句時，可
譯成"呢"。 "哉" is an interjection expressing an emphatic
exclamatory tone; it can be translated as "啊" in spoken Chinese.
When "哉" is used in conjunction with the question word "何" to
form a genuine or rhetorical question, it can be translated as "呢"
in spoken Chinese.

◆ 感嘆詞　　　　　　an interjection
　gǎntàncí

相關的成語

滿招損，謙受益 mǎnzhāosǔn qiānshòuyì

自滿 (驕傲 jiāoào) 招致損失，謙虛 (qiānxū) 受到利益。
Haughtiness invites loss, while modesty brings gain.

自以為賢　　　zìyǐwéixián

覺得自己才德比別人高
One deems oneself as way above others in terms of talents and virtue.

31

第九課

盜鍾(鐘)

注解

1. 盜 dào 　【動詞】偷　to steal

　　　　　　　【名詞】賊(zéi)；小偷　a thief

2. 鍾 zhōng 　【名詞】通"鐘"，樂器，用銅(tóng)或鐵(tiě)製成
a comprehensive term for metal musical instruments, usually of bronze or iron; here, a bell with a clapper. (The characters "鍾" and "鐘" were interchangeable in early classical Chinese.)

　　　　◆ 通 tōng 　　　[of characters] to be interchangeable [with one another]

3. 范氏
Fàn shì 　【名詞】此處指春秋時代晉國六卿之一，范吉射
(Jíshè).　Here 范氏 (lit. surnamed Fàn) refers to Fàn Jíshè, one of the six chief ministers of the state of Jin.

　　　　◆ 晉國 Jìnguó 　　A state that flourished from the twelfth century to 376 B.C. and occupied parts of present day Shānxī, Shǎnxī, Hénán and Héběi provinces.

　　　　◆ 卿 qīng 　　a high official in ancient times; a minister

4. 敗 bài 　【動詞】失敗；在戰爭或競爭中失敗，跟勝(shèng)字相對

to fail; to be defeated in war or in a contest, the opposite of "勝" (to be victorious)

范氏之敗　指范吉射在公元前490年被晉國另一位卿趙簡子
Fàn shì zhī bài 　打敗而言

"Fàn's defeat" refers to Fàn Jíshè's defeat at the hands of Zhào Jiǎnzǐ, another minister of the state of Jìn, in 490 B.C.

5. 竊 qiè 　【動詞】偷　to steal

6. 負 fù 【動詞】 背 (bēi) to carry on the back

7. 走 zǒu 【動詞】 跑；逃跑 to run away

8. 鎗 qiāng 【象聲詞】 玎玎璫璫地 clang

◆ 象聲詞 an onomatopoeia
xiàngshēngcí

9. 然 rán 【詞尾】 用作形容詞詞尾時，白話可翻譯成
"的"；用作副詞詞尾時，白話可翻譯成"地"

When it is used as an enclitic particle following an adjective or an adverb, it is somewhat similar to the suffix "-like" or "-ly" in English and means "in [such] a way or manner."

◆ 詞尾 cíwěi a suffix

鎗然 【副詞】 玎玎鏜鏜地；聲音響亮悅耳地
qiāngrán resonantly; clangorously

◆ 響亮 xiǎngliàng resonant and reverberating

◆ 悅耳 yuèěr pleasant to the ear

10. 懼 jù 【動詞】 害怕；恐懼 to be afraid; to fear

11. 聞 wén 【動詞】 聽見 to hear

12. 遽 jù 【副詞】 急忙；趕緊 quickly; at once

13. 掩 yǎn 【動詞】 遮蓋 (zhēgài)；遮掩 (zhēyǎn) to cover up
捂 (wǔ) 住；用手遮住 to cover with one's hands

14. 憎 zēng 【動詞】 憎恨；厭惡 to hate; to abhor

15. 可 kě 【動詞】 有"認可"的意思，可譯成"可以"
或"行"。
As a verb it means "to sanction" or "to approve." It can be translated into spoken Chinese as "可以" or "行" and into English as "to be acceptable," or "to be all right."

33

——→ 還算說得過去　to be acceptable/permissable

——→ 還算有點儿道理　to be reasonable

16. 也　yě　【助詞】用在句末表示判斷的語氣　a final particle used here to convey a tone of judgment or decision

17. 悖　bèi　【形容詞】違背道理；荒謬 (huāngmiù)；荒唐 ridiculous; absurd

18. 矣　yǐ　【助詞】用在句末表示感歎的語氣，通常用在形容詞的後面，，與‘啦’(了啊合音)相當例如："久矣"(很久啦)。

The word "矣" is a final particle used here as an interjection; it usually follows an adjective and adds an emphatic tone to the word it follows. It is roughly equivalent to the interjection ‘啦’(lā: 了 + 啊) in spoken Chinese. For example, the phrase "久矣" can be put into spoken Chinese as "很久啦"(so very long). Such interjectory elements can be rendered into English by the use of an exclamation mark or by adding such intensifying words as "so," "very," "how," "indeed," etc. (e.g., "How ridiculous!" or "Ridiculous indeed!").

◆ 感歎語氣　mood of emphatic interjection
gǎntànyǔqì

成語

掩耳盜鈴　yǎněrdàolíng

LITERALLY: "To cover one's ears when stealing a bell."

捂著耳朵偷鈴。

比喻自己欺騙自己，明明遮 (zhē) 掩不了的事，偏要設法遮掩。

To deceive oneself. This phrase is used as a metaphor to describe situations where one is attempting to deceive oneself into thinking that there is a way to cover up something that clearly cannot be covered up.

34

第十課

鄭人買履

注解

1. 鄭 Zhèng 【名詞】國名 A state that flourished from 806 to 375 B.C. and occupied parts of present-day Shǎnxī and Hénán provinces.

2. 買 mǎi 【動詞】買 to buy

3. 履 lǚ 【名詞】鞋 shoes

4. 且 qiě 【副詞】將要；打算 to be going to or about to [do something]; to be on the verge/brink of [doing something]

5. 先 xiān 【副詞】指事情、行為發生在前 first

6. 自 zì 【代詞】自己 oneself (himself, herself, itself)

7. 度 duò 【動詞】量 to measure
   dù 【名詞】尺寸 (chǐcùn)；尺碼 (chǐmǎ) measurement; size

8. 足 zú 【名詞】腳 foot; feet

9. 置 zhì 【動詞】放 to put; to place

10. 之 zhī 【代詞】它；此處指尺碼 it; here, "it" refers to the measurement

11. 座 zuò 【名詞】座位 seat

12. 至 zhì 【介詞】介紹時間，在句中的作用像副詞，相當於白話中的 "[等]到…[的時候]" ， (見 楊樹達 《詞詮》卷一頁九： "比" (bǐ)；卷五頁十二：

35

"至"。)

The word "至" functions here as a preposition used to introduce a temporal clause. It resembles an adverb in this sentence and is roughly equivalent to the phrase "[等]到 … [的時候]" in spoken Chinese and to "when," "reaching the point when..." "at the time that..." in English. These meanings are derived from the basic denotation of the verb "至", "to reach or arrive at a place." Compare note 23 below. (*See Yáng Shùdá's Cí Quán, ch. 1, p. 9, "bǐ"; ch. 5, p. 12, "zhì".*)

14. 市 shì 　【名詞】交易物品的場所；買賣東西的地方；市場 markets; a marketplace
臨時或定期集中在一地方進行的貿易活動／交易的活動 the act of gathering together on a regular or temporary basis to trade; commerce; commercial activities

◆ 貿易 màoyì 　　trade

15. 忘 wàng 　【動詞】忘記 to forget

16. 操 cāo 　【動詞】拿 to hold; to take

17. 已 yǐ 　【副詞】已經 already

18. 乃 nǎi 　【副詞】才 then; only then

19. 持 chí 　【動詞】拿 to grasp; to take
此處：帶 to take along; to carry along

20. 反 fǎn 　【動詞】轉 to turn
此處：轉身 to turn oneself around

21. 歸 guī 　【動詞】回去 to return
此處：回家 to go home

22. 取 qǔ 　【動詞】拿 to fetch; to pick up; to get

23. 及 jí 　【介詞】介紹時間。在句中的作用像副詞，用法

36

與"至"字相同。相當於白話的"[等]到…[的時候]
。"(見楊樹達《詞詮》卷四頁九:"及"。)

The word "及" functions here as a preposition used to introduce a
temporal clause. It resembles an adverb in this sentence and is
used like the word "至". It is roughly equivalent to the phrase
"[等]到…[的時候]" in spoken Chinese and to "when," "at the
point when," etc., in English. These meanings are derived from
the basic denotation of the verb "及", "to reach a place."
(*See Yáng Shùdá's Cí Quán, ch. 4, p. 9, "jí".*)

24. 罷 bà 【動詞】停止 to cease
此處:結束;終止 to close; to finish

25. 遂 suì 【副詞】於是;就 then; thereupon

26. 試 shì 【動詞】試一試 to try [on]

27. 以 yǐ 【介詞】用 Literally: to use; here, with; by [means of]

28. 寧 nìng; níng 【助動詞】寧可;寧願 would rather; to prefer

29. 信 xìn 【動詞】相信 to believe in or to trust in

30. 無 wú 【副詞】表示否定,此處與"不"相同
The word "無" functions here as an adverb that indicates negation
of what follows it; here, it is equivalent in meaning to "不" (not).

31. 自信
zì xìn 【動詞語】自己信自己;相信自己 to believe in
oneself; to trust one's own judgment

32. 也 yě 【助詞】用於句末表示堅決的語氣 a final
particle used here to indicate a tone of resolution

相關成語

墨守成規　mòshǒuchéngguī

固守舊法，不肯改變。
to adhere blindly to established conventions

死抱住老法子不肯改進。
to fall into a rut; to get into a rut

第十一課

仁義

注解

1. 仁 rén 　　【名詞】仁愛　benevolence; humanity; mercy; kindness; charity

2. 義 yì 　　【名詞】正道；正義　righteous ways; righteousness

3. 昔 xī 　　【時間詞】從前　formerly; once upon a time

4. 昆弟 kūn dì 　　【名詞語】兄弟　elder and younger brothers

5. 游 yóu 　　【動詞】游玩　to play; to go for a ramble; to roam
　　　　　　　　　　　旅行　to travel
　　　　　　　　——→ 外出／離家求學　to go out to seek learning
　　　　　　　　——→ 到…去求學 to travel to...to seek learning

6. 齊 Qí 　　【名詞】周朝國名，在今山東省

The name of a vassal state of the Zhōu dynasty that flourished from the twelfth century to 221 B.C. and occupied part of present-day Shāndōng province.

◆ 周朝 *Zhōucháo*　　the Zhōu dynasty (the 12th century - 256 B.C.)

7. 魯 Lǔ 　　【名詞】周朝國名，領土大部分在今山東南部並包括江蘇 (sū) 安徽 (huī) 的一小部分

The name of a vassal state of the Zhōu dynasty that flourished from 1108 to 249 B.C. and occupied the southern part of present-day Shāndōng province as well as a small part of Jiāngsū and Ānhuī provinces.

◆ 領土 *lǐngtǔ*　　　　territory

39

◆ 包括 *bāokuò*   to include; to comprise

8. 間 *jiān*   【名詞】中間   middle; in between [of]

之間   【名詞語】的中間   within a specific space [of]
zhījiān   ⟶ 一帶 the area [of]

9. 從 *cóng*   【動詞】跟隨   to follow

10. 同 *tóng*   【形容詞】同樣的   the same kind
          ⟶ 同一位 the same person

11. 師 *shī*   【名詞】老師   a teacher

12. 進 *jìn*   【動詞】同 "盡"（根據朱駿聲《說文通訓定聲》的說法）

According to the explanation given by Zhū Jùnshēng in his book *Shuōwén Tōngxùn Dìngshēng*, here it is equivalent to "盡"；"完" to exhaust

13. 道 *dào*   【名詞】道理   doctrine; philosophy

14. 進仁義之道   【動詞語】學完仁義的道理   to finish studying the doctrine of benevolence and righteousness
jìn rén yì zhī dào   ⟶ 把仁義的道理學完了 had finished studying the doctrine of benevolence and righteousness
       ⟶ 把仁義的道理學得很透徹了 had thoroughly and exhaustively studied the doctrine of benevolence and righteousness

15. 若何   【準繫詞語】如何；像什麼；怎麼樣？ like what? what is it like?
ruò hé

16. 伯 *bó*   【名詞】大兒子   the eldest son

17. 愛 *ài*   【動詞】愛惜   to cherish

18. 身　shēn　　【名詞】身體　the body

⟶ 自身；自己的生命
one's body ; one's own life

《孝經》：" 身體髮膚，受之父母，不敢毀傷。"
ALLUSION: *The classic of filial piety:* "Our body, with hair and skin, [is what we] receive from our parents, [we] do not dare to allow it to be injured [in any way]."

愛身
ai shēn　　【動詞語】愛惜自身　to cherish one's body

⟶ 看重自己的生命
to value one's own life

19. 後　hòu　　【名詞】時間或位置在後的，與 "先" 或 "前"

相對　In a series of things or sequence of events, "後" refers to those which occur later in order or in time; it is used in contradistinction to "先", which refers to those that precede in order or time. (*See also L. 14, no. 22, p. 58*)
後面；後頭 (與前面、前頭相對) the back (as opposed to the front)

20. 名　míng　　【名詞】名聲　reputation

21. 後名
hòu míng　　【動詞語】以名聲為後　to take reputation as that which comes after (i.e., second)

以為 (認為) 名聲在後頭
to hold that reputation is secondary

覺得名聲不重要　to think/feel that
reputation is unimportant

⟶ 看輕名聲　to disdain reputation

22. 仲　zhòng　　【名詞】二兒子　the second son

23. 殺　shā　　【動詞】殺死　to kill

殺身
shā shēn　　【動詞語】犧牲 (xīshēng) 自己的生命
to sacrifice one's own life

41

《論語 · 衛靈公》："志士仁人，無求生以害仁，有殺身以成仁。"

LOCUS CLASSICUS: *Analects*, Chapter 15: " The determined scholar and the man of virtue will not seek to live at the expense of injuring their virtue. They will even sacrifice their lives (They will kill themselves) to preserve their virtue complete."

[Legge, *The Chinese Classics*, Vol. 1, p. 297.]

24. 以 yǐ 　　【連詞】來　in order to; so as to

25. 成 chéng 　　【動詞】完成；成就　to accomplish; to achieve
　　　　　　　　——→ 建立 to establish

成名
chéng míng 　　【動詞語】成就名聲　to achieve repute
　　　　　　　　——→建立名聲　to establish one's reputation

26. 叔 shū 　　【名詞】三兒子　the third son

◎ 季 jì 　　【名詞】最小的兒子　the youngest son

27. 並 bìng 　　【副詞】一起；一同　together
　　　　　　　此處：[兩個]都　both

28. 全 quán 　　【動詞】保全；不受傷害　to assure the safety of; to protect or guard; to keep intact

並全
bìng quán 　　【動詞語】都保全；都不受傷害　to keep both intact; to keep both from harm's way

《詩經 · 大雅 · 烝民》："既明且哲，以保其身。"

ALLUSION: *The book of odes* , "The greater odes"; Ode 260: "Intelligent is he and wise, protecting his own person;" [Legge, *The Chinese Classics*, Vol. 4, p. 543.]

29. 彼 bǐ 　　【指示詞】那(遠指)，與 "此"(近指：這)相對　that; those; (this word is the opposite of "此" (this) and always refers to what is distant or remote. [in English usage "these" often sounds more natural, whereas in Chinese "those" sounds better].

42

30. 術 shù 　【名詞】學說；道理　theory; teaching; doctrine

31. 相 xiāng 　【副詞】互相　each other; mutually

32. 反 fǎn 　【動詞】違 (wéi) 反；違背
　　　　　　　to run counter to; to be contrary to

　　相反 　【動詞語】互相違反；彼此衝突　to be contrary to
　　xiāng fǎn 　each other; to be mutually contradictory ; to contradict each other

33. 於 yú 　【介詞】從　from

34. 儒 rú 　【名詞】儒家　the Confucian school

35. 孰 shú 　【疑問代詞】誰；哪個　who; which one

36. 是 shì 　【形容詞】對　to be right; to approve/agree

37. 非 fēi 　【形容詞】不對；錯　to be wrong; to disapprove/disagree

38. 耶 yé 　【助詞】呢　an interrogative particle

相關成語

殺身成仁 shāshēnchéngrén

犧牲自己來成就仁德

to die to achieve virtue -- to die for a righteous cause.

捨生取義 shěshēngqǔyì

LITERALLY: "To cast away life *in order to* pick up righteousness"

為正義真理不惜犧牲生命

This saying is used to describe the behavior of someone who is willing to do what is right and just at any cost, even the cost of his own life.

明哲保身 míngzhébǎoshēn

LITERALLY: "Perspicuity [and] intelligence preserve body."

聰明人能居安避險 (bìxiǎn),保全其身

A wise person knows how best to keep himself from harm and safeguard his personal security.

第十二課

蘇代諫趙王

注解

1. 蘇代
Sū Dài

【名詞】洛陽人，戰國時代 (403 - 221 B.C.) 著名的
縱橫家之一

A man from Luòyáng who lived during the Warring States period
(403 - 221 B. C.), he was one of the most renowned political
strategists of his day.

◆ *縱橫家*
zōnghéngjiā

political strategists (of the Warring States
period)

2. 諫 jiàn

【動詞】規勸；勸諫；用言語或行動勸告別人
（君主、尊長或地位比自己高的人）改正錯誤，
或勸阻別人不要做不應該做的事

To admonish; to urge another person by word or deed (usually a
ruler, a senior, or person of higher status than the speaker) to mend
his faults; or to dissuade another person from doing something
that ought not be done. Here: to remonstrate with [a superior].

◆ 勸告 *quàngào*   to advise; to urge

◆ 君主 *jūnzhǔ*   a sovereign; a monarch; a ruler

◆ 尊長 *zūnzhǎng*   an older person; an elder; a senior

◆ 勸阻 *quànzǔ*   to dissuade [someone] from

3. 趙 Zhào

【名詞】戰國時代國名，統有今河北省南部及山
西省北部

The name of a state during the Warring States period. It flourished
from 326 to 228 B.C. and controlled the southern part of present-
day Héběi province and the northern part of Shānxī province.

45

4. 且 qiě 　　【副詞】將要　to be going to or about to [do something]; to be on the verge/brink of [doing something]

5. 伐 fá 　　【動詞】進攻 (gōng)；攻打 to attack

6. 燕 Yān 　　【名詞】周代諸侯國，戰國時為七雄之一，在今河北北部和遼寧一帶

Originally one of the feudal fiefdoms of the Zhōu dynasty, the state of Yān became one of the seven most powerful states contending for hegemony during the Warring States period; it occupied the northern part of present-day Héběi province and part of Liáoníng province. The capital city of Yān occupied the site of modern Běijīng.

　　◆ 周代 Zhōudài 　　the Zhōu dynasty (the 12th century - 256 B.C.)

　　◆ 諸侯國 zhūhóugúo 　　the fiefs of the feudal lords subject to the kings of Zhōu.

7. 為 wèi 　　【介詞】替；給；為　for; on behalf of

8. 惠王 Huìwáng 　　【名詞】趙惠文王；姓趙，名何，"惠文"是他的諡號 King Huì (r. 299 - 267 B.C.) was surnamed Zhào and had the given name Hé; "Huìwén" was his posthumous honorific title.

　　◆ 諡號 shìhào 　　a posthumous honorific title

9. 者 zhě 　　【助詞】跟表示時間的詞結合成名詞語，表示某一段時間，這樣的"者"有的可譯成"…的時候"，有的須選擇適當的時間詞譯成白話（詳見第一課、生字六，第二頁）

When used in conjunction with a time word (or temporal clause), the word "者" indicates or demarcates a certain period of time. (for detail, see L. 1, no. 6, p. 2)

今者 jīn zhě 　　【時間詞】這次 this time; on this occasion; at present

10. 臣 chén 【名詞】官吏、百姓對君主的自稱，秦漢以前在
一般人面前表示謙卑 (qiān bēi)，也可以自稱 "臣"

This term was used exclusively by officials and subjects to refer to
themselves when addressing their ruler, king, or emperor.
However, prior to the Qín-Hàn period, this word was used as a
self-deprecatory term by the speaker to refer to himself when
addressing others (including superiors) to express a polite or
modest tone.
LITERALLY: "[your] servant." It can simply be rendered in
English as "I ".

11. 過 guò 【動詞】渡 (dù)過 to cross [a river or ocean]; here, to ford

12. 易水 【名詞】河名，在今河北省的易縣。易水以北是
Yì Shuǐ 燕國，以南是趙國

The Yì River in Héběi province. The state of Yān was situated to
the north of the Yì River, the state of Zhào to the south of it.

13. 蚌 bàng 【名詞】蚌；生活在淡水裡的一種軟體動物名，
介殼長圓形，黑褐色 a clam; a fresh water mollusk with
a dark brown, elliptical, hinged shell

14. 方 fāng 【副詞】正在，表示動作在進行中 just; in the
process of; in the course of. This word indicates that the action of
the verb following it is taking place.

15. 曝 pù 【動詞】曬 (shài) [太陽]
to expose to sunlight; to bask in the sun

16. 鷸 yù 【名詞】鳥名 a snipe

17. 啄 zhuó 【動詞】鳥用嘴取食 [of a bird] to peck
此處：啄住 to clamp down on [with the beak]

18. 合 hé 【動詞】合攏 (lǒng) to close

19. 箝 qián 【動詞】夾 (jiā)住 to hold with tongs; to clamp down on

20. 喙 huì   【名詞】鳥嘴 a beak ; a bill

21. 雨 yǔ   【動詞】下雨 to rain

22. 即 jí   【連詞】就；便

23. 死 sǐ   【形容詞】死的；死了的 dead

24. 亦 yì   【副詞】也 also; as well; too

25. 兩者   【名詞語】兩個 N (指蚌和鷸) "these two",
liǎng zhě   referring here to the clam and the snipe (*cf. L. 5, no. 26, p. 20*)

26. 肯 kěn   【助動詞】願意 to be willing

27. 相 xiāng   【副詞】互相 mutually; each other

28. 舍 shě   【動詞】同"捨"，放棄 (qì)；捨棄
      to give up; to relinquish; to let go

29. 漁父   【名詞語】年老的漁人 an old fisherman
yú fù   捕 (bǔ)魚的老頭儿
      an old man who was catching fish

30. 得 dé   【動詞】獲 (huò) 得；得到 to get; to obtain;
      此處：遇到 to encounter；發現 to find

31. 擒 qín   【動詞】捕捉 (zhuō) to catch

32. 久 jiǔ   【副詞】長久 for a long time

33. 支 zhī   【動詞】支撐 (zhīchēng)；撐持 (chēngchí) to set against
      撐拒 (chēngjù) to be at a standoff

相支
xiāng zhī

【動詞語】a. 互相撐持 to set against each other
b. 互相撐拒 to be deadlocked
c. 雙方用盡力氣地對抗 to be at a standoff or at an impasse

34. 以 yǐ

【連詞】以致；結果 with a result that; consequently (usually indicating an unpleasant result)

35. 敝 bì

【形容詞】疲乏 (pífá) exhausted; weary; worn out

36. 大眾
dà zhòng

【名詞語】廣大的群 (qún)眾 a large crowd [of people]
此處：人民；民眾 the common people; the masses

37. 恐 kǒng

【動詞】怕 to fear; to be afraid that;
擔心 (dānxīn) to worry

38. 強 qiáng

【形容詞】強大 powerful and strong

39. 為 wéi

【動詞】成為；變成 to become

40. 也 yě

【助詞】出現在複合句前一個分句的後面，表示停頓的語氣，用來引起下文，可譯成"啊"

When the particle "也" appears at the end of the first clause of a compound sentence, it expresses a tone of reflective caesura which is intended to mark the transition to the text immediately following it. This tone can be expressed in spoken Chinese by the word "啊". In English, somtimes "filler words" like "so" serve the same function in a sentence.

41. 故 gù

【連詞】所以 consequently; therefore

42. 願 yuàn

【動詞】希望 to hope; to wish

43. 熟 shú

【副詞】仔細地 carefully or painstakingly [study, survey, inspect, etc.]
周密 (zhōumì)地 circumspectly

44. 計 jì 　　【動詞】計慮；考慮 to consider

45. 也 yě 　　【助詞】用在敘述句的句末，表示祈使 (希望
　　　　　　、請求)、禁止或命令的語氣。此處表示祈使，
　　　　　　可譯成 "啊" 或不譯出。

When the particle "也" is used at the end of a narrative sentence, it expresses a tone of exhortation, prohibition, or command. Here it expresses a tone of exhortaion which can be expressed in spoken Chinese by the word "啊" or left unexpressed. In English, this tone can be expressed by adding such modal auxiliary verbs as "should", "can", "must" etc., or by using the imperative mood of the verb.

◆ 祈使 qíshǐ 　　　　to request; to entreat

◆ 禁止 jìnzhǐ 　　　　to forbid; to prohibit

46. 善 shàn 　　【形容詞】好 good; excellent

此處；應答之詞，表示同意
a rejoinder used to express agreement or concurrence

47. 乃 nǎi 　　【副詞】就 thereupon; then

48. 止 zhǐ 　　【動詞】停止 to stop; to cease

成語

鷸蚌相爭，漁翁得利 yùbàngxiāngzhēng-yúwēngdélì

LITERALLY: "When the snipe fights with the clam, it is the old fisherman who gains the advantage."

比喻雙方相爭，結果第三者得利。

This proverb is used as a metaphor to describe a situation where a third party benefits from the struggle between two other parties.

第 十 三 課

郢書燕說

注解

1. 郢 Yǐng 　　　【名詞】古地名。春秋戰國時楚國的國都，在今
　　　　　　　　湖北省北邊

An ancient place name. Yǐng was the capital city of the state of
Chǔ during the Spring and Autumn and Warring States periods;
it was situated in the northern part of present-day Húběi province.

2. 書 shū 　　　　【名詞】信　　　　　a letter; a missive

　　　　　　　　　【動詞】寫 [信]　　　to write [a letter]

3. 燕 Yān 　　　　【名詞】周代諸侯國，戰國時為七雄之一，在今
　　　　　　　　河北北部和遼寧一帶

Originally one of the feudal fiefdoms of the Zhōu dynasty, the
state of Yān became one of the seven most powerful states
contending for hegemony during the Warring States period; it
occupied the northern part of present-day Héběi province and part
of Liáoníng province. The capital city of Yān occupied the site of
modern Běijīng.

4. 說 shuō 　　　　【動詞】解說；解釋 to explain; to interpret;
to expound [on it]

5. 遺 wèi 　　　　【動詞】給予；送給；送交 to send; to give to
[Note: when it is read as "yí", this character means "to leave behind" or "to
pass down".] *(See L. 33, no. 9, P. 134)*

6. 相國
　　xiàng guó 　　【名詞】輔佐君主掌管國事的最高官吏。秦以後
叫丞 (chéng)相或宰 (zǎi)相，現代叫總理。（參看第一
課、生字二，第一頁）

A title of distinction normally given only to senior officials in a
ruler's central administration who personlly assisted him in
governing the state. After the Qín dynasty (the first unified

Chinese empire), such officials were known as councilors-in-chief (丞 (chéng) 相) or grand councilors (宰 (zǎi)相). These titles are loosely translated as "prime minister" and are roughly equivalent to the contemporary title "premier." (*See L. 1, no. 2, p. 1*)

◆ 秦 *Qín*　　　　the Qín dynasty (221 - 206 B.C.)

◆ 輔佐 *fǔzuǒ*　　to help; to assist

7. 夜 yè　　【名詞】晚上　　　　[at] night

夜書　　【動詞語】在晚上寫信　to write a letter at night
yè shū

8. 火 huǒ　　【名詞】燈光或燭光　lamplight or candlelight

◆ 燈光 *dēngguāng*　the light of an oil lamp

◆ 燭光 *zhúguāng*　the light of a candle

9. 明 míng　【形容詞】明亮　bright
[Note: brightness is used as a metaphor for intelligence, which penetrates and illuminates human affairs.]

【名詞】明智；智慧　wisdom

10. 謂 wèi　【動詞】告訴…；對…說　to tell; to speak to

11. 持 chí　【動詞】拿　to take; to hold

12. 燭 zhú　【名詞】蠟燭　a candle

13. 舉 jǔ　【動詞】舉起；把…舉高一點　to raise; to raise up

14. 云 yún　【動詞】說　to speak; to say

15. 過 guò　【副詞】錯誤地　mistakenly; by mistake

過書　　【動詞語】錯誤地寫 to have written by mistake
guò shū　　──→不小心寫錯 to have carelessly written

52

16. 非 fēi 　【否定繫詞】不是　　not [to be]; is/was not

◆ 否定繫詞　　a negative linking verb
　　fǒudìngxìcí

17. 書意　【名詞語】信裡的意思　　the meaning of the letter
shū yì

18. 受 shòu 　【動詞】接受；接到　　to receive

19. 之 zhī 　【代名詞】第三人稱代詞，他、她、牠、它。此
處為"它"，指信中的"舉燭"二字
Here it stands for the third person pronoun: he; she; it; "it" refers to the two characters "舉燭".

20. 者 zhě 　【助詞】表示停頓
a particle used here to indicate a pause.

◆ 停頓 tíngdùn 　　to pause

21. 尚 shàng 　【動詞】崇 (chóng) 尚；注重
to revere, to esteem; to consider important

尚明　【動詞語】崇尚光明；注重光明
shàng míng 　　to esteem brightness; to consider brightness
[i.e., intelligence] important
—→ 崇尚明智 to esteem wisdom
—→ 敬重明智的人 to value intelligent men

22. 也者　【助詞】用在主語後表示提頓，引出下面的解釋
yě zhě 　文字
When the modal expression "也者" follows a subject, it expresses a tone of reflective caesura which serves to focus attention on the subject or topic of the sentence while anticipating the explanatory remarks immediately following it. This tone can sometimes be expressed in English by such introductory phrases as, "as for..." or "as to..."

◆ 提頓 tídùn 　　to mention with a pause

23. 舉 jǔ 　　【動詞】推舉；推薦　to recommend

24. 賢 xián 　　【形容詞】有道德、有才能　virtuous and talented

【名詞】有道德、有才能的人　men of virtue and talent

舉賢
jǔ xián 　　【動詞語】推舉賢人；推舉有道德、有才能的人
LITERALLY: "to raise up the worthy"; to put forward worthy men; to select people of virtue and talent

25. 任 rèn 　　【動詞】任命；任用　to appoint; to employ

26. 白 bái 　　【動詞】稟 (bǐng) 告　to report to one's superior

27. 說 yuè 　　【形容詞】同"悅"，高興　the word "說" is interchangeable with the word "悅" here: pleased; happy

大說
dà yuè 　　【形容詞語】大悅；非常高興　very pleased

◆ 形容詞語　　　an adjectival phrase
xíngróngcíyǔ

28. 以 yǐ 　　【介詞】因　because [of it]; thereby

29. 治 zhì 　　【動詞】治理　to govern; to put in order

【形容詞】治理得好；太平　well-governed; peaceful

30. 則 zé 　　【連詞】倒〔是〕，表示姑且承認一件事情，預備下句指出問題或缺點
...is..., [but]...; a conjunction used to express provisional acceptance of what it connects so as to point out a problem or drawback with it in the following clause. It is used in a sentence pattern analogous to: "Fair is fair, but this is going too far!" in English.

31. 似 sì 　　【準繫詞】像　to be like; to be similar to

◆ 準繫詞   a pseudo-copula (linking verb)
zhǔnxìcí

[Note: a pseudo-copula functions in a sentence like a copula (e.g., to be), but does not have all the grammatical characteristics of a copula.

32. 此 cǐ   【指示代詞】這 this

33. 類 lèi   【名詞】種類 kind; type; sort

成語

郢書燕說 Yǐngshū Yānshuō

LITERALLY: "The letter of Yǐng [and] the explanation of Yān" -- to draw a forced analogy or to make a farfetched interpretation

比喻牽強附會(qiānqiǎngfùhuì)的解釋－－把沒有這種意思的話硬說成有這種意思的解釋

This metaphor is now used to characterize a distorted interpretation or a forced analogy used to make something accord with one's own ideas or views.

第十四課

狐假虎威

注解

1. 狐 hú 　　【名詞】狐狸 a fox

2. 假 jiǎ 　　【動詞】借 to borrow; to make [unauthorized] use of

3. 虎 hǔ 　　【名詞】老虎 a tiger

4. 威 wēi 　　【名詞】威風；強大的、使人畏懼的力量
　　　　　　power and prestige; awesome power and influence

5. 求 qiú 　　【動詞】尋(xún)求；尋找 to look for; to seek

6. 獸 shòu 　　【名詞】四足、全身生毛的哺乳動物；[野生]動
　　　　　　物 four-footed, hairy, and mammal creatures; [wild] animal

　　百獸 　　【名詞語】各種[野生]動物 all kinds of [wild] animals
　　bǎi shòu

7. 食 shí 　　【動詞】吃 to eat

8. 敢 gǎn 　　【助動詞】敢 dare

9. 天帝 　　【名詞】上帝 the Lord-on-high; the emperor of Heaven
　　tiān dì 　　　　　老天爺(yé) Heaven

10. 長 zhǎng 　　【名詞】領導人；領袖(xiù) a leader

　　　　　　【用作動詞】領導 to lead
　　　　　　　　做領袖 to be the leader [of]

長百獸　【動詞語】領導百獸 to lead the various wild animals
zhǎng bǎi shòu　　做百獸的領袖；做各種動物的領袖
to be the leader of the various wild animals

11. 今 jīn　【時間詞】現在 [要是]　now; [if] now; now [if]
[Note: this word can sometimes have a suppositional as well as a temporal meaning, although the suppositional meaning is implied and can only be understood from the context]

12. 是 shì　【指示代詞】同 "此"，這；這個；這樣　here, the same as "此", this; this one; this way

13. 逆 nì　【動詞】違背 to go against; to disobey; to contravene

14. 命 mìng　【名詞】命令 command; order; mandate

15. 以 yǐ　【介詞】用；拿；此處應譯作 "把" to take; here it functions like the word "把" in colloquial Chinese

16. 為 wéi　【動詞】作為；當作 to regard as; to consider [to be]

17. 信 xìn　【形容詞】信實；誠實 honest; trustworthy; of good faith

18. 為 wèi　【介詞】為；給；替 for; on behalf of

19. 先 xiān　【名詞】時間或位置在前的，與 "後" 相對
In a series of things or sequence of events, "先" refers to those which occur first in order or in time; it is used in contradistinction to "後", which refers to those that follow in order or time. (See L. 11, no. 19, p.41)

【副詞】在前面 in front of; ahead of; before

20. 行 xíng　【動詞】走 to walk

21. 隨 suí　【動詞】跟隨 to follow

22. 後 hòu   【名詞】指與前相對的方位；後面
                   the back (as opposed to the front) of something
                   (*See L. 11, no. 19, p.41*)

                   【副詞】在後面 behind

23. 觀 guān   【動詞】看   to see; to observe

24. 走 zǒu   【動詞】逃跑 to flee

25. 乎 hū   【助詞】用在句末，表示疑問或反問，相當於白
                   話中的"嗎？"
                   When it appears at the end of a sentence, the particle "乎"
                   expresses an interrogative or rhetorical tone; it is roughly
                   equivalent to the colloquial Chinese question word "嗎？"

26. 也 yě   【助詞】出現在複合句前一個分句的後面，表示
                   停頓的語氣，用來引起下文，可譯成"啊"
                   When the particle "也" appears at the end of the first clause of a
                   compound sentence, it expresses a tone of reflective caesura which
                   is intended to mark the transition to the text immediately following
                   it. This tone can be expressed in spoken Chinese by the word
                   "啊". In English, somtimes "filler words" like "so" serve the
                   same function in a sentence.

27. 以為   【動詞】認為；覺得 to regard; to consider [to be]
    yǐ wéi

28. 與 yǔ   【介詞】跟 together with

29. 皆 jiē   【副詞】都 all

30. 畏 wèi   【動詞】畏懼 (jù)；害怕；怕 to fear; to be afraid of

31. 也 yě   【助詞】用在敘述句句末，表示確認一種事實或
                   情況，使聽的人信服，含有指示兼誇張的語氣。
                   白話中可譯成"吶"。 A particle used at the end of a
                   narrative sentence, expressing an acknowledgement of a certain
                   fact or situation, so as to convince the listener. It usually carries

58

an indicative and exaggerative tone. It can be rendered intro spoken Chinese as "呐".

成 語

狐假虎威　　húijiǎhǔwēi

LITERALLY: "The fox borrows the tiger's awesomeness."

比喻倚仗別人的勢力來欺壓 (qīyā)人。

This proverb is akin to the English saying "an ass in a lion's skin." It is used as a metaphor to describe situations where one person relies upon associations with powerful and influential people to bully or cheat the weak and defenseless.

第十五課
攫金

注解

1. 攫 jué 【動詞】奪取 (duóqǔ)；搶 (qiǎng)
to take by force; to snatch; to grab

2. 金 jīn 【名詞】金子 gold

3. 欲 yù 【動詞】想要 to desire; to long for; to lust after

欲金者 【名詞語】想要金子的人
yù jīn zhě one who desires or lusts after gold

4. 清 qīng 【形容詞】清爽 (shuǎng) refreshing; exhilarating

5. 旦 dàn 【時間詞】天明；早晨 dawn; morning

清旦 【時間詞】天剛亮時；清晨；清早 early in the
qīng dàn morning; bright and early in the morning

6. 衣 yī 【名詞】衣服 clothes

yì 【用作動詞】穿衣服 to put on clothes

7. 冠 guān 【名詞】帽子 a cap; a hat

guàn 【用作動詞】戴 (dài) 帽子 to put on a cap

8. 適 shì 【動詞】往；到…去 to go to [a place]
此處：至；到達；到了
to reach; to arrive [at]

9. 鬻 yù 【動詞】賣 to sell

60

鬻金者　【名詞語】賣金子的人　one who sells gold
yù jīn zhě

10. 所 suǒ　【名詞】處所；地方　a location; a place

11. 因 yīn　【副詞】於是；就　thereupon; see L.3, note 13
此處：即刻 forthwith; straightaway

12. 去 qù　【動詞】離開　to leave　to run away
跑走；跑了 to run away

13. 吏 lì　【名詞】低級的官吏；小官 an official of low rank
此處：警(jǐng)官 a police officer; a constable

14. 捕 bǔ　【動詞】捉；逮(dǎi)　to catch; to arrest

捕得　【動詞語】捉到；逮著　to have caught
bǔ dé

15. 問 wèn　【動詞】問　to ask; to question

16. 焉 yān　【指示代詞】等於"於是"，"是"指代處所
The word "焉" is equivalent in meaning to "於是" [at the place
in question], where "是" refers to a location.

17. 見 jiàn　【動詞】看見　to see

18. 徒 tú　【副詞】只　only

相關成語

利令智昏　　lílìngzhìhūn

LITERALLY: "Profit makes wisdom dimwitted."

金錢私利使頭腦發昏(變得很糊塗)以致什麼不合理或違
法的事都敢做。

The desire for gain or profit can turn even a wise man into a dimwit. This
proverb is used as a metaphor to describe someone who is blinded by the lust
for gain or befuddled by greed to the point of being willing to do virtually
anything to satisfy it.

第十六課

君子慎所藏

注解

1. 君子
   jūnzǐ
   【名詞】品德高尚的人　a man of high moral character; a perfect or true gentleman; a man of virtue

2. 慎 shèn
   【形容詞】慎重；小心
   cautious; careful; prudent; circumspect

3. 所 suǒ
   【代詞】指代地方、人、或事物　a relative pronoun that can refer to people, places, or things (*See sentence analysis*)

   【指示詞】那個　a demonstrative pronoun meaning these; those; this; that

4. 藏 cáng
   【動詞】隱藏　to conceal; to hide
   此處：指藏身、居住
   here it means to keep oneself; to dwell

   所藏
   suǒ cáng
   【動詞語】藏身之地；居住之地
   the place of keeping; the place of living;
   here it means where one lives

5. 孔子
   Kǒng zǐ
   【名詞】(551 - 479 B.C.) 姓孔，名丘 (Qiū)，字仲尼 (Zhòngní)，春秋時代魯國人。創立儒家學派，提倡仁愛的道理。他的學說影響深遠，至今還廣受尊崇，世世代代的人都稱他為 "至聖 (shèng) 先師。"
   Kǒng Qiū (551 - 479 B.C.) (known also by his courtesy name Zhòngní) was a man from the state of Lǔ who lived during the Spring and Autumn period. He founded the Confucian School, which advocated and promoted the doctrine of benevolence. His thought has had a profound and far-reaching influence, and his teachings are widely accepted and revered throughout East Asia even today. For generations, he has been known as "the greatest sage and teacher".

6. 視 shì　　【動　詞】看　to look at; to observe or inspect

7. 友 yǒu　　【名　詞】朋友　a friend

　　　　　　　【動　詞】結交　to associate with; to befriend

　所友　　　【名詞語】結交的人；結交的朋友
　suǒ shǐ　　　　　　　the person whom one befriends

8. 君 jūn　　【名　詞】君主　a sovereign; a monarch; a ruler

9. 使 shǐ　　【動　詞】派遣 (pàiqiǎn)；差遣　to dispatch

　所使　　　【名詞語】派遣的人
　suǒ shǐ　　　　　　　the person whom one dispatches; the emissary

10. 善 shàn　　【形容詞】善良；好　virtuous; good

　善人　　　【名詞語】善良的人；好人　a kind-hearted and
　shàn rén　　benevolent fellow; a good person

11. 居 jū　　【動　詞】居住　to reside; to dwell; to live [in]

12. 如 rú　　【準繫詞】如同；像；好像是 to be similar; to be like

13. 蘭 lán　　【名　詞】一種香草　a kind of fragrant grass; fragrant
　　　　　　　thoroughwort; orchid

14. 芝 zhī　　【名　詞】一種香草　a kind of fragrant herb; a kind of
　　　　　　　purplish fungus symbolizing nobility

15. 室 shì　　【名　詞】屋子　a room

蘭芝之室【名詞語】充滿蘭芝芳香的屋子，比喻清潔的地
lán zhī zhī shì　方、良好的環境或品德高尚的人聚集的場所
　　　　　LITERALLY: a room suffused with the natural fragance of sweet-
　　　　　scented herbs and grasses. This phrase is a metaphor for a very

clean place, a morally uplifting environment, or a gathering place for virtuous individuals.

16. 久 jiǔ　　【副詞】時間長；長久　for a long time

17. 聞 wén　　【動詞】用鼻子嗅 (xiù)　to smell

18. 香 xiāng　　【名詞】香氣；香味儿　fragrance

19. 則 zé　　【副詞】就 [是]　then [it is...]

20. 化 huà　　【動詞】變化；[無形中] 改變
　　　　　　　　to change; to change [imperceptibly]

◎ 薰染 xūn rǎn　　【動詞】薰之使有香，染之使有色　to fumigate and make aromatic, to dye and make colorful
薰陶 (xūn táo) 習染 (rǎn)；耳濡 (rú) 目染；長期接觸的人、事物、或環境對生活習慣逐漸產生某種影響
to exert a gradual uplifting or degrading influence on one's habits and lifestyle through prolonged association or contact with persons, things, and/or one's environment

21. 惡 è　　【形容詞】邪惡；不善良；壞　malevolent; evil; bad

惡人 è rén　　【名詞語】邪惡的人；壞人
　　　　　　　a malevolent person; a miscreant

22. 鮑魚 bào yú　　【名詞】醃 (yān) 魚；鹹 (xián) 魚　salted fish

23. 肆 sì　　【名詞】市場　marketplace；鋪子　a store; a shop

鮑魚之肆 bào yú zhī sì　　【名詞語】賣鹹魚的市場，比喻髒臭的地方、惡劣的環境或小人聚集的場所
LITERALLY: a market for salted fish. This is a metaphor for a filthy place, a bad or objectionable environment, or a gathering place for small-minded persons of ill repute.

65

24. 丹 dān 【名詞】丹砂 (shā) cinnabar
朱紅色 cinnabar red; vermillion

【形容詞】朱紅 vermillion

25. 藏 cáng 【動詞】儲 (chǔ) 藏；收藏 to keep

所藏者 【名詞語】儲藏的那個東西 those things kept
suǒcángzhě

26. 赤 chì 【形容詞】紅 bright red; scarlet

【動詞】變紅 to turn red; to redden

27. 烏 wū 【名詞】烏黑色 raven black

【形容詞】烏黑 raven black

28. 黑 *hè*, hēi 【形容詞】黑 black

【動詞】變黑 to turn black; to blacken

相關諺語

近朱者赤，近墨者黑 jìnzhūzhěchì-jìnmòzhěhè

LITERALLY: "He who nears vermillion becomes red; he who nears ink becomes black."

比喻接近好人使人變好，接近壞人使人變壞。

This proverb is used as a metaphor that means good companions have a beneficial influence, while bad ones have a deleterious influence.

◆ 諺語 *yànyǔ*   a proverb; a saying

第十七課

刻舟求劍

注解

1. 刻 kè　　【動詞】刻　to cut; to carve; to notch

2. 舟 zhōu　　【名詞】船　a boat; a ship
　　　　　此處：船邊；船舷 (xián)
　　　　　the side of a boat

3. 求 qiú　　【動詞】尋 (xún) 求；尋找；找　to look for; to search for

4. 劍 jiàn　　【名詞】劍　a sword

5. 涉 shè　　【動詞】渡 (dù)；過　to cross [a river by boat]; to ford

6. 江 jiāng　　【名詞】河　a river

7. 自 zì　　【介詞】從　from

8. 墜 zhuì　　【動詞】掉　to fall; to drop

9. 遽 jù　　【副詞】急速；趕緊　at once; forthwith; immediately

10. 契 qì　　【動詞】刻；刻〔記號〕　to carve out; to cut [a notch]

11. 是 shì　　【指示代詞】此；這裡　here; it is equivalent to the word
　　"此" (this [place]).

12. 從 cóng　　【介詞】從　from

13. 行 xíng　　【動詞】走　to move ahead

移 (yí) 動 to move

14. 若 ruò 　　　【準繫詞】像是　to be like

15. 此 cǐ 　　　【指示代詞】這樣　this

若此 　　　【準繫詞語】像這樣 to be like this
ruò cǐ
　　　　　　【用作副詞】像這樣 like this

16. 惑 huò 　　　【形容詞】糊塗　dim-witted; addle-brained

17. 乎 hū 　　　【助詞】嗎　an interrogative particle

成語

刻舟求劍 kèzhōuqiújiàn

LITERALLY: "To notch the boat in order to find the sword."

比喻牢守一種方法，不知情況已經發生變化。形容固執
(gùzhí)不通，用愚蠢(yúchǔn)的方法做事。

To cut a notch on the side of the boat to indicate where a sword fell into the
river in order to be able to know where to look for it later. This is a metaphor
for holding tenaciously to a certain way of thinking or of doing things no
matter how illogical or senseless it may be, for being stubbornly set in one's
ways, and for doing things in a very stupid, clumsy way.

第十八課

和氏之璧

注解

1. 氏 shì 【名詞】姓 a surname; a family name

   和氏 【名詞語】姓和的人 a man surnamed Hé
   Hé shì

2. 璧 bì 【名詞】平而圓、中心有孔／洞的玉 a round flat piece of jade with a hole in its center

3. 得 dé 【動詞】獲得； to obtain
   此處：發現；得到 to get; to have gotten

4. 玉璞 【名詞語】含著玉的石頭
   yù pú a stone containing [a piece of] jade [inside it]

5. 奉 fèng 【動詞】兩手捧著 to hold up with both hands (to show respect); to offer to a superior

6. 獻 xiàn 【動詞】恭敬地把東西送給人 to present respectively

7. 厲王 【名詞】姓芈 (Miē)，名熊眴 (Xióngxuàn) King Lì of Chǔ
   Lì wáng (r. 758 - 741 B.C.)

8. 使 shǐ 【動詞】命令 to order or command

9. 玉人 【名詞】玉匠；切開玉璞、雕琢玉、用玉作器物
   yù rén 的工人 a jade worker; an artisan who cuts open stones containing jade, carves and polishes jade, and makes implements or objects of jade

10. 相 xiàng 【動詞】仔細看、估定價值；鑑 (jiàn)定 to examine carefully and assess the value of [something]; to appraise

11. 石 shí 【名詞】石頭 a stone

12. 誑 kuáng 【動詞】欺騙 to cheat; to deceive

　　　　　　　【名詞】騙子 a liar

13. 刖 yuè 【動詞】砍斷腳 to cut off the foot [as a punishment]

14. 薨 hōng 【動詞】古代稱侯王死為薨 to die (said of a feudal lord)

15. 武王
　　Wǔ wáng 【名詞】姓羋 (Miē)，名熊通 (Xióngtōng)，厲王之弟
　　　　　　　King Wǔ of Chǔ (r. 740 - 690 B.C.)

16. 即 jí 【動詞】就；到…去 to go to [a place]

17. 位 wèi 【名詞】王位；君位 here: the throne

　　即位
　　jí wèi 【動詞語】到君位上去；登上君位；做君主
　　　　　　to accede to the throne; to take the throne; to become the ruler

18. 文王
　　Wén wáng 【名詞】姓羋 (Miē)，名熊貲 (Xióngzī)，武王之子
　　　　　　　King Wén of Chǔ (r. 689-675 B.C.)

19. 乃 nǎi 【副詞】就；於是 then; thereupon

20. 抱 bào 【動詞】用手臂圍住；抱著
　　　　　　　to hold in the arms; to cradle

21. 淚 lèi 【名詞】眼淚 tears

22. 盡 jìn 【動詞】完；光 to exhaust; to have consumed entirely

23. 繼 jì 【動詞】繼續 to continue

24. 奚 xī 【疑問副詞】何；為什麼 why

25. 悲 bēi 【形容詞】悲痛；傷心 grieved

70

【動詞】悲痛 to grieve

26. 非 fēi 　【副詞】用在動詞、形容詞之前，表示對行為、動作和性質、狀態的否定，可譯成“不”
used before a verb or an adjective to negate the following predicate, it functions like the adverb "not."

27. 夫 fú 　【助詞】表感嘆，可譯成“啊！”
an exclamatory particle that can be rendered "啊" in spoken Chinese, and it is analogous to "oh!" in English.

28. 寶 bǎo 　【形容詞】寶貴 precious

　　寶玉 　【名詞語】寶貴的玉
　　bǎoyù 　　　　　　　　a valuable piece of jade

29. 題 tí 　【動詞】題名 to label
　　　　　　稱…作；給…起名字叫…
　　　　　　to give a name to ...

30. 貞 zhēn 　【形容詞】忠誠正直 loyal and upright
　　　　　　有操守　　virtuous

　　貞士 　【名詞語】忠誠正直的人 a loyal upright man
　　zhēn shì 　　　　　有操守的人　　a man of virtue/integrity

31. 名 míng 　【動詞】命名 to name
　　　　　　給…取名叫… to give a name to ...

32. 理 lǐ 　【動詞】治玉；切開、磨光玉；把玉切開、磨光 to work [jade]; to cut and polish jade

33. 焉 yān 　【指示代詞】於是；在那兒；從那兒
in it; from it (here: from the stone) See Lesson 15, no.16

34. 命 mìng 　【動詞】命名；取名；叫…名字作…；給…取名叫… to name...; to make up a name for [something/someone]

第十九課

東周欲為稻

注解

1. 東周
Dōng Zhōu

【名詞】周朝自 (441 B.C.) 起分為東西二君。東周的首都是下都，在洛陽的東邊。傳至 (249 B.C.)被秦國給消滅了。

After 441 B.C. the territory of the ancient kingdom of Zhōu was divided between two rulers: the king in the east ruled the Eastern Zhōu, with its capital at Xiàdū, east of Luòyáng. The Eastern Zhōu kingdom was vanquished and annexed by the state of Qín in 249 B.C.

- ◆ 周朝 *Zhōucháo*   the Zhōu dynasty
- ◆ 首都 *shǒudū*   capital city
- ◆ 消滅 *xiāomiè*   to exterminate; to vanquish [of states]

2. 欲 yù
【動詞】想要 to desire; to long for

3. 為 wéi
【動詞】做 to do; to make
此處：種 to plant

4. 稻 dào
【名詞】稻子
rice, especially rice grown in flooded paddy fields

5. 西周
Xī Zhōu

【名詞】周考王 (r. 440 - 431 B.C.) 在 441 B.C. 封他的弟弟揭 (Jiē) 為河南公，也稱西周君。首都在洛陽。傳至 （255 B.C.）被秦國給消滅了。

In 441 B.C., King Kǎo of Zhōu (r. 440-431 B.C.) installed his younger brother, Jiē, as the Duke of Hénán; also known as "The Lord of the Western Zhōu," he was the first ruler of the Western Zhōu kingdom, which made Luòyáng its capital city. In 255 B.C. the Western Zhōu kingdom was vanquished and annexed by the state of Qín.

6. 下 xià　　【名　詞】位置在低處 the lower place; the bottom

　　　　　　　【用 作 動 詞】　使⋯到低處去；使⋯下
　　　　　　　　　　　　　to make [something] go downward
　　　　　　　放下 to send down

　下水　　　　【動 詞 語】使水流下 to make the water flow down-
　xià shuǐ　　　　　　　　stream
　　　　　　　　　　　放水　to let the water go/flow downstream

7. 蘇子　　　　【名　詞】姓蘇，名秦，字季子，（317 B.C.卒）洛
　Sūzǐ　　　　陽人。戰國時代著名的縱橫家。

　　　　　　　Sū Qín (also known by his courtesy name Jìzǐ) [d. 317 B.C.], a
　　　　　　　native of Luòyáng, was one of the renowned political strategists of
　　　　　　　the Warring States period.

8. 君 jūn　　　【名　詞】君主；國君 the ruler; ruler of a state

9. 請 qǐng　　【表 敬 副 詞】表示請求的敬詞：請讓我⋯

　　　　　　　a polite expression used to introduce a request: 請讓我 "please
　　　　　　　let me ...."

　　　　　　　◆ 請求 qǐngqiú　　　to request

　　　　　　　◆ 敬詞 jìngcí　　　　a polite expression

10. 往 wǎng　【動　詞】到⋯去 to go to [a place]

11. 謀 móu　　【名　詞】計謀；計策 a scheme; a plan

12. 所以　　　【名 詞 語】用來⋯的方法；⋯的方法
　suǒyǐ　　　the means whereby [something can be done]; the way [to do
　　　　　　　something]

13. 富 fù　　　【形 容 詞】富足 rich; affluent

　　　　　　　【用 作 動 詞】使⋯富足 to make ...rich; to enrich

73

富東周　　【動詞語】使東周富足　to make the Eastern Zhōu rich; to
fù Dōng Zhōu　enrich the Eastern Zhōu kingdom

14. 民 mín　　【名詞】人民；老百姓　the people; the common people

15. 皆 jiē　　【副詞】都　all

16. 種 zhòng　　【動詞】種　to plant

17. 麥 mài　　【名詞】麥子　wheat

18. 無 wú　　【副詞】不　not

19. 他 tuō　　【代詞】別的　other

無他種　　【動詞語】不種別的　lit. nought else plant; do not plant
wú tuō zhòng　other [edible grains]

20. 若 ruò　　【連詞】假若；如果；要是　if; supposing

21. 害 hài　　【動詞】損害；傷害　to spoil; to injure

22. 不若　　【準繫詞語】不如
bú ruò　　　　　　　　not as good as...; can do no better than ...

23. 一 yī　　【名詞】一次　once; one time

24. 為 wèi　　【介詞】給；替　for

25. 病 bìng　　【動詞】損害　to harm; to damage

26. 必 bì　　【副詞】必定；一定　certainly

27. 奪 duó　　【動詞】奪取；搶奪　to take by force

奪之　　　　　【動詞語】搶奪它　to take it back by force
duó zhī
　　　　　　　　　　──→搶奪水　to take the water away by force
　　　　　　　　　　──→斷絕水源　to cut off the water at its source
　　　　　　　　　　──→停止放水　to stop letting the water flow down

28. 是　shì　　　【指示代詞】此　this

　　若是　　　　【準繫詞語】如此；像這樣　like this; in this way
　　ruò shì

29. 則　zé　　　【連詞】就　then

30. 令　lìng　　【動詞】命令；使　to command; to order

31. 一　yī　　　【副詞】完全　completely; totally

32. 仰　yǎng　　【動詞】仰仗；依賴；依靠　to look to [somebody for support]; to depend on

33. 受　hòu　　　【動詞】接受　to receive; to accept

34. 命　mìng　　【名詞】命令　a command; an order

35. 於　yú　　　【介詞】從　from

36. 善　shàn　　【應答詞】好，表示同意　excellent; a responding word used to express agreement or concurrence with someone

　　　　　　　　◆ 應答詞 yìngdácí　a responding word

37. 金　jīn　　　【名詞】金子；金錢　gold; money
　　　　　　　　　　此處：酬金　[monetary] reward; compensation

第二十課

結草報恩

注解

1. 結 jié 　　【動詞】打結　to tie a knot; to knot

2. 草 cǎo 　　【名詞】草　grass

結草
jié cǎo
【動詞語】把草結起來。把草打成結　to tie up [the tips of] grass; to tie grass into knots

Note: This phrase is sometimes understood to mean "to make ropes of grass"; but it can also be understood to mean to tie together the top part of tall grasses in order to obstruct the passage of men or horses and chariots.

3. 報 bào 　　【動詞】報答　to repay; to requite

4. 恩 ēn 　　【名詞】恩惠　a favor; grace; kindness

5. 左傳
Zuǒ zhuàn
【名詞】書名。是一本解釋《春秋》經義的書，周左丘明撰

LITERALLY: *Zuǒ's commentary*. This book is an exegetical commentary by Zuǒ Qiūmíng of the Zhōu dynasty on the *Spring and Autumn Annals* 《春秋》, a work traditionally said to have been edited by Confucius.

　　◆ 撰 *zhuàn*　　　　to write; to compile

6. 宣公
Xuāngōng
【名詞】魯國的君主，姓姬 (Jī) 名俀 (Tuǐ)，在位十八年。"宣" 是他的諡號。

The ruler of the state of Lǔ; his surname was Jī "姬" and his given name Tuǐ "俀". He ruled for 18 years and was given the posthumous title Xuān "宣"

　　◆ 諡號 *shìhào*　　　　a posthumous honorific title

宣公十五年　　the fifteenth year of Duke Xuān's reign: 594 B.C.
Xuāngōng shíwǔnián

7. 初 chū　　【副詞】起初，多用於追述往事時
originally; at first; at the outset; this word is often used to introduce a recounting of past events

8. 魏武子　　【名詞】姓魏，名犫 (Chóu)，春秋時代晉國的六
Wèi Wǔzǐ　　卿之一。"武"是他的諡號。
Wèi Chóu was one of the six chief prime ministers of the state of Jìn during the Spring and Autumn period. He was given the posthumous honorific title "Wǔ".

9. 嬖 bì　　【動詞】寵愛　to favor

嬖妾　　【名詞語】愛妾；寵愛的姨太太　a favorite concubine
bì qiè

10. 子 zǐ　　【名詞】孩子　child

11. 疾 jí　　【動詞】患病；生病　to be ill

12. 命 mìng　　【動詞】命令　to order; to instruct; to command

13. 顆 Kē　　【名詞】魏顆，魏武子的兒子
Wèi Kē, Wèi Wūzǐ's son.

14. 必 bì　　【副詞】必須；一定要　must; have to

15. 嫁 jià　　【動詞】出嫁；女子結婚
此處：把…嫁出去；讓…跟人結婚
to marry off (said of women only).

16. 是 shì　　【指示代詞】此；這個女人　this [one]; this woman

嫁是　　【動詞語】把這個女人嫁出去；把她嫁出去；
jià shì　　讓她跟別人結婚

77

to give this [woman] away in marriage [to someone]; to marry this [woman] to somebody

17. 病 bìng 【動詞】病勢轉重 to worsen (said of an illness); (to become) severely ill

疾病
jí bìng
【動詞語】病重；病得很重 to be severely ill; to become critically ill

18. 則 zé 【連詞】卻 on the contrary

19. 殉 xùn 【名詞】陪葬的人或物 a person or thing to be buried together with the deceased as part of the funeral offerings

20. 及 jí 【介詞】〔等〕到…〔的時候〕 when; at the time of ...

21. 卒 zú 【動詞】死 to die

22. 則 zé 【連詞】就 then

23. 亂 luàn 【形容詞】昏亂；神智不清 confused; not to be in one's right mind

24. 從 cóng 【動詞】聽從 to obey; to comply with

25. 治 zhì 【形容詞】神智清醒 to be in one's right mind

26. 輔氏
Fǔshì
【名詞】地名，春秋時代屬於晉國，在今陝西省 A place located in present day Shǎnxī province that belonged to the territory under the control of the state of Jìn during the Spring and Autumn period.

27. 役 yì 【名詞】戰役 a battle; an engagement

輔氏之役 【名詞語】在輔氏發生的戰役。左傳[魯]宣公十
Fǔshì zhī yì 五年："秦桓公伐晉，次於輔氏"

The battle at Fǔshì. This battle is recorded in the *Zuǒ's Commentary* under the 15th year of Duke Xuān. "In autumn, in the 7th month, Duke Huán of Qín invaded Jìn, and halted his army at Fǔshì." (Legge, *The Chūn Qiū with the Zuǒ Zhuàn*, p. 328).

◆ 秦桓公　　　　　the posthumous title of Duke Huán of Qín
　 Qín Huángōng　　(r.603-575 B.C.)

◆ 伐 *fá*　　　　　to attack; to invade

◆ 次 *cì*　　　　　to station troops; to halt one's army

28. 亢　*kàng*　　【動詞】攔阻 (lánzǔ)　 to block; to impede

29. 杜回　　　　　【名詞】人名，秦國的大力士　 a great military figure
　 Dù Huí　　　　　from the state of Qín.

30. 躓　*zhì*　　　【動詞】絆 (bàn)；走路時腳遇到阻礙 (zǔ aì) 碰上它
　　　　　　　　　to trip [on something]; to have one's foot bump into or catch on
　　　　　　　　　some obstacle while walking; to stumble.

31. 顛　*diān*　　【動詞】跌倒　 to fall; to tumble down.

　 躓而顛　　　　【動詞語】絆了一下就跌倒了　 to stumble and fall
　 zhì ér diān

32. 獲　*huò*　　　【動詞】俘 (fú)獲；捉住　 to capture

33. 夜　*yè*　　　【名詞】夜晚；夜裡　 the night

34. 夢　*mèng*　　【動詞】作夢；夢見　 to dream; to see
　　　　　　　　　[someone/something] in a dream

35. 余　*yú*　　　【代詞】我　 first person pronoun; I

36. 而　*ěr*　　　【代詞】同"爾"，你　 "而" has the same meaning as
　　　　　　　　"爾" here: second person pronoun; you

37. 婦人　　　　　【名詞】已婚女子；女人　 a married woman
　 fù rén

38. 先人　　　　【名詞】祖先　refering to one's ancestors as a group
xiān rén　　　　　　　此處：去世的父親 [your] deceased father

39. 治命　　　　【名詞語】神志清醒時的命令　an order given by
zhìmìng　　　someone while he is in his right mind

40. 是以　　　　【介詞語】以是；因此　because of that; for this reason
shì yǐ

　　　　　　　　◆ 介詞語　　　　a prepositional phrase
　　　　　　　　　jiecíyǔ

成語

結草報恩　　jiécǎobàoēn

LITERALLY: "Knot grass to repay a kindness"

把草打成結來報答恩惠

含意是死後報恩：說話的人表示感激 (gǎnjī) 到極點，若活著時不能報答恩惠，死後也要設法報答。

To repay a favor after death. This proverb is used as a metaphor for the sincerest expression of thanks and gratitude; it means a person is so grateful that even if he is unable to repay a kindness or favor while living, he will find a way to do so from beyond the grave.

第二十一課

歧路亡羊

注解

1. 歧 qí   【形容詞】分岔 (chà) 的 forked

               【名詞】岔路 forked paths

2. 路 lù   【名詞】道路 roads; paths

   歧路   【名詞語】岔路；從大路上分出來的小路 a path
   qí lù   branching out from the main road; a fork in th road; side roads;
               forked paths

3. 亡 wáng   【動詞】失去；丟 (diū) 掉；丟了 to lose; to have lost

4. 羊 yáng   【名詞】羊 a sheep

5. 列子   【名詞】戰國時代鄭 (Zhèng) 國人。姓列，名禦寇
   Lièzǐ   (Yùkòu)，哲學家。他的思想出於老子，跟莊周很相
            近，是道家第三位大師。歷來老莊并稱或莊列并
            稱。

            Lièzǐ (450?-375? B.C.) was a philosopher from the state of Zhèng
            who lived during the Warring States period. He was surnamed Liè
            and had the given name Yùkòu. His thought was based in the
            doctrines of Lǎozǐ and was similar to that of Zhuāng Zhōu. He
            was the third most important figure in the Taoist philosophical
            school, which has for centuries been referred to as either the school
            of "Lǎo and Zhuāng" or the school of "Zhuāng and Liè."

          ◆哲學家   a philosopher
           zhéxuéjiā

          ◆老子 Lǎozǐ   a philosopher; the founder and patriarch of
                       the Taoist school.

◆ 莊周 *Zhuāng Zhōu*　　a philosopher; the second most important figure in the Taoist school.

◆ 道家 *Dàojiā*　　the Taoist school of thought

◆ 歷來 *lìlái*　　since ancient times; for a long time

◆ 大師 *dàshī*　　a master

6. 楊子
   Yáng Zǐ

【名詞】戰國時代衛(wèi)國(今河北、河南的一部分)人，名朱，字子居，哲學家。他的書沒流傳下來，他的學說只能從《孟子》、《列子》中看到一部分。他主張"為我"；"拔一毛利天下而不為。"

Yáng Zhū was a philosopher from the state of Wèi (located in parts of present-day Hénán and Héběi provinces) who lived during the Warring States period. He is also known by his courtesy name Zǐjū. His works are no longer extant, and his doctrines can only be partially reconstructed from passages preserved in the *Mencius* and the *Lièzǐ*. He advocated the doctrine of "self-interest" (為我) and is famous for his remark, "Even if by plucking a single hair from my body I could benefit the whole world, I would not do it."

◆ 流傳 *liúchuán*　　to transmit or to be transmitted from person to person, or from generation to generation

◆ 學說 *xuéshuō*　　a theory; a doctrine

◆ 主張 *zhǔzhāng*　　to hold a view; to advocate

◆ 為我 *wèiwǒ*　　[to do something] for oneself

◆ 拔一毛 *bá yìmáo*　利天下 *lì tiānxià*　而不為 *ér bùwéi*　　Even if by plucking a single hair from my body I could benefit the whole world, I would not do it.

7. 鄰人
   lín rén

【名詞語】鄰居　neighbors; the people next door

8. 既 *jì*

【連詞】"既…又…"連用的時候，"既"表示兩種情況同時存在，或兩件事情同時進行
When it is used as a conjunction in the pattern "既…又…", the

82

word "既" indicates that two conditions or actions co-exist or are going on simultaneously. It functions here like the construction "both ... and [also] ..." does in English.

【副詞】已經　already

9. 率　shuài　【動詞】率領 (lǐng)；帶領　to lead; to bring

10. 黨　dǎng　【名詞】親屬 (shǔ)　relatives; family members

11. 請　qǐng　【動詞】請求　to request; to ask; to implore

12. 豎　shù　【名詞】童僕 (tóngpú)；小廝 (sī)；十幾歲的男用人　a house boy; a young male servant

13. 追　zhuī　【動詞】追趕　to pursue; to chase after

14. 嘻　xī　【感嘆詞】表示驚嘆，咦 (yí)　an interjection indicating surprise: Well! Hey!

15. 何　hé　【疑問副詞】為什麼　why

16. 眾　zhòng　【形容詞】眾多；多　many

17. 反　fǎn　【動詞】同 "返"，回來　Here it has the same meaning as the word "返": to return.

18. 獲　huò　【動詞】得到　to get; to obtain
　　　　　此處："找到" "to find"

19. 乎　hū　【助詞】表示疑問，相當於白話的 "嗎" 或 "呢"
A particle used to indicate an interrogative tone, it is roughly equivalent to the words "嗎" or "呢" in spoken Chinese.

20. 矣　yǐ　【助詞】用於句末表示情況改變或新情況發生了，相當於白話的 "了"

83

When it occurs at the end of a sentence, the particle "矣" usually indicates that a situation has changed or that a new state of affairs has come about: it functions like the word "了" in spoken Chinese. It can often be expressed by the perfect tense in English.

21. 奚 xī 【疑問副詞】何；為什麼 why

22. 中 zhōng 【名詞】中間；裡面；裡頭 within; inside of

23. 焉 yān 【助詞】用在敘述句句末，指示或強調當前的事實，不必翻譯

A particle used at the end of a narrative sentence to emphasize or draw attention to the present or existing situation described in the sentence. It need not be translated into spoken Chinese; here, it can be translated into English as "even" to express an emphatic tone.

24. 之 zhī 【動詞】往；到⋯去 to go to

25. 所 suǒ 【指示詞兼代詞】 a demonstrative word that can function both as an adjective and as a pronoun (see sentence analysis 9)

【代詞】指代地方、人、或事物 a relative pronoun that can refer to people, places, or things (see sentence analysis 9)

【指示詞】那個 a demonstrative pronoun meaning these; those; this; that

26. 所以 suǒ yǐ 【連詞】用如白話中的"所以"（詳見句析九）

A conjunction equivalent in meaning to the word "所以" in spoken Chinese; it is equivalent to "therefore" in English. (For more details, see sentence analysis 9)

27. 戚然 qī rán 【副詞】憂傷地；難過地 morosely; sadly

28. 容 róng 【名詞】臉色；臉上的神情 one's facial expression or demeanor

變容
biàn róng
【動詞語】改變了臉色；改變了臉上的神情
to change one's facial expression or demeanor

29. 言 yán
【動詞】說話 to speak

30. 移 yí
【動詞】移動；經過 to shift; to pass; to lapse

移時
yí shí
【動詞語】過了好一會儿 after some [considerable] time had passed;

【副詞】很久 for a long time

31. 竟 jìng
【動詞】終竟；窮盡 to end; to exhaust

竟日
jìng rì
【動詞語】終日；過完一天 throughout the day

【副詞】一整天 the entire day; for a whole day

成語

歧路亡羊 qílùwángyáng

LITERALLY: "Because there were too many forks in the road the sheep was lost."

因為岔路太多結果丟掉了羊。比喻一種學說的根本相同，發展到後來有很多不同的解釋，研究這種學說的人常常不小心迷失了方向，走上錯路。

This is a metaphor used to describe a situation where the basic precepts of a school of thought or a theory are later subjected to a variety of different interpretations. Confronted with this welter of conflicting interpretations, people studying the theory or doctrine not infrequently can lose their proper sense of direction and, if they are not careful, unwittingly go down the wrong path.

相關成語

誤入歧塗   wùrùqítú

不慎走上錯誤的道路

to erroneously go down the wrong path; this proverb can be used to describe how one who seeks truth is apt to get confused when confronted with too many choices.

被引進錯誤的道路

to be led astray; to misguidedly take the wrong path

第 二 十 二 課

揠苗

注解

1. 揠 yà 　【動詞】拔起 [一點兒]；往上拔 [一點兒] to pull upward [a bit]

2. 苗 miáo 　【名詞】剛長出來的稻或麥 seedlings of cereal crops; sprouts or shoots of rice or wheat

3. 閔 mǐn 　【動詞】憂慮 (yōulù)；擔心 to worry about; to be concerned about

4. 芒芒然 mángmáng rán 　【副詞】疲憊 (bèi) 地；疲倦 (juàn) 地；精疲力盡地 wearily; exhaustedly

5. 病 bìng 　【形容詞】非常疲乏；累 [壞] extremely tired; exhausted [to the point of collapse]

6. 矣 yǐ 　【助詞】用在形容詞後可加強語氣。相當於白話的"了啊"或"啦"

This particle is placed after an adjective to reinforce or intensify its meaning. It is equivalent to the words "了啊" or "啦" in spoken Chinese.

7. 予 yú 　【代詞】我 first person pronoun: "I"

8. 助 zhù 　【動詞】幫助 to aid; to help

9. 趨 qū 　【動詞】很快地走 to go quickly; to hasten; to hurry along 此處：跑 to run

10. 往 wǎng 　【動詞】到…去 to go to [a place]

11. 則 zé　【連詞】卻；原來已經 (表示出乎意料之外，沒想到) however; on the contrary (it indicates that what follows is unexpected or unanticipated)

12. 槁 gǎo　【形容詞】枯；乾枯 withered

13. 矣 yǐ　【助詞】用於句末表示情況改變或新情況發生了，相當於白話的 "了"

A final particle equivalent in meaning here to the word "了" at the end of a sentence in spoken Chinese; it indicates (among other things) a change of situation or that some new condition or state of affairs now pertains.

14. 天下 tiānxià　【名詞語】天下的人；世界上的人 "[all the people] under heaven"; all the people in the world; the whole world

15. 寡 guǎ　【形容詞】少 few

16. 益 yì　【名詞】利益；好處 advantage

17. 舍 (捨) shě　【動詞】放棄；丟下不管 to abandon; to throw away and pay no heed to

18. 耘 yún　【動詞】除去田裡的野草 to weed [a field]

19. 非徒 fēi tú　【副詞】不僅；不但 not only

20. 又 yòu　【副詞】還；更 also; moreover

21. 害 hài　【動詞】傷害 to injure; to harm

22. 之 zhī　【代名詞】它 it /them (the pronoun here refers back to the sprouts)

88

成語

揠苗助長　　yàmiáozhùzhǎng

LITERALLY: "To pull up the seedling, hoping to make it grow faster"

逐字譯成白話是：把苗拔高一點儿，幫助它長

比喻違反事物的發展規律，急於求成，反而壞事。

This metaphor is used to describe a situation in which a person disregards something's natural or intrinsic pace of growth or development and as a result of excessive enthusiasm to bring the matter to a speedy resolution, on the contrary, ruins everything.

第二十三課

燕人

注解

1. 燕 Yān 【名詞】國名 The name of a state (*see L. 12, no. 6, p. 46*)

2. 生 shēng 【動詞】出生 to be born

3. 長 zhǎng 【動詞】長大 to grow up

4. 楚 Chǔ 【名詞】國名 the name of a state (*see L. 7, no. 3, p. 24*)

5. 及 jí 【介詞】至；到 to reach (*see L. 10, no. 23, p. 36*)

6. 老 lǎo 【形容詞】年老 aged; old

   及老 jí lǎo 【介詞語】等到老了〔的時候〕 upon reaching old age; when he was old

7. 還 huán 【動詞】回 to return to

8. 本 běn 【形容詞】本來的；一個人自己的 original; one's own...

   本國 běn guó 【名詞語】他自己本來的國家；家鄉；老家 one's native country; one's homeland

9. 晉 Jìn 【名詞】國名 the name of a state (*see L. 9, no. 3, p. 32*)

10. 同 tóng 【副詞】共同；一起 together

11. 行 xíng 【動詞】走 to walk; to travel

同行者　【名詞語】一起走的人　a fellow traveller
tóng xíng zhě

12. 誑　kuáng　【動詞】騙；欺騙　to cheat; to trick; to deceive

13. 指　zhǐ　【動詞】指　to point at; to be pointing at

14. 城　chéng　【名詞】城市；城牆　a city; a city wall
(LITERALLY: the four walls of a city and the area that they enclose)

15. 愀然　【副詞】很難過地；怏怏不樂地　glumly
qiǎo rán

16. 容　róng　【名詞】臉上的神情　facial expression; demeanor

變容　【動詞語】改變臉色；改變臉上的神情
biàn róng　　　　to change one's facial expression

17. 若　ruò　【人稱代詞】第二人稱代詞；你或你的
a second person pronoun; you or your

18. 里　lǐ　【名詞】古代一種居民組織，先秦以二十五家為里，後來泛指村莊、鄉里
Originally, in pre-Qín times, this term referred to a neighborhood of 25 families; later it came to be used as a generic term for local communities: a village

19. 社　shè　【名詞】土地廟　an altar to the local god of the soil

20. 喟　kuì　【動詞】嘆息　to sigh

喟然　【副詞】嘆息地　sighingly
kuì rán　　此處：傷感地；悲哀地
heavy-heartedly; wistfully

21. 嘆　tàn　【動詞】嘆氣　to sigh

91

22. 舍 shè 【名詞】房屋；房子 a house; a building

23. 先人 xiān rén 【名詞】祖先 one's ancestors

24. 廬 lú 【名詞】茅(máo)廬；茅舍 a rustic dwelling
茅草頂的房子 a cottage; a thatched hut

25. 涓 xuàn 【動詞】通"泫"：流淚 to shed tears

涓然 xuàn rán 【副詞】簌簌地 (sùsù.dē)；眼淚紛紛 (fēn) 落下地
streaming; in a stream (said of tears); in rivulets

26. 壠 lǒng 【名詞】墳堆；墳墓 tumuli
Note: This word was a dialectical variant for "塚" and was used at that time in the region controlled by the states of Qín and Jìn.

27. 塚 zhǒng 【名詞】墳墓 grave mounds

28. 禁 jīn 【動詞】抑(yì)制；克(kè)制 to restrain [oneself]
停止 to stop

不自禁 bú zì jīn 【動詞語】[自己]克制不住自己；止不住自己
cannot stop [doing something]; cannot stop oneself from [doing something]

29. 啞然 è rán 【副詞】哈哈大笑地 "guffaw-like"; an onomatopoetic adverb used to express the sound of boisterous laughhter

30. 昔 xī 【時間詞】從前 generally this word means "in the past"
此處：剛才 here it means: "just now."

31. 紿 dài 【動詞】欺騙；騙 to cheat; to deceive; to trick

32. 耳 ěr 【助詞】而已；只不過…罷了 an elided form of
"而已"：simply; only; nothing more than

33. 慚 cán　　【形容詞】慚愧　[to feel] ashamed; [to be] mortified

34. 悲 bēi　　【形容詞】悲傷；悲痛　grief-stricken

　　悲心　　【名詞語】悲傷的心情；悲痛的心情
　　bēi xīn　　　　　　grief; feelings of grief

35. 更 gèng　　【副詞】更加　even (more, less)

36. 微 wēi　　【形容詞】輕微；微少　slight; tenuous

　　更微　　【形容詞】更輕微；輕微多了 slighter; even less [*than before*].
　　gèngwēi

93

第二十四課

畫蛇添足

注解

1. 畫 huà 　　【動詞】畫　to paint or draw [a picture]

2. 蛇 shé 　　【名詞】蛇　a snake

3. 添 tiān 　　【動詞】增 (zēng) 加；添上；加上　to add [on]

4. 足 zú 　　【名詞】腳　feet

5. 祠 cí 　　【動詞】祭祀 [神或祖先] to offer sacrifices [to the spirits or ancestors]

6. 賜 cì 　　【動詞】賞 (shǎng) 賜；賜給 (上級給下級或長輩給晚輩)　to bestow [upon]; to give (used only when someone of superior status gives something to someone of inferior status, or when someone of a senior generation gives something to someone of a junior generation.)

　　　◆ 上級 *shàngjí*　　the higher authorities; one's superiors

　　　◆ 下級 *xiàjí*　　[one's] subordinates or inferiors

　　　◆ 長輩 *zhǎngbèi*　　elders of a family; the older generation

　　　◆ 晚輩 *wǎnbèi*　　the juniors in a family; the younger generation

7. 舍人 shèrén 　　【名詞】門客
LITERALLY: "Gate guests"; also known as "retainers". In classical times, retainers, advisors, and consultants were maintained and housed at the expense of wealthy, influential persons, usually persons of rank, and were dependent on them for their livelihoods. By extension, the term came to include all kinds of hangers-on attached to the households of the aristocracy.

8. 巵 zhī 　【名詞】古時一種盛酒的圓形器皿；一種酒杯
a cylindrical vessel used for drinking wine; a beaker; a goblet

◆ 器皿 qìmǐn 　food containers, including plates, dishes, bowls, cups, etc.

9. 酒 jiǔ 　【名詞】酒　liquor; spirits; wine; brewed or distilled alcoholic beverages
Note: Wine made from the fermented juice of grapes was not known in classical times and was first introduced from Central Asia only in the Táng dynasty (609-960 A.D.)

巵酒
zhī jiǔ 　【名詞語】一杯酒　a beaker of spirits; a goblet of liquor

10. 數 shù 　【形容詞】幾　several

數人
shù rén 　【名詞語】幾個人　several persons

11. 飲 yǐn 　【動詞】喝　to drink

12. 足 zú 　【形容詞】夠　sufficient

不足
bù zú 　【形容詞語】不夠　insufficient; not enough

13. 餘 yú 　【名詞】剩 (shèng) 餘　the remains; the remainder

有餘
yǒu yú 　【動詞語】有剩餘　to have a surplus

　【形容詞語】太多　too much

14. 請 qǐng 　【表敬副詞】表示建議的敬詞：讓我們；讓咱們
a polite expression used to introduce a suggestion: "let us ...."

◆ 建議 jiànyì 　to suggest

15. 地 dì 　【名詞】土地；地面　the ground

95

畫地　【動詞語】畫[於]地；[在]地面上畫
huà dì　　　　　　　to draw ... on the ground

16. 為　wéi　【動詞】成為　to become; to turn into

17. 成　chéng　【動詞】完成；完　to complete; to finish

18. 引　yǐn　【動詞】拿過[來]　to draw [to oneself]; to take

19. 且　qiě　【副詞】將要　to be going to; to be about to

20. 乃　nǎi　【副詞】卻　but; however

21. 左　zuǒ　【形容詞】左邊的　the left [side]; on the left

22. 持　chí　【動詞】拿〔著〕；端〔著〕　to hold; holding

23. 右　yòu　【形容詞】右邊的　the right [side]; on the right

24. 未　wèi　【副詞】[還]沒有　not yet; still not

25. 奪　duó　【動詞】搶(qiǎng)奪；搶[走]
　　　　　　　　to take [by force]; to snatch [away]

26. 固　gù　【副詞】本來　originally (by nature); naturally

27. 安　ān　【疑問副詞】何；怎麼　how

28. 遂　suì　【副詞】於是；就　hereupon; then

29. 終　zhōng　【副詞】終於　finally; eventually; in the end

30. 亡　wáng　【動詞】失掉　to lose

成 語

畫蛇添足 huàshétiānzú

LITERALLY: "Draw a snake and add feet to it."

比喻做多餘的事 (不必做的事) 不但没有好處，反而有壞處

This proverb is used as a metaphor for doing something to excess (or doing more than is required) so that not only is no advantage gained, but may result in disadvantages instead.

第二十五課

濠梁之遊

注解

1. 濠 Háo 　　【名詞】水名，在今安徽省鳳陽縣附近

The name of a river located in present-day Ānhuī province near Fèngyáng district.

2. 梁 liáng 　　【名詞】橋 (qiáo) a bridge

濠梁 Háo liáng 　　【名詞語】濠水的橋 the bridge over the Háo River

3. 遊 yóu 　　【動詞】閒遊 to stroll

4. 莊子 Zhuāngzǐ 　　【名詞】姓莊，名周，戰國時代宋國蒙 (Méng) 縣（今河南省商邱縣）人。他認為世上無絕對的標準，反對人為的禮法制度，主張隨順自然，逍遙自適。與老子同為道家學派的宗師，著有《莊子》三十三篇。

Zhuāng Zhōu (365?-290 B.C.) was a man from the district of Méng in the state of Sòng (located in present-day Shāngqiū district of Hénán province). He held that there are no absolute standards in this world and denied the validity of such man-made prescriptions for social order as ritual, advocating instead that people should act with natural spontaneity and lead a carefree and easy-going life. He is, along with Laǒzǐ, considered to be one of the intellectual patriarchs of the Taoist school of thought. The *Zhuāngzǐ*, a work of 33 chapters, is attributed to him.

◆ 逍遙 *xiāoyáo*　　free and unfettered; carefree

◆ 自適 *zìshì*　　make oneself comfortable and at ease

◆ 道家 *Dàojiā*　　The Taoist school (a school of thought that flourished during the Spring and Autumn and the Warring States periods, 770 - 221 B.C.)

98

◆ 宗師 *zōngshī*   a master of great learning and integrity; a patriarch or founder of a school of thought

5. 惠子   【名詞】姓惠，名施(Shī)，戰國時宋國人，曾做過
　　Huìzǐ   梁國的相。他喜歡讀書，善於辯論，注重邏輯思
　　　　　　考，是中國思想史中名家的代表人物。他是莊子
　　　　　　的好友，也是他辯論的對手。

Huì Shī was a man from the state of Sòng who lived during the Warring States period; he once served as a councillor in the state of Liáng. He was fond of study, excelled in argument and emphasized the importance of logical thinking. In the history of Chinese thought, he is considered to be an exemplar of the School of Names (sometimes also called the School of Logicians). He was both Zhuāngzǐ's friend and his adversary in argument.

◆ 辯論 *biànlùn*   to argue; to debate

◆ 邏輯 *luójí*   logic

◆ 名家 *Míngjiā*   the School of Names (i.e., Logicians)

◆ 對手 *duìshǒu*   opponent (in a contest); adversary

6. 鰷 tiáo   【名詞】一種白色的小魚，也叫白鰷
　　　　　　minnow, a small white fish

7. 游 yóu   【動詞】動物在水裡游動；游泳　to swim

　　出游   【動詞語】浮出水面或在水中游動；時隱(yǐn)
　　chū yóu   時現地游動 to dart [in and] out of the water [while] swimming, appearing and disappearing as they swim

8. 從容   【副詞】不慌(huāng)不忙地 carefree and leisurely
　　cōng róng   此處：自由自在地
　　　　　　free and easy; leisurely and contentedly

9. 是 shì   【代詞】此；這 this

10. 樂 lè   【形容詞】快樂 happy

99

【名詞】快樂　happiness

11. 非 fēi　【否定繫詞】不是　is not; not to be

12. 安 ān　【疑問副詞】表示反問，怎麼…？　how; it is used to express a rhetorical question (i.e., how do you know this?).

【疑問代詞】代處所，何處；哪裡　it also means "where?" (i.e., where did you come to know this?)

安知
ān zhī　【動詞語】怎麼〔能〕知道　How do/can you know this?
於何處知？從哪裡知道　Where did you come to know this?

Note: It is intended to be ambiguous here.

13. 固 gù　【副詞】固然，表示先承認某種事實或看法，但是後面還要加以否定
indeed; admittedly (admitting a certain fact or opinion at first, yet denying it afterward.)

【副詞】本來　originally (by nature); naturally

14. 矣 yǐ　【助詞】用在句末表示堅信，或用在形容詞後加強語氣。相當於白話的"了啊"或"啦"
This particle is placed at the end of a sentence to show strong conviction or after an adjective to reinforce or intensify its meaning. It is equivalent to the words "了啊"or "啦" in spoken Chinese.

15. 全 quán　【形容詞】齊全；充足　complete; sufficient
此處：百分之百；毫無疑問
without doubt; absolutely sure

16. 循 xún　【動詞】順 (shùn) [著] to follow; to abide by

17. 本 běn　【名詞】根本　the root; the origin

其本
qí běn　【名詞語】它之根本；辯論的起點　the original issue; the beginning of the argument; the heart of the matter

100

18. 云 yún 　【助詞】用於分句的句末，表示停頓
　　　　　　　　a particle indicating a pause

19. 者 zhě 　【助詞】用於分句的句末，表示停頓
　　　　　　　　a particle indicating a pause

20. 既 jì 　【副詞】表示動作、行為、或狀況已經產生，可
　　　　　　　譯成"已經" an adverb used to indicate that an action, deed,
　　　　　　　or situation has already occurred; it is equivalent to "已經" in
　　　　　　　spoken Chinese and the verb that follows it generally should be
　　　　　　　translated in a perfect tense in English.

21. 已 yǐ 　【副詞】已經　already

　　既已　　【副詞】既已兩字連用，還是"已經"的意思
　　jì yǐ　　　　a compound adverb meaning "already"

22. 而 ér 　【連詞】才　then; only then

23. 濠上　　【名詞語】濠[梁]之上；濠水的橋上
　　Háoshàng　　　　on [the bridge over] the Háo River

宋　蘇軾　　觀魚臺詩
Sòng　Wū Shì　　Guān Yú Tái Shī

欲將同異論錙銖，肝膽猶能楚越如。

Yù jiāng tóng yì lùn zī zhū, gān dǎn yóu néng Chǔ Yuè rú.

若信萬殊歸一理，子能知我我知魚。

Ruǒ xìn wàn shū guī yì lǐ, Zǐ néng zhī wǒ wǒ zhī yú.

想要拿最細微的差別來討論同與不同，

Xiǎngyào ná zuì　xì.zhì .dē　chābié lái　tǎolùn tóng yǔ bù tóng,

肝膽還能像楚國越國一樣遠；

Gān dǎn háinéng xiàng Chǔguó Yuèguó yíyàng yuǎn;

要是相信萬種不同的物類回歸到同一個原理，

Yàoshì xiāngxìn Wànzhǒng Bùtóng .dē wùlèi　huíguī dào tóng　yígè　yuánlǐ,

您能了解我，我也能了解魚。

Nín néng liǎojiě wǒ,　wǒ yě néng liǎojiě yú.

Sòng　Sū Shì　　A Peom on the Fish-Observing Terrace

If you want to discuss similarities and differences in their minute detail,

Liver and gall-bladder then will seem as far apart as the states of Chǔ and Yuè.

If you believe that 10,000 distinctions all converge in one principle,

Then, you can understand me, and I understand fish.

第二十六課

齊桓公使管仲治國

注解

1. **齊桓公**
   Qí Huángōng

【名詞】人名 (r. 685-643 B.C.) 。姓姜 (Jiāng)，名小白，"桓"是他的諡號。春秋時代齊國的君主，在位四十二年，是五霸中的第一位。

Duke Huán of Qí (r. 685-643 B.C.) was surnamed Jiāng and had the given name Xiǎobái. Huán is his posthumous honorific title; this title is used when he is referred to in historical records. King of the state of Qí during the Spring and Autumn period, he reigned for 42 years and was the leader of the Five Hegemons who held real political and military power in the final years of the Zhōu dynasty.

◆ **諡號** *shìhào*   a posthumous honorific title

◆ **五霸** *wǔbà*   The Five Hegemons of the Spring and Autumn period:

齊桓公 (Qí Huángōng),

晉文公 (Jìn Wéngōng),

宋襄公 (Sòng Xiānggōng),

秦穆公 (Qín Mùgōng), and

楚莊王 (Chǔ Zhuāngwáng)

2. **使** shǐ

【動詞】命令 to order

3. **管仲**
   Guǎn Zhòng

【名詞】人名 (d. 644 B.C.)。姓管，名夷 (yí) 吾，字仲。春秋時代齊國的宰相，幫助齊桓公成就霸業。

Guǎn Zhòng (d. 644 B.C.) was surnamed Guǎn, had the given name Yíwú, and the courtesy name Zhòng. As chief councillor to the Duke of Qí during the Spring and Autumn period, he helped Duke Huán of Qí achieve the status of hegemon.

◆ **成就** *chéngjiù*   to achieve; to accomplish

103

◆ 霸業 *bàyè*   the enterprise of establishing oneself as a powerful hegemon among the feudal lords of the Spring and Autumn period.

4. 治 zhì   【動詞】治理；管理   to govern; to administer

【形容詞】治理得好；太平
well-governed; peaceful and orderly

治國
zhì guó   【動詞語】管理國政   to administer the affairs of state

5. 賤 jiàn   【形容詞】卑賤；地位低下；地位低
lowly; of low status

6. 臨 lín   【動詞】從高處往低處看 to look down from a high place towards a low place
此處：從上監視(jiān shì)下；統治
it also has the connotative sense of "supervising from above" or "to rule"; "to govern"

7. 貴 guì   【形容詞】顯貴；地位崇高；地位高   of high status; highly-placed; highly-ranked

8. 卿 qīng   【名詞】古代高級官名

A term used generically (or with particularizing prefixes) to refer to eminent officials. During the Zhōu dynasty, the "卿" comprised the highest ranked category of officials serving the king and the feudal lords. The term is generally translated into English as "minister" (Hucker, *Dictionary of official titles in imperial China*, p. 173).

上卿
shàng qīng   【名詞語】卿的第一級；地位最高的卿

a minister of the first grade; the minister holding the highest position; the chief minister

9. 貧 pín   【形容詞】貧窮；沒有錢   poor; impoverished

10. 使 shǐ   【動詞】使喚(shǐhuàn) to order [a person] about; to tell people to carry out orders

支使 (zhīshǐ)　to engage the services or labor of [someone]

差遣 (chāiqiǎn)　to dispatch or send [a person on an errand, etc.]

11. 市租　【名詞】市場的稅收　the revenue from taxes levied on
shì zū　　　　　　　　　　　　　commercial transactions

　　　　　　　　貨物稅　a commodity tax

12. 疏 shū　　【形容詞】疏遠　distant (said of familial or social relations)

13. 制 zhì　　【動詞】控制　to control

　　　　　　　約束 (yuēshù)　to restrain

14. 親 qīn　　【形容詞】親近　intimate; closely related; close

15. 立 lì　　【動詞】登上帝王或諸侯的位置
　　　　　　to be installed as [a king, etc.]; to ascend the throne
　　　　　　[said of a king or feudal lord]

　　　　　　此處：升登某一高位
　　　　　　here: to be raised up to a high position

16. 仲父　【名詞】春秋時代齊桓公對他的大臣管夷吾的尊
Zhòng fù　　稱。"仲"是夷吾的字，"父"的意思是像尊敬
　　　　　　父親一樣地尊敬他。

This polite form of address was used by Duke Huán of Qí when he spoke with his official Guǎn Yíwú (Guǎn Zhòng). "仲" was Guǎn Yíwú's courtesy name; the word "父" indicates that the Duke intended to show him the same degree of honor and respect that he would show his own father. This appellation can be translated as "Venerable Zhòng" or "Uncle Zhòng."

◆ 尊稱 zūnchēng　　a respectful form of address; honorific title

17. 大 dà　　【副詞】表示程度深；非常；極度　greatly; fully;
in a big way; on a large scale

18. 安 ān　　【形容詞】安定　stable

105

大安
dàān

【形容詞語】非常安定；非常太平
very peaceful; totally peaceful

19. 霸 bà　【名詞】諸侯的盟主；諸侯的領袖 a hegemon; a leader among the feudal lords during the Spring and Autumn Period

【動詞】稱霸；做諸侯的盟主；做諸侯的領袖
to be acknowledged as a hegemon; to head the alliance of the feudal lords; to lead the feudal lords

◆ 諸侯 zhūhóu　the feudal lords who nominally acknowledged the suzerainty of the king of the Zhōu dynasty

◆ 盟主 méngzhǔ　the leader of an alliance or covenant (among the feudal lords)

20. 賢 xián　【形容詞】有道德　virtuous; worthy
有才幹　capable; talented

21. 權 quán　【名詞】權力　power; authority
權勢　influence derived from holding high rank or an important position

22. 者 zhě　【助詞】表示假設的語氣，可譯成 “要是…[的話]”

Here the particle "者" expresses a subjunctive mood in the clause it is attached to; it can be translated into spoken Chinese as "要是 …[的話]" and into English as "if" or with the subjunctive mood of the verb. (cf. L. 36, no. 35, p. 152)

23. 亦 yì　【副詞】也　as well

24. 南 nán　【方向詞】南邊；南方　south; southern; the South

25. 面 miàn　【名詞】臉　face

【動詞】臉對著　to face [a certain direction]

106

南面
nán miàn

【動詞語】面南；面向南；臉對著南邊。古代君主的座位放在朝廷中的北邊，當君主坐著時，臉一定對著南邊，所以用"南面"比喻做君主，或做領袖。

LITERALLY: "to be facing south", or "to face the south".
In traditional China, the ruler's throne was placed at the northern end of the hall used for court audiences; and when the ruler sat on his throne, ritual prescribed that he sit facing the south. This term came to mean by extension "the one who is sitting facing south" and is used as a metaphor for a leader or ruler (or for leading and ruling).

26. 矣 yǐ

【助詞】用於句末表示理論上或事實上一定會產生的後果，可譯成"了"。

Here the particle "矣" is used to express a tone of certainty or conviction: it indicates that something will or must occur on the basis of the situation or principles described in the sentence.

第二十七課

知音

注解

1. 知 zhī 　【動詞】知曉 (xiǎo)；了解 to understand

2. 音 yīn 　【名詞】音律 the principle of music

知音
zhī yīn
【動詞語】a.知曉音律 to understand the principle of music
b.能從對方所彈奏出的樂聲中了解他的志趣並賞識他的才華 able to discern and comprehend the feelings and intents expressed in music and appreciate the talents of the performer

【名詞語】知音的人 one who understands music

⟶ 能從對方所彈奏出的樂聲中了解他的志趣並賞識他的才華的人 a person who is able to discern the feelings and intents expressed in music performed by someone and also appreciate his talents

⟶ 能從一個人的言語、作品中了解他的志趣並賞識他的才華的人 a person who is able to understand the purpose and interest of someone from what he says and writes, and thus apprecaite his talents

⟶ 志趣相同、彼此了解、互相賞識的人 friends who have the same ideal and inclination, thus understand and appreciate each other

3. 伯牙
Bó Yá
【名詞】春秋時代人。擅 (shàn) 長作曲，彈琴的技術非常精妙；是中國古代最著名的音樂家。

Bó Yá lived during the Spring and Autumn period. He excelled in composition and was wonderfully skilled at playing the lute; he is considered the most outstanding musician of ancient times.

4. 鼓 gǔ 　【動詞】彈奏 (tánzòu) to play [a musical instrument]

108

5. 琴 qín　　【名詞】樂器，有五弦或七弦
　　　　　　　　a Chinese lute having five or seven strings

6. 鍾子期　　【名詞】春秋時代楚國人。是中國歷史上最著名
　 Zhōng Zǐqī　的了解音律的人。

Zhōng Zǐqī was a man from the state of Chǔ who lived during the Spring and Autumn period. He is renowned in Chinese history for his understanding of the laws of harmonics.

7. 方 fāng　　【介詞】正在…[的時候] while; at the time when [an action is in progress]

8. 志 zhì　　【名詞】意念；心思　state of mind; intent; thought
　　　　　　《詩‧大序》："詩者，志之所之也。在心為志
　　　　　　，發言為詩。"——詩歌是意念去的地方。存在
　　　　　　心中時它是意念，用文字言語表達出來就是詩。

"Popetry is the product of earnest thought. Thought [chreished] in the mind becomes earnest; exhibited in words, it becomes poetry." (*Legge, Chinese Classics*, Vol. 4, p.34)

　　◆ 詩 Shī　　　　the *Book of Odes*, one of the five Confucian classics.

　　◆ 大序 Dàxù　　the Great Preface, appended to the first ode, believed to have been written down by a Han scholar on the basis of a long tradition.

9. 太山　　　【名詞】山名，也寫作"泰山"，是中國著名的
　 Tàishān　 五嶽(yuè)之一。相傳孔子登泰山而小天下 (孔子登
　　　　　　　上泰山的山頂，看到很遠的地方，覺得天下很
　　　　　　　小)，可以想像它有多麼高。

The name of a mountain, also written as "泰山". Mount Tài was one of the famous "five sacred peaks." It is said that Confucius ascended Mount Tài and thought all the world small (When Confucius reached the summit of Mount Tài and could see remote and distant places, and he felt that the world was small); from this one can imagine its great height.

　　◆ 五嶽 wǔyuè　　　the five sacred peaks

◆ 中嶽嵩山　　　　Mount Sōng, the central peak
　Zhōngyuè Sōngshān

◆ 東嶽泰山　　　　Mount Tài, the eastern peak
　Dōngyuè Tàishān

◆ 西嶽華山　　　　Mount Huà, the western peak
　Xīyuè Huàshān

◆ 南嶽衡山　　　　Mount Héng, the southern peak
　Nányuè Héngshān

◆ 北嶽恆山　　　　Mount Héng, the northern peak
　Běiyuè Héngshān

10. 善　shàn　　【形容詞】好；美妙　good; marvelous; superb

11. 哉乎　　　　【助詞】啊，表示讚歎 (zàntàn)　a particle combination
　zāi hū　　　used to express a tone of admiration, appreciation, or approbation

12. 巍巍　　　　【形容詞】山勢高大雄偉的樣子　the imposing
　wēi wēi　　quality of a great mountain
　　　　　　　　　　　此處：借以描述樂聲的雄壯、肅穆
　　　　　　　used here to describe the majestic and solemn sound of the music

◆ 山勢 shānshì　　the physical features of a mountain

◆ 高大 gāodà　　lofty and grand

◆ 雄偉 xióngwěi　　majestic; awesome

◆ 雄壯 xióngzhuàng　　majestic; powerful

◆ 肅穆 sùmù　　solemn; grave

13. 乎　hū　　【助詞】此處用作形容詞的語尾，有加強語氣的
　　　　　　　作用，可譯成 "啊"
　　　　　　The word "乎" is used here as an enclitic particle attached to an
　　　　　　adjective to intensify or emphasize its meaning.

14. 若　ruò　　【準繫詞】像…[一樣]；好像是…[一樣]
　　　　　　to be like [something]

15. 少選　　　　【時間詞】須臾 (yú)；片刻　a short while; a moment
　　 shǎoxuǎn

　　少選之間　　【名詞語】很短的時間內；過了一會儿
　　 shǎo xuǎn zhī jiān　　　　within an instant; a moment later

16. 流 liú　　　　【動詞】流動　to flow

　　流水　　　　【名詞語】流動的河水
　　 liú shuǐ　　　　　　fast flowing water; a swift current

17. 湯湯　　　　【形容詞】水流盛大的樣子；洶湧澎湃
　　 shāng shāng　　the quality of an imposing expanse of fast-flowing water; surging and crashing
　　　　　　　　　　　此處：借以描述琴聲的高低起伏、連綿不絕 used here to describe the never-ending variation in the rhythm of the music

　　　　　　◆ 洶湧 xiōngyǒng　　surging

　　　　　　◆ 澎湃 pēngpài　　crashing

18. 破 pò　　　　【動詞】摔破
　　　　　　　　　　to break something by dashing it on the ground

　　破琴　　　　【動詞語】摔破琴；把琴摔破
　　 pò qín　　　　　　to dash the lute on the ground

19. 絕 jué　　　　【動詞】斷絕；折斷　to break off; to snap

20. 絃 xián　　　　【名詞】琴絃(弦)　the strings [of a lute]

　　絕絃　　　　【動詞語】折斷琴絃。把琴絃折斷
　　 jué xián　　　　　　to snap in two the strings [of a lute]

21. 終 zhōng　　　　【動詞】窮盡　to come to the end

　　終身　　　　【動詞語】終竟一生；窮盡一生；過完一生
　　 zhōng shēn　　　　to come to the end of one's life

111

【副詞】一輩 (bèi) 子
all one's life; to the day of one's death
(for detail, see L. 1, no. 27, p. 5)

22. 世 shì 【名詞】世界 (jiè) the world
此處：世上 in the world

23. 足 zú 【形容詞】足夠；夠得上 enough; sufficient
值得 to be worth; to be deserving of

相關的成語

高山流水，得遇知音 gāoshānliúshuǐdéyùzhīyīn

LITERALLY: "High mountains - flowing water", to be able to encounter one who understands my music!"

這個成語用來比喻志趣相同者之間的心靈 (líng) 契合，或描寫一個人對另一個人的才華極度的讚賞 (zàn shǎng)

This proverb is used as a metaphor to describe the sympathetic interaction between like-minded individuals or to characterize a friend keenly appreciative of one's talent.

第二十八課

曾子辭邑

注解

1. 曾子
   Zēngzǐ
   【名詞】孔子的弟子。姓曾，名參，字子輿 (Yú)
   One of Confucius' disciples surnamed Zēng, with the given name
   Shēn, and the courtesy name Zǐyú (*See L. 5, no. 7, p. 17*)

2. 辭 cí
   【動詞】推辭　to decline (an appointment, invitation, offer,
   etc.); to refuse; to rebuff

3. 邑 yì
   【名詞】封地　a grant of arable land with the people who
   worked it; a benefice; a fief

4. 弊 bì
   【形容詞】　壞；破損　bad; tattered
   　　　　　此處：破舊　worn out

   弊衣
   bì yī
   【名詞語】破舊的衣服　old, threadbare clothing

5. 耕 gēng
   【動詞】耕田；用犁把土翻鬆　to till; to plough; to use
   a plow to turn and loosen the soil

   ◆ 犁 lí　　　　　　a plough

   ◆ 翻鬆 fānsōng　　　to turn up and loosen [soil]

6. 野 yì
   【名詞】田野　open fields

7. 魯 Lǔ
   【名詞】春秋時代國名。在今山東省
   The name of a state that flourished during the Spring and Autumn
   period and occupied part of present-day Shāndōng province. (*See
   L. 11, no. 7, p. 39*)

113

8. 致 zhì　　【動詞】給予；送給　to give [to]; to present [to]; to bestow [upon]

致邑
zhì yì　　【動詞語】送給封地；送給…一塊封地
to give [someone] a [grant of] land and people; to give [someone] a [gift of] land and people; to bestow a benefice upon [someone]

9. 焉 yān　　【指示代詞】此處：“於之”（於曾子）
here: "to him" (to Zēngzǐ), *see sentence analysis 2*

10. 固 gù　　【副詞】堅決地　steadfastly; firmly; resolutely

11. 或 huò　　【虛指代詞】有人　someone

12. 求 qiú　　【動詞】乞(qǐ)求　to seek; to petition [for]; to entreat

13. 奚 xī　　【疑問副詞】何；為什麼　an interrogative adverb equivalent in meaning to the word "何" (what → for what; why) here it means "why."

14. 施 shī　　【動詞】施捨；給人財物　to bestow; to give someone something of value

　　【名詞】施舍的財物　alms; things given as a charity

受人施者【名詞語】接受別人施舍的人
shòu rén shī zhě　　those who receive a benefaction from others

15. 常 cháng　　【副詞】常常 often；通常 usually

16. 畏 wèi　　【動詞】畏懼；怕　to fear; to be afraid

17. 與 yǔ　　【動詞】贈與；送給　to give [to]

與人者
yǔ rén zhě　　【名詞語】給人東西的人　those who give things to others; benefactors

18. 驕 jiāo　【形容詞】驕傲；自高自大；看不起別人
arrogant; self-important and overbearing; haughty

驕人　【動詞語】對人表示驕傲的態度　to act in an
jiāo rén　arrogant manner towards someone (*see Sentence Analysis 5.1*)

19. 縱 zòng　【連詞】縱然；即使；就算是　even if; even though
用在複合句的前一個分句，表示假設性的讓步；
下一個分句由於有這種假設的情況，而出現相應
的結果或結論

The conjunction "縱", meaning "given that," "even if,"
"notwithstanding," etc., is used in the initial subordinate clause
of a **compound sentence** to express a hypothetical condition; the
consequence or conclusion that results from this hypothetical
situation appears in the main clause that follows it.

20. 賜 cì　【動詞】賞 (shǎng) 賜；賜給　to bestow [upon]
(*For detail, see L. 24, no. 6, p. 94*)

　　　【名詞】賞賜；賞給的東西
a benefaction; the things bestowed on someone

21. 豈 cì　【副詞】怎麼…呢；難道…嗎　how...,usually used
with an interrogative particle to form a rhetprcal question (*see also
L.33, no. 30, p.137, and L. 37, no. 51, p. 163*)

22. 孔子　【名詞】(551 - 479 B.C.) 姓孔，名丘 (Qiū)，字仲尼
Kǒngzǐ　(Zhòngní)，春秋時代魯國人。（詳見第十六課，生
字五，六十三頁。）

Kǒng Qiū (551 - 479 B.C.) (known also by his courtesy name
Zhòngní) was a man from the state of Lǔ who lived during the
Spring and Autumn period. (*For detail, see Lesson 16, note 5,
p.63.*)

23. 足 zú　【形容詞】足夠　to be sufficient; to be adequate

24. 以 yǐ　【介詞】用　to use; to be used [for the purpose of]

115

足以　　　　【合成詞】足夠用來　　to suffice to be used [for the
zú yǐ　　　　　　purpose of]

◆ 合成詞　　　　　a composite word
héchéngcí

25. 全　quán　　　【動詞】保全；保護使…不受傷害　　to preserve; to
preserve [something] from harm or injury

26. 節　jié　　　　【名詞】節操　integrity; moral fortitude

第二十九課

孔子猶江海

注解

1. 猶 yóu 　【準繫詞】如同；像是　to be the same as; to be like

2. 江 jiāng 　【名詞】江　a river

3. 海 hǎi 　【名詞】海　a sea
　　　　　　　　(usually applied to a very large body of water)

4. 趙簡子 　【名詞】春秋時晉國六卿之一。姓趙，名鞅
　 Zhào Jiǎnzǐ　(Yāng)，字志父，諡簡子。

　　Zhào Jiǎnzǐ was one of the six chief ministers of the state of Jìn during the Spring and Autumn period. His given name was Yāng, his courtesy name Zhìfù, and his posthumous honorific title, Jiǎnzǐ.

5. 子貢 　【名詞】姓端木，名賜，字子貢。他是孔子的著
　 Zǐgòng 　名弟子之一。長於言語，是有名的政治家、外交
　　　　　　　家，也是個成功的商人。

　　Zǐgòng was surnamed Duānmù, had the given name Cì, and the courtesy name Zǐgòng. One of Confucius' most renowned disciples, he excelled in discourse, was famous as a political thinker and diplomat, and was in addition a successful merchant and trader.

6. 為人 　【動詞語】做人　to conduct oneself [in a certain fashion];
　 wéi rén 　to behave

　　　　　　【名詞】做人的態度　conduct; behavior

7. 何如 　【準繫詞語】像什麼　what like ——→ like what
　 hé rú 　　　　　　　怎麼樣　how; in what manner

117

8. 賜 Cì 　　【名詞】子貢稱自己的名字，是一種表示禮敬的
　　　　　　方式　Zǐgòng refers to himself here by using his given name: this
　　　　　　is a polite usage.

9. 識 shì 　　【動詞】了解　to know; to understand; to comprehend

10. 說 yuè 　　【形容詞】同"悅"，高興　the word "說" is
　　　　　　interchangeable with the word "悅" here: pleased; happy

不說 　　【形容詞語】不高興　displeased; unhappy
bú yuè

11. 夫子 　　【名詞】舊時對學者的尊稱，可譯成"先生"或
fūzǐ 　　　　"您"
　　　　　　a term of respect used in ancient China to address men of learning;
　　　　　　it can be translated into spoken Chinese as "先生" or "您" and
　　　　　　into English as "sir" or simply as "you".

12. 事 shì 　　【動詞】事奉；侍奉　to wait on; to serve
　　　　　　　　此處：追隨　to follow

事師 　　【動詞語】事奉老師；從師求學
shì shī 　　　　　　to follow a teacher to study with him

13. 業 yè 　　【名詞】書冊之版；書籍　originally the wooden slips
　　　　　　used for writing which were tied together to form books; books
　　　　　　　　　此處：學業　by extension, it means "the books
　　　　　　studied" or "one's studies"

　　　　◆ 版 bǎn 　　　　the wooden slips used for writing in ancient
　　　　　　　　　　　　China

終業 　　【動詞語】完成了學業；念完了書　to have
zhōng yè completed one's studies; to bring one's studies to completion

14. 去 qù 　　【動詞】離開　to leave; to depart from

15. 寡人 　　【名詞】寡德之人，古時君主自稱之謙 (qiān) 辭；
guǎ rén 　　我

118

This term is a truncated form of the phrase "寡德之人" ([This] person of little/meagre virtue); it is a polite, self-deprecatory form of address used in ancient times by rulers when they referred to themselves. Although ostensibly a self-effacing epithet, it is somewhat akin to the royal "we" in tone, since its use was prescribed. It can simply be translated as a first person pronoun (i.e., I, me).

◆ 謙辭 qiāncí   a polite expression; a polite self-deprecatory or self-effacing expression

16. 何 hé   【疑問代詞】什麼 an interrogative pronoun meaning "what" or "why"

17. 也 yě   【助詞】與疑問詞 "何" 字合用時表示疑問的語氣，可譯成 "呢" When it is used in conjunction with the interrogative pronoun "何", the final particle expresses an interrogative tone and functions like the final word "呢" in spoken Chinese.

18. 譬 pì   【準繫詞】譬如；好比 can be compared to; can be likened to

19. 渴 kě   【形容詞】口渴 thirsty

渴者 kě zhě   【名詞語】口渴的人 one who is thirsty; a thirsty person

20. 飲 yǐn   【動詞】喝[水] to drink [water]

飲江海 yǐn jiāng hǎi   【動詞語】飲[於]江海；在江或海那儿喝水 to drink from a river or a sea

21. 足 zú   【形容詞】夠；滿足 sufficient; ample; enough

知足 zhī zú   【動詞語】知道夠了 to know when [something] is enough
覺得夠了 to feel that one has had an ample amount [of something]

22. 而 ér   【連詞】就 and then

23. 已 yǐ 　　　【動 詞】停止　to stop

◎ 經驗
jīng yàn 　　　【名 詞】　experience

◎ 學識
xué shì 　　　【名 詞】　leraning; erudition; knowledge

24. 則 zé 　　　【連 詞】卻，表示與預期的情況相反 on the contrary; yet. Usually the word "則" is used to introduce a clause containing a statement or assertion contrary to the speaker's or the reader's expectations.

25. 奚 xī 　　　【疑 問 副 詞】何？怎麼…[呢]？哪裡…[呢]？
How? How [come] ... ? How [could] ... ?
The word "奚" is an interrogative particle placed at the beginning of a sentence or an independent clause to introduce a rhetorical question.

26. 足 zú 　　　【形 容 詞】足夠　to be sufficient; to suffice

27. 以 yǐ 　　　【介 詞】用　to use; to be used [for the purpose of]; for

足以
zú yǐ 　　　【合 成 詞】足夠用來　to suffice to be used [for the purpose of]

奚足以
xī zú yǐ 　　　【合 成 詞】以反問的語氣表示否定的意思，可譯成：
Here a rhetorical question is used to express a negative meaning; it can be translated as follows:
a. 怎麼夠[被]用來…呢？
how could it suffice [to be] used [for the purpose of]
不夠[被]用來…
[it] does not suffice [to be] used [for the purpose of]
b. 怎麼夠得上…呢？
how could ... suffice to
夠不上…
[it] does not suffice to

第三十課

苛政猛於虎

注解

1. 苛 kē 　　【形容詞】苛刻；暴虐 harsh; tyrannical

2. 政 zhèng 　　【名詞】政治 government; administration

   苛政 　　【名詞語】苛刻的政治；暴虐 (bàonuè) 的政治
   kē jèng 　　harsh and oppressive government; by extension, tyranny

3. 猛 měng 　　【形容詞】凶猛；凶殘 ferocious

4. 虎 hǔ 　　【名詞】老虎 a tiger

5. 孔子 　　【名詞】(551 - 479 B.C.) 姓孔，名丘 (Qiū)，字仲尼
   Kǒngzǐ 　　(Zhòngní)，春秋時代魯國人。（詳見第十六課，字
   　　　　　　彙五，第六十三頁）

   　　　　　　Kǒng Qiū (551 -479 B.C.) (known also by his courtesy name
   　　　　　　Zhòngní) was a man from the state of Lǔ who lived during the
   　　　　　　Spring and Autumn period. (*for detail, see lesson 16, no. 5,
   　　　　　　p.63*)

6. 過 guò 　　【動詞】經過 to pass; to go by

7. 泰山 　　【名詞】山名。在山東省，為五嶽之一 Mount Tài, a
   Tài shān 　　famous mountain in Shāndōng province; one of the "five sacred
   　　　　　　peaks" in China (*see Lesson 27, no. 9, p.109*).

8. 側 cè 　　【名詞】旁邊 the side; on the side

9. 婦人 　　【名詞】已婚的女子 a married woman
   fù rén

10. 哭 kū 【動詞】因悲傷、痛苦或情緒激動而流淚發聲
to sob and shed tears in expressing sorrow, pain, etc.

11. 墓 mù 【名詞】墳墓 a grave

12. 哀 āi 【形容詞】悲痛；傷心 dolorous

哭哀
kū āi 【動詞語】哭得很悲痛
to cry/weep dolorously

13. 夫子
fū zǐ 【名詞】先生，此處指孔子
here, "the master", referring to Confucius

14. 式 shì 【名詞】同"軾"，古代車廂前用作扶手的橫木
The word "式" should be read here as "軾"--the horizontal
wooden crosspiece at the front of a carriage.
這裡用如動詞"扶軾"：扶著軾敬禮；把手放
在車前橫木上敬禮。 In this sentence, it is used as a verb
meaning "to rest one's hands on the wooden crosspiece."
古人乘車，遇到應表敬意的人或事時，乘者就低
頭扶軾。在這裡，孔子扶軾是表示對婦人在墓前
哀哭的注意和關心。
In the classical period, when someone riding in a carriage
encountered a situation where courtesy dictated that he make a
show of respect, the rider bowed his head and rested his hands on
the carriage's railing. Here Confucius, by resting his hands thus is
expressing his concern about and attentiveness to the dolorous
crying of the woman in front of the grave.

15. 使 shǐ 【動詞】派 to dispatch

16. 子路
Zǐlù 【名詞】姓仲，名由，子路是他的字。孔子的著
名弟子之一。
Zǐlù was surnamed Zhòng and had the given name Yóu; Zǐlù was
his courtesy name. He was one of Confucius' principal disciples.

17. 壹 yī 【副詞】實在；的確 truly; indeed

18. 似 sì 【準繫詞】好像是… to seem to be

19. 重 chóng 　【副詞】重複 (fù) 地；好幾次地 repeatedly

20. 憂 yōu 　【名詞】 憂傷；傷心的事 grief; troubles

21. 者 zhě 　【代詞】之狀；的樣子 　-looking [one]

似…者 　【固定結構】像…似的；好像是…的樣子
sì … zhě 　　　　to seem to be; to seem like

◆ 固定結構 　　a formal construction
gùdìngjíegòu

壹似重有憂者：
　的確像是好幾次遇到傷心事似的；
　的確像是遭遇過好幾件傷心事的樣子
Indeed [you] seem to have repeatedly encountered misfortune.

22. 然 rán 　【形容詞】對的；是的 　true; right

23. 昔 xī 　【時間詞】從前 formerly; in the past

24. 舅 jiù 　【名詞】此處指丈夫的父親；公公 father-in-law

25. 焉 yān 　【指示代詞】於之 in it; from it; by it

26. 何為 　【介詞語】為何；為什麼？
hé wèi 　　　　what for? for what reason? why?

27. 去 qù 　【動詞】離去；離開 to leave; to depart

28. 小子 　【名詞】年輕人；弟子們 young men; disciples
xiǎo zǐ

29. 識 zhì 　【動詞】同 "誌"：記住 to take note of; to remember
(used here in the imperative mood: Remember!)

123

成語

苛政猛於虎   kēzhèngměngyúhǔ

LITERALLY: "Tyrannical government is more ferocious than even a tiger."

暴虐的政治比老虎還凶猛。

Tyrannical government is more ferocious than even a tiger.

第三十一課

曳尾於塗中

注解

1. 曳 yè 　　【動詞】拖　to drag

2. 尾 wěi 　　【名詞】尾巴　a tail

   曳尾
   yè wěi 　　【動詞語】拖尾巴　to drag [its] tail

   　　　　　【用如副詞】拖著尾巴　dragging [its] tail

3. 塗 tú 　　【名詞】泥　mud

4. 釣 diào 　　【動詞】釣魚　to fish

5. 濮水
   Pú shuǐ 　　【名詞】河名，在今河南省
   　　　　　name of a river in present day Hénán province

6. 使 shǐ 　　【動詞】命令　to order
   　　　　　　　　 此處：派；派遣 to send; to dispatch

7. 大夫
   dài fū 　　【名詞】爵名，比卿低，比士高；在戰國時代常
   　　　　　指文官，分上、中、下三級
   "Grand master." An official title and noble rank used during the
   Zhōu dynasty to designate the second highest category of officials,
   below minister (卿) and above serviceman/gentleman (士); it
   comprised three grades: senior grandmaster (上大夫); ordinary
   grandmaster (中大夫); and junior grandmaster (下大夫).
   During the Warring States period, this title was generally conferred
   on civil rather than on military officials. (Hucker, *Dictionary of
   official titles in imperial China*, p. 465.)

   ◆ 文官 *wénguān* 　　civil officials

125

◆ 武官 *wǔguān*   military officials

8. 先 xiān   【動詞】先容 (先去見) ；一件事發生以前，先去為人介紹、說明、安排…

to prevene; to anticipate; before something happens, to first go and courteously introduce to, explain to, or make arrangements on behalf of a third party.

9. 願 yuàn   【動詞】希望 to wish; to desire

10. 竟 jìng   【名詞】同 "境" ，國境 here it is equivalent to the character "境" meaning border; boundary

竟內
jìng nèi   【名詞語】四境之內 ；國內 ；全國 within the four borders [of the realm]; the realm; the entire country

11. 累 lèi   【動詞】麻煩 ；煩勞
to bother [sb.] with; to burden [sb.] with; to trouble sb. to do sth.

12. 矣 yǐ   【助詞】用於句末表示事實上的既成狀態，可譯成 "了"

Here the particle "矣" expresses a tone of finality: the action of the sentence has been completed and as a result a new state or condition pertains. This tone can be expressed by "了" in spoken Chinese and by the use of a perfect tense or by the addition of an adverb like "now" in English. The sense is similar to "it has/had come to pass".

13. 持 chí   【動詞】拿 to hold

14. 竿 gān   【名詞】釣竿 a fishing pole

持竿
chí gān   【動詞語】拿釣竿 to hold a fishing pole

【用如副詞】拿著釣竿 holding a fishing pole

15. 顧 gù   【動詞】回頭看 to turn round/around and look at ...

16. 神 shén 【形容詞】神異 preternatural; divine

靈驗；預測能夠應驗
of a prediction: accurate; reliable

17. 龜 guī 【名詞】烏龜 a tortoise

神龜
shén guī 【名詞】靈龜 (guī)；靈驗的烏龜 "a divine tortoise"
whose shell (carapace) can be used for prognostication

18. 歲 suì 【名詞】年 a year

19. 巾 jīn 【名詞】包東西的布 cloth; a piece of cloth used to wrap things

【動詞】用布包著 to wrap up in a piece of cloth

20. 笥 sì 【名詞】竹簍 a rectangular bamboo basket

【動詞】放在竹簍中 to place in a bamboo basket

21. 藏 cáng 【動詞】藏 to store
珍藏 to treasure

22. 廟堂
miào táng 【名詞語】宗廟的大堂 the great hall of the ancestral temple

23. 寧 nìng; níng 【助動詞】寧可；寧願 would rather; to prefer

24. 留 liú 【動詞】遺留；留下 to leave behind

25. 骨 gǔ 【名詞】背骨 back bone
在本文內指龜甲 (jiǎ)，用來占卜 (zhānbǔ)
here: the hard shell (carapace) of a tortoise used for prognostication

留骨
liú gǔ 【動詞語】留下背骨 to leave [its] backbone [for posterity]
⟶ 留下龜甲 to leave [its] shell [for posterity]

127

26. 貴 guì 　【形容詞】珍貴；寶貴　valuable; precious

在本文內，"貴"是形容詞用作動詞，意動用法：
"以為寶貴"；而且根據上下文的意思，應解
釋作："被以為寶貴"，含意是"受重視"。

In this passage, "貴" is an adjective that functions as a putative verb (i.e., it means "以為寶貴" [to think it is precious]) and given the context it should be understood as a passive construction meaning "被以為寶貴" [to be thought of as precious], which can be taken to mean by implication "受重視" [to be highly thought of/regarded].

27. 矣 yǐ 　【助詞】用於句末表示一種命令的語氣，可譯成
"吧"

Here the particle "矣" expresses an imperative tone; it can be translated into spoken Chinese as "吧" and into English by using the imperative mood (i.e., as a command or order).

成語

曳尾塗中　　yèwěitúzhōng

LITERALLY: "To crawl in the mud dragging its tail."

比喻寧願過貧賤但自由的生活，也不願去作官。

This is a metaphor used to indicate that a person would rather lead a poor but carefree life than serve as an official.

第三十二課

塞翁失馬

注解

1. **塞** sài 【名詞】邊界上險(xiǎn)要的地方 strategic locations along the frontier

2. **翁** wēng 【名詞】年老的男子；老頭兒 an old man

3. **失** shī 【動詞】失去 to lose; to have lost

4. **馬** mǎ 【名詞】馬 a horse

5. **術** shù 【動詞】占卜 (zhānbǔ) to prognosticate

   【名詞】占卜 prognostication

6. **亡** wáng 【動詞】逃走；逃跑 to run away

7. **入** rù 【動詞】進入；進⋯去（來） to enter; to go into

8. **胡** hú 【名詞】中國古代西北部民族的統稱，秦漢時多指匈奴

   This term is used as a general appellation for the various nomadic tribes living to the north and northwest of Chinese territory in antiquity (as well as in later times). During the Qín and Hàn periods, "胡" usually refers to the Xiōngnú people. It is common to translate "胡" into English as "barbarian(s)," but it could also be rendered as "northern nomads". (It almost always has a pejorative connotation).

   入胡 rù hú 【動詞語】進入胡人的領土；進入胡人的地方 to enter the [northern] barbarians' territory

9. 弔 diào 【動詞】弔慰(wèi)；慰問 [遇到不幸的人] to offer condolences; to console [someone who has met with misfortune]

10. 何 hé 【疑問副詞】怎麼 Why (or how) ...?

11. 遽 jù 【副詞】就，通常與副詞 "豈"、"何"、"奚" 等合用，構成反問句

The adverb "遽" meaning "就" or "then" is generally used in combination with the adverbs "豈", "何", "奚", etc. in rhetorical interrogative sentences; e.g., "何遽", which literally means "what then...?" "why then...?" or "how then... ?"

何遽…乎 【固定結構】怎麼就 [不]…呢？
hé jù...hū 難道就 [不]…嗎？
why would [it not]...?

12. 為 wéi 【動詞】成為；變成 to become; to turn into

13. 福 fú 【名詞】福氣 good fortune

14. 將 jiāng 【動詞】帶領 to lead

15. 駿馬 【名詞語】好馬 a thoroughbred; a fine horse
jùn mǎ

16. 賀 hè 【動詞】慶賀；向…道賀 to congratulate; to offer congratulations to [someone]

17. 禍 huò 【名詞】災禍 misfortune; disaster

18. 良 liáng 【形容詞】好 good

19. 好 hào 【動詞】愛好；喜歡 to be fond of; to like

20. 騎 qí 【動詞】騎馬 to ride [on horseback]

21. 墮 duò 【動詞】落；掉下來；摔(shuāi)下來 to fall down (off)

130

22. 髀 bì 　【名詞】胯(kuà)骨　the thighbone

23. 大 dà 　【副詞】大規模地；大量地
　　　　　　　　　　on a large scale; in great numbers

24. 舉 jǔ 　【動詞】發動〔軍隊〕 to mobilize [troops]

　　大舉 　【動詞語】大規模地發動軍隊
　　dà jǔ 　　　　　　　to mobilize on a large scale

25. 入 rù 　【動詞】侵入　to invade

26. 丁 dīng 　【名詞】成年男人　an adult male

27. 壯 zhuàng 　【形容詞】強壯；健壯　strong; robust

28. 引 yǐn 　【動詞】開弓 to draw a bow
　　　　　　　此處：拉過來；取過來；拿起來
　　　　　　　to pull over; to pick up; to take up

29. 弦 xián 　【名詞】弓弦　bowstring
　　　　　　　此處：弓　bows

　　引弦 　【動詞語】拉開弓弦 to draw a bowstring
　　yǐn xián 　　　　　此處：拿起弓來 to take up [their] bows

30. 戰 zhàn 　【動詞】作戰；打仗　to fight [in battle]

31. 獨 dú 　【副詞】單獨地　alone

32. 跛 bǒ 　【形容詞】瘸(qué) lame; lamed

33. 保 bǎo 　【動詞】保全；使…不受傷害 to secure; to keep secure;
　　　　　　　to save from danger

34. 化 huà 　【名詞】變化　change

131

35. 極 jí　　　　【名詞】極點；盡頭　the extreme; the end

　　　　　　　　【動詞】窮究；推究到極點；推究到盡頭
　　　　　　　　to ascertain to the extreme; to explore to the end

化不可極　【動詞語】變化得不能(沒法子)推究到盡頭
huà bù kě jí　　the ultimate ending of this transforming can never be ascertained

36. 深 shēn　　　【形容詞】深奧 (aò)　deep; profound

37. 測 cè　　　　【動詞】測量　to fathom; to measure

深不可測　【形容詞語】深得不能(沒法子)測量
shēn bù kě cè　　so deep as to be beyond any means of measuring;
　　　　　　　　of unfathomable depth

成 語

塞翁失馬，焉知非福　sàiwēngshīmǎ-yānzhīfēifú

逐字譯成白話是："邊境的老頭儿丟掉了馬，怎麼知道不是福？"

LITERALLY: "When the old man on the frontier lost his horse, how could it be known to not be good fortune?"

比喻遇到災禍、失敗，可能會轉變成福氣、成功。

This is used as a metaphor for situations in which apparent disaster, defeat, or loss may turn into or lead to good fortune or success. It is used in the same way that the saying "a blessing in disguise" is used in English, but with the sense of "a loss may turn out to be a gain."

132

相關成語

深不可測 shēnbùkěcè

深得没法子測量

of unfathomable depth

第三十三課
齒亡舌存

注解

1. 齒 chǐ 【名詞】牙齒 teeth

2. 亡 wáng 【動詞】a.不存在；不在 to not exist
   b.失去；沒有 to lose; to have lost; to not have

3. 舌 shé 【名詞】舌頭 the tongue

4. 存 cún 【動詞】存在；在 to exist

5. 常摐 【名詞】人名，相傳為老子之師
   Cháng Chuāng personal name, traditionally said to have been Lǎozǐ's teacher

6. 疾 jí 【名詞】病 illness; sickness
   【動詞】生病 to be ill; to be sick

7. 老子 【名詞】姓李，名耳，字聃，相傳為春秋時期
   Lǎozǐ 思想家，道家的創始人
   Traditionally said to have been a philosopher who lived during the Spring and Autumn period and the founder of the Taoist School of philosophy. His surname was Lǐ (李), his given name Eˇr (耳) and his courtesy name Dān (聃).

8. 問 wèn 【動詞】問候 to enquire after

9. 遺 yí 【動詞】遺留；留 to leave behind; to pass on
   【形容詞】遺留下來的 left behind; here: bequeathed

10. 教 jiào 【名詞】教誨(huì)；教導 instuctions; teachings

遺教 【名詞語】留下來的教誨 teachings to pass on
yí jiào

11. 語 yù 【動詞】告訴 to tell

12. 諸 zhū 【兼詞】是代詞"之"和介詞"於"的合音"之於"。用於句中；如果"諸"前有動詞，它後面一定是名詞或名詞語

This combined word is formed by the elision of the pronoun "之" and the preposition "於"（之於）. When "諸" is used in the middle of a sentence, if there is a verb preceding it, a noun or noun phrase must follow it. Its meaning depends on the context in which it is used; literally it means "it to".

◆ 兼詞 jiāncí　　a combined word

13. 雖 suí 【連詞】雖然 although
即使 even if

14. 過 guò 【動詞】經過；走過 to go past; to pass by

15. 故鄉 【名詞】出生或長期居住過的地方；家鄉 one's
gù xiāng place of origin; native place; one's family's village

16. 下車 【動詞語】從車上下來 to dismount;
xià chē to step down from a carriage or a chariot

17. 謂 wèi 【動詞】說 to say

18. 故 gù 【形容詞】a.舊（與"新"相對）；舊有的
old (in contrast to new);
b.原來的（與"後來的"相對）
original (in contrast to later); former (in contrast to subsequent)

【用如名詞】故舊
a.故交；舊友；老朋友 old friend
b.故物：從前的人留下來的東西
old things; things left by earlier people

19. 耶 yé 【疑問詞】嗎 (in English, this is usually represented by a question mark)

20. 嘻 xī 【歎詞】啊，表示讚賞 an exclamation used to express approval and appreciation

21. 是 shì 【形容詞】正確；對 true; right;
與 "非" 相對 the opposite of "非"（is not true)

22. 已 yǐ 【助詞】用於句末，同 "矣"，了，表示十分肯定的語氣 a final particle used here to express a strong affirmative tone

是已 shì yǐ 【形容詞】對了啊；對啦 that is right

23. 喬 qiáo 【形容詞】高 high; tall

24. 木 mù 【名詞】樹 tree

喬木 qiáomù 【名詞】高大的樹
lofty, mighty trees -- as in "the mighty oak"

25. 趨 qū 【動詞】很快地走 to walk hurriedly
小步快走 [表示恭敬] to walk by hurriedly in small steps [as a way of showing respect]

26. 敬 jìng 【動詞】尊敬 to respect

27. 老 lǎo 【形容詞】年老 old; aged
【用如名詞】年老的人、物 old persons or things

敬老 jìng lǎo 【動詞語】尊敬年老的〔人或物〕
to respect what is aged

136

28. 張 zhāng 【動詞】張開 to open

29. 示 shì 【動詞】給…看 to show ...to

30. 豈 qǐ 【副詞】難道 is it not? used in written language; usually before a negative word to form a rhetorical question

豈非…耶 【固定結構】難道不是…嗎 could [it] not be ...?
qǐ fēi ... yé would [it] not be ...?

31. 柔 róu 【形容詞】柔軟；柔弱 soft; flexible; tender

32. 剛 gāng 【形容詞】堅硬；剛強 hard; stiff; rigid

33. 事 shì 【名詞】事情；事理人情
principles of hman behavior/relations

34. 盡 jìn 【形容詞】窮盡 exhausted
達到盡頭 reaching to the end
此處：完全包含在內
here: to be encapsulated in; to be summed up completely

相關成語

柔舵克剛 róunéngkègāng

LITERALLY: "The soft will conquer the hard."

柔弱的能勝過剛強的－比喻用柔和的方式能克服剛強的人。

The soft will conquer the hard - Soft and subtle approach can disarm a man of hot temper.

137

第 三 十 四 課

晏子與楚王論盜

注解

1. 晏子
Yànzǐ
【名詞】人名。姓晏，名嬰，春秋時齊國的大夫
A personal name. Yànzǐ was surnamed Yàn and had the given name Yīng; he was a high official in the state of Qí during the Spring and Autumn period.

2. 與 yǔ
【連詞】和；同；跟 and

3. 楚 Chǔ
【名詞】國名 the name of a state (*see L. 7, no. 3, p. 26*)

4. 論 lùn
【動詞】談論 to discuss; to talk about

5. 盜 dào
【動詞】偷竊；竊盜；偷東西 to steal; to rob

【名詞】盜賊；偷東西的人 robber; thief

6. 使 shì
【動詞】出使；接受君命到…去做大使
to be appointed as a diplomatic envoy to ...; to receive an appointment as an ambassador to [a place]; to serve as an envoy

7. 聞 wén
【動詞】聽到 to hear [of]

8. 左右
zuǒyòu
【名詞】在兩旁侍候的近臣；侍從
LITERALLY: "those to the left and right [of the king]"; those in close attendance; his retinue

9. 習 xí
【形容詞】嫻習；善於 accomplished; adept at

10. 辭 cí
【名詞】言辭；辭令 diction; rhetoric; oratory

138

習辭
xí cí

【動詞語】嫻習辭令 to be accomplished in rhetoric
善於辭令 to be good with words
很會說應對得體的話 able to use
language appropriate for the occasion

11. 方 fāng 【副詞】將要；快要 to be about to [do something];
to be on the verge of [doing something]

12. 辱 rù 【動詞】侮辱；羞辱 to insult; to humiliate

13. 何以
hé yǐ

【介詞語】疑問代詞"何"用作賓語，倒放在介
詞"以"之前，意思是"以何"；用什麼法子

In this phrase, the interrogative pronoun "何" functions as the
object of the preposition "以", so it has been transposed in front
of the preposition; it means:
LITERALLY: "what with = with what ?"
→ "rely on what?"; use/employ what [means/method] [to do this]?;
how can this be done?

14. 為 wèi 【介詞】用同"於"：當；在

"為" functions here like the preposition "於" (at); it means at the
time when → when; while

15. 請 qǐng 【表敬副詞】請讓我 please allow me; please let me (a
polite form of speech used to introduce a request)

16. 縛 fù 【動詞】捆綁 to bind; to tie up

17. 過 guò 【動詞】經過 to pass by

18. 行 xíng 【動詞】走 to walk

19. 何為
hé wéi

【動詞語】疑問代詞"何"用作賓語，倒放在動
詞"為"之前，意思是"為何"；做什麼

In this phrase, the interrogative pronoun "何" functions as the
object of the verb "為", so it has been transposed in front of the
verb; it means:

LITERALLY: "What do?"→ "do/did what?"; What does/did [he] do?

20. 齊 Qí 【名詞】國名，在今山東 the name of a state located in present-day Shāndōng province (*see L. 11, no. 6, p. 39*)

21. 坐 zuò 【動詞】犯…罪 to commit a crime (or offence)

何坐
hé zuo
【動詞語】犯了什麼罪 What commit?
LITERALLY: What [crime] did he commit?

坐盜
zuò dào
【動詞語】犯了竊盜罪；犯了偷東西的罪
to have commited [the crime of] robbery

22. 賜 cì 【動詞】賞賜（上給下） to bestow on (used only when a person of superior rank or status gives something to a person of inferior rank or status)

23. 酣 hān 【形容詞】半醉 half drunk

[喝得]很盡興 pleasantly inebriated

[喝得]很暢快 [to drink] to one's heart's content

24. 吏 lì 【名詞】低級的官吏；小官
a sub-official functionary or a low-ranked civil official. This generic term usually refers to those government employees who performed clerical and menial tasks in various government and court offices and who had no formal status in the civil service hierarchy; the term can be variously translated into English as clerk, servant, functionary, minor official, etc., depending on the context in which it appears (Hucker, *A dictionary of official titles in imperial China,* p. 302)

25. 詣 yì 【動詞】前往；到…去
to go to [a place]; to arrive at [a place]

26. 曷 hé 【疑問代詞】同 " 何 " an interrogative particle; here it is equivalent in meaning to the interrogative particle " 何 " [what]

27. 視 shì 【動詞】看 to look at

28. 避 bì 【動詞】避開 to get away from; here, to leave [the mat]

29. 席 xí 【名詞】座位 a mat; a seat

避席
bì xí 【動詞語】古人席地而坐，離席起立，以示尊敬
ancient people set a mat on ground and sat on it; they usually left the mat and stood up to show respect to others

30. 橘 jú 【名詞】橘樹 the mandarin (mandarin orange) tree (*Citrus reticulata*), a small, spiny Chinese orange tree

橘子 mandarin (mandarin orange), a small flattened deep-colored orange with sweet pulp and thin easily separable rind

31. 生 shēng 【動詞】生長 to grow

32. 淮 Huái 【名詞】水名。淮河，發源於河南，流經安徽，至江蘇入海

the Huái River, which begins in Hénán province, runs through Ānhuī, and empties into the sea on the Jiāngsū coast

33. 淮南
Huáinán 【名詞】淮河南邊 the region south of the Huái River

34. 淮北
Huáiběi 【名詞】淮河北邊 the region north of the Huái River

35. 枳 zhǐ 【名詞】枳樹；一種像橘樹的樹
the citron tree (*Citrus medica*)
枳子，一種像橘子，但沒有橘子那麼甜、那麼好吃的水果；像橘子但比橘子酸的水果 a variety of citrus fruit similar to the orange, but without the orange's sweetness and tastefulness; variously called the citron (*citrus medica*) or trifoliate orange

36. 葉 yè 【名詞】葉子 a leaf; leaves

37. 徒 tú 【副詞】徒然；白白地 uselessly

141

38. 相似　　　【動詞語】互相像；彼此很像　to resemble each other;
　　 xiāngsì　　　to be similar to each other

39. 實　shí　　　【名詞】果實　fruit

40. 味　wèi　　　【名詞】味道　flavor; taste

41. 土　tǔ　　　【名詞】土壤　soil

　　 水土　　　【名詞語】一個地方的水跟土，即指自然環境和
　　 shuǐtǔ　　　氣候
　　　　　　　LITERALLY: "water and soil"; a metaphor for the natural
　　　　　　　environment, climate, and particular local conditions of a
　　　　　　　place

得無…耶／乎【固定結構】表示懷疑或推測，白話可譯成：
dé wú ...　ye/hū
　　　　　　　莫非是…嗎？ Could it not be that ...?
　　　　　　　別是…吧？　 It isn't [because] ..., is it?
　　　　　　　恐怕是…吧？　I fear it is ..., isn't it?"
　　　　　　　大概是…吧？　Probably it is ..., isn't it?"

成語

橘逾淮則為枳　Júyùhuáizéwéizhǐ

LITERALLY:　"When orange trees pass the Huai River, they then become
citron trees."

逐字譯是橘樹過了淮河就變成枳樹

比喻人或事物會隨生存環境的改變而改變。

This saying is used as a metaphor to describe how people and other things
will change as their living conditions change (i.e., they will adapt to the
circumstances in which they find themselves).

第三十五課

彌子瑕

注解

1. **彌子瑕**
   Mí Zǐxiá

   【名詞】春秋時代衛靈公的幸臣，是古代著名的美男子之一

   A favourite courtier of Duke Líng of Wèi [r. 535-493 B.C.], he lived during the Spring and Autumn period and was renowned as one of the male beauties of antiquity.

   ◆ **衛靈公**
   Wèi Línggōng

   One of the rulers of the state of Wèi during the Spring and Autumn period, he was surnamed Jī (姬) and had the given name Yuán (元). He reigned for 42 years from 535 to 493 B.C.

   ◆ **幸臣** xìngchén   a favorite courtier

2. **寵** chǒng   【動詞】寵愛   to favor; to be favored

3. **衛** wèi   【名詞】春秋時國名，在今河北省南部及河南省北部

   A state in the Spring and Autumn period, situated in the southern part of present-day Héběi province and the northern part of present-day Hénán province.

4. **君** jūn   【名詞】君主   the ruler; the sovereign

   衛君
   Wèi jūn   【名詞】衛國的君主，指衛靈公   the ruler of the state of Wèi, here referring to Duke Líng of Wèi.

5. **法** fǎ   【名詞】法律(lǜ)   laws

6. **竊** qiè   【動詞】偷   to steal

   【副詞】偷偷地；偷著   covertly; illicitly

143

7. 駕 jià 　【動詞】駕駛 (shǐ) to drive [a vehicle]

8. 車 jū, chē 　【名詞】車子 a vehicle; a carriage; a chariot

9. 罪 zuì 　【名詞】罪過；犯法的行為
　　　　　　　　a category of offense; a criminal offense

　　　　　　【名詞】懲 (chéng) 罰；刑罰
　　　　　　　　the punishment for a criminal offense

10. 刖 yuè 　【動詞】砍斷腳 to cut off the foot [as a punishment]

11. 母 mǔ 　【名詞】母親 mother

12. 病 bìng 　【動詞】生病 to fall ill; to become ill

13. 告 gào 　【動詞】告訴 to tell

14. 矯 jiǎo 　【動詞】假託 to feign
　　　　　　　此處：矯命；假託君命；
　　　　　　　騙人說是君主的命令 to feign permission
　　　　　　　by decree; to pretend to have an order authorizing ...

矯駕君車 【動詞語】騙人說是君主命令地駕駛君主的車子
jiǎo jià jūn jū 　to feign permission to drive; to pretend to have an order authorizing
　　　　　　him to drive the ruler's carriage

15. 賢 xián 　【形容詞】有道德；高尚 worthy

賢之 　【動詞語】以之為賢；認為他很高尚；
xián zhī 　　　　　　to think him worthy; to consider him worthy
　　　　　　──→ 誇獎他 to praise him

16. 孝 xiào 　【形容詞】孝順 filial

17. 哉 zāi 　【助詞】用在形容詞後，表示讚美的語氣，可

144

譯成 "啊"
an interjective particle used after an adjective to express a tone of admiration and approbation

18. 犯 fàn 【動詞】觸犯；違背 to violate [regulations or laws]

犯罪
fàn zuì
【動詞語】違反法律；做出犯法的、應受處(chǔ) 罰的行為 to violate the law; to commit a criminal offense

犯刖罪
fàn yuè zuì
【動詞語】犯了砍斷腳的罪 to commit a criminal offense punishable under the category of punishment requiring the cutting off of one foot

19. 異 yì 【形容詞】不同 different

異日
yì rì
【時間詞】另一天 another day

20. 遊 yóu 【動詞】遊逛(guàng)；閒遊 to stroll

21. 果 guǒ 【名詞】果實；水果 fruit

22. 園 yuán 【名詞】種蔬(shū)菜、花果、樹木的地方 an area of land used to grow vegetables, flowers, and trees

果園
guǒ yuán
【名詞語】種植果樹，出產水果的園子 an orchard

23. 食 shí 【動詞】吃 to eat

24. 桃 táo 【名詞】桃子 a peach

25. 甘 gān 【形容詞】甜 sweet
此處是形容詞的意動用法：以為甜；覺得很甜
Here the adjective is used in a putative sense: to think [it] sweet; to consider [it] sweet

26. 半 bàn 【名詞】半；一半 one half; a half

27. 啗 dàn 【動詞】吃 to eat

此處動詞 "啗" 是動詞的使動用法：使…吃
Here the verb "啗" is used in a causative sense: to make ... eat; to cause ... to eat

啗君
dàn jūn
【動詞語】使君啗——→給君吃 to cause the ruler to eat; to give to the ruler to eat (on the causative use of the verb in this phrase, *see sentence analysis 7*)

28. 味 wèi 【名詞】味道 taste; flavor

29. 寡人
guǎ rén
【名詞語】寡德之人；古代國君自稱的謙詞
"This person of meagre virtue"; a self-effacing term used by rulers in ancient times to refer to themselves (*see L. 29, no. 15, p. 119*)

30. 色 sè 【名詞】美色；美貌 sensual or physical beauty;
此處：美的容貌 good looks

31. 衰 shuāi 【動詞】衰退 to decline

色衰
sè shuāi
【主謂】美貌衰退 [his] good looks declined
——→變老變醜(chǒu)了 [he] became old and ugly

32 愛 ài 【名詞】愛情 affection; ardor

33. 弛 chí; shǐ 【動詞】鬆(sōng)弛 to slacken; to relax
——→減弱；減少 to decrease; to grow cool (of emotions)

愛弛
ài chí
【主謂】愛情鬆弛 [the ruler's] affection slackened
——→愛情減弱了 [the ruler's] ardor cooled
——→愛情減少消失了
[the ruler's] ardor grew increasingly cool

34. 得 dé 【動詞】得到；獲(huò)得 to get; to obtain

35. 罪 zuì 　【動詞】責怪 to reproach

　　　　　　　　【名詞】譴 (qiǎn) 責；責怪 reproach

得罪　　【動詞語】得到責怪 to get reproach
dé zuì　　　　──→ 被責怪；受責怪 to be reproached

36. 是 shì　【指示代詞】此；這個 [人] this; this [person]

37. 嘗 cháng　【副詞】曾經…過　once (used to indicate that something did transpire in the past at least one time)

38. 餘 yú　【形容詞】剩下的　leftover

39. 故 gù　【副詞】本來　from the beginning; all along

40. 行 xíng　【名詞】行為　behavior

41. 變 biàn　【動詞】改變　to change

42. 初 chū　【名詞】當初；先前　the beginning; the outset

43. 以前　【副詞】從前　previously; heretofore
yǐ qián

44. 見 jiàn　【助動詞】表示被動，相當於 "被"

The word "見" functions here as a passive marker equivalent in meaning and function to the passive marker "被".

見賢　　【動詞語】被以為賢；被認為賢 to be considered
jiàn xián　　　　worthy; to be thought to be worthy;
　　　　　──→被誇獎；受誇獎 to be found praiseworthy

45. 獲 huò　【動詞】獲得；得到　to capture; to get

147

獲罪　　　【動詞語】得到責怪 to get reproach
huò zuì　　　　　——→被責怪；受責怪 to be reproached

46. 憎　zēng　　【動詞】憎惡(wù)；厭惡　to detest

成　語

色衰愛弛　　　sèshuāiàichí

LITERALLY: "Looks decline, love slackens."

[一個人的]美貌衰退，[別人對他的]愛情就鬆弛
(減弱)了

As a person's outward appearance declines, so does the feeling of affection for that person grow increasingly cooler.

第三十六課

楚莊王不殺絕纓者

注 解

1. 楚莊王
   Chǔ
   Zhuāngwáng
   【名詞】楚國的明君，公元前616至591年在位，為春秋時代五霸(五位諸侯之長)之一。
   A famous ruler of the state of Chǔ, King Zhuāng (r. 616-591 B.C.) was one of the Five Hegemons (leaders of the feudal lords) during the Spring and Autumn Period (*On the Five Hegemons, see L. 26, no.1, p. 103*)

2. 殺 shā 【動詞】殺；處死 to kill; to put to death

3. 絕 jué 【動詞】斷絕 to break
   此處：拉斷；揪斷 to be broken

4. 纓 yīng 【名詞】帽帶子；繫冠的帶子；把兩條絲帶繫在帽子的兩端，以便結在頷(hán)下 a capstring (the two cords attached to the base of the cap and tied under the chin to hold the cap in place).

   絕纓者
   juéyīngzhě
   【名詞語】斷了帽帶子的人；被揪斷了帽帶子的人 the one with a broken capstring; the one whose capstring was broken

5. 群 qún 【形容詞】眾；很多的 in groups; in large numbers

6. 臣 chén 【名詞】臣子 officials under a feudal ruler

   群臣
   qún chén
   【動詞】眾臣；眾多的臣子；臣子們
   a group of officials; [all] the officials; the entire body of ministers

7. 暮 mù 【時間詞】傍晚；日落時；天黑了的時候
   dusk; evening; the period when the sun is going down and it grows dark

149

日暮
rì mù
【主謂句】太陽將落；天快黑的時候 sunset; dusk

8. 酣 hān
【形容詞】半醉 half drunk; pleasantly inebriated

酒酣
jiǔ hān
【動詞語】喝酒喝得很暢快 to reach a point of pleasant inebriation when drinking; to drink to one's heart's content

9. 燈 dēng
【名詞】油燈 a lamp (usually this refers to a small bowl or saucer with a wick floating in oil.)

10. 燭 zhú
【名詞】蠟燭 a candle

11. 滅 miè
【動詞】熄滅 to extinguish; to be extinguished; to put out; to be put out

12. 乃 nǎi
【副詞】竟然；竟 to one's surprise; unexpectedly

13. 引 yǐn
【動詞】拉 to pull

14. 美人
měirén
【名詞語】美麗的女子 a beauty; a beautiful woman
此處指楚王的妾 a concubine of the king

15. 援 yuán
【動詞】拽 (zhuài) to pull; to haul; to drag
揪 (jiū) to clutch; to grasp with the hand; to seize

援絕
yuánjué
【動詞語】揪斷 to seize and break [off]

16. 冠 guān
【動詞】帽子 a cap

17. 援得
yuándé
【動詞語】揪到 to grab; to grasp

18. 持 chí
【動詞】拿 [著] to hold; to grasp

19. 趣 cù 　　【動詞】催促　to urge

趣火
cù huǒ 　　【動詞語】催促火；趕緊叫人拿火來
LITERALLY: to press for fire; to have someone bring fire [to light the lamps] right away

20. 上 shàng 　　【動詞】點燃 (rán)；點上 [燈、燭] to light up [the lamps and candles]

21. 視 shì 　　【動詞】看　to look at; to see

22. 醉 zuì 　　【形容詞】喝醉　to be drunk; to be tipsy

23. 失 shī 　　【動詞】失掉　to lose

24. 禮 lǐ 　　【名詞】禮貌　politeness; etiquette

失禮
shī lǐ 　　【動詞語】失掉禮貌　to commit a breach of etiquette
——→做出不合禮貌的事來　to do something discourteous

25. 奈何
nài hé 　　【副詞語】怎麼　how...?
為什麼 why...?

奈何…乎
nài hé 　 hū 　【固定結構】為什麼…呢？　why...?
怎麼 [可以]…呢？　how can...?

26. 欲 yù 　　【動詞】想要　to want; to desire

27. 顯 xiǎn 　　【動詞】顯示；明顯地表現；誇耀 (kuāyaò)
to illustrate; to make a display of; to show off

28. 婦人
fùrén 　　【名詞語】已婚的女子　a married woman

29. 節 jié 　　【名詞】貞節　virtue; chastity (especially when used with reference to women)

30. 辱 rù 【動詞】侮辱 to disgrace; to insult; to humiliate

31. 士 shì 【名詞】有學問、有才幹的讀書人 learned and talented scholar

辱士
rù shì
【動詞語】侮辱有學問、有才幹的讀書人
to humiliate a person of learning and talent

32. 乎 hū 【助詞】與 "奈何" 同用在一句中，表示反問的語氣，可譯成 "呢"

When "乎" is used in conjunction with "奈何" in the same sentence, it expresses a rhetorical interrogative tone; it can be translated into spoken Chinese as "呢". (see no. 25, p.151)

33. 命 mìng 【動詞】命令 to order; to command

34. 飲 yǐn 【動詞】喝酒 to drink

35. 者 zhě 【助詞】表示假設的語氣，可譯成 "要是…[的話]"

Here the particle "者" expresses a subjunctive mood in the clause it is attached to; it can be translated into spoken Chinese as "要是…[的話]" and into English as "if" or with the subjunctive mood of the verb. (cf. L. 26, no. 22, p. 106)

36. 歡 huān 【形容詞】歡樂；快樂；高興
merry; happy; joyous; gay

37. 卒 zú 【副詞】終於 finally; in the end

38. 盡 jìn 【動詞】達到盡頭；達到極點；達到頂點
to the utmost

盡歡
jìnhuān
【動詞語】使歡盡；使歡樂達到頂點；玩到最歡樂的程度 to enjoy to the utmost; to cause [someone] to enjoy to the utmost; to have the best time possible

39. 罷 bà 【動詞】停止 to stop; to cease

152

此處：結束 to end; to finish; to wind up

分散；散去 to disperse

40. 居 jū 【動詞】用於時間詞前，表示相隔了一段時間，可譯成＂過〔了〕＂ as a verb used before words indicating a period of time to express that so much time has elapsed, it's usually rendered as ＂過〔了〕＂ in modern Chinese.

居三年 jū sān nián 【動詞語】過了三年 three years later; after three years

41. 戰 zhàn 【動詞】打仗；作戰 to fight; to battle

42. 合 hé 【動詞】會戰 to meet; to engage [the enemy] in combat

43. 奮 fèn 【動詞】奮勇；提起勇氣 to muster [one's] courage

44. 首 shǒu 【副詞】首先 first

此處：領先 to be in the lead

45. 卻 què 【動詞】後退 to step back; to retreat;

使…後退 to force ...to retreat; to repulse

46. 敵 dí 【名詞】敵人 the enemy

卻敵 quèdí 【動詞語】使敵人後退；打退敵人 to repulse the enemy

47. 勝 shèng 【動詞】戰勝 to win a victory; to triumph

勝之 shèngzhī 【動詞語】戰勝他們 to vanquish them [i.e., the enemy or the enemy's army]

48. 德 dé 【名詞】道德 virtue

49. 薄 bó 【形容詞】微少 meagre; slight

德薄　　　【主謂】道德微少；没什麽道德　[my] virtue is
dé bó　　　meagre → I am a person without merit; I am not worthy

　　　　　◆ 主謂 zhǔwèi　　　　subject and predicate

50. 未嘗　　【副詞】從來没…過　never before [has there been]
wèicháng

51. 異 yì　　【形容詞】奇特；與衆不同　special; distinctive

異子　　　【動詞語】以子為異；認為你與衆不同
yì zǐ　　　to see you as special; to consider you to be extraordinary
　　　　　——→ 對待你特別好　to treat you especially well

52. 出死　　【動詞語】出去死——→冒死
chū sǐ　　go out to die [for someone/something]; to risk death

53. 疑 yí　　【動詞】遲疑；打不定主意　to hesitate

不疑　　　【動詞語】不遲疑(不打不定主意；打定主意)
bù yí　　　to not hesitate; to not vacillate (having made up one's mind; not
　　　　　vacillating); resolutely

54. 如是　　【準繫詞語】如此；像這樣　like this
rúshì

55. 往者　　【時間詞】從前　in the past
wǎngzhě

56. 隱 yǐn　　【動詞】隱藏　to conceal; to hide from view

57. 忍 rěn　　【動詞】忍耐　to endure; to restrain oneself; to tolerate

隱忍　　　【動詞語】忍耐著不動聲色；控制自己的感情不
yǐnrěn　　表現出來 to bear an insult, affront, grievance, etc. with patience
　　　　　and self-control; to contain one's emotions and refrain from any
　　　　　display of anger

58. 加 jiā 　【動詞】加上；放上　to add to; to put on

此處： 施加　to impose

59. 誅 zhū 　【動詞】責罰；懲罰　to punish

【名詞】責罰；懲罰　punishment

60. 也 yě 　【助詞】出現在複合句前一個分句的後面，表示停頓的語氣，用來引起下文，可譯成"啊"

When the particle "也" appears at the end of the first clause of a compound sentence, it expresses a tone of reflective caesura which is intended to mark the transition to the text immediately following it. This tone can be expressed in spoken Chinese by the word "啊". In English, somtimes "filler words" like "so" serve the same function in a sentence.

61. 終 zhōng 　【副詞】終於；到底　ultimately

62. 蔭 yìn 　【動詞】庇護；保護　to shelter; to protect

63. 蔽 bì 　【動詞】遮擋；遮掩　to cover up

蔭蔽 yìnbì 　【動詞語】庇護　to protect

64. 德 dé 　【名詞】恩德；恩惠　favor; kindness

65. 顯 xiǎn 　【副詞】明顯地；公開地　overtly; openly; publicly

66. 報 bào 　【動詞】報答　to repay

67. 也 yě 　【助詞】用於句末表示堅決的語氣

A particle used at the end of a narrativ sentence, expressing a tone of resolution or finality.

68. 常 cháng 　【副詞】經常　constantly

—→ 一直　always; all along

155

69. 肝腦 gān naǒ 　【名詞】肝和腦　liver and brains; guts

70. 塗 tú 　【動詞】塗抹　to splatter

塗地 tú dì 　【動詞語】塗抹在地上　to splatter on the ground

71. 頸 jǐng 　【名詞】脖子　the neck

72. 血 xuè, xiě 　【名詞】血　blood

73. 濺 jiàn 　【動詞】噴射；噴濺　to spurt out

濺敵 jiàn dí 　【動詞語】噴濺敵人　to spurt out onto the enemy [in combat]

74. 也 yě 　【助詞】用於判斷句的句末，對主語和謂語間的同一關係加以認定

When it is used at the end of a determinative sentence, "也" re-asserts the equivalency between the subject and predicate, i.e., that A is B, it is! This tone can sometimes be expressed in English by adding "always".

75. 遂 suì 　【副詞】終於；最後　eventually; finally

76. 敗 bài 　【動詞】打敗　to defeat

77. 軍 jūn 　【名詞】軍隊　armed forces; army; troops

78. 強 qiáng 　【動詞】變強；變得很強大　to become very powerful

成 語

盡歡而罷　jìnhuānérbà

盡歡而散　jìnhuānérsàn

LITERALLY: "To enjoy to the utmost and then stop."

使歡樂達到頂點才停；玩到最快樂的程度才散
To disperse only after each has enjoyed himself to the utmost

肝腦塗地　gānnǎotúdì

LITERALLY: "To splatter one's liver and brains on the ground."

準備〔在戰場上〕慘烈地犧牲自己的生命
[Ready to] die the gruesome death on the field of battle.

盡忠竭力，不惜一死來報答別人的恩惠
To try one's best to serve someone, even at the expense of one's own life.

相 關 成 語

感恩圖報　gǎnēntúbào

LITERALLY: "To feel grateful and intend to repay"

感激他人對自己所施的恩惠而設法報答
To feel grateful for a kind act and plan to repay it.

第三十七課

子羔為衛政

注解

1. 子羔
   Zǐgāo

   【名詞】人名，孔子弟子。姓高，名柴，字子羔，曾作過衛國的士師

   Zǐgāo was the courtesy name of Gāo Chái, a disciple of Confucius who once served as the chief judge in the state of Wèi.

   ◆士師 shìshī   a chief judge

2. 為政
   wéi zhèng

   【動詞語】管理政事   to administer government affairs

3. 衛 wèi

   【名詞】春秋時國名，在今河北省南部及河南省北部

   A state in the Spring and Autumn period, situated in the southern part of present-day Héběi province and the northern part of present-day Hénán province.

4. 刖 yuè

   【動詞】砍斷腳   to cut off a foot [as a pinishment]

5. 君臣
   jūn chén

   【名詞】國君跟臣子；此處指"政府"   ruler and ministers; here it is used as a metaphor for "the administration" or "the government"

6. 亂 luàn

   【形容詞】混亂；不安寧 disorderly; not at peace

   【動詞】亂了；發生了變亂   to be in turmoil;

   ——→發生了亂事   to raise a revolt

   ——→發生了政變   to be in a state of political crisis

158

衛之君臣亂　【敘述句】蒯聵 (Kuǎikuì)（姓姬，名蒯聵）是衛
Wèi zhī -　　靈公姬元之子，原被立為世子，後因得罪其父，
jūn chén luàn　懼禍出亡。靈公薨，國人立蒯聵之子姬輒 (Jī Zhé)
（史稱出公）為君。至出公十二年（紀元前四八零
年），蒯聵潛回衛國，脅迫執政大臣孔悝 (Kǒng Kuī)
幫助他與兒子爭位。出公姬輒 (Jī Zhé) 不願與生父
爭位，出奔魯國，蒯聵如願地做了衛國的君主，
在位四年，史稱衛莊公。衛之君臣亂，即指這次
政變而言。詳見左傳哀公十四年。

Kuǎikuī had originally been installed as heir apparent by his father, Duke Líng of Wèi. However, fearing recrimination because he had offended his father, Duke Líng, Kuǎikuì fled into exile. Upon Duke Líng's death, Jī Zhé (the son of Kuǎikuì and grandson of Duke Líng) succeeded him as Duke Chū. In 480 B.C., the 12th year of Duke Chū's reign, Kuǎikuì secretly returned to Wèi and coerced Kǒng Kuī, the chief executive of the government, to help him usurp the dukedom from his own son. Unwilling to contend for the sovereignty with his own father, Duke Chū (Jī Zhé) fled to the state of Lǔ, and his father, Kuǎikuì, became the duke of Wèi, just as he had wished. He reigned for four years and was known to history as Duke Zhuāng of Wèi. In this context, the phrase "衛 之君臣亂" refers to the political crisis of 480 B.C.. *For further details, see the Zuǒ Zhuàn, the 14th year of Duke Aī.*

7. 走 zǒu　【動詞】逃跑 [到]　to flee [to]

8. 郭 guō　【名詞】外城；古代在城的外圍加築的一道城
牆　the outer city wall in ancient times

郭門　【名詞語】外城的城門　the gates of the outer city wall
guō mén

9. 閉 bì　【動詞】關；關上 [了]　to close; to be closed

10. 刖者　【名詞語】被砍斷腳的人　foot-cut-off one
yuèzhě　　　──→ the one whose foot was cut off

11. 守 shǒu　【動詞】把守　to guard

守門　　　【動詞語】把守郭門
shǒu mén　　　　　　　to guard the gate [of the outer city wall]

12. 彼 bǐ　　　【指示代詞】那邊；那裡　there; that place

於彼　　　【介詞語】在那儿；在那邊　over there; at that place
yú bǐ

13. 缺 quē　　　【名詞】缺口　a breach; a gap

14. 君子　　　【名詞】品德高尚的人
jūn zǐ　　　　　　　　a man of noble character; a gentleman

15. 踰 yú　　　【動詞】越過［牆］；跳過［牆］
　　　　　　　　　　　to climb or jump over [a wall]

16. 竇 dòu　　　【名詞】孔穴(xùe)；洞　a hole

17. 隧 suì　　　【動詞】鑽［洞］；從洞穴通道走出　to go through [a hole] ; to burrow [through]

18. 此 cǐ　　　【指示代詞】這；這裡　here; this place

於此　　　【介詞語】在這儿　over here; at this place
yú cǐ

19. 室 shì　　　【名詞】屋子　a room

20. 追 zhuī　　　【動詞】追趕　to chase; to pursue

追者　　　【名詞語】追趕的人　the chasing ones; the ones chasing; the pursuers
zhuī zhě

21. 罷 bà　　　【動詞】歸；回去　to turn back; to return

22. 去 qù　　　【動詞】離開　to leave

將去
jiāng qù
【動詞語】將要離開　[to be] about to leave

23. 虧損
kuī sǔn
【動詞】損害 to impair
此處：不遵守 not to abide by

24. 主 zhǔ
【名詞】君主　lord; ruler

25. 法令
fǎlìng
【名詞】法律政令　laws and orders

26. 親 qīn
【副詞】親自　personally; [by] oneself

27. 難 nàn
【名詞】災難　disaster; calamity; distress

28. 報 bào
【動詞】報復　to pay back

29. 怨 yuàn
【名詞】怨恨；仇 (chóu) 恨 hatred; a grudge

報怨
bào yuàn
【動詞語】報復仇怨；報仇　to avenge a grievance

30. 時 shí
【名詞】時機　opportunity; chance

31. 逃 táo
【動詞】逃走　to escape

逃我
táo wǒ
【動詞語】使我逃走 to cause me to [be able to] escape
讓我逃走 to let me escape

32. 斷足
duàn zú
【動詞語】砍斷腳 to cut off a foot; to have a foot cut off

33. 固 gù
【副詞】本來　all along; truly; indeed

34. 罪 zuì
【名詞】該受的刑罰
the due punishment for the offense

161

35. 無可奈何 【動詞語】沒有法子能對它作什麼
　　 wúkěnàihé　　　　　　　There is no way one can do anything about it.
　　　　　　　　　 ——→ 沒辦法只好這麼作
　　　　　　　　　　　　 There is nothing to do but ...

36. 治 zhì 　　【動詞】治罪；懲治 (chéngzhì)；to punish
　　　　　　　　　 依應得的罪處 (chǔ)罰犯罪的人
　　　　　　　　　 to punish the offense according to the law

37. 傾側　　　 【動詞】斜；歪；傾斜　to tilt
　　 qīngcè

　　　　　　　 ◆斜 xié　　　　　　　 to slant to one side

　　　　　　　 ◆歪 wāi　　　　　　　 to skew

　傾側法令 【動詞語】使法令傾側 to slant and skew the laws and
　 qīngcèfǎlìng　　　　　　 orders
　　　　　　 ——→ 把法令歪 (wāi)到這邊歪到那邊 [地
　　　　　　 看] to tilt and turn the law this way and that
　　　　　　 ——→ 從各種角度研究法令
　　　　　　　　 to consider the laws from every angle

38. 先後臣 　【動詞語】以臣為先，以臣為後
　　 xiānhòu chén　 ——→ 把我放在前面或把我放在後面
　　　　　　　　 ——→ 仔細地衡量(考慮) 我的罪
　　　　　　　　　　 to put me ahead [the law] or to put me after [the
　　　　　　　　　　 law]; to deliberate my case very carefully

　　　　　　 ◆衡量 héngliáng　　 to weigh; to measure; to judge

39. 免 miǎn 　　【動詞】免除　to exempt [someone] from

40. 法 fǎ 　　　【名詞】刑；刑罰；犯罪應受的懲罰
　　　　　　　　 here: the prescribed punishment

　免於法 　【動詞語】從刑罰中免除；免掉受刑罰 to be
　 miǎn yú fǎ　 exempted from punishment under the law

162

41. 獄　yù　【名詞】罪案　an inquest; the details of a criminal case

42. 決　jué　【動詞】判決　to decide; to ascertain

43. 罪　zuì　【名詞】罪名　the offense; the category of punishment

44. 定　dìng　【動詞】決定；確定　to decide; to be decided

45. 臨　lín　【介詞】在即將/快到…的時候
　　　　　　　　　　　　on the point of ...; just before ...

46. 當　dāng　【助動詞】應當；該　ought to

47. 論　lùn　【動詞】衡量；判決；　to weigh; to judge

　　論刑　【動詞語】判刑；依罪定刑；根據罪名決定刑罰
　　lùnxíng　to pass sentence; to decide on a fitting punishment

48. 愀然　【副詞語】很憂傷地；很難過地
　　qiǎorán　　　　　　pained [looking]; glumly

49. 不樂　【形容詞語】不快樂；不高興
　　bú lè　　　　　　　　unhappy

50. 見　xiàn　【動詞】"現"的古字：顯現；流露
　　　　　　　　　　　　to reveal; to manifest

51. 顏色　【名詞】臉色；神色；表情
　　yán sè　　　　　　one's facial expression; one's demeanor

52. 豈　qǐ　【副詞】難道…　is it possible...; could it be possible...

53. 私　sī　【動詞】偏袒；偏愛　to be partial to; to show favor to

54. 天生　【形容詞】天生來的
　　tiān shēng　　　　naturally endowed by Heaven

163

55. 仁人　【名詞語】仁愛的人
　　rén rén　　　　　　　　a humane person; a benevolent person

56. 固　gù　【副詞】本來　originally; innately

57. 然　rán　【指示代詞】如此；像這樣；這樣
　　　　　　　　　　　　to be like this; to be so

固然　【形容詞語】本來如此
gù rán　　　　　　　　[was] always like this;　[was] ever so

58. 脫　tuo　【動詞】逃脫；逃出　to escape [from]

59. 君　jūn　【名詞】對對方的敬稱，相當於“您”
　　　　　　A polite and respectful form of address used as an equivalent of
　　　　　　“you” in direct address, it is roughly equivalent to the archaic
　　　　　　English form of address “my lord” or “milord”.

脫君　【動詞語】使您逃脫；放您逃走
tuō jūn　　LITERALLY: to cause you [to have the means whereby] to escape
　　　　　　(causative usage); to let you escape

第三十八課

鄒忌諷齊王納諫

注解

1. 鄒忌
Zōu Jì

【名詞】人名，戰國時代齊國人。憑藉彈琴的技藝求見齊威王，很受賞識，被任命為臣。後來升遷到宰相的地位，受封為成侯。

Personal name. A native of Qí during the Warring States Period, Zōu Jì excelled at paying the lute. He sought an audience with King Wēi of Qí on the basis of his talent and was greatly appreciated. He received a number of official posts, the highest being prime minister, and was later enfeoffed as the Marquis of Chéng.

◆ 憑藉 *píngjiè*　　　to rely on; to depend on

◆ 技藝 *jìyì*　　　skill; artistry

◆ 求見 *qiújiàn*　　　to request an audience; to petition for an audience

◆ 賞識 *shǎngshì*　　　to recognize the worth of; to appreciate (the virtues in sb.)

◆ 任命 *rènmìng*　　　to appoint

◆ 升遷 *shēngqiān*　　　to promote; to advance (to a higher position or rank)

◆ 封 *fēng*　　　to confer (a title, territory, etc.); to enfeoff

◆ 候 *hóu*　　　a marquis

2. 諷 fěng; fèng 【動詞】用委婉、含蓄的話勸告　to advise with tact and indirection; to advise or criticize in a roundabout way

◆ 委婉 *wěiwǎn*　　　mild and roundabout; tactful; indirect

◆ 含蓄 *hánxù*　　　implicit; veiled

3. 齊王
Qíwáng

【名詞】即齊威王 (r. 358 - 320 B.C.)，姓田，名因齊，"威"是諡號。他是齊桓公田午的兒子，即位後不久，就派兵到西邊去攻打趙國、衛國，又打敗了強大的魏國，自稱為王。他統治齊國近四十年，政治清明，國家安定，沒有一個諸侯敢去侵略。

This refers to King Wēi of Qí (r. 358 - 320 B.C.). Surnamed Tián, his given name was Yīnqí and his posthumous honorific title was Wēi; he was the son of Duke Huán of Qí (Tián Wǔ, not Jiāng Xiǎo bái). Not long after he had ascended the throne, he dispatched troops westward to attack the states of Zhào and Wèi; moreover, he attacked and defeated the great and powerful state of Wèi and took for himself the title of king. He reigned for nearly four decades, during which time the administration of the government was enlightened, the state was at peace internally, and not one of the feudal lords dared to invade his territory.

◆ 即位 *jí wèi* — to ascend the throne

◆ 自稱 *zìchēng* — to call oneself; to claim to be

4. 納 nà 【動詞】接受 to accept

5. 諫 jiàn 【動詞】諫正；規勸 to remonstrate

【名詞】諫言；規勸的話 remonstrance

6. 修 xiū 【名詞】長；高；身高 long; high; of persons, height

7. 尺 chǐ 【名詞】長度單位，十寸 (cùn) 為一尺 a unit of length comprised of ten *cùn* and varying from 22.38 to 23.75 cm in length

8. 餘 yú 【名詞】表示整數後不定的零 (líng) 數 more than; in excess of. This word is used after a round number to represent an unspecified remainder.

八尺有餘
bāchǐ yòuyú
【數量詞】八尺多 more than eight *chǐ* (this would be equivalent to saying "more than six feet tall" if modern units of measurement were used.)

9. 而 ér 　　　【連詞】而且 and; [not only]...but

10. 形貌
xíng mào 　　　【名詞】外形；相貌　the appearance of a person; countenance

11. 昳 yì 　　　【形容詞】光艷(yàn)；明亮　radiant

12. 麗 lì 　　　【形容詞】好看；美麗　good-looking; beauteous

昳麗
yì lì 　　　【形容詞】有神采、很俊美 radiantly beauteous
　　　　　　　　　　　〔非常〕英俊　[extremely] handsome

◆ 英俊 yīngjùn　　handsome (of men)

13. 朝 zhāo 　　　【時間詞】早晨　morning; in the morning

14. 服 fú 　　　【動詞】此處：佩戴；穿[衣]戴[帽]
　　　　　　　　　　to wear; to put on [clothes]

15. 衣 yī 　　　【名詞】衣服　clothing; clothes (technically this word refers only to the upper garment)

16. 冠 guān 　　　【名詞】帽子　cap

17. 窺 kuī 　　　【動詞】暗中偷看 to peek; to look covertly
　　　　　　　　　　此處：照 to observe

18. 鏡 jìng 　　　【名詞】鏡子　a mirror

窺鏡
kuījìng 　　　【動詞語】照鏡子 to look into the mirror; to observe oneself in the mirror

19. 孰與
shú yǔ 　　　【固定結構】"A孰與B...？"；A與B[比]，
誰(哪一個)…？
A compared with B, who ...? which one ...?

167

20. 城北　城北邊　the north of the city
chéngběi　【處所詞】

　　　　◆ 處所詞　chùsuocí　　a place word

21. 徐　xú　【名詞】姓　a surname

22. 公　gōng　【名詞】對別人的尊稱，相當於白話的"先生"
a respectful form of address toward others, it is roughly equal to
"先生" in spoken Chinese, and to "sir" or "master" in modern
spoken English.

城北徐公【名詞語】城北邊的徐先生　Master Xú of the north of
chéngběi Xúgōng　　　　　　　the city

23. 妻　qī　【名詞】妻子；太太　a wife

24. 君　jūn　【名詞】對對方的尊稱，相當於"您"
A polite and respectful form of direct address meaning "you", it is
roughly equivalent to the archaic English usage "my lord" or
"milord".

25. 及　jí　【動詞】趕上　to catch up with; to come up to
此處：比得上　to be compared favorably with

26. 復　fù　【副詞】又　a second time; [the] next [time]

27. 旦日　【時間詞】明日；第二天　the following day
dàn rì

28. 客　kè　【名詞】客人　a visitor; a guest

29. 若　ruò　【準繫詞】如；像　[to be] like

不若　【準繫詞語】不如；不像；比不上 to be not like...;
bú ruò　　to be not as good as ...; to be not equal to ...

30. 熟　shú; shóu【副詞】仔細　closely; carefully

168

31. 視 shì 【動詞】看 to look at

熟視 shúshì 【動詞語】注目細看；仔細地看 to look at carefully

32. 自視 zì shì 【動詞語】自己看自己；看自己 to look at oneself

33. 遠 yuǎn 【形容詞】距離長；時間久（跟近相對）
DENOTATION: to be far separated in time or space (the opposite of "近" -- near; close); distant; remote; far away
此處：差距(jù)大；如"遠不及"，"遠超過"
CONNOTATION: to differ greatly in degree, as in "遠不及"(to be far inferior to), "遠超過"(to far exceed)

遠甚 yuǎnshèn 【形容詞語】遠得很；非常遠；遠遠地
very far; to a very great degree or extent

不及遠甚 bùjí yuǎnshèn 【動詞語】遠遠不及；遠遠趕不上
LITERALLY: not reach [by] very far [distance]; far inferior to

34. 寢 qǐn 【動詞】睡；臥；躺下休息 to go to bed; to lie down and rest

35. 思 sī 【動詞】思索；考慮 to ponder; to think over

36. 美我 měi wǒ 【動詞語】以我為美；認為我美 to think that I am handsome; to consider me handsome
——→ 說我美 to say that I am handsome

37. 者 zhě 【被飾代詞】…之故；…的原因 the reason for ...

38. 私 sī 【動詞】偏愛 to be partial to

39. 畏 wèi 【動詞】畏懼(jù)；害怕 to fear

40. 求 qiú 【動詞】要求 to request

【用作名詞】要求　here the verb functions as a nominal meaning "request"

有求　　【動詞語】有要求
yǒuqiú　　　　　　　　to have a request

41. 入 rù　　【動詞】進入　to enter

42. 朝 cháo　　【名詞】朝廷　the court; the administration

43. 誠 chéng　　【副詞】確實　truly; sincerely

44. 以 yǐ　　【動詞】認為 to think; to be of the opinion

45. 地 dì　　【名詞】國土；領土　territory

46. 里 lǐ　　【量詞】長度的單位 lǐ, a Chinese unit of length (= 1/2 kilometre)

　　　NOTE: in ancient times, a lǐ was defined as 1,800 chǐ, which roughly equals 418 m. (See A.F.P. Hulsewé, *Remnants of Ch'in Law*, p. 19)

47. 方里　　【量詞】長、寬各一里；一平方里　　a square each
fāng lǐ　　side of which is one lǐ; a square lǐ

方千里　　【名詞語】長、寬各一千里；一百萬平方里
fāng qiān lǐ　　an area each side of which is one thousand lǐ; one million square lǐ

48. 宮 gōng　　【名詞】君主的房屋；宮殿 (diàn) a residential palace used by the ruler or his consorts

49. 婦 fù　　【名詞】婦女；已婚女子　married women

宮婦　　【名詞語】君王的姬妾；選入宮中侍奉王的美
gōng fù　　女　palace ladies; beautiful women who had been selected to enter the palace to wait on the king

　　　◆ 侍奉 shìfèng　　　to wait on; to serve

170

50. 左右　【名詞】身邊跟從的人；侍從
zuǒ yòu　LITERALLY: those to his left and right, (i.e. in his retinue); personal attendants

51. 莫 mò　【無指代詞】沒有一個；沒有一個人 no one; none
跟 "或" 相反 the opposite of "或", which means someone; some

52. 朝廷　【名詞語】君主視朝聽政的地方 a royal or imperial
cháo tíng　court; the place where the ruler holds court audiences and governs the country

53. 臣 chén　【名詞】官員　officials

朝廷之臣　【名詞語】朝廷中的官員 officials under a feudal ruler;
cháotíng zhī chén　court officials

54. 境 jìng　【名詞】邊境；國境　a border; a boundary

四境　【名詞語】四邊國境
sì jìng　the border on four sides; the four borders

55. 由 yóu　【介詞】從 from

由此　【介詞語】從這個 [情形]
yóu cǐ　from this [situation]

56. 觀 guān　【動詞】觀察；看　to view; to look [at]

57. 蔽 bì　【動詞】蒙蔽　to obfuscate; to delude

【動詞】被蒙蔽；受蒙蔽
to become obfuscated; to become deluded

58. 令 lìng　【名詞】命令 an order; a command

下令　【動詞語】下命令　to issue an order; to order [an inferior]
xià lìng　to [do something]

171

59. 吏 lì　【名詞】低級官員；小官　functionaries; minor officials

60. 民 mín　【名詞】平民；百姓（與"君"、"官"對稱）
the common people; people (as opposed to the ruler or the government)

61. 面 miàn　【副詞】當面　face to face [with...]; to [my] face

62. 刺 cì　【動詞】指責　to point out and chide

63. 過 guò　【名詞】過失；過錯　faults

64. 受 shòu　【動詞】接受　to receive

65. 賞 shǎng　【動詞】賞賜　to bestow a reward; to reward

【名詞】獎賞　a reward; an award

上賞
shàng shǎng　【名詞語】上等的獎賞
the highest reward

66. 上 shàng　【動詞】呈上；呈獻 (xiàn)　to submit [a document to a superior]; to present [something] to one's superior

67. 書 shū　【名詞】書信；但寫給王看的書信，通常稱為奏 (zòu)章
a piece of writing; a letter, in general, anything in writing submitted to the king by an inferior was called a memorial

上書
shàng shū　【動詞語】上奏章　to submit a written memorial; to memorialize

68. 中賞
zhōng shǎng　【名詞語】中等的獎賞　the middle reward

69. 謗 bàng　【動詞】公開的指責　to point out and chide in public
此處：批評　to criticize

172

70. 議 yì 【動詞】議論 to discuss

71. 朝市
cháo shì 【名詞語】朝廷與市場
[at] the royal court or [in] the marketplace

72. 耳 ěr 【名詞】耳朵 the ear; ears

73. 下賞
xià shǎng 【名詞語】下等的獎賞
the lowest reward

74. 初 chū 【副詞】剛剛 at the outset; at first

75. 進諫
jìn jiàn 【動詞語】進獻諫言
to present remonstrances

76. 門 mén 【名詞】大門 a door; a gate
此處：門前 in front of the gate

77. 庭 tíng 【名詞】庭院；院子 the front courtyard

78. 若市
ruò shì 【準繫詞語】像市場一樣 like a marketplace
此處：像市場一樣[擠]
as [crowded as] a marketplace

79. 數 shù 【形容詞】幾個 several; a few; a number of

80. 時時
shí shí 【副詞】常常；時常 often; frequently
有時候兒 from time to time; at times

81. 間 jiàn 【副詞】間或；偶然 occasionally; once in a while

82. 期年
jī nián 【名詞語】一週年 [on the] anniversary; a full year later

83. 韓 Hán 【名詞】國名，在今河南省西北及陝西省東部之地

173

The name of a state that existed during the Warring States period and occupied the northwestern part of present-day Hénán and the eastern part of present-day Shǎnxī provinces.

84. 魏 Wèi 【名詞】國名，在今河南省北部及山西省西南部之地

The name of a state that existed during the Warring States period and occupied the northern part of present-day Hénán and the southwestern part of present-day Shānxī provinces.

85. 皆 jiē 【副詞】都 all

86. 朝 cháo 【動詞】朝見；到朝廷來見君主
LITERALLY: to go to the court of a ruler and to accept his sovereignty; to pay court

87. 所謂 suǒ wèi 【名詞語】所說的 that called; what is called

88. 戰 zhàn 【動詞】打仗 to do battle

89. 勝 shèng 【動詞】勝利 to win

戰勝 zhàn shèng 【動詞語】打勝；獲得勝利 to battle and win; to win a victory; to triumph

成語

門庭若市 méntíngruòshì

LITERALLY: "At the gate and in the courtyard it was as crowded as a marketplace."

大門前和庭院中擠得像市場一樣，形容來往的人很多
This phrase is used to describe a place bustling with social activity, where many people are constantly coming and going.

第三十九課

魏節乳母

注解

1. 魏 Wèi 　【名詞】魏國 (369-225 B.C.)　the name of a state that flourished during the Warring States period and was situated in present-day Hénán province

2. 節 jié 　【名詞】節操　uprightness

　　　　【形容詞】節烈；肯為正義、國家、君主死 upright; willing to die for righteousness, for one's country, or for one's sovereign

3. 乳母 rǔmǔ 　【名詞】奶媽　a wet nurse

4. 公子 gōngzǐ 　【名詞】諸侯的兒子叫公子　a princeling; a general term used to refer to any son of a feudal lord

5. 秦 Qín 　【名詞】秦國 (338-206 B.C.)　the name of a state that flourished during the Warring States period and was situated in present-day Shǎnxī province

6. 破 pò 　【動詞】打破；打敗 to break; to destroy; to defeat

7. 魏王瑕 Wèiwáng Xiá 　【名詞】戰國時代魏國的最後一位君主 the last ruler of the state of Wèi: King Xiá of Wèi (r. 227-225 B.C.)

8. 諸 zhū 　【形容詞】眾多　numerous; many

9. 令 lìng 　【動詞】命令；下命令 to order; to issue an order

10. 鎰 yì 　【量詞】古代的重量單位，20兩為一鎰，一說24兩為一鎰 an ancient unit of weight = 20 or 24 taels

11. 匿 nì 【動詞】藏匿 to conceal; to hide

12. 罪 zuì 【名詞】懲罰 (chéng fá) punishment

13. 夷 yí 【動詞】滅族；殺死整個家族 to exterminate an entire family or clan

14. 與 yǔ 【介詞】跟 and

15. 俱 jù 【副詞】一起 together

16. 逃 táo 【動詞】逃走 to flee; to run away

17. 故臣 gù chén 【名詞語】舊臣；從前的臣子 former ministers

18. 識 shì 【動詞】認識 to recognize

19. 恙 yàng 【名詞】憂慮 anxiety；禍患 adversity

無恙 wúyàng 【動詞語】沒有禍患；平安無事 LITERALLY: free from adversity/affiliction ; safe and sound

20. 嗟呼 jiē hū 【歎詞】咳！唉！表示挫 (cuò) 折或失望 alas! (an interjection used to express frustration and disappointment)

21. 奈…何 nài … hé 【動詞語】怎麼辦；把…怎麼辦 What to do with ...; What shall I do about ...?

22. 安 ān 【疑問代詞】何處；哪裡；哪儿 where

安在 ān zài 【動詞語】在何處；在哪裡 to be at/in what place? 在哪儿 where is ... ?

23. 倘 tǎng 【連詞】倘若；假如；要是 suppose; if

24. 可 以
   kě yǐ
   【助動詞】 可以；能 can

25. 言 yán
   【動詞】 說 to speak; to tell

26. 金 jīn
   【名詞】 古代計算貨幣的單位，先秦以二十兩為一鎰，一鎰又稱一金 a solid piece of gold weighing 20 or 24 taels

27. 昆弟
   kūn dì
   【名詞語】 兄弟 elder and younger brothers

28. 類 lèi
   【名詞】 族類；同族；同族的人 kinsfolk

   無類
   wú lèi
   【動詞語】 沒有[遺留下的]同族的人
   not have kinsfolk [left alive]
   ——→同族的人都被殺死 kinsfolk will all be slaughtered

   昆弟無類
   kūndì wúlèi
   【敘述句】 〔在〕兄弟〔中〕沒有[遺留下的]同族的人／兄弟
   [among] elder-younger brothers not-have kinsfolk left alive
   ——→ 沒有〔遺留下的〕同族兄弟
   there is no elder-younger brothers in the clan left alive
   ——→ 兄弟都被殺死
   brothers will all be killed

29. 吁 xū
   【歎詞】 唉，表示悲傷
   oh! alas! (an interjection used to express sorrow or dismay)

30. 處 chù
   【名詞】 處所；地方 place; whereabout

31. 亦 yì
   【副詞】 也 also; too

32. 終 zhōng
   【副詞】 到底 after all; to the end; in the end

177

33. 亡 wáng 【動詞】滅亡 to perish; to be destroyed; [of a state] to fall

34. 族 zú 【名詞】家族；同姓的親屬 clan; kinsfolk

35. 滅 miè 【動詞】消滅 to exterminate; to wipe out

36. 為 wèi 【介詞】為 for

37. 利 lì 【名詞】利益 benefit

38. 反 fǎn 【動詞】反叛；背叛 to revolt; to rebel; to turn against

39. 上 shàng 【名詞】等級、地位高的人；君主 one's superior 此處指小公子，實指魏王 here it refers to the little prince, and in fact, to the deceased king of Wèi

40. 逆 nì 【形容詞】叛逆 treasonous

【名詞】叛逆 treason

41. 也 yě 【助詞】用在判斷句末 a final particle used at the end of a determinative sentence

42. 畏 wèi 【動詞】畏懼；怕 to fear; to dread

43. 棄 qì 【動詞】拋棄 to throw away; to abandon

44. 義 yì 【名詞】道義；正義 what is fitting and proper; righteousness

45. 亂 luàn 【形容詞】昏亂；愚蠢 muddled; confounded

【名詞】昏亂；愚蠢 folly

46. 持 chí 【動詞】拿；憑藉 to hold onto; to rely on

47. 以 yǐ 【介詞】[靠它]來 thereby to...

48. 求 qiú   【動詞】謀求 to seek [to]

49. 為 wéi   【動詞】做；幹 to do

50. 也 yě   【助詞】用於句末表示堅決的語氣 a final particle
expressing a tone of resolution

51. 且 qiě   【連詞】而且 and; moreover

52. 夫 fú   【指示代詞】那個；那些 that; those

53. 養 yǎng   【動詞】養活；使…能活下去
to raise; to sustain the life of ...

養子   【動詞語】養活孩子；照顧孩子
yǎngzǐ   to raise a child; to care for a child

54. 務 wù   【動詞】致力；盡力；把力量都用在…方面
to do one's utmost to ...

55. 生 shēng   【動詞】生存；活 to live; to be alive

生之   【動詞語】使之生；使他生存；使他活著
shēng zhī   to make him live; to keep him alive; to preserve his life

56. 賞 shǎng   【名詞】賞賜；賞賜的東西或錢財
a reward; a gift of goods or cash

利賞   【動詞語】以賞賜為利益 to consider the reward as [a
lì shǎng   source for personal] profit
——→貪圖賞賜；極力希望得到賞賜
to covet a reward; to exert oneself in the hope
of obtaining a reward

57. 誅 zhū   【動詞】殺死 to kill; to be killed

畏誅   【連詞】畏懼被殺死；怕被殺死 to fear being killed
wèi zhū

58. 廢 fèi 　　【動詞】廢棄　to discard; to abandon; to cast aside

　　廢正義　【動詞語】廢棄正義　to abandon what is right and proper
　　fèi zhèngyì

59. 行 xíng 　　【動詞】實行；做　to practice; to do

60. 逆 nì 　　【動詞】違反；違背　to counter; to go against

　　逆節　【動詞語】違背節操 to go against moral principles
　　nì jié

　　　　　　　【名詞】違背節操 [的事] things or actions that go against moral principles

　　行逆節　【動詞語】做違背節操 [的事]　to go against what is
　　xíng nìjié 　right and proper (moral); to do what is not right and proper

61. 哉 zāi 　　【助詞】與副詞 "豈" 合用，構成反問句：
　　　　　　　"豈…哉？" 譯成白話是 "怎麼…呢？"
　　　　　　　a final particle used in conjunction with the adveb "豈" to form a
　　　　　　　rhetorical interrogative sentence "豈…哉？" which can be
　　　　　　　rendered in spoken Chinese as "怎麼…呢？" and in English
　　　　　　　as "How...."

62. 令 lìng 　　【動詞】使；讓　to let; to cause; to allow

63. 擒 qín 　　【動詞】捉　to capture; to arrest; to be captured

64. 遂 suì 　　【副詞】就　then; thereupon

65. 抱 bào 　　【動詞】抱 [著]　to hold or carry enfolded in the arms;
　　　　　　　to cradle [in the arms]

66. 深 shēn 　　【形容詞】從外面到裡面的距離很大　deep; of great
　　　　　　　distance from the interior to the exterior

67. 澤 zé 　　【名詞】窪(wā)地；低濕的地方
　　　　　　　a fen; a marsh; a low lying land

深澤
shēn zé
【名詞語】窪地的深處　deep in the fens

68. 告　gào
【動詞】報告　to report to

69. 追　zhuī
【動詞】追趕　to chase; to pursue

70. 爭　zhēng
【動詞】搶[著]；搶先
to strive to be the first [to do something]

71. 射　shè
【動詞】射箭　to shoot [with arrows]

72. 身　shēn
【名詞】身體；身子　the body; the trunk [of the body]

73. 蔽　bì
【動詞】遮蔽；遮擋　to cover; to shelter

74. 矢　shǐ
【名詞】箭　an arrow

75. 著　zhuó
【動詞】射中 (zhòng)　to hit [a mark or target]

76. 數十
shù shí
【數詞】幾十枝　several tens [of arrows]; scores [of]

77. 貴　guì
【形容詞用作動詞】以…為貴　to consider
[something] valuable or precious
⟶ 敬重　to respect; to esteem

78. 守　shǒu
【動詞】保持　to maintain ; to preserve

79. 忠　zhōng
【形容詞】忠誠　loyal; devoted; faithful

【名詞】忠心　a sense of loyalty

守忠
shǒuzhōng
【動詞語】保持忠心　to preserve [one's] sense of loyalty

181

80. 死義　sǐ yì 　【動詞語】為義而死；為道義而犧牲自己　to die for a righteous cause; to sacrifice oneself for a moral principle

◆ 犧牲 xīshēng　　a sacrifice; to sacrifice

81. 卿　qīng 　【名詞】古代高級官名，地位相當於秦以後的宰相　a court minister; a royal chamberlain

82. 禮　lǐ 　【名詞】禮儀；儀式　rites; a ceremony

83. 葬　zàng 　【動詞】埋葬　to bury; to inter

以卿禮葬之　【動詞語】以[葬]卿之禮葬之；用埋葬卿的禮
yǐ qīnglǐ zàngzhī　　儀埋葬她（節乳母）　to bury her with the rites befitting a great minister; to inter her with the ceremony appropriate for a great minister

84. 祠　cí 　【動詞】祭祀　to sacrifice; to offer a sacrifice to ...

85. 太牢　tàiláo 　【名詞】祭祀用的動物，包括豬、牛、羊　the Great Offering (sacrificial animals included the ox, sheep or goat, and the pig); this was the most elaborate sacrificial offering.

86. 寵　chǒng 　【動詞】恩賜　to favor; to bestow favor on
授給⋯官位　to bestow an official post
封給⋯爵 (jué) 位　to give an honorific post

87. 五大夫　wǔ dàifū 　【名詞】爵位名，通常賞賜給有功的人
LITERALLY: grand master of five: Grandee of the Ninth Order, 12th highest of 20 titles of honorary nobility (chüeh; jüé) conferred on deserving subjects. [Hucker, *Dictionary of official titles in Imperial China*, p. 573.]

相關成語

貪生怕死 tānshēngpàsǐ

LITERALLY: "Greedy for life; fearful of death"

當死而不死，對生命過於留戀

This saying is a metaphor used to criticize a person for fearing to do what he ought to do because he values his own safety above all else.

見利忘義 jiànlìwàngyì

LITERALLY: "See profit; forget righteousness"

為圖自己的私利而不顧道義

This saying is used to describe the behavior of people who scheme to profit from something without any regard for what is right or just.

捨生取義 shěshēngqǔyì

LITERALLY: "To cast away life *in order to* pick up righteousness"

為正義真理不惜犧牲生命

This saying is used to describe the behavior of someone who is willing to do what is right and just at any cost, even the cost of his own life.

第四十課

子産不毀鄉校

注解

1. 子産
Zǐchǎn

【名詞】人名。春秋時代鄭國的大夫公孫僑，子產是字。他博學多聞，長於治國。執掌國政二十餘年，對內實行寬厚但不失嚴明的政策；對外尊重當時正在爭霸的晉楚兩大強國，但絕不接受他們不合理的要求。因此鄭國雖弱小，卻能保持安定，不受侵略。鄭國的老百姓很愛戴他，晉楚等國的君主也都很敬重他。是中國古代最傑出的政治家之一。

Zǐchǎn was a high minister (grandee) of the state of Zhèng during the Spring and Autumn period. His name was Gōngsūn Qiáo; Zǐchǎn was his courtesy name. He was erudite, broadly-experienced, and accomplished at statecraft. He was in charge of the government for more than twenty years. In domestic affairs, he put into practice policies that were tolerant and generous, yet stern and fair; in diplomacy he paid homage to the two principal states contending for hegemony, the states of Jìn and Chǔ, but refused to accept any unreasonable demands from either state. For these reasons, though Zhèng was a weak and small state, it remained sound, stable, and free from foreign invasion. The people of Zhèng respected and supported Zǐchǎn, and the rulers of Jìn and Chǔ also respected him. He was one of ancient China's outstanding statesmen.

◆ 博學 *bóxué*　　learned; erudite

◆ 多聞 *duōwén*　　to have broad experience; broadly-experienced

◆ 長於 *chángyú*　　to be good at; to be accomplished at

◆ 寬厚 *kuānhòu*　　tolerant and generous

◆ 嚴明 *yánmíng*　　stern and fair

◆ 爭霸 *zhēngbà*　　to contend for hegemony; to strive for supremacy

184

◆ 愛戴 *àidài*   to respect and support

◆ 傑出 *jiéchū*   outstanding; eminent

2. 毀 huǐ   【動詞】毀壞；拆毀   to destroy; to pull down

3. 鄉 xiāng   【名詞】古代行政區域的名稱，一萬二千五百家為一鄉   the name of an ancient admimnistrative unit nominally comprised of 12,500 households

     ◆ 行政區域   a district; an administrative area
     xíngzhèngqūyù

4. 校 xiào   【名詞】學校   a school

     鄉校   【名詞語】鄉間的學校 a local school
     xiāngxiào

5. 論 lùn   【動詞】評論   to comment on

6. 執 zhí   【動詞】執掌 (zhǎng)；掌管 to be in charge of; to conduct

7. 政 zhèng   【名詞】政權   political power; the government

     執政   【動詞語】執掌政權；掌管國家政事
     zhí zhèng   to hold political power; to conduct the government

     【名詞語】執掌政權的人   those who hold political power; those who conduct the government

8. 然明   【名詞】人名。姓鬷 (Zōng)，名蔑 (Miè)，字然明，
     Ránmíng   鄭國的大夫 Zōng Miè (courtesy name Ránmíng) was a high official of the state of Zhèng.

9. 何如   【準繫詞語】如何？怎麼樣？ lit: What like ⟶
     hérú   Like what? What do you think of it? How about it?

10. 何為   【介詞語】為什麼？ What for? Why?
     héwèi

11. 夫 fú 【助詞】放在句首，表示將發議論 When it is used at the beginning of a sentence, this particle usually indicates that the speaker or subject is offering what follows as a personal comment, observation or criticism.

12. 朝 zhāo 【名詞】早晨 the morning

13. 夕 xī 【名詞】傍 (bàng) 晚 the evening

朝夕 【名詞語】早晨跟傍晚 morning and evening
zhāo xī 此處：時常；經常 often; frequently

14. 退 tuì 【動詞】返 (fǎn) 歸 (guī)；返回 to go back to; to come back to; to return
此處：工作完了回來 to return ... after work

15. 議 yì 【動詞】議論 to discuss critically; to comment on

16. 善 shàn 【形容詞】好；妥善
good; appropriate

17. 否 fǒu 【副詞】用在肯定否定式表示選擇的句子裡，表示否定的一面。例如：是否＝是不是
When it is used in an interrogative sentence asking for a simple affirmative or negative response (an A or not-A question), this word stands for the negative part of the question.
For example: 是否：to be true or to be untrue

善否 【形容詞語】妥善不妥善；妥不妥善
shàn fǒu to be appropriate or inappropriate

18. 其所善者 【名詞語】人民認為妥善的那些政令
qísuǒshànzhě those government policies and ordinances which people regard as good

19. 行 xíng 【動詞】實行；推行 to carry out; to implement [policies, etc.]

20. 其所惡者 【名詞語】人民認為不妥善的那些政令
    qísuǒèzhě   those government policies and ordinances which people regard as inappropriate

21. 改 gǎi   【動詞】更改；改正 to change; to correct

22. 是 shì   【指示代詞】此；這個 this; these
    此處：指鄉校及鄉校中人民的評論
    "This" here refers to the entire description of the village school and its functions in the foregoing passage.

23. 師 shī   【名詞】老師 a teacher

24. 若之何 【疑問副詞】為什麼？怎麼可以？
    ruòzhīhé   how could...? so how can...?

25. 忠 zhōng   【形容詞】忠誠；盡心竭力 loyal; devoted; to devote one's total mental and physical energies [to some person, cause, task, etc.]

   忠善 【動詞語】忠 [於] 善 devoted to good; dedicated to good
   zhōngshàn   忠於為善 devoted to doing good
   對於 [實行] 妥善的政令盡心竭力
   with respect to implementing good government policies, to do one's utmost
   ⟶ 盡心竭力地實行妥善的政令
   to do one's utmost to implement good government policies.

26. 損 sǔn   【動詞】減少 to decrease; to slacken; to lessen

27. 怨 yuàn   【動詞】怨恨 to hold a grudge against; to harbor resentment toward somebody

   【名詞】怨恨 ill-will

   損怨 【動詞語】減少怨恨 to decrease [the feeling of] ill-will
   sǔn yuàn

187

28. 作 zuò 　【動詞】表現　to display; to make a show of

29. 威 wēi 　【名詞】威力　might; prestige

作威 zuò wēi 　【動詞語】表現威力；作出令人畏懼的事來
to display one's might and power; to cow others
by a display of might; to make a show of force
此處：採取嚴厲 (yánlì) 的措 (cuò) 施
to use harsh measures

30. 防 fáng 　【動詞】堵 (dǔ) 住　to block up; to prevent

防怨 fáng yuàn 　【動詞語】防堵怨恨　to block [the feeling of] ill-will

31. 豈 qǐ 　【副詞】難道…？用反問表示肯定　Would it not ...?
Don't you mean to say...?
An adverb used at the head of a rhetorical question to indicate
that the speaker anticipates a response to the contrary.

32. 遽 jù 　【副詞】急速 (sù) 地；很快地　quickly

33. 止 zhǐ 　【動詞】制止　to prevent; to check; to stop

34. 川 chuān 　【名詞】河流　a river; runing water

35. 決 jué 　【動詞】[堤防]潰 (kuì) 決；水把堤防衝 (chōng) 破
to breach the dike; to overflow

◆ 堤防 dīfáng 　dikes or embankments

大決 dà jué 　【動詞語】大規模地衝破堤岸
to breach the dike on a large scale

36. 犯 fàn 　【動詞】侵犯；危害　to ravage; to endanger
此處：淹 (yān) 没　to inundate

37. 傷 shāng 　【動詞】傷害　to injure; to hurt; to harm

188

38. 克 kè 【助動詞】能夠　to be able to [succeed, overcome]

39. 救 jiù 【動詞】拯(zhěng)救　to save; to rescue

40. 小決 xiǎojué 【動詞語】小規模地衝開堤防
to breach the dike on a small scale
此處：[給河堤] 開一個小口
to make a small breach in the dike

41. 道 dǎo 【動詞】通 "導(dǎo)"，疏(shū)通
to dredge a river in order to channel the water

使道 shǐ dǎo 【動詞語】使河水[被]引導出去；使河水[暢順地]
流出去　to make the water flow out freely [in a channel]

43. 藥 yào 【名詞】藥物　medicine
【用作動詞】以…為藥；把…當作藥
here the noun functions as a verb: to regard ... as medicine; to medicate [oneself]
【動詞】治療　to cure; to treat

藥之 yào zhī 【動詞語】以之（民評）為藥；把百姓的評論當
作良藥（好藥）　to take people's criticism as a good
medicine [for curing the political illness]

42. 蔑 Miè 【名詞】人名，就是然明。古人對人說話時自稱
名字而不用代詞 "吾"，表示尊敬聽話的人
Miè is Zōng Miè's given name; his courtesy name was Ránmíng
(see no. 8). In antiquity, when a person referred to himself in
speech or in a dialogue, he used his given name, instead of the
personal pronoun "I", as a mark of respect toward the listener.

43. 今而後 jīn ér hòu 【時間詞】從今以後　LITERALLY: today and after
[today]; from now on; henceforth

44. 吾子 wúzǐ 【代詞】您　you; sir; my dear sir
對人稱 "吾子"，有表示親近的含意

189

When used in direct address, the term "吾子" implies some familiarity or intimacy between the speaker and the person so addressed. It is roughly equivalent to the archaic English form of address "my dear sir" or "good sir."

45. 信 xìn 【副詞】確實；的確 truly; indeed

46. 可 kě 【助動詞】適宜 suitable; fit
値得 worthy of

47. 事 shì 【動詞】事奉；侍奉；追隨 to serve; to follow

可事 kě shì 【動詞語】值得敬佩追隨 fit to respect and follow

48. 小人 xiǎo rén 【名詞語】地位卑賤、見識短淺的人。此處是然明自謙之稱，意思是"我"。

LITERALLY: a small person; a small-minded person; someone of mean status and limited experience. Ránmíng uses this derogatory term here as a polite, self-deprecatory way of referring to himself: "this small person ⟶ this small-minded person = I"

◆ 自謙 zìqián to be self-deprecatory

49. 實 shí 【副詞】確實；的確；實在 truly; really; actually

50. 才 cái 【名詞】才能 ability
【動詞】有才能 to have ability; to be capable

不才 bù cái 【動詞語】沒有才能 without ability
此處："見識短淺"、"見事不明"、"看事看得不透徹"
shallow; lacking in perspicuity; short-sighted

51. 果 guǒ 【副詞】果真 really; truly

190

52. 其 qí 【代詞】通常代第三身 "他" 或 "他們的" ，偶或代第二身 "你" 或 "你們的" 跟第一身 "我" 或 "我們的" 。此處根據上下文應代第一身

The word "其" is generally encountered as a third person (singular and plural) pronoun (equivalent to he, she, it, they) and as a third person (singular and plural) possessive pronoun (his, hers, its, theirs). It is occasionally also used as a first and second person (singular and plural) pronoun (I, we, you) and possessive pronoun (my, our, your). From the context, the word "其" should be understood here as a first person possessive pronoun (my, our).

其鄭國
qí Zhèngguó
【名詞語】我們的鄭國 our state of Zhèng

53. 賴 lài 【動詞】依賴；依靠 to rely on; to depend on

54. 唯 wéi 【副詞】只；只有；只是 only; merely

55. 二三 èr sān 【數詞】泛指複數；兩三個；幾個 a general term for plural mumber; two-or-three; several

◆泛指 fànzhǐ   to make a general reference [to something]

◆複數 fùshù   plural mumber

56. 臣 chén 【名詞】臣子 officials serving under a feudal ruler; court officials

二三臣
èr sān chén
【名詞語】兩三個臣子；幾個臣子 two or three officials
——→我們這些臣子 a few of us court officials; we

57. 仲尼 Zhòngní 【名詞】孔子的字 Confucius' courtesy name

58. 語 yǔ 【名詞】言論；話 speech; words

58. 觀 guān 【動詞】看 to look at; to view

59. 謂 wèi 　　【動詞】說，用於評論人或物　to say, used to introduce another person's point of view, criticism, or opinion about sb. or sth.

60. 仁 rén 　　【形容詞】仁愛　kind-hearted; benevolent; humane
此處：愛人民
kind to the people [governed]; caring

61. 信 xìn 　　【動詞】相信　to believe

相關成語

防民之口，甚於防川 fángmínzhīkǒu shènyúfángchuān

LITERALLY: "Blocking up the people's mouths is worse than blocking up the rivers."

逐字譯成白話是："堵住人民的嘴，比防堵河流還嚴重。"

實際的意思是："制止人民的議論，比堵住河流更有害。"

"It is worse (more damaging) to stop the people from voicing critical opinions than to block up the rivers."

作威作福 zùowēizuòfú

濫用權威，專橫獨斷。
tyrannically abuse one's power;
to over-exert one's power and position by acting imprudently

CLASSICAL CHINESE
A BASIC READER

ANALYSES

袁乃瑛　　唐海濤　　蓋杰民
Naiying Yuan　Haitao Tang　James Geiss

PRINCETON UNIVERSITY PRESS
PRINCETON, NEW JERSEY

句析目錄

句析目錄

句析目錄

句析目錄

List of Errata to the Analyses

page	line	was	should be
		was	should be
10	5	be robbed	(shift right)
59	6	the preposition…	(close up)
68	23	togethere	together
97	10	複句中。	複句。
102	10	ha cannot	he cannot
120	17	"之"	"哭"
130	12	賓語倒	賓語常倒
130	16	(don't)	(none)
139	8	grass to	(shift right)
195	10	prep	adv
231	21	s v o	(shift right)
232	16	ancestral	(shift left)
232	17	temple	(shift right)
233	4	basket	(shift right)
235	15	v conj	(shift right)
252	5	showthe	show the
261	4	這個人	(shift right)
265	20	實在	卻
266	1	實在	卻
279	4	介紹；	介紹，
284	11	adj mod. pron	(shift right)
327	19	s	(shift right)
355	4	鄉校，	鄉校
361	23	\prep o/	(shift right)
361	23	\adv adj/	(shift right)
361	27	堤坊	堤防
362	3	堤坊	堤防
373	20	adjectiveto	adjective to

鄭相卻魚

句子分析

一. 鄭相 卻 魚
        v o
  s   p

鄭相拒絕魚。

Zhèng minister refuse fish.

⟶ 鄭國宰相拒絕魚。

The prime minister *of the* state *of* Zhèng refus*ed a gift of* fish.

⟹ 鄭國宰相拒絕魚。

The prime minister of the state of Zhèng refused a gift of fish.

※鄭相卻魚 :

這是個標準的**敘述簡句**，由一個主語及一個動詞性的謂語兩部分構成。謂語本身又包含動詞及賓語。文言敘述句的基本詞序是主語在前、接著是動詞、動詞後才是賓語。

This is a typical **Narrative Simple Sentence** that comprises of two parts: the subject and the verbal predicate. The predicate is in turn composed of a verb and its object. The standard word order of a narrative sentence is Subject-Verb-Object.

二. ［於］昔者　　有 餽魚於 鄭相者，
   ［prep］o   v o prep o n
             adi. mod n
    s   p

※有　　　　　【動詞】含有"領有""存在"兩種意思，因此結構"N1有N2"(A式)和結構"［於］N1

（時／地／群）有 N2"（B式）稍微不同。中國語
言學家通常把A式叫作"有無句"，把B式叫
作"存在句"來表示它們的區別。(見呂叔
湘，《中國文法要略》六六至六九頁)。當
"有"字出現在表示時間的"介詞語"後面
時，意思是"在…時候…存在。""[於]昔者
有…"意思是"在從前的時候有／存在…。"
為了分析和解釋時方便，在本書中把這種介詞
語"[於]N1"稱作"主語"。

The verb "有" has both a possessive and a durative aspect.
Thus, the construction "N1 有 N2" (Type A) and the
construction "[於] N1 (time/location/group) 有 N2"
(Type B) are slightly different. To draw this distinction, Chinese
linguists usually call Type A a "**possessive sentence**" and
Type B an "**existential sentence**". (See Lǚ Shūxiāng's
Zhōngguó Wénfǎ Yàolüè pp. 66-69.) When "有" appears after a
temporal prepositional phrase, it means "at such a time
something existed." "[於]昔者有...." means "At a time in the
past there existed/Once there was..." For convenience in analysis
and explanation, prepositional phrases "[於] N1" that occur in
Type B sentences will be treated as "subjects" in this book.

※…者　　　　【名詞語】"…者" "…之N（…之人）"

饋 魚 於 鄭相 者
　v　o　prep　o
　　adjectival modifier　　　pronoun

The entire construction preceding the pronoun "者" is an
adjectival modifier: here "者" means "a person who..."; it
transforms the construction into a noun phrase.

從前有贈送魚給鄭相的人，

Past have present-fish-to-Zhèng-minister one,

⟶ [在]從前有個贈送魚給鄭國宰相的人，

[In] *the* past *there was* a person *who* present*ed a gift of fish* to *the* prime
minister *of the* state *of* Zhèng;

⟹ 從前有個贈送魚給鄭國宰相的人，

Once there was a person who presented a gift of fish to the prime minister of
the state of Zhèng;

三. 鄭相 不 受。
　　　　　　＼adv v／
　　s　　　　　p

鄭相不接受。

Zhèng minister not accept.

⟶ 鄭國宰相不接受。

the prime minister *of the* state *of* Zhèng *did* not accept *it* (i.e., *the* gift).

⟹ 鄭國宰相不接受。

the prime minister of the state of Zhèng did not accept it.

四. 或 謂鄭相 曰：“子嗜魚，何故不受?”
　　　　＼v o／ ＼v　　　　　　　　　o　　　　／
　　s　　 p1　　　　　　　　　p2

“子[既]嗜魚，[則][以] 何故不受?”
　　　[conj] ＼v o／ [conj] ＼[prep]　o　adv v／
　　s　　　　　　p1　　　[conj]　　　　p2

※ 謂…曰 “謂”，“曰”都是“說”的意思，後面都
　　　　　 有所說的話。但“謂”不與所說的話緊接，
　　　　　 而“曰”則與所說的話緊接。“謂”後可緊
　　　　　 接一間接賓語“某人”，然後再接上“曰”
　　　　　 ，構成“謂…曰”句型

　　　　　 "謂" and "曰"both mean "to say" and are both used to
　　　　　 introduce a direct quotation. However, whereas "曰"
　　　　　 always precedes the first word of the direct quotation, "謂"
　　　　　 does not necessarily have to; it can sometimes be followed by
　　　　　 an indirect object, and then followed by "曰"to form the
　　　　　 pattern "謂 [a person] 曰" (address [a person] saying).

※ 既…則… “既”跟“則”都是連詞，“既”用在上一
　　　　　 分句提出某一事實作為前提，“則”字用在
　　　　　 第二分句，根據前提所提出的事實作一合理
　　　　　 的推論。白話可譯成“既然…那麼…”，構

成標準的推論複句。但有時"既"省略，
有時"既"、"則"都省略。

"既" (since) and "則" (then) are both conjunctions. "既" is used in the first clause stating a fact as the premise, and "則" is used in the second clause to draw a reasonable inference from it. In spoken Chinese this can be rendered as "既然…那麼…", comstituting a typical **Inferential Complex Sentence**. Either or both these conjunctions can be omitted without substantially changing the meaning of the sentence.

有人告訴鄭相説："您愛好魚，什麼緣故不接受？"

Someone address Zhèng minister say: "Gentleman relish fish, what reason not accept?"

⟶ 有人對鄭國宰相説："您[既然]非常喜歡吃魚，[那麼] [因爲]什麼緣故不接受呢？"

Someone address*ed the* prime minister *of the* state *of* Zhèng, say*ing*: "[Since] you relish eat*ing* fish, [then] [for] what reason *did you* not accept *the gift of fish* ?"

⟹ 有人對鄭國宰相説："您既然非常喜歡吃魚，那麼因爲 什麼緣故不接受呢？"

Someone addressed the prime minister of the state of Zhèng saying: "Since you relish eating fish, why then did you not accept?"

五. [鄭相] 對 曰：" "
　　[s]　　　p

回答説：

Reply, say:

⟶ [鄭國宰相]回答説：

[*The* prime minister *of the* state *of* Zhèng] repl*ied*, say*ing*:

⟹ 他回答説：

He replied, saying:

五．一　　　"吾　以　嗜　魚　故　不　受。
　　　　　　　prep ＼ v　o ／ conj ＼adv v ／
　　　　　　　s　　　　p1　　　　　p2

"我因爲愛好魚，所以不接受。

"I for relish fish reason not accept.

⟶　"我因爲非常喜歡吃魚，所以才不接受。

"I, because *of* relish*ing* fish, consequently *did* not accept *the gift of fish.*

⟹　"我因爲非常喜歡吃魚，所以才不接受。

"Because I relish eating fish, I thus did not accept.

※ 以…故…是標準的因果複句，"以"是個介詞，用在上一分句，介紹原因或理由，"故"是個連詞，用在下一分句，說明它的後果。白話可譯成"因爲…所以…"。

This is a typical **Causal Complex Sentence.** The first or subordinate clause states a cause or reason, which is here introduced by the preposition "以" (because); the main clause which follows is usually introduced by the conjunction "故" (therefore) to express its effect or consequence. This can be translated into spoken Chinese as "因爲…所以…" and into English as "because..., thus..."

五．二　　　[吾][若] 受魚 [則] 失祿，[則] 無以食魚；
　　　　　　　[conj] ＼v　o／ [conj] ＼v　o／ [conj] ＼v o v o／
　　　　　　　[s]　　　p1　　　　　p2　　　　　　　p3

※ 若…則…是標準的假設複句，"若"是連詞，用在上一分句，提出一個假設，"則"也是連詞，用在下一分句，說明假設的後果。白話可譯成"要是…就／那麼／那麼就…"。文言的這種句式，往往省略"若"或"若"、

"則"都省略，但白話譯文為求意思清楚，
仍須譯出"要是…就／那麼／那麼就…"。

This is a typical **Hypothetical Complex Sentence.**
The first or subordinate clause expresses a hypothetical
statement, which is here introduced by the conjunctions "若"
(if) ; the main clause which follows is usually introduced by
the conjunction "則" (then) to state a fact or condition
contingent on the hypothetical statement expressed in the first
clause (if A, then B). Both conjunctions can be omitted in
some cases.

接受魚，失掉薪俸，沒有法子吃魚。

Accept fish, lose salary, not-have wherewith eat fish.

⟶ [我][假若]接受了魚，[就]會失掉薪俸，[那
麼][就]沒有法子吃魚了。

[If I] *were to* accept *the* fish, [then] *I might* lose *my* official salary,
[and so] *I would* not have any way *at all to* eat fish.

⟹ 我假若接受了魚，就會失掉薪俸，那麼就沒有法
子吃魚了。

If I were to accept the fish, I might lose my official salary; then I
would have no way at all to eat fish.

五.三　[吾]不受[魚][則]得祿，[則]終身食魚。"
　　　　　 \adv v [o]/ [conj]\v o/ [conj] \v o v o/
　　　　 [s]　　 p1　　　　 p2　　　　　　 p3

＊終身　　　過完一生
　　　　　 ⟶一輩子
　　　　　 "終身"本來是動賓結構，此處用來描寫
　　　　　 "食魚"，在句中的地位降低，作用像個副詞
　　　　　 ，故可直接翻譯成"一輩子。"

"終身" is by itself a verb-object construction meaning "to
live to the end of one's life". Here it is used to describe a second
verb-object construction, "食魚" (to eat fish). In this sentence,
it modifies the verb-object phrase it is describing and functions
like an adverbial phrase. Hence it can be translated
into spoken Chinese as "一輩子" and into English as "until the
end of [one's] life."

6

不接受，得到薪俸，一輩子吃魚。”

Not accept, get salary, whole life eat fish."

⟶ ［我］不接受［魚］吶，［就］能得到薪俸，［那麼］
［就］一輩子都能吃到魚。”

If [I] *do* not accept [*the* fish], [then] *I* can get *my* official salary,
[and so] can eat fish *until the* end *of my* life."

⟹ 我不接受魚吶，就能得到薪俸，那麼就一輩子
都吃得到魚。”

If I do not accept, I can get my official salary and so can eat fish
until the end of my life."

7

第二課

宋有富人

句子分析

一. ［於］宋 有富人，
\［prep］o / \ v o /
　　s　　　 p

　　　　　　　※有　　　　在存在句中（見第一課，句子分析二）"有"字出現在處所性"介詞語"（如：［於］宋有…）時，意思是"在N1（地）有／存在N2"。

　　　　　　　　　　　　In an existential sentence (*see Lesson 1, sentence analysis 2*), when "有" appears after a prepositional phrase indicating location (e.g., ［於］宋有 ...), it means "at a certain place (**N1**) there was **N2**" or "There was **N2** at/in **N1**."

　　　　宋有有錢人，

　　　　Sòng have wealthy person.

　　——→［在］宋國有個很有錢的人，

　　　　[In] *the* state *of* Sòng *there was* a very rich person.

　　===> 宋國有個很有錢的人，

　　　　In the state of Sòng there was a wealthy person.

二. 天 雨 牆 壞。
　　∨　 ∨
　　s　p　s　p

　　　　　　　※壞　　　"壞"本是形容詞，但在本句內用作動詞，不可以翻譯成"很壞"，得翻譯成"變壞"或"壞了"，"了"表示經過變化，產生了新的情況。

8

"壞" primarily functions as an adjective in classical Chinese; however, in this sentence it functions as a verb and cannot be translated as "very bad." It must be translated as "become damaged" or "be ruined" in English and as "壞了" in spoken Chinese, where "了" indicates that because of some change a new situation has arisen.

天下雨，牆壞。

Heaven rain, wall be-damaged.

———> 天下雨，他家的牆壞了。

It rain*ed, and the* wall *around* his house *was* damag*ed.*

===> 天下雨，他家的牆壞了。

It rained, and the wall around his house was damaged.

三． 其子曰：" 不築，必將有盜。"
   s   p

   [父] [若] 不 築， [則] 必 將 有 盜。
        [conj] \adv v/   [conj] \adv aux v o/
   [s]   p1   p2

他的兒子說： " 不修理，一定會有賊。"

His son say: "Not build, certainly will have robber."

———> 他的兒子說： " [您] [要是] 不修理牆， [那麼] 一定會有賊。"

His son sa*id*: "[If] [you] *do* not repair *the* wall, [then] *we* will certainly have robber*s*."

===> 他的兒子說： " 您要是不修理牆，那麼一定會有賊。"

His son said: "If you do not repair the wall, we will definitely be robbed."

四． 其鄰人之父 亦 云 [： " 不築，必將有盜。"]
             \adv v   [o]
   s   p

9

他的鄰居的老頭儿也說。

Their neighbors' old man too say.

⟶ 他的鄰居的老頭儿也說 [："不修理，一定會有賊。"]

The old man next door also sa*id* [: If *you* don't repair it, *you* will   definitely *be* rob*bed*).

⟶ 他的鄰居的老頭儿也這麼說。

The old man next door **said so** too.

⟹ 他的鄰居的老頭儿也這麼說。

The old man next door said so too.

五.　　　[及] 暮　而 [富人] 果 大 亡 其財。
　　　　　\[prep] o/　conj　[s]　\adv adv v　o/
　　　　　adv　　　　　　　**p**

※而　　　"而"字連接介詞語和動詞語時，"而"字前
　　　　介詞語的用處像是一個副詞，描寫"而"字後
　　　　的動詞語，在這種情形下，"而"字不必翻譯
　　　　。

When it links a prepostional phrase and a predicate, the prepositional phrase preceding the word "而" functions like an adverb describing the predicate following the word "而". In such cases, the word "而" need not be literally translated into spoken Chinese. In English it can be rendered as "and" or incorporated into an adverbial phrase (i.e., when it got dark).

天黑果然大量丟失他的錢。

Evening -- as expected big lose his money.

⟶ [到了]天黑了[的時候]，[有錢的人]果然大量地失掉他
的錢財。

[When] *it got* dark, [*the* wealthy man], as expected, *lost* his money *in* great amount.

—→ [到了]天黑了[的時候]，[有錢的人]果然丟了很多他的錢。

[When] *it got* dark, [*the* wealthy man], as expected, **lost *a* great amount *of* his money.**

==⟹ 到了天黑了的時候，有錢的人果然丟了很多他的錢。

When it got dark, the wealthy man, as expected, lost a great amount of his money.

六． 其家 甚 智 其子， 而 疑 鄰人之父。
　　　　　\adv (adj)v　o/　conj \v　　o/
　　　s　　　p1　　　　　　　　p2

※其家甚智其子，而疑鄰人之父：

這是**轉折式複句**。上下兩分句不但意思相對立，而且在邏輯上也衝突，或軼出常識與期望之外。通常用"而"字或"然"字連接兩個分句，可譯成白話的"可是"或"卻"。

The is a **Contradictive Compound Sentence**. The two clauses are not only contrary in meaning, but they also express a contradiction in logic, common sense, or expectation. The second clause is often linked to the first one with the conjunction "而"or"然", which can be translated into spoken Chinese as "可是"or"卻".

※智　　　"智"形容詞用作動詞，意動用法。

The word "智" is an adjective that functions here as a **putative verb** (i.e., to think N Adj.). Here it means:

智其子：　1)以其子為智
took their son to be bright

2)以為(認為)其子智
considered their son to be bright

3)覺得他們的孩子聰明
thought their son bright

※而　　　"而"字連接兩個謂語，逆接，前後兩個謂語有相背的關係，可譯成"可是"，"卻"或"反倒"。

11

When the word " 而 "connects two predicates that are mutually contrary, it can be translated into spoken Chinese as " 可是 ", 卻 " or " 反倒 " and into English as "but," "yet," "on the contrary."

那家人很聰明他們的孩子，可是懷疑鄰居的老頭儿。

That family muchly bright their child, but suspect neighbors' old man.

⟶ 那家人以為他們的孩子很聰明，可是都懷疑鄰居的老頭儿。

The people *in* that family **considered their child very bright**, but suspected *the* old man next door.

⟹ 那家人覺得他們的孩子很聰明，可是都懷疑鄰居的老頭儿。

That family thought their child very bright, but suspected the old man next door.

第三課

守株待兔

句子分析

一． [於]宋人 有 耕者。
　　　\prep　o／ \v　o／
　　　　　s　　　　p

　　　　　　　　※有　　　　在存在句中（見第一課，句子分析二）
　　　　　　　　　　　　　　"有"字出現在表示一群體的介詞語後面（如[
　　　　　　　　　　　　　　於]宋人有...者）時，意思是"[在]N1[中]有
　　　　　　　　　　　　　　／存在 N2"。

　　　　　　　　　　　　　　In an **existential sentence** (See Lesson 1, sentence
　　　　　　　　　　　　　　analysis 2), when "有" appears after a prepositional phrase
　　　　　　　　　　　　　　delimiting a group (e.g., [於]宋人有…者), it means "In a
　　　　　　　　　　　　　　certain group (**N1**) there was **N2**" or "There was **N2** among
　　　　　　　　　　　　　　N1."

　　　　宋人有耕田的人。

　　　　Sòng people have till-field one.

　　──→　[在]宋國人[裡]有個耕田的人。

　　　　[Among] *the* people *of the* state *of* Sòng, *there was* a person *who was* till*ing*
　　　　his field.

　　══⟹　有個耕田的宋國人。

　　　　There was a person in the state of Sòng who was tilling his field.

二． [於]田中 有 株，
　　　\prep o／ \v o／
　　　　s　　　p

　　　　田裡有樹樁，

　　　　Field middle have stump,

⟶ [在]田裡有截樹樁子,

[In] *the* field *there was* a *tree* stump.

⟹ 在田裡有截樹樁子,

In the field there was a tree stump.

三.　兔 走 觸 株，折 頸 而 死，

先/因　　　後/果

s　p1　p2　　p3　conj　p4

※兔走觸株,折頸而死:

這是**連續式複句**。這種複句的謂語部分連用兩個或兩個以上的動詞來表示同一主語的一連串有一定順序的動作／行動,呈現一極簡明、緊湊的風格。

This is a **Sequential Compound Sentence**. Tis type of sentence has a predicate that contains two or more verbs to show a series of sequential actions by the same subject. It is a terse and compact style.

※而

"而"字連接兩個謂語,順接,前後兩謂語有先後或因果的關係,"而"字可譯成
"就"。

When the word " 而 " links two predicates in a sequential, temporal, or causal manner, the word " 而 " can be translated into spoken Chinese as " 就 " and into English as "and," "and then," "and so," etc.

兔子跑碰樹樁,折斷脖子就死,

Hare run hit stump, break neck and die,

⟶ 一隻兔子跑過來,碰到樹樁子上,碰斷了脖子就死了,

A hare r*an by*, dash*ed into the tree* stump, br*oke its* neck, *and* then d*ied*;

⟹ 一隻兔子跑過來,碰到樹樁子上,碰斷了脖子就死了,

14

A hare ran by, dashed into the tree stump, broke its neck, and then died;

行動　　　　目的
四． ［耕者］因　釋其耒而　守株，冀復得兔。
　　　　　　adv　＼ v　o／ conj ＼ v　o／ ＼ v　　o　／
　　　s　　　　　　 **p1**　　　　　 **p2**　　　　 **p3**

　　　　　　　　　　　　　　　　　　　　　[s] adv　v　o
　　　　　　　　　　　[耕者]冀 ［己］復　得　兔
　　　　　　　　　　　　　　[s]　　 v　　　　o

※ 耕者因釋其耒而守株，冀復得兔：

> 這是目的式複句。第二分句（主要分句）表示目的。第一分句（從屬分句）指出藉以達到目的的方法。通常在第二分句前用一"而"字或"以"字，可譯成白話的"來"或"去"。

This is a **Purposive Complex Sentence**. The second (main) clause expresses a purpose or goal, and the first (subordinate) clause indicates or describes the means whereby this purpose or goal is to be attained. The connective "而" or "以" is generally used to introduce the second clause. The connective is equivalent to "來" or "去" in spoken Chinese.

※而

> "而"字連接兩個謂語，順接，前一謂語表示行動，後一謂語表示目的，"而"字可譯成"來"或"去"。

The conjunction "而" links two predicates in sequence: the first predicate states an action; the second predicate shows the purpose of that action. When "而" is used in this way, it can be rendered as "來" or "去" in spoken Chinese and as an infinitive complement (to + verb) in English.

※復得兔

> "復得兔"是動賓結構，它前面省略[或隱藏著]主語"己"字，全都寫出來應該是"[己]復得兔"作動詞"冀"字的賓語，這種句子中包含著另一個句子的結構，稱為包孕(yùn)句。

The phrase "復得兔" is a verb-object (**v-o**) construction; the subject "己" (he himself) is understood and omitted. In its fullest form, the sentence would read "[己]復得兔". The entire sentence serves as the object of the verb "冀". This type of sentence construction, in which an independent clause

15

functions as a grammatical element in a complex sentence, is called an **embedding sentence** construction ("包孕句" lit., a **pregnant sentence**).

就放下他的犁去守樹椿，希望再得兔子。

whereupon let-go his plough to guard stump, hope again get hare.

⟶ [耕田的人]就放下他的犁去守著樹椿子，希望再得到兔子。

[*the* person till*ing the* field] then put down his plough *in order* to watch *the* tree stump, hop*ing* to get *a* hare again.

⟹ 耕田的人於是放下他的犁去看守樹椿子，希望再得到兔子。

The person tilling the field then put down his plough to watch the tree stump, hoping to get a hare again.

五． 兔 [__] 不 可 復 得 ， 而 身 為 宋 國 笑 。
　　　 \o [s] adv aux adv v/ conj \prep o v/
　　　　　　　 p1　　　　　　 s　　　 p2

[耕者] 不 可 復 得 兔 ， 而 身 為 宋 國 笑 。
　　　　 \adv aux adv v o/ conj \prep o v/
　　 [s]　　　 p1　　　　　　 s　　 p2

※兔　　　"兔"在句子的前頭，好像是句子的主語，其實它本是句中動詞"得"的賓語，提到句子的前頭，是為了表示強調。

The word "兔" at the head of this sentence appears to be the subject of the sentence; in fact it is the object of the verb "得"; it has been placed at the beginning of the sentence for emphasis.

※身為宋國笑：被動句句式之一

這種被動句的句式是"N1(patient or receiver) 為 N2 (agent or doer) V"。本句中"為"是介詞，引進

16

施事者 N2 (agent or doer) ，可譯成白話的 "被" ；
N1是 "身" （耕者自己）；介詞引進的 N2 (doer)
是 "宋國" （宋國人）；動詞是 "笑" （嘲
笑）。

This is one of the **passive sentences**. This sentence pattern
is: "N1 為 N2 V", where N1 is the receiver or patient of the
verb and N2 is the doer or agent of the **verb**. The preposition
" 為 " here introduces N2, the doer. In this sentence, "**N1**" is
"身", the tiller himself; the **verb** is "笑", to laugh at or to
deride. The preposition "為", which can be rendered as "被" in
spoken Chinese, both serves as a passive sentence marker and
introduces N2, or the agent of the **verb**, "宋國", meaning "the
people of the state of Sòng."

兔子不能再得，可是自身被宋國笑。

Hare not can again get, but himself by Sòng state deride.

⟶ 兔子 [他] 再也得不到，他自己反倒被宋國人嘲笑了。

A hare **he *could*** **not get again**; instead, he himself *was* derid*ed* by *the*
people *of the* state *of* Sòng.

⟹ 兔子他再也得不到，他自己反倒被宋國人嘲笑了。

A hare he could not get again; instead, he was derided by the people of the
state of Sòng.

第四課

逐臭

句子分析

一．　[於]人 有 大臭 者，

人有非常臭的人，

People have big-stink one,

——→ [在]人 [裡]有個非常臭的人，

[Among] *all the* people *there was* a very stinky one.

===⟹ 有個非常臭的人，

There was a very foul-smelling person.

二．　[於] 其親戚、兄弟、妻妾、知識 無 能 與[之]居 者。

他的親戚、哥哥、弟弟、太太、姨太太、朋友沒有能跟居住的人。

His blood/in-law relatives, elder/younger brothers, wife/concubines, acquaintances not-have can-with-live one.

——→ [在]他的親戚、哥哥、弟弟、太太、姨太太和朋友[中]沒有能跟 [他]一塊儿居住的人。

[Among] his relative*s by* blood *and by* marriage, *his* elder *and* younger brother*s, his principal* wife, concubine*s, and* friend*s, there was* not one *who could stand to* live with [him].

====⟹ 他的親戚、哥哥、弟弟、太太、姨太太和朋友沒有能跟
他一塊儿居住的。

None of his relatives by blood and by marriage, his elder and younger
brothers, his principal wife, concubines, and friends could stand to live with
him.

三. 　[大臭者] 自 苦 而 居 [於] 海上。
　　　　　　 adv adj conj \ v [prep]　o /
　　　　　 \(pron)(v)/
　　　 s　　 p1　　　　 p2

※自苦　　　"苦"是形容詞用作動詞，意動用法。跟第
二課"智其子"，第五課"榮之"相同。不同
的地方是它的賓語由它的副詞"自"兼任。"
自"除了副詞的作用外，還兼有代詞的性質。
"自苦"即"苦自"。其實在文言中並沒有"
苦自"這種結構，"自"必須得放在"苦"之
前。

The word "苦"is an adjective that functions here as a
putative verb (i.e., to think oneself to be [something]). It
differs from other putative constructions (See Lesson 2, "智其
子" and Lesson 5, "榮之") insofar as its adverbial modifier
"自" also serves as the object of the putative verb. In addition
to its adverbial function, the word "自" has the characteristics of
a **pronoun** (i.e., it is a reflexive pronomial object like "himself
"). Hence, "自苦" (lit. "himself embittered") means the same
thing as "苦自" (lit. "he feels himself embittered"), although
the second construction is not possible in classical Chinese
because "自" can only be placed in front of a putative verb. It
means:

1) 自以為苦
　himself take [it, i.e., this situation] to be embittering

2) 自己以為自己很苦惱
　personally consider oneself to be very embittered

3) 自己覺得自己很苦惱
　himself feel oneself to be very embittered

4) 自己感到自己很苦惱
　himself find oneself very embittered

5) 自己感到很苦惱
　himself feel very embittered

19

自己苦惱就住海邊上。

Himself bitter so live sea by.

⟶ [非常臭的人]自己感到很苦惱就住[到]海邊上[去]。

[*The* stinky person] himself *felt* very *embittered*, so ***he went to*** live by ***the seashore***.

⟹ 他自己感到很苦惱就到海邊上去住。

He himself felt very embittered and so went to live by the seashore.

四． [於] 海上人 有 說其臭者，
＼[prep] o ／ ＼v o／
             s   **p**

（上方：v o n / adj mod n）

海上人有喜歡他的臭味的人，

Sea-by people have like-his-stink one(s).

⟶ [在]海邊上的人[裡]有喜歡他的臭味的人，

[Among] *the* people by *the* seashore, *there were* those *who* liked his stink.

⟹ 海邊上的人有喜歡他的臭味的，

There were people at the seashore who liked his stink.

五． [說其臭者] [於]晝夜 隨 之 而 弗 能 去。
               ＼[prep o ／ v o conj ＼adv aux v／
                 ＼ adv ／
       [s]   **p1**   **p2**

※而　　連詞，連接兩個謂語，在本句內在兩個謂語之間，沒有甚麼特定的關係 (既不是順接，也不是逆接)，"而"字只有調節音節、使句

20

子聽起來悅耳的作用，不必翻譯。

Here the conjunction "而" simply links two predicates. In this sentence, the two predicates do not have a specific relation (i.e., they are neither sequential nor antithetical), so the conjunction "而" serves only to make the sentence more euphonic; it need not be literally translated into spoken Chinese. In English, it can be translated as an adverbial phrase.

白天晚上跟隨他不能離開。

Day night follow him and not can leave.

⟶ [喜歡他的臭味的人]白天夜裡都跟隨著他，不能離開他。

[*The* people *who* lik*ed* his stink] follow*ed* him day *and* night, *being* not able *to* leave him.

⟹ 他們白天夜裡都跟隨著他，不能離開他。

They followed him day and night, unable to leave.

第五課

先王之義勝

句子分析

一. <u>子夏</u> <u>見曾子</u>。
     s   v o
             p

     子夏拜訪曾子。

     Zǐxià visit Zēngzǐ.

    ⟶ 子夏去拜訪曾子。

     Zǐxià *paid a* visit *to* Zēngzǐ.

    ⟹ 子夏去拜訪曾子。

     Zǐxià paid a visit to Zēngzǐ.

二. <u>曾子</u> <u>曰</u>："[子]何肥也?"
     s   v   o
             p

     "[子] 何 肥 也?"
           adv (adj) part
                 v
         s   p

    ※肥   此處"肥"字用作動詞，意思是"變胖"，"了"字表示新情況，因此白話文可以說"胖了。"

In this sentence the adjective " 肥 " functions as a verb meaning "to get fat." It can be translated into spoken Chinese as " 胖了 ", where the word " 了 " indicates a change of situation. This meaning can be conveyed in English by using a past perfect form of the verb (e.g., have gotten).

22

※ 也　　　　句末語氣詞，與疑問副詞"何"相呼應，"
　　　　　　　　何…也？"表示疑問的語氣，相當於白話中的
　　　　　　　　"呢"。可譯成白話的"為什麼…呢？"或"
　　　　　　　　怎麼…呢？"

The final particle "也" functions here in conjunction with the interrogative adverb "何"："何…也"; it expresses an interrogative tone (i.e., it marks a question) and corresponds to the word "呢" in the spoken Chinese construction "為什麼…呢?" or "怎麼 …呢?" It should be translated into English as an interrogative sentence; the particle "也" can be represented by a question mark.

曾子説："為什麼胖呢？"

Zēngzǐ say: "How fat? "

——→　曾子説："[您]怎麼胖了呢？"

Zēngzǐ sa*id*: "How *did* [you] *get so* fat?"

===→　曾子説："您怎麼胖了呢？"

Zēngzǐ said: "How did you get so fat?"

三.　　[子夏] 對 曰："[吾][以]戰勝，故肥也。"
　　　　　　 ⌄　⌄　　　○
　　　s　　　　　　p

"[吾] [以] 戰 勝，　故　　肥　　也。"
　　　　 [conj] v comp/　conj　\(adj)v/　part
　　 [s]　　　 p1　　　　　　　p2

※ 也　　　　句末語氣詞，表示解釋的語氣，相當於白話中
　　　　　　　　的"啊"。當"了啊"連用時，可譯成"啦
　　　　　　　　"。因此"胖了啊"可直接譯成"胖啦。"

The final particle "也" expresses an explanatory tone; it corresponds to the word "啊" in spoken Chinese.　When "了" and "啊" are used together, they become the contraction "啦". Thus, "胖了啊" can simply be translated as "胖啦".

回答説："打仗勝，所以胖啊。"

23

Reply say: "Battle win, therefore fatten."

⟶ ［子夏］回答説："［我］［因爲］打仗打勝了，所以胖了啊。"

[Zǐxià] repl*ied*, say*ing*: "[I] [Because] *of* win*ning a* battle, *have* therefore *gotten* fat."

⟹子夏回答説："我因爲打仗打勝了，所以胖啦。"

Zǐxià replied, saying: "I have gotten fat bacause I won a battle."

四． 曾子 曰："［此］何謂也?"

"［此］何謂也?"

※ 何　　　　疑問代詞，意思是"什麼"。在本句中用作動詞"謂"的賓語。在文言中，疑問代詞用作賓語時應倒放在動詞之前。

"何" is an interrogative pronoun, meaning "what". In this sentence it functions as the object of the verb "謂" (to say; to mean). **In classical Chinese, when "何" functions as an object, it is usually placed immediately in front of the verb.**

若還原成敘述句的正常詞序，則為：

If this interrogative sentence were recast according to the conventional word order of a narrative sentence, it would be written as:

⟶ "［此］謂何也?"

曾子説："説什麼呢?"

Zēngzǐ say: "Say what?"

⟶ 曾子説："［這句話］是什麼意思呢?"

24

Zēngzǐ said: "What *does* [your remark] *mean*?"

===⇒ 曾子說：" 這句話是什麼意思呢？"

Zēngzǐ said: "What do you mean by that?"

五． 子夏 曰：　　"吾入見先王之義則榮之，

<u>s</u>　　　<u>p</u>　　　出見富貴之樂又榮之，

　　　　　　　　兩者戰于胸中，

　　　　　　　　未知勝負，故臞。

　　　　　　　　今先王之義勝，故肥。"

子夏說：
Zǐxià said:

五．一　　　"吾　入　見　先王之義 [於][書]　則　榮之，
　　　　　　　v　v　o　[prep] [ol]　coni　v　o
　　　　　<u>s</u>　　　　　<u>p1</u>　　　　　　<u>p2</u>

※　則　　連詞，它連接的後一部分是前一部分導致的結
　　　　　果，可譯成 " 就 "。

When the action of the second part of the sentence results from
the action of the first part, the conjunction " 則 " can be translated
into spoken Chinese as " 就 " and into English as "and then,"
"and so," "and thus," etc.

※　榮　　形容詞用作動詞，意動用法。

An adjective used as a verb (**putative usage**): to take x to be
y; consider x y.

※　榮之　　以之為榮
　　　　　　以為它榮
　　　　　　take (consider, think) it to be splendid
　　　　　　認為它榮
　　　　　　覺得它榮
　　　　　　consider it splendid

"我進入看到古代聖王的正道就覺得它崇高；

"I enter see ancient kings' righteousness, then magnificate it,

⟶ "我進入家門，[在書上]看到古代聖王的正道，就覺得它(那些正道)很崇高；

Zǐxià said: "*When* I enter*ed the* gate *of my* home (i.e., return*ed* home), *I* saw [*written* in books] *the* righteous way*s of the* sage king*s of* antiquity, *and* then *I thought* them magnificent;

⟹ "我從外面回到家裡，在書上看到古代聖王的正道，就覺得那些正道很崇高；

Zǐxià said: "When I returned home, I saw written in books the righteous ways of the sage kings of antiquity and thought them magnificent;

五.二   [吾] 出 見 富貴之樂 [於] [塗] 又 榮 之。
             \v v   o   [prep] [o]/ \adv v o/
      [s]   **p1**   **p2**

出去看到有錢有地位的快樂又覺得它榮耀。

exit see wealth/rank's pleasure, too aggrandize them.

⟶ [我]出了家門，[在路上]看到有錢有地位的快樂，又覺得它(那種快樂)很榮耀。

When [I] went out (i.e., *left* home), *I* saw [*in the* streets] *the* pleasure*s* of wealth *and* rank, *and thought* them splendid too.

⟹ 我從家裡出去，在路上看到有錢有地位的快樂，又覺得那種快樂很榮耀。

When I left home, I saw in the streets the pleasures of wealth and rank and thought them splendid as well.

五.三   兩者 戰 于 [吾] 胸中，
               \v prep [mod]   o/
            s   **p**

※者	"者"字用在數詞後面構成名詞語，它所指代的對象一般見於上文。"者"字不能譯成"…的"，而須在數詞與它指代的對象之間加進相應的量詞和名詞。

When the pronoun "者" directly follows a numeral to form a pronominal phrase, its antecedent (i.e., the noun it refers to) usually appears in the previous text. In such cases, the modified pronoun "者" can be translated into spoken Chinese as "個", "樣", "種", etc., and into English as a demonstrative pronoun (i.e., these, those).

兩個在胸中打仗，

The two battle in breast middle,

⟶ 兩種感覺在[我]心裡打仗，

These two feeling*s fought against each other* in [my] heart;

⟹ 兩種感覺在我心裡打仗，

These two feelings fought against each other in my heart;

$$\text{五．四} \quad [以][吾] 未 知 [孰] 勝 [孰] 負 ， 故 [吾] 臞 。$$

	[s]	p(v)	[s]	p(v)		
conj		adv v	o		conj	adj
[s]		p1			[s]	p2

※包孕句	勝、負都是動詞，它們前面各省略了一個主語"孰"，全都寫出來該是"孰勝孰負"，作動詞"知"字的賓語。這種句中包含著另一個小句子的結構稱為包孕(yùn)句。

Both "勝" (to triumph) and "負" (to be defeated) are verbs; before each verb the subject "孰" (which one) is understood and omitted. In its fullest form, this sentence would read: "[孰]勝[孰]負." The two sentences together serve as the compound object of the verb "知" This type of sentence construction, in which an independent clause (i.e., a complete sentence) functions as a grammatical element or clause in a complex sentence, is called an **embedding sentence construction** (包孕句, lit: "**pregnant sentence**").

還不知道勝敗，所以瘦。

27

not-yet know triumph defeat, therefore skinny.

⟶ [因爲][我]還不知道[哪個]勝[哪個]敗所以[我]很瘦。

[because I] still *did* not know [which] *would* triumph *and* [which] *would be* defeat*ed*, consequently, [I] *got* skinny.

⟹ 因爲我還不知道哪個勝哪個敗，所以我很瘦。

I did not yet know which would triumph and which would be defeated; as a result, I got skinny.

五.五　今 [以]先王之義　勝[於吾胸中]，　故 [吾]　肥。"
　　　　adv [conj]　　　　　\v [prep ol/　　conj　　\(adj)v/
　　　　　s　　　　　　　　　　p　　　　　　　　　　[s]　　　p

現在古代聖王的正道打勝，所以胖。"

Now ancient kings' righteousness triumph, therefore fat."

⟶ 現在[因爲]古代聖王的正道[在我心裡]打勝了，所以[我]就胖了啊。"

Now [because] *the* righteous way*s* of *the* sage king*s* *of* antiquity *have* triumph*ed* [in my heart], consequently [I] *have gotten* fat."

⟹ 現在因爲古代聖王的正道在我心裡打勝了，所以我就胖啦。"

Now the righteous ways of the sage kings of antiquity have triumphed in my heart, and as a result I have gotten fat."

第六課

梟逢鳩

句子分析

一． 梟逢鳩。

$$\underset{\text{s}}{梟}\ \underset{\text{p}}{\underset{\text{v}\quad\text{o}}{逢\ 鳩}}。$$

貓頭鷹遇見斑鳩。

Owl meet ringdove.

——→ 貓頭鷹遇見斑鳩。

An owl *met a* ringdove.

==⟹ 貓頭鷹遇見斑鳩。

An owl met a ringdove.

二． 鳩曰："子將安之?"

$$\underset{\text{s}}{鳩}\ \underset{\text{p}}{\underset{\text{v}\qquad\qquad\text{o}}{曰："子將安之?"}}$$

"子 將 安 之?"

$$\underset{\text{s}}{子}\ \underset{\text{p}}{\underset{\text{aux}\quad\text{o}\quad\text{v}}{將\ 安\ 之?}}$$

※ 安　疑問代詞，意思是"何處"、"哪裡"、"哪兒"或"什麼地方"。在本句中作動詞"之"字的賓語。在文言中，疑問代詞用作賓語時，應倒放在動詞之前。

An interrogative pronoun, the word "安" means "what place," "where," or "whither". In this sentence, it serves as the object of the verb "之" (to go to). **In classical Chinese, when an interrogative pronoun functions as the object of a verb, it is generally placed in front of the verb.**

斑鳩説：“您將要到哪裡去？”

Ringdove say, "Sir shall where go?"

⟶ 斑鳩説：“您打算到哪兒去？”

The ringdove sa*id*: "Where *do* you intend *to* go?"

⟹ 斑鳩説：“您打算到哪兒去？”

The ringdove said: "Where do you intend to go?"

三． 梟 曰：“我將東徙。”

"我 將 東 徙"

※ 東　　　　方向詞。在文言中，方向詞應放在動
　　　　　　詞之前。例如：“東流”、“西下”、“南
　　　　　　來”、“北往”。

**In classical Chinese, a directional word is
generally placed in front of the verb that governs it.**
For example, "東流" (east flow / to flow east), "西下" (west
go down / to go down in the west), "南來" (south come / to
come from the south), "北往" (north go / to go to the north).

貓頭鷹説：“我將要向東邊搬。”

Owl say: "I going east move."

⟶ 貓頭鷹説：“我打算搬到東邊去。”

The owl sa*id*: "I *am* goi*ng to* move to *the* east."

⟹ 貓頭鷹説：“我打算搬到東邊去。”

The owl said: "I am going to move to the east."

四．　鳩曰："[子][以]何故[東徙]?"
　　　s　　　　　　　　p

"[子][以]何故[東徙]?"
　　　　　　　[prep] o [adv v]
[s]　　　　　p

斑鳩説："什麼緣故?"

Ringdove say: "What reason?"

⟶ 斑鳩説："[您][因爲]什麼緣故[向東邊搬]呢?"

The ringdove sa*id*: "[For] what reason *are* [you] [mov*ing* to *the* east]?"

⟹ 斑鳩説："因爲什麼緣故呢?"

The ringdove said: "For what reason?"

五．　梟曰："鄉人皆惡我鳴，[吾]以[此]故東徙。"
　　　s　　　　　　　　　　p

"鄉人　皆惡我鳴，[我] 以 [此]故東徙。"
　　　adv v o　　　prep o adv v
　　s　　p　　　　[s]　　p

※ 我鳴　　是主謂結構(有的文法學家稱它爲句子形
式)本是獨立的句子，但是在"鄉人皆惡我鳴
"句中，"我鳴"是作主要動詞"惡"的賓
語，在全句的結構中只起一個詞的作用，因而
失掉了獨立性。這種主要動詞的賓語是主謂結
構的句子，稱作包孕句，而且是最典型的包
孕句。另外還有其他形式的包孕句，見第五
課，句子分析五、四"未知勝負"；第八課，
句子分析六、一"吾不知其美"；第十課，句
子分析四"吾能持度"。

"我鳴" (I cry: here, "I screech") is a **subject-predicate** (s-

31

p) construction. (Some grammarians would call this construction an **independent clause**.) This construction is by itself an independent sentence; but in the sentence "鄉人皆惡我鳴" (The villagers all detest [that] I screech), "我鳴" functions as the object of the main verb "惡". In terms of the construction of the entire sentence, it functions as a dependent clause and cannot be construed as an independent element. This construction should, strictly speaking, be translated into English as a dependent clause (i.e., [that] I screech) rather than as a noun phrase (i.e., my hoot). This type of sentence, in which a subject-predicate clause serves as the object of the main verb, is called an **embedding sentence** construction (包孕句, lit: **pregnant sentence**). This is the most typical **embedding sentence** construction; in addition, there are other forms of the **embedding sentence**: see *Lesson 5, sentence analysis 5.4* "未知勝負"; *Lesson 8, sentence analysis 6.1* "吾不知其美"; *Lesson 10, sentence analysis 4* "吾忘持度".

※此 | 指示代詞，相當於白話中的"這個"。在本句內"此"有修飾"故"的作用，像是個形容詞。其實，"此"還是指代前面"鄉人皆惡我鳴"那句話。

A demonstrative pronoun, the word "此" corresponds to "這個" in spoken Chinese and to "this" in English. In this sentence, the word "此" seems to function like an adjective modifying the word "故". In fact, the word "此" in the phrase "此故" (lit: This [being the case], consequently = for this reason) refers to the entire preceding sentence ("The villagers all detest that I screech.")

貓頭鷹說："鄉村裡的人都討厭我叫，因為緣故向東邊搬。"

Owl say: "Country people all detest I screech, for reason east move."

⟶ 貓頭鷹說："鄉村裡的人都討厭我叫，[我]因為[這個]緣故才向東邊搬。"

The owl sai*d*: "*The* villager*s* all detest *that* I screech; for [this] reason, [I] *am* mov*ing* to *the* east."

⟹ 貓頭鷹說："鄉村裡的人都討厭我叫，因為這個緣故我才搬到東邊去。"

The owl said: "The villagers all detest that I screech; consequently, I am moving to the east."

六． 鳩曰："[若]子能更鳴，[則]可矣；
　　　　　　　　v　　o
　　s　　p　　[若][子]不能更鳴，[則][縱][子]東徙，

　　　　　　　[鄉人]猶惡子之聲。"

六．一　　"[若]子 能 更 鳴，[則] 可 矣；
　　　　　[conj]　　aux　v　o　[conj]　v　part
　　　　　　　s　　　　p1　　　　　　p2

斑鳩説："您能改變叫聲，可以了；

Ringdove say: "You can change cry, do allow;

────→　斑鳩説："[要是]您能改變叫的聲音，那[就]行了
　　　　；

The ringdove sa*id*: "[If] you can change *the* sound *of your* cry,
[then] that *is* acceptable;

════⟹　斑鳩説："要是您能改變叫的聲音，那就行了；

The ringdove said: "If you can change the sound of your cry,
then it will be all right;

六．二　　[若][子] 不 能 更 鳴，[則][縱][子] 東 徙，
　　　　　[conj]　　adv aux v　o　[conj][conj]　　adv v
　　　　　[s]　　　　　p　　　　　　　　[s]　　　p

[人] 猶 惡 子之聲。"
　　　adv　v　　o
[s]　　　p

※ "若… 則… 縱… 猶…"

假設式複句（若…則…）中的主要小句中包
含著另一容認式複句（縱…猶…）。

This is a **compound suppositional sentence** (若…則…
/ if...then...). The principal independent clause forms another

dependent **concessive sentence** (縱⋯猶⋯ / granted that ... still...).

NOTE: In Chinese grammatical usage, no formal distinction is drawn between what are referred to as compound and complex sentences in English. A compound sentence containing a **subordinate clause** (偏正結構) corresponds to what would be called a complex sentence in English (i.e., a sentence that has a main clause and a subordinate clause).

※縱 zòng   連詞，縱然，可翻譯成 "即使"，"就算是" 或 "就是"，用來引出容認式複句 (縱然⋯可 是還⋯)中的從屬小句。

The word "縱" is a subordinate conjunction meaning "even though". It can be translated into spoken Chinese as "即使", "就是" or "就算是" and into English as "even if," "granted that," " notwithstanding," etc. It is used to introduce the dependent clause of a compound sentence.

不能更改叫聲，東邊搬，仍然厭惡您的聲音。"

not can change cry, east move, still detest sir's sound."

⟶ [要是][您]不能改變叫的聲音，[那麼][即使][您]搬到東 邊去，[那儿的人]還是會討厭您的叫聲。"

[if] [you] cannot change *the* sound *of your* cry, [then] [even if] [you] move to *the* east, [*the* people there] *will* still detest *the* sound *of* your cry."

⟹ 要是您不能改變叫的聲音，那麼就是您搬到東邊去，那 儿的人還是會討厭您的叫聲。"

if you cannot change the sound of your cry, then even if you move to the east, the people there will still detest your cry."

第七課

矛盾

句子分析

一.

[於]楚人 有 賣盾與矛者，
[prepl o / \ v o \
　　s　　　　　　　　p

※與　　　　【連詞】相當於白話中的"和"或"跟"，此
　　　　　處連接"盾"、"矛"兩個名詞。

The word "與" functions here as a conjunction equivalent to
the words "和" and "跟" in spoken Chinese; here it connects
the words "盾" and "矛". It is equivalent to "and" in English.

楚人有賣盾和矛的人，

Chǔ people have sell-shields-and-spears one.

──→ [在]楚國人[裡]有個賣盾和矛的人，

[Among] *the* people *of the* state *of* Chǔ *there was* one *who sold* shields and
spears.

══⟹ 有個賣盾和矛的楚國人，

There was a man of the state of Chǔ who sold shields and spears.

二.　　[賣盾與矛者] 譽之 曰："　　"
　　　　[s]　　　　 \ v o / \ v o /
　　　　　　　　　　　 p1　　　 p2

誇它說：

Vaunt them say:

──→ [賣盾和矛的人]誇他的盾說：

35

[*The* person sell*ing* shield*s* and spear*s*] brag*ged about* them (i.e., his shield*s*) say*ing*:

⟹ 他誇他的盾說：

He bragged about his shields, saying:

"吾盾之 堅， ［於］物 莫 能 陷 ［之］ 也。"
   ___s__［之］ p(adj)/ \［prep］ o pron/ \aux v ［o］/ part
      s   **p**   **s**   **p**

※ 之	把句子變成主謂短語的符號。所謂主謂短語是在主語和謂語的中間加上"之"字，使句子變成近似名詞語的結構，通常用作包孕句(bāoyùn jù)中的主語或賓語，但有時它也可用作複合句(fùhé jù)中的半獨立分句。試比較下面兩種結構：

The word "之" functions here as a grammatical marker that transforms the independent clause (i.e., **s-p** construction or complete sentence) in which it stands into a **clausal phrase**. When the particle "之" is placed between a subject and a predicate, it changes the independent clause into a grammatical construction that resembles a noun phrase: this is the so-called 主謂短語; literally, a phrase containing a subject and a predicate. **Clausal phrases** often serve as subjects and objects in **embedding sentences**. Sometimes a clausal phrase can function as a semi-independent clause in a **compound sentence**. For example, compare sentences (1) and (2) below:

1. 吾盾 堅   （句子）
    s   p(adj)   (a sentence)

我的盾很堅固。
My shields are very strong.

（話中的意思已完足）
(The meaning is complete).

2. 吾盾 之 堅
    s 之 p(adj)

我的盾的堅固

The hardness of my shields,

————→ 我 的 盾 堅 固 的 程 度

The degree of hardness of my shields,

====⇒ "我 的 盾 那 麼 堅 固"

"My shields being so hard,"

(話 中 的 意 思 還 沒 完，聽 的 人 會 問 怎 麼 樣？說 話 的 人 必 須 得 說 出 下 一 句 才 能 使 聽 的 人 完 全 明 白 。)

(The meaning is incomplete; the listener will ask what is meant. The speaker must complete the rest of the sentence before the listener will be able to completely understand the meaning.)

※ 莫　　　無 指 代 詞，沒 有 什 麼，沒 有 一 個

An indeterminate pronoun, the word "莫" means "[there is] nothing" or "[there is] not one [thing]".

※物莫能陷

[於]物莫能陷

[在]物中沒有什麼能刺穿
Among all things, there is nothing that can pierce through

————→ 沒有什麼東西能刺穿
there is nothing that can pierce through

====⇒ 沒有一個東西能刺穿

（無　　物　　能 陷 〔吾盾〕）

there is not one thing that can pierce through [my shields]

"我 的 盾 的 堅 固，東 西 沒 有 什 麼 能 刺 穿 啊 。"

"My shields, of hardness, not-have thing can pierce."

————→ "我 的 盾 那 麼 堅 固，[在]東 西 [中]沒 有 什 麼 能 刺 穿 [它]啊 。"

"My shields *being of* such hardness, [among] thing*s* none can pierce through [them]."

————→ "我 的 盾 堅 固 得 沒 有 一 個 東 西 刺 得 穿 啊 。"

37

"My shields *are so* **hard** *that* **nothing can pierce through them.**"

⟹ "我的盾堅固得沒有一個東西刺得穿啊。"

"My shields are so hard that nothing can pierce through them."

三. [賣盾與矛者] 又 譽 其 矛 曰 ： "   "
　　　　　　　　　　　＼adv v　o／ ＼v　　o／
　　　　[s]　　　　　　　 p1　　　　 p2

又誇他的矛説：

additionally, vaunt his spears, say:

⟶ [賣盾和矛的人]又誇他的矛説：

[*The* person sell*ing* shields and spears] bragg*ed about* his spears as well, say*ing*:

⟹ 他又誇他的矛説：

He bragged about his spears as well, saying:

"吾矛 之　 利，[吾矛] 於 物 無 不 陷 也。"
＼ s　[之] p(adj)／　　　＼prep o v adv v／ part
　s　　　　　p　 [s]　　　　　　　p

※ "無 … 不 …" = "每 … 皆 …"
　　　　雙 否 定 表 示 肯 定

A double negative construction is used here to indicate affirmation. It is equivalent in meaning to the construction "每 … 皆 … " (whenever/every time...always...); (whatever/everything...always...)

※ 於物無不陷

[我的矛]對於東西沒有不能刺穿的
[My spears] in respect of things not have not pierce through ones.
In respect of things, there is nothing [my spears] cannot pierce through.

⟶ [我的矛]沒有一個東西不能刺穿

[My spears] do not have one thing *they* cannot pierce through.
There is not one thing they can not pierce through.

⟹ [我的矛]沒有一個東西刺不穿
There is not one thing that my spears do not pierce through.

〔吾矛〕（無物　　不陷）
There is nothing that my spears do not pierce through.

"我的矛的鋒利，對於東西沒有不能刺穿的啊。"

"My spears, of sharpness, among things not-have not pierce."

⟶ "我的矛那麼鋒利，[我的矛]沒有一個東西不能刺穿啊。"

"My spears *being of* such sharpness, *there are* no thing*s* [my spears] cannot pierce through."

⟶ "我的矛鋒利得沒有一個東西刺不穿啊。"

"My spear*s* *are so* sharp *that there is* **nothing they cannot pierce through**."

⟹ "我的矛鋒利得沒有一個東西刺不穿啊。"

"My spears are so sharp that there is nothing they cannot pierce through."

四． 或 曰："以子之矛陷子之盾，何如？"

"[若][人] 以 子之矛陷子之盾，[則][子之矛與子之盾]何如？"

※何如： "如"是個準繫詞，"何"是個疑問代詞，合起
來意思是"像什麼？"引申為"怎麼樣？"，"是什
麼樣的？"在本句中，可譯成"會怎麼樣？"

The word "如" (to be like) is a pseudo-copula (i.e., a word that resembles a linking verb such as "to be" but which can be used as a copula only in certain contexts. The word "何" (what) is an interrogative pronoun. The combination "何如？" literally means

"像什麼？"(is like what?); this sense has come by extention to mean "怎麼樣？" ("how?" or "how is it...?") and "是什麼樣的？" ("What kind [is it]?" or "of what quality [is it]?"). In this context, it means "what would it be like?" , "how would it be?" or "what would happen?"

有人説：" 用您的矛刺您的盾像什麼？"

One say: "Use you of spear pierce you of shield, what like?"

⟶ 有人説：" [要是][有人]用您的矛來刺您的盾，[那麼][您的矛和您的盾]會怎麼樣？"

*Some*one sa*id*: "[If] [someone] uses *one of* your spear*s to* pierce *one of* your shield*s*, [then] how *would it come out* like *for* [your spear*s* and shield*s*]?

⟹ 有人説：" 要是有人用您的矛來刺您的盾，那麼會怎麼樣？"

Someone said: "What would happen if one were to use your spears to pierce your shields?"

五． 其人 弗 能 應 也。
　　　　\adv aux v part/
　　s　　　　　p

那個人不能回答啊。

That person not can respond!

⟶ 那個人可就回答不出來了啊。

That person then *could* not answer!

⟹ 那個人可就回答不出來啦。

That person could not answer!

六．　夫 不可陷之盾與無不陷之矛　不　可 [於] 同世 而 立。
　　　part　　　　　　　　　　　　　　　　＼adv aux [prep] o conj v／
　　　　　　　　　s　　　　　　　　　　　　　　　p

不能刺穿的盾和沒有東西不能刺穿的矛不能同時存在。

Then, not-can-pierce of shields and not-have-not pierce of spears not can same world and exist.

⟶ 不能刺穿的盾和沒有一個東西不能刺穿的矛不能 [在] 同時存在。

So, not-can-pierce shield*s* and nothing-can-not-pierce spear*s* cannot exist [in] *the* same time *and* place.

⟶ 刺不穿的盾和什麼東西都刺得穿的矛不可能同時存在。

Now, shield*s* *that* cannot *be* pierced through and spear*s* *that* can pierce through anything cannot exist at once.

⟹ 刺不穿的盾和什麼東西都刺得穿的矛不可能同時存在。

Now, shields that cannot be pierced through and spears that can pierce through anything cannot exist at once.

第八課

逆旅二妾

句子分析

一． 陽子 之宋，宿 於逆旅。
           v   o   v prep o
     s   p1   p2

    陽子到宋去，住在旅館。

    Yángzǐ go Sòng, overnight at inn.

  ⟶ 陽子到宋國去，住宿在旅館裡。

    Yángzǐ *went* to *the* state *of* Sòng *and* spent *the* night in *an* inn.

  ⟹ 陽子到宋國去，住宿在旅館裡。

    Yángzǐ went to the state of Sòng and spent the night in an inn.

二． 逆旅人 有妾二人，
             v   o
      s   p

               ※妾二人   "妾二人"等於"二妾"。在文言中，名詞的量詞通常放在名詞之後。例如："書萬卷"、"酒一壺"、"淚千行"，翻譯成白話是"一萬卷書"、"一壺酒"、"一千行淚"。

                       "妾二人" is equivalent to "二妾". **In classical Chinese, enumerators for nouns are generally placed after the noun and followed by a measure word/AN.** For example, "書萬卷" (books ten thousand roles = ten thousand roles/volumes of books); "酒一壺" (wine one pot = one pot of wine); "淚千行" (tears one thousand streams = a thousand streams of tears). Such phrases can be translated into spoken Chinese as "一萬卷書" (ten thousand volumes of books), etc.

旅館人有姨太太二人，

Inn person have concubine two persons,

⟶ 旅館的主人有兩個姨太太，

The innkeeper ha*d* two concubine*s*,

⟹ 旅館的主人有兩個姨太太，

The innkeeper had two concubines,

三．　其一人　美，其一人　惡。
　　　　　　　＼adj／　　　　　＼adj／
　　　s　　　**p**　　　　**s**　　　**p**

※其　　　【代詞】等於 "N + 之"，"其一人" 等於 "N 之一人"。此句中的 N 指妾，故 "其一人" 的意思是 "妾之一人"；說得更清楚一點是 "二妾中之一人"。譯成白話是 "兩個妾裡的一個人"。但是這樣說話太囉嗦了，故習慣上白話只把 "其一" 翻譯成 "其中的一個" 就可以了。

The word "其" is a pronoun equivalent in meaning to the construction " **noun (N)** + 之 (**possessive marker**)." In this sentence, N refers to the antecedent "妾". Hence, "其一人" means "妾之一人" and can be translated into spoken Chinese as "兩個妾裡的一個人"(one of the two concubines). This is too wordy, however, and it usually suffices to translate "其一" into spoken Chinese as "其中的一個"(one of them). "其" can usually be translated into English as a pronoun; here, "其一" means "one of them."

她們的一個人美麗，她們的一個人醜陋。

the one person beautiful; the one person ugly.

⟶ 其中的一個很美麗，其中的一個很醜陋。

One of them *was* very beautiful; *the other* one *was* very ugly.

====⇒ 其中的一個很美麗，其中的一個很醜陋。

One of them was very beautiful; the other one was very ugly.

四． 惡者 貴 而 美者 賤。

adj conj　　　　adj
＼ⅴ　　　　　＼ⅴ
  s   p   s   p

※者 　　【被飾代詞】等於"之＋N"，"惡者"等於"惡之N"。此句中之"N"指妾，故"惡者"的意思是"醜陋的妾"；同理，"美者"的意思是"美麗的妾"。

The word "者" is a pronoun that must always be modified ; it is equivalent in meaning to the combination "之 (connective marker) + noun (N)". "惡者" is equivalent to "惡之N", where N refers to the antecedent "妾". Hence "惡者" means "醜陋的妾"(the ugly concubine); likewise, "美者" means "美麗的妾"(the beautiful concubine). In this usage, the word "者" can generally be translated into English as an indefinite pronoun (one: "the ugly one," "the beautiful one") or a relative pronoun (who: "the one who was ugly").

※貴 　　【形容詞】地位高。此句中形容詞用作動詞，意動用法。根據上下文的需要，又有被動的意思："被以為貴"意思是"被重視"，較自然的說法是"受重視"，而用來描述夫與妾的關係說"受寵"是最恰當的。

The word "貴" is an adjective meaning "of high rank or status." In this sentence, the adjective "貴" functions as a putative verb (i.e., to think someone or something has high rank or status). Given the context in which "貴" appears, it must also be construed here as a passive construction: "被以為貴" (was thought to be of high rank or status), which means "被重視" (was highly regarded) or in more colloquial spoken Chinese "受重視" (lit: to receive high regard). When it is used to describe relations between a man and his concubine, "貴" is best translated into spoken Chinese as "受寵" (was favored), where "受" is used to mark the passive construction. It can be translated into English as "to be held in high regard" or "to be favored."

※賤 　　【形容詞】地位低。在句中的用法跟前面的"貴"相同，意思是"被以為賤"，"被輕

視"。較自然的說法是："不受重視"，"不受寵"。

The word "賤" is an adjective meaning "of low rank or status." In this sentence, the adjective "賤" functions as a putative verb (i.e., to think someone or something has low rank or status). Like "貴", it must be construed here as a passive construction meaning "被以為賤" (was thought to be of low rank or status), i.e., "被輕視" (was held in low regard), or in more colloquial spoken Chinese "不受重視" (was not highly regarded), "不受寵" (was not favored).

——→ 醜的人貴，可是美的人賤。

Ugly person dear, but beautiful person cheap.

——→ 醜的姨太太受寵，可是美的姨太太不受寵。

The ugly concubine *was* favor*ed*, but *the* beautiful concubine *was* not favor*ed*.

===> 醜的受寵，美的反倒不受寵。

The ugly one was favored; the beautiful one, on the contrary, was not favored.

五. 陽子 問其故

s   p

※其故   它之故

LITERALLY: "its reason" ——→ "the reason for it," where "it" refers to the situation described in the preceding sentence.

陽子問它的緣故，

Yángzǐ ask its reason.

——→ 陽子問這個情況的緣故，

Yángzǐ ask*ed about the* reason *for* this situation.

45

⟶ 陽子問為什麼這樣，

Yángzǐ ask*ed* **why this** *was*;

⟹ 陽子問爲什麼這樣，

Yángzǐ asked why this was;

六. 逆旅小子 對 曰： " "

s p1 p2

旅館小伙子回答説：

Inn young man reply, say:

⟶ 旅館的小伙子回答説：

The young man *who kept the* inn repl*ied*, say*ing*:

⟹ 旅館的小伙子回答説：

The young man who kept the inn replied, saying:

                                s 之 p(adj)
                                  她 之 美

六.一 其美者 自美，吾 不 知 其美 也；

            adv adj   adv v o part

            pron

            s   p   s   p

※自美   在 "自＋v" 的結構中， "自" 兼有副詞和反身代名詞的作用。逐字譯成白話是 "自以為美"； "自己認為自己很美"； "自己覺得自己很美"。

In the grammatical construction " 自 + **v** ", the word " 自 " functions both as an adverb and a reflexive personal pronoun (lit: herself thought herself). Literally translated into spoken Chinese character by character, this means " 自以為美 ", which means : " 自己以為自己很美 " (*She* herself thought herself

46

very beautiful) or "自己以為（認為、覺得）自己很美"
(*She* felt *that she* herself was *very* beautiful).

<table>
<tr><td>※其</td><td>【代詞】"N＋之"。"其美"，"N之美"，"美者之美"。試比較"美者美"與"美者之美"就可發現前者是意思完足的句子，後者是名詞語化了的主謂短語"s 之 p"。"s 之 p"沒有獨立性，只能作句中動詞"知"字的賓語。這種主謂短語中的"之"字在翻譯成白話時不必譯。</td></tr>
</table>

In the phrase "不知其美", "其" is a pronoun equivalent in meaning to the construction " **noun (N) + 之 (clausal phrase marker)**". "其美" means "N 之美" = "美者之美". If one compares the two constructions "美者美" (The beautiful one is beautiful) and "美者之美" (that the beautiful one is beautiful), it can be seen that the first is an independent sentence; it makes sense as it stands. The second has been transformed into a noun phrase by using a clausal phrase construction "s 之 p" and cannot stand by itself; the second can only be construed as the object of the verb "知". In such clausal phrases, the word "之" need not be translated into spoken Chinese. Strictly speaking, this construction should be translated into English as a dependent clause (i.e., " that she is beautiful") and not as a pronoun and noun (i.e., " her beauty."). Note: In the preceding phrase "其美者", the word "其" functions like a demonstrative pronoun (i.e., that).

那個美麗的妾自以為美，我不覺察她美；

That beautiful one herself beautify; I not know she's beautiful;

⟶ 那個美的覺得她自己很美，可是我並不感到她美；

That beautiful concubine think*s* herself very beautiful, but I definitely *do* not think *that* she *is* beautiful;

⟹ 那個美的覺得她自己很美，可是我並不感到她美；

That beautiful concubine considers herself very beautiful, but I definitely do not feel that she is beautiful;

六.二　　　　　　　　　　　　　　　　　　　　s 之 p(adj)
　　　　　　　　　　　　　　　　　　　　她 之 惡
　　　　　　其惡者 自惡，吾 不 知 其惡 也。
　　　　　　　　adv adj　　　_adv_ v　o_/　part
　　　　　　　\pron adj/
　　　　　　　　s　　p　　　s　　　　p

　　　　※自惡　　　"自惡" 結構與前句 "自美" 相同。

　　　　　　　　　　The construction "自惡" in this sentence is the same as the
　　　　　　　　　　construction "自美" in the preceding sentence.

　　　　※其惡　　　"其惡" 結構與前句 "其美" 相同。

　　　　　　　　　　The construction "其惡" in this sentence is the same as the
　　　　　　　　　　construction "其美" in the preceding sentence.

那個醜陋的妾自以爲醜，我不覺察她醜。

That ugly one herself uglify; I not think she's ugly.

———→ 那個醜的覺得她自己很醜，可是我並不感到她醜。

That ugly concubine think*s* herself very ugly, but I definitely *do* not think
that she *is* ugly.

══➤ 那個醜的覺得她自己很醜，可是我並不感到她醜。

That ugly concubine considers herself very ugly, but I definitely do not feel
that she is ugly.

七.　　陽子曰："　　　"
　　　　　　_v___o_/
　　　　s　　　p

陽子說："　　　"

Yángzǐ said:

七.一　　　弟子 記之，
　　　　　　_v__o_/
　　　　　s　　p

48

※之　　　　　　【代名詞】它，代下面這句話。可譯成
"這句話"，也可不譯出。

The word "之" is a pronoun which here stands for "this sentence" (i.e., the sentence that follows the word "之"). It could be translated into spoken Chinese as "這句話" or left untranslated. It could simply be translated into English as "this," or more explicitly as "these words."

"徒弟們記住它，

"Disciples, note it,

⟶　"徒弟們記住這句話，

"Disciples, mark these words:

⟹　"徒弟們記住這句話，

"Disciples, remember these words:

七．二　　"[若] [人] 行 賢 而 去 自賢之心，
　　　　　　[conj] [s]　∖ v　o ╱ conj ∖ v　　o ╱
　　　　　　　　　　　　　　p　　　　　　p

"做高尚的事，卻去掉自以爲賢的心理，

"Do good yet eschew himself good of sense,

⟶　"[要是] [一個人] 做高尚的事，卻去掉自己覺得自己很高尚的心理，

"[If] [one] does good deeds while ridding himself of a sense of smugness,

⟹　"要是一個人做高尚的事，卻去掉覺得自己很高尚的心理，

"If a person does good deeds without being smug about it,

七.三 　　　 [則] [人] 安 往 而 不 愛 哉 ?"
　　　　　　 [conj] ＼o　v／ conj ＼adv　v／ part
　　　　　　　　[s] 　　p 　　　　p

※不愛　　 此處應看作**被動結構**"不被愛"它不像第三課中的"身為宋國笑"有明顯的**被動句**的符號"為"字，它的被動的意思是從上下文的結構中讀出來的。在文言中有些動詞不分主動被動形式，須由上下文來決定。

Here the phrase "不愛" should be construed as a **passive construction**: "不被愛" (not [be] well-liked/loved). This usage differs from the **passive construction** introduced in Lesson 3, "身為宋國笑" (He himself was ridiculed by the people of Sòng), where the passive voice is clearly indicated by the passive-voice marker "為". Here the passive mood must be inferred from the context. In classical Chinese, some verbs have both an active and a passive voice. Given the context, the phrase "不愛" (not liked/loved) should be construed as here "不被愛" (not be well-liked/loved).

※而　　 【連詞】它連接的兩個謂語在時間上不分先後，在事理上也不相因或相逆，它的作用只在配合句子的音節，譯成白話時通常省略不譯。

Here the word "而" is a conjunction linking two predicates that have neither a sequential/temporal relation nor a complementary/opposing causal relation. Here "而" simply joins two independent clauses and adds to the euphony of the sentence. It need not be translated into spoken Chinese; it can be translated into English as "and".

※安往而不 [被] 愛哉？
反問表示肯定。意思是"往何處皆 [被] 愛"

Here a rhetorical question is used to express affirmation: "Where can he go and not be loved/well-liked?" (i.e., Wherever he goes he [will] be well-liked).

到哪裡去不被人愛呢？"

where go-ing not by-people love?"

——→ [那麼] [他] 到哪裡去不受歡迎呢？"

[then] where *could* [he] go *and* not *be* welcom*ed*?"

50

⟶ 那麼他無論到什麼地方去都會受歡迎。"

then **wherever he go**es**, he** *will always be* **welcome**d."

⟹ 那麼他無論到什麼地方去都會受歡迎。"

then wherever he goes, he will always be welcomed."

第九課

盜鍾(鐘)

句子分析

一.

※范氏之敗

"范氏敗"是一個獨立的句子,在主語"范氏"與謂語"敗"之間加上一個"之"字就變成主謂短語,失掉了獨立性,作被省略了的介詞"於"的賓語,組成一個介詞語,"於…"意思是"在…的時候",在全句中提示事情發生的時間,作用等於一個狀語,或稱時間分句,即時間式複句中的上一分句。

"范氏敗" is an independent clause (i.e., it could stand as a complete sentence). The addition of the character "之" between the subject and predicate transforms the sentence into a dependent **clausal phrase** which functions here as the object of an omitted temporal preposition like "於" (when; at the time of). The entire construction can be understood as an adverbial clause meaning "When Fàn was defeated" or "At the time of Fàn's defeat"; it functions in the complete sentence as an adverbial modifier or a temporal adverbial clause indicating when the events that follow transpired. It is actually the first clause in a **Temporal Complex Sentence.**

范吉射打敗,

Fàn Jíshe's defeat,

⟶ [當]范吉射[被趙簡子]打敗了[的時候],

[When] Fàn Jíshè *was* defeat*ed* [by Zhào Jiǎnzǐ],

⟹ 當范吉射被打敗了的時候,

52

When Fàn Jíshè was defeated,

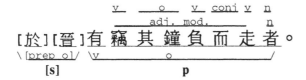

[於] [晉] 有竊其鐘負而走者。

        ※ "竊其鐘，負 [之] 而走"

這本是連動結構，此處用來描寫代詞 "者" 字
，只有定語的作用。

The phrase "竊其鐘，負 [之] 而走" is by itself a
compound predicate; here it modifies the pronoun "者" (a
person who....) and in this sentence should strictly be construed
as an adjectival modifier.

        ※ "負 [之] 而走"

"而" 字連接兩個動詞語，但是兩個動詞語的
地位並不平等。"負 [之]" 雖然本是動賓結
構，但是此處只用來描寫怎麼 "走"，地位變
低，作用近似一個狀語。"而" 字不必翻譯。

Here the word "而" links two predicates of unequal weight.
Although the phrase "負 [之]" is itself a verb-object
construction, in this context it serves only to modify the verb "
走" (i.e., fled in what manner -- carrying bell on back) ; it
functions here like an adverbial phrase and does not carry the full
force of a compound predicate construction. In such cases, it is
not necessary to literally translate the word "而" into spoken
Chinese. Such phrases can be translated into English as verbals
(e.g., an adjectival participle, "<u>carrying</u> [the bell] on his back").

有偷他的鐘背著逃跑的人。

have steal-his-bell-backbear-and-flee one.

⟶ [在晉國] 有個偷了他的鐘背著 [它] 逃跑的人。

[in *the* state *of* Jìn] *there was a* stole his bell, *on his* back *carry*ing [it] flee*ing*
one.

⟹ 有個偷了他的鐘背著它逃跑的人。

53

there was a person who stole his bell and fled carrying it on his back.

二．　　[鐘] 鎗然 有聲，
　　[s]　　＼adv　v　o／
　　　　　　　　　p

玎鐺地有聲音，

Clang-like have sound,

⟶　[鐘] 玎玎鐺鐺地發出聲音來，

[*The* Bell] *gave out a* clang*ing* sound.

⟹　鐘玎玎鐺鐺地發出聲音來，

The bell was clanging.

三．　　[竊鐘者] 懼 人聞之，　遽 掩 其耳。
　　[s]　　＼v　o／　　＼adv　v　o／
　　　　　　　p　　　　　　　p

　　　　　　　　　　　　v　o
　　　　　　　　　s——
　　　　　　　　　　p
※ " 懼 人 聞 之 "：
　　v　　o

"人聞之"既有主語"人"又有謂語"聞之"
，本是個獨立的句子，但是此處用來作動詞"
懼"字的賓語，構成一個包孕句，在全句中
的作用像個詞，文法學家稱它為"句子形式
"(s-p construction)。

The expression "人聞之" is an independent clause comprised of a subject (人) and a predicate (聞之): it can stand by itself as a complete sentence. However, in this context it functions as the object of the verb "懼" and forms part of an **embedding sentence** construction; it should be construed as a dependent clausal phrase in the complete sentence. Grammarians also refer to this type of object a **"subject-predicate (s-p) construction"**.

害怕人聽見它，趕緊搗他的耳朵。

Fear people hear it; quickly cover his ears.

⟶ [偷鐘的人]害怕別人聽見鐘聲，趕緊搗住他自己的耳朵。

[*The* one *who stole the* bell] fear*ing* other people *would* hear *the* sound *of the* bell; cover*ed* his own ear*s* quickly.

⟹ 賊害怕別人聽見鐘聲，趕緊搗住他自己的耳朵。

Fearing that other people would hear it, he covered his own ears quickly.

四．　[竊鐘者]憎 人 聞 之 ，[此] 可 也；

憎惡人聽見它，可以啊；

Hate people hear it, do allow;

⟶ [偷鐘的人]厭惡別人聽見鐘聲，[這]還算說得過去；

For [*the* one *who stole the* bell] *to* hate other people hear*ing* it, [this] **can be regarded as** permissable,

⟹ 偷鐘的人厭惡別人聽見鐘聲，還算說得過去；

To hate other people hearing it is reasonable,

[竊鐘者] 自 掩 其耳，[此]悖 矣。

自己搗他的耳朵，荒唐了啊。

himself cover his ears, absurd so!

⟶ [偷鐘的人]自己捂住他自己的耳朵，[這]太荒唐了啊。

for [*the* man *who stole the* bell] *to* cover up his own ear*s*, [that] *is* so absurd!

⟹ 偷鐘的人自己捂住自己的耳朵，太荒唐啦。

but how absurd of him to cover up his own ears!

第十課

鄭人買履

句子分析

一.

鄭人有將要買鞋的人，

Zhèng people have presently-buy-shoes-one.

⟶ ［在］鄭國人裡有個打算買鞋的人，

[Among] *the* people *of the* state *of* Zhèng *there was* a person *Who was going to* buy *a pair of* shoes.

⟹ 有個打算買鞋的鄭國人，

There was a man from the state of Zhèng who was going to buy a pair of shoes.

二.　　　［買履者］先 自 度 其足，而 置 之［於］其座，
　　　　　　　　　\adv adv v　o/　conj \v　o [prep] o/
　　　　[s]　　　　　　　　p 1　　　　　　　p2

　　　※而　　　"而"字連接兩個謂語，前後兩事，在時間上
　　　　　　　　有先後之別，"而"字相當於白話的"就"。
　　　　　　　　Here the word "而" connects two predicates that state two things
　　　　　　　　in a temporal sequence. The "而" in this usage corresponds to
　　　　　　　　the word "就" in spoken Chines.

　　　※ 省略　　文言中介紹處所的介詞"於"有時省略
　　　　　　　　In classical Chinese, the preposition "於" is sometimes
　　　　　　　　omitted before place words and locative phrases (i.e., his seat).

先自己量他的腳，就放它他的座位上。

Prior self measure his feet, then put it his seat.

⟶ [買鞋的人]先自己量一量他自己的腳，然後就把量好的尺碼放[在]他的座位上。

[*The* man buy*ing* shoe*s*] first measure*d* his own feet *him*self; afterwards *he* then put *the* measurement [on/by] his seat.

⟹ 買鞋的人先自己量一量他自己的腳，然後就把量好的尺碼放在他的座位上。

First he measured his feet; then he put the measurement on his seat.

三. [買履者之] <u>至</u> [其] v o <u>之市</u> 而 [買履者] <u>忘</u> <u>操之</u>。
　　　 prep 　　 o 　　 conj 　 [s] 　 v 　　 o

　　　 ※　　買履者 之市 ⟶ 句子 This is a complete sentence
　　　　　　　s　　　p　　　　　　(independent clause)

　　　　　 N+之 = 其

　　　　　 買履者 + 之 = 其

　　　　　 其 + 之 市
　　　　　　　　 v 　o

　　　　　 買履者 [之] 之市 ⟶ 主謂短語 clausal phrase
　　　　　　　　　　　 v 　o 　　　　(dependent clause)
　　　　　　　s　　　　p

　　※主謂短語

　　　　句子的主語謂語之間加上一個"之"字就把句子變成主謂短語(作用像個名詞語)，作介詞"至"的賓語。"之"字只是把句子變成主謂短語的符號，不必翻譯。

The **subject-predicate (s-p) construction** or **clausal phrase:**

58

When the word "之" is placed between the subject and the predicate of an independent clause (i.e., a sentence), it is transformed into a dependent **clausal phrase**. In a complex sentence, such **clausal phrases** function like noun phrases. In this sentence, the **clausal phrase** serves as the object of

the preposition "至". In this construction, the word "之" only serves as a marker to indicate that the independent clause (sentence) has been changed into a **clausal phrase**. Such phrases can be translated into English as infinitive, participial, gerund, verb or absolute phrases; when they function as the object of a preposition (as in this case), they can be rendered as adverbial clauses (i.e., when it was time for him to go to the marketplace).

※而　　　"而"字連介詞語(至[買履者之]之市)與動詞語(忘操之)時，介詞語在句中的作用像副詞，"而"字不必翻譯。

When the word "而" connects a prepositional phrase (至[買履者之]之市) and a predicate (忘操之), the prepositional phrase functions like an adverbial element in the sentence and the word "而" need not be translated as a conjunction; it simply serves to link the prepositional phrase to the predicate.

到到市場去忘記拿它。

At go market-ing forget take it.

⟶　等到[買鞋的人]到市場去的時候[他]忘記了帶尺碼。

At *the* time [*the* man buy*ing* shoe*s*] *went* to *the* marketplace, [he] forg*ot* *to* take it (i.e., *the* measurement) along.

⟹　等到他到市場去的時候儿忘了帶尺碼。

When it was time to go to the marketplace, he forgot to take it along.

四．　[買履者] 已 得 履，乃 曰： "吾 忘 持度。"

※乃　　　"乃"是副詞，用在主要小句的謂語之前，表示在附屬小句提到的情況下，又出現了另外的情況。相當於白話的"才"。

59

"乃" is an adverb which is used in the main clause of a complex sentence to indicate that the condition stated in the subordinate clause is a prerequisite. It is equivalent to "才" in spoken Chinese.

已經得鞋，才說：“我忘記帶尺碼。”

Already get shoes, then say, "I forget carry measure."

⟶ ［買鞋的人］已經得到鞋了，才想起來說：“我忘記了帶尺碼。”

When [*the* man buy*ing* shoe*s*] *had* already *gotten his* shoe*s, only* then *did he* think *of* it *and* say: "I forg*ot* *to* bring *the* measurement along."

⟹ 他已經拿到鞋了，才想起來說：“我忘了把尺碼帶來。”

Only when he had already gotten his shoes did he think of it and say, "I forgot to bring along the measurement."

五. ［買履者］ 反 歸 而 取 之 。
　　　　　　　action（行動）　purpose（目的）
　　　　　　　＼adv v／ conj＼v　o／
　　　［s］　　　p1　　　　p2

轉身回去拿它。

Turn return to get it.

⟶ ［買鞋的人］轉身回家去拿尺碼。

[*The* man buy*ing* shoe*s*] turn*ed* around, *and went* back home *to* get *the* measurement.

⟹ 他轉身回家去拿尺碼。

He turned around and went back home to get the measurement.

```
         [s]   之 p(v)
       買履者之
```

六．　及 [其]　　反，市罷，[買履者] 遂 不 得 履。
　　　＼prep　　ｏ／　　 ＼v／　　　　＼adv adv v ｏ／
　　　　　　　　　　　　　ｓ　ｐ　　 [s]　　　 ｐ

等到回來，市場停止，就不能得到鞋。

By return, market close, so not get shoes.

⟶　等到 [買鞋的人] 回來的時候，市場上的交易已經終止了，
　　[買鞋的人] 就得不到鞋了。

By [*the* time] [*the* man buy*ing* shoe*s*] *had* return*ed*, *the* market *was* close*d*, so [*the* man buy*ing* shoe*s*] *did* not get (i.e., buy) *any* shoe*s*.

⟹　等到他回來的時候，市已經收了，他就沒買到鞋。

By the time he had returned, the market was closed, so he didn't get any shoes.

七．　人 曰：“ [子] 何不試之以足？”
　　　　＼v　　　　　　ｏ　　　　／
　　　　ｓ　　　　　　 ｐ

七．一　　“ [子] 何 不 試 之 以 足？”
　　　　　　　 ＼adv adv v ｏ prep ｏ／
　　　　　　　 [s]　　　 ｐ

人說：“爲什麼不試它用腳？”

Person say: "How not try it by foot?"

⟶　有人說：“ [您] 爲什麼不用腳來試一試它呢？”

A person sa*id* : "How *is it that* [you] *did* not try it/them (i.e., *the* shoes) by *means of your* foot?"

⟹　有人說：“您爲什麼不用腳來試一試鞋呢？”

Someone said: "Why didn't you use your feet to try them on?"

八． [<u>買履者</u>] <u>曰</u>：" 　　　　"
　　　　　　　　　　\v＿＿o／
　　　　[s]　　　　　 p

八．一　　" [<u>吾</u>] <u>寧 信 其 度</u>， <u>無 自 信</u> 也。"
　　　　　　　　　 \aux v　o／　 \adv adv v／ part
　　　　　　 [s]　　　 p1　　　　　　 p2

※ " 寧 A 無（不 / 毋 / 勿）B "

這是個取捨式複句。比較兩種情況，然後決定取捨，通常在表示"取"的小句裡用一"寧"字。

This is a **Preferential Compound Sentence**. When comparing two sets of circumstances and then deciding which is preferable, the word " 寧 " is placed in front of the phrase describing the preferable choice, and the less preferable alternative is preceded by the word " 無 " (or 不 / 毋 / 勿).

※ <u>自 信</u>　　<u>自己 相信自己</u>
　 adv v　　　 adv　 v　 o
　 pron　　　 pron

　————＞　　　 相信自己

說："寧可相信那尺碼，不相信自己啊。"

Say: "Rather believe that measure, do not self believe."

————＞ [<u>買鞋的人</u>]說："[我]寧可相信那個尺碼，也不相信我自己啊。"

[*The* man buy*ing* shoe*s*] sa*id*: "[I] *would* rather trust *in* that measurement *and do* not trust myself."

＝＝＝＞ 買鞋的人說："我寧可相信那個尺碼，也不相信我自己啊。"

The person buying shoes said: "I would rather trust in that measurement than trust in myself!"

第十一課

仁義

句子分析

一． [於] 昔 有昆弟三人，
　　　\\[prep] o/　\\v　o/
　　　　　s　　　　　p

　　　從前有兄弟三人，

　　　Past have brothers three persons;

　──→[在]從前有三兄弟，

　　　[In] *the* past *there were* three brother*s*;

　══>從前有三兄弟，

　　　Once upon a time, there were three brothers;

二． [昆弟三人] 游 [於] 齊魯之間，
　　　　　　　　\\v　[prep]　o/
　　　[s]　　　　　　　p1

　　　出游齊魯之間，

　　　roam Qí-Lǔ's midst;

　──→[三兄弟]離家[到]齊魯一帶[去]求學，

　　　[*The* three brother*s*] *left* **home** *and* roam*ed through the* region *of* Qí *and* Lǔ [to] seek learning,

　　　[*The* three brother*s*] *left* **home** *and* travel*led* in *the* region *of the* state*s of* Qí *and* Lǔ *to* seek learning,

63

⟹ 三兄弟離家到齊魯一帶去求學，

They left home and travelled in the region of the states of Qí and Lǔ to seek learning,

[從] 同 師 而 學 。
\[prep] o conj v/
    p2

同 老師 學習 。

same teacher to study.

⟶ [跟隨著]同一位老師學習。

and stud*ied* [with] *the* same teacher.

⟹ 跟隨著同一位老師讀書。

and studied with the same teacher.

※　比較：
COMPARE the following pattern 同 **N** 而 **V**:

A.[從]同師而學
to study [with] the same teacher

B. [於]同世而立 . *(see L. 7, sentence analysis 6, p. 41)*
to stand (exist) [in] the same world

進 仁義之道 而 歸 。
\v_____o/ conj \v/
   p3   **p4**

窮盡仁義的道理就回去。

exhaust benevolence/righteousness's path, then return.

⟶ 把仁義的道理學得很透徹就回家了。

They had exhaust*ed their* study *of the* teaching of benevolence *and* righteousness *and* then return*ed* home.

Hav*ing* exhaustively stud*ied the* doctrine of benevolence *and* righteousness, *they* return*ed* home.

⟹ 把仁義的道理學得很透徹就回家了。

When they had exhaustively studied the doctrine of benevolence and righteousness, they returned home.

三. 其父曰：“仁義之道若_何？”
　　s　　　　　p

仁義之道 若 何
　s　　　　p

※若何： “若”是準繫詞，“何”是疑問代詞。“A若何？”是疑問準判斷句。逐字譯成白話是“A像什麼？”但為求語氣自然，通常譯成“A怎麼樣？”

“若”is a pseudo-linking verb (i.e., it functions like "to be" but is limited in its use -- in this case to similies); “何”is an interrogative pronoun. “A若何？”is the inter-rogative form of a pseudo-determinative sentence (i.e., it expresses a judgement but does so without the force of a regular determinative sentence “A者B也”). This sentence can be translated into spoken Chinese word by word as “A像什麼？” (A is like what?), but a more natural translation would usually be“A怎麼樣？”(What is A like?).

他們的父親說：“仁義的道理如何？”

Their father say: "Benevolence/righteousness's path like what?"

⟶ 他們的父親說：“仁義的道理像什麼？”

Their father said: "*The* teaching of benevolence *and* righteousness *is* like what?"

⟹ 他們的父親說：“仁義的道理怎麼樣？”

Their father said: "What is the doctrine of benevolence and righteousness like?"

65

四． 伯旦：“仁義使我愛身而後名。”

仁義 使 我 愛身而 後名

※我： “我”是“使”的賓語，也是“愛身而後名”的主語。它有兩種功用。這種句子叫“**兼語式**”結構。“我”是**兼語**。

The word "我" functions here both as the object of the verb "使" and as the subject of the phrase "愛身而後名"; it serves a dual function. This usage, in which one word simultaneously fills two grammatical functions in the same sentence is called a **pivotal construction**. In this sentence, the word "我" is the **pivotal element.**

※而： 表示前後兩個謂語一意相因，即“而”前後兩謂語說法不同，表達的意思卻類似或相同。在白話中不必譯出。

Here the word "而" indicates that the predicate preceding it is linked to the predicate that follows it as a single interconnected thought; that is, the two verbs linked by "而" express essentially the same meaning or a similar meaning in different words. In such cases, "而" need not be translated into spoken Chinese as a conjunction; in English it can simply be rendered as "and."

※後名： 名詞用作動詞，**意動用法**。

In this phrase, the word "後" (the back) functions like a verb and is used in a putative sense (i.e., to think that something comes after other things); this phrase should be construed here as a **verb-object (v-o) construction:**

1) 以名為後
   to take (i.e., regard) reputation as that which comes after (i.e., second)

2) 以為(認為)名聲在後面
   to hold that reputation comes after [other things]

3) 覺得名聲不重要
   to think/feel that reputation is not important

4) ──→看輕名聲
   to disdain reputation

Note: Only nouns and adjectives can be used as putative verbals. In this sentence, "後" must be construed as a noun that has a putative verbal sense (i.e., think that it should come second).

大的說："仁義使我愛惜身體看輕名聲。"

Eldest say: "Benevolence/righteousness cause me love body while seconding reputation.

⟶ 大兒子說："仁義使我愛惜自己的生命看輕名聲。"

The eldest son sa*id*: "Benevolence *and* righteousness cause*s* me *to* cherish *my* own life while put*ting* reputation second."

⟹ 大兒子說："仁義使我看重自己的生命看輕名聲。"

The eldest son said: "Benevolence and righteousness would make me value my life and put my reputation second."

五.   仲曰："仁義使我殺身以成名。"

仁義使我殺身以成名

※以：   基本上是介詞，但有時用作連詞。用作連詞時與"而"字的作用相同，連接兩個謂語，前一謂語表示一個行動，後一謂語表示那個行動的目的或後果。表示目的，"以"字可譯成"來"或"去"（如本課）；表示後果，"以"字可譯成"以致⋯"或"結果⋯"。
（如第十二課）

The word "以" generally functions as a preposition, but sometimes it can serve as a conjunction. When it is used as a conjunction, it functions like the word "而" does when it is used to connect two predicates. The first predicate states an action; the second predicate describes the purpose or the consequence of that action. When the second predicate describes the purpose, "以" can be rendered as "來" or "去" in spoken Chinese and as "in order to", "so as to", "for the purpose of", "thereby", etc., in English. (*as in this lesson*).

When the second predicate describes the consequence, "以" can be rendered as "以致" or "結果" in spoken Chinese and as "consequently", "as a consequence", etc., in English. (*as in lesson 12*).

二的説："仁義使我殺死自己來成就名聲。"

Second say, "Benevolence/righteousness cause me kill body to achieve reputation."

⟶ 二兒子説："仁義使我犧牲自己的生命來建立名聲。"

The second son sa*id*, "Benevolence *and* righteousness cause*s* me *to* sacrifice *my* own life *in order* to attain *a* reputation."

⟹ 二兒子説："仁義使我犧牲自己的生命來建立名聲。"

The second son said, "Benevolence and righteousness would make me sacrifice my life in order to establish my reputation."

六． 叔 曰："仁 義 使 我 身 名 並 全。"

仁 義 使 我 身 名 並 全

※身名並全：賓語提前，表示強調，比較 "兔不可復得"

In this phrase, the object (身名) is placed before the verb (全) for emphasis. Compare this construction with the similar construction "兔不可復得" in Lesson 3; *see sentence analysis 5. p.16.*

三的説："仁義使我生命名聲一齊保全。"

Third say: "Benevolence/righteousness cause me body-reputation togethrer preserve."

⟶ 三兒子説："仁義使把我生命和名聲都保全住。"

The third son sa*id*: "Benevolence *and* righteousness cause*s* me *to* preserve both *my* life and *my* reputation intact."

===> 三兒子說："仁義使我把生命和名譽都保全住。"

The third son said: "Benevolence and righteousness would make me preserve both my life and my reputation intact."

七．　彼三術　相反，　而　同　出　於　儒，孰是孰非　耶？
　　　　\adv　v/　conj　\adv　v prep　o/　\ s　p s　p/　part
　　　s　　p1　　　　　　p2　　　　　　p3

　　　　　※孰是孰非：

　　　　　　　是兩個主謂小句子，此處用作全句的主語
　　　　　　　"彼三術"的謂語。這種句子叫做主**謂謂語
　　　　　　　句**，是比較特殊的一種包孕句。

　　　　　　This construction is comprised of two independent clauses; it functions in this sentence as the principal predicate for the subject "彼三術". This kind of sentence is called a **clausal predicate sentence**; that is, the principal predicate (P3) itself is made up of two independent clauses. This is an unusual type of **embedding sentence** construction.

那三種道理互相違反，可是一同出來從儒家，哪個對哪個錯呢？

These three doctrines one-another contradict, yet alike come out of Confucians; which right, which wrong so?

——> 那三種道理互相衝突，可是都從儒家發展出來，哪個對哪個錯呢？

These three doctrine*s* contradict one another, yet all *alike* originate from *the teachings of the* Confucians: *so*, which *is* right, *and* which *is* wrong?

===> 那三種道理互相衝突，可是都從儒家發展出來，哪個對哪個錯呢？

These three doctrines are mutually contradictory, yet they all come from the teachings of the Confucian school. Which of them is right, which wrong?

第十二課

蘇代諫趙王

句子分析

一. <u>趙 且 伐 燕</u>，
　　　　\adv　v　o/
　　s　　　　p

　　趙將要攻打燕，

　　Zhào soon attack Yān,

　　⟶ 趙國將要攻打燕國，

　　When the state *of* Zhào *was* about *to* attack *the* state *of* Yān,

　　⟹ 趙國將要攻打燕國，

　　When the state of Zhào was on the verge of attacking the state of Yān,

二. <u>蘇代 為 燕 謂 惠王 曰</u>： "　　　"
　　　　　\prep　o　v　o/　\v　　　o/
　　s　　　　　p1　　　　　p2

　　蘇代為燕告訴惠王說：

　　Sū Dài for Yān address Huì King, say:

　　⟶ 蘇代為燕國對趙惠王說：

　　Sū Dài address*ed* King Huì *of* Zhào on behalf *of the* state *of* Yān, say*ing*:

　　⟹ 蘇代為燕國對趙惠王說：

　　Sū Dài spoke to King Huì of Zhào on behalf of the state of Yān, saying:

70

三. "今者 臣 來， 過 易水，
　　　adv　　\v\　　\v　o/
　　　　s　　p1　　　p2

"這次臣來，渡過易水，

"Current-ly, servant come, cross Yì waters,

⟶ "這次臣到趙國來，渡過易水，

"On this occasion, *when your* servant *came* to *the* state *of* Zhào, *and was* cross*ing the* Yì River,

⟹ "這次我到趙國來，渡過易水，

"This time when I came to the state of Zhào and was crossing the Yì River,

蚌 方 出 曝， 而 鷸 啄 其肉。
　\adv　v　v/　conj　　\v　o/
　s　　　p　　　　　s　　p

蚌正出來曬太陽，鷸啄住牠的肉。

clam just out sunning when snipe peck its flesh.

⟶ 一個蚌正出來曬太陽，一隻鷸啄住牠的肉。

a clam *had* just *come* out *of the water to* sun *itself*, when a snipe beg*an* peck*ing at* its flesh.

⟹ 一個蚌正出來曬太陽，一隻鷸啄住牠的肉。

a clam had just come out of the water to sun itself, when a snipe pecked at its flesh.

四. 蚌 合 而 箝 其喙。
　　\v/　conj　\v　o/
　s　p1　　　　p2

蚌合攏就夾牠的嘴。

Clam clos-ing clamp its beak.

71

——→ 蚌合攏起來就夾住牠的嘴。

The clam close*d* up and clamp*ed* down *on* its beak.

===⇒ 蚌合攏起來夾住牠的嘴。

The clam closed up and clamped down on its beak.

五．　鷸曰：‘　　　’
　　　　　 ＼ ⌵ 　ｏ ＿／
　　　[s]　　　ｐ

‘今日[天]不雨，明日[天]不雨，即　有死蚌。’
　adv　　＼adv ⌵/　adv　　＼adv ⌵/　conj　＼⌵ ｏ/
　　　[s]　　ｐ　　　　[s]　　ｐ　　　　　ｐ

※ 即　　　　“即”表示在某種條件或情況下自然會怎麼
　　　　　　樣。與“則”同 So, then.

The word “即” indicates that under certain conditions or
circumstances [A], a certain consequence [B] naturally or
spontaneously follows. It functions in the same way as “則”.

A 即 B
A 就會 B.
A [and] [so] then B.

鷸説：‘今天不下雨，明天不下雨，就有死蚌。’

Snipe say, 'Current day not rain, next day not rain, then have dead clam.'

——→ 鷸説：‘今天老天不下雨，明天老天也不下雨，就會有曬
死了的蚌。’

The snipe said: '*If* today *it does* not rain, *and if* tomorrow *it* also *does* not
rain; then *there will be a* dead clam (i.e., *a* clam dead *from* exposure *to the*
sun).'

===⇒ 鷸説：‘今天老天不下雨，明天老天也不下雨，就會有
曬死了的蚌。’

The snipe said: 'If today it does not rain, and if it also does not rain
tomorrow, then there will be a dead clam.'

72

六. 蚌 亦 謂 鷸 曰： ' '
　　　\adv v o/　\v　o/
　　　s　p1　　p2

' 今日 [汝喙] 不 出， 明日 [汝喙] 不 出， 即 有 死鷸。'
　adv　　\adv v/　adv　　\adv v/　conj　\v o/
　　　[s]　p　　　　[s]　p　　　　p

蚌也告訴鷸說：'今天出不去，明天出不去，就有死
鷸。'

Clam too address snipe, say: 'Current day not out, next day not out, then
have dead snipe.'

⟶ 蚌也對鷸說：'今天 [你的嘴] 拔不出去，明天 [你的嘴] 也
拔不出去，就會有夾死了的鷸。'

The clam too address*ed the* snipe, say*ing*: '*If* today your bill/beak *can* not *be*
pull*ed* out; *and if* tomorrow your bill/beak also *can* not *be* pull*ed* out, then
there will be a dead snipe (i.e., *a* snipe starv*ed to* death because *it could* not
free its bill *to* eat).'

⟹ 蚌也對鷸說：'今天你的嘴拔不出去，明天你的嘴也拔
不出去，就會有夾死了的鷸。'

The clam too addressed the snipe, saying: 'If your bill can not be pulled out
today and also can not be pulled out tomorrow, then there will be a dead
snipe.'

七. 兩者 不 肯 相 舍， 漁父 得 而 并 擒 之。
　　\adv aux adv v/　　\v/ conj \adv v o/
　　s　　　p　　　　s　p　　　　p

兩個不願意互相捨棄，捕魚的老頭儿得到就一齊捉住牠
們。

The two not willing one another let go; old fisherman find then together catch
them.

⟶ 雙方不願意互相放開，捕魚的老頭儿發現了牠們就把牠
們倆一齊捉住了。

73

These two *were* not will*ing to* let one another go; *an* old fisherman *found* them and *caught* them both.

⟶ 雙方誰也不願意放開誰，捕魚的老頭兒發現了牠們就把牠們倆一齊捉住了。

Neither *was* will*ing to* let *the* other go; *an* old fisherman *found* them and *caught* both *of* them at once.

⟹ 雙方誰也不願意放開誰，捕魚的老頭兒發現了牠們就把牠們倆一齊捉住了。

Neither was willing to let the other go; an old fisherman found them and caught both of them at once.

八．　今　趙　且　伐　燕，
　　　adv　　\adv　v　o/
　　　s　　　　　p

現在趙將要攻打燕，

Present Zhào soon attack Yān.

⟶ 現在趙國將要攻打燕國，

Now *the* state *of* Zhào is *on the* verge *of* attack*ing the* state *of* Yān.

⟹ 現在趙國將要攻打燕國，

Now the state of Zhào is on the verge of attacking the state of Yān.

九．　燕趙　久　相　支　以　敝　大眾，
　　　　　\adv　adv　v/　conj　\(adj)v　o/
　　　s　　　　p1　　　　　　　p2

　　　　※ "敝　大眾"：
　　　　　　(adj)　o
　　　　　　　v

使大眾敝。形容詞用作動詞，使動用法。

"to cause the masses to become worn out". Here the adjective "敝" functions as a causative verb (i.e., to cause or make [something] happen). This is called **causative usage.**

燕趙長久互相撐持以致疲乏人民，

Yān and Zhào long-time one another prop against so wear out the masses,

⟶ 燕國趙國長久地互相撐拒結果使老百姓疲乏，

If the states *of* Yān *and* Zhào *are at a* standoff *for a* long time, fight*ing to the* point *where the* common people *become worn* out,

⟹ 燕國趙國長久地互相撐拒結果使老百姓疲乏，

If the states of Yān and Zhào are at a standoff for a long time, fighting to the point where the common people become worn out,

十． 臣恐強秦之為漁父也；

臣怕強秦的成爲漁父啊；

servant fear powerful Qín's becoming old fisherman;

⟶ 我擔心強大的秦國會成爲捕魚的老頭啊；

I fear *that the* powerful state *of* Qín *will become the* old fisherman;

⟹ 我擔心強大的秦國會成爲捕魚的老頭啊；

I fear that the powerful state of Qín will become the old fisherman;

十一． 故［臣］願王熟計之也。"

所以希望大王仔細計慮它啊。"

therefore hope great king thoroughly plan it."

⟶ 所以［我］希望大王周密地考慮一下這件事啊。"

75

therefore, [I] hope *that* your majesty *will* consider this matter thoroughly."

====> 所以希望大王周密地考慮一下這件事啊。"

therefore, I would like your majesty to consider this carefully."

十二. 惠王 曰:"善。" [趙] 乃 止 [伐燕]。
　　　　 s　　 p　　　　　　 [s]　　 p

惠王說:"好。" 就停止。

King Huì say: "Fine." Whereupon stop.

——> 趙惠王說:"好。" [趙]就不去攻打[燕]了。

King Huì *of* Zhào sa*id*: "All right." And so [*the* state *of* Zhào] halt*ed the planned* attack *on* [*the* state *of* Yān].

====> 趙惠王說:"好。" 趙國就不去攻打燕國了。

King Huì of Zhào said: "Agreed." Whereupon Zhào stopped the attack on Yān.

第十三課

郢書燕說

句子分析

一.

　　　郢人有送給燕相信的人，

　　　Yǐng people have send-Yān-prime-minister-letter one;

　━━━→ [在]郢都人[裡]有個送給燕國宰相一封信的人，

　　　[Among] *the* people *in the* capital city *of* Yǐng *there was* one *who* sent a letter to *the* prime minister *of the* state *of* Yān.

　═══> 有個送給燕國宰相一封信的郢都人，

　　　There was a man from the capital city of Yǐng who sent a letter to the prime minister of the state of Yān.

　　　　※遺　　　　雙賓語動詞，含有 " 交 A 給 B " 的意思。
　　　　　　　　　普通的及物動詞只要有一個賓語就可以把句子
　　　　　　　　　的意義完全表達出來了。雙賓語動詞卻必須得
　　　　　　　　　有兩個賓語－－直接賓語（A，指所給的物）和
　　　　　　　　　間接賓語（B，指受物的人）－－才能把句子的
　　　　　　　　　意義完全表達出來。因這類動詞本質上有 "
　　　　　　　　　交 A 給 B " 的意思，必須說出兩個賓語才能使
　　　　　　　　　句意完足。如本句 " 書 " 是直接賓語， " 燕相
　　　　　　　　　國 " 是間接賓語。這類雙賓語的動詞，除了 "
　　　　　　　　　遺 " 以外，還有 " 與 " (yǔ) " 予 " (yǔ) " 授
　　　　　　　　　" (shòu) " 贈 " (zèng) " 賜 " (cì) 等。

The verb "遺" takes two objects: it conveys the meaning "pass [down]/bestow **A** to/on **B**." In general, a transitive verb can completely convey its meaning in a sentence by taking a single direct object. A **double object verb** must take two objects to convey its complete meaning, because these verbs inherently contain the sense of giving something (**A** = direct object) to someone (**B** = indirect object). Only when both a direct and an indirect object are named can the full meaning of the verb be expressed in the sentence. In this sentence, "書" (a letter) is the direct object and "燕相國" (the prime minister of Yān) is the indirect object. In addition to the word "遺", the following **double object verbs** are frequently encountered: "與" (yǔ) (to give [something] to [someone]); "予" (yǔ) (to give [something] to [someone]); "授" (shòu) (to confer [something] on [someone]); "贈" (zèng) (to give [something] as a gift to [someone]); "賜" (cì) (to bestow [something] to [someone]).

二． 　[郢人]　[於] 夜 書，
　　　　　　　　　\[prep] o　v/
　　　　 [s]　　　　　　　　p

晚上寫信，

night write,

⟶ [郢都人][在]晚上寫信，

[*The* man *from* Yǐng] *wrote the* letter [in] *the* evening;

⟹ 郢都人在晚上寫信，

He wrote the letter in the evening;

三． 　火 不 明，
　　　　 \adv adj/
　　　 s　　　p

火光不亮，

flame not bright,

⟶ 燭光不夠亮，

the candlelight *was* not bright enough,

78

===> 燭光不夠亮，

the candlelight was not bright enough,

四． ［郢人］因 謂 持燭者 曰：" 舉 燭。"
　　　　　　adv　　v　　o　　　v　　o
　　[s]　　　　　　p1　　　　　p2

就告訴拿蠟燭的人說：" 舉高蠟燭。"

thereupon address hold-candle one say: "Raise candle."

——> ［他］就告訴拿蠟燭的人說：" 把蠟燭舉高一點儿。"

so [he] sa*id* to *the* one hold*ing the* candle: "Raise up *the* candle a bit."

===> 他就告訴拿蠟燭的人說：" 把蠟燭舉高一點儿。"

so he said to the person holding the candle: "Raise up the candle a bit."

五． ［郢人］云 而 過書 " 舉 燭。"
　　　　　　v　conj　adv　v　o
　　[s]　　p1　　　　　p2

說就誤寫 " 舉燭 " 。

speak-ing wrongly write "Raise candle."

——> ［郢都人］因說這句話結果就錯誤地寫上了 " 舉燭 " 這兩個字。

Because *he* sa*id* these word*s* , as a result, [*the* man *from* Yǐng] mistakenly *wrote* in *the* two characters: "Raise candle."

===> 郢都人因說這句話結果就錯誤地寫上了 " 舉燭 " 這兩個字。

As a result of saying these words he mistakenly wrote in the two characters : "Raise candle."

六．　　“舉燭” 非 書意 也。
＼v　o／　＼n-l.v.　o／ part
　　　s　　　　　　　p

　　“舉燭”不是信的意思啊。

"Raise candle" not be letter intent surely.

　──→ “舉燭”並不是信裡的意思啊。

"Raise up *the* candle" *was* not meant *to be* in *the* letter.

　══> “舉燭”並不是信裡的意思啊。

"Raise up the candle" was not meant to be in the letter.

七．　燕相受書而說之，曰：“　　”
　　＼v　o／conj＼v　o／　＼v　　o／
　　s　　p1　　　p2　　　　p3

　　燕相接到信就解釋它，說：

Yān councillor receive letter and interpret it, say:

　──→ 燕國宰相接到了這封信就解釋它，說：

The prime minister *of the* state *of* Yān receive*d* the letter, and interpret*ed* it, sa*id*:

　══> 燕國宰相接到了這封信就解釋這兩個字，說：

When the prime minister of the state of Yān received the letter, he expounded on these two characters and said:

七．一 “‘舉燭’者，[乃] 尚明 也。
　　　　　part　＼l.v.l v　o／ part
　　　　s　　　　　p

　　“‘舉起蠟燭’啊，崇尚光明啊。

" 'Raise candle': esteem bright surely.

⟶　"　'舉燭'〔是〕崇尚光明啊。

" 'Raise *up the* candle' [is] *to* esteem brightness (i.e., intelligence);

⟹　"　'舉燭' 是崇尚明智的意思。

"'Raise up the candle' means to esteem wisdom;

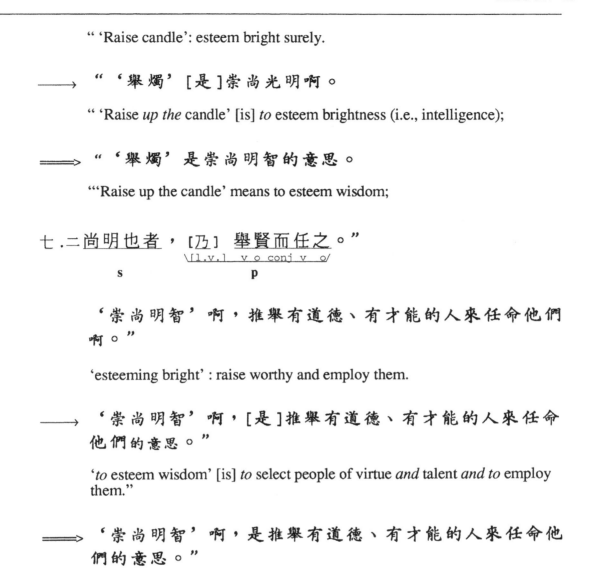

七．二尚明也者，〔乃〕舉賢而任之。"

'崇尚明智' 啊，推舉有道德、有才能的人來任命他們啊。"

'esteeming bright' : raise worthy and employ them.

⟶　'崇尚明智' 啊，〔是〕推舉有道德、有才能的人來任命他們的意思。"

'*to* esteem wisdom' [is] *to* select people of virtue *and* talent *and to* employ them."

⟹　'崇尚明智' 啊，是推舉有道德、有才能的人來任命他們的意思。"

'to esteem wisdom' means to select people of virtue and talent and to employ them."

八．　燕相〔以　之〕白王，〔王〕大　說，國　以〔之〕治。

燕相稟告王，非常高興，國家因而治理得好。

Yān councillor inform king, greatly pleased; state thereby ordered.

——→燕國宰相［把他的解釋］稟告給燕王，燕王非常高興，燕國因［此］治理得很好。

The prime minister *of the* state *of* Yān report*ed* [his interpretation *of this phrase*] to *the* king *of* Yān, *who was* greatly please*d by it; the* king *of* Yān then use*d this policy of* selecting virtuous *and* talented people *to govern the* state *well and the* state *was* because of this well-govern*ed*.

====＞燕國的宰相把他的想法稟告給燕王，燕王非常高興，燕國因爲舉用賢人就變得很太平。

The prime minister of the state of Yān reported his interpretation of this phrase to the king of Yān, who was greatly pleased by it; the king of Yān then used this policy of selecting virtuous and talented people to govern the state well and the state was consequently well-governed.

九．　［燕］　治　　則　〔爲〕　治　矣，　［］　　非　　書　意　　也。
　　　　　　　 \adj/　\adv [l.v.]　adj/ part.　　　\n-l.v.　　n　/ part.
　　　　　　[s]　　 p1　　　　　p2　　　　　　[s]　　　　　　p

※則：　　　"則"字的基本性質是連詞，但當它用在 "是則…也"或"Adj.則Adj.矣，然非／不…"句式之內，只能看作是繫詞"乃"（見楊樹達《詞詮》卷六、則字，二七四頁），可譯為白話的"是"。楊伯峻《文言常用虛詞》及呂叔湘、朱自清、葉聖陶《文言讀本》則認為在這兩種文言句式內的"則"字可看作副詞兼有繫詞的作用，依上下文的需要，可譯成"就是"、"卻是"、或"倒是"。

編者認為這種用法的"則"字既然可譯成"就是"、"卻是"、或"倒是"，就不妨把它看作單純的副詞，在後面省略了一個繫詞"為"。

本句"治則治矣，非書意也。"譯成白話是"太平倒是太平了，可是不是信裡的意思啊。"上一小句表示讓步，承認太平這個事實，下一小句用否定詞否認這個事實的價值及意義。這種"Adj.則Adj.矣，然非／不…"句式在白話中還大量使用著，如：“好倒是好，可是太貴”，“便宜倒是便宜，可是不好看。”

The word "則" basically functions as a conjunction, but when it appears in the **paradigms** "是則…也" or " Adj. 則 Adj. 矣，然非／不…", certain Chinese grammarians hold that it can only be construed as a linking verb (copula), that it functions like the word "乃", and that it should consequently be translated into spoken Chinese as "是" (to be). (See Yáng Shùdá, *Cí Quán*, Ch. 6, on "zé", p. 274). Others scholars like Yáng Bójùn (in his *Wényán Chángyòng Xūcí*), Lǔ Shūxiāng et. al., (in their *Wényán Dúběn*) , treat the word "則" in such sentences as an adverb that simultaneously functions as a linking verb and hold that it can, depending on the context, be variously translated into spoken Chinese as "就是" (is just)、 "卻是" (is but)、 或 "倒是" (is, to be sure/is indeed).

While arguing that in this usage the word "則" can be translated into spoken Chinese as "就是"、 "卻是"、 or "倒是," we think it can nonetheless still be construed as a simple adverb modifying a linking verb like "為" that is understood and hence omitted. Thus the sentence "治則治矣，非書意也" can be translated into spoken Chinese as "太平倒是太平了，可是不是信裡的意思啊。" (Well-governed is to be sure well-governed/ Great peace is indeed great peace, but that is not what was meant in the letter). The first clause makes a concession (i.e., that a state of great peace or good government does indeed exist); the second clause then negates its significance with respect to the particular situation described therein (i.e., it is in no sense a result of what the author of the letter was talking about when he mistakenly wrote "raise candle"). This type of classical Chinese sentence pattern is still commonly seen in spoken Chinese in such examples as "好倒是好，可是太貴。" (Good is to be sure good, but this is too expensive), or "便宜倒是便宜，可是不好看。" (Cheap is cheap, but this is ugly). In English, this paradigm occurs in such common expresssions as, "Fair is fair, but ..."

太平倒太平了，不是信的意思啊。

orderly nay orderly indeed; is not letter intant surely.

⟶ [燕國]太平倒是太平了，可是[燕國宰相的解釋]並不是信裡的意思啊。

As for[the state *of* Yān] *being* well-govern*ed*, it is cetainly well-govern*ed*, but [*the* prime minister *of* Yān's explanation of *the* phrase] *was* not *what the* letter mean*t*.

⟹ 燕國太平倒是太平了，可是燕國宰相的解釋並不是信裡的意思啊。

Now for the state of Yān to acheive orderly government is one thing, but the prime minister of Yān's interpretation of the phrase was not what the letter meant.

十． ［於．］ 今世學者 多 似 此類。
　　　\ [prep]　　　o　 /　 \p-l.v.　 n /
　　　　　　extp-s　　　　s　　　p

現代學者多像這類。

Current-generation-learned-ones, most like this sort.

⟶ ［在］現代的學者［中］多數像這類的人。

[Among] contemporary scholars, *the* great majority resemble this sort of people.

⟶ ［在］現代的學者［中］多數像燕國宰相這類的人。

[Among] contemporary scholars, *the* great majority resemble the sort of *this* **prime minister** *of* **Yān**.

⟹ 在現代的學者中多數像燕國宰相這類的人。

Among contemporary scholars, the majority are like the sort of this prime minister of Yān.

第十四課

狐假虎威

句子分析

一． 虎　求百獸　而　食之，　得狐。

<pre>
        \ v o /   conj \ v o /   \ v o /
   s   p1   p2   p3
</pre>

老虎尋找各種野獸來吃牠們，得到狐狸。

Tiger seek various animals to eat them; get fox.

⟶ 老虎尋找各種動物來吃牠們，得到了一隻狐狸。

A tiger *was* look*ing* for various kind*s* *of wild* animals *to* eat them; *he* got a fox.

⟹老虎尋找各種動物來吃牠們，得到了一隻狐狸。

A tiger was looking for all sorts of wild animals to eat; he got a fox.

二． 狐　曰：　"　"

<pre>
        \ v   o /
   s   p
</pre>

狐狸說：

Fox say:

⟶ 狐狸說：

The fox sa*id*:

⟹ 狐狸說：

The fox said:

二.一　　　　　"子　無　敢　食　我　也，
　　　　　　　　　＼adv　aux　v　o／　part
　　　　　　　　　s　　　　　p

"您不敢吃我啊，

"You not dare eat me surely:

——→ "您絕不敢吃我，

"You certainly dare not eat me:

===⟹ "您絕不敢吃我，

"You certainly dare not eat me:

二.二　　　　天帝　使　我　長百獸，
　　　　　　　　　　　　　　v　　o
　　　　　　　　　　＼v　o/s　　p　／
　　　　　　　　　s　　　　　p

老天爺使我領導各種動物，

Heaven ruler order me head various animals;

——→ 老天爺使我做各種動物的領袖，

Heaven *has made* me *the* **leader of all** *the* **wild animals**;

===⟹ 老天爺使我做各種動物的領袖，

Heaven has made me the leader of all the wild animals;

　　　　　　　　　　　　　　　　　v　　o　　[n]
　　　　　　　　　　　　　　　　adj. mod. [n]
二.三　　　　今　子食我，是　[乃]　逆天帝命[者]也。
　　　　　　　adv　v　o/　＼[l.v.]　　pn　／　part
　　　　　　　　s　p　s　　　　　p

※"N1 [乃] N2也"

　　　　　是標準的判斷句，"N [乃] v-o 也"（是
　　　　　[乃]逆天帝命也）是判斷句的變式，或者可以

說是簡化了的判斷句。"V-O"(逆天帝命)後
可以加上一個"者"字,使自己的地位變低,
成為"者"字的定語。此處"者"字可以譯成
"之行為。"

N1 [乃] N2 也 is a typical **determinative sentence**
pattern. N [乃] V-O 也 (the pattern in the sentence "是[乃
]逆天帝命也") is a variant form of the determinative sentence;
it can also be described as a simplified form of the determinative
sentence. The **V-O** element following the copula (乃) --in this
example the phrase "逆天帝命"-- can be followed by the
particle "者". The addition of this particle changes the
grammatical function of the phrase by transforming it into an
adjectival modifier. The whole construction can then be
construed as a noun phrase. In this construction, the word "者"
functions as a pronoun and can be translated as "*conduct* that
goes against the orders of Heaven." As a **V-O** construction, it
can simply be translated into English with an infinitive phrase
(e.g., "This is to go against the orders of Heaven"). As an
adjectival modifier -- particle "者" construction, it can be
translated with a dependent clause (e g., "This is what goes
against the orders of Heaven." or "This is *behaviour* that goes
against the orders of Heaven.")

現在您吃我,這違背天帝的命令啊。

now you eat me; this disobey Heaven ruler command surely.

——→ 現在您要是吃我,這[是]違背老天爺命令的行為
啊。

now, *if* you eat me, this [is] conduct *that goes* against *the*
command *of* Heaven.

══⟹ 現在您要是吃我,這是違背老天爺命令的行為
啊。

now, if you eat me, it goes against the command of Heaven.

二.四   子 以 我 為 <u>不 信</u>,
                              adv adj

您把我當作不誠實,

87

You take me to be not credible,

——→ [要是]您把我當作是不誠實的,

If you regard me as *being* not trustworthy,

===> 要是您認爲我不誠實,

If you think me untrustworthy,

* "以…爲…" : 意動繁句 *putative complex sentence.*

"以"、"爲"是意動繁句中一同用的動詞。兩個字可以分開來用也可以合起來用。分用時"以"是動詞,"爲"是繁詞,意思是"拿A當B",其中的 A 一定是個名詞,B 則可以是名詞或形容詞。B 爲名詞時意思是"拿什麼當什麼",B 爲形容詞時意思是"拿什麼當怎麼樣〔的〕"。本句是 B 爲形容詞的例子。

In a **putative complex sentence** the verbs"以"and "爲"are used in conjunction. These two verbs can be conjoined as"以爲"or separated, as in the paradigm"以A 爲 B." When they appear separated, "以" should be construed as a verb and "爲" as a copula (linking verb). The entire construction "以A 爲 B " should be understood to mean "take A as B" where A must be a noun (or noun phrase) while B can be either a noun or an adjective. When B is a noun, the meaning is simply: "take A as B", "take [someone/something] and consider him/it to be (think him/it to be) [someone/ something else]"; when B is an adjective, the meaning is: "take [someone/something] and consider him/it to be (think him/it to be) <u>like</u> [some descriptive adjective]." The sentence under discussion is an example of the type where B is a descriptive adjective.

如果把"以""爲"兩個字合併在一塊儿寫成"以爲",那麼"以爲"就變成了一個有認定意味的動詞。"以爲AB"意思是"認爲(覺得)A [是]B",B中所說的不是事實,而只是存在於主語心中的一種想法,B仍有名詞或形容詞的兩種可能。若把本句中分開用的"以"、"爲"合起來用,就成了:"子以爲我不信"

If the words are conjoined and written as "以爲", this "以爲" should be construed as a single compound verb that conveys a sense of stipulating, contending or determining something, some condition, or some abstract statement to be the case (with or without respect to evidence). The verbal phrase "以為 A B " then means "to regard/consider A as B," or "to hold that A is B", where the statement comprised by B (a noun/noun phrase or an adjective/adjectival phrase) is not presented as a fact but rather only as a thought existing in the mind of the subject "子". In this construction (i.e., when 以為 functions as a single compound verb), A is always a noun/noun phrase, while B can be either a noun/noun phrase or an adjective/adjectival phrase. In the sentence under discussion, "以為" is used as a single compound verb; A is a noun (我) and B is a predicate adjective or adjectival phrase (不信).

[若]子 以為 我 不 信。
[conj]　　 v　o/s　p
s　　　　　　　p

"我"是"以為"的賓語，同時也是"不信"的主語，"我"在句中負有兩種責任，因此，"我"是所謂的"兼語"，整個句子稱為"意動繁句"。

In this sentence, the word "我" functions both as the object of "以為" and as the subject of the predicate "不信". The word "我" thus serves two distinct grammatical functions in the sentence; Chinese grammarians refer to words that function like "我" does in this sentence as **pivotal words** (兼語), and to such sentences as **putative complex sentences** (意動繁句).

1)　您以為我不誠實
You take me to be untrustworthy.

2)　[要是]您認為我不誠實
[If] you consider me to be untrustworthy,

3)　要是您覺得我不誠實
If you think me untrustworthy,

二.五　吾 為 子 先 行，
　　　 prep o adv v
s　　 p

我為您先走，

I for you first walk,

⟶ 我為您在前頭走，

89

I *will* **walk ahead for you**;

⟹ 我爲您在前頭走，

I will walk ahead of you;

二.六　　　子　隨　[於]我後，
　　　　　　　　＼ v　[prep]　o ／
　　　　　　s　　　　p

您跟隨我後頭，

you follow me after,

⟶ 您跟隨[在]我後頭，

you follow behind me,

⟹ 您跟隨在我後頭，

you follow behind me,

　　　　　　　　　　　v　o　conj　aux adv v
　　　　　　　　　　s　之　p1　　　p2
二.七　　　[子]觀　百獸　之　見我　而　敢　不走乎？"
　　　　　　　＼v　　　　　o　　　　　　　／ part
　　　　　　[s]　　　　　　p

※ "百獸之見我而敢不走乎？"
　　是用反問句來表示肯定的意思。

In this sentence, a **rhetorical question** is used to express affirmation:

1) "各種野獸看見我卻還敢不逃跑嗎？"
"[When] the various animals see me, do they nevertheless still dare not flee?"

2) "各種動物看見我不敢不逃跑。"
"[When] the various animals see me, they dare not not flee."

3) "各種動物看見我一定會逃跑。"
"[When] the various animals see me, they most certainly will flee."

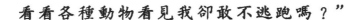

看看各種動物看見我卻敢不逃跑嗎？"

observe: various animals seeing me and dare not flee?"

⟶ 您看看各種動物看見我卻還敢不逃跑嗎？"

and observe: *when the* various animal*s* see me, *do they* nevertheless still dare not flee?"

and observe: dare *any of the* wild animal*s* see me and not flee.

⟹ 您看看各種動物看見我卻還敢不逃跑嗎？"

and observe: whether any wild animals see me and dare not flee."

三． 虎以為[其言]然， 故 遂 與之行，
　　　＼ v　 o / s adj/　 conj ＼adv prep o　v /
　　　 s　　　 p1　　　　　　　 p2

老虎以為對，所以就跟牠走，

Tiger think right, so just with him go.

⟶ 老虎認為[牠的話]很對，所以就跟牠一塊走，

The tiger *thought* [*the* fox's word*s*] *were* reasonable, so *he went* right along with him.

⟹ 老虎覺得狐狸的話很有道理，所以就跟牠一塊走，

The tiger thought the fox's words reasonable, so he just went along with him.

四． 獸 見之 皆走。
　　　＼v　 o / ＼adv v/
　　　 s　 p1　　 p2

野獸看見狐狸跟老虎都逃跑。

Wild beasts see them (i.e., the fox and the tiger), all flee.

⟶ 野獸看見狐狸跟老虎都逃跑了。

91

When the wild animal*s saw them* (i.e., *the* fox and *the* tiger), all fl*ed.*

⟹ 動物看見牠們倆都逃跑了。

When wild animals saw these two, they all fled.

五. 虎不知獸畏己而走也，以為［獸］畏狐也。

※也： 語氣詞，用在複句的前一小句末，表示停頓

Here the word "也" functions as a rhetorical particle; it is placed at the end of the first clause of a compound sentence to mark the end of the clause and to indicate a rhetorical pause, which is intended to emphasize the statement made in the first clause.

老虎不知道野獸怕自己才逃跑啊，以為怕狐狸吶。

Tiger not know wild beasts fear himslef and flee, think fear fox.

⟶ 老虎不知道動物因為怕自己才逃跑啊，還以為［動物］怕狐狸吶。

The tiger *did* not know *that the* wild animal*s* fl*ed* only from fear *of* him; *it thought* (*the* wild animal*s*) fear*ed the* fox!

⟹ 老虎不知道動物因為怕自己才逃跑啊，還以為牠們怕狐狸吶。

The tiger, thinking they feared the fox, did not know that only because the wild animals feared him did they run away!

第十五課

攫金

句子分析

一. ［於］昔　　［於］齊人　　有 欲金者。
　　＼[prep] o／　＼[prep]　o／　＼v　　o／
　　　　adv　　　　　　s　　　　　　p

從前齊人有想要金子的人。

Earlier, Qí people have lusting-after-gold one.

⟶ ［在］從前［在］齊國人［裡］有個想要金子的人。

[In] *the* past, [among] *the* people of *the* state *of* Qí *there was* a *person who* lust*ed after* gold.

⟹ 從前有個想要金子的齊國人。

Once there was a man from the state of Qí who lusted after gold.

二. ［於］清旦，［欲金者］衣　冠　而　之市，　適 鬻金者之所，
　　＼[prep] o／　　　　　＼v／＼v／conj＼v o／　＼v　　　o／
　　　adv　　　　　［s］　　p1　p2　　　p3　　　　　p4

　　　　　　　　　　　　　因　攫其金　而　去。
　　　　　　　　　　　　＼v　o／conj＼v／
　　　　　　　　　　　　adv　p5　　　p6

清早，穿衣服，戴帽子就到市場去，到賣金子的人的地
方，於是搶他的金子就跑走。

Early morn, robe and cap himself, and go to market, reach sell-gold one's
place, whereupon snatch his gold and leave.

——→[在]大清早，[想要金子的人]穿上衣服，戴上帽子就到市場去了，到了賣金子的人的地方，於是搶了他的金子就跑走了。

Early [in] *the* morning, [*the* man *who* lust*ed after* gold] *put* on *his* cloth*es*, don*ned the* cap, and *went* to *the* marketplace. *Upon* reach*ing the* place *where a* man *was* sell*ing* gold, *he* thereupon snatch*ed up the* man's gold *and ran off*.

===⟹ 在大清早，他穿上衣服戴上帽子就到市場去了，到了賣金子的人的鋪子，即刻搶了他的金子就跑了。

Bright and early one morning, he donned his cap and gown and went to the marketplace; upon arriving at a goldsmith's shop, he straightaway snatched up the man's gold and fled.

三．　更 捕得之， 問 [之] 曰："人皆在焉，子攫人之金何？"
　　　　　\ v comp o /　\v [o]/　\v ⎯⎯⎯⎯⎯⎯⎯o/
　　　s　　p1　　　p2　　　　　p3

警官逮住他，問説："　"

Constable catch hold him; question, say:

——→ 警官逮著他，問 [他] 説："　"

The constable *had caught* him *and* question*ed* [him], say*ing*:

===⟹ 警官逮著了他，問他説："　"

After the constable had caught him, he questioned him, saying:

三．一　　"人 皆 在 焉，
　　　　　　　\adv v prep-o/
　　　s　　　　p

　　　※焉　　　用作指示代詞時，等於"於是"。"是"指代
　　　　　　　　處所，在本文中，"是"指代"鬻金者之所"
　　　　　　　　，也就是"賣金子的鋪子"或"金店"，可以
　　　　　　　　簡單地譯成"那個地方"或"那裡"

When the word "為" functions as a demonstrative pronoun, it is equivalent in meaning to "於是"(in this place). In this usage, "是" refers to a place; in the text "是" refers to "鬻金者之所" (the place of the seller of gold; i.e., the goldsmith's shop or the gold store). "為" can be translated into colloquial Chinese as "那個地方" or "那裡" and into English as "at that place" or "there".

"人都在那裡，

"people all present there;

⟶ "別人都在那裡，

"*There were* other people there;

⟹ "別人都在那裡，

"There were other people there;

三.二
<u>子 攫 人之金</u> 何 ？"

S V O

s   p

※ 何 是疑問副詞，通常置於句中動詞之前，但本文作者卻把"何"從句中移到句末，使它升格擔負謂語的責任，把簡句變成包孕句了。這種化簡為繁的寫法，目的在加強語氣。文言中這種置句中副詞於句末用作謂語，甚至把這種謂語倒置在主語之前以加強語氣，是常見的一種修辭方式；例如：《論語、述而》：

When the word "何" functions as an interrogative adverb (i.e., why, how), it usually appears in the middle of the sentence in front of the verb. However, by moving "何" to the end of the sentence, the author of this text employs it in a sense that goes beyond its usual adverbial function; here it serves as the main predicate of the sentence and thereby changes the simple sentence that precedes it into an **embedding sentence**. This style of writing, in which a simple pattern is made complex or ornate, is used to strengthen the emotive or oratorical tone of a sentence. Such transpositions (i.e., moving an adverb from the middle of a sentence to make it function as a predicate at the end of the sentence, or even putting the predicate in front of the subject to intensify the emotive or oratorical tone of the sentence) rank

95

among the more common rhetorical devices employed in classical Chinese. Consider, for example, the following line from the *Analects*:

子曰：“甚矣吾衰也，久矣吾不復夢見周公。”

The master said: "Extreme is my decay; for a long time, I have not dreamed, as I was wont to do, that I saw the Duke of Chou." (Legge, *The Analects of Confucius*, p. 196)

若把兩個包孕句中的謂語“甚”及“久”放回句中就變成兩個簡句如下：

If the predicates of the two embedding sentences ("甚" and "久") were returned to the middle of the sentence, the complex sentence would be transformed into two simple sentences like the following:

子曰：“吾甚衰矣，吾久不復夢見周公矣。”

The master said: "I have become much weakened; I have long stopped dreaming of the Duke of Chou."

然而兩種句式語氣的強弱則有顯著的區別。

However, the relative strength and weakness of the emphatic or oratorical tone in these two sentences can be clearly distinguished. It is paralleled in the difference between Legge's translation ("Extreme is my decay"), where the word "extreme" is emphasized by transposing it to the beginning of the sentence, and a more pedestrian version like "I am very tired," which lacks an oratorical or emphatic tone.

您搶人的金子，爲什麼？”

You grab man's gold -- why?"

——→ 您搶人家的金子，爲什麼？”

You grab*bed the* man's gold -- why?"

====> 您搶人家的金子，爲什麼？”

You grabbed the man's gold -- why?"

96

四. [欲金者] 對 曰："   "
　　　　[s]　　p1　　　　p2

回答説：

Respond say:

⟶ [想要金子的人]回答説：

[*The* man *who* lust*ed after* gold] repl*ied*, say*ing*:

⟹ 他回答説：

He answered, saying:

四.一　"[於] 取金之時，[余] 不見人，徒見金。"
　　　　　[prep]　o　　[s]　adv v o　adv v o
　　　　　　　adv　　　　　p1　　　　p2

※ 取金之時〔余〕不見人，徒見金。

這是對待式複句中。這種複句中的前後兩分句一正一反，意思互相對立。其中的一個分句含有否定詞。

This is an **Antithetical Compound Sentence**. In this type of sentence the two clauses oppose each other, one in the positive, and the other in the negative sense. One of the two clauses must contain a negative word.

"拿金子的時候，沒看見人，只看見金子。"

"Take-gold time, not see people, only see gold."

⟶ "[在]拿金子的時候，[我]沒看見什麼人，只看見了金子。"

"[At] *the* time *I* took *the* gold, [I] *did*n't see any people, *I* only *saw* gold."

⟹ "在拿金子的時候，我沒看見什麼人，只看見了金子。"

"When I took the gold, I didn't see any people, I only saw gold."

97

第十六課

君子慎所藏

句子分析

一． <u>君子</u> <u>慎</u> [<u>於</u>] <u>所藏</u>。

```
        adj [prep]   o
          \___v____/
   s           p
```

※ 所   用在及物動詞之前，組成一個名詞語（所 + v =
n），表示"v 的 n"。動詞後沒有用作賓語的
名詞時，"所"字的作用好像是代替名詞充當
動詞後的賓語，在這種情況下，這個"所"字
可以看作是代詞。"所藏"譯成白話是"藏
匿的地方"引申的意思是"居住的地方"或"
生活的環境"。

When the word "所" occurs before a transitive verb, the
combination "所 + v" functions like a phrase (所 + v = n).
This phrase is equivalent in meaning to the construction **n** of **v**
(e.g., 所藏 = where kept = place of keeping [N of V]). When
the transitive verb is not followed by a noun that functions as its
object, the word "所" serves both as a pronoun and as the object
of the verb, much like the word "where" does in English. In this
context, the word "所" can be construed as a pronoun. Here "所
藏" can be rendered into colloquial Chinese as "藏匿的地方"
(LITERALLY: place of keeping), which is used as a metaphor
for a person's place of residence or living conditions. Here "所"
can be translated into English as a relative pronoun like "where,"
as in "where he keeps [himself]." The "所 + v" construction
can be translated into English in a number of different ways,
depending on the context (e.g., with relative pronouns, dependent
clauses, noun or infinitive phrases, gerundives).

品德高尚的人慎重居住的地方。

Morality-noble person is circumspect where he dwell.

——→ 品德高尚的人[對於]他居住的地方很慎重。

A person of high moral character *is* very circumspect [about] *the* place *in which he* live*s*.

⟶ 品德高尚的人對於選擇自己生活的環境採取非常慎重的態度。

A person of high moral character adopts *an* exceedingly circumspective attitude toward selec*ting* his living condition*s*.

⟹ 品德高尚的人對於選擇自己生活的環境非常慎重。

A person of high moral character is exceedingly circumspect about selecting his living conditions.

二.孔子曰：" . "
　　　＼v＿＿o＿／
　s　　　p

孔子說："　　　"

Confucius said: "　　　"

二.一　　　"[人][若] 不 知 其 子，[則] 視 其 所 友；
　　　　　　 [conj] ＼adv v o ／ [conj] ＼v o ／
　　　　　　 [s]　　　 p1　　　　　　　p2

※其所友　其子之所友，"之"字儘管有所有格"的"的性質，但為了避免白話翻譯中有太多"的"字，不妨把它看作只有連接兩個詞的作用，不必譯出。

"whom his son befriends." Although the word "之" does have a possessive sense, in this case, it can also be **simply understood to function as a link between the two phrases** "其子" and "所友", in which usage it need not be translated into spoken Chinese as "的".

"不了解他的孩子，看他的孩子結交的人；

"Not understand one's child, look-at his child make-friend ones.

——→ "[人要是]不了解他自己的孩子，[那麼就]看看他的孩子
結交的人；

"[If one] *does* not understand one's own child, *one* [need only] observe
whom one's child befriend*s*.

===⟹ "一個人要是不了解他自己的孩子，那就看看他的孩子結
交的朋友；

"If one does not understand one's own child, one need only observe whom
one's child befriends.

二.二   [人] [若] 不 知 其 君， [則] 視 其所使。"
　　　　　　　[conj]\adv v o /   [conj]\ v o /
　　　　　　　[s]   p1   p2

　　　　　　　※其所使：其君之所使
　　　　　　　　　　　　"whom his ruler dispatches"

不了解他的君主，看他的君主派遣的人。"

Not understand one's ruler, look-at one's ruler dispatching ones."

——→ [人要是]不了解他自己的君主，[那麼就]看看他的君主派
遣的人。"

[If one] *does* not understand one's ruler, *one* [need only] observe *what kind
of* men one's ruler dispatch*es*."

===⟹ 一個人要是不了解他自己的君主，那就看看他的君主派
遣的人。"

If one does not understand one's ruler, one need only observe whom one's
ruler dispatches."

三.   [孔子]又 曰： "   "
　　　　　　　\adv v   o /
　　　　[s]   p

又說： "   "

Also say:

⟶ ［孔子］又說：" "

[Confucius] also sa*id*:

⟹ 孔子又說：" "

Confucius also said:

三・一 " [人] 與 善人居， 如 [人] 入 蘭芝之室，

※ A 如 B: 是典型的準判斷句。"如"是準繫詞，譯成白話是"好像是"。A跟B可以是名詞、名詞語、或半獨立性小句。 A跟B是半獨立性小句時，由準繫詞"如"連接而構成的全句就是一種習見的準判斷包孕句。

This is a typical **pseudo-determinative sentence**. "如" is a pseudo-linking verb, and can be rendered in spoken Chinese as "好像是" (is like). Both A and B can be nouns, noun phrases, or semi-independent clauses. The last type of sentence --"A (clause) 如 B (clause)" is a very common **pseudo-determinative embedding sentence**.

"跟善良的人住，好像是進入蘭芝的屋子，

"With good person live is like enter room of fragrant plants:

⟶ "［一個人］跟善良的人在一塊儿住，好像是進入了養蘭芝的屋子一樣，

"*When* [a person] live*s* together with *a* person of good character, *it* is as if *he* enter*ed a* room *in which* sweet-scented grass*es and* herb*s were* be*ing* cultivat*ed*:

⟹ "一個人跟善良的人在一塊儿住，好像是進入了養蘭芝的屋子一樣，

"Living together with a person of good character is like going into a room where sweet-scented plants are being raised:

三.二　　　[人] [居] 久　而　不　聞　其　香，
　　　　　　　　　\[v] comp/　conj　\adv　v　o /
　　　　　　　[s]　p1　　　　　　p2

長久就不會聞見它的香氣，

long time, then not can smell their fragrance;

⟶ [人] [待] 久了就聞不見蘭芝的香氣了，

after *having stayed a good* while, [he] cannot smell *the* fragrance of *the* sweet-scented plant*s* any*more*;

⟹ 人待久了就聞不見蘭芝的香氣了，

after having stayed a long while, ha cannot smell the fragrance of the sweet-scented plants amymore;

　　　　　　　　　　　　　　prep　o　v
　　　　　　　　　　　　[g]　‾‾‾‾‾‾‾‾
三.三　　　[此]　則　[為]　[人] 與　之　化　矣；
　　　　　　[s]　adv　[l.v.]　　　　p　　part

※則：　　"則"字的基本性質是連詞，但當它用在 "是則…也"或"ADJ. 則 ADJ矣，然非／不…"句式之內，只能看作是繫詞"乃"（楊樹達《詞詮》卷六、則字），可譯為白話的"是"。楊伯峻《文言常用虛詞》及呂叔湘、朱自清、葉聖陶《文言讀本》則認為在這兩種文言句式內的"則"字可看作副詞兼有繫詞的作用，依上下文的需要，可譯成"就是"、"卻是"、或"倒是"。

編者認為這種用法的"則"字既然可譯成"就是"、"卻是"、或"倒是"，就不妨把它看作單純的副詞，在後面省略了一個繫詞"為"。

本句 "［此］則［為］［人］與之化矣。" 即屬於 "是則 … 也。" 句型，譯成白話是 "這個就是人跟它一塊儿變化了。" "就是" 表示一種確定兼解釋的語氣。

The word "則" basically functions as a conjunction, but when it appears in the PARADIGM "是 則 … 也" or "ADJ. 則 ADJ. 矣 , 然 非／不 …" certain Chinese grammarians hold that it can only be construed as a linking verb (copula), that it functions like the word "乃", and that it should consequently be translated into spoken Chinese as "是" (to be). (See Yáng Shùdá, *Cí Quán*, Ch. 6, on "zé").

Others scholars like Yáng Bójùn (in his *Wényán Chángyòng Xūcí*), Lǚ Shūxiāng et. al., (in their *Wényán Dúběn*) treat the word "則" in such sentences as an adverb that simultaneously functions as a linking verb and hold that it can, depending on the context, be variously translated into spoken Chinese as "就是" (is just), "卻是" (is but), or "倒是" (is, to be sure/is indeed).

While arguing that in this usage the word "則" can be translated into spoken Chinese as "就是"、"卻是"、or "倒是," we think it can nonetheless still be construed as a simple adverb modifying a linking verb like "為" that is understood and hence omitted.

This sentence "［此］則［為］［人］與之化矣。" is a variant of the "是 則 … 也" pattern. It can be rendered in spoken Chinese as "這個就是人跟它一塊儿變化了。" (This then is [to say] [that] the person has changed along with them/the sweet-scented plants.) Here, the words "就是" (the counterpart of "則" in spoken Chinese) express an affirmative and explanatory tone.

就跟它變化了；

then with them transformed.

⟶ ［這］就是［人］跟蘭芝一起變化了；

[this] then is [*the* person] *has* changed along with *the* sweet-scented plant*s*.

⟶ 這就是人受到薰染變得跟蘭芝一樣香了；

this is because *the* person **has been changed** by *the* **influence of *the* environment *and has* become as fragrant as *the*** sweet-scented plant**s**.

⟹ 這就是人受到薰染變得跟蘭芝一樣香了；

103

this is because the person has been changed by the influence of the environment and has become as fragrant as the sweet-scented plants.

三.四　　　[人] 與 惡人居，如 [人] 入 鮑魚之肆，

跟邪惡的人住，好像是進入鹹魚的鋪子，

With malevolent-person live is like entering salted fish store:

——→ [一個人]跟邪惡的人在一塊儿住，好像是進入了賣鹹魚的鋪子一樣，

When [a person] live*s* together *with a* malevolent person, *it* is as if he *went* into *a* store *that sells* salted fish:

===⇒ 一個人跟邪惡的人在一塊儿住，好像是進入了賣鹹魚的鋪子一樣，

Living with a malevolent person is like going into a store that sells salted fish:

三.五　　　[人] [居] 久 而 不 聞其臭，

長久就不會聞見它的臭味，

long time, then not can smell its stench (i.e., *the* stench of *the* salted fish);

——→ [人] [待]久了就聞不見鹹魚的臭味了，

after having stayed a good while, [he] cannot smell *the* stench of *the* salted fish any*more*;

===⇒ 待久了就聞不見鹹魚的臭味了，

after having stayed a long while, he cannot smell the stench of the salted fish anymore;

104

三.六　　　[此] 則 [為]. [人] 亦 與 之 化 矣。"
　　　　　　[s]　adv　[l.v.]　　　p　　　part

（adv prep o v / p）

就也跟它變化了。"

then also with it transformed."

──→ [這]就是[人]也跟鹹魚一起變化了。"

[this] then is [*the* person] *has* also chang*ed* along with *the* salted fish."

──→ 這就是人受到薰染也變得跟鹹魚一樣臭了。"

this too is *because the* person *has been* changed by *the* influence of *the* environment *and has* become as malodorous as *the* salted fish."

══⇒ 這就是人受到薰染也變得跟鹹魚一樣臭了。"

this too is because the person has been changed by the influence of the environment and has become as malodorous as the salted fish."

四.　　 故 [人] 曰：" 　　　　"
　　　conj　　　　 v　　　o
　　　　[s]　　　p

所以說：" 　"

Therefore say：" 　"

──→ 所以[有人]說：" 　"

So [*it has been*] *said*：" 　"

══⇒ 所以有人說：" 　"

So it has been said：" 　"

105

四 .一

"丹之所藏者 赤；烏之所藏者 黑。"
　　　　　　　adj　　　　　　　　adj
　　　　　　　\v/　　　　　　　　\v/
　　s　　　　p　　　s　　　　　p

✳丹之所藏者赤；烏之所藏者黑：

這是平行式複句。這種句子的各分句字數相等、句構相同、意義相關，平列在一起顯示一種整齊之美。

This is a **Parallel Compound Sentence**. This type of sentence s made of two or more clauses of equal length, identical structure, and related meaning. This form is traditionally considered stylistically pleasing.

✳所藏者

動詞後有名詞或代詞"者"時，"所 + v"組成的短語只含有形容詞的性質，"所"字的作用只像是指示詞"那個"。"所藏者"最清楚、正確的譯法應該是"儲藏的那個／些個東西"，但如果譯成"所儲藏的東西"，也不能算錯，因白話中這樣的表達方式仍存在。

When the verb is followed by a noun or by the pronoun "者", the phrase formed by the combination "所 + v" has an adjectival quality only (i.e., it functions as an adjectival modifier); in such cases, the word "所" functions like the demonstrative pronoun "那個" [that, those]. This is most clearly seen in the example at hand (所藏者): the clearest and most precise translation of this phrase into spoken Chinese should be "儲藏的那個／些個東西" [those things kept], but it would also be correct to render it as "所儲藏的東西" because this usage of "所" still exists in modern spoken Chinese. A distinction can be drawn in English by saying "those things kept" or "that which is kept" to stress the demonstrative quality of "所" in this usage, and the construction "所 + v" should be rendered in this case as "what is kept" or "things kept".

"朱紅色儲藏的那個東西紅；烏黑色儲藏的那個東西黑。"

"Cinnabar-red-keep thing redden; raven-black-keep thing blacken."

——➞ "朱紅色中儲藏的那個東西會變紅；烏黑色中儲藏的那個東西會變黑。"

"Those thing*s* store*d in* cinnabar red *will* become red; those thing*s* ke*pt in* raven black *will* become black."

==⟹ "朱紅色中儲藏的那個東西會變紅；烏黑色中儲藏的那個東西會變黑。" "

"That which is kept in cinnabar red reddens; that which is kept in raven black blackens."

五. <u>君子</u> <u>慎</u> [於] <u>所藏</u>。
      adj [prep] o
        v
  s   p

品德高尚的人慎重居住的地方。

Morality-noble person is circumspect where he dwell.

⟶ 品德高尚的人[對於]他居住的地方很慎重。

A person of high moral character *is* very circumspect [about] *the* place *in which he* live*s*.

⟶ 品德高尚的人對於選擇自己生活的環境採取非常慎重的態度。

A person of high moral character adopts *an* exceedingly circumspective attitude toward select*ing* his living condition*s*.

==⟹ 品德高尚的人對於選擇自己生活的環境非常慎重。

A person of high moral character is exceedingly circumspect about selecting his living conditions.

第十七課

刻舟求劍

句子分析

一．

楚人有個渡河的人，

Chǔ people have cross-river one;

⟶ [在]楚國人[中]有個渡河的人，

[Among] *the* people *of the* state *of* Chǔ *there was* one *who was* cross*ing a* river;

⟹ 有個渡河的楚國人，

There was a man from the state of Chǔ who was crossing a river;

二．

$$\underset{\text{s}}{其劍} \quad \underset{\text{p}}{\underset{\text{prep o v prep o}}{自舟中墜於水}}。$$

他的劍從船裡掉到水裡。

his sword from boat's interior drop in water.

⟶ 他的劍從船上掉到水裡去了。

his sword from *the* boat drop*ped* into *the* water.

⟹ 他的劍從船上掉到水裡去了。

108

his sword dropped from the boat into the water.

三. ［涉江者］遽 契其舟 曰：" 是吾劍之所從墜。"
　　　　　　　　＼adv　v　o／　＼v　　　　　　o　　　／
　　　　s　　　　　　p1　　　　　　　　　p2

趕緊 刻那條船說：

Forthwith notch that boat, say:

⟶ ［渡河的人］趕緊刻那條船說：

[*The* person cross*ing the* river] at once cut *a notch on the* boat, say*ing*:

⟶ 渡河的人趕緊在那條船邊上刻了個記號說：

[*The* person cross*ing the* river] immediately **cut *a notch on the* side *of
the* boat** , say*ing*:

⟹ 渡河的人趕緊在那條船邊上刻了個記號說：

He immediately cut a notch on the side of the boat , saying:

三.一 " 是 ［乃］ 吾劍之所從墜。"
　　　　　　＼[l.v.]　　　　pn／
　　　　s　　　　　p

※句型變換： SENTENCE TRANSFORMATION:

1.吾劍　　　　墜　　　　（敘述句）
　s　　　　　　p
　My sword　　dropped.　　(a narrative sentence)

2.吾劍 從 是 墜　　　　（敘述句）
　　　＼prep　o　v／
　s　　　　　p
　My sword from this (place) dropped.　(a narrative sentence)

3.是 ［乃］ 吾劍之所從 墜 （判斷句）
　　＼[l.v.]　(noun phrase)／
　s　　　　　　p

109

This [is] my sword's dropping from place.
This [is] wherefrom/whence my sword dropped place.
(a determinative sentence)

※ 所從墜：

所從 [ ] 墜

所 + 介詞 [ ] + 動詞 = 名詞語

所 + prep [ ] + verb = noun phrase

"所" 字在此處代表介詞 "從" 後的
賓語，同時也代表動詞 "墜" 後的
賓語；指示事情從那儿發生的地方

Here the word "所" stands for the object of the
preposition "從" (from) as well as the object of
the verb "墜". That is, "所" simultaneously
refers to "the place" it dropped into the water and
"where" it dropped into the water. The distinction
between "所墜" and "所從墜" in classical
Chinese is equivalent to the distinction between "the
place it dropped" and "the place where [from] it
dropped" in English. It can be translated:
"wherefrom VERB"

所從 [ ] verb

a. 從 〔那儿〕 V 〔之處〕
   wherefrom VERB place

b. 從那儿 V 的地方
   place where/from which [SUBJECT] VERB

所從 [ ] 墜

a. 從 〔那儿〕 墜 〔之處〕
   wherefrom dropped [my sword] place

b. 從那儿掉下去的地方
   the place where/from which [my sword] dropped

"這我的劍從那儿掉下的地方。"

"This -- my sword wherefrom drop place."

⟶ "這個地方 [是] 我的劍從那儿掉下去的地方。"

"This place [is] *the* place wherefrom my sword drop*ped*."

⟹ "這裡是我的劍從船上掉下去的地方。"

"This is the place where my sword dropped from the boat."

110

四. 舟 止，
    s **p**

船停，

Boat stop,

——→ 等到船停了的時候，

When *the* boat *had* stop*ped*,

===> 船停了，

When the boat had stopped,

五.　[涉江者] 從 其所契者 入 水 求 之。
               \prep   o   v o v o/
        [s]   **p**

※ 其所契者

1. " 其 " = noun / pronoun + 之
2. " 所 " + verb + " 者 "
" 所 " 字用在動詞之前，動詞後所謂的賓語
" 者 " 字已出現，故 " 所 " 字在此處只有指
示形容詞的作用，意思是 " 那個 " 。

When " 所 " appears in front of a verb and the **pronominal object** " 者 " immediately follows the verb, the word " 所 " functions solely as a demonstrative adjective (i.e., this/that; these/those). The difference between " 所契 " and " 所契者 " roughly corresponds to the difference between "**what** [was] **cut**" and "**that which** [was] **cut**" in English, "that which" being more emphatic than "what" because of the demonstrative adjective "that".

所契者 :　刻的那個地方
           "that place which [was] cut"
    ——→　"that place where [it was] cut"

" 所契 " :　" 所契 " 的作用是作 " 者 " 字
          的定語 – " 刻的那個 " " 地方 "

Here " 所契 " (that notched) functions as an adjectival modifier of " 者 " (the place) = "that place.where it was cut"

111

其所契者： 他 [的] 刻的那個地方

他刻的那個地方

"that place which he cut"

⟶ "that place where he had cut [a mark]"

從他刻的那個地方跳進水裡找它。

from the notch-ing place enter water look-for it.

⟶ [渡河的人] 從他刻記號的那個地方跳進水裡去找它。

[*the* person cross*ing the* river] jump*ed* into *the* water to look *for* it from that place *where* he *had* cut *the notch.*

⟹ 他從他刻記號的那個船邊跳進水裡去找劍。

he jump*ed* into *the* water to look *for* it from **the boat side** *where he had* cut *the* notch.

⟹ 他從他刻記號的那個船邊跳進水裡去找劍。

he jumped into the water to look for it from the place where he had cut the notch.

六. 舟 已 行 矣， 而 劍 不 行。

      \adv　v/　part　conj　\adv　v/

      s   p   s   p

船已經走了，可是劍沒走。

Boat already move, but sword not-yet move.

⟶ 船已經往前走了，可是劍並沒移動。

The boat *had* move*d* ahead, but *the* sword *had* not.

⟹ 船已經往前走了，可是劍並沒移動。

The boat had moved ahead, but the sword had not.

七 a.　[涉江者] 求 劍 若 此，　不 亦 惑 乎？
　　　　　　　　　　　l.v. pron
　　　　　　\v o comp/　\adv adv adj/ part
　　　[s]　　　p1　　　　　　p2

七 b.　[涉江者] 若 此 求 劍，不 亦 惑 乎？
　　　　　　　l.v. pron
　　　　　　\adv. v o/　\adv adv adj/ part
　　　[s]　　　p1　　　　　p2

　　※ "若此" :

　　　　　　這是由準繫詞 "若" 和指示代詞 "此" 結合而
　　　　　成的 "合成詞"，意思是 "像這樣"。它的
　　　　　作用像個副詞，表示性狀和程度，可用來修飾
　　　　　動詞、形容詞或另一副詞。如用在這些詞之前
　　　　　，可譯成 "像這樣子地⋯，" 如用在這些詞之
　　　　　後，可譯成 "⋯得像這樣子。"

The phrase "若此" is a **composite word** made up of
the pseudo-linking verb "若" (to be like) and the demonstrative
pronoun "此" (this); it means "[It is] like this," or "in this
way," "in this manner." It functions as an adverb and is used to
express quality or degree; it can modify a verb, an adjective, or
another adverb. If it appears in front of one of these words, it
can be translated into spoken Chinese as "像這樣子地⋯"; if
it appears after one of these words, it can be rendered as "⋯得像
這樣子." In English it can be translated as "like this" or "in this
way" in both cases.

　　　　　　儘管 "若此" 在文言中多半是用在它所修飾的
　　　　　詞之後，譯成白話時還可搬到它所修飾的詞之
　　　　　前，如 "求劍若此" 譯成 "找劍找得像這樣子
　　　　　"，就沒有譯成 "這樣地找劍" 聽起來自然。

Although "若此" appears after the word or clause it modifies
(which is more common in classical Chinese), it can be
translated into spoken Chinese in the pre-verbal or adverb
position (i.e., "像這樣子地⋯") rather than in the post-verbal
or complement position (i.e., "⋯得像這樣子.") because the
adverbial construction sounds more natural. Hence "求劍若此
" should be rendered as "這樣地找劍" in spoken Chinese. This
is not a problem in English, since English sentence structure
only allows the phrase "like this" or "in this manner" to follow
the words or clauses it modifies (i.e., "to look for the sword like
this/in this manner" is the only translation possible).

　　※ "不亦⋯乎？"

113

用反問的方式委婉地表示肯定的意思。目的在讓讀者自己思索、判斷來加強肯定的意味。

A rhetorical question is used here to indirectly express the writer's affirmative point of view or opinion. The object of this usage is to draw the reader into considering or judging the statement himself, which in turn has the effect of making the tone of the statement more emphatic; the question "Is it not ...?" invites the reader to agree with the writer.

A. 找劍像這樣，不也糊塗嗎？

Look-for sword like this, isn't also dim-witted?

⟶ [渡河的人]找劍找得像這樣子，不也很糊塗嗎？

[*The* person cross*ing the* river] *in* look*ing for his* sword like this *is being* very dim-witted, isn't *he*?

⟶ 他找劍像這樣找法，不也很糊塗嗎？

In **looking for his sword like this** he *is being* very dim-witted, isn't he?

⟹ 他找劍像這樣找法，不也很糊塗嗎？

In looking for his sword like this he is being very dim-witted, isn't he?

B. 像這樣地找劍，不也糊塗嗎？

Thus look-for sword isn't also dim-witted?

⟶ [渡河的人]這樣地找劍，不也很糊塗嗎？

[*The* person cross*ing the* river] **look*ing in* this way *for the* sword** *is* very dim-witted, isn't *it*?

⟹ 他這樣地找劍，不也很糊塗嗎？

Looking for the sword like this is very dim-witted, is it not?

第十八課

和氏之璧

句子分析

一. <u>楚人和氏</u> 得 玉璞 [於] 楚山中， 奉 而 獻 之 [於] 厲王。
　　　　　　＼v　o　[prep]　o　／＼v/adv conj v o [prep] o／
　　　s　　　　　　　p1　　　　　　　　　　p2

楚人和氏得到含玉的石頭楚山裡，捧著獻它厲王。

Chǔ person surname of Hé get jade-stone Chǔ mountains, hand-holding present it King Lì.

——→ 楚國人和氏 [從]楚國的山裡得到了一塊含著玉的石頭，他就捧著玉石去獻 [給]厲王。

There was a man *from the* state *of* Chǔ surname*d* Hé *who* got a piece of stone containi*ng* jade [from] *the* mountai*ns* of Chǔ and present*ed the* stone containi*ng* jade *with both* hand*s* raise*d* [to] King Lì *of Chǔ.*

===→ 楚國人和氏從楚國的山裡得到了一塊含著玉的石頭，他就捧著去把它獻給厲王。

A man from the state of Chǔ surnamed Hé got a stone containing jade from the mountains of Chǔ and respectfully presented it to King Lì of Chǔ.

　　　　　　　　　　　　　　　　　　　[s]　[l.v.]　pn part
二. <u>厲王</u> 使 玉人 相 之，玉人 曰："[此][乃] 石 也。"
　　＼v　o/s　v　o／　　　　＼v　　　　　　o　／
　　s　　　　p　　　　　s　　　　　　p

厲王教玉匠鑑定它，玉匠說："石頭啊。"

King Lì order jade artisan appraise it; jade artisan say, "Stone."

——→ 厲王命令玉匠鑑定那塊玉石，玉匠說："[這][是]普通的石頭啊。"

115

King Lì order*ed a* jade worker *to* examine this *piece of* stone contain*ing* jade; *the* jade worker sa*id*: "[This] [is] ordinary stone."

⟹ 厲王命令玉匠鑑定那塊玉石，玉匠說："這是普通的石頭。"

King Lì ordered a jade worker to appraise it; the jade worker said: "This is ordinary stone."

三． 王 以 和 為 誑，而 刖 其 左 足。

王以爲和氏是騙子，就砍斷他的左腳。

King think Hé liar and cut off his left foot.

⟶ 厲王以爲和氏是個騙子，就砍斷了他的左腳。

King Lì *thought the* man surname*d* Hé *was* a liar, and so *he* cut off his (i.e., Hé's) left foot.

⟹ 厲王認爲和氏是個騙子，就砍斷了他的左腳。

The king thought Hé a liar and so cut off his left foot.

四． 及 厲王薨，武王 即 位，[和氏] 又奉其璞而獻之[於]武王。

到厲王死，武王登上王位，又捧著那塊玉石去獻它武王。

Till King Lì die, King Wǔ accede throne, again hand-holding that jade-stone present it King Wǔ.

⟶ 等到厲王死了，武王登上了王位，[和氏]又捧著那塊玉石去把它獻[給]武王。

Upon King Lì's death, King Wǔ acceded *to the* throne; [*the* man surname*d* Hé] again rais*ing the* jade-bear*ing* stone *with both hands* present*ed* it [to] King Wǔ.

⟹ 等到厲王死了，武王登上王位，和氏又捧著那塊玉石去把它獻給武王。

When King Lì died, King Wǔ acceded to the throne; Hé again respectfully presented the stone containing jade to King Wǔ.

五. 武王使玉人相之，[玉人]又曰：＂[此][乃]石也。＂

[s] [l.v.] pn part

武王教玉匠鑑定它，又說：＂石頭啊。＂

King Wǔ order jade-worker appraise it; again say, "Stone."

⟶ 武王命令玉匠鑑定那塊玉石，[玉匠]又說：＂[這][是]普通的石頭啊。＂

King Wǔ order*ed a* jade worker *to* appraise this piece *of* stone contain*ing* jade; [*the* jade worker] again sa*id*: "[This] [is] ordinary stone."

⟹ 武王命令玉匠鑑定那塊玉石，玉匠又說：＂這是普通的石頭。＂

King Wǔ ordered a jade worker to appraise it; again he said: "This is ordinary stone."

六. 王又以和為誆，而刖其右足。

adj adj n

王也以爲和氏是騙子，就砍斷他的右腳。

King [Wǔ] also think Hé liar, so cut off his right foot.

⟶ 武王也以爲和氏是個騙子，就砍斷了他的右腳。

King Wǔ also *thought the* man surname*d* Hé *was a* liar, so *he* cut off his right foot.

⟹ 武王也認爲和氏是個騙子，就砍斷了他的右腳。

The king also thought Hé a liar and so cut off his right foot.

七． 武王薨，文王即位，
       ╲ v   ╲ v o ╱
       s   p   s   p

武王死，文王登位，

King Wǔ die, King Wén accede throne.

⟶ 武王死了，文王登上了王位，

When King Wǔ die*d*, King Wén accede*d to the* throne.

⟹ 武王死了，文王登上了王位，

When King Wǔ died, King Wén acceded to the throne.

八． 和乃抱其璞，而哭於楚山之下，
     adv ╲ v o ╱ conj v prep   o
             adv
     s   p

和氏就抱著那塊玉石，哭在楚山的下面，

Hé then cradle the stone jade and cry at foot of Chǔ mountains.

⟶ 和氏就抱著那塊玉石，在楚國的山下哭，

[*The* man surname*d*] Hé then cradled the stone jade *in his arms and* cried at *the* foot *of the* mountain*s of* Chǔ.

⟹ 和氏就抱著那塊玉石，在楚國的山下哭，

The man surnamed Hé then cradled the stone jade in his arms and cried at the foot of the mountains of Chǔ.

九． ［哭］三日三夜，淚盡 而 ［和氏］繼 ［之］ 以 血。
　　　［v］　comp　　　　ｖ coni　　［s］　ｖ ［o］ comp

三天三夜，眼淚盡了，就用血來繼續。

three days three nights, tears exhaust and follow with blood.

⟶ ［哭了］三天三夜，他的眼淚都哭完了，［他］接著哭出血來。

[cried *for*] three day*s and* three night*s*, his tears *were* all *cried* out, and [he] **continue***d to* **cry** *with* ***tears of*** **blood**.

⟹ 哭了三天三夜，他的眼淚都哭光了，接著哭出血來。

He cried for three days and three nights; when he had cried out all his tears, he kept on crying with tears of blood.

十． 王 聞之， 使人 問其故，曰：" 。"
　　ｖ ｏ　　ｖ ｏ/s ｖ ｏ　　ｖ ｏ
　 s　 p1　　　　p2　　　　　p3

王聽到它，派人問他的緣故，說：

King hear it; send a person ask its reason; say:

⟶ 文王聽到這件事，派人去問他痛哭的緣故，說：

King Wén, *upon* hear*ing of* this matter, sen*t a* person to ask *the* reason *for* it (i.e., his great wail*ing*], *who* said:

⟹ 文王聽到這件事，派人去問他痛哭的緣故，說：

Upon hearing of this, the king sent a person to ask about the reason for his great wailing, who said:

十.一 天下之刖者 多矣，子 奚哭之悲 也？"
　　　　 adj part　　adv v comp part
　　　　 s　 p　　 s　 p

※子奚哭之悲也：

這是感嘆詢問句，在詢問中帶有感嘆語氣，是一種嘆疑兼半的句子，用來表達 "為什麼那麼…" "怎麼那麼…" 的意思。

This is an **Exclamatory Interrogative Sentence**, and it conveys a sense of "why ... so ..."

這種句子的結構是主語＋疑問詞＋動詞＋之＋補語＋也。

The typical structure of this type of sentences is Subject + a question word +verb + the strucural particle 之 + the complement+ the interrogative particle 也。

"奚" 是疑問詞，在句中用作狀語，表示詢問 "為什麼？" ；"哭" 是動詞；"悲" 是形容詞，用作補語，表示哭的程度；"之" 是結構助詞，用在動詞和補語之間，作用和白話的 "得" 字相同。

"奚 "is an interrogative adverb, asking why? "之" is the main verb. "悲" is an adjective, serving as the complement of the verb, indicating the intensity or degree of the verb; "之" is a structual particle used between the verb "哭" (to cry) and the complement "悲" (grievous). It functions in the same way as "… 得…" does in spoken Chinese.

類似的例子見於《史記‧項羽本紀》："羽豈其苗裔也？何興之暴也？"

A similar example can be found in the *Records of the Grand Historian*, at the end of *The Annals of Xiàng Yǔ*: "Is Yǔ a descendent of him (Shùn)? Why did he rise to power so suddenly?"

天下的斷腳的人多啦，您為什麼哭得那麼悲痛呢？

"In this world there are many foot cut off ones; why do you cry so grievously?"

──→ 天下的被砍斷腳的人多啦，您為什麼哭得那麼悲痛呢？

"In this world *there* are many *who have had* a foot cut off; why *do* you cry so grievously?"

====> 天下的被砍斷腳的人多啦，您為什麼哭得那麼悲痛呢？

"In this world there are many who have had a foot cut off; why do you cry so grievously?"

十一. 和　曰：“　　”
　　s　　　　p

和氏說：

The person surnamed Hé said:

十一.一　　吾　非悲刖也，
　　　　　s　　　　p　part

※非：　　　“非”字用在名詞謂語前時，是個否定繫詞，可譯成白話的“不是”。此處它是用在動詞謂語之前，中國語法學家一般認為它是個副詞，意思是“不”。但在本句中，它和“也”字合用，有很強的解釋或申辯語氣，譯成白話時，仍須譯成“我並不是因為腳被砍斷而悲傷”。

When the word "非" is used before a noun predicate, it is usually a negative linking verb. Here it is used before a verbal predicate. Chinese grammarians, in general, regard it as an adverb. However, in this sentence it is used in conjunction with the particle "也" and carries a strong explanatory tone. As such, it is more appropriate to translate it as "我並不是因為腳被砍斷而悲傷" in spoken Chinese, and as "It's not that I grieved for my feet being cut off" or "I **do** not grieve for my feet being cut off" in English.

※悲刖：　　“悲”字是個不及物動詞，本不應該下接賓語。“悲刖”這個所謂的“動詞語”是由“為刖而悲”簡化而來的一種特殊結構，譯成白話是“因為腳被砍斷而悲傷”。

"悲" is basically an intransitive verb. Usually intransitive verbs do not take an object, but here the verbal phrase "悲刖" is derived from a fuller expression "為刖而悲" and constitutes a special construction. It can be rendered in spoken Chinese as "因為腳被砍斷而悲傷" (grieved by [his] feet having been cut off).

我不是悲痛被砍掉了腳，

I not grieve have feet cut off.

121

⟶ 我並不是因爲被砍掉了腳而悲痛，

I *do* not grieve because *my feet have been* cut off.

⟹ 我並不是因爲被砍掉了腳而悲痛，

I do not grieve because my feet were cut off.

十一.二　　[吾] 悲 夫！[璞] [乃] 寶玉 而 [玉人] 題 之 以 石，
　　　　　　　\adj/ part　　　\l.v.l　p/ conj　　　\v　o　prep o/
　　　　　　[s]　p　　[s]　　p　　　[s]　　p

悲痛啊！寶貴的玉，可是拿石頭來給它起個名字，

Oh [what] grief! precious jade, yet name it as ordinary stone;

⟶ [我]悲痛啊！[玉石][是]塊寶貴的玉，可是[玉匠]叫它
作石頭，

I grieve, *for* [this stone] [is] a piece *of* precious jade, yet [*the* jade worker]
calls it ordinary stone;

⟹ 我悲痛啊！玉石是塊寶貴的玉，可是玉匠叫它作石頭，

Oh! I grieve because this stone is a piece of precious jade, yet the jade worker
calls it ordinary stone;

十一.三　　[吾] [乃] 貞士 而 [王] 名 之 以 誑，
　　　　　　　\l.v.l　np/ conj　\v　o　prep o/
　　　　　　[s]　　p　　[s]　　p

忠誠正直的人，可是拿騙子來給他取名字，

loyal, upright person, yet name him liar,

⟶ [我是]個忠誠正直的人，可是[王]叫我作騙子，

[I am] a loyal, upright person, yet [*the* king] **calls me *a* liar**,

⟹ 我是個忠誠正直的人，可是王叫我作騙子，

I am an upright man, but am called a liar by the king;

十一．四　　　此 [乃] 吾 所 以 悲　也 。"
　　　　　　　　　　＼l.v.　　 np 　／　part
　　　　　　　s　　　　　p

※ 此吾所以悲也：

這是一個典型的判斷句 "A[乃]B也。" 其中主語A和謂語B都是名詞或名詞語。指示代詞 "所" 跟後面的介詞加動詞結合構成一個名詞語。

This is a typical determinative sentence:

A　　　 [乃]　　 B　　 也
[noun]　　　　　 [noun]

In this sentence pattern both the subject and the predicate are nouns or noun phrases. The word "所", taken together with the preposition and/or verb immediately following it (in this case "以悲") constitutes a noun phrase.

※ "所以悲" ： the reason for which [I] grieve

1) 所＋介詞＋動／形＝名詞語

2) 所＋Prep.＋V/Adj.＝ NP

3) 所＋以＋悲

4) 以＋之＋悲＋之故

"所" 字在此處代表介詞 "以"（因）後的賓語，同時也代表動詞 "悲" 後的賓語，表示事情因之而發生的緣故。

Here the word "所" stands for the object of the preposition "以" (for) as well as the object of the verb "悲" (grieve), and indicates the reason or cause for which an event occurred. It can be literally translated into English as "wherefor grieve" or "what for [I] grieve" (i.e., "grieve for what [reason]") and hence by extension as "the reason for which [I] grieve" or more simply as "why I grieve".

※ 句型變換 ： SENTENCE TRANSFORMATION

吾以此悲　　　　　　　　　　　　　　 敘述句
I for/because of this grieve.　　　　　　 narrative

此[乃]吾所以悲也　　　　　　　判斷句
This [is] I what for/because of grieve.　　determinative

此[乃]吾以之[而]悲之故也　　　　判斷句
This [is] I for/because of it [so] grieve reason. determinative

這--我所以悲痛啊。"

this--I wherefor grieve!

——→ 這才是我因爲它而悲痛的緣故啊。"

this alone is *the* reason wherefor I grieve!

===> 這才是我悲痛的緣故啊。"

this alone is why I grieve!"

十二．王　乃　使玉人理其璞，而　得　寶　焉，
　　　　　adv \v　o/s　v　o/　conj \v　o prep-[o]/
　　　s　　　　　　p1　　　　　　　　　　　p2

王就教玉匠切開那塊玉石，就從石中得到一塊寶玉，

King then order a jade worker cut open this stone containing jade and get from it a piece of precious jade.

——→文王於是命令玉匠切開那塊玉石，結果從石中得到一塊寶玉，

The king then order*ed a* jade worker *to* cut open this piece *of* stone contain*ing* jade and consequently g*ot* from it a piece *of* precious jade.

===> 文王於是命令玉匠切開那塊玉石，結果從石中得到一塊寶玉，

The king then ordered a jade worker to cut open this piece of stone containing jade and consequently got from it a piece of precious jade.

十三．[王] 遂 命 [之] 曰：" 和氏之璧。"
　　　　　\adv　v　[o/s]　v　　　　　　o/
　[s]　　　　　　　　p

※遂命曰 " 和氏之璧 " ：

這是兼語結構中的命名式：上一小句通常
用 " 命 " 、 " 謂 " 、 " 名 " 、 " 稱 " 諸字，下
一小句通常用 " 為 " 、 " 曰 " 等字。

This is a **Denominative Construction**: A verb such as
" 命 ", " 謂 ", " 名 ", " 稱 " is used in the first clause, and a verb
such as " 為 " or " 曰 ", is used in the second clause. This is
one type of the **Pivotal Sentences**.

於是取名叫 " 和氏之璧 " 。

Thereupon name "The pierced jade disk of the man surnamed Hé."

⟶ [王] 於是就叫它作 " 和氏之璧 " 。

Thereupon [*the* king] name*d* it *"The* pierce*d* jade disk of *the* man surname*d*
Hé."

⟹ 王於是就給它取名叫 " 和氏之璧 " 。

Thereupon the king named it "The pierced jade disk of the man surnamed
Hé."

第十九課

東周欲為稻

句子分析

一. 東周 欲 為 稻，
　　　　　v　o
　　s　　p
　　　　v　o

　　東周想要種稻子，

　　Eastern Zhōu want planting rice;

　──→ 東周想要種稻子，

　　The Eastern Zhōu *kingdom* want*ed to* plant rice;

　══⟹ 東周想要種稻子，

　　The Eastern Zhōu kingdom wanted to plant rice;

二. 西周 不 下 水，
　　　　adv v o
　　s　　p

　　西周不放下水，

　　Western Zhōu not let down water,

　──→ 西周不放下水來，

　　the Western Zhōu *kingdom would* not let *the river* water *flow* down*stream,*

　══⟹ 西周不放下水來，

　　the Western Zhōu kingdom would not let the river water flow downstream,

三. 東周 患 之。
　　　　v　o
　　s　　p

東周擔心它。

Eastern Zhōu worry it (i.e., this situation).

⟶ 東周擔心這個情形。

and the Eastern Zhōu *ruler was* worr*ied about* this situation.

⟹ 東周擔心這個情形。

and the Eastern Zhōu ruler was worried about this situation.

四． 蘇子 謂 東周君 曰： " 　　 "

蘇子告訴東周君說：

Sūzǐ tell Eastern Zhōu ruler say:

⟶ 蘇子對東周君說：

Sūzǐ *spoke* to *the* Eastern Zhōu ruler say*ing*:

⟹ 蘇子對東周君說：

Sūzǐ spoke to the Eastern Zhōu ruler saying:

四．一 " 臣 請 使 西周 下 水 ，可 乎 ？ "

"請讓臣使西周放下水，可以嗎？"

"Servant ask make Western Zhōu let-down water, permissable?"

⟶ "請讓臣／我使西周放下水來，可以嗎？"

"Your servant/I ask*s that you* allow him/me *to* make *the* Western Zhōu let *the river* water flow down*stream*; *is it* allow*ed*?"

==⟹ "我請您讓我使西周君放下水來，可以嗎？"

"I ask that you allow me to make the Western Zhōu let the river water flow downstream; may I?"

五. [蘇子] 乃 往 見 西周之君，曰："   "
      [s]   adv v v   o   v   o
              p1   p2

就去見西周的君主說：

Straightaway go see Western Zhōu ruler, say:

⟶ [蘇子]就去見西周的君主說：

[Sūzǐ] *went* straightaway *to* see *the* Western Zhōu ruler *and said*:

==⟹ 蘇子就去見西周的君主說：

Sūzǐ then went to see the ruler of the Western Zhōu and said:

五. 一   "君之謀 過 矣。
           s   p part

"您的計劃錯啦。

"Your plan erroneous.

⟶ "您的計劃錯啦。

"Your plan *is* wrong.

==⟹ "您的計劃錯啦。

"Your plan is wrong.

五. 二 今 [君] 不 下 水，[乃] [君之] 所 以 富 東周 也。
          adv [s] adv v o   [l.v.]   np   part
                      s   p

※"所以富東周"：

128

LITERALLY: that [which is/was/will be] used to enrich the Eastern Zhōu, *or*
the means by which [you] enrich the Eastern Zhōu kingdom

1) 所＋介詞＋動詞＋賓語＝名詞語

所＋以＋ｖ＋ｏ＝ NP

所＋以＋富＋東周＝名詞語

2) 用它來ｖ-ｏ之法

用它來富東周之法

3) 用來ｖ-ｏ的方法

用來富東周之法

"所"字在此處代表介詞"以"(用)後的賓
語，表示事情或行為用它來實現的方法。

Here the word "所" stands for the object of the preposition
"以" (to use) and indicates the means by which a certain thing
is/was/will be done. It can be literally translated into English as
"that used to enrich the Eastern Zhōu," (i.e., "that [which
is/was/will be] used to enrich the Eastern Zhōu) and hence by
extension as "the means by which/whereby [you] enrich the
Eastern Zhōu."

※所＋介詞＋動詞＋賓語＝名詞語

※所　以　富　東周＝名詞語

※句型變換 : SENTENCE TRANSFORMATION

君 以 不 下 水 富 東 周   敘述句
　　\prep　　ｏ　　ｖ　ｏ／   narrative
ｓ　　　　　　　　ｐ

不下水 [乃]君之所以富東周   也   判斷句
　　　\[l.v.]　　　　np　　　　　／   part   determinative
ｓ　　　　　　　　ｐ

現在不放下水，用來使東周富的辦法啊。

Now not let down water, whereby enrich Eastern Zhōu.

⟶ 現在[您]不放下水去，這[是][您]用來使東周富足
的辦法啊。

129

If [you] now *do* not let *the* water *flow* down*stream*, that [is] *the* means *by which* [you] enrich *the* Eastern Zhōu *kingdom*.

⟹ 現在您不放下水去，這是您用來使東周富足的辦法啊。

If you now do not let the water flow downstream, that will be your way to enrich the Eastern Zhōu kingdom.

五．三　今 其 民 皆 種 麥，無 他 種 矣。
　　　　adv \adj n/ \adv v　o/ \adv o - v/ part
　　　　　　　s　　　　p1　　　　　　p2

※ "其民無他種"：

文言敘述句的正常詞序是 "SP(V-O)"；但句中若有否定詞 "不"、"無" 或 "莫" 而且賓語又是代詞時，詞序就變成 "SP(O-V)"，也就是在文言的否定句中，代詞賓語倒放在動詞之前。

In classical Chinese, the normal word order of a narrative sentence is "sp(v-o)". But when the predicate has a negative word like "不"(not), "無"(no) or "莫"(don't) and the object is a pronoun, then the word order changes to "sp(o-v)". In other words, **in classical Chinese the pronominal object in a negative sentence always precedes the verb.**

現在東周的人民都種麥子，不種別的了。

Now their people all plant wheat nought else plant.

⟶ 現在東周的百姓都種麥子，不種別的糧食了。

Now *the* common people of *the* Eastern Zhōu all plant wheat *and* plant no other food grain*s*.

⟹ 現在東周的百姓都種麥子，不種別的糧食了。

Now the Eastern Zhōu people all are planting wheat and nothing else.

五.四 　　君 若 欲 害 之，[不下水] 不 若 一為下水，
　　　　　　conj ＼v o／　　＼[A] adv l.v.　B ／
　　　　　　s　　　p1　　　　　　　p2

A. [君]不 下 水　　　　B. [君] 一 為 [之]下 水
　　＼adv v o／　　　　　　　＼adv prep [ol] v o／
　　[s]　p1　　　　　　　[s]　　　p2

　　　　　(東周之)
以 病 其 所種。
conj ＼v o／
　　p3

　　※ "A不若B"：

　　　　　"A不若B"="A不如B"，是否定性的準
　　　　判斷句，表示比較。意思是"A不像是B"，
　　　　"A不像B一樣[adj.]"，"A沒有B那麼[adj.]"，
　　　　"B比A[adj.]"，"B比較[adj.]"。這種句子結構
　　　　中的"A"往往根據上文省略，但讀者還能清楚
　　　　地了解句子的含意。本句中"A"是"不下水"
　　　　，"B"是"一為下水"，若全寫出應是"不下
　　　　水不若一為下水。"逐字譯成白話是"不下水
　　　　不像／沒有一次為〔東周〕放下水一樣／那麼
　　　　好。"或"一次為〔東周〕放下水比不放下水
　　　　好。"意思雖然極清楚，但未免太囉嗦。文言
　　　　省略A，只寫出B，逐字譯成白話是"不如一
　　　　次為〔東周〕放下水。"意思也很清楚易懂，
　　　　因為這種省略A只說B的句構，在白話中也是
　　　　習見的用法。

"A不若B"="A不如B" This is a **negative pseudo-determinative sentence** that expresses a comparison. It means "A不像是B" (A is not like B); "A不像B一樣[adj.]" (A is not [adj.] to the same degree as B); "A沒有B那麼[adj.]" (A is not as [adj.] as B); "B比A[adj.]" (B is more [adj.] than A); "B比較[adj.]" (B is comparatively more [adj.]). In this type of sentence pattern, "A" often refers to a statement in the preceding text and is therefore omitted from the comparison, but the reader can still clearly comprehend the implied meaning of the sentence. In this sentence, "A" refers to "不下水" (not let down water); "B" refers to "一為下水" (once let down water for [ ]). If the implied comparison were fully expressed, the sentence would be written as "不下水不像／沒有一次為〔東周〕放下水一樣／那麼好" (Not letting water flow down (A) is

131

not as good as letting water flow down for once for [the Eastern Zhōu] (B)) or "一次為〔東周〕放下水比不放下水好" (It is better to let the water flow down one time for [the Eastern Zhōu] than not to let the water flow down). Although the meaning is absolutely clear, this version is rather wordy. The classical Chinese sentence thus omits "A" and only expresses "B". Literally translated into spoken Chinese it means: "不如一次為〔東周〕放下水" (it would not be as good as letting the water flow down one time for [the Eastern Zhōu]) The meaning here is also quite clear and easy to understand, because this kind of sentence structure, in which "A" is omitted and only "B" is expressed, is also a common usage in spoken Chinese. It is frequently encountered in English usage as well.

您假若想要害他們，不如一次爲放下水來損害他們種的。

You if want harm them, better once for them down water to spoil what they plant.

⟶ 您假若想要害東周，不如給他們放一次水來損害他們種的麥子。

If you wish *to* harm *the* Eastern Zhōu, *it would be* better *to* let *the* water *flow* down*stream* once so as *to* spoil *the* wheat *that* they *have* plant*ed*.

⟹ 您假若想要害東周，不如給他們放一次水來損害他們種的麥子。

If you wish to harm the people of the Eastern Zhōu, it would be better to let the water flow downstream once to spoil the wheat that they have planted.

五.五　[君][若] 下水，則東周 必 復種稻；

放下水，那麼東周一定再種稻子；

Let down water, then Eastern Zhōu certainly once again plant rice;

⟶ [您][要是]放下水去，那麼東周一定會再種稻子；

132

[If you] let *the* water *flow* down*stream*, then *the* Eastern Zhōu *people* certainly will plant rice once again;

⟹ 您要是放下水去，那麼東周一定會再種稻子；

If you let the water flow downstream, the Eastern Zhōu will certainly plant rice again;

五.六　[東周]種 稻，而 [君] 復 奪 之。
　　　　　　＼ v o／ conj　　＼adv v o／
　　　[s]　　　p　　　 [s]　　　p

種稻，就再奪水。

plant rice, then again take away water.

⟶ [東周]種稻子，[您]就再不放水。

when [*the* Eastern Zhōu *people*] *have* plant*ed* rice, then once again [you] *do* not let *the* water *flow* down*stream*.

⟹ 東周種稻子，您就再停止放水。

when they have planted rice, then you stop it again.

五.七　若 是，則 東周之民 [君] 可 令 一仰 西周，
　　　l.v. pron conj　　o/s　　aux v ＼adv v o／
　　　　p(n)　　　　o/s　　[s]　　　　p1

　　　而 受 命 於 君 矣
　　conj＼v o prep o／ part
　　　　　　p2

※兼語提前：TRANSPOSITION OF THE PIVOTAL PHRASE
兼語如果比較複雜，可以提到第一個動詞之前。一方面引起讀者的注意，同時也有加強語氣的效果。

If the pivotal phrase is relatively long or complex, it is often transposed to the head of the sentence. This transposition effectively highlights the phrase by placing it at the head of the sentence and thus intensifies its rhetorical impact.

133

如果把句中被提前的兼語放回原來的位置，就成了：

If the transposed pivotal phrase is returned to the typical object position, the resulting sentence is:

[君] 可 令 東周之民 一 仰 西周，
　　 \aux v　 o/s　 　adv v　 o /
[s]　　　　　 　 p1

而 受 命 於 君 矣。
conj \v　o prep o/ part
　　　　 p2

※ 受命於君：

逐字譯成白話是"從君主這儿接受命令"或"從您這儿接受命令"，聽起來很生硬；因此這種"受N1於N2"的結構通常採取意譯的方式。"受命於君"譯成自然的白話是"接受君主的命令"。

Literally translated into spoken Chinese this means "從君主這儿接受命令" (to accept an order from the ruler) or "從您這儿接受命令" (to accept an order from you). This sounds awkward, so the pattern "受N1於N2" is generally translated into spoken Chinese according to its sense; thus, "受命於君" can be translasted into spoken Chinese more naturally as "接受君主的命令" (to accept the ruler's orders /the orders of the ruler). This does not present a problem in English, and either translation is acceptable.

像這樣，那麼東周的人民就能使完全仰仗西周，而接受命令從您了。"

Like this, then Eastern Zhōu people can be made completely dependent on Western Zhōu and accept orders from you."

⟶ 如果像這樣，那麼[您]就能使東周的百姓完全依賴西周，而接受您的命令了。"

[If] *you do it* this way, [you] **can make *the* people of *the* Eastern Zhōu depend completely on *the* Western Zhōu** and *they will start having to* **accept order**s **from you**."

⟹ 如果像這樣，那麼您就能使東周的百姓完全依賴西周，結果就接受您的命令了。"

If you do it this way, you can make the people of the Eastern Zhōu depend completely on the Western Zhōu and as a result accept orders from you."

六．　西周君曰："善。"

西周君說："好。"

Western Zhōu ruler say: "Excellent!"

⟶　西周君說："好極了。"

The Western Zhōu ruler sa*id*: "Excellent!"

⟹　西周君說："好極了。"

The Western Zhōu ruler said: "Excellent!"

七．　蘇子亦得兩國之金也。

蘇子也得到兩國的金啊。

Sūzǐ also get two kingdoms' money.

⟶　蘇子也得到兩國君主的酬金啊。

Sūzǐ also *got a* reward from both kingdoms' ruler*s*.

⟹　蘇子也得到兩國君主的酬金啊。

Sūzǐ also received compensation for his services from both kingdoms' rulers.

第二十課

結草報恩

句子分析

一．　初，魏武子 有 嬖妾，［嬖妾］無 子。

　　起初，魏武子有寵愛的妾，沒有孩子。

First, Wèi Wǔzǐ have favoured concubine, no children.

⟶ 起初，魏武子有個寵愛的姨太太，［她］沒有孩子。

At first, Wèi Wǔzǐ *had a* favorite concubine; [she] *had* no children.

⟹ 起初，魏武子有個寵愛的姨太太，她沒有孩子。

Originally, Wèi Wǔzǐ had a favorite concubine; she had no children.

二．　武子 疾，命 顆 曰："［汝］必 嫁 是。"

　　武子生病，命顆說："一定嫁掉這個。"

Wǔzǐ become ill; order Kē say: "Must marry-off this."

⟶ 武子病了，命令他的兒子魏顆說："［你］一定要把這個妾嫁出去。"

Wǔzǐ bec*ame* ill; *he* order*ed* his son Wèi Kē say*ing*: "[You] must marry off this concubine."

⟹ 武子病了，命令他的兒子魏顆說："你一定要把這個妾嫁出去。"

When Wǔzǐ fell ill, he ordered his son Wèi Kē saying: "You must marry her off."

三.　[武子] 疾 病 則 曰： "[汝] 必 以 [之] 為 殉。"

病重卻説： "一定用來作爲陪葬的人。"

Illness grow critical; however say: "Must use as burial sacrifice."

⟶ [武子]病重了卻説： "[你]一定要用[她]來作陪葬的人。"

[Wǔzǐ] became critically ill; instead *he* said: "[You] must use [her] *for a* burial sacrifice."

⟶ 武子病重了卻説： "你一定要用她來給我陪葬。"

When Wǔzǐ became severely ill, *he* said instead: "You must *have* [her] **buried with** me *as a* **sacrificial offering.**"

⟹ 武子病重了卻説： "你一定要用她來給我陪葬。"

When Wǔzǐ became severely ill, he said instead: "You must have her buried with me as a sacrificial offering."

四.　及 [武子]卒，顆 嫁 之，

到死，顆嫁掉她，

At death, Kē marry off her.

⟶ 等到[武子]死了，魏顆把那個姨太太嫁了出去，

At [Wǔzǐ's] death, Wèi Kē marri*ed* off this concubine.

137

⟹ 等到武子死了，魏顆把她嫁了出去，

When Wǔzǐ died, Wèi Kē married her off.

五．　[顆]曰："　　　"
　　　　　＼v　　　o∘＿／
　　　[s]　　　p

五、一　　"[人] 疾 病 則 亂，吾 從 其 治 [命] 也。"
　　　　　　　　　　　　　　　　　　　　pron adj [n]
　　　　　　＼v comp／conj ＼v／　＼v　　o∘＿／ part
　　　　　[s]　　p1　　conj　p2　　s　　　　p

説："病重就昏亂，我聽從他神志清醒啊。"

say: "Illness critical then disordered; I follow his right mind."

⟶ [魏顆]説："[人]病重了就神志不清了，我聽從他神志清醒時的[命令]啊。"

[Wèi Ke] said: "When a [person] becomes critically ill, his faculties are disordered; I will obey his right-minded [order]."

Wèi Kē said: "When a person is so severely ill, his senses are disordered; I obeyed the charge he gave when his mind was right."

⟹ 魏顆説："人病重了就神志不清了，我聽從他神志清醒時的命令啊。"

Wèi Kē said: "When a person is so severely ill, his senses are disordered; I obeyed the charge he gave when his mind was right."

六．　及 輔氏之役，顆 見 老人 結 草 以 亢 杜回。
　　　　　　　　　　　　　　　　s　v　o conj v　o
　　　　　　　　　　　　　　　　　　p1　　　　p2
　　　＼prep　　o∘＿／　　＼v　　o∘＿＿＿＿＿／
　　　　adv　　　　　　　　s　　　　　p

到 '輔氏之役'，顆見老人結草來攔阻杜回。

At 'battle of Fǔshì' Kē see old person tie-up grass to impede Dù Huí.

138

⟶ 等到 '輔氏之役' 的時候，魏顆看見一個老人把草打成結
來攔阻杜回。

At *the* time *of* '*the* battle of Fǔshì', Wèi Kē *saw* an old person ty*ing* up grass *to* impede Dù Huí.

⟹ 等到 '輔氏之役' 的時候，魏顆看見一個老人把草打成
結來攔阻杜回。

At the time of 'the battle of Fǔshì', Wèi Kē saw an old man knotting up grass to impede Dù Huí.

七． 杜回　躓　而　顛，　故 [顆]　獲之。
　　　 s　 \v conj v/　conj [s]　\v o/
　　　　　　p　　　　　　　　　 p

杜回絆就跌倒，所以俘獲他。

Dù Huí stumble and fall, therefore capture him.

⟶ 杜回絆了一下就跌倒了，所以 [魏顆] 俘獲了他。

Dù Huí stumbl*ed and* fell *down*; therefore [Wèi Kē] capture*d* him.

⟹ 杜回絆了一下就跌倒了，所以魏顆俘獲了他。

Dù Huí stumbled and fell down; therefore Wèi Kē captured him.

八． [於] 夜 [顆] 夢之曰：" 　　　 "
　　 [prep] o　\v o/s v　　o/
　　　　　[s]　　　 p

夜裡夢見他說：

Night; dream of him, say:

⟶ [在] 夜裡 [魏顆] 夢見那個老人說：

[In] *the* night [Wèi Kē] dream*t* of the old man, *who* sa*id*:

⟹ 夜裡魏顆夢見那個老人說：

At night, Wèi Kē dreamt he saw this old man, who said:

八．一 　　"余 [乃] 而 所嫁 婦人 之 父 也，
s [l.v.]　　　　p(n)　　　　part

"余 [乃] 　　　　　　　　父 也，
s [l.v.]　　　　　　　p(n) part

"余 [乃] 　　　　婦人 之 父 也，
s [l.v.]　　　　　p(n)　　　part

"余 [乃] 而 所嫁 婦人 之 父 也，
s [l.v.]　　　　p(n)　　　　part

pron　adj　n
adjectival mod.　　n

※ 所嫁 婦人：

動詞後有名詞作賓語時，所＋動詞組成的短語
"所嫁"只含有形容詞的性質，此種結構中"
所"字的作用像是一個指示詞"那個"。

When the verb is followed by a noun as its object, then the
phrase composed of "所" + verb "所嫁" has only an adjectival
quality, and in this usage "所" serves as a demonstrative
adjective (that).

"我 -- 你嫁掉的那個女人的父親啊。

"I, father to that woman you marry off.

⟶ "我 [就是] 你嫁出去的那個女人的父親啊。

"I [am] father to that woman *whom* you marr*ied* off.

⟹ "我是你嫁出去的那個女人的父親啊。

"I am the father of that woman whom you married off.

八.二　　　　爾 用 先人 之 治命，余 是 以 報。"

你用先人的神志清醒時的命令，我因此報答。"

You use ancestor's right-minded order, I therefore repay."

⟶ 你用你父親生前神志清醒時的命令，我因此報答你。"

You use*d* your decease*d* father's right-mind*ed* order, I repay you because *of* that."

You follow*ed the* order *that* your decease*d* father g*a*ve *when* he *was in* his right mind; for this I *am* repay*ing* you."

⟹ 你用你父親生前神志清醒時的命令，我因此報答你。"

You followed the order that your deceased father gave when he was in his right mind; for this I am repaying you."

第二十一課

歧路亡羊

句子分析

一． <u>楊子之鄰人</u> 亡羊，
　　　　s　　　　 _v _o
　　　　　　　　 p

　　　楊子的鄰居丟羊，

　　　Yángzǐ's neighbor lose sheep;

　──→ 楊子的鄰居丟了一隻羊，

　　　Yángzǐ's neighbor los*t* a sheep;

　══⟹ 楊子的鄰居丟了羊，

　　　Yángzǐ's neighbor lost a sheep;

二． [楊子之鄰人] 既 率 其 黨 [追 之]，
　　　　[s]　　　 \conj adv [v o]/
　　　　　　　　　　　　 p1

　　　　　 又 請 楊子之豎 追 之 。
　　　　　 \adv v o/s v o/
　　　　　　　　 p2

※ [楊子之鄰人] 既率其黨，又請楊子之豎追之：

這是加合式複句。這種句子的上一分句用
"既"說明一種事實或描述一種情況，下一分句
用"又"、"且"來加強上一分句的意思，形成
"既…又／且…"的句式，含有"不但A而且還
B"、"不但A同時還B"的意思。

This is an **Additive Compound Sentence**. In this type of
sentence, the first clause is usually introduced by the adverb

142

"既" (already) to state a fact or to describe a situation, and the second clause contains the adverb "又" or "且" to add to what is said in the first clause, forming a paradigm "既⋯又⋯", meaning "not only A, but also B" or "not only A, but at the same time B"

※ "既⋯又⋯" :

表示兩種情況同時存在

The construction "既⋯又⋯" is used to indicate that two states or conditions co-exist. It functions like the construction "both . . . and [also]" does in English.

※ 率其黨 [追之] :

"率其黨" 本來是動詞加賓語，但在本文中地位降低，成為 "追之" 二字的狀語；而 "追之" 則蒙下省略

When it stands alone, the phrase "率其黨" functions as a v-o meaning "to lead his family members", but in this sentence it has a subsidiary grammatical function, serving instead as an adverbial phrase describing the main verb-object (v-o) phrase "追之", which is omitted here to avoid repetition.

※ 請楊子之豎追之 :

兼語結構：本句中 "楊子之豎" 既是動詞 "請" 的賓語，又是謂語 "追之" 的主語

This sentence is a **pivotal construction** in which the noun phrase "楊子之豎" serves both as the object of the verb "請" and as the subject of the predicate "追之."

既率領他的親屬，又請楊子的小廝追趕牠。

both lead his family members and ask Yángzǐ's servant boys to chase after it.

⟶ [鄰居]既率領著他的親屬[追趕跑掉的羊]，又請求楊子的小廝一塊儿去追趕跑掉的羊。

[the neighbor] not only led his own relatives [to chase after the lost sheep], but also asked Yángzǐ's young servant boys to go together with them to chase after the lost sheep.

⟹ 鄰居既率領著他的親屬，又請求楊子的小廝一塊儿去追趕跑掉的羊。

143

the neighbor not only led his relatives, but also asked Yángzǐ's young servant boys to go together with them to chase after the lost sheep.

三.　　楊子曰："嘻!亡一羊,何追者之眾?"

※ 1) 追者眾。(句子)

"追的人很多。"意思已經完足

The construction "追者眾" (chasing ones many) is an independent clause (i.e., a simple sentence) which means, "Those people chasing after [the sheep] were many." The meaning of the sentence is clear and complete as it stands.

※ 2) 追者之眾:

句子中主語、謂語間加一"之"字,變成主謂短句,用作主語。"追的人的多的程度" →"追的人那麼多",意思還沒完,需要別的句子成分(謂語)來補足。

When the particle "之" is added to this sentence between the subject and the predicate, the sentence is transformed into a clausal phrase which literally means "the 'many-ness' of the chasing people." (i.e., "such a great many people chasing"). The meaning of the phrase "such a great many people chasing" is incomplete; it must be completed by the addition of a predicate.

※ 3) 追者之眾 何?

"追[牠]的人那麼多為什麼?"
副詞"何"移到句子的後面,作用像謂語。

"Such a great many people chasing [it], why?" In this sentence, when the interrogative adverb "何" [why] is moved to the end of the sentence, it functions as the predicate for the clausal phrase "追者之眾."

※ 4) 何 追者之眾 ? (詢問兼感嘆)

為什麼追 [牠] 的人那麼多？

"Why such a great many people chasing [it]?" The predicate "何" has been moved to the beginning of the sentence for emphasis. (This rhetorical device is discussed in *L. 15, sentence analysis 3.2, p. 95*)

楊子説：" 咦！丟一羊，爲什麼追的人多？"

Yángzǐ say: "Hey! Lose one sheep, why chase-it ones many?"

⟶ 楊子説：" 咦！丟了一隻羊，爲什麼追牠的人那麼多？"

Yángzǐ said: "Hey! You've los*t* one sheep, why *are* so many people chas*ing after* it*?*"

⟹ 楊子説：" 咦！丟了一隻羊，爲什麼追牠的人那麼多？"

Yángzǐ said: "Hey! You've lost one sheep, why are so many people chasing after it?"

四．　鄰人 曰："[以] 多 [於] 歧路。"

＊ 多歧路：

多 [於] 歧路
adj [prep]　o

⟶ [在] 歧路 [方面] 多
[in respect of] by-ways, many

⟹ 有很多歧路
there were many forked paths

他例　　　　：多才多藝
OTHER EXAMPLES:　多 [於] 才多 [於] 藝

⟶ [在] 才 [方面] 多，[在] 藝 [方面] 多。
[in respect *of*] talents, many; [*in respect of*] skills, many

⟹ 有很多才藝
to have many talents and skills

鄰居説："多岔路。"

145

Neighbor say: "Many forked paths."

⟶ 鄰居説：" [因爲] 多 [於] 岔路。"

The neighbor sa*id*: "[because] [*in* respect *of*] fork*ed* path*s are* many ."

⟹ 鄰居説："因爲有很多岔路。"

The neighbor said: "Because there are many forked paths."

五．　[鄰人] 既 反，
　　　　　　　　adv　v
　　[s]　　　　p

　　　已經回來，

　　Already return,

⟶ [鄰居] 已經回來了，

[*The* neighbor] *had* already return*ed*,

⟶ [鄰居] 回來了以後，

After [*the* neighbor] ha*d* return*ed*,

⟹ 鄰居回來了以後，

After the neighbor had returned,

六．　[楊子] 問：" 獲 羊 乎？"
　　　　　　　　v　o　part
　　[s]　　　v　　　o
　　　　　　　　p

　　　問："得羊嗎？"

　　ask: "Get sheep?"

146

⟶ [楊子]問：＂找到羊了嗎?＂

[Yángzǐ] ask*ed*: "*Did you* find *the* sheep?"

⟹楊子問：＂找到羊了嗎?＂

Yángzǐ asked: "Did you find the sheep?"

七．　[鄰人]曰：＂亡之矣。＂
　　　[s]

說：＂丟牠了。＂

Say: "Lose it ."

⟶ [鄰居]說：＂丟了羊了。＂

[*The* neighbor] sa*id*: "*I have* los*t* it (i.e., *the* sheep)."

⟹鄰居說：＂把羊給丟了。＂

The neighbor said: "I have lost the sheep."

八．　[楊子]曰：＂奚亡之?＂
　　　[s]

說：＂爲什麼丟牠 ?＂

Say: "Why lose it ?"

⟶ [楊子]說：＂爲什麼丟了羊呢 ?＂

[Yángzǐ] sa*id*: "Why *did* you lose it (i.e., *the* sheep)?"

⟹楊子說：＂爲什麼把羊給丟了呢 ?＂

Yángzǐ said: "Why did you lose it?"

九．　　〔鄰人〕　曰：" 　　"
　　　　　　　　　　＼v＿＿o／
　　　[s]　　　　　　 p

説：

Say:

——→[鄰居]説：

[*The* neighbor] sa*id*:

====>鄰居説：

The neighbor said:

九．一　　　　" 歧路之中 又 有 歧 焉，
　　　　　　　　　　　　＼adv　v　o／ part
　　　　　　　　 s　　　　　 p

" 岔路的裡面又有岔路，

"forked paths within have forked-paths;

——→ " 在岔路的裡面又有岔路，

"Among fork*ed* path*s* *are even more* fork*ed* path*s*;

===> " 岔路裡又有岔路，

"There are even more forked paths in the forked paths;

148

                                    ___s___ [l.v. p(n)]
                                   (羊之)
九．二   吾 不 知 [其] 所之 [為 何]，所以 反 也。"
              \adv v   o   / conj \v/ part
              s   p1   p2

※ 所 V ：   所 ＋ V ＝ N
※ 所之 ：   所 ＋ 之 ＝ N
           所之＝往之處   place [it] went to
           到那儿去的地方   the place where [it] went

※ "所以反也"

是 " [此乃吾之] 所以反也 " 之省寫。此句中 "
所以" 的用法是從文言的 "所以"（代詞 "所
" ＋介詞 "以" －－ "因之而 v 之故"，"因為
它而 v 的緣故"，"…v 的緣故"）的用法轉變
為白話中連詞性的 "所以" 的用法的重要樞紐
和例證，在文言中極罕見，應特加注意。

The phrase "所以反也" is an abbreviated version of the full
sentence "[此乃吾之] 所以反也" ([This is my] *for/because of
it* returned = [this is my] *why returning reason* = [this is] *why* [I]
returned --> *therefore* [I] *returned*). The way that "所以" is used
in this sentence marks an important turning point in the
development of the Chinese language: it is from this classical
usage of "所" as a pronoun and "以" as a preposition -- "因
之而 v 之故" "*because of it* V " = "*because of it/this* [I]
returned" -- that the modern spoken Chinese conjunction "所以"
meaning "therefore" is derived. This use of "所以" is an
extremely early and rare example of the sense that ultimately
passed into spoken Chinese, and as such it is worth pointing
out.

NOTE: In classical Chinese "所以" does not always mean "because of
             it" -->"therefore." It could mean "[that] whereby" = "the way
             that" or " [that] wherefor" = "the reason for"

我不知道到那儿去的地方，所以回來啊。"

I not know where go to; therefore, return."

——→ 我不知道 [牠] 去的地方 [是什麼地方]，所以就回來了啊
     。"

I *do* not know *the* place [it/*the* sheep] *went to* [is what place]; therefore, *I* return*ed*."

⟶ 我不知道牠跑到哪條岔路上去了，所以就回來啦。"

I *do* not know **down which path it ra*n***; therefore, I return*ed*."

⟹ 我不知道牠跑到哪條岔路上去了，所以就回來啦。"

I do not know down which path it ran; therefore, I returned."

十. 楊子戚然變容，不言者移時，不笑者竟日。
　　　s　　　p1　　　　　p2　　　　　　p3

※ 者： 語氣詞，表示句中停頓，相當於白話的 "啊"

The word "者" functions here as a rhetorical particle. It marks a pregnant pause in the sentence that is intended to emphasize or draw attention to what immediately follows it. This use of "者" is roughly equivalent to the use of the spoken Chinese word "啊" in the middle of a sentence. It can be expressed in English by using such emphatic adverbs as "indeed" or "verily."

楊子憂傷地改變臉色，不說話啊很久，不笑啊一整天。

Yángzǐ morosely change facial expression; not speak, indeed, very long; not laugh, verily, a whole day.

⟶ 楊子很憂傷地改變了臉色，沈默了很久，一整天都不笑。

Yángzǐ, deject*ed*, chang*ed his* demeanor; **indeed,** *for a* long time he *was* **silent,** *and for* an entire day *he did* not laugh even once.

⟹ 楊子很憂傷地改變了臉上的神情，沈默了很久，一整天都不笑。

Yángzǐ's expression became very morose; he was silent then for a long time and did not laugh even once the whole day.

第二十二課

揠苗

句子分析

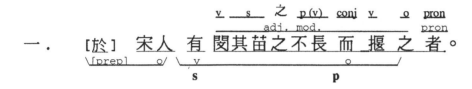

一. [於] 宋人 有 閔其苗之不長 而 揠之 者。

      ※其苗之不長：

> "其苗不長"是意思完足的敘述簡句。在主語"其苗"與謂語"不長"之間加上"之"字，就變成"主謂短語"，做動詞"閔"字的賓語。"之"字只是化句子為主謂短語的記號；不必翻譯也不應翻譯成"的"，因翻譯出來會使白話的語氣笨拙、不自然。因此"其苗之不長"只須譯成"他的苗不長"就可以了。

> "其苗不長" is a complete narrative sentence. Adding "之" between the subject "其苗" and the predicate "不長" transforms it into a **clausal phrase** that serves as the object of the verb "閔". "之" is used here only as a marker for this transformation; it need not and should not be rendered as "的" in spoken Chinese, for that would sound awkward and unnatural. Therefore "其苗之不長" need only be rendered as "他的苗不長" in spoken Chinese to convey the meaning.

宋人有擔心他的苗不長就拔高苗的人，

Sòng people have a worry about his sprouts not growing tall and pull them up one,

⟶ [在]宋國人[裡]有個擔心他的苗長不大就去把苗拔高一點的人，

[Among] Sòng people *there was* one *who was* concern*ed of* his sprouts not grow*ing* tall and pull*ed* them up a bit,

151

===> 有個擔心他的苗長不大就去把苗拔高一點的宋國人，

There was a person from the state of Sòng who was concerned that his sprouts would not grow tall and so pulled them up a bit.

二. [_]芒芒然歸，謂 其人曰："   "
    _adv__v/ _v__o/ _v____o_/
[s]   **p1**   **p2**   **p3**

很累地回家，告訴他的人說：

Exhaustedly return home, speak to his folks say:

——> [他]很累地回家，告訴他家裡的人說：

[He] return*ed* home exhaust*ed*, sp*oke to* his family member*s* say*ing*:

===> 他很累地回家，告訴他家裡的人說：

He returned home exhausted and spoke to the people in his family saying:

二.一 "今日[ ] 病 矣！予 助苗長矣！"
   adv   _adj/ part _v_o/s_v/ part
        [s] **p**   **s** **p**

"今天累壞了啊！我幫助苗長了！"

"Today become dead tired. I help sprouts lengthen!"

——> "今天[我]可累壞啦！我剛才幫助苗長高了！"

"Today [I] *have become* tire*d* out; I just *have* help*ed the* sprout*s* grow taller!"

===> "今天我可累壞啦！我剛才幫助苗長高了！"

"Today I am tired out! I have just helped the sprouts grow taller!"

三. 其子 趨 而 往視之，苗 則 槁 矣。
　　　(v) conj ＼v　v　o／ conj (adj) part
　　　＼adv／
　　s　　p　　　　p　　s　　p

※趨：　　本來是動詞，在本句中地位變低，用作副詞，
　　　　　描寫怎麼"往"。

When it stands alone, the word "趨" functions as a verb meaning "To rush [towards]", but in this sentence it has a subsidiary grammatical function, serving instead as an adverb describing the main verb "往" [to go to]--in this case describing how or in what manner he went. Here the word "而" simply links the adverb and the verb. This construction can be translated into English with an adverb and a verb (e.g. "went hastily") or a verb and a present participle (e.g., "went rushing").

※則：　　"則"字是連詞，作用是連接兩個謂語，即兩
　　　　　件事前後相繼。通常是第一件事略先，第二件
　　　　　事略後；這種用法的"則"字應譯成"就"或
　　　　　"便"；但是也有第二件事發生在前，直到第
　　　　　一件事發生時第二件事才被發現的情形。這種
　　　　　用法的"則"字，一定用在第二件事的主語之
　　　　　後，應譯成"原來已經"（表示出乎發現者意
　　　　　料之外）。如本句："其子趨而往視之，苗則
　　　　　槁矣。""苗槁"這件事本發生在"其子趨而
　　　　　往視之"之前，但它被發現卻在"往視"之後
　　　　　。"其子"發現"苗槁"這一事實時一定會有
　　　　　出乎意外之感，因此把"則"譯成"原來已經
　　　　　"比只譯成"卻"更能生動地傳達出其子吃驚
　　　　　的程度。

"則" is a conjunction connecting two predicates stating two events that happened sequentially; usually the first event happened earlier and the second later. In such cases, "則" should be rendered as "then," or "thereupon." Sometimes the second event took place earlier, yet it was not known until the first event had happened. In such cases the word "則" always follows the subject of the second event, and it should be rendered as "it turned out that..." to indicate a tone of surprise. In this sentence: "the sprouts withered" took place earlier than "the son went rushing to look at them", but it was discovered after "the son went rushing to look at them." When the son finds that the sprouts have already withered, he will certainly be surprised. And to vividly bring out this feeling of surprise, it is better to render "則" as "it turned out that...." than to simply render it as "however."

他的兒子跑去看它，苗卻枯了。

His son rushing go see them; sprouts, however, wither.

——→ 他的兒子跑著到田裡去看苗，苗原來已經都枯了。

His son *went* rush*ing to the* field *to* look *at the* sprout*s*, but *the* sprout*s*, *it* turn*ed* out, *had* wither*ed*.

===> 他的兒子跑著到田裡去看苗，苗原來都已經枯了。

His son ran to the fields to look at the sprouts; but it turned out that the sprouts had all withered.

四.
<pre>
       adj. mod.   pron
 _____
 天下之不助苗長者 寡 矣。
                  \adj/ part
      s   p
</pre>

天下的不助苗長的人少了啊。

World people not help sprouts grow -- few indeed!

——→ 天下的不幫助苗長的人太少啦。

The people *in the* world *who do* not help *their* sprout*s* grow *are* few indeed!

===> 天下不幫助苗長的人太少啦。

The people in the world who do not help their sprouts grow are few indeed!

五.
<pre>
    因   果
    v   [o/s]   v o conj v o pron   adv v o   pron
 _____   _____
 以為 [_] 無益   而舍之者 [乃] 不耘苗 者 也；
 \   adj. mod.   pron/   \adj. mod. pron/ part
          s   [l.v.]   pn
</pre>

認為沒有好處就放棄它的人，不替苗除野草的人啊；

154

Think have no advantage and thus abandon it/them ones, not for-sprouts weed ones;

⟶ 認爲培養它沒有好處就放棄它的人 [是] 不替苗除掉野草的人；

The people *who* think *there is* no advantage *in* nurtur*ing* something and thus abandon it [are] *the* people *who do* not weed *their* sprouts;

⟹ 認爲培養它沒有好處就放棄它的人是不替苗除掉野草的人；

The people who think there is no advantage in nurturing something and thus abandon it are the people who do not weed their sprouts.

六．
<pre>
    v o/s v   pron   v   o   pron
    助之長   者 [乃]   揠苗   者 也。
    \adj.mod. pron/   \adj.mod. pron/ part
         s   [l.v.]   pn
</pre>

幫助它長的人，拔苗的人啊。

Help it (i.e. something) grow ones, pull sprouts ones.

⟶ 幫助它長的人 [是] 把苗拔高一點儿的人。

The people *who want to* help something grow [are] *the* people *who* pull *their* sprout*s* up a bit.

⟹ 幫助它長的人是把苗拔高一點儿的人。

The people who want to help something grow are the people who pull their sprouts up a bit.

七．
<pre>
        [v o]
   [揠苗] 非 徒 無益，而 又 害之。
              \adv adv v o/ conj \adv v o/
     [s]   p1   p2
</pre>

不僅沒有好處，反而還害它。

Not only have no advantage, contrarily in addition harm them.

⟶ ［揠苗］這種做法不僅沒有好處，反而還害了它。

This method [*of* pull*ing* up *the* sprouts] not only has no benefit; on the contrary, *it* also harms them.

⟹ 揠苗這種做法不僅沒有好處，反而還害了它。

This method of pulling the sprouts up a bit not only has no benefit, but on the contrary also harms them.

第二十三課

燕人

句子分析

一.　燕人 生 於 燕，長 於 楚，及 老 而 還 本國。
　　　　　\v prep o/　\v prep o/　\prep o conj v　o/
　　　　s　　 p1　　　　p2　　　　　　　p3

燕人生在燕，長在楚，到老回本國。

Yān person born in Yān, grow in Chǔ, reaching old return original country.

——→ 有一個燕國人在燕國出生，在楚國長大，等到老了的時候回他自己的老家去。

There was a man *of the* state *of* Yān *who was* born in Yān, grew up in *the* state *of* Chǔ, *and* when he grew old, return*ed to his* native land.

——→ 有一個燕國人在燕國出生，在楚國長大，等到老了的時候回他自己的老家去。

There was a man of the state of Yān who was born in Yān, grew up in the state of Chǔ, and when he grew old, returned to his native land.

二.　[_] 過 晉國，同行者 誑 之，指城 曰：" 此燕國之城。"
　　　　\v o/　　　　\v o/　\adv v　o/
　[s]　p　　　 s　　 p1　　　 p2

" 此 [乃] 燕國之城 "
　s　[l.v.]　　pn

經過晉國，一起走的人騙他，指城牆說："這-燕國的城牆。"

157

Pass through Jìn, going-with-him one trick him, point city wall, say: "This -- city wall of Yān state."

⟶ 在［他］經過晉國的時候，跟他一起走的人騙他，指著城牆說：“這［是］燕國的城牆。”

When [he] pass*ed* through *the* state *of* Jìn, *the* person travel*ling* together with him point*ed at the* city wall, say*ing*: "This [is] *the* city wall *of the* state *of* Yān."

⟹ 在他經過晉國的時候，跟他一起走的人騙他，指著城牆說：“這是燕國的城牆。”

While he was passing through the state of Jìn, the person travelling together with him tricked him; pointing at the city wall, he said: "This is the city wall of the state of Yān."

三. 其人 愀然 變容。

那個人難過地改變臉色。

This person glumly chang expression.

⟶ 那個燕國人很難過地改變了臉上的神情。

This man *from* Yān glumly chang*ed his* expression.

⟹ 那個燕國人很難過地改變了臉上的神情。

This man from Yān glumly changed his expression.

四. ［同行者］指社曰：“此［乃］若里之社。”

指土地廟說：“這－你村子的土地廟。”

Point local soil-god-altar, say: "This--your village's local soil-god-altar."

—→ [一起走的人]指著土地廟說："這[是]你村子裡的土地廟。"

[*The* person travel*ling with* him] point*ed at an* altar *to the* local god *of the* soil, say*ing*: "This [is] your village's altar *to the* local god *of the* soil."

==⇒ 一起走的人指著土地廟說："這是你村子裡的土地廟。"

The person travelling with him pointed at an altar to the local god of the soil and said: "This is your village's altar to the local god of the soil."

五． [其人] 乃 喟然 而 歎。
        \adv adv conj v /
[s]   p

就傷感地歎氣。

Then wistfully sigh.

—→ [那個燕國人]就很傷感地歎氣。

[*The* man *from* Yān] then sigh*ed* wistfully.

==⇒ 那個燕國人就很悲哀地歎氣。

The man from Yān then sighed heavy heartedly.

六． [同行者] 指舍 曰："此[乃] 若先人之廬。"
            v o   s [l.v.]   pn
[s]   \adv v   o /
                          p

指房子說："這 — 你祖先的茅舍。"

Point house, say, "This -- your ancestors' thatched cottage."

—→ [一起走的人]指著房子說："這[是]你祖先的茅舍。"

[*The* person travel*ling with* him] point*ed at a* house, sa*id*, "This [is] your ancestors' thatched cottage."

===⟹ 一起走的人指著房子説："這是你祖先的茅舍。"

The person travelling with him, pointing at a cottage, said: "This is your ancestors' thatched cottage."

七． ［其人］乃 涓然 而 泣。
　　　　　　　\adv　adv　conj　v/
　　　　[s]　　　　　　　　p

就眼淚簌簌地哭。

then tears falling in rivulets-like cry.

⟶ ［那個燕國人］就眼淚紛紛落下地哭了。

[*The* man *from* Yān] then, tears fall*ing* in rivulets *as it were*, so cr*ied*.

[*The* man *from* Yān] then cr*ied*, *the* tears stream*ing* in rivulets *down his face*.

===⟹ 那個燕國人就眼淚紛紛落下地哭了。

The man from Yān then cried, the tears streaming in rivulets down his face.

八． 　　　　　　　v　o　　　　　s [l.v.]　　　　pn
　　　［同行者］指塿 曰："此 ［乃］ 若先人之塚。"
　　　　　　　\adv　v　　　　　　　　　　　o/
　　　[s]　　　　　　　p

指墳堆説："這你祖先的墳墓。"

Point tumuli, say: "These--your ancestors' grave mounds."

⟶ ［一起走的人］指著一片墳堆説："這［是］你祖先的墳墓。"

[*The* person travel*ling with* him] point*ed at* some tumuli, say*ing*: "These [are] your ancestors' grave mound*s*."

===⟹ 一起走的人指著一片墳堆説："這是你祖先的墳墓。"

The person travelling with him pointed at some tumuli and said: "These are your ancestors' grave mounds."

九．　其人哭　不自　禁。

那個人哭不能止住自己。

This person cry, not able stop himself.

⟶　那個燕國人哭得止不住自己。

This person *from* Yān cr*ied*, unable *to* stop himself.

⟹　那個燕國人哭得止不住自己。

This person from Yān could not stop himself from crying.

十．　同行者　啞然大笑　曰："予昔給若，此[乃]晉國耳。"

同行的人哈哈大笑說："我剛才騙你，這裡一晉國罷了。"

Travelling together one guffaw-like laugh, say: "I just fool you, this--Jìn state only."

⟶　跟他一起走的人哈哈大笑說："我剛才騙你，這裡只不過[是]晉國罷了。"

The person travel*ling* together with him, guffaw*ing*, sa*id*: "I trick*ed* you just now, this [is] only *the* state *of* Jìn."

⟹　跟他一起走的人哈哈大笑說："我剛才騙你，這裡只不過是晉國罷了。"

The person travelling with him spoke with a guffaw, said: "Just now I tricked you; this is only the state of Jìn."

十一. 其人 大 慚。
　　　 　　\adv adj/
　　　 s　　 p

那個人非常慚愧。

This person extraordinarily embarrassed.

⟶ 那個燕國人非常慚愧。

This person *from* Yān *was* extremely embarrass*ed*.

⟹ 那個燕國人非常慚愧。

This man from Yān was mortified.

十二. 及 [燕人] 至 燕， 真 見 燕國之城社， 真 見 先人之廬塚，
　　　 prep 　　 \v o/ \adv v　 o/　　 \adv v　 o/
　　　　 [s]　 p1　　 p2　　　　　　 p3

　　 [其] 悲心 更 微。
　　 \[adj] n/ \adv adj/
　　　 s　　 p

等到到燕國，真看見燕國的城牆土地廟，真看見祖先的
茅廬墳墓，悲哀的心情更輕微。

Upon reaching Yān, truly see city walls, soil-god-altar of Yān state; truly see thatched cottage, grave mounds of ancestors: grief feeling even slighter.

⟶ 等到 [燕國人] 到了燕國的時候，真看見了燕國的城牆跟土
地廟，真看見了祖先的茅廬跟墳墓，[他的] 悲傷的心情
反倒輕微多了。

When [he] arrive*d in the* state *of* Yān, *he* truly s*aw* city wall*s* and *the* altar *to the* local god *of the* soil *of the* state *of* Yān; *he* truly s*aw the* thatched hut and grave mound*s of his* ancestors: [his] feeling*s* of grief instead *were* even less *intense than before.*

⟹ 等到他到了燕國的時候，真看見了燕國的城牆跟土地廟
，真看見了祖先的茅廬跟墳墓，他的悲傷的心情反倒輕
微多了。

162

When he arrived in the state of Yān and truly saw the state of Yān's city wall and altar to the local god of the soil and truly saw his ancestors' thatched cottage and grave mounds, his feelings of grief were instead even less intense than before.

第二十四課

畫蛇添足

句子分析

一．　　　[於] 楚　有　祠者，
　　　　　　\[prep] o / \ v　o /
　　　　　　　　　　s　　　　p

　　　　　　楚有祭祀的人，

　　　　　　Chǔ have sacrificing one;

　　　　　⟶　[在]楚國有個祭祀的人，

　　　　　　[In] *the* state *of* Chǔ *there was* a person perform*ing a* sacrifice;

　　　　　⟹　楚國有個祭祀的人，

　　　　　　In the state of Chǔ there was a person performing a sacrifice;

二．　　　[祠者] 賜　其舍人　卮酒。
　　　　　　　　　\ v　oi　　　Od /
　　　　　[s]　　　　　　　p

　　　　　※賜　　　　雙賓語動詞，含有“交 A 給 B”的意思。
　　　　　　　　　　　普通的及物動詞只要有一個賓語就可以把句子
　　　　　　　　　　　的意義完全表達出來了。雙賓語動詞卻必須得
　　　　　　　　　　　有兩個賓語－直接賓語（A，指所給的物）和間
　　　　　　　　　　　接賓語（B，指受物的人）－才能把句子的意義
　　　　　　　　　　　完全表達出來。因這類動詞本質上有“交 A
　　　　　　　　　　　給 B”的意思，必須說出兩個賓語才能使句意
　　　　　　　　　　　完足。如本句“卮酒”是直接賓語，“舍人”
　　　　　　　　　　　是間接賓語。這類雙賓語的動詞，除了“賜”

164

以外，還有"與"（yǔ）"予"（yǔ）"授"（shòu）
"贈"（zèng）"遺"（wèi: 送給）等。

The verb "賜" takes two objects: it conveys the meaning "pass [down]/bestow **A** to/on **B**." In general, a transitive verb can completely convey its meaning in a sentence by taking a single direct object. A **double object verb** must take two objects to convey its complete meaning, because these verbs inherently contain the sense of giving something (**A** = direct object) to someone (**B** = indirect object). Only when both a direct and an indirect object are named can the full meaning of the verb be expressed in the sentence. In this sentence, "卮酒" (a goblet of liquor) is the direct object and "舍人" (retainers) is the indirect object. In addition to the word "賜", the following **double object verbs** are frequently encountered: "與" (to give [something] to [someone]); "予" (to give [something to someone]); "授" (to confer [something] on [someone]); "贈" (zèng) (to give [something] as a gift to [someone]); "遺" (wèi) (to give [something] as a gift to (someone]).

賜他的門客一杯酒。

offer his retainers a goblet liquor.

⟶ [祭祀的人]賜給他的門客一杯酒。

[*the* person perform*ing the* sacrifice] offer*ed* his retainer*s* a goblet *of* liquor.

⟹ 他賜給他的門客一杯酒。

he offered his retainers a goblet of liquor.

三． 舍人 相 謂 曰 : " "

s　　　p1　　　p2

adv v　v　　o

　※ 相謂　　互相告訴；你告訴我，我告訴你；引申為
　　　　　　　"一塊儿商量"

"相謂" means "to say to one another": you tell me, I tell you. It has the connotative sense of "discussing together" or "talking over among themselves."

門客互相告訴說：

Retainers to-one-another speak say:

⟶ 門客們一塊儿商量説：

The retainer*s* discuss*ed this among* themselve*s* say*ing*:

⟹ 門客們一塊儿商量説：

The retainers discussed this among themselves saying:

三.一　"數人飲之，[酒]不足；一人飲之，[酒] 有 餘。
　　　　　\v o/　　　\adv adj/　　\v o/　　　　\v o/
　　　　　s　　p　　[s]　p　　s　　p　　[s]　　p

※ 數人飲之，不足；一人飲之，有餘：

這是個補充式複句。句構像平行式，但上下兩分句的意思互相補充。兩分句中多數含有反義詞。

This is a **Complementary Compound Sentence.** In such a sentence the two clauses complement each other in meaning. Usually an antonym of a word in the first clause appears in the second clause.

"幾人喝它，不夠；一人喝它，有餘。

"Several people drink it, not enough; one person drink it, have excess.

⟶ "幾個人喝這杯酒，[酒]不夠；可是一個人喝這杯酒，[酒]又有剩餘。

"*With* several people drink*ing* it (i.e., this goblet), [*the* liquor] *will* not suffice; *with* one person drink*ing* it (i.e., this goblet), [*the* liquor]*will* more *than* suffice.

⟹ "幾個人喝這杯酒，酒不夠；一個人喝它，卻又太多。

"With several people drinking this goblet, the liquor will not suffice; with one person drinking it, there will be more than enough.

166

三.二　　[吾] 請 畫 [於] 地 為 蛇，先成者 飲 酒。"
　　　　　　　 ＼adv　v　[prep]　o　v　o／　　　＼v　o／
　　　[s]　　　　　　　p　　　　　　　　s　　p

※ 畫地為蛇：

畫[於]地為蛇，"畫"與"為"看起來都是動
詞，實際上"為"是"畫"的結果補語。試
把這個句子的詞序改成"於地畫為蛇"或

"畫為蛇於地"就可以證明。類似的例子
如"畫地為牢 (láo)" 司馬遷《報任少卿書》

In the phrase "畫地為蛇" (to draw [on] the ground making a
snake), the words "畫" (to draw) and "為" (to make) appear at
first glance to be verbs; but, in fact, "為" functions in this
phrase as the **resultative complement** of the verb "畫" (i.e.,
it describes the result or outcome of the action of the principal
verb). This function can be seen if the order of the sentence is
changed to "於地畫為蛇" (on the ground to draw [with the
result being] a snake) or "畫為蛇於地" (to draw [with the
outcome being] a snake on the ground). A similar example is "
畫地為牢"(to draw on the ground [with the outcome being] a
jail). (*Sīmǎ Qiān*, "*A letter in response to Rén Shàoqīng*").

讓我們畫地成蛇，先完成的人喝酒。"

Let's draw ground make snake; first-finishing one drink liquor."

⟶　讓我們 [在] 地面上畫作一條蛇，先畫完的人喝酒。
　　"

Let us *each* draw a snake [on] *the* ground; *the* person *who*　finish*es*
draw*ing* first drink*s the* liquor."

⟹ 讓咱們在地面上畫作一條蛇，先畫完的人喝酒。"

Let us each draw a picture of a snake on the ground; the one who
finishes first drinks the liquor."

四.　　　一人 蛇 先 成。
　　　　　　　　　 adv　v
　　　　　　　　＼s　　p／
　　　　 s　　　　　　p

167

※ 蛇先成：本身是主謂結構，"蛇"是主語，"先成"是謂語，在全句中降格用作主語"一人"的謂語。類似的句構如"莊周家貧"《莊子·外物》。"莊周"是主語，"家貧"是謂語，而"家貧"本身也是一個主謂結構；"家"是主語，"貧"是謂語。這種主謂結構的子句降格作謂語的句式是一種比較特殊的包孕句。

This sentence should not be taken to mean " One person's snake was finished first." The phrase "蛇先成" is in itself a **s-p construction** (i.e., an **independent clause** or a sentence) in which "蛇" is the subject and "先成" is the predicate. This **independent clause** has a subsidiary grammatical function inside the larger sentence, where it serves as the predicate of the subject "一人". The sentence "莊周家貧" (Zhuāng Zhōu was poor), *Zhuāngzǐ*, "External Things", exhibits the same pattern. "莊周" is the subject, and "家貧" (the household is poor) is the predicate. However, "家貧" is in itself an **s-p construction** (i.e., a sentence): "家" is the subject, and "貧" is the predicate. This type of sentence, in which an **independent clause (s-p construction)** is made to fill a subsidiary grammatical function as the predicate of a longer sentence, constitutes a special case of the **embedding sentence**.

※ 蛇先成：主語"蛇"是謂語"先成"動作的對象，從邏輯上說應看作是被動句，但是句中沒有表示被動的詞，如"為"、"被"、"見"、"於"等。類似的例子如"狡 (jiǎo) 兔死、走狗烹 (pēng)"《史記·淮陰侯列傳》。這是中國語文中一種力求簡約的方法：即使句子的意思是被動的，如能藉上下文的含義表達出來，就不用表示被動的詞。

In this sentence, the subject "蛇" is the target or object of the action described by the predicate "先成" [to (be) complete first]. It should logically be construed as a **passive sentence** [i.e., "The snake *was* finished first." not "The snake finished first."], but the sentence contains no passive marker (e.g., "為", "被", "見", or "於") to indicate this. For example, another sentence which should logically be construed as a passive construction but which contains no passive marker is: "狡兔死，走狗烹" [(When) the sly rabbits have died/are dead, the running (i.e., hunting) dogs **are/(will) be boiled**]. (Sīmǎ Qiān, *Shǐjì*, "The biography of the Marquis of Huáiyīn."). The ommission of a passive marker is one device used in classical Chinese to attain a concise and laconic mode of expression. If the sentence should be construed in the passive and this can be ascertained from its immediate context, it is not necessary to add a passive marker to indicate this.

一人蛇先成。

One person snake first finish.

⟶ 一個人蛇先畫成了。（一個人先畫成了蛇）

One person finish*ed* draw*ing a* snake first.

⟹ 一個人蛇先畫成了。

One person finished drawing a snake first.

五． ［其人］引 酒 且 飲，
　　　　　[s]　　　p1　　　p2

乃 ［以］左手 持 卮，［以］右手 畫 蛇 曰： " "

※ "持卮"、"畫蛇"：

都是**動賓結構**，在本句內降格用作副詞，形容 "曰"

The phrases "持卮" (hold[ing] the goblet) and "畫蛇" (draw[ing] the snake) are **verb-object (v-o)** constructions; but in this sentence, they play a subsidiary grammatical role, functioning solely as adverbial clauses modifying the verb "曰" (to speak): speaking in what manner, or in this case, while doing what.

拿過酒將要喝，卻左手拿酒杯，右手畫蛇說：

Draw-over liquor, about to drink, but left hand hold goblet, right hand draw snake, say:

⟶ ［那個人］拿過酒來將要喝，卻［用］左手拿著酒杯［用］右手畫著蛇說：

[That person] *took* up *the* liquor *and was* about *to* drink, but hold*ing the* goblet [in] *his* left hand *and* [us*ing*] *his* right hand *to* draw *the* snake, *he* said:

⟹ 他拿過酒來將要喝，卻用左手端著酒杯，用右手畫著蛇說：

He took up the liquor and was about to drink, but using his left hand to hold the goblet while drawing the snake with his right, he said:

五．一　　　 "吾　能　為　之　足。"
　　　　　　　　　 ＼aux　prep　o　　v／
　　　　　　　 s　　　　　　 p

　※足：　　　本來是名詞"腳"，但根據它在本句內的地位和作用，應把它看作是**動賓結構**，意思是"加上腳"或"添上腳"。

In classical Chinese, the word "足" is primarily encountered as a noun meaning "腳" [feet/foot]; but given its position and function in this sentence, it must be construed as a verb meaning "to add/put feet onto" and functions as such in the **v-o** construction "加／添足" (LITERALLY: "footed it," i.e., "put feet on it").

"我能爲它添腳。"

"I can for it add feet."

⟶ "我能替它添上腳。"

"I can add feet *to* it (i.e., *the* snake)."

⟹ "我能給它添上腳。"

"I can add feet to the snake."

六．　　[其蛇足] 未 成，一人之蛇 成。
　　　　　　　　　＼adv　v／　　　　　 ＼v／
　　　　 [s]　　　 p　　　 s　　　 p

沒有完成，一人的蛇完成。

Not have finish, one person's snake finish.

⟶ [他的蛇足]還沒有畫完，另一個人的蛇畫成了。

[His snake's feet] *were* not yet completely draw*n when* another person's snake *was* complete*d*.

⟹ 他的蛇腳還沒有畫完，另一個人的蛇畫成了。

His snake's feet were not yet completed, when another person's snake was completed.

七． ［其人］奪其巵曰：" "
　　[s] 　 p1 　 p2

搶那酒杯説：

Grab that goblet, say:

⟶ ［那個人］搶過那隻酒杯説：

[That person] grab*bed the* goblet away *and* said:

⟹ 那個人搶過那隻酒杯説：

That person grabbed the goblet away and said:

七．一 "蛇固無足，子安能為之足？"
　　　 s　p　　 s　　　 p

"蛇本來沒有腳，您怎麼能為它添腳？"

"Snake originally not have feet; you how able for it add feet?"

⟶ "蛇本來沒有腳，您怎麼能替它添上腳呢？"

"*A* snake by nature *has* no feet; how can you make feet for it?"

171

===⟹ "蛇本來沒有腳，您怎麼能給它添上腳呢？"

"A snake by nature has no feet; how can you add feet to it?"

八． 　[此人] 　遂 飲 其酒。
　　　　　　　＼adv　v　o／
　　　[s]　　　　　　p

就喝那酒。

Thereupon drink that liquor.

⟶ [那個人]就喝了那杯酒。

[That person] thereupon drank that *goblet of* liquor.

===⟹ 他就把那杯酒喝掉了。

Thereupon, he drank the liquor.

九． 　為蛇足者 　終 亡 其酒。
　　　　　　　　＼adv　v　o／
　　s　　　　　　p

為蛇添腳的人終於失掉他的酒。

For-snake-add-feet one in-the-end lose his liquor.

⟶ 替蛇添腳的人終於失掉了他的酒。

In *the* end, *the* person *who* add*ed* feet to *the* snake los*t* his liquor.

===⟹ 給蛇添腳的人終於失掉了他的酒。

In the end, the one who added feet to his snake lost his liquor.

第二十五課

濠梁之遊

句子分析

一． 莊子與惠子　遊　於　濠梁之上。
　　　　s　　　　　v　prep　o
　　　　　　　　　　　　p

　　莊子跟惠子閒遊在濠的橋上。

　　Zhuāngzǐ and Huìzǐ stroll on Háo bridge's top.

　　──→　莊子跟惠子在濠水的橋上閒遊。

　　Zhuāngzǐ and Huìzǐ *were* stroll*ing* on *the* Háo River bridge.

　　══→　莊子跟惠子在濠水的橋上閒遊。

　　Zhuāngzǐ and Huìzǐ were strolling on the Háo River bridge.

二． 莊子　曰：" 　　　　"
　　　s　　v　　o
　　　　　　　p

　　莊子說：

　　Zhuāngzǐ said:

二．一　　"儵魚　出　游從容，
　　　　　　s　　v　v　comp
　　　　　　　　　　p

　　"鰷魚出來、游動自在，

　　"Minnows come out, swim contentedly --

173

——→ "鰷魚浮出水面或在水中游動得很自在,

"*The* minnows *dart* in and out *of the* water, leisurely and contentedly swim*ming* --

===⟹ "鰷魚浮出水面或在水中游動得很自在,

"The minnows dart in and out of the water, leisurely and contentedly swimming --

二.二 是 [乃] 魚之樂 也。"

※魚之樂 "魚樂" 是意思完足的 **描寫簡句**:主語是 "魚" ,謂語是 "樂" ,譯成白話是 "魚很快樂。" 在主語謂語之間加上 "之" 字,句子就變成主 **謂短語** ,作繫詞 "乃" 字的名詞謂語 。 "之" 字只有化句子為主 **謂短語** 的符號的作用,不必譯成 "的" 。

"魚樂 "(the fish are happy) is a complete and fully comprehensible sentence: the subject is "魚 " and the predicate is "樂." It can be translated into spoken Chinese as "魚很快樂 " (The fish are *very* happy). When the particle "之 " is added between the subject and the predicate, this sentence is transformed into a **clausal phrase** that serves as the predicate nominative of the understood copula "乃." The particle "之 " functions solely as a grammatical marker indicating that the sentence has been transformed into a **clausal phrase**; it should not be translated as a possesive marker. This phrase does *not* mean "the happiness of fish" in English: it can be more precisely translated as a noun phrase ("fish being happy") or as a clause ("that the fish are happy").

這,魚快樂啊。"

This -- fish happy."

——→ 這 [是] 魚快樂啊。"

This [is] fish *being* happy."

174

⟹ 這是魚快樂啊。"

This is fish being happy."

三. 惠子 曰: "   "
　　　　　　　＼v　　o／
　　　s　　　　　p

惠子說:

Huìzǐ said:

三.一 "子 非 魚, [子] 安 知 魚之樂?"
　　　　　＼n-l.v. p(n)／　＼adv v o／
　　　　　s　　p　　　[s]　　　p

"您不是魚，怎知魚快樂？"

"You are not fish, how know fish happy?"

⟶ "您不是魚，[您]怎麼知道魚快樂呢？"

"You are not *a* fish; how *do* [you] know *that the* fish *are* happy?"

⟹ "您不是魚，您怎麼知道魚快樂呢？"

"You are not a fish; how do you know that the fish are happy?"

四. 莊子 曰: "   "
　　　　　　　＼v　　o／
　　　s　　　　　p

莊子說:

Zhuāngzǐ said:

四.一 "子 非 我, [子] 安 知 我之不知魚之樂?"
　　　　　＼n-l.v. p(n)／　＼adv v o／
　　　　　s　　p　　　[s]　　　p

175

$$\underset{\text{s} \quad 之 \quad \text{p}}{\underset{我 \; 之}{} \quad \underset{\overset{\backslash\text{adv} \; \text{v} \quad \text{o}/}{不 \; 知}}{\overset{\overset{\text{s}\;之\;\text{p}}{}}{魚 \; 之 \; 樂}}}$$

※ 我之不知魚之樂

　　這是主謂短語中又含有主謂短語的結構。
　　"我不知魚之樂"是包孕句：主語是"我"
　　，謂語是"不知魚之樂"。在主語和謂語之間
　　加上"之"字，這個包孕句就變成了主謂
　　短語作全句"〔子〕安知我之不知魚之樂"中
　　動詞"知"字的賓語；而謂語"不知魚之樂"
　　也是一個主謂短語的結構。
　　（參看句子分析2.2及3.1）。

This **clausal phrase** itself contains an **embedded clausal phrase**. "我不知魚之樂"is an **enbedding sentence**. The addition of the clausal phrase marker "之"between the subject "我" and the predicate "不知魚之樂" transforms this sentence into a **clausal phrase** that functions within the complete sentence "〔子〕安知我之不知魚之樂" as the object of the verb"知." The predicate "不知魚之樂" is likewise comprised of a verb which takes as its object the **clausal phrase**"魚之樂" (See *sentence analyses* 2.2 and 3.1, pp. 172-3)

"您不是我，怎知我不知魚快樂？"

"You are not I, how know I not know fish happy?"

⟶ "您不是我，您怎麼知道我不知道魚快樂呢？"

"You are not I, *so* how *do* you know *that* I *do* not know *the* fish *are* happy?"

⟹ "您不是我，您怎麼知道我不知道魚快樂呢？"

"You are not I, so how do you know that I do not know the fish are happy?"

五．　$\underset{\text{s}}{惠子} \quad \underset{\overset{\backslash\text{v} \quad \text{o}/}{\underset{\text{p}}{曰：" \quad 。"}}}{}$

惠子説：

Huìzǐ said:

五.一　　"我　非　子，[我]　固　不　知　子　矣；
　　　　　＼n-l.v. p(n)/　　＼adv adv v　o/ part
　　　　　　s　　p　　　[s]　　　　　p

　　　"我不是您，固然不知您啦；

　　　"I am not you; indeed, not know you,

⟶　　"我不是您，[我]固然不知道您啦；

　　　"I am not you; indeed, [I] *do* not know you,

⟹　　"我不是您，我固然不知道您啦；

　　　"I am not you; indeed I don't know you;

五.二　　子　固　非　魚　也，
　　　　　＼adv n-l.v. p(n)/ part
　　　　　　s　　　p

　　　您本來不是魚啊，

　　　you by nature are not fish:

⟶您本來不是魚啊，

　　　you by nature are not *a* fish:

⟹您本來不是魚啊，

　　　you by nature are not a fish:

五.三　　子之不知魚之樂　全　矣。"
　　　　　　　　s　　　　　　p part

177

子 之 不 知 魚之樂
s 之   \adv v o/
    s 之   p

您不知魚快樂，完全啦。"

you not know fish happy, complete."

⟶ 您不知道魚快樂的根據，很充足啦。"

the grounds *for arguing that* you *do* not know *that the* fish *are* happy *must already be* sufficient."

⟶ 您不知道魚快樂，是毫無疑問的了。"

there **is absolutely no question** *that* you *don't* know *that the* fish *are* happy."

⟹ 您不知道魚快樂，是毫無疑問的了。"

there is absolutely no question that you don't know that the fish are happy."

六.   莊子 曰："   "
          \v o/
     s   p

莊子説：

Zhuāngzǐ said:

六.一   "[ ] 請 循 其本。
           \adv v o/
      [s]   p

"請順它的本。

"Please follow its origin.

178

⟶ "讓咱們回到辯論的起點。

"Let's **go back to** *the* star**ti**ng point *of our* argument.

⟹ "讓咱們回到辯論的起點。

"Let's go back to the starting point of our argument.

六.二

子曰'汝安知魚樂'云者，
```
      s  adv v  o
```
```
 v        o       part
```
s   p

[子] 既 已 知 吾 知 之 而 問 我，
```
         s  v  o
```
```
\adv adv v   o  conj v  o/
```
[s]   p

※安知⋯　可以是反問句，也可以是疑問句
1.子安知魚樂？意思是"知魚樂"是不可能的
，你怎麼（怎麼會／能）"知魚樂"呢？
2.子安知魚樂？意思是我承認你"知魚樂"，
但是請告訴我你是怎麼（用什麼法子／從哪
兒）"知魚樂"的？

How can/do..It functions in a rhetorical question or in a genuine question.
1. "How *can* you know that fish are happy?" *Can* this
knowledge exist at all? How *can* you know?
2. "How *do* you know that fish are happy?" Presumably you
know that fish are happy, but "How (by what means/whence) *do*
you know?"

您说'你怎知魚快樂啊？'已知我知它才問我，

you say 'You how know fish happy': already know I know it
so ask me.

⟶ 您说'你怎麼知道魚快樂啊'[您]已經知道我知道
魚快樂了，然後才問我從哪儿知道魚快樂的？

When your said: 'How *do* you know *that the* fish *are* happy':
[you] already *had to have* known I knew it; only then *could
you have* asked me **how** *I* came *to* know/**where** *I* knew it *from
that the* fish *are* happy.

179

⟹ 您説‘你怎麼知道魚快樂啊？’您已經知道我知道魚快樂了，才問我從哪儿知道魚快樂的，

When you said: 'How did you come to know this,' you already had to have known that I knew the fish are happy, only then could you have asked me where I knew it from.

六.三　我 知 之 [於] 濠[梁之]上 也。”

我知它濠水上頭啊。”

I know it Háo River top."

⟶ 我知道它 [在] 濠水的 [橋] 上啊。”

I *came to* know it *from being* on [*the* bridge] *over the* Háo River."

⟹ 我在濠水的橋上知道魚快樂的啊。”

I came to know it from being on the bridge over the Háo River."

* This exchange plays on the two meanings of the word "安", which means both "how" in a rhetorical question and "where/from where/whence" in a literal sense, (e.g., Where does this come from?)

※請循其本…

莊子反駁惠子的法子是：

1.子能知我，我自然也能知魚。因為莊子的思想基本上是認為萬物是能彼此相通的：對此宋朝學者蘇軾曾作詩闡明

2.他故意利用＂安＂字兩種不同的含意，＂怎麼＂、＂從哪裡＂巧妙地混淆惠子問題的含意（從＂怎麼＂改到＂從哪裡＂）來機智地回答他

Let's return to the original question...

This is how Zhuāngzǐ rebuffed Huìzǐ:

1. "You can know me, so it naturally follows that I can know the fish." Because in Zhuāngzǐ's philosophy, he believes that all things in the world can communicate with and understand each other.

2. He deliberately played with the double meanings of the word "安" (meaning either the rhetorical "how" or the interrogative "wherefrom/whence") to ingeniously switch the meaning of Huìzǐ's original question (from "how" to "wherefrom/whence") and made a rather amusing and witty response.

蘇軾　　觀魚臺詩

欲將同異論錙銖，肝膽猶能楚越如。

Yù jiāng tóng yì lùn zī zhū, gān dǎn yóu néng Chǔ Yuè rú.

若信萬殊歸一理，子能知我我知魚。

Ruò xìn wàn shū guī yì lǐ, Zǐ néng zhī wǒ wǒ zhī yú.

Sū Shì　　A Peom on the Fish-Observing Terrace

If you want to discuss similarities and differences in their minute detail,

Liver and gall-bladder then will seem as far apart as the states of Chǔ and Yuè.

If you believe that 10,000 distinctions all converge in one principle,

Then, you can understand me, and I understand fish.

181

第二十六課

齊桓公使管仲治國

句子分析

一．　齊桓公 使 管仲 治 國。
　　　　　　＼ v o/s v o／
　　　s　　　　　　p

齊桓公命令管仲治國。

Duke Huán of Qí order Guǎn Zhòng govern state.

⟶齊桓公命令管仲管理國政。

Duke Huán *of* Qí order*ed* Guǎn Zhòng *to* administer *the* affairs *of* state.

⟹齊桓公命令管仲管理國政。

Duke Huán of Qí ordered Guǎn Zhòng to administer the affairs of state.

二．　管仲 對 曰："　　"
　　　　　＼ v v o／
　　　s　　　p

管仲回答説：

Guǎn Zhòng respond, say:

⟶管仲回答説：

Guǎn Zhòng respond*ed*, say*ing*:

⟹管仲回答説：

Guǎn Zhòng responded, saying:

二. 一 　　“賤 [者] 不 能 臨 貴 [者]。”
　　　　　　　　　　 \adv aux v o/
　　　　　　 s 　　　　　　　 p

※ 　賤　在文言中，形容詞用作名詞時，通常拿表示性質或特徵的詞來代表具有那種性質或特徵的人或事物。

In classical Chinese, adjectives that also function as nouns usually describe a characteristic or special quality of someone or something that can be used to stand for the person or thing possessing that quality or characteristic.

例如：　賤【形容詞】“卑賤、地位低”根據它在本句中的位置及功用，應看作是名詞語“賤者”下文的“貴”、“貧”、“富”、“疏”、“親”，都是這種用法。

EXAMPLE: The adjective "賤" means "lowly" or "of low rank and status". Given this word's position and function in this sentence, it should be construed as an adjectival noun meaning "the lowly," or as a noun phrase meaning "persons of low social status," "humble people," or "those who are poor." In the following passage, the adjectives "貴", "貧", "富", "疏" and "親" are all used in this manner.

“地位低不能統治地位高。”

"Rank low not able rule rank high."

⟶ “地位低 [的人] 不能統治地位高 [的人]。”

"[People *of*] low rank cannot rule *over* [people *of*] high rank."

⟹ “地位低的人不能統治地位高的人。”

"Those of low rank cannot rule over those of high rank."

三. 　桓公 以 [管仲] 為 上卿，而 國 [猶] 不 治。
　　　　 \v o/s v o/ conj \[adv] adv adj/
　　　 s 　　　　　 p 　　　　 s 　　　 p

※ 桓公以 [管仲] 為上卿：

這句話在形式上雖然像是意動繁句的結構 "S 以 [N1]為 N2",但是因為句中的主語 S "桓公" 已使兼語 [N1] (管仲)的身分有了變化,而不只是 存在主語心裡的一種想法,在性質上更接近於 使動繁句。文法學家乾脆就把這類的 "以… 為…" 句列在使動用法項下;並說:"以 此 (N1)為彼 (N2)" 如見之於事實就有 '致 使' (即使動) 的意思,如只存在心中就 有 '意謂' (即意動) 的意思。"(見 呂叔湘《中國文法要略》九八、九九頁。)在 這種含有致使意味的 "S 以 [N1]為 N2" 的結構中, "以" 字必須得譯成 "用",而絕不能譯成 " 把"。本句 "桓公以 [管仲]為上卿" 譯成白話應是 "桓公用 [管仲] 作上卿" 或 "桓公任命 [管仲]作上卿"。

Although this sentence has the syntactic structure of a typical **putative complex sentence** (S 以 [N1] 為 N2), the subject "桓公" caused the status of the pivotal term (N1) "管仲" to change: thus, it cannot be understood as expressing a thought which exists solely in the subject's mind; it is much closer in character to a **causative complex sentence**. Grammarians simply classify this type of "以[N1]為 [N2]" sentence under the category of **causative usage** with the addendum that if the action in the construction "以此 (N1)為彼 (N2)" is actualized in word or deed it has a **causative sense** (i.e., it expresses something that was in fact made to happen), whereas if the action exists solely in the subject's mind as thought, it has a **putative sense** (i.e., it expresses something brought before the mind as a thought or idea). (See Lǚ Shūxiāng, *Zhōngguó Wénfǎ Yàoluè*, pp. 98, 99). In "S 以 [N1] 為 N2" constructions that express a causative sense, the word "以" must be translated as "用" (to use or employ) and cannot be rendered as "把" (take or hold [someone] *to be*). The sentence under discussion (桓公以 [管仲] 為上卿) should be translated into spoken Chinese as "桓公用 [管仲] 作上卿" (Duke Huán used [Guǎn Zhòng] as prime minister) or "桓公任命 [管仲] 作上卿" (Duke Huán appointed [Guǎn Zhòng] prime minister).

桓公用作上卿可是國不太平。

Duke Huán use [ ] as prime minister, yet state not peaceful and orderly.

⟶ 桓公任命[管仲]作上卿,可是國家[還]不太平。

184

Duke Huán appoint*ed* [Guǎn Zhòng] first minister, yet *the* state [*of* Qí] *was* [still] not peaceful and orderly.

===> 桓公任命管仲作上卿，可是國家還不太平。

Duke Huán appointed Guǎn Zhòng the chief minister, yet still the state of Qí was not peaceful and orderly.

四. 桓公 曰：" "
　　　　　s　　　　p

桓公説：

Duke Huán said:

四.一　　　" [國]　[以]何故 [而] [猶] [不] [治]？ "

" 什麼緣故？ "

"What cause?"

——> " [國家] [因爲]甚麼緣故[還] [不] [太平]呢？ "

"[For] what cause *is* [*the* state] [still] [not] [peaceful and orderly]?"

===> " 國家因爲什麼緣故還不太平呢？ "

"Why is the state not yet peaceful and orderly?"

五. 管仲 對 曰：" "
　　　　　s　　　　p

管仲回答説：

Guǎn Zhòng responded, saying:

五．一　　　"貧[者] 不 能 使 富[者]。"
　　　　　　　　　　　　　　　adv aux v o
　　　　　　　　　　s　　　　　　　　p

"貧窮不能使喚富足。"

"Poor cannot order about rich."

⟶ "貧窮[的人]不能支使富有[的人]。"

"Poor [people] cannot order *about* rich [people]."

⟹ "貧窮的人不能差遣富有的人。"

"Those who are poor cannot order about those who are rich."

六．　　桓公 賜 之 齊國市租一年 ，而 國 [猶] 不 治。
　　　　　　v oi　　od　　　　conj　　　[adv] adv adj
　　　s　　　　　　p　　　　　　　　s　　　p

桓公賜他齊市場稅金一年，可是國不太平。

Duke Huán bestow on him Qí markets tax for one year, yet state not peaceful and orderly.

⟶ 桓公賜給他齊國一年的貨物稅，可是國家[還]不太平。

Duke Huán bestow*ed on* him *the* proceed*s from the* commodity tax*es of the* state *of* Qí *for* one year, yet *the* state *was* [still] not peaceful and orderly.

⟹ 桓公賜給他齊國一年的貨物稅，可是國家還不太平。

Duke Huán bestowed on him the proceeds from the commodity taxes of Qí for one year, yet the state was still not peaceful and orderly.

七．　　桓公 曰："　　"
　　　　　　　v　　o
　　　s　　　p

桓公說：

186

Duke Huán said:

七.一　　　　 "［國］ ［以］ 何故 ［而］［猶］［不］［治］？"
```
              [prep]  o
      [國]  [以]  何故  [而]  [猶]  [不]  [治] ？
              adv   [conj][adv][adv][adj]
      [s]                    p
```

Same as sentence analysis 4.1, p. 183.

八.　 ［管仲］ 對 曰 ： " "
```
      [管仲]  對  曰 ： "    "
               v   v    o
      [s]        p
```

回答說：

Respond, say:

⟶ ［管仲］回答說：

[Guǎn Zhòng] respond*ed*, say*ing*:

⟹ 管仲回答說：

Guǎn Zhòng responded, saying:

八.一　　　 "［與］［君］疏［者］不能制 ［與］［君］親［者］。"
```
          prep  o  adj pron           prep  o  adj pron
             adj mod                      adj mod
     "［與］［君］疏［者］不能 制 ［與］［君］親［者］。"
                    adv aux  v            o
              s                     p
```

※ 疏、親：

指人跟人的關係，根據上下文的意思，應補上
［與］［君］二字。

The words "疏"(distant; remote) and "親" (close; intimate)
refer to interpersonal relations; from the context, it is clear that
these terms describe relations with the ruler; so, the phrase
"［與］［君］" (distant [*from the ruler*]; close [*to the ruler*], intimate
[*with the ruler*]) should be understood before the words "疏" and
"親".

"疏遠不能控制親近。"

"Far removed cannot control near at hand."

⟶ "［跟］［君主］關係疏遠［的人］不能控制［跟］［君主］關係親近［的人］。"

"[People] distant *from* [*the* ruler] cannot control [people] close *to* [*the* ruler]."

⟹ "跟君主關係遠的人不能控制跟君主關係近的人。"

"Those distant from the ruler cannot control those close to the ruler."

九.　桓公 立 ［之］ 以 ［之］ 為 仲父，

　　s　　p1　　　　p2

※ 立：

【動詞】升登高位。在本句內是動詞的使動用法：使［　］升登高位。

"立" is a verb meaning "[to be] installed in a high position". In this sentence it is used causatively to mean: "cause [someone] to be installed in a high position."

※ 桓公以［管仲］為仲父：

意動繁句 "S以[N1]為N2"，一般的譯法是 "S把N1看作N2" (S takes N1 for N2)或 "S認N1為N2" (S regards N1 as N2). 本句中主語S是 "桓公"，N1是 "管仲"，N2是 "仲父"，逐字譯成白話是 "桓公把管仲看作仲父"，含意是 "桓公認管仲作仲父"，管仲身分之改變，完全憑桓公主觀的意願而決定，但卻影響到別人對管仲的態度。可看作是一種介乎 "意動" 與 "使動" 之間的繁句。根據桓公極力尊崇管仲的態度來考慮，這句話最恰當的白話翻譯應為 "桓公尊稱他（管仲）作仲父。"

The **putative complex sentence** " S 以 [N1]為 N2" is usually translated into spoken Chinese as " S把 N1看作 N2" (S takes N1 as/to be N2) or as "S認 N1為 N2" (S regards N1 as N2). In this sentence, the subject S is "Duke Huán"; N1 is "Guǎn Zhòng"; and N2 is "Uncle Zhòng". Translated literally character by character into spoken Chinese, this sentence means

"桓公把管仲看作仲父"(Duke Huán took Guǎn Zhòng to be Uncle Zhòng), which means by implication "桓公認管仲作仲父"(Duke Huán regarded Guǎn Zhòng as *his* Uncle Zhòng) This change in Guǎn Zhòng's status was decided solely on the basis of Duke Huán's subjective volition (i.e., how the duke personally thought of him) but was actualized in fact in how he was treated by other people. Thus, this sentence can be understood as a type of complex sentence that contains both putative and causative elements. In light of the fact that Duke Huán spared no effort in honoring Guǎn Zhòng, the most apt translation of this sentence into spoken Chinese would be "桓公尊稱他[管仲]作仲父。"(Duke Huán bestowed on him the honorific appellation Uncle Zhòng).

※按： "以N1為N2"的句式在語意上可以有一些細微的分別，關鍵在"以"字的含意和N1, N2之間的關係。這個句式基本上是**意動繁句**，如："王以和為誑。"有時可以看作是一種介乎"意動"與"使動"之間極特殊的繁句－兼有意動與使動的意思在一起的繁句，如："桓公以[管仲]為仲父。"但有時也可看作是**使動繁句**，如："桓公以[管仲]為上卿。"
意動繁句的標準句型"S以[N1]為N2",有時竟可直接看作使動繁句，可能就是由這種兼意動與使動的繁句過渡而來的。因此可以說：1)"王以和為誑"是純粹的意動繁句：即"王以和為誑"而和並不因此而真地為誑；2)"桓公以[管仲]為仲父"，管仲真地成了[桓公所謂的]仲父，換句話說，管仲的身分確實因桓公主觀的意願而有了些改變；所以"意動"和"致使"的意味同時存在並表現出來，可稱之為意動兼使動的繁句。
至於3)"桓公以[管仲]為上卿。"桓公的行為使管仲的身分有了改變，跟**使動繁句**"S使[N1]為N2"的用法毫無分別，可直接把它看作是使動繁句了。這些細微的分別與語意學及語用學有關，已超出語法形式（句型、句構）的範圍。但要徹底了解文言，同一句型中這些細微的區別還是很值得注意的。

NOTE:

The meaning of the sentence pattern "以 N1 為 N2" can subtly differ depending on the semantic sense of the verb "以" and the relation between the two nouns N1 and N2. Three principal distinctions in usage can be drawn. First, this is the basic sentence pattern for a **putative complex sentence** such as "王以和為誑" (The king thought Hé a liar). Second, it can be used in certain contexts to express a meaning that contains both putative and causative elements, as in the sentence "桓公以〔管仲〕為仲父" (Duke Huán thought of/regarded [Guǎn Zhòng] -- *and thus caused him to be thought of/regarded* -- as *his* Uncle Zhòng). Third, it can sometimes also be used as the sentence pattern for a **causative complex sentence** such as "桓公以〔管仲〕為上卿。" (Duke Huán used [Guǎn Zhòng] as *his* prime minister), in which the subject makes or causes something to happen to someone or something. In such cases, the typical **putative complex sentence** pattern "S 以 [N1] 為 N2" can be understood to have a purely causative sense: this usage can be seen as an extension of the sense already present in sentences that simultaneously express both putative and causative meanings. The following distinctions in the usage of this sentence pattern can be drawn:

1) **pure putative usage** expresses the thought of the subject and refers to mental activity. For example, the sentence "The king thought Hé a liar" merely states what the king *thought* about Hé: Hé did not in fact become a liar because the king thought him one.

2) **factive putative usage** expresses the thought of the subject *and* the real changes or conditions caused by it: this type of sentence contains both putative and causative elements. For example, in the sentence "Duke Huán regarded [Guǎn Zhòng] as *his* Uncle Zhòng", Guǎn Zhòng's actual status changed because the duke thought of him or regarded him as his uncle: the duke's subjective opinion had actual, tangible consequences -- he *caused* other people to treat Guǎn Zhòng with respect *by thinking* of him in this way. In this usage, the subject causes something to happen by thinking in a certain way.

3) **causative usage** simply expresses that the subject *caused* or *made* something happen to someone or something. In the sentence "Duke Huán used [Guǎn Zhòng] as *his* prime minister", Duke Huán's action literally caused Guǎn Zhòng's status to change. The sense expressed in this usage is identical to that expressed by the typical **causative complex sentence** "S 使 N1 為 N2", and such sentences can be understood as causative sentences, even though they use what appears to be a **putative complex sentence** pattern. While such fine distinctions in meaning are germane to the study of semantics and pragmatics, they transcend the scope of the basic syntactical constructions being introduced in this text. However, to understand the nuances of usage in classical Chinese thoroughly, such fine distinctions in the meanings of sentences with the same syntax should be noted.

桓公使登高位，以爲仲父，

Duke Huán have [ ] raise to high position , take [ ] to be Father Zhòng.

190

⟶ 桓公使[他]登上高位，尊稱[他]爲仲父，

Duke Huán cause*d* [him] *to be* raise*d up to a* high position *and* **referred to him** *with* respect *as* venerable *as my* father Zhòng.

⟹ 桓公把他升到極高的地位，尊稱他爲仲父，

Duke Huán raised him up to the highest position, and with all due respect called him Uncle Zhòng.

十. 齊國 大 安，而 遂霸 [於] 天下。
     adv adj/ conj _adv v [prep] o_/
    s   p1   p2

齊國非常安定，就終於霸天下。

Qí state extremely peaceful and in the end achieve hegemony (i.e., leadership) over all under Heaven.

⟶ 齊國就變得非常太平，終於稱霸[於]天下。

The state *of* Qí became extremely peaceful and orderly *and in the* end beca*me* know*n as the* hegemon *of* all under heaven.

⟶ 齊國就變得非常太平，終於成爲全天下諸侯的領袖。

Then *the* state *of* Qí beca*me* very peaceful and orderly and in *the* end **gain*ed* control** *over* all *the* feudal lord*s on* **earth.**

⟹ 齊國就變得非常太平，終於成爲全天下諸侯的領袖。

Then the state of Qí became a totally peaceful and orderly state and in the end gained control over all the feudal lords on earth.

十一. 孔子 曰：" "
       _v   o_/
    s   p

孔子說：

Confucius said:

191

十一.一　　　　“ [以] 管仲 之 賢，
　　　　　　　　　　　＼ s 　　 p ／
　　　　　　　[prep]　　　 o

“管仲的有才幹，

“Guǎn Zhòng's having ability,

⟶ “[憑]管仲那麼有才幹，

“[Rely*ing on*] one **hav*ing* such ability** *as* Guǎn Zhòng,

⟹ “憑管仲那麼有才幹，

“Even someone with Guǎn Zhòng's capability,

十一.二　　　　[管仲] 不 得 此 三權 者，
　　　　　　　　　＼adv v adj　 o ／ part
　　　　　　　[s]　　　　 p

※ 者：　　　 語氣詞，表示假設的語氣：
　　　　　　　　 “要是…啊，”

　　　　　　 A modal partical indicating a supposition:
　　　　　　 "supposing that..."

要是不得這三權啊，

if not get these three powers,

⟶ [管仲]要是得不到這三種權勢啊，

had [Guǎn Zhòng] not *been* able *to* get these three kind*s of* power,

⟹ 要是他得不到這三種權勢啊，

had he been unable to get these three kinds of power,

十一.三　　[則] 亦 不 能 使 其 君 南 面 而 霸 矣。”
　　　　　　[conj] \adv adv aux v o/s adv conj v/ part
　　　　　　　　　　　　　　　　　　　　　p

※ 面：　　【名詞】臉：用作動詞，面向，臉對著。“南
　　　　　　面”即“面南”方位詞作動詞賓語時通
　　　　　　常倒置在動詞之前。
　　　　　　“南面”在本句中又降格為副詞作動詞“霸
　　　　　　”的狀語。

　　　　　　As a noun, "面" means "face" or "visage"; when used as a
　　　　　　verb, it means "to face" or "to be facing"."南面" (south facing)
　　　　　　means the same thing as "面南" (facing south). **When
　　　　　　directional words function as the object of a verb,
　　　　　　they are generally placed immediately in front of the
　　　　　　verb rather than after it, as most objects are.** In this
　　　　　　sentence, the v-o construction "南面" functions as an adverbial
　　　　　　modifier describing the verb "霸" (i.e., "to be facing south acting
　　　　　　as hegemon). The word "而" simply links the adverbial phrase
　　　　　　to the verb in a subordinate grammatical relation.

※ 霸：　　在本句中用作動詞，“稱霸”；“作諸侯的領
　　　　　　袖”。

　　　　　　In this sentence, the word "霸" (which is also encountered as a
　　　　　　noun meaning "hegemony" or "hegemon") functions as a stative
　　　　　　verb: "to be called/acclaimed the hegemon [of the feudal lords];"
　　　　　　that is, "to be the leader of the feudal lords."

也不能使他的君主面南稱霸了。”

too not able cause his ruler facing south, bocome hegemon."

⟶ [那麼]也就不能使他的君主面向南方稱霸了。”

[then] certainly *he* too *would have been* unable *to* cause his ruler *to be
fac*ing south, acclaim*ed the* hegemon."

⟶ 那麼也就不能使他的君主面對著南方成爲諸侯的領
袖了。”

would, indeed, not *have been* able *to have* cause*d* his ruler *to be
fac*ing south, acknowledge*d* as *the* leader of *the* feudal prince*s*."

=⟹ 那麼也就不能使他的君主面對著南方成爲諸候的領
袖了。"

would, indeed, not have been able to have caused his ruler to be
facing south, acknowledged as the leader of the feudal princes."

第二十七課

知音

句子分析

一. <u>伯牙子 鼓琴</u>，<u>鍾子期 聽之</u>。

s   v o   s   v o

     p   p

伯牙先生彈琴，鍾子期聽它。

Master Bó Yá play lute; Zhōng Zǐqī listen it.

⟶ 伯牙先生彈琴，鍾子期聽他彈奏出來的曲子。

Master Bó Yá *was* play*ing the* lute; Zhōng Zǐqī *was* listen*ing to* it (i.e., *the* tune he *was* play*ing*).

⟹ 伯牙先生彈琴，鍾子期聽他彈奏出來的曲子。

Master Bó Yá was playing the lute; Zhōng Zǐqī was listening to the tune he was playing.

二. [<u>伯牙子</u>] <u>方 鼓 [琴] 而 志 在 太山</u>。

              v [o]

[s]   prep o conj s v o

        adv   p

正彈奏著意念在太山。

Just playing and intent on Mount Tài,

⟶ [伯牙先生]在彈著[琴]的時候，心思在太山那儿。

While play*ing*, [Bó Yá's] intent fix*ed on* Mount Tài.

⟶ 伯牙先生在彈著琴的時候，心裡想著泰山。

While play*ing*, Bó Yá's **thoughts dwelt on** Mount **Tài**,

195

===> 伯牙先生在彈著琴的時候，心裡想著泰山。

While playing, Bó Yá's thoughts dwelt on Mount Tài,

三． 鍾子期 曰：" "
　　　 s　　　 p

鍾子期說：

Zhōng Zǐqí said:

三．一　　　"善哉乎，[子][之]鼓琴。
　　　　　　　 p　　　　　 s

　　　 ※"善哉乎，鼓琴"：

　　　　　　 這是一句典型的倒裝句。"善哉乎"是謂語
　　　　　　 "善"再加上助詞"哉乎"，把它放在主語
　　　　　　 "[子][之]鼓琴"之前，表示強烈的讚嘆語氣
　　　　　　 。類似的例子，如："大哉孔子。" "善哉，
　　　　　　 子貢之言也"。

　　　　　　 This sentence is a representative example of **transposed
　　　　　　 sentence order**. The predicate "善哉乎" (Marvelous indeed!)
　　　　　　 has been moved to the head of the sentence, in front of the
　　　　　　 subject ([子][之]鼓琴/[your] lute playing) to accentuate the
　　　　　　 tone of exclamatory approbation. Another representative example
　　　　　　 of the **transposed sentence** (倒裝句) appears in the
　　　　　　 Confucian Analects: "大哉孔子。" "Great indeed is the
　　　　　　 philosopher Kung (Kǒng)!" (Legge, *The Confucian Analects*, p.
　　　　　　 216).

　　　 "真好啊！彈琴。

"Oh! how superb lute playing!

——— "真美妙啊！[您]彈琴。

"Oh! how superb [your] lute play*ing is*!

===> "真美妙啊！您彈琴。

196

Oh! how superb your lute playing is!

※句型變換：SENTENCE TRANSFORMATION:

[子][之] 鼓琴 善 哉乎
s 之   v o \adj/ part
         p
         s   p

您彈琴[的技巧]真好啊！

Your [skill at] playing the lute, oh! how superb!

"善哉乎，[子之]鼓琴。"可以還原成
"子之鼓琴善哉乎！"主語"子之鼓琴"是一
主謂短語，加上形容詞謂語"善"，構成一
個描寫繁句。為了翻譯成通順自然的白話文
，不妨把全句轉換成敘述句"子鼓琴善。"

If the word order in the transposed sentence "善哉乎，[子之]鼓琴" is changed back to the standard order of subject-predicate (s-p), the result is a **complex descriptive sentence** in which the word "善" functions as a predicate adjective: "子之鼓琴[s]善哉乎[p]." In this sentence, the clausal phrase "[子之]鼓琴" can be translated into English as a noun phrase "[your] lute playing". In order to translate this sentence into fluent spoken Chinese, it could be transformed into a simple narrative sentence by eliminating the clausal phrase construction: "子鼓琴善" ("You play the lute superbly.")

[子] 鼓 琴 善 哉乎 ！
    \v o comp/ part
[s]   p

彈琴彈得好啊！

Play lute - oh! how superb.

⟶ [您]彈琴彈得真美妙啊！

[Your] lute play*ing*, oh! how superb!

⟹ 您彈琴彈得真美妙啊！

Oh! How superb your lute playing is!

197

三.二　　　[琴聲] 巍巍乎 若 太山。"

[s]　　　　　p

高大雄偉像太山。"

mighty imposing like Mount Tài."

——→ [琴聲] 雄壯肅穆得像太山一樣。"

[*The* sound *of the* lute] *is* majestic *and* solemn like Mount Tài."

==⇒ 琴聲雄壯肅穆得像太山一樣。"

The sound of the lute is majestic and solemn like Mount Tài."

四.　　　[於] 少選之間，而 [伯牙之]志 在 流水。

adv　　　　　conj　　　[s]　　　p

短時內心思在流水。

Moments later, intent on flowing water.

——→[在]很短的時間內[伯牙的]心思轉到流水那儿去了。

[In] *a* few moment*s*, [Bó Yá's] intent turn*ed to* flow*ing* water.

==⇒ 過了一會儿，伯牙的心思轉到流水那儿去了。

A moment later, Bó Yá's thoughts turned to flowing waters.

五.　　鍾子期 復 曰："　　"

s　　　　　p

鍾子期又說：

Zhōng Zǐqī again said:

五.一   "善哉乎，[子][之]鼓琴。

See sentence analysis 3.1, pp. 194-6

五.二   [琴聲]湯湯乎 若 流水。"

洶湧澎湃像流水。"

Surging, crashing like flowing water."

⟶ [琴聲]洶湧澎湃得像流水一樣。"

[*The* sound *of the* lute] is surg*ing and* crash*ing* like *a* torrent."

⟹ 琴聲洶湧澎湃得像流水一樣。"

The sound of the lute is surging and crashing like a torrent."

六.   鍾子期死，

鍾子期死，

Zhōng Zǐqī die,

⟶ 鍾子期死了，

After Zhōng Zǐqī die*d,*

⟹ 鍾子期死了，

After Zhōng Zǐqī died,

七．　伯牙 破 琴 ，絕 絃 ，終身 不 復 鼓 琴 ，
　　　　　　ˇ ○　　 ˇ ○　　 　 ˇ ○
　　　　　　＼v ○／　＼v ○／　＼adv adv adv v ○／
　　　　s　　 p1　　　　 p2　　　　　　p3

伯牙摔破琴，折斷絃，一輩子不再彈琴，

Bó Yá destoy lute, break strings, for the rest of his life not again play lute,

——→ 伯牙把琴摔破，把絃折斷，一輩子再也不彈琴了，

Bó Yá smash*ed his* lute, snap*ped the* string*s, and to the* day *of* his death **never again** play*ed the* lute,

===> 伯牙把琴摔破，把絃折斷，一輩子再也不彈琴了，

Bó Yá smashed his lute, snapped the strings, and to the day of his death never again played the lute,

　　　　　　　　　　　　aux prep [○]　 v ○
　　　　　　　　　　　　　　 adj. mod.　　　　pron
七．一　　 以為 世 無 足 為 ［之］鼓 琴 者。
　　　　　　＼v　○/s　v　　　　　 ○　　　　／
　　　　　　　　　　　　　　 p4

認為世上沒有值得為彈琴的人。

think world not have worth-playing-lute-for one.

——→ 認為世上再也沒有值得給 [他]彈琴的人了。

for he felt that there was no longer anyone *in the* world worth play*ing* for.

===> 認為世上再也沒有值得為他彈琴的人了。

for he felt that there was no one left in the world worth playing for.

第二十八課

曾子辭邑

句子分析

一. 曾子 [衣] 弊衣 而耕 於 魯 ，
　　　　 \[v] 　o / conj \v prep o/
　　　　 _____adv_____ / p
　　s p

曾子破衣耕在魯，

Zēngzǐ wear old clothes and till in Lǔ.

——→ 曾子 [穿著] 破舊的衣服在魯國耕田，

Zēngzǐ *was* wear*ing* old, threadbare cloth*es, and* till*ing his* field*s in the* state *of* Lǔ.

══⇒ 曾子穿著破舊的衣服在魯國耕田，

Zēngzǐ was wearing threadbare clothes, and tilling his fields in the state of Lǔ.

　　　　　　　　　　　　　　[於之]
二. 魯君 聞 之 而 致 邑 焉 。
　　　　 \v o/ conj \v o prep-[o]/
　　s p1 p2

※ 焉： 指示代詞，指代範圍或方面，"焉"字等於"於之"（指人、物），"於是"（指地）。此處指人（曾參）。

The word "焉" is a demonstrative pronoun used to stand for a certain aspect of something or to delimit a general reference to persons, things, or places. It is equivalent to the prepositional phrase "於之" (LITERALLY: in/by/to/for/on him/her/it) when used in respect of persons or things, and to the phrase "於是"

(LITERALLY: in/at this/that [place]) when used in respect of location. Here "焉" means "於之" "[gave] *to him*" or "[bestowed] *on him*", where "him" refers to Zēngzǐ.

魯君聽它就送封地給他。

Lǔ's ruler hear it and bestow land on him.

⟶ 魯國的君主聽到這件事就送一塊封地給他。

The ruler *of the* state *of* Lǔ hear*d about* this matter and bestow*ed a grant of* land *and the people farming it on* him.

⟹ 魯國的君主聽到這件事就送給他一塊封地。

The ruler of the state of Lǔ heard about this matter and bestowed a benefice on him.

三． 曾子 固 辭 不 受 [邑]。
　　　　　\adv v adv v [ol]/
　　　s　　　　p

曾子堅決推辭不接受。

Zēngzǐ steadfastly decline, not accept.

⟶ 曾子堅決地推辭不接受那塊[封地]。

Zēngzǐ steadfastly declin*ed and did* not accept *the* [land] *and people*.

⟹ 曾子堅決地推辭不接受那塊封地。

Zēngzǐ steadfastly declined to accept the benefice.

四． 或 曰： " "
　　　　\v　　o/
　　s　　p

有人說：

Someone said:

四.一　"[此] 非 子之求[之]，[乃] 君 自 致之，

[子] 奚 固 辭 也？"

"不是您乞求，國君自己給它，爲什麼堅決推辭呢？"

"Not your seeking, ruler himself bestow it; what for steadfastly decline?"

⟶ "[這]不是您乞求[它]的，[是]國君自動送封地給您的，[您]爲什麼要堅決地推辭呢？"

"[This] is not something you *sought; it* is something *the* ruler gave you *on* his own; why *do* [you] steadfastly decline *to accept it*?"

⟹ "這不是您乞求的，是國君自動把封地送給您的，您爲什麼要堅決地推辭呢？"

"It is not that you sought it; the ruler bestowed it on you of his own volition; why do you so steadfastly decline it?"

五.　曾子曰："　"

曾子說：

Zēngzǐ said:

五.一　"吾 聞：'受人施者常畏人，與人者常驕人。'

203

我聽説：

I have heard:

```
        v   o    pron                    v  oi  [od]    pron
      adj.mod. pron                    adj. mod.    pron
‘ 受 人 施 者  常 畏 人 ；  與 人 [物] 者  常 驕 人 。’
            \adv v  o/                      \adv v  o/
      s          p              s              p
```

※ 驕：　　　【形容詞】驕傲。在本句中，用作動詞。

The word "驕" is usually encountered as an adjective meaning "haughty", "arrogant" or "overbearing"; but in this sentence it functions as a stative verb (i.e., it describes a state or condition -- to be overbearing [toward someone]).

※ 驕人：　對人表現出驕傲[的態度]。

Hence, the **v-o** construction "驕人" means "to be overbearing [toward] people"; that is, "[to exhibit a] haughty, arrogant [attitude] [toward] people."

'接受別人施捨的人常怕人，給別人的人常驕傲人。'

'Accept-other's-bestowal one often fear other; give-other one often overbearing other.'

——→ '接受別人施捨的人常懼怕施捨東西給他的人；送給別人[東西]的人常常對接受東西的人表現出驕傲的態度。'

'People *who* accept bestowal *from* another person often fear *the* donor; people *who* give [thing*s*] *to* others often *are* overbeari*ng* toward *the* people *who* accept them.'

===⟹ '接受別人施捨的人常常懼怕施捨的人；送給別人東西的人常常對接受東西的人表現出驕傲的態度。'

'Those who receive a benefaction often fear the benefactor; those who give things to others often treat the recipient with arrogant disdain.'

204

五．二　　　縱 君 有 賜 [於] [我]　不 我 驕 也，
　　　　　　conj \v o [prep] [o]/ \adv o v/ part
　　　　　　　s　　　 p1　　　　　　　 p2

※不我驕：在否定句中，代詞性賓語倒置在動詞
　　　　　之前。本句"不我驕"的意思是"不驕我
　　　　　"，但在文言中不用"不驕我"的詞序。

In negative sentences, pronominal objects (in this sentence the first person pronoun "我") are transposed from their usual position in the sentence following the verb and placed immediately in front of the verb that governs them. In this sentence, "不我驕" (not [to] me being arrogant) is equivalent in meaning to "不驕我" (not being arrogant [to] me, i.e., does not treat me with arrogant disdain/ is not overbearing toward me), but in classical Chinese the word order "不驕我" is **not** used in negative sentences.

縱然國君有賞賜，不驕傲我，

Even if ruler have grant, not overbearing me,

⟶ 即使國君有賞賜[給][我]，不對我表現出驕傲的態
度，

Even if *the* ruler ha*d a* benefaction [for me] *and was* not overbear*ing* toward me,

⟹ 即使國君有賞賜給我，不對我表現出驕傲的態度，

Even if the ruler were to bestow a benefice on me without displaying a haughty attitude,

五．三　　　吾 豈 能 勿 畏 [之] 乎？"
　　　　　　\adv aux adv v [o]/ part
　　　　　　 s　　　　 p

我豈能不畏嗎？"

I how able not fear?"

⟶ 我難道能不怕[他]嗎？"

205

how *could* I not fear [him]?"

⟹ 我難道能不怕他嗎 ？"

how could I not fear him?"

六.　孔子 聞 之 曰：" 　　 。"
　　　　ⱽ　ᵒ　ⱽ　　ᵒ
　　　s　　　　　p

孔子聽它說：

Confucius hear it (i.e., about this incident), say:

孔子聽到這件事說：

When Confucius hear*d about* this incident, *he* sa*id*:

孔子聽到這件事說：

When Confucius heard about this incident, he said:

六.一　"參之言 足 以 [之] 全 其節 也。"
　　　　　　　aux prep [o] ⱽ ᵒ part
　　　　s　　　　　　　p

＊"足以"：

這是由形容詞"足"（夠）和介詞"以"（用）結合而成的"合成詞"，作用像是個"助動詞"，譯成白話是"足夠用[它]來…"。因"足以"基本上用在表示被動性的主語之後，故最準確的譯法應該是"足夠被用來…"。由於句子的被動性很明顯，儘管省略了被字，聽的或看的人還是能了解，所以習慣上還是把它譯成"足夠用來…"或進一步簡化譯成"夠得上…"，聽起來更自然。但這時介詞"以"的意思也就淡化以至于消失了。

This is a **composite word** comprised of the adjective "足" (sufficient) and the preposition "以" (with/by); it functions in a sentence like an auxiliary verb and can be translated into spoken Chinese as "足夠用 [它] 來…" (enough to use [it] to/for...). Since this expression is almost always used after a subject conveying a passive sense, it should be rendered more precisely as "足夠被用來…" ([it] suffices to be used for..../sufficient to be used to....). Because the passive nature of such a sentence is obvious to the reader or listener whether the word "被" is expressed or not, the sense of this word is usually translated into spoken Chinese as "足夠用來…" (enough to use for) or even more simply as "夠得上…," (reaches/is up to [a certain standard or quantity]) This simple translation sounds even more natural, but the sense of the preposition "以" (with/by) in the original word "to suffice [to use] for" is lost.

"不足以…"

否定式："不足以…"，準確的逐字語譯應為"不夠被用來…"，簡化後可譯成"不夠用來…"甚至於譯成"夠不上 [用來]…"

The negative form of this word is "不足以…" (not to suffice for..../not be sufficient to...); this is rendered into spoken Chinese most precisely as (not sufficient to be used for.../to...) and more simply as (not suffice to use for.../not enough to use for...) or even just as (not up to [being used for...]).

"參的話夠用來保全他的節操啊！"

"Shēn's words suffice for keeping whole his integrity."

——➝ "曾參的話足夠被用來保全他的節操啊！"

"Zēng Shēn's remark *will be* sufficient *to be* use*d to* preserve his integrity."

===➝ "曾參的話夠得上保全他的節操啊！"

"What Zēng Shēn has said will suffice to preserve his integrity."

第二十九課

孔子猶江海

句子分析

一. 趙簡子 問 子貢 曰："   "

趙簡子問子貢說：

Zhào Jiǎnzǐ ask Zǐgòng, say:

⟶ 趙簡子問子貢說：

Zhào Jiǎnzǐ question*ed* Zǐgòng, say*ing*:

⟹ 趙簡子問子貢說：

Zhào Jiǎnzǐ questioned Zǐgòng, saying:

一.一.　　"孔子 為 人 何 如？"

| | ※為人： | "做人"是個動賓結構，但在本句中用作"何如"的主語，在此處的作用像是個名詞語，意思是"做人的態度"。 |

"做人"(to conduct oneself) is a verb-object construction, but here it is used as the subject of "何如"(what like?); it functions as a noun phrase meaning "the way one conducts oneself".

※何如：　　"如"是個準繫詞，"何"是個疑問代詞，合起來意思是"像什麼？"引申為"怎麼樣？"，"是什麼樣的？"

The word "如"(to be like) is a pseudo-copula (i.e., a word that resembles a linking verb like "to be" but which can be used as a copula only in certain contexts, e.g., in comparisons, as is the case with "如"), and the word "何" (what) is an interrogative pronoun. The combination "何如?" literally means "像什麼?" (is like what?); this sense has come by extention to mean "怎麼樣?" ("how?" or "how is it...?") and "是什麼樣的?" ("What kind [is it]?" or "of what quality [is it]?")

※為人何如：

"為人何如"本身是個小句，用作主語孔子的謂語。這類句子文法學家稱之為主謂謂語句，是包孕句的一種。（參看第二十四課《畫蛇添足》句析四，一六七頁）

"為人何如" (conducting oneself like what) is an independent clause (i.e., a sentence) that serves as the predicate of "孔子" (Confucius). Grammarians call this type of sentence an **s-p predicate sentence**, which in turn is itself a type of **embedding sentence**. (*Cf. L. 24, sentence analysis 4, p.167*).

"孔子做人怎麼樣？"

"Confucius conduct-himself what like?"

⟶ "孔子做人的態度怎麼樣？"

"Confucius' conduct *is* like what?"

⟹ "孔子做人的態度怎麼樣？"

"How does Confucius conduct himself?"

二． 子貢 對 曰："賜不能識也。"

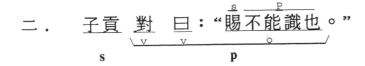

子貢回答說：

Zǐgòng responded, saying:

209

二.一   "賜 不 能 識 [之] 也。"
                   \adv aux v [o]/ part
              s   p

"賜不能了解啊。"

"Cì cannot understand."

⟶ "我不能了解[他]啊。"

"I cannot fathom [him] (i.e., Confucius)."

⟹ "我不能了解孔子啊。"

"I cannot fathom Confucius."

三.   簡子 不 悅 ，曰： "   "
                 \adv adj/ \v   o/
              s   p   v   p

簡子不高興，説：

Jiǎnzǐ, not pleased, say:

⟶ 簡子很不高興，説：

Jiǎnzǐ, not at all pleased, said:

⟹ 簡子很不高興，説：

Jiǎnzǐ, not at all pleased, said:

三.一   "夫子 事 孔子 數十年，
                    \v o   comp/
              s   p

"先生事奉孔子幾十年，

"Sir wait-on Confucius several decades;

⟶ "您追隨孔子追隨了幾十年，

"You accompan*ied* Confucius *for* several decade*s*;

===> "您追隨孔子追隨了幾十年，

"You accompanied Confucius for several decades;

三.二　　　[夫子]終業而去之；
　　　　　　　　　\v　o/　conj　\v　o/
　　　　　　　　　　　\p　　　　　　\p/
　　　　　　　s　　　　　　　p

完成學業才離開他；

complete studies and leave him.

——→ [您]完成了學業才離開孔子；

only *when* [you] complete*d your* stud*ies did you* leave Confucius.

===> 您完成了學業才離開他；

only when you had completed your studies did you leave him.

三.三　　　　寡人問[孔子][於]子，
　　　　　　　　　\v　[od]　　[prep]　oi/
　　　　　s　　　　　　　　p

※ 於：　　　介詞，介紹雙賓語句中的間接賓語
　　　　　　　"S 問 O1 於 O2"（S 向 O2 問 O1）
　　　　　　　是雙賓語句最完整的形式

The preposition "於" is used to introduce the indirect object in a **double-object sentence** (i.e., a sentence in which the verb must take both a direct and an indirect object to fully convey its meaning). Compare the following paradigms:

S 問 O1 於 O2 equals S 向 O2 問 O1

The paradigm "subject (S) asks of/about direct object (O_1) from indirect object (O_2)" is equivalent in meaning to the paradigm "subject (S) from indirect object (O_2) asks of/regarding direct object (O_1)." Thus, the full form of the **double-object sentence pattern** is:

S (subject) 問 O_1 (direct object) 於 O_2 (indirect object)

S (subject) asks of/about O_1 (direct object) from O_2 (indirect object)

211

本句"寡人問子"是"寡人問孔子於子"的省
寫。類似的句子如"葉公問孔子於子路，子路
不對。"《論語·述而》

The sentence "寡人問子" is a truncated version of the full
version of the sentence: "寡人問[孔子][於]子" [I asked
of/about [Confucius] (O₁) [from] you (O₂) = I asked you (O₂)
about [Confucius] (O₁). It is understood here from the context
that the question refers to Confucius. A model example of the
full form of the **double object sentence** pattern appears in
the following line from the *Confucian Analects*:
"葉公 (s) 問孔子 (o₁) 於子路 (o₂)，子路不對" "Duke Shè
(s) inquired of Confucius(o₁) from Zǐlù (o₂) , Zǐlù did not
answer back."
"The Duke of Shè asked Zǐlù about Confucius, and Zǐlù did
not answer him" (Legge, *Confucian Analects*, p. 210)

寡人問您，

Meagre virtue person question you;

⟶ 我 [向] 您問 [孔子]，

I ask*ed* you *about* [Confucius];

⟹ 我向您問孔子，

I asked you about Confucius;

三.四　　子 曰．[子] 不 能 識 [之]，

您說不能了解，

you say: 'Not can fathom.'

⟶ 您說 [您] 不能了解[他]，

you sa*id that* [you] *could* not fathom [him].

⟹ 您說您不能了解他，

212

you said that you could not fathom him.

三.五 [此] [為] 何 也？"
          \ [l.v.] pron/ part
     [s]   p

※ 何： "何"字是指事物或處所的疑問代詞，相當於白
        話的"什麼"。"何"字單獨用作謂語時，主要用
        來詢問原因，後面常跟著"也"、"哉"等語氣詞
        。可以根據上下文的語氣譯成"是什麼緣故呢
        ？"或"為什麼呢？"

        The word "何"is an interrogative pronoun used to refer to
        inanimate things and places. (It *never* serves as a personal
        interrogative pronoun, e.g., "who"). It roughly corresponds to
        the phrase "什麼" ("what") in spoken Chinese. When the word
        "何" functions as an independent predicate, it is used primarily
        to inquire about the reason for something and is generally
        followed by such particles as "也" or"哉." Depending on the
        context, it can be translated into spoken Chinese as "是什麼緣
        故呢？" (What is the reason for this?) or "為什麼呢？"
        (Why?)

什麼呢？"

What?"

——→[這緣故][是]什麼呢？"

What [is *the* reason]?"

===> 這是什麼緣故呢？"

Why?"

四 子貢 曰："   "
     s   \ v   o /
           p

子貢說："   "

Zǐgòng said: "   "

213

四.一　　"賜[之][事][孔子] 譬 渴者之飲[於]江海，

s ［之］［v］［o］　　　　　　s 之 v [prep] o

l.v.　　　o

s　　　　　　　　　p1

※賜譬渴者之飲江海：

"賜譬渴者之飲江海" 是準判斷繁句 "A (s [之] p) 譬 B (s[之] p)" 簡化了的寫法。如把省略的部分補出來，應該是 "賜[之][事孔子]譬渴者之飲[於]江海"。同樣的句型見於第十六課《君子慎所藏》句析三·一，一零一頁："[人之]與善人居，如[人之]入蘭芝之室"。

"賜譬渴者之飲江海" is a simplified version of the **pseudo-determinative complex sentence** pattern: " A (s [之] p) 譬 B (s [之] p). " If the omitted portion of this sentence were replaced, the sentence would read: "賜 [之] [事孔子] 譬渴者之飲 [於] 江海" (Cì's following Confucius is like a thirsty one's drinking from river/sea). *The same sentence pattern also appears in L. 16, sentence analysis 3.1, p.101:* "[人之]與善人居，如 [人之] 入蘭芝之室。"

"賜好比口渴的人喝江海，

"Cì is like thirsty one drinking river, sea;

——→ "我 [追隨孔子] 好比口渴的人在江海邊喝水，

"My [accompany*ing* Confucius] *can be* like*ned to a* thirsty person drink*ing at the* bank *of a* river, *or the* shore *of a* sea;

===⇒ "我追隨孔子好比口渴的人在江海邊喝水，

"My accompanying Confucius can be likened to a thirsty man drinking at the bank of a river or the shore of a sea:

四.二　　　知 足 而 已。

v o/ conj \v/

p2　　　p3

知道滿足就停止。

know enough, then stop.

214

——→ 覺得滿足了就停了。

One knows *one has had* enough *to drink* and *so* stops.

══⇒ 覺得夠了就停了。

When he has had enough, he stops.

四.三　　孔子　猶　江海　也，
　　　　　　＼p-l.v.　　pn／　part
　　　　　　s　　　　p

※猶：　　"猶"是個準繫詞，譯成白話是 "如同" 或 "像是"
　　　　　。"A (N1) 猶 B (N2) 也" 是標準的準**判斷句**，
　　　　　譯成白話是 "A (N1) 像是 B (N2) 啊，" 或根據比
　　　　　喻詞 B (N2) 的特點，進一步譯成 "A (N1) 像是 B
　　　　　(N2) 一樣 Adj. 啊"。

The word "猶"is a pseudo-copula equivalent in meaning to
"如同" (is the same as) or "像是" (is like) in spoken Chinese.
"A (N1) 猶 B (N2)也" is a standard **pseudo-determinative
sentence** pattern: it can be translated into spoken Chinese as
"A (N1) 像是 B (N2) 啊" (A (N1) is like B(N2)), or, if the
particular characteristic for which B(N2) stands as a metaphor is
expressed, more precisely as "A (N1)像是 B (N2)一樣 Adj.啊" (
"A (N1) is as Adj. as B(N2)" or "A(N1) is Adj. like B(N2)").

※孔子猶江海也：
　　　　　本句中"孔子"是"A (N1)", "江海"是"B (N2)". 江海的
　　　　　特點是深廣，故本句可譯成"孔子像是江海啊"
　　　　　或進一步譯成"孔子像是江海一樣深廣啊！"。

In this sentence, "孔子"is "A (N1)" and "江海" is "B
(N2)": the special characteristic singled out for comparison is the
deep and vast quality of a sea or a river. Therefore, the sentence
in question can be translated into spoken Chinese as
"孔子像是江海啊" (Confucius is like a river, a sea) or more
fully as "孔子像是江海一樣深廣啊" ("Confucius is as deep
and vast as a river, a sea", or "Confucius is deep and vast like a
river, a sea).

孔子像江海啊，

Confucius is like river, sea.

215

⟶ 孔子像是江海一樣深廣啊，

Confucius is deep *and* vast like *a* river *or a* sea.

⟹ 孔子像是江海一樣深廣啊，

Confucius is deep and vast like a river or a sea.

四.四　　　賜 則 奚 足 以 [ ] 識 之 ？ ”
　　　　　conj \adv adj prep [o] v o/
　　　　　　s　　　　　　　p

※ 足以：　　本句中介詞"以"字後省掉的賓語，即是和主語
　　　　　　相同的"賜"，含義是"賜之學識經驗"，在實際
　　　　　　的語言當中就簡化成"賜"。

In the sentence "奚足以[賜]識之", the object omitted after
the preposition "以" (to use/using; to take/taking; to rely
on/relying on; by/by means of) is "賜" (i.e., Zǐgòng), the
subject of the entire sentence. As the object of the preposition "
以", this proper name should be understood to mean by
extension *the experience and erudition of Cì.* To preserve a
laconic style of expression, this implied meaning would be
simply conveyed by referring to the person's name.
Synecdoche (a figure of speech by which a part is put for the
whole, the whole for a part, species for genus, genus for species,
name of material for things made from it.) and **metonymy** (use
of one word for another it might be expected to suggest) are
rhetorical tropes frequently encountered in classical Chinese.
Hence, the full import of this sentence (賜則奚足以識之？–
Cì, however, how enough to be used for knowing him?) is:
"How [could] it suffice to rely on [Cì's experience and erudition]
to fathom him?"

※ "奚足以 / 何足以"

"奚足以 / 何足以"準確的逐字語譯應為"怎麼
夠[被]用來…？"，簡化後可譯成"怎麼夠得上
…？"這是用反問的語氣表示否定："不足以
…"，"不夠用來…"，"夠不上〔用來〕…"

"奚足以 / 何足以"can be literally translated into spoken
Chinese character by character as "怎麼夠[被]用來…？"
(How could it suffice to [be] use[d] to/for), which can be more
simply put as "怎麼夠得上…？" (How could it suffice [to be
used] to/for?). Here a rhetorical question is used to express a
negative meaning. In classical Chinese style, an indirect
rhetorical expression of negation is generally preferred over a

216

simple negative statement such as "不足以⋯" (does not suffice [to be used] to...).

※ 賜則奚足以識之？

用反問句的結構 "S奚足以V - O?" 來表示否定的意思，"S不足以V - O" 目的在使聽者或讀者自己思索出這句話的真實含意，以加深印象及加強認同感；同時也可達到修辭上委婉、曲折、饒有餘味的目的。

This sentence uses a rhetorical interrogative sentence pattern (S 奚足以V - O?) to express a negative meaning (S 不足以V - O). A rhetorical question leads the listener or reader to infer for himself what answer is really intended or implied by the rhetorical question; it thus deepens the impact of the point being made and strengthens the listener or reader's sense of identification with the speaker. At the same time, by virtue of its indirect and euphemistic rhetorical tone, its subtle implications linger and resonate in the listener or reader's mind.

賜　則　奚　足以　識　之？"
conj \adv aux prep v o/
s　　　　　　　p

賜卻怎麼夠用來了解他？"

Cì, however, how enough for understanding him?"

⟶ 我的經驗跟學識卻怎麼夠被[　]用來了解他呢？"

Cì's experience *and* erudition, however, how *could it* suffice *to be* use*d to* understand him?"

⟹ 我卻怎麼夠得上（足夠用來）了解他呢？"

However, how could I ever be up to fathoming him?"

五．　簡子曰："　　　"
　　　　　　v　　　o/
s　　　　p

簡子説："　　"

Jiǎnzǐ said: "   "

五．一　　　善　哉　！　子貢之言　也。
　　　　　　　\adj/　part　　　　　　　part
　　　　　　　　p　　　　　　　s

※ 哉：　　感嘆詞。通常用在當作謂語用的形容詞後表
　　　　　示感嘆的語氣。中文的詞序基本上是主語在前
　　　　　，謂語在後。但感嘆句有時把謂語提到主語之
　　　　　前以加強感嘆的語氣。這種句子叫"倒裝句"。
　　　　　本文"善哉！子貢之言也。"是典型的例子。其
　　　　　他的例子如："大哉孔子！"《論語・子罕》參
　　　　　看第二十七課，句析三・一，一九六頁。

The word "哉" is an interjection that frequently appears after a predicate adjective (i.e., an adjective that completes the meaning of the verb, generally used after a copula (linking verb - "to be/乃") to identify or comment on the subject of the sentence. It emphasizes or intensifies the meaning of the adjective while conveying an exclamatory tone. In classical Chinese, the basic word order of a declarative or narrative sentence is subject-predicate (**s-p**). However, in an **exclamatory sentence** the predicate is sometimes transposed to the head of the sentence, in front of the subject. The **predicate-subject** word order intensifies the exclamatory tone by putting the predicate (in this case the predicate adjective "善") in the most prominent position in the sentence. This type of sentence (in which the usual word order is changed) is called a **transposed sentence** (倒裝句). One example of transposed word order appears in this lesson: "善哉！子貢之言也" (Admirable indeed [are] Zǐgòng's words). This is a representative example of the transposed sentence pattern. *Another model example appears in the Confucian Analects: (See also L. 27, sentence analysis 3.1, p.196)*

大 哉 (predicate adjective) 孔 子 (subject) !
"Great indeed is the philosopher Kǒng!"
(Legge, *Confucian Analects*, p. 216)

The rhetorical effect of the original sentence is mirrored in Legge's translation.

好啊！子貢的話啊。

Oh, superb, Zǐgòng's words!

——→ 子貢的話說得真好啊！

Zǐgòng's words *are* well s*aid* indeed!

218

⟶ 子貢的話真有道理啊！

What Zǐgòng *have said is* **indeed true**!

⟹ 子貢的話真有道理啊！

What you have said is indeed true!

第三十課

苛政猛於虎

句子分析

一． 孔子 過 泰山側，

　　　 s　　 v　　 p

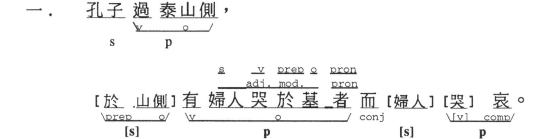

[於 山側] 有 婦人 哭 於墓 者 而 [婦人] [哭] 哀。

※ "婦人哭於墓者"：定語後置

文言中的名詞語通常是"定語＋中心詞"
(adjectival modifier + noun)，定語在前，被修飾
的中心詞在後，但有時作者要突顯中心詞，或
因定語太長，往往把中心詞提前而把定語放到
中心詞的後面去，然後再加上一個"者"字來
複指那個中心詞。例如："千里馬"是個名詞
語。"千里"是定語，"馬"是被修飾的中心
詞。為了突顯中心詞"馬"，把它提到前面來
，而把定語"千里"放在它後面，再加一"者
"複指中心詞"馬"，寫成"馬之千里者"，
或省寫成"馬千里者"。中心詞"馬"與定語
"千里"間的關係好像是分母（馬）與分子（
千里者）的關係。"馬之千里者"一字一字地
譯成白話應為："馬裡的每天能跑一千里的馬
"或"馬裡的每天能跑一千里的"，聽起來很
囉嗦。為求通順自然，仍然可以譯成"每天能
跑一千里的馬。"同理，"婦人哭於墓者"是
典型的定語後置的結構。"婦人"是被飾中心
詞，"哭於墓"是描寫"婦人"的定語。作者

要突顯中心詞 "婦人" ，同時定語 "哭於墓"
也較長，所以採取定語後置的方式寫成 "婦人
之哭於墓者" ，其實這個名詞語若照正常的詞
序寫成 "哭於墓之婦人" 也未嘗不可，只是表
達的方式比較平淡， "婦人" 一詞引人注意的
力量不那麼強罷了。

In classical Chinese, a noun phrase usually comprises an
adjectival modifier and the noun it modifies, with the adjectival
modifier preceding the modified noun. However, if a writer
wishes to highlight the noun in the sentence, or if the modifier
is too long, the modified noun is frequently placed in front of the
adjectival modifier, which then, instead of preceding it,
immediately follows the modified noun. In such cases, the
modified pronoun " 者 " is attached to the adjectival modifier to
refer back to or reiterate the modified noun. For example, " 千里
馬 " (a thousand *li* horse) is a noun phrase in which " 馬 ", the
modified noun, is modified by " 千里 ". If a writer wished to
highlight the word " 馬 ", he could move it in front of the
adjectival modifier " 千里 " and add the pronoun " 者 "
immediately after the adjectival modifier to refer back to or
reiterate the modified noun (馬). This construction (**noun +
adjectival modifier + 者**) would yield the following phrase:
" 馬之千里者 " (of/among horses a thousand *li* one). In the
noun phrase " 馬之千里者 ", the relation between the adjectival
modifier and the noun is comparable to that between a general
class or genus (馬) and a sub-class or species (千里); that is,
the modifier defines or delimits a class or group inside the
general category defined by the noun. Translated into spoken
Chinese, the noun phrase " 馬之千里者 " literally means " 馬裡
的每天能跑一千里的馬 " (of/among horses the can run one
thousand *li* every day ones) or " 馬裡的每天能跑一千里的 "
(of/among horses those able to run one thousand *li* every day).
In this construction, the relation between the adjectival modifier
and the modified noun is the reverse of the usual arrangement:
instead of sub-class [千里] modifying general class [馬], the
general class [馬] precedes the sub-class [之千里者]. For the
sake of smoothness, the wordy literal translation can still be
simply rendered in spoken Chinese as " 每天能跑一千里的馬
" (horses that can run one thousand *li* every day). " 婦人之哭
於墓者 " is likewsie a typical example of the "**noun +
adjectival modifier + 者** " construction. " 婦人 " (a married
woman) is the noun being modified and " 哭於墓 " (crying at the
grave) is the adjectival modifier describing " 婦人 " . Since the
writer wished to highlight the noun " 婦人 " in this sentence, and
since the adjectival modifier (哭於墓) is not short, he used the
"**noun + adjectival modifier + 者** "pattern and wrote " 婦
人之哭於墓者 " (of/among women the crying at a grave one).
This noun phrase could of course also be cast in the conventional
adjectival modifier-noun pattern as " 哭於墓之婦人 " (a
weeping-at-a/the-grave woman = a woman weeping at a grave);
but this mode of expression is rather bland, and the rhetorical
emphasis on the noun " 婦人 " is relatively diminished in this
construction.

孔子經過泰山旁邊，有婦人在墳前哭的而且悲痛。

Confucius pass Mount Tài's side. There is woman crying in front of grave, and dolorous.

——→ 有一次孔子乘車經過泰山旁邊的時候，遇見一個在墳前哭的婦人而且婦人哭得很悲痛。

Once when Confucius *was* pass*ing along* side Mount Tài *in a* carriage, *he* encounter*ed a* mar*ried* woman weep*ing* at *a* grave mound, and *the* woman *was* weep*ing* dolorously.

===→ 有一次孔子乘車經過泰山旁邊的時候，遇見一個在墳前哭的婦人而且她哭得很悲痛。

Once when Confucius was passing along side Mount Tài in a carriage, he came upon a married woman weeping at a grave mound, and weeping dolorously.

二.　　夫子 軾　而 聽 之，使 子 路 問 之 曰：" . "
　　　　＼v/adv conj v o/ ＼v o/s v o/ ＼v o/
　　　　s　　　p1　　　　p2　　　　　p3

夫子扶軾聽它，派子路問她説：

Master rest on railing and listen it. Send Zǐlù inquire her, say:

——→ 孔子扶著軾聽她哭，派子路去問她説：

Rest*ing his* hand*s on the* front rail *of the* carriage, Confucius listen*ed to* her wail*ing* , *and then* sen*t* Zǐlù *to* question her *by* say*ing*:

Confucius rest*ed his* hand*s on the* front rail *of the* carriage and listen*ed to* her weep*ing, and* sen*t* Zǐlù *to* question her *by* say*ing*:

===→ 孔子扶著軾聽她哭，派子路去問她説：

Confucius rested his hands on the front rail of the carriage and listened to her weeping, and then sent Zǐlù to question her by saying:

222

二．一　　"子之哭也，壹似［子］［之］重有憂者。"

※ 似…者：

這是個固定結構，由被飾代詞"者"與"似"、"若"等準繫詞配合，表示比擬(nǐ)，可譯成"好像是…似的"或"像是…的樣子"。

"似…者" is a formal construction in which the modified pronoun "者" is paired with such pseudo-copulas as "似" and "若" to express a comparison or simile. It can be translated into spoken Chinese as "好像是…似的"or"像是…的樣子"and into English as "to seem to be..." or "to seem like/as if...".

"您的哭啊，實在好像是重複有憂傷的事似的。"

"Your crying truly seem have had multiple troubles."

⟶ "您哭的程度啊，實在像是遭遇過好幾次傷心事的樣子。"

"Your so cry*ing* truly seem*s* like you *have* **repeatedly encounter*ed* msfortune.**"

⟹ "您那麼痛哭啊，實在像是遭遇過好幾次傷心事的樣子。"

"From the way you are crying, it truly seems like you have repeatedly encountered misfortune."

三．　　［婦人］［聞］［之］而曰："　　"

就說：

Then say:

⟶ ［那個婦人］［聽見］［這話］就說：

[That woman] [hear*d*] [it] *and* then sa*id*:

223

⟹ 那個婦人就説：

That woman then said:

三.一　　　　"[子之言] 然。昔者 吾舅 死 於 虎，
　　　　　　　　　　　　　　　　adv　　　＼v prep o／
　　　　　　　　[s]　　　p　　　　s　　　　　p

　　※死於虎："死在老虎口中。"也可看作被動結構："被
　　　　　　　老虎咬死。"

　　　　The phrase "死於虎" literally means "died in/from/by a tiger".
　　　　Here the implied sense of the passage is "died in the mouth of a
　　　　tiger." or "died in a tiger's jaws". This phrase can also be
　　　　construed as a passive construction meaning "was bitten to death
　　　　by a tiger" = "was killed by a tiger."

　　　"對，從前我的公公死在虎口，

　　"True. Past, my father-in-law die from/by tiger.

⟶ "[您的話]説得很對。從前我的公公被老虎咬死了，

"[What you say] *is* true. Earlier, my father-in-law *was **bitten to
death** by **a tiger***;

⟹ "您説的很對。從前我的公公被老虎咬死了，

"You are right. Before this, my father-in-law was bitten to death by
a tiger;

三.二　　　　吾夫 又 死 焉，
　　　　　　　　　＼adv v comp／
　　　　　　s　　　　　p

　　※焉：　　　指示代詞，指代範圍或方面。也有文法學家稱
　　　　　　　它為 "兼詞"，因為它兼有介詞 "於" 和代詞
　　　　　　　"是"（指地）、"之"（指人或物）的作用
　　　　　　　。此處 "焉" 是 "於之"，也就是 "於虎。"
　　　　　　　參看第二十八課，句析二，二零一頁。

　　　　The word "焉" is a demonstrative pronoun that refers to scope
　　　　or aspect (i.e., among a certain group or in a certain place).
　　　　Some grammarians refer to it as a **composite word** because it

combines the functions of the preposition "於" and the pronoun "是" (referring to a place) or "之" (referring to persons or things). Here "焉" means "於之" (from it/by it); "之" (it) refers to a tiger. "死焉" thus means "died from it/ by it" (i.e., was killed by a tiger). *See also L. 28, sentence analysis 2, p.201.*

我的丈夫又死在虎口，

my husband also die from/by it,

⟶ 後來我的丈夫又被老虎咬死了，

later, my husband *was* also **bitten *to* death by *a* tiger,**

⟹ 後來我丈夫又被老虎咬死了，

later, my husband was also bitten to death by a tiger;

三.三　　今　吾子　又　死　焉。"

今 = adv

吾子 = s

又 死 焉 = adv v comp / p

現在我的兒子又死在虎口。"

now, my son also die from/by it."

⟶ 現在我兒子又被老虎咬死了。"

now, my son *has* also *been* **bitten *to* death by *a* tiger.**"

⟹ 現在我兒子又被老虎咬死了。"

now, my son has also been bitten to death by a tiger."

四．　夫子曰："[汝]　何　為　不　去　也？"

夫子 = s

曰 = v

[汝] = [s]

何 為 不 去 也 = o prep adv v part

何...也 = o / p

※ 何為 ：　"何為" 是介詞語，"何" 是疑問代祠，意思是 "什麼"，作介詞 "為" 的賓語。文言中一般介詞語的詞序是介詞在前，賓語在後，如第十課 "子何不試之以足？" "足" 是普通名詞，應放在介詞語之後；"何" 是疑問代詞，用作介詞賓語時必得倒放在介詞之前；正如疑問代詞用作動詞賓語時必得到放在動詞之前一樣：如第六課："子將安之？" 但 "何為" 譯成白話時仍須譯成 "為什麼" 而不能譯成 "什麼為"。這是文言、白話間少數詞序不同的例子之一，值得特別注意。

"何為" is a prepositional phrase: "何" is an interrogative pronoun meaning "什麼" (what) that serves as the object of the preposition "為" (for). In classical Chinese, the usual word order in a prepositional phrase is *preposition - object*, as in "[子]何不試之以足？" (Lesson 10). "足" is a common noun, so it should be placed after the preposition "以". "何" is an interrogative pronoun; when it functions as the object of a preposition, it must be transposed in front of the preposition. When an interrogative pronoun serves as the object of the verb, it must likewise be placed in front of the verb, as in "子將安之？" (Lesson 6). However, when translating "何為" into spoken Chinese, it must still be translated as "為什麼" and cannot be translated as "什麼為". This is one example of the small number of differences in word order between classical and spoken Chinese and as such is worth noting. Although "何為" corresponds exactly to the word order of "what for" in English, it is better translated as "why" in most cases.

孔子説 ："為什麼不離開呢？"

Confucius say: "What for not leave?"

⟶ 孔子説 ："[你]為什麼不離開這兒呢？"

The master sa*id*: "Why *do* [you] not leave here?"

⟹ 孔子説 ："你為什麼不離開這兒呢？"

The master said: "Why do you not leave?"

226

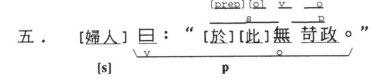

五．　[婦人] 曰："[於][此]無 苛政。"

　　說："沒有苛政。"

Say: "Not have harsh government."

⟶ [婦人]說："[在這儿]沒有暴虐的政治。"

[*The* woman] sa*id*: "[Here] *there is* no tyrannical government."

⟹ 婦人說："這儿沒有暴虐的政治。"

The woman said: "There is no tyrannical government here."

六．　夫子曰："小子識之，苛政猛於虎也。"

＊苛政猛於虎：

"N1 adjective 於 N2" 是文言中常見的描寫句句型。用作謂語的形容詞後面的介詞"於"字介紹比較的對象。"N1 adjective 於 N2" 的意思是"N1比 N2 還／更 adjective"。"苛政猛於虎"意思是"暴虐的政治比老虎還凶猛"。類似的例子如："米貴於玉"，"米比玉還貴"。

" N1 adjective 於 N2 " is a descriptive sentence pattern frequently encountered in classical Chinese comparisons, where N1 is compared with N2 in respect of some quality or characteristic (adjective). The preposition "於", which always follows the adjective in the predicate of the sentence, is used to introduce the target or object of comparison (N2). The meaning of the construction "N1 adjective 於 N2" is equivalent to the meaning of the spoken Chinese construction N1 比 N2 還／更 adjective.

N1 adj 於 N2 = N1 比 N2 還／更 adj
N1 adj 於 N2 = N1 is more adj than N2

227

The meaning of the sentence "苛政 (N1) 猛 (adj) 於虎 (N2)" in spoken Chinese is "暴虐的政治 (N1) 比老虎 (N2)還凶猛 (adj)" and in English "Harsh and oppressive government (N1) is more ferocious (adj) than a tiger (N2)." Another typical example of this pattern occurs in the sentence "米 (N1) 貴 (adj) 於玉 (N2)", which corresponds to "米 (N1)比玉 (N2)還貴 (adj)" in spoken Chinese and to "Rice (N1) is dearer/more expensive (adj) than jade (N2)" in English.

孔子説：“弟子們記住它，苛刻的政治比老虎更凶猛啊。”

Master say: "Young men, remember these words: harsh and oppressive government is more ferocious than tiger."

⟶ 孔子説：“弟子們記住這句話，暴虐的政治比老虎更凶猛可怕啊。”

The master sa*id*: "Young men, *take* note *of* this: tyrannical government *is* more ferocious *and* fearsome than even *a* tiger."

⟹ 孔子説：“弟子們記住這句話，暴虐的政治比老虎更凶猛可怕啊。”

The master said: "Young men, take note of this: tyrannical government is more ferocious and fearsome than even a tiger."

第三十一課

曳尾於塗中

句子分析

一．　莊子　釣　於　濮水，
　　　　　　　＼_v_prep_o_／
　　　s　　　　p

　　　莊子釣魚在濮水，

　　　Zhuāngzǐ fish at Pú River.

　　⟶　莊子在濮水邊釣魚，

　　　Zhuāngzǐ *was* fish*ing* by *the* Pú River.

　　⟹　莊子在濮水邊釣魚，

　　　Zhuāngzǐ was fishing by the Pú River.

二．　楚王　使　大夫二人　往　先　焉，
　　　　　　　＼v　o/s　　　v　v　prep-o／
　　　s　　　　　p

　　　　　※焉：　　指示代詞，在本句內同時含有"於是"、
　　　　　　　　　　"於之"兩層意思。，"是"指地（濮水）；
　　　　　　　　　　"之"指人（莊子）。

　　　　　　　　In this sentence the word "焉" functions as a demonstrative pronoun that simultaneously conveys the sense of the two prepositional phrases: "於是" where "是" refers to a place (i.e., the Pú River); and "於之" where "之" refers to a person (i.e., Zhuāngzǐ).

　　　楚王派大夫二人到濮水那兒去向他先容，

　　　Chǔ king dispatch two high officials to prevene him there,

229

⟶ 楚王派遣兩位大夫到濮水那儿去先見莊子說明他的願望，

The king of Chǔ sen*t* two high official*s to* go *to the* Pú River first *to* meet Zhuāngzǐ *and* make *the* king's wish*es* know*n*.

⟹ 楚王派遣兩位大夫到濮水那儿去先去見莊子說明他的願望，

The king of Chǔ sent two high officials to go there first to see Zhuāngzǐ and to make the king's wishes known.

三. [二大夫] 曰：＂願以竟內累矣。＂

說：

say:

⟶ [兩位大夫] 說：

[*The* two high official*s*] sa*id*:

⟹ 兩位大夫說：

The two high officials said:

三.一 ＂[楚王] 願 以 竟內 [之][事] 累 [先生] 矣。＂

＂希望拿國內煩勞了。＂

"Wish with inside the borders to burden."

⟶ ＂[楚王]希望拿楚國國內[的][事情]來煩勞[您]了。＂

"[*The* king *of* Chǔ] *has* now wish*ed* with [*the* affairs] *of the* realm *of* Chǔ *to* trouble [you].

⟶ "楚王希望請您到楚國來作宰相，管理全國的政事了 。"

"*The* king *of* Chǔ *has* now express*ed a* desire *to* **invite you** *to* **Chǔ** *as* **prime minister** *to* **supervise** *the* **administration** *of the* **whole kingdom**."

⟹ "楚王希望請您到楚國來作宰相，管理全國的政事 。"

"The king of Chǔ has now expressed a desire to invite you to Chǔ as prime minister to supervise the administration of the whole kingdom."

四． 莊子持竿不顧，曰："   "
　　　　　　ꞈv o／ ꞈadv v／ ꞈv   o／
　　　s　adv　　　p1　　　　p2

莊子拿釣竿不回頭看，說：

Zhuāngzǐ, hold fishing pole, not turn round, say:

⟶莊子拿著釣魚竿不回頭看，說：

Zhuāngzǐ, hold*ing his* fishing pole *and* not turn*ing the* head *round to* look *at them*, sa*id*:

⟹莊子拿著釣魚竿不回頭看，說：

Zhuāngzǐ, holding his fishing pole and not turning round to look at them, said:

四．一　　　"吾聞楚有神龜，
　　　　　　　　　　ꜱ v o
　　　　　　　ꞈv   o／
　　　　　　s　　p

231

"我聽說楚有神龜，

"I hear Chǔ have divine tortoise,

⟶ "我聽說楚國有隻靈驗的烏龜，

"I *have* heard *that the* state *of* Chǔ *has* a divine tortoise,

⟹ "我聽說楚國有隻靈驗的烏龜，

"I have heard that the state of Chǔ has a divine tortoise,

四.二　　　　　[神龜] 死 已 三千歲 矣，
　　　　　　　　　　　　　＼v　adv　comp／　part
　　　　　　　　[s]　　　　　　p

死已經三千年了，

die already three thousand years;

⟶ [牠]死了已經三千年了，

[it] *must have* died *more than* three millennia ago;

⟹牠死了已經三千年了，

that must have died more than three millennia ago;

四.三　　　　王 巾 [之] 笥 [之] 而 藏 之 [於] 廟堂之上。
　　　　　　＼v [o]／ ＼v [o]／ conj ＼v o [prep]　　　o　／
　　　　　　＼adv　　adv　　　　　　　　p
　　　　　　　s　　　　　　　　　　p

王用手巾包放在竹簍裡藏牠宗廟大堂的裡面。

king, wrap and put in a bamboo basket, treasure it in hall of　ancestral temple.

——→ 楚王用手巾包著［牠］放［牠］在竹簍裡地把［牠］珍藏
［在］宗廟大堂的裡面。

the king, wrap*ping* [it] *in a piece of* cloth，and put*ting* [it] in *a*　bamboo
basket, treasure*d* it [in] *the* hall *of the* ancestral temple.

===⟹楚王用手巾包著放在竹簍裡地把牠珍藏在宗廟大堂
的裡面。

the king wrapped it in a piece of cloth, put it in a rectangular bamboo
basket, and treasured it in the hall of the ancestral temple.

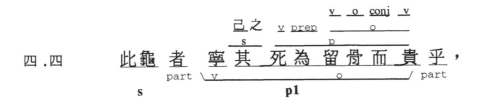

四．四

※句型

SENTENCE　　　S　寧　A　乎　　　寧　B　乎
PATTERN:　　　**S RATHER/PREFER A OR RATHER/PREFER B**

這是典型的選擇問句。前後兩分句各帶一寧
字，比較兩件事或兩種情況的利害得失，然後
決定選擇哪一種來行動。這個句型譯成白話是
"S寧願A呢，還是寧願B呢？

When two clauses in sequence each begin with the word
"寧", the advantages and disadvantages, merits and drawbacks of
the two situations or possibilities stated in these two clauses are
being compared in order to subsequently select one of them as a
course of action. This sentence pattern can be translated into
spoken Chinese as " S寧願A呢,還是寧願B呢？" (*Would* S
rather A or [rather] B?) This pattern can also be translated into
English as "*Would* S prefer A or [*would* S prefer] B?

此龜者寧其死為留骨而貴乎，寧其生而曳尾於塗
中乎？

龜　　寧願 A呢，還是寧願B呢？
Would the tortoise rather A or [would it] [rather] B?

A.　　其死為留骨而貴
其dying for leaving behind its shell to be honored

233

牠之死為留骨而貴
its being dead and having its shell left behind to be honored

牠之為留骨而貴 [而] 死
[rather] die for leaving behind its shell to be honored

B.　其生而曳尾於塗中
its living and dragging tail in the mud

牠之生而曳尾於塗中
its being alive and dragging [its] tail through the mud

牠自己活著在泥裡拖 [著] 尾巴 [爬]
[rather] live and crawl, tail dragging in the mud.

這隻龜啊，寧願牠自己為了留下背骨受重視死掉呢？
Now this tortoise, would it rather be dead and having its shell left behind to be honored,

還是寧願牠自己活著在泥裡拖尾巴呢？
or would it rather be alive and crawling, dragging its tail through the mud?

這龜啊，寧願牠死為留下背骨受重視呢，

This tortoise, would it rather die for leaving behind *its* shell to be honored,

——→ 這隻烏龜啊，寧願牠自己為了留下背骨受重視死掉呢，

Now this tortoise, would it rather be *dead and* have its shell left behind *to be* honor*ed*,

=====> 這隻烏龜啊，寧願牠自己為了留下背骨受重視死掉呢，

Now this tortoise, would it rather die in order to have its shell left behind to be honored,

四.五　　[ ] 寧其 生而 曳尾 於塗中 乎？"

寧願它自己活著拖尾巴在泥裡呢？"

234

rather live and drag tail in mud?"

⟶ 還是寧願牠自己活著在泥裡拖著尾巴爬呢？"

or would it rather *be* alive *and* crawl*ing*, drag*ging its* tail *through the* mud?"

⟹還是寧願牠自己活著在泥裡拖著尾巴爬呢？"

or would it rather be alive and crawling, dragging its tail through the mud?"

五．　二大夫　曰：" "
　　　　s　　v　　o
　　　　　　　p

兩位大夫說：

Two high officials say:

⟶兩位大夫說：

The two high officials sa*id*:

⟹兩位大夫說：

The two high officials said:

　　　　　　　　　　v　conj　v　o　prep　o
五．一　　　"[此龜] 寧 生 而 曳 尾 於 塗中 。" "
　　　　　　　[s]　　v　　　　　o
　　　　　　　　　　　　　p

"寧願活著拖尾巴在泥裡。"

"Would rather live and drag tail in mud."

⟶ "[這隻烏龜]寧願活著在泥裡拖著尾巴爬。"

"[The tortoise] *would* rather *be* alive *and* crawl*ing*, drag*ging its* tail *through the* mud."

235

===⟹ "這隻烏龜寧願活著在泥裡拖著尾巴爬。"

"The tortoise would rather be alive and crawling, dragging its tail through the mud."

六．　　莊子曰："　　"
　　　　　　　＼ v ＿＿ o ／
　　　　　s　　　　p

莊子說：

Zhuāngzǐ said:

六．一　　　"[子] 往 矣，吾 將 曳 尾 於 塗中。"
　　　　　　　＼ v ／ part　　＼aux v o prep o／
　　　　　　[s]　 p　　 s　　　　　p

"走吧，我要拖尾巴在泥裡。"

"Begone! I will drag tail in mud."

——⟶ "[你們]走吧，我要在泥裡拖著尾巴爬。"

"[You] Leave! I am go*ing to* drag *my* tail *through the* mud as I crawl."

===⟹ "你們走吧，我要在泥裡拖著尾巴爬。"

"Leave! I am going to drag my tail through the mud."

第三十二課

塞翁失馬

句子分析

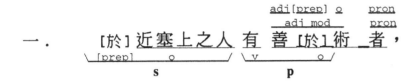

一． [於] 近塞上之人 有 善 [於] 術 者，

s　　　　　　　　p

※ 善術：　善[於]術
to excell at prognostication

在占卜方面很好
to be good at prognosticating

⟶ 很會占卜
to be *very* skilled at prognostication

其他例子：

OTHER
EXAMPLES:　善繪畫
to excel at painting [pictures]

善[於]繪畫
to be good at painting [pictures]

⟶ 很會畫畫
to be *very* skilled at painting [pictures]

近塞上的人有很會占卜的人，

Near-frontier people have good-at-prognosticating one,

⟶ [在]靠近邊界上的人[裡]有個很會占卜的人，

[Among] *the* people near *the* frontier, *there* was one person skill*ed at* prognostication,

⟹ 靠近邊界上的人裡有個很會占卜的人，

Among the people near the frontier, there was one skilled at prognostication.

237

二　　[其]馬 無 故 亡 而 入 胡，人 皆 弔 之。

馬無故逃進胡地，人都來慰問他。

horse, no reason, run away and enter the barbarians; people all console him.

⟶　[他的]馬無緣無故地逃跑進胡人的領土去了，別人都來慰問他。

[his] horse, *for* no reason, ran *off* and entered *the* territory *of the* northern barbarians; *the* other people all consoled him.

⟹　他的馬無緣無故地逃跑進胡人的領土去了，別人都來慰問他。

For no reason, his horse ran off into the territory of the northern barbarians; the other people all consoled him.

三.　　其 父 曰："此 何 遽 不 能 為 福 乎？"

他的父親說："這怎麼就不能成福呢？"

His father say: "This -- why then can't become good fortune?"

※　遽：　副詞，意思是"就"，通常與副詞"豈"、"何"、"奚"等合用，構成反問句。

The adverb "遽" meaning "就" or "then" is generally used in combination with the adverbs "豈"、"何"、"奚" etc. in rhetorical interrogative sentences; e.g., "何遽" which literally means "what then...?" "why then...?" or "how then...?"

※　何遽不能…乎？：
　　怎麼就不能…呢？　Why can't . . . ?
　　難道就不能…嗎？　Can it not be that. . . ?

⟶ 他的父親說：" 這件事怎麼就不能變成福呢？ "

His father said: "*As for* this, why then can't *it* become good fortune?"

⟹ 他的父親說：" 這件事怎麼就不能變成福呢？ "

His father said: "As for this, why then can't it become good fortune?"

四． 居 數月，其馬 將 胡駿馬 而 歸，人 皆 賀 之。

過幾月，他的馬帶胡人的好馬回來，人都賀他。

Pass a few months, his horse leading barbarian fine horses return; people all congratulate him.

⟶ 過了幾個月，他的馬帶著胡人的好馬回來了，別人都來向他道賀。

After several month*s had* pass*ed*, his horse return*ed* lead*ing* some fine barbarian horse*s*; *the* other people all congratulat*ed* him.

⟹ 過了幾個月，他的馬帶著胡人的好馬回來了，別人都來向他道賀。

After several months had passed, his horse returned leading some fine barbarian horses; the other people all congratulated him.

五． 其父 曰：" 此 何 遽 不能 為 禍 乎？ "

他的父親說：" 這怎麼就不能變成禍呢？ "

His father said: "This -- why can't become misfortune?"

239

⟶他的父親説："這件事怎麼就不能變成災禍呢？"

His father said: "*As for* this, why can't *it* become misfortune?"

⟹他的父親説："這件事怎麼就不能變成災禍呢？"

His father said: "As for this, why can't it become misfortune?"

六. 家 富 [於] 良馬，其子 好 騎，墮 而 折其髀，人 皆 弔 之

```
   \adj [prep] o /        \v  o /  \v conj\v   o /      \adv v o /
    s      p          s     p1    p2    p3      s    p
```

※富[於]良馬：

在良馬方面很富
wealthy [*in respect of*] fine horses

⟶ 有很多良馬
had many fine horses

其他例子：

OTHER
EXAMPLES:　富[於]才學
rich [in] talent and learning

在才學方面很豐富
rich [*in respect of*] talent and learning

⟶ 有很多才學
has a great deal of talent and learning

家裡多好馬，他的兒子好騎，摔下，摔斷他的髀骨，人都慰問他。

Household have many good horses: his son like riding, fall off, and break his thighbone; people all console him.

⟶ 家裡有很多好馬，他的兒子喜歡騎馬，從馬上摔下來，摔斷了他的髀骨，別人都來慰問他。

There were *now* many good horse*s in the* household: his son like*d to* ride, fe*ll* off *a* horse, *and* br*oke* his thighbone; *the* other people all console*d* him.

⟹ 家裡有很多好馬，他的兒子喜歡騎馬，從馬上摔下來，
摔斷了他的胯骨，別人都來慰問他。

There were now many good horses in the household: his son liked to ride, fell off a horse, and broke his thighbone; the other people all consoled him.

七． 其父曰；"此 何遽 不 能 為 福 乎？"

他的父親說："這怎麼就不能變成福呢？"

His father said: "This, why can't become good fortune?"

⟶ 他的父親說："這件事怎麼就不能變成福呢？"

His father said: "*As for* this, why can't *it* become good fortune?"

⟹ 他的父親說："這件事怎麼就不能變成福呢？"

His father said: "As for this, why can't it become good fortune?"

八． 居 一年，胡人 大舉 入塞，丁壯者 引 弦 而 戰。

　　　※ 丁壯者：名詞語，是 "丁[之]壯者" 的省寫
　　　This noun phrase is a short form of "丁[之]壯者"

丁[之]壯者
of/among adult males those [adult males] who are robust

⟶ 壯丁
robust adult males

相似的例：馬之千里者
⟶ 千里馬

SIMILAR
EXAMPLES: of/among horses those [horses] that can run 1000 *li* [in a day]

241

———→ a "thousand *lǐ*" horse

參看第三十課，句析一，"婦人哭於墓者"
的說明。二二零頁。

See Lesson 30, p. 220, the grammar note under **sentence analysis** 1.

過一年，胡人大規模入塞，壯丁拿弓去戰。

After a year, barbarians on large scale enter the frontier; adult males take up bows to fight.

———→ 過了一年，胡人大規模地發動軍隊侵入邊界，成年的男
人都拿起弓來去打仗。

After a year, *the* barbarian*s* mobilize*d* on *a* large scale *and* enter*ed the* frontier; all *the* adult male*s took* up their bow*s to* do battle.

═══→ 過了一年，胡人大規模地發動軍隊侵入邊界，成年的男
人都拿起弓來去打仗。

After a year, the barbarians mobilized on a large scale and entered the frontier; all the adult males took up their bows to do battle.

九.　　近塞之人，死者 十九，
　　　　s　　　　　　　s　　p
　　　　　　　　　　　　p

※死者十九：

"十九"是"十分之九"，不是"十九個"。
文言若說"十九個"，須寫作"十有（讀又）
九"，意思是整數"十"之外再加上零數"九
"，共"十九個"。

"十九" means "十分之九" or "of ten, nine," that is, "nine *out* of *every* ten" or ninety percent; it does not mean "十九個" or "nineteen". If one wishes to write "nineteen" in classical Chinese, it would have to be written as "十有 (read as 又 in the fourth tone) 九"; this literally means to the integer ten add nine, to get a total of nineteen.

※十九：

“十九”是名詞，意思是“十分之九”，在本句中用作謂語；譯成白話時必須得加上動詞“有”字。

“十九” is a noun phrase meaning “[of] ten, nine = nine out of *every* ten”. In this sentence it functions as a predicate; when the phrase is translated into spoken Chinese the verb “有” must be added and in English the verb “to be” must be added (The ones who died *were* nine out of ten).

近塞的人，死的十九，

people near frontier, dead nine of ten.

⟶ 靠近邊界的人，死掉的有十分之九，

Of the people near *the* frontier, nine *out of* ten die*d*.

⟹ 靠近邊界的人，死掉的有十分之九，

Of the people near the frontier, nine out of ten died.

十．　此　獨　以　[子]　跛之故，父子相保。

這個獨因瘸的緣故，父子相保。

This alone, by reason of being lame, father-son mutually safe.

⟶ 這個人家，單獨因為[兒子]瘸了的緣故，父親跟兒子彼此都沒受到傷害。

This family *was the* only *one*, by reason of *the* [son's] *being* lame, *with neither* father *nor* son injured.

⟶只有這家人因為兒子瘸了的緣故，父子還能平安地活在一塊儿。

Because of the son's be*ing* lame, *in* this family alone *were* father and son **still together safe and sound**.

243

===⟹ 只有這家人因爲兒子瘸了的緣故，父子還能平安地活在
一塊儿。

Because of the son's being lame, in this family alone were father and son still
together safe and sound.

十
一. 故 福 之 爲 禍 ， 禍 之 爲 福 ， 化 不 可 極 ， 深 不 可 測 也 。
    conj s 之 p(v-o)　　s 之 p(v-o)　　v ＼adv aux v/　adj＼adv aux v/ part
                                    comp.　　　　　comp.
                        s　　　　　　　　　p1　　　　　　　p2

故福變禍，禍變福，化不能窮，深不能測啊。

Consequently, fortune become misfortune, misfortune become fortune, this
transformation cannot exhaust; deep it is beyond fathoming!

——⟶ 所以福變成禍，禍變成福，變化得不能推究到盡頭，深
得不能測量啊。

Thus, *as to how* fortune become*s* misfortune *and* misfortune become*s*
fortune, *the* ultimate end*ing of* this transformation *is* unascertainable; *it is
of* unfathomable depth.

===⟹ 所以福變成禍，禍變成福，變化得不能推究到盡頭，深
得不能測量啊。

Thus, as to how fortune becomes misfortune and misfortune becomes
fortune, the ultimate ending of this transformation is unascertainable; it is
of unfathomable depth.

第三十三課

齒亡舌存

句子分析

一. <u>常摐</u> 有 疾，
　　 s　　 p

　　常摐有病，

　　Cháng Chuāng have illness.

　　——→ 常摐生病了，

　　Cháng Chuāng *fell* ill.

　　===> 常摐生病了，

　　Cháng Chuāng fell ill.

二. <u>老子</u> 往 問焉，曰 " "
　　 s　　　 p　　　 p

　　老子去他那儿問病，说：

　　Lǎozǐ go there to ask about it, say:

　　——→ 老子到他那儿去問候他，说：

　　Lǎozǐ *went to* him *to inquire after* him. *He said:*

　　===> 老子到他那儿去問候他，说：

　　Lǎozǐ went to him to inquire after him. He said:

二.一　　　　　"先生 疾 甚 矣，
　　　　　　　　　　　＼v　comp／　part
　　　　　　　　　　　s　　p

"先生病重了，

"Master, very sick now,

⟶ "先生病得很重了，

"Master, *you must be* very sick now.

⟹ "先生病得很重了，

"Master, you must be very sick now.

二.二　　　　　　　　　　　ex.o aux prep[o]　v ___ o　pron
　　　　　　　　　　　　　　　　adi. mod.　　　　　　　pron
　　　　[先生] 無 遺教可以 [之]語諸弟子者 乎？"
　　　　　　　　　　＼v _____ o _____／　　　part
　　　　[s]　　　　　　　p

沒有留下的教誨可以告訴它給弟子的嗎？"

Do you not have teaching to bequeath that can be told to disciple?"

※ 定語後置 ： POSTPOSITIONAL MODIFIER

　　　　名詞語通常是定語在前，中心詞（被描寫的名
　　　　詞）在後：如"良馬"，但是定語如太長，就
　　　　往往移置在中心詞之後，加一個"者"字來複
　　　　指中心詞。如本句定語"可以語諸弟子"移置
　　　　在中心詞"遺教"之後，加"者"字複指，就
　　　　是典型的定語後置的用法。參看第三十課《苛
　　　　政猛於虎》中"婦人哭於墓者。"本句還原為
　　　　正常的詞序應如下：

In a noun phrase, the adjectival modifier usually precedes the
noun being modfied, as for example in the phrase " 良馬 " (fine
horses); but when the modifier is considered too long, it is
frequently moved after the noun being modified and followed by
the word " 者 ", which functions as a pronoun that refers back to
the noun being modified and delimits the modifying phrase.

In this sentence, the modifier "可以語諸弟子" has been placed after "遺教", the noun phrase it modifies, and is followed by the pronoun "者". This is a typical example of the postpositional modifier construction (N + **modifier** + 者). *See Lesson 30,* "婦人哭於墓者." If this sentence were recast in the conventional word order of modifier + noun, it would be written as follows:

[先生] 無　可以語諸弟子之 遺教 乎？"

 ⟶ 您沒有什麼可以把它告訴給弟子的遺教嗎？"

Do you not have some teaching *to* transmit *to* posterity *that* can *be told* to *your* disciple?"

 ⟶ 您沒有什麼可以告訴給弟子的遺教嗎？"

Do you not have some **teaching *to* pass *on* that** can *be told* to *your* **disciple?"**

 ⟹ 您沒有什麼可以告訴給弟子的遺教嗎？"

Do you not have some teaching to pass on that can be told to your disciple?"

三．常摐曰："　　　　"

常摐說：

Cháng Chuāng said:

三.一　　"子雖　不問，吾將　語子。"

※雖：　　連詞，用在**讓步句**中，連接從句與主句。它出現在從句（前一分句）中，表示承認甲的存在，主句（後一分句）又說乙事實仍可

能發生或進行。如果是純粹地表示讓步，“
雖”字可譯成“雖然”；如果是一方面表示讓
步、一方面又表示誇張的假設，來加強主句語
氣的力量，就應譯成“即使”。根據上下文，
本句中的“雖”字譯成“即使”比較恰當。

The conjunction "雖" is used in **concessive sentences** to link the main and the subordinate clauses. It appears in the subordinate clause (the first clause) to express that although/even if the existence of fact/situation A is conceded, fact/situation B, stated in the main clause (the second clause) still can occur or continue to develop. If the sentence is purely concessive, the conjunction "雖" can be translated into spoken Chinese as "雖然"(although). If the subordinate clause is partly concessive and partly a hyperbolic supposition meant to intensify the expressive power of the main clause, then the conjunction "雖" should be translated into spoken Chinese as "即使" and into English as "even if". Given the context of this sentence, the more felicitous translation would be "even if."

"你雖然不問，我將要告訴你。"

"You though not ask, I will tell you."

——➝ "即使你不問，我也打算告訴你。"

"Even if you *did* not ask, I *was going to* tell you."

==➝ "即使你不問，我也打算告訴你。"

"Even if you did not ask, I was going to tell you."

四．　　常摐曰：“　　　”
　　　　　　　　　　\v_____o/
　　　　　　　　s　　　　p

常摐說：

Cháng Chuāng said:

　　　　　　　　　　v　o　conj v　o
　　　　　　　　[s]　‾‾‾‾‾‾‾‾‾‾‾‾‾‾
　　　　　　　　　　p
四．一　　"[人] 過 故鄉 而 下_車，　子 知 之 乎?"
　　　　　　　　extraposed object　　　\v_o/　part
　　　　　　　　　　　　　　　　　　　s　p

248

"過故鄉就下車，你知道它嗎？"

"Pass by ancestral village and dismount carriage; you know it?"

⟶ "[人]經過故鄉就下車，你知道這樣做的緣故嗎？"

"*When* pass*ing their* ancestral village [people] dismount *from their* carriage*s, do* you know *the* reason *for* it?"

⟹ "人經過故鄉就下車，你知道這樣做的緣故嗎？"

"When people pass their ancestral village, they dismount from their carriages; do you know the reason for it?"

五．老子曰："   "
　　　　　s　　　　p

老子說：

Lǎozǐ said:

五．一 "〔人〕過 故 鄉 而 下 車，非 謂 其 不 忘 故 耶？"

"過故鄉就下車，不是說他不忘舊嗎？"

"Pass ancestral village and dismount carriage, is not say one not forget origin?"

⟶ "[人]經過故鄉就下車，不是說他不忘故舊嗎？"

"*When* pass*ing by the* ancestral village, [*a* person] dismount*s from the* carriage; is *it* not *to* say one *does* not forget *one's* origin*s*?"

⟹ "過故鄉就下車，不是說一個人不忘故舊嗎？"

"To dismount from the carriage when passing by one's ancestral village, is this not to say one does not forget one's origins?"

六． 常摐曰：" 嘻！是已。"
　　　　　　　　　　exc.　adj　part
　　　　　\v_____o/

常摐説："啊！對啦。"

Cháng Chuāng say : "Ah! Right."

——→ 常摐説："啊！對啦。"

Cháng Chuāng said : "Yes it is, indeed!"

===→ 常摐説："啊！對啦。"

Cháng Chuāng said : "Yes it is, indeed!"

七． 　常摐 曰：" 　　"
　　　　　　　\v_____o/
　　　　　s　　　p

常摐説：

Cháng Chuāng said:

　　　　　　　　v　o　conj v
　　　　[s]　_____
　　　　　　　　　p
七・一 "［人］過 喬木 而 趨， 子 知 之 乎？"
　　　　extraposed object　　　　\v o/　part
　　　　　　　　　　　　　　　s　　p

"過大樹就小步快走，你知道它嗎？"

"Pass tall tree and walk hurriedly in small steps, you know it?"

—— "［人］經過大樹就邁著小步快快地走過去，你知道
　　這樣做的緣故嗎？"

"Passing by a mighty old tree [a person] walks by hurriedly with small steps; do you know the reason for this?"

===→ "人經過大樹就邁著小步快快地走過去，你知道
　　這樣做的緣故嗎？"

"When passing a mighty tree, one walks by hurriedly with small steps, do you know the reason why?"

八 . 老子 曰 ："   "
        \v   o   /
    s   p

老子說 ：

Lǎozǐ said:

八 .一   "[人] 過 喬木 而 趨 ， 非 謂 .敬老 耶 ？"

"Pass tall tree and walk hurriedly with small steps, is not say respect what is old?"

⟶   "[人] 經過大樹就邁著小步快快地走過去，不是說尊敬年長的人或物嗎？"

"Passing *by a* mighty *old* tree [one] walk*s by* hurriedly *with* small steps, is *this* not *to* say *such is* respect*ing the* old?"

⟹   "經過大樹就邁著小步快快地走過去，不是說敬老嗎？"

"To pass by a mighty old tree one walks by hurriedly with small steps, is that not to say one pays respect to what is aged?"

九 . 常摐 曰 ："嘻 ！ 是已 。"
               exc.   adj part
        \v   o/
     s   p

常摐說 ："啊 ！ 對啦 。"   (same as sentence 6)

Cháng Chuāng said : "Yes it is, indeed!"

251

十. 〔常摐〕張 其口 而 示 老子 曰: " "
\v o conj v o/ \v o/
[s] p1 p2

張開他的嘴來給老子看,說:

Open his mouth to show Lǎozǐ, say:

⟶ [常摐]張開他的嘴來給老子看,說:

[Cháng Chuāng] opened his mouth *to show the inside to* Lǎozǐ, say*ing*:

⟹ 常摐張開他的嘴來給老子看,說:

Cháng Chuāng opened his mouth and showed the inside to Lǎozǐ, saying:

十.一 "吾舌 存 乎?"
\v/ part
s p

"我的舌在嗎?"

"My tongue, exist?"

⟶ "我的舌頭還在嗎?"

"My tongue, *does it* still exist?"

⟹ "我的舌頭還在嗎?"

"Does my tongue still exist?"

十一 老子 曰: "然。"
\v o/
s p

老子說:"是的。"

Lǎozǐ say: "Yes."

⟶ 老子説：" 在。"

Lǎozǐ said: "Yes, *it does*."

⟹ 老子説：" 是的。"

Lǎozǐ said: "Yes."

十二　　　"吾齒　存 乎？"
　　　　　　　\ᵛ/　part
　　　　　s　　p

" 我的牙齒在嗎？"

"My teeth, exist?"

⟶ " 我的牙齒還在嗎？"

"My teeth, *do they* still exist?"

⟹ " 我的牙齒還在嗎？"

"Do my teeth still exist?"

十三　　　老子 曰：" 亡。"
　　　　　　　\ᵛ　　°/
　　　　s　　p

老子説：" 不在。"

Lǎozǐ say: "Not exist."

⟶ 老子説：" 不在了。"

Lǎozǐ said: "*They do* not exist *any more*."

⟹ 老子説：" 不在了。"

Lǎozǐ said: "They don't exist any more."

十四　　　　　常摐曰：“子知之乎？”

常摐说：“你知道它吗？”

Cháng Chuāng say: "You know it?"

——→ 常摐说：“你知道這樣子的緣故嗎？”

Cháng Chuāng sa*id*: "*Do* you know *the* reason *for* this?"

==⇒ 常摐说：“你知道這樣子的緣故嗎？”

Cháng Chuāng said: "Do you know why this is?"

十五　　　　　老子曰：“　　　”

老子说：

Lǎozǐ said:

十五、一　　　“夫舌之存也，豈非以其柔耶？

"舌在，難道不是因爲它軟嗎？

"Tongue exist, could not be from its soft?

——→ "舌頭還在，難道不是因爲它柔軟嗎？

"Now, *the* tongue's *still* exist*ing*, *would* it not *be* from its *being* soft?

==⇒ "舌頭還在，難道不是因爲它柔軟嗎？

"Now the tongue's still existing, is it not because it is soft?

十五、二　　齒 之 亡 也，豈 非 以 其 剛 耶？"
　　　　　　\s 之 v/ part \adv l.v. prep o/ part
　　　　　　　　s　　　　　　　　p

牙齒不在，難道不是因爲它堅硬嗎？"

Teeth not exist, could not be from their hard?"

——→牙齒沒有了，難道不是因爲它堅硬嗎？"

As for the teeth's not exist*ing, would* it not *be* from their be*ing* hard?"

===→牙齒沒有了，難道不是因爲它堅硬嗎？"

As for the teeth's not existing, is it not because of their being hard?"

十六　　　　常摐曰："嘻！是已。　(same as sentence 6)
　　　　　　　　　　　exc. adj part
　　　　　　　　　　　\v　　　o/
　　　　　　s　　　　　　p

常摐說："啊！對啦。

Cháng Chuāng said : "Yes it is, indeed!

十六．一　　　　天下之事 已 盡矣
　　　　　　　　　　　\adv adj/ part
　　　　　　　　s　　　　p

天下的事情已經窮盡了，

All matters under heaven have now been exhausted.

——→天下的事理人情都已經說完了，

All *the* principle*s of* human relation/behavior under heaven *have* already *been* thoroughly discuss*ed*,

——→天下的事理人情已經全都包含在內了，

255

All *the* principle*s of* human behavior in *the* world *have* **already**
been encapsulat*ed in* **this;**

⟹ 天下的事理已經全都包含在內了，

All the principles of human behavior in the world have already been
encapsulated in this;

十六．二　　　[吾] 無 ．.[所] 以 復 語 子 哉 ！"

(annotation above: [o] prep adv v o)
(annotation below: \v——————o——/ part)
[s]　　　　p

※ 無以：　是 "無 [所] 以 v-o" 的省寫，意思是 "沒有用來 v-o
的 N"。參看第一課，句析五．二，無以食魚，
第六頁。

"無以" is an abridged form of "無所以 v-o" (to have
nothing wherewith to...) *See L.1, sentence analysis 5.2, [I
would] have no way thereby to eat fish. p.6.*

※ 有以：　是 "有 [所] 以 v-o" 的省寫，意思是 "有用來 v-o 的
N"。

"有以" is an abridged form of "有所以 v-o" (to have
something wherewith to...)

沒有拿來再告訴你的啦！"

Nothing wherewith again tell you, truly!

⟶ [我] 沒有什麼拿 [它] 來再告訴你的 [話] 啦！"

[I] *do* not have anything more *to* say *to* you, truly!

⟹ 我沒有什麼拿來再告訴你的話啦！"

I do not have anything more to tell you!

256

第三十四課

晏子與楚王論盜

句子分析

一. 晏子 將 使 [於]楚。
　　　　\adv　v　[prep] o /
　　　s　　　　　p

　　　晏子將要出使楚。

　　　Yànzǐ about to envoy Chǔ.

　　⟶ 晏子將要出使 [到] 楚國去。

　　　Yànzǐ *was* about *to* go [to] *the* state *of* Chǔ *as an* envoy.

　　⟹ 晏子將要出使到楚國去。

　　　Yànzǐ was about to go to the state of Chǔ as an envoy.

二. 楚王 聞 之 ，謂 左右 曰：" "
　　　　　\v　o /　\v　o　v　　o /
　　　s　　p1　　　　　　p2

　　　楚王聽到它，告訴侍從說：

　　　Chǔ king hear it, tell retainers, say:

　　⟶ 楚王聽到這個消息，告訴侍從們說：

　　　When the king *of* Chǔ hear*d* this news, *he spoke to his* retainers say*ing*:

　　⟹ 楚王聽到這個消息，對侍從們說：

When the king of Chǔ heard this news, he spoke to his retainers saying:

二·一　"晏嬰 [乃] 齊之習 [於] 辭者 也。

"晏嬰齊的嫻習辭令的人啊。

"Yàn Yīng, Qí's good-with-words one.

⟶ "晏嬰 [是] 齊國的嫻習 [於] 辭令的人。

"Yàn Yīng [is] a man of the state of Qí skilled [at] rhetoric.

⟹ "晏嬰是齊國嫻習辭令的人。

"Yàn Yīng is a man of the state of Qí accomplished in rhetoric.

二·二　今 [晏嬰] 方來，吾 欲 辱 之，[吾] 何 以 也？"

現在快要來，我想辱他，用甚麼呢？"

Now about-to come; I want humiliate him: what use?"

⟶ 現在 [他] 快要來了，我想要羞辱他，[我] 應該用甚麼法子呢？"

Now [he] is about to come to Chu. I want to humiliate him; what means should [I] employ to do this?"

⟹ 現在他快要來了，我想要羞辱他，我應該用甚麼法子呢？"

Now he is about to come; I want to humiliate him: what means should I employ to do this?"

258

三．

侍從回答說：

Attendant respond, say:

⟶ 一個侍從回答說：

One *of the* attendant*s* respond*ed*, say*ing*:

⟹ 一個侍從回答楚王說：

One of his attendants responded, saying:

三．一 "為其來也，臣請縛一人，過王而行。

"當他來啊，臣請捆一個人，過大王走。

"At his coming, servant please let have bound a person, pass by king walk.

⟶ "當他來的時候啊，請大王讓我捆綁一個人，從大王面前走過。

"When he come*s*, please let your servant (i.e., me) *have* a person tie*d up and have him* **walk past your majesty** (i.e., you).

⟹ "當他來的時候啊，請大王讓我捆綁一個人，從您面前走過。

"When he comes, please let me have a man tied up and have him walk past you.

三.二　王曰：‘[此][乃] 何為 ＿者 也？’
　　　　　[s] [l.v.] adj mod pron part

大王説：‘幹什麼的人啊？’

Great king say: 'Do what one?'

⟶ 大王説：‘[這個人][是]幹什麼的啊？’

Your majesty *will* say: '[This person] [is] one *who* do*es* what?'

⟹ 您説：‘這個人是幹什麼的啊？’

You will say: 'What is this person doing?'

[臣] 對 曰：‘[此][乃] 齊人 也。’
　　 [s] [l.v.] p(n) part
[s]

回答説：‘齊人。’

Respond, say: 'Qí person.'

⟶ [臣] 就回答您説：‘[這個人][是]齊國人。’

[Your servant/I] *will* then respond *to* you say*ing*: '[This person] [is] *a* person *from the* state *of* Qí.'

⟹ 我就回答您説：‘這個人是齊國人。’

I will respond saying: 'This is a person from the state of Qí.'

三.三　王曰：‘[此] 何 坐？’，[臣] 曰：‘[此] 坐盗。
　　　　　　　　[s] p　　　　　　　　　[s] p

260

王説：'犯什麼罪？' 説：'犯偷東西的罪。'"

King say: 'What charge?'; say: 'charge robbery.'"

⟶ 大王説：'[這個人]犯了什麼罪？'[臣]説：'[這個人]犯了偷東西的罪。'"

Your majesty *will* say: 'What *is* [this person] charg*ed with* ?'; [your servant] *will* say: '[This person] *is* charg*ed with* robbery.'"

⟹ 您説：'他犯了什麼罪？' 我説：'他犯了偷東西的罪。'"

You will say: 'What is he charged with?' I will say: 'He is charged with robbery.'"

四． 晏子至，楚王賜晏子酒。

晏子到，楚王賜晏子酒。

Yànzǐ arrive; Chǔ king offer Yànzǐ wine.

⟶ 晏子到了，楚王賜給晏子酒喝。

Yànzǐ arriv*ed*; *the* king *of* Chǔ offer*ed* Yànzǐ wine *to* drink .

⟶ 晏子到了，楚王擺酒招待晏子。

Yànzǐ arriv*ed*, *the* king *of* Chǔ **lai***d* **out** *a* **banquet** *to* **entertain** him.

⟹ 晏子到了，楚王擺酒招待晏子。

Yànzǐ arrived. The king of Chǔ laid out a banquet to entertain him.

五． [至][飲]酒酣，吏二人縛一人詣王。

酒暢快，二小官儿捆一人到王前。

Wine happy, two officers tie up a person, bring to king.

⟶ [到] 他們喝酒喝到很暢快的時候，兩個小官儿捆著一個人到楚王面前來了。

When they *had drunk to* their hearts' content, two minor official*s* tie*d up* a person *and brought* him before *the* king.

⟹ 在他們喝酒喝到很暢快的時候，兩個小官儿捆著一個人到楚王面前來了。

When they had drunk to their hearts' content, two minor officials tied up a person and brought him before the king of Chǔ.

六. 王 曰："　　。"
　　 s　v 　　o

王説：

King say:

⟶ 楚王説：

The king *of* Chǔ sa*id*:

⟹ 楚王説：

The king said:

"縛者 [乃] 曷 為 者 也？"
　　　　　 o　v
　 \ l.v. p(n) part /
　 \ s 　　　 p 　/

"捆的人幹什麼的人啊？"

"Bound one - do what one?"

⟶ "捆著的人 [是] 幹什麼的人啊？"

"*The* bound man [is] one *who* does what?"

⟹ "捆著的人是幹什麼的啊？"

"What is the bound man doing?"

七． [吏] 對 曰： "[此][乃] 齊人 也， 坐盜。"

回答說： "齊人，犯偷東西的罪。"

Respond, say: " Qí person, charge robbery."

⟶ [兩個小官兒] 回答說： "[這個人][是]齊國人，犯了偷東西的罪。"

[*The* two minor official*s*] responde*d*, say*ing*: "[This person] [is] *a* person *from the* state *of* Qí *who is* charge*d with* robbery."

⟹ 兩個小官兒回答說： "這個人是齊國人，犯了偷東西的罪。"

The two minor officials responded, saying: "This is a man from the state of Qí who is charged with robbery."

八． 王 視 晏子 曰： "齊人 固 善 [於] 盜乎？"

王看晏子說： "齊人本來善偷嗎？"

The king, look Yànzǐ, say: "Qí people naturally good rob?"

263

⟶ 楚王看著晏子説："齊國人本來就很善[於]偷東西嗎？"

The king *of* Chǔ, look*ing at* Yànzǐ, sa*id*: *"Are the* people *of the* state *of* Qí innately skill*ed* [at] rob*bing?"*

⟹ 楚王看著晏子説："齊國人本來就很善於偷東西嗎？"

The king of Chǔ, looking at Yànzǐ, said: "Are the people of the state of Qí innately skilled at robbing?"

九．　晏子 避 席 對 [王] 曰："　"

s　　　　　p

晏子離座回答説：

Yànzǐ leave mat, respond, say:

⟶ 晏子離開了座位回答楚王説：

Yànzǐ le*ft his* seat *and* respon*ed to* him, say*ing*:

⟹ 晏子離開了座位回答説：

Yànzǐ left his seat and responded, saying:

九．一　　"嬰 聞 之，

s　　p

嬰聽説，

Yīng (i.e., I) hear it

⟶ 我聽説，

I hear*d* it (i.e., this *that* I *am* about *to* tell you)

⟹ 我聽説，

I have heard that ...

九.二 　橘 [若] 生 於 淮南 則 為 橘；[若] 生 於 淮北 則 為 枳。
　　　　　[conj]\v prep o/ conj\v o/ [conj] \v prep o/ conj \v o/
　　　　 s　　　 p1　　　 p2　　　　　 p3　　　 p4

橘樹生長在淮南就成爲橘樹；生長在淮北就變成枳
樹。

Mandarin orange trees grow in Huái south then become mandarin
trees; grow in Huái north then become citron trees.

⟶ 橘樹[如果]生長在淮河以南就成爲橘樹；[如果]
生長在淮河以北就變成枳樹了。

[If] *the* mandarin orange tree grow*s* south *of the* Huái River, then *it*
become*s a* mardarin orange tree;　[if] *it* grow*s* north *of the* Huái River,
then *it* become*s a* citron tree.

⟹ 橘樹如果生長在淮河以南就成爲橘樹；如果生長
在淮河以北就變成枳樹了。

If the mandarin orange tree grows south of the Huái River, then it
becomes a mandarin orange tree;　if it grows north of the Huái River,
then it becomes a citron tree.

九.三 　[其]葉 徒 相似，其實 味 不 同。
　　　　　　\adv adv v/　　　\ s adv adj/
　　　　 s　　 p1　　 s　　 p2

葉子白相像，它們的果實味道不同。

Leaves uselessly each other resemble; their fruits tastes not same.

⟶ [兩種樹的]葉子白白相像，它們的果實味道實在不
同。

[*The* two plants'] leave*s* uselessly resemble each other, *for the* taste*s*
of their fruit*s are* not *the* same.

===> 兩種樹的葉子白白相像，它們的果實味道實在不
同。

Their leaves uselessly resemble each other, for their fruits do not taste
the same.

九.四

[其] 所 以 然 者 [為] 何？

[其 所 以 然 者][乃] 水 土 異 也。

因之如此之故什麼？水土不同啊。

Wherefore like this reason what? Water, soil different.

※ 1) [其] 所以然者〔為〕何？
[Their] wherefore like this reason [is] what?

2) [其] 所以如此之故是什麼？
The wherefore like this reason is what?

3) [它們] 如此之故是什麼？
The they are beacuse of it like this reason is what?

4) [它們] 這樣的緣故是什麼？
The reason they are like this is what?

5) [它們] 為什麼這樣？
Why are they like this? (Why is this?)

※ [其所以然者][乃] 水土異也 = 是[乃] 水土異也
[Their wherefore like this reason] [is] water, soil differnt.

[這樣的緣故] 是因為 [淮南淮北的] 水土不同
[The reason for this] is that [south of the Huái River and north of the
Huái River] the water and soil are different.

這樣的緣故什麼？水土不同啊。

Like this reason what? Water, soil different.

266

⟶ ［它們］這樣的緣故［是］什麼？這［是］因為淮南淮北
的水土不同的緣故啊。

Why *are* [they] like this? This [is] because south *of the* Huái
River *and* north *of the* Huái River *the* water *and* soil *are* different.

⟶ 橘子變成枳子的緣故是什麼？這是因為淮南淮北的
自然環境不同啊。

Why *do* mandarin oranges become citrons？ Because the
natural environments north *and* south *of the* Huái River *are* different.

⟹ 橘子變成枳子的緣故是什麼？這是因為淮南淮北的
自然環境不同啊。

Why do mandarin oranges become citrons？ Because the natural
environments north and south of the Huái River are different.

九.五
今 民 生長 於齊 不盜 ， 入楚則盜，
adv ＼ v prep o adv v／ ＼v o conj v／
s   p1   p2

今民生長在齊不偷，入楚卻偷，

Now people grow up in Qí not rob; enter Chǔ then rob.

⟶ 現在人民生長在齊國不偷東西，進了楚國卻偷東
西了，

At present, people *who* grow up in *the* state *of* Qí *do* not rob; after
they have enter*ed the* state *of* Chǔ though, then *they start to* rob.

⟹ 現在人民生長在齊國不偷東西，進了楚國卻偷東
西了，

At present, people who grow up in the state of Qí do not rob; after
they have entered the state of Chǔ though, then they start to rob.

267

九.六   得無 楚之水土 使 民 善 [於] 盜 耶？"
            adv   ＼ v o/s adj [prep] v/o ／ part
                 s   p

＊ 得無…耶？

用推測的語氣委婉地表示肯定的意思：

A tone of supposition is used here to express an
affirmative meaning indirectly.

得無…乎？
Could not be...?

莫非…嗎？
Can it not be that ...?

別是…吧？
It isn't because ..., is it?

恐怕是…吧？
I fear it is ..., isn't it?

大概是…吧？
Probably   it is ..., isn't it?

莫非楚的水土使民善盜嗎？"

Could not be Chǔ's water, soil cause people good at robbing?"

——→恐怕 [是] 楚國的環境使人民很善 [於] 偷東西吧？"

I fear it [is] the environment of the state of Chǔ that causes people to
be particularly skilled [at] robbing."

====> 大概是楚國的環境使人民特別會偷東西吧？"

Probably it is the environment of the state of Chǔ that causes people to
be particularly skilled at robbing, isn't it?"

第三十五課

彌子瑕

句子分析

一. <u>昔者</u> <u>彌子瑕</u> <u>有 寵 於 衛君</u>。
　　adv　　　　　　＼v　o　prep　o／
　　　　　s　　　　　　　　　p

※ 寵：　　本來是動詞，在本句內用作名詞。"有寵"：
　　　　　"得寵"；"受寵"。"有寵於衛君"，逐字
　　　　　譯成白話是："從衛君那裡得到寵愛"；為求
　　　　　通順自然，通常改譯成"得到衛君的寵愛"或
　　　　　"很受衛君的寵愛"。比較"受命於君"，第
　　　　　十九課，句析五‧七，第一三四頁。

The word "寵" is generally encountered as a verb meaning " to [show] favor [to]", but in this sentence it functions as a noun (object) in the **v-o** construction "有寵" (to have favor [with]), which is equivalent in meaning to "得寵" (to get/obtain favor [from]) or "受寵" (to receive favor [from]), in spoken Chinese. Hence, in this sentence, the phrase "有寵" can be literally translated into spoken Chinese as "從衛君那裡得到寵愛" (to [have] obtained favor from the ruler of Wèi = was favored by the ruler of Wèi). To achieve a smoother, more natural tone, it is generally translated instead as "得到衛君的寵愛" (to be favored by the ruler of Wèi) or "很受衛君的寵愛". Compare this construction with the similar construction "受命於君" (to receive an order from the ruler = to be ordered by the ruler [to do something]). *Discussed in Lesson 19, **sentence analysis** 5.7, p. 134.*

從前彌子瑕從衛君得寵。

Formerly, Mí Zǐxiá from Wèi ruler get favor.

——→ 從前彌子瑕得到衞國君主的寵愛。

Formerly, Mí Zǐxiá **obtain**ed *the* favor of *the* ruler *of the* state *of* Wèi.

269

===> 從前彌子瑕很受衛國君主的寵愛。

Once, Mí Zǐxiá was well-loved by the ruler of the state of Wèi.

二　　衛國之法：竊駕君車者，罪刖。
　　　　s　　　　　　　　p

※ ：　　　是標點符號中所謂的"冒號"，在句子裡用來
　　　　提示下文。如果在冒號前有主語 (subject) 與動詞
　　　　(verb) 如 "子曰"，那麼冒號後的部分就是動詞
　　　　"曰" 的賓語 (object)；如果在冒號前只有一個
　　　　名詞 (noun) 如 "彌子瑕" 或有一個名詞語 (noun
　　　　phrase) 如 "衛國之法"，那麼這個冒號在句中
　　　　的作用就大致相當於繫詞 "是"，用來說明 "n
　　　　" 是什麼樣子的。

The colon is used in contemporary punctuation of classical
Chinese to grammatically set off the grammatical element that
precedes it (usually the subject or the topic of the sentence) from
what follows it (usually the predicate or comment on the topic);
that is, it divides the sentence into grammatical units. If a
subject and a verb precede the colon (e.g., " 子 (s) 曰 (p)"/ the
master said), then what follows it should be construed as the
object of the verb (in this case, the verb " 曰 "). If a noun (e.g.,
"彌子瑕") or a noun phrase (e.g., "衛國之法") precedes the
colon, then the colon functions like a copula (a linking verb,
e.g. "乃") and is used to separate the noun or noun phrase from
its qualifier (Note: Classical Chinese was originally written
without punctuation. Modern punctuation is used to help clarify
the structure of a classical sentence--in the second example (i.e.,
"衛國之法")by using the colon (:) to indicate where a linking
verb was understood but not expressed in the sentence.)

衛國的法：

Wèi state's law:

——> 衛國的法律是 …

According to the law *of* Wèi:

===> 衛國的法律是 …

According to the law of Wèi:

二.一
    竊　駕　君車　者，　[其]罪　[為]　刖

（adv　v　o　pron / adj.mod. pron）

偷著駕駛君主車子的人刑罰砍斷腳。

illicitly drive ruler's carriage one, punishment - cut off foot.

⟶ 偷著駕駛君主車子的人 [他的] 刑罰 [是] 砍斷腳。

One *who* drive*s the* ruler's carriage illicitly, [his] punishment *shall* [be] *the* cut*ting* off *of* one foot.

⟹ 偷著駕駛君主車子的人，他的刑罰是砍斷腳。

Whosoever drives the ruler's carriage illicitly shall be punished by having one foot cut off.

三.
    彌子瑕　母病，人聞 [之] ，有夜告彌子 [者] 。

（adv　v　o　[pron] / adj. mod [pron]）

彌子瑕母親病，人聽到，有在夜裡告訴彌子。

Mí Zǐxiá's mother sick, people hear; have at night tell-Mízǐ one.

⟶ 彌子瑕母親病了，別人聽到了 [它／這個消息] ，有個在夜裡告訴彌子 [的人] 。

When Mí Zǐxiá's mother bec*ame* ill, people hear*d* [*about* it/*the* news]; ha*d* a *told* Mízǐ during *the* night [person].

⟹ 彌子瑕母親病了，別人聽到了這個消息，有人在夜裡告訴彌子。

When Mí Zǐxiá's mother became ill, someone who had heard the news told Mízǐ during the night.

271

四．　彌子 矯 駕 君 車 以 出 [於] [宮]。
　　　　　＼adv v o／ conj ＼[prep] [o]／
　　　　　　＼　adv　／　　　　v [compl]／
　　　s　　　　　　　　　p

　　　　　　　　　※以：　　本來是介詞，但在本句中的作用與"而"字相
　　　　　　　　　　　　　　同，用作陪從連詞。"以"前面的部分 (矯駕
　　　　　　　　　　　　　　君車) 雖然本來是動詞語(動賓結構)，但降格為
　　　　　　　　　　　　　　副詞，用來描寫"以"字後面的動詞(出)。

　　　　　　　　　　　　The word "以" is primarily encountered as a preposition
　　　　　　　　　　　　meaning "in", "by", "through", "by means of", "so as to", "in
　　　　　　　　　　　　order to", etc.; but it can also serve as a coordinating
　　　　　　　　　　　　conjunction. When it is used as a conjunction, it functions like
　　　　　　　　　　　　the word "而" does when it links an adverbial modifier to a verb.
　　　　　　　　　　　　Although the clause preceding the word "以" (矯駕君車 / to
　　　　　　　　　　　　feign permission to drive the ruler's carriage) is a complete
　　　　　　　　　　　　predicate (i.e., a verb-object (**v-o**) construction), it plays a
　　　　　　　　　　　　subsidiary grammatical role in this sentence, serving only as an
　　　　　　　　　　　　adverbial phrase modifying the verb immediately following the
　　　　　　　　　　　　word "以" (in this case, 出 / to go out). This construction
　　　　　　　　　　　　(**adverbial phrase/v-o** + 以 + **verb**) can be translated into
　　　　　　　　　　　　English by rendering what precedes the conjunction "以" as a
　　　　　　　　　　　　participial phrase (left [the palace] *having feigned permission to
　　　　　　　　　　　　drive the ruler's carriage*)

　　　　　彌子假託命地駕君主的車子出去。

　　　　　Mízǐ feign permission drive ruler's carriage, exit.

　　　⟶　彌子騙人説是君主的命令地駕著君主的車子 [從] [宮裡]
　　　　　出去了。

　　　　　Mízǐ, feign*ing* permission *to* drive *the* ruler's carriage, exit*ed* [from] [*the*
　　　　　palace].

　　　⟹　彌子騙人説是君主的命令地駕著君主的車子從宮裡出去
　　　　　了。

　　　　　Having feigned permission to drive the ruler's carriage, Mízǐ left the palace.

五．　君 聞 [之] 而 賢 之 曰："　　"
　　　　＼v [o]／ conj ＼adj/v o／＼v　　o／
　　　s　　p1　　　　　　p2　　　　p3

272

君主聽到就以之爲賢説：

Ruler hear and think him worthy, say:

⟶ 君主聽到[它]就認爲彌子很高尚説：

The ruler hear*d of* [this] *and* consider*ed* Mízǐ *to be* worthy, say*ing*:

⟹ 君主聽到這件事就誇獎彌子説：

The ruler heard of this and found him praiseworthy, saying:

五.一 " 孝哉！[彌子瑕]
　　　　 p　　　[s]

" [彌子瑕] 孝　哉！
　　　　　　　　\adj/ part
　[s]　　　p

" 孝順啊 !

"Filial!

⟶ " [彌子瑕]真孝順啊 !

"[Mí Zǐxiá] *is* indeed filial!

⟹ " 彌子瑕真孝順啊 !

"How filial he is!

　　　　　　　　　　　　　　 他之. v o
　　　　　　　　　　　　　 s [之]　 p
五.二　 [彌子瑕] 爲 母之故，忘 其 犯 刖 罪。"
　　　　　　　　 \prep o　 v　　 o
　　　[s]　　　　　　　　p

爲母親的緣故，忘記他犯砍斷腳的罪。"

For mother's sake, forget his committing offense punishable by cutting off one foot."

273

——→ ［彌子瑕］為了母親的緣故，忘記他自己犯了砍斷腳的罪。"

On account of *his* mother, [Mí Zǐxia] forg*ot that* he *was* commit*ting an* offense punishable by *the* cut*ting* off *of* one foot."

===⟹他為了母親的緣故，忘記自己犯了砍斷腳的罪。"

On account of his mother, he forgot that he was committing an offense punishable by having one foot cut off."

六． 異日［彌子瑕］　與　君　遊　於　果園。
　　　　adv
　　　　　　［s］　　　 prep　o　v　prep　o
　　　　　　　　　　　　　　　　　p

另一天，跟君主在果園閒遊。

Another day, with ruler stroll in orchard.

——→ 另一天，［彌子瑕］跟君主一塊儿在果園裡閒遊。

One day, *when* [Mí Zǐxiá] *was* stroll*ing* with *the* ruler in *an* orchard.

===⟹另一天，彌子瑕跟君主一塊儿在果園裡閒遊。

One day, Mí Zǐxiá was strolling through an orchard with the ruler.

七． ［彌子瑕］食　桃　而　甘［之］，不　盡［之］，　以　半　啗　君。
　　　　　　　 v　o　conj　v　[o]　adv　v　[o]　prep　o　v　o
　　　　　　［s］　 p1　　　　p2　　　　p3　　　　p4

　　　＊ 甘：　　 本來是形容詞，在本句內用作動詞，意
　　　　　　　　 動用法，它後面省略了賓語"之"。"甘
　　　　　　　　 ［之］"："以之為甘"，"以為它甜"。

The word "甘" is usually encountered as an adjective meaning "sweet", but in this sentence it is being used as a putative verb (i.e., to think [something] to be sweet), the object "之" being understood and omitted. Hence the full form of the predicate would be

274

"甘[之]", which is equivalent in meaning to "以之為甜" (think it to be sweet), or in spoken Chinese "以為它甜" (think [to oneself that] it/the peach is sweet).

※ 啗：　動詞，吃。"啗君"從本句的上下文看當然不是"吃君主"，而是"使君主吃"。這是動詞使動用法的佳例。

The word "啗" is a verb meaning "to eat". Viewed in the context of this passage, the phrase "啗君" certainly cannot be taken to mean "ate his lord"; "啗" must be construed as a causative verb (i.e., to cause or make [someone]). Here it means "caused/made the ruler eat [the peach]." **This is an excellent example of the causative use of a transitive verb.**

吃桃子，以爲甜，不吃完，拿半個使君主吃。

Eat peach and think sweet, not finish, with half make ruler eat.

⟶ [彌子瑕]吃桃子，覺得[它]很甜，不吃完[它]，拿半個給君主吃。

[Mí Zǐxiá] *was eating* a peach *and thought* [it] *tasted* quite sweet; *he did* not finish [it]; with *the* half *of it leftover he fed the* ruler.

⟹ 彌子瑕吃桃子，覺得桃子很甜，不把它吃完，拿半個給君主吃。

He was eating a peach which he thought tasted quite sweet; not finishing it, he fed the other half to the ruler.

八. 君曰："愛我哉！忘其口味，以啗寡人。"
　　　　　s　　　　　p

君主說：

The ruler said:

八.一　　　"愛我哉！[彌子瑕]
　　　　　　　　p　　　　　[s]

"[彌子瑕] 愛我 哉！
　　　　　　　＼ v　o ／ part
　s　　　　　　p

"愛我啊！

"Love me, truly!

⟶ "[彌子瑕]真愛我啊！

"[Mí Zǐxiá] truly loves me!

⟹ "彌子瑕真愛我啊！

"Truly, he loves me!

八.二　　　[彌子瑕] 忘 其口味，以 [之] 啗 寡人。"
　　　　　　　　　　＼v　o／　＼prep [o]　v　o／
　　　　　[s]　　　　　p 1　　　　　　p2

忘他的口味拿來使寡人吃。"

Forget his mouth's good taste, with it cause meagre virtue person eat."

⟶[彌子瑕]忘了他嘴裡的甜美的味道拿[它]來給我吃。"

[Mí Zǐxiá], forget*ting the* sweet taste in his *own* mouth, **with [it] fed this person *of* meagre virtue**."

Forget*ting the* sweet taste in his *own* mouth, he *fed* me with it."

⟹ 彌子瑕忘了他嘴裡的甜味儿拿桃子來給我吃。"

Forgetting the sweet taste in his own mouth, he fed me with it."

　　　　　　　　　　s　p　　　　　　s　p
　　　　　　　　　s　　p　　[s]　　　p
九.　　及 彌子瑕 色 衰，[君] 愛 弛，[彌子瑕] 得罪 於 君。
　　　＼prep　　　　　　　o／　　　　＼v　o prep o／
　　　　　　　　adv　　　　　　　[s]　　　　p

到彌子瑕美貌衰退，愛情鬆弛，從君主那裡得到責怪。

When Mí Zǐxiá's good looks decline, affection decrease; get reproach from ruler.

⟶ 等到彌子瑕美麗的容顏衰退的時候，[君主]愛情鬆弛了，[彌子瑕]受到君主的責怪。

When Mí Zǐxiá's good looks fade*d*, [*the* ruler's] ardor cool*ed and* [Mí Zǐxiá] *was* **reproach*ed by the*** **ruler**.

⟹ 等到彌子瑕美麗的容顏變老變醜的時候，君主愛情減少消失了，他受到君主的責怪。

When Mí Zǐxiá's good looks faded, the ruler's ardor cooled, and he was reproached by the ruler.

十.　君曰：＂是固嘗矯駕吾車，又嘗啗我以餘桃。＂

君主說：

The ruler said:

十.一　＂是 固 嘗 矯 駕 吾 車 ，又 嘗 啗 我 以 餘 桃。＂

＂這個本來曾經假託我的命令地駕駛過我的車子，又曾經拿剩下的桃子使我吃過。＂

"This in fact once feign permission to drive my carriage; also once feed me with leftover peach."

⟶ ＂這個人本來曾經騙別人說是我的命令地駕駛過我的車子，又曾經把吃剩的桃子給我吃過。＂

"This person actually once feign*ed* permission *to* drive my carriage *and* also fe*d the* remain*s* of *a* peach *that he had eaten from to* me."

===⟹ "這個人本來曾經騙別人説是我的命令地駕駛過
我的車子，又曾經把吃剩的桃子給我吃過。"

"This person actually once feigned permission to drive my carriage and also fed the remains of a peach that he had eaten from to me."

十
一.　　故 彌子之行 　未 變 於 初 也，
　　　　adv　　　　　　　＼adv v prep o／ part (pause)
　　　　　　　s　　　　　　　　p

本來彌子的行為跟當初沒有變啊，

All along Mízǐ's behavior from outset not have change;

——⟶ 本來彌子的行為跟當初比並沒有什麼改變啊，

Comparing Mízǐ's behavior all along, *there was* no change from *the* begin*ning*,

===⟹ 本來彌子的行為跟當初比並沒有什麼改變啊，

Mízǐ's behavior never changed from what it had been all along since the beginning,

　　　　　[s]　adv 之 adv　 v　　 conj adv v o pron　　[君]_s_ 之 _p_
　　　　　　　　　　　adj. mod.　　　　　　　　 pron　 s　　 p
十　　而 [彌子] 以前之所以見賢，而後 獲罪者，[乃] 愛憎之變 也。
二.　 ＼conj　　　　　　　　　　　　　　　　　／ ＼l.v.　　　　　　 part／
　　　　　　　　　　　　　s　　　　　　　　　　　　　　　　　p

※見：　　本來是動詞，看見；用作結構助詞時跟被動的
　　　　 符號 "被" 字的意思和用法一樣，後面常省略
　　　　 了被動句中的施事者。如本句中的 "見賢" 意
　　　　 思是：

　　　　　　　　被 [君主] 以為賢

　　　　　　 ——⟶ 被 [君主] 認為賢

　　　　　　 ——⟶ 被 (受) [君主] 誇獎

The word " 見 " is usually encountered as a verb meaning "to see" or "to look and see"; when it is used as a structual particle , it functions like the passive marker " 被 ". It often implies an omitted or understood **agent**, or source of the action, in a

278

passive sentence. In this sentence "見賢" means "was seen as worthy" = "was thought worthy [*by the ruler* (**agent**)]"

有時動詞的施事者也在句中出現，通常由介詞"於"來介紹：如"昔者彌子瑕見愛於衛君。"《史記‧老莊申韓列傳》

Sometimes the **agent** of the **verb** also appears in the sentence, it is usually introduced by the preposition "於" : for example, "昔者彌子瑕見愛於衛君" (Formerly, Mí Zǐxià was well loved by the ruler of Wèi.) (*Records of the Grand Historian, Biographies of Lǎozǐ, Zhuāngzǐ, Shēn Búhài, and Hán Fēi*)

※n 之所以 v 者：
n v 之故

(nv 的緣故)
(the reason for **nv**)

The pattern "**n** 之所以 **v** 者" is equivalent in meaning to the pattern "**nv** 之故". Here, for example, "[彌子] (**n**) 之所以見賢 (**v**) 者" (that reason for which [Mízǐ] was thought worthy) is equivalent in meaning to "[彌子] (**n**) 見賢 (**v**) 之故" (The reason [Mízǐ] was thought worthy), which can be rendered in spoken Chinese as "彌子被認為高尚的緣故" and in English as "the reason why Mí Zǐ was thought worthy."

※n 所以 v：彌子所以見賢
彌子被以為賢之故

Mízǐ wherefor/what for seen *as* worthy
= Why Mízǐ *is* seen *as* worthy

※n 之所以 v：彌子之所以見賢
彌子[之]被以為賢之故

Mízǐ's wherefor/what for seen *as* worthy
= The reason why Mízǐ is seen as worthy

※n 之所以 v 者：彌子之所以見賢者
彌子[之]被以為賢的[那個]緣故

Mízǐ's wherefor/what for seen *as* worthy thing
= Mízǐ's wherefor/what for seen *as* worthy reason
= Mízǐ's that for *which* seen *as* worthy
= Mízǐ's that reason for which seen *as* worthy
= that reason for which Mízǐ *is* seen *as* worthy
= **that reason why** Mízǐ *is/was* seen *as* worthy

以前彌子之所以見賢而後獲罪者　　乃　〔君〕愛憎之變也
                B   A

At first Mízǐ's what for was seen as worthy and later got blamed thing (=reason)   was   the change from affection to revulsion *toward him* [in the ruler].

以前彌子被以爲賢後來卻獲罪之故，是愛憎之變啊。

Wherefore Mízǐ is previously seen worthy and later get blamed is change from affection to revulsion.

———→ 以前彌子受到誇獎、後來卻得到責怪的緣故，是君主寵愛跟憎惡的感情改變了啊。

The reason *why* he *was* prais*ed* for it at first *and was* reproach*ed* for it later is *that the* ruler's feelings *for him* chang*ed from* feelings *of* affection *to* feelings *of* revulsion.

═══⇒ 以前彌子受到誇獎、後來卻得到責怪的緣故，是君主寵愛跟憎惡的感情改變了啊。

The reason why he was praised for it at first and was reproached for it later is that the ruler's feelings for him changed from feelings of affection to feelings of revulsion.

句型變換 : SENTENCE PATTERN TRANSFORMATION

(from narrative sentence paradigm to determinative sentence paradigm)

以前 At first   而後 and later on

彌子以色見賢　(敘述句)   彌子以色衰獲罪 (敘述句)
Mízǐ by *virtue of* his good looks was seen   Mízǐ by *virtue of* his good look's declining
as worthy.   (narrative sentence)   got reproached.   (narrative sentence)

色乃　彌子以前之所以見賢 (判斷句)   色衰乃　彌子而後之所以獲罪 (判斷句)
Good looks was what for/why at first Mízǐ   His good looks declining was what for/why Mízǐ
was seen as worthy. (determinative sentence) got reproached later. (determinative sentence)

彌子以君愛見賢   彌子以君憎獲罪
Mízǐ by *virtue of* the ruler's affection was seen Mízǐ by *virtue of* the ruler's revulsion got
as worthy.   (narrative sentence)   reproached   (narrative sentence)

君愛乃　彌子以前之所以見賢   君憎乃　彌子而後之所以獲罪
The ruler's affection was what for/why at first The ruler's revulsion was what for/why Mízǐ
Mízǐ was seen as worthy. (determinative sentence) got reproached later.   (determinative sentence)

(色) (Good looks)			見賢 seen as worthy	
君愛 The ruler's affection	以前 at first			
乃 was		彌子之 所以 Mízǐ's what for/why		者也 thing/reason
(色衰) (Good looks decline)				
君憎 The ruler's revulsion	而後 later		獲罪 got reproached	

把以上四小句結合起來就成為 :

These four short sentences can be combined to form the following determinative sentence:

君愛──→君憎　乃　以前彌子之所以見賢而後獲罪者也
      A   B
The ruler's affection   was   at first Mízǐ's what for seen as worthy and later got blamed
[becoming] the ruler's   reason.
revulsion

The ruler's affection [becoming] the ruler's revulsion was the reason why at first Mízǐ was seen as
worthy and later got reproached.

第三十六課

楚莊王不殺絕纓者

句子分析

一. 楚莊王 賜 群臣 酒。

　　　　＼v　oi　od／
　s　　　　　p

楚莊王賜臣子們酒。

Chǔ King Zhuāng bestow body-of-officials wine.

⟶ 楚莊王賜給臣子們酒喝。

King Zhuāng *of* Chǔ offer*ed his* official*s* wine *to* drink.

⟹ 楚莊王賜給臣子們酒喝。

King Zhuāng of Chǔ offered his officials wine to drink.

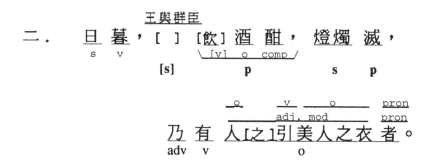

二. 日 暮，[　]［飲］酒 酣，燈燭 滅，

　s　v　　　＼[v]　o　comp／　s　p
　　　　　[s]　　　　p

乃 有 人［之］引美人之衣 者。
adv　v　　　o

※有人引美人之衣者：

　　　　"有N…者"是定語後置的用法。本句中定語是
　　　　"引美人之衣"，移到中心詞"人"之後，加
　　　　被飾代詞"者"複指那個中心詞"人"。還原
　　　　成正常的詞序，應是"有引美人之衣之人"。

The phrase "有人引美人之衣者" is a postpositional adjective constuction based on the paradigm "有 N···者". In this sentence the adjectival modifier "引美人之衣" has been moved after the modified noun "人" and the modified pronoun "者" has been added after the adjectival modifier to refer back to the modified noun "人". If this phrase were rewritten in the conventional word order of "adjectival modifier + noun", it would be: "有引美人之衣之人." (there was a pulled on concubine's clothing person).

※ 比較　（一）

COMPARE　馬之千里者＝馬千里者＝千里馬

of/among horses those horses that run 1000 *li* in a day = a 1000 *li* [a day] horse

丁壯者＝壯丁

of/among adult males the ones who are robust = robust adult males. (*Lesson 32*)

（二）

有婦人哭於墓者＝有哭於墓之婦人

of/among women one crying in front of a grave
= There is a woman crying in front of a grave. (*Lesson 30*)

天黑，喝酒暢快，油燈蠟燭滅，竟有拉美人的衣服的人。

Sky darken, get pleasantly inebriated, lamps and candles out; whereupon have pull-at-beautiful-women's-clothing one.

⟶ 天黑了，[王跟臣子們]喝酒喝得很暢快，油燈蠟燭滅了，竟有個拉美人的衣服的人。

After it ha*d* become dark *and* [everyone] *was* pleasantly inebriat*ed, the* lamp*s and* candle*s went* out; whereupon a person pull*ed at the* clothing of *one of the king's* beautiful wom*en* (i.e., concubine*s*).

⟹ 天黑了，大家喝酒喝得很暢快，油燈蠟燭滅了，竟有個拉美人的衣服的人。

When it got dark and everyone was pleasantly inebriated, the lamps and candles went out; whereupon a person pulled at the clothing of one of the king's concubines.

三. 美人 援 絕 其冠纓, 告 王 曰: " "

      \v comp o/ \v o v o/
    s   p1   p2

美人揪斷他的帽帶子,告訴王説:

Beautiful woman grab and break his capstring; inform king, say:

⟶ 美人揪斷了他的帽帶子,告訴王説:

The concubine grab*bed and* br*oke off the* man's capstring; *she* inform*ed the* king, say*ing*:

⟹ 美人揪斷了他的帽帶子,告訴王説:

The concubine grabbed and broke off his capstring and informed the king saying:

                           v o   pron
                          adj. mod. pron

三.一 " 今者 燭 滅, [於 席] 有 引妾衣 者,

   adv   \v/ \ [prep o]/ \v   o/
     s   p   [s]   p

" 現在燭滅,有拉妾的衣服的人,

"now candles out, there is one pulling concubine's clothing;

⟶ "現在蠟燭滅了,[在席間]有個拉我衣服的人,

"Just now *when the* candle*s went out*, someone [among *the* guest*s*] pull*ed at* my clothing;

⟹ "現在蠟燭滅了,席間有個拉我衣服的人,

"Just now when the candles went out, one of the guests pulled at my clothing;

三.二 妾 援 得 其冠纓 持 之。

      \v comp o/ \v o/
    s   p1   p2

妾揪到他的帽帶子，拿著它。

concubine pull his capstring, hold it.

⟶ 我揪到他的帽帶子，拿著它。

I pull*ed at* his capstring *and* held it.

⟹ 我揪到他的帽帶子，拿在手裡。

I pulled at his capstring and held it in my hand.

三.三 [王] 趣 火 來 上 [火] 視 絕 纓 者。"

趕緊拿火來點上，看看揪斷帽帶的人。"

Quickly have fire brought, light, see break-capstring one."

⟶ [大王] 趕緊叫人拿火來點上 [燈]，看看那個被揪斷了帽帶子的人。"

[Your majesty], quickly *have* fire *brought* in *and* light [*the* lamp*s*] *so that we can* see *the* one with *the* brok*en* capstring."

⟹ 大王趕緊叫人拿火來點上燈，看看那個被揪斷了帽帶子的人。"

Quickly have fire brought in to light the lamps so that you can see the one with the broken capstring."

四. 王曰："[寡人] 賜 人 酒，使 [人] 醉 失 禮，

奈 何 欲 顯 婦人 之 節 而 辱 士 乎?"

285

※ "奈何…乎?":

"奈何"是副詞,譯成白話是"為什麼","怎麼"。"乎"是疑問語氣詞,譯成白話是"呢"。兩詞用在同一句中,彼此呼應,構成帶有反問語氣的固定句型"奈何…乎?"譯成白話是"為什麼…呢?"用反問來表示強烈的否定的語氣。因為不贊成得那麼強烈,也可轉譯成"怎麼[可以]…呢?"

"奈何" is an adverbial phrase that can be translated into spoken Chinese as "為什麼" (why) or "怎麼"(how/ how *could*). "乎" is an interrogative particle equivalent in function and meaning to "呢" in spoken Chinese. When "奈何" and "乎" are used in conjunction in a sentence, they form a fixed sentence pattern that expresses a rhetorical question: "奈何…乎?" which can be translated into spoken Chinese as "為什麼…呢?" (why?). A rhetorical question is used to express a strong negative tone; since it expresses such strong disapproval, this sentence pattern could by extension be translated into spoken Chinese as "怎麼[可以]…呢?" (How [could]...?) In English this negative tone of disapproval can also be expressed by such rhetorical questions as "Could it be that...?", "Do [you] want to...?", "Why would..." etc.

王說:"賜人酒,使喝醉失掉禮貌,為什麼想要顯示婦人的貞節去羞辱有學問有才幹的讀書人呢?"

King say: "Offer people wine, make drunk, breach etiquette; why want display lady's virtue and disgrace scholar?"

⟶ 王說:"[我]賜給人酒喝,使[人]喝醉了做出不合禮貌的事來,怎麼可以因為想要顯示婦人的貞節去羞辱有學問有才幹的讀書人呢?"

The king sa*id*: "[I] offer*ed* wine *to* someone, g*ot him* drunk, *and* ma*de him* **commit a breach of etiquette**; how *could* I want *to* display your virtue *and in so doing* disgrace *a* scholar *of* learning *and* ability?"

⟹ 王說:"我賜給人酒喝,使人喝醉了做出不合禮貌的事來,怎麼可以為了要顯示婦人的貞節去羞辱有學問有才幹的讀書人呢?"

286

The king said: "I offered wine to someone, made him drunk, and made him commit a breach of etiquette; how could I disgrace a scholar just for the sake of making a display of your virtue?"

五． ［王］乃 命 左右 曰： " "
\adv v o v o/
[s] p

就命令侍從們說：

Then command attendants, say:

⟶ ［王］就命令他的侍從說：

[*The* king] then command*ed his* attendant*s*, say*ing*:

⟹王就命令侍從們說： " "

The king then commanded his attendants, saying:

五．一 "今日［群臣］與 寡人 飲，
adv \prep o v/
[s] p1

不 絕 冠 纓 者 ［則］［寡人］不 歡。"
\adv v o/ part [conj] \adv v/
p2 [s] p

※ 不絕冠纓者：

"者"是助詞(語氣詞)，表示假設的語氣，譯成白話是"要是…的話"、"要是…"、或" …的話"。

Here the particle "者" functions as a suppositional marker: it indicates that the phrase preceding it should be understood as a contingent or conditional element of the sentence. This sense can be expressed in spoken Chinese by "要是…的話" (if), or"要是…" and " …的話" used independently. It can also be expressed in English by using the subjunctive mood.

"今天跟我喝酒，不揪斷帽帶子的話不高興。"

"Today drink with me; not break off capstrings, not happy."

⟶　"今天［你們］跟我一塊儿喝酒，要是你們不揪斷帽帶子的話［我］［就］不高興。"

"Today [you] *are* all drink*ing* with me; if you *don't* break off *your* capstrings, [I *will*] not *be* happy."

⟹　"今天你們跟我一塊儿喝酒，要是你們不揪斷帽帶子的話我就不高興。"

"Today you are all drinking with me; if you don't break off your capstrings, I will not be happy."

六．　群臣 百有餘人 皆絕 其冠纓，而 ［人］上 火，
　　　s　　p1　　　adv v　o　conj　　v o
　　　　　　　　　　　p2　　　　　　　　［s］　p

　　［君臣］ 卒盡歡而罷。
　　　　　　adv v　o conj v
　　　［s］　　　p

　　　※ 群臣百有餘人：

　　　　　"有"讀作"又"，表示整數"百"後再加上零數"餘"，全句譯成白話是"臣子們有一百餘人"，或"臣子們有一百多個人"。（參看第三十二課《塞翁失馬》中句析九，"死者十九"，第二四二頁）。

In this context, the word "有" should be read as "又" (also), meaning after the round number one hundred add some unspecified figure "in excess of" one hundred. The entire phrase can be translated into spoken Chinese as "臣子們有一百餘人" (over a hundred officials) or as "臣子們有一百多個人" (more than a hundred officials). In English, this could also be translated as "a hundred odd" or "a hundred some." (*See L. 32, sentence analysis 9,* "死者十九", *p.242*)

群臣一百多人都揪斷他們的帽帶子，才點上燈，最後玩儿到最歡樂的程度才停止。

Group of officials one hundred and more all break their capstrings, then set fire; in end enjoy utmost, then disperse.

⟶ 臣子們有一百多個人都揪斷了他們的帽帶子，然後才點
上燈，最後［大家］玩兒到最歡樂的程度才散。

His officials, more *than* one hundred *in all*, all br*oke* their capstring*s*; only
then *did people* light *the* lamp*s: and in the* end [they] enjo*yed themselves* to
the utmost, only then dispers*ing*.

⟹ 臣子們有一百多個人都揪斷了他們的帽帶子，然後才點
上燈，最後大家玩兒到最歡樂的程度才散。

His officials, more than one hundred in all, all broke their capstrings; only
afterwards were the lights lit: in the end they all enjoyed themselves to the
utmost, and only then dispersed.

七． 居 三 年，晉 與 楚 戰。 ［楚］有 一 臣 常 在 前，

　　　 ＼v　comp／　　　　　＼v／　　　 ＼v　o/s　adv　v　o／
　　　 　 adv　　　　　 s　 p　 ［s］　　　　　　　 p

　［晉與楚］五 合 ［楚臣］ 五 奮　首 卻 敵，卒 得 勝 之。
　　　　　＼adv　v／　　　　＼adv　v／　＼adv　v　o／　＼adv　aux　v　o／
　　 ［s］　　 p　 ［s］　　 p1　　　　p2　　　　　p3

　　　　※ 有一臣常在前：

這是一句典型的有無繁句。有無繁句的特
點是一個有無簡句後融接著一個敘述句。
也就是有無簡句的賓語後緊接著另一個動詞
，同時也兼作這個動詞的主語。一個最好的例
子是《論語・學而》中的"有朋自遠方來
"，"朋"既是"有"的賓語，又是"自遠方
來"中動詞"來"的主語。"朋"字具有兼語
的性質。這種有無繁句中的"有"字帶有一
種介紹的作用：因為全句的主語是上文沒有提
過的，帶有或多或少的無定性質，需要介紹一
下。（詳見呂叔湘《中國文法要略》頁一零一
）。本句"有一臣常在前"中的"臣"就是這
種有無繁句中的兼語，它既是"有"字的
賓語，又是"在前"的主語。

289

This is a representative example of the **complex existential sentence** (有無繁句) pattern. The distinguishing characeristic of this sentence pattern is that it attaches a narrative sentence to the end of a simple existential sentence (i.e., a sentence containing "有" or "無" as the main predicate) In addition, the object (or in English sentences, the predicate nominative) of the verb 有/無 is a **pivotal word** that serves as the subject of the predicate in the attached narrative sentence as well as the object (predicate nominative) of the verb in the simple existential sentence. (Here the pivotal word is "臣"). An excellent example of this sentence pattern occurs in the *Analects*: "有朋自遠方來" (There are like-minded persons *who* come from afar.)《論語 · 學而》. In this sentence, the word "朋" serves both as the object of the verb "有" and the subject of the predicate "來" in the attached narrative sentence "朋自遠方來".(Like-minded persons come from afar). In such complex existential sentences, the verb "有" is used to introduce the subject of the entire sentence; because the subject has not appeared in the preceding text, it remains to some degree uncertain and hence must be introduced at this point. (See Lǚ Shūxiāng, *Zhōngguó Wénfǎ Yàoluè*, p. 101).

In the sentence "有一臣常在前", "臣" is the pivotal word in the complex existential sentence: it serves both as the object of the verb "有" and the subject of the predicate "在前" in the attached narrative sentence. This sentence pattern can often be translated into English as "There was/were N *who/that* ...": in this case, "There was one official *who* was usually at the front."

過三年，晉國跟楚國打仗。有一個臣子常常在前面，五會戰，五奮勇領先打退敵人，終於能夠戰勝他們。

Three years pass; Jìn and Chǔ battle. Have one official usually at front: five times meet, five times muster courage, at the head repulse enemy, finally can conquer them.

⟶ 過了三年，晉國跟楚國打仗。[楚國]有一個臣子常常在前面，[晉楚]五次會戰，[那個臣子]五次奮勇領先打退敵人，終於能夠戰勝了他們。

Three years pass*ed*; *then* the state*s of* Jìn and Chǔ *went to* war. *There was* one official [from *the* state *of* Chǔ] *who was* always at *the* front *of the ranks*; *in* five engagement*s* [*between the* force*s of* Jìn *and* Chǔ], five time*s* [*that* official] mustered *his* courage *and led the army of Chǔ to* repulse *the* enemy; *in the* end *he was* able *to* vanquish them.

⟹ 過了三年，晉國跟楚國打仗，楚國有一個臣子常常在前面，晉楚五次會戰，那個臣子五次奮勇領先打退敵人，終於能夠戰勝了他們。

Three years passed; then the states of Jìn and Chǔ went to war. There was one official of Chǔ who was always at the front of the ranks; in five engagements between the forces of Jìn and Chǔ, five times he mustered all his courage and led the army of Chǔ to repulse the enemy; in the end, he was able to vanquish them.

八. 莊王 怪 而 問 [之] 曰："　"
　　　　 \adj/v conj v [o] v 　　 o /
　　　 s 　　　　　 p

莊王覺得奇怪就問説：

King Zhuāng think extraordinary so question, say:

——→ 莊王覺得很奇怪就問 [他] 説：

King Zhuāng *thought it* extraordinary *and* so question*ed* [him], say*ing*:

===⇒ 莊王覺得很奇怪就問他説：

King Zhuāng thought it extraordinary and so questioned him, saying:

八.一 　　　"寡人 德 薄，又 未嘗 異 子，
　　　　　　　 \s p/ \adv adv v o /
　　　　　 s 　 p1 　　　 p2

※ 寡人德薄：

這是個描寫繁句：主語是"寡人"，謂語是"德薄"。"德薄"本身也是一個描寫簡句，"德"是主語，"薄"是形容詞用作謂語。同樣的句子如"莊周家貧。"《莊子‧外物》。類似的句子如第二十四課《畫蛇添足》中的"一人蛇先成"，第一六八頁。

This is a **complex descriptive sentence** in which the subject is "寡人" and the predicate "德薄". "德薄" is in itself a **simple descriptive sentence** comprised of the subject "德" and the adjective "薄", which functions as the predicate (in English this would be the predicate adjective, i.e., "is meagre"). The structure of the sentence "莊周家貧"《莊子‧外物》is identical. The structure of the sentence "一人蛇先成" in L. 24,《畫蛇添足》is similar but not identical. (*See L. 24, sentence 4, p. 168*)

291

※未嘗異子：

"異"是形容詞用作動詞，意動用法。"異子"意思是"以子為異"，譯成白話是"認為你奇特"或"認為你與眾不同"。根據上下文，最恰當的白話譯文應是"待你特別好。"（參看第二課《宋有富人》中，句析六，"其家甚智其子"，第十一頁）。

The word "異" (special) is an adjective used here as a putative verb (i.e., to think/consider to be special). The phrase "異子" means "以子為異" (take you to be special), which can be translated into spoken Chinese as "認為你奇特" (consider you to be special) or "認為你與眾不同" (consider you unlike the rest). In this context, the most apt translation into spoken Chinese would be "待你特別好" (treat you especially well). (Cf. the sentence "其家甚智其子" in L. 2 《宋有富人》, sentence analysis 6, p. 11).

"我德少，又又未曾以子爲異，

"My virtue meagre; moreover, have never take you especial.

"我道德微少，又從來沒對待你特別好過，

"My virtue *as a ruler is* meagre; moreover, *I have* never treat*ed* you especially well.

"我道德微少，又從來沒對待你特別好過，

"My virtue as a ruler is meagre; moreover, I have never treated you especially well.

八.二　　子 [以] 何故 出死 不疑 如 是？"
　　　　　\[prep] o　v　v　adv v　comp/
　　　　s　　　　　　　　p

※如是：　這是準繫詞"如"與代詞"是"結合而成的，通常用作準判斷句"A(S-N1)如B (P-N2)"中的謂語，如第二十九課《孔子猶江海》。但是一個句子的謂語中若已出現了動詞，"如是"在它

後面就降格為補語，如本句"不疑如是"，譯
成白話是"不遲疑得像這樣"。
要是把"如是"移到動詞"不疑"之前，就
用作副詞，"如是不疑"譯成白話是"像這樣
地不遲疑"。（參看第十七課《刻舟求劍》句
析七b，"求劍若此"，第一一三頁）。

This is a verb phrase comprised of the pseudo-copula "如" (to
be like) and the demonstrative pronoun "是" (this) that often
serves as the predicate of pseudo-determinative sentence based on
the pattern "A (S/N1) 如 B (P/N2)". (See L. 29 《孔子猶江海
》 on this sentence pattern.) However, if a verb has already
appeared in the predicate of the sentence and the phrase "如是"
follows it, then its grammatical function in the sentence is
diminished, and it serves simply as a verbal complement. In this
sentence, the phrase "不疑如是" can be translated into spoken
Chinese as "不遲疑得像這樣" (to not hesitate in this way). If
"如是" is placed in front of the verb "不疑", then it functions
as an adverbial phrase; "如是不疑" would be translated into
spoken Chinese as "像這樣地不遲疑" (in this way to not
hesitate). In both cases, "如是" would be translated into
English as an adverbial phrase meaning "in this way", "to this
extent/degree". (*See also sentence analysis 7b*, "求劍若此" *in
Lesson 17* 《刻舟求劍》*, p. 113*).

你什麼緣故出去死不遲疑像這樣？"

You what reason go to die not hesitate like this?"

⟶ 你[因爲]什麼緣故出去冒死的危險不遲疑得像
這樣呢？"

[For] what reason *did* you resolutely go out *and* risk death like
this?"

⟹ 你因爲什麼緣故出去冒死的危險不遲疑得像這樣
呢？"

Why did you resolutely go out and risk death like this?"

293

句型變換一：   SENTENCE TRANSFORMATION ONE

子 [以] 何故 出 死 如是 不疑 ？"

你什麼緣故出去死像這樣不遲疑？"

You what reason go to die like this not hesitant?"

⟶ 你 [因為]什麼緣故出去冒死的危險冒得像這樣不遲疑呢？"

You [for] what reason *went* out *and* risk*ed* dy*ing* so resolutely?"

⟹ 你因為什麼緣故出去冒死的危險冒得像這樣不遲疑呢？"

Why did you go out and risk death so resolutely?"

句型變換二：   SENTENCE TRANSFORMATION TWO

子 [以] 何故 如是 不疑 出 死 ？"

你什麼緣故像這樣不遲疑出去死？"

You what reason like this not hesitant go to die?"

⟶ 你 [因為]什麼緣故像這樣不遲疑地出去冒死的危險呢？"

You [for] what reason so resolutely *went* out *and* risk*ed* dy*ing*?"

⟹ 你因為什麼緣故這樣不遲疑地出去冒死的危險呢？"

Why did you so resolutely go out and risk death?"

九． ［臣］對曰："　"
　　　　　＼ v　v　　○／
　［s］　　　　p

回答說：

Respond, say:

⟶ ［那個臣］回答說：

[*The* official] respond*ed*, say*ing*:

⟹ 那個臣回答說：

The official responded saying:

九．一　　"臣 當 死。往者［臣］醉 失 禮，
　　　　　＼aux v／　adv　　　　＼v　v　○／
　　　　　s　　p　　　　　　［s］　　　p

王隱忍不加［臣］［以］誅 也。
＼v　adv v　[o]　[prep] ○ part／
s　　　　　　　p

＊加誅：

這個詞組看起來像個簡單的動詞語（動詞"加"＋賓語"誅"），其實它是整個謂語"動詞語（動詞＋賓語）＋介詞語（介詞＋賓語）"的省寫。這個句構全部都寫出來應是"N1加N2以N3"（主語＋動詞＋賓語＋介詞＋賓語）；也可改變詞序寫成"N1以N3加N2"（主語＋介詞＋賓語＋動詞＋賓語），譯成白話是"N1把N3加到N2上"。

如果"N3"是動詞在句中活用為名詞的字，那麼這個句構就可以簡單地譯成"N1 V(N3) N2"如本句"君不加誅"全寫出應是"君不加臣以誅"，改變詞序後可以寫成"君不以誅加臣"，譯

295

成白話是 "君主不把懲罰加在臣子身上"。
"誅" 本是動詞 "懲罰" ，在本句中活用為名詞 "懲罰" ，所以本句也可恢復 "N3" 的動詞性，改譯成 "君主不懲罰臣"。
現在白話中常見的句構 "N1對N2加以N3" ，簡單直接地可說成 "N1 V(N3) N2." 就是從文言中這種句構發展出來的。

This phrase might at first glance appear to be a simple verbal phrase (**v-o**) composed of the verb " 加 " and the object " 誅 "; in fact, it is an abbreviated way of writing the complete predicate of the sentence, which consists of a verbal phrase (v-o/verb and object) and a prepositional phrase (preposition and its object). If it were written out in full, this sentence pattern would be "N1 加 N2 以 N3" (N1 does to N2 with N3) (noun + verb + object + preposition + object) and would correspond to the pattern "N1 把 N3 加到 N2上 " (N1 takes N3 and applies it to N2).

If "N3" is a verb that is serving in the capacity of a noun, this sentence pattern can be even more simply translated as "N1 V(N3) N2". For example, if the sentence " 君不加誅 " [Ruler not do punishment/The ruler does not apply punishment] were written out in full it would be " 君不加臣以誅 " (Ruler not do to official with punishment/The ruler does not apply to the official punishment = does not punish official); if the word order of this sentence were changed slightly it would be written as " 君不以誅加臣 " (Ruler not with punishment do to official/The ruler does not apply punishment to the official). This last sentence could be translated into spoken Chinese as " 君主不把懲罰加在臣子身上 " (The ruler does not take the punishment and apply it to the subject's person).

" 誅 " is basically a verb meaning " 懲罰 " (to punish), which is used in this sentence pattern in the capacity of a noun meaning "punishment"; therefore, in this sentence if N3 is restored to its verbal function, the sentence can be re-translated as " 君主不懲罰臣 " (The ruler *did* not punish the official).

In modern spoken Chinese, the sentence pattern "N1 對 N2 加以 N3 " is frequently encountered; it can be simply and directly restated as "N1 V(N3) N2". This usage in modern spoken Chinese developed out of the classical Chinese sentence structure discussed above.

"臣應當死。從前喝醉失掉禮貌，王忍耐著不動聲色，沒加懲罰。

"Servant deserve to die. Heretofore, drunk, breach etiquette. King conceal feelings, tolerate, not apply punishment.

—→ "臣應當死。從前 [臣] 喝醉了做出不合禮貌的
事來。王忍耐著不動聲色，沒把懲罰加到臣身
上來（沒懲罰臣）。

"Your servant deserves *to* die. Once [I] *got drunk and* **committed a
breach of etiquette**. Your majesty ***bore it*** without *any* show
of **displeasure** *and did* not punish *me*.

⟹ "臣應當死。從前臣喝醉了做出不合禮貌的事來
，王忍耐著不動聲色，沒懲罰臣。

"Your servant deserves to die. Once I got drunk and committed a
breach of etiquette. Your majesty bore it without any show of
displeasure and did not punish me.

九.二　　臣 終 不 敢 以 [受][王] 蔭蔽之德 而 不 顯 報王也。"
　　　　　\adv adv aux prep[v]　　　　　　o　　conj adv adv v o part/
　　　　s　　　　　　　　　　　　　　p

※不敢不：

用雙否定表示肯定來加強肯定的意思。"不敢
不"是"一定得"、"必須得"的強調說法。

A double negative is used here to express affirmation in order
to stress the affirmative meaning. "不敢不" (not dare not)
means "一定得" (certainly must) or "必須得" (absolutely
must). It is used as a rhetorical device to intensify the tone of
affirmation.

※以A而不B：

因為A就不B

because of A, then not B

※不敢以A而不B：

按照雙否定的結構逐字譯成白話是"不敢因為
A就不B"，實際上要表達的意思是"雖然A但
是還必須得B"，語氣是極端肯定的。

This double negative construction can be literally translated
into spoken Chinese character by character as "不敢因為A就
不B" (not dare because of A then not B); what this in fact
means is "雖然A,但是還必須得B" (Although A, must still

297

B nonetheless), and it expresses a tone of absolute affirmation. This rhetorical tone can be expressed in English by such phrases as "can not help but", "must by all means". etc.

臣終於不敢因為庇護的恩惠就不公開地報答王啊。

Servant ultimately dare not for kindness of protection just not openly repay king.

⟶ 臣到底不敢因為[受了王]暗中庇護的恩惠就不公開地報答王啊。

[*Having* received] *the* favor *of* [your] covert protection, *your* servant ultimately just dare*d* not not openly repay your majesty.

⟹ 臣到底不敢因為受了王暗中庇護的恩惠就不公開地報答王啊。

Having received the favor of your covert protection, your servant ultimately just dared not not openly repay your majesty.

九.三 [臣] 常 願 [以] 肝腦塗地， 用 頸血 濺 敵 久矣。

```
        adv v \[prep]  o   v  o/  \prep  o   v   o/
\[s]              o1              o2        / \adj/ part
                  s                              p
```

※久矣： 把句中副詞搬到句末（或提到句首）作謂語，表示強調。（參看第十五課，句析三·二，第九十五頁）

In classical Chinese, an adverb (or an adverbial clause) can be transposed to the end (or to the head) of a sentence; it then functions as the predicate of the sentence. This rhetorical device is used to emphasize the word or clause that has been transposed and to highlight its importance in the sentence. (*See L. 15, sentence analysis 3.2, p. 95*)

子曰："甚矣，吾衰也；
　　　　　p　　s

久矣，吾不復夢見周公。"《論語·述而》
p　　　s

The master said: "Extreme is my decay; for a long time, I have not dreamed, as I was wont to do, that I saw the Duke of Chou." (Legge, *The Analects of Confucius*, p. 196)

還原成正常的詞序如下：

This sentence can be recast in the conventional word order as follows:

吾衰也，　甚矣；
　s　　　　p
My decay is extreme.

吾不復夢見周公　，久矣。"
　s　　　　　　　　p
My no longer dreaming of the Duke of Chou has been long.

吾　甚　衰　矣，
　　\adv adj part/
s　　　p
I *am/have become* much weakened.

吾　久　不　復夢見周公 矣。"
　\adv adv adv v　o part/
　　s　　　　　p
I have long stopped dreaming of the Duke of Chou.

本句也可還原成正常的詞序如下：

The sentence under discussion can also be recast in the conventional word order as follows:

[臣]久 常 願 [以] 肝腦塗地，用頸血濺敵 矣。
　\ adv adv v　　　　　　o　　　　　/ part
[s]　　　　　　　　p

為了保持原句強調的語氣，此處仍按原來的
詞序翻譯如下：

For the sake of preserving the emphatic tone in the classical text, the following translation is formulated in the original word-order.

常願肝跟腦塗地，用頸血噴濺敵人久啦。

Constantly wish brain liver to splatter ground, use neck's blood to spurt out onto enemy, long oh so very.

⟶ ［臣］一直希望［拿］肝和腦塗抹在地上，在戰場上慘烈地犧牲，用脖子裡的血噴濺敵人已經很久啦。

For such a long time [*your* servant] ha*s* constantly wish*ed to* splatter *his* brain*s and* liver (his guts) *on the* ground *and to* spurt *the* blood *out from his* neck *onto the* enemy *to repay you.*

⟹ 臣一直希望把肝和腦塗抹在地上，用脖子裡的血噴濺敵人已經很久啦。

For such a long time, I have constantly wished to splatter my brains and liver on the ground and to let my blood spurt out from my neck onto the enemy to repay you.

九．四　臣　乃　夜絕纓者　也。"
　　　　　＼l.v.　p(n)／　part
　　　　 s　　　 p

臣就是晚上揪斷帽帶子的人啊。"

Servant is night break-capstring one."

⟶ 臣就是那天晚上被揪斷了帽帶子的人啊。"

Your servant is *the* one *whose* capstring **was broken** that night."

⟹ 臣就是那天晚上被揪斷了帽帶子的人啊。"

Your servant is the one whose capstring was broken that night."

十．　［楚］遂　敗　晉軍，楚　得　以［此］強。
　　　　 ＼adv　v　o／　　＼aux prep [o]　v／
　 [s]　　　 p　　　 s　　　 p

終於打敗晉國的軍隊，楚國能夠因而強大。

Eventually defeat Jìn armies; Chǔ able thereby to grow strong.

⟶ 終於打敗了晉國的軍隊，楚國能夠因［這次戰爭］變得很強大。

Eventually, *he* defeat*ed the* arm*ies of the* state *of* Jìn, *and the* state *of* Chǔ *was* able *to* grow strong *as a result of* [this battle].

⟹ 終於打敗了晉國的軍隊，楚國能夠因這次戰爭變得很強大。

Eventually, he defeated the armies of the state of Jìn, and the state of Chǔ was able to grow strong as a result of this battle.

第三十七課

子羔為衛政

句子分析

一． 子羔 為 衛政，刖 人之足。
　　　　s　　p1　　　p2

子羔治理衛國的政事，砍斷人的腳。

Zǐgāo administer Wèi goverment, cut off person's foot.

⟶ 子羔治理衛國的政事的時候，砍斷了一個犯人的腳。

When Zǐgāo *was* administer*ing the* goverment *of the* state *of* Wèi, *he had* a person's foot cut off *as punishment for a crime.*

⟹ 子羔治理衛國的政事，砍斷了一個犯人的腳。

When Zǐgāo was administering the goverment of the state of Wèi, he had a person's foot cut off as punishment for a crime.

二． 衛之君臣 亂，子羔 走 [於] 郭門，郭門 閉。
　　　s　　　p　s　v [prep]　o　　s　　p

衛國的君臣亂，子羔逃外城門，外城門關閉。

Ruler and ministers of Wèi in turmoil; Zǐgāo flee outer city wall gate; outer city wall gate closed.

⟶ 衛國的君臣之間發生了變亂，子羔逃到外城的城門，外城的城門已經關上了。

During the turmoil among *the* ruler *and* ministers of *the* state *of* Wèi, Zǐgāo fle*d* to *the* outer city wall gate, *but the* outer city wall gate *was* already close*d*.

===⟹ 衛國的政府發生了政變，子羔逃到外城的城門，外城的
城門已經關上了。

During the political crisis in the state of Wèi, Zǐgāo fled to the outer city wall gate; the outer city wall gate was already closed.

三. 刖者 守門 ， 曰： " "
      ⎵v o⎵   ⎵v o⎵
    s   p   p

斷腳的人把守門，說：

Foot-cut-off one guard gate, say:

———⟶ 那個被砍斷腳的人正把守著外城的城門，對子羔說：

The person *whose* foot *had been* cut off *was* guard*ing the* outer city wall gate; *he* said *to* Zǐgāo:

===⟹ 那個被砍斷腳的人正把守著外城的城門，對子羔說：

The person whose foot had been cut off was guarding the gate of the outer city wall; he said to Zǐgāo:

三.一 " 於 彼 有 缺。"
        ⎵prep o⎵ ⎵v o⎵
         s   p

"在那兒有缺口。"

"At that place is breach."

———⟶ "在那邊牆上有個缺口。"

"Over there *there is* a breach *in the* wall."

===⟹ "在那邊牆上有個缺口。"

303

"Over there is a breach in the wall."

四．　子羔曰：" 君子不踰。"

子羔說："君子不跳。"

Zǐgāo say: "Gentleman not climb over."

⟶ 子羔說："君子不跳牆。"

Zǐgāo sa*id*: "A man of noble character *does* not climb over *the* wall *to escape*."

⟹ 子羔說："君子不跳牆。"

Zǐgāo said: "A man of noble character does not climb over the wall to escape."

五．　[刖者]曰：" 於彼有寶。"

說："在那兒有洞。"

Say: "At that place is hole."

⟶ [被砍斷腳的人]說："在那邊有個洞。"

[*The* man *whose* foot *had been* cut off] sa*id*: "Over there *there is* a hole *beneath the wall*."

⟹ 被砍斷腳的人說："在那邊有個洞。"

The man whose foot had been cut off said: "Over there is a hole beneath the wall."

六．　子羔　曰：" 君子 不 隧。"

子羔說：" 君子 不 鑽。"

Zǐgāo say: "Gentleman not go through."

子羔說：" 君子 不 鑽洞。"

Zǐgāo sa*id*: "A man of noble character *does* not go through *a* hole *under the wall to escape*."

子羔說：" 君子 不 鑽洞。"

Zǐgāo said: "A man of noble character does not go through a hole under the wall to escape."

七．　[刖者] 曰：" 於 此 有 室。"

說：" 在這兒有屋子。"

Say: "At this place is room."

⟶　[被砍斷腳的人] 說：" 在這裡有間屋子。"

[*The* man *whose* foot *had been* cut off] sa*id*: "Over here *there is* a room."

⟹　被砍斷腳的人說：" 在這裡有間屋子。"

The man whose foot had been cut off said: "Over here there is a room."

八．　子羔　入 [室]，追者　罷。

305

子羔進入，追趕的人回去。

Zǐgāo enter; chasing-ones stop.

⟶ 子羔進 [屋子] 去了，追趕的人回去了。

Zǐgāo enter*ed* [*the* room] *and his* pursuer*s went* back.

⟹ 子羔進屋子去了，追趕的人回去了。

Zǐgāo entered the room; his pursuers left.

九． 子羔　將去，謂 刖者 曰：" ＂
　　　　　　　＼adv　v／ ＼v　o　v　　　o／
　　　　s　　p1　　　　p2

子羔將要離開，對砍斷腳的人說：

Zǐgāo, about leave, address cut-off-foot one, say:

⟶ 子羔將要離開的時候，對被砍斷腳的人說：

When Zǐgāo *was* about *to* leave, *he* sp*oke* to *the* person *whose* foot **had been** cut off, say*ing*:

⟹ 子羔將要離開的時候，對被砍斷腳的人說：

When Zǐgāo was about to leave, he spoke to the person whose foot had been cut off, saying:

九．一 "吾 不 能 虧損 主之法令，而 親 刖 子之足。
　　　　＼adv aux　v　　　o／ conj ＼adv v　o／
　　　　s　　　p1　　　　　　　　　p2

"我不能損害君主的法令，才親自砍斷你的腳。

"I can not impair ruler's laws and orders; thus, I myself cut off your foot.

306

——→ "我不能破壞君主的法令，才親自下令砍斷了你的腳。

"I *am* not able *to* violate *the* laws and orders of *the* ruler, so I myself *had to* give *the* order *to* cut off your foot.

——→ "我不能不遵守君主的法令，才親自下令把你的腳砍斷了。

"**I can not disobey** *the* laws and orders of *the* ruler, so I *had to have* your foot cut off.

===⇒ "我不能不遵守君主的法令，才親自下令把你的腳砍斷了。

"I can not disobey the laws and orders of the ruler, so I had to have your foot cut off.

九.二　　吾 在 難中，此 乃 子之報怨 時 也。

我在災難裡，這是你的報仇時機啊。

I in distress; this is your pay-back-grudge chance.

——→ 我在災難裡，這正是你的報仇時機啊。

Now I *am* in distress; this then is your chance *for* revenge.

===⇒ 我在災難裡，這正是你的報仇時機啊。

Now I am in distress; this then is your chance for revenge.

九.三　　[子] [以] 何故 逃 我？"

307

什麼緣故使我逃？"

What reason escape me?"

⟶ [你][因為]什麼緣故讓我逃走呢？"

[For] what reason *did* [you] cause me *to be able to* escape?"

⟹ 你為什麼讓我逃走呢？"

Why did you let me escape?"

十.　　刖者 曰：" "
　　　　 s　　 p

砍斷腳的人說：

Foot-cut-off one say:

被砍斷腳的人說：

The person *whose* foot ***had been*** cut off sa*id*:

被砍斷腳的人說：

The person whose foot had been cut off said:

十.一　　"斷足 固 [為] 我罪 也，[君] 無 [計] 可 奈 [之] 何。
　　　　 s　　　　　　　p　　　　 [s]　　　　　　 p

"砍斷腳本來我的罪，沒有能對怎麼樣。

"Cutting off foot all along my offense;　not have what-to-do.

⟶　 "砍斷腳本來 [是] 我的罪，[您] 沒有 [辦法] 能
　　 對 [它] 怎麼樣。

308

"*The* cut*ting* off *of* my foot [was] all along *for* my offense: *there was* no [way] [you] *could* do *anything* [about it]?

⟹ "砍斷腳本來是我的罪，您沒有法子能對它做什麼
。

"The cutting off of my foot was all along for my offense: you could do nothing about it.

十.二　　君 之 治 臣 也，　[君] 傾 側 法令，
　　　　　　　　\v o/ part　　　　[s]　　\v/　 p
　　　　　　s　之　　p

先 後 臣 以 法，
\v　v　o　prep o/
　　　　p

欲 臣 之 免 於 法 也，臣 知 之。
\v　s 之 v prep o/ part　　\v o/
　　　p　　　o　　　　　　s　　p

您懲治臣啊，使法令傾斜，憑藉法律以臣為先，以
臣為後，想要臣免於刑罰，臣知道它。

Lord's punishing servant, slant and skew laws and orders, put servant ahead of and after with respect to the law, want servant's exempted from law, servant know this.

⟶ 當您懲治我的時候啊，[您]把法令歪到這邊側到那邊
地看，根據法律把我放在前面或把我放在後面，想
要我免掉刑罰，我知道這個。

As for your punish*ing* me, [you] tilt*ed* and turn*ed the* laws this way *and* that, put me ahead *of the law and* after *the law*, want*ed* my be*ing* exempt*ed* from punishment; I know it.

⟶ 當您懲治我的時候啊，[您]從各種角度來研究法令
，根據法律來慎重衡量我的罪，想要我免受刑罰，
這我知道。

As for your punish*ing* me, **[you] considered *the* laws from every angle, prudently deliberate*d* my case against *the* law**, and want*ed* me exempt*ed* from punishment; **I know this**.

⟹ 當您懲治我的時候啊，您從各種角度來研究法令，根據法律來慎重衡量我的罪，想要我免受刑罰，這我知道。

As for your punishing me, you considered the laws from every angle, prudently deliberated my case against the law, and wanted me exempted from punishment; I know this

十.三

獄 決 罪 定， 臨 當 論 刑，

罪案判決，罪名確定，接近應當衡量刑罰，

Facts of case ascertained, category of offense determined; approaching ought to weigh sentence,

⟶ 案子判決了，罪名確定了，接近該判決刑罰的時候，

The facts *of the* case *had been* ascertain*ed*; *the* category *of the* offense *had been* determin*ed*; *when the* time *to* pass sentence dr*ew* near,

⟹ 案子判決了，罪名確定了，快到該依法決定刑罰的時候，

The facts of the case had been ascertained; the category of the offense had been determined; when the time to pass sentence drew near,

十.四

君 愀然 不 樂， [憂] 見 於 顏色，臣 又 知 之。

您憂傷不樂，顯現在臉上，臣也知道它。

310

lord despondent and unhappy, reveal in facial expression; servant too know it .

⟶ 您很憂傷地不快樂，[憂傷的心情]在臉上顯現出來，這我也知道。

you *were* pain*ed* and unhappy *looking*; [your pain] *was* reveal*ed* in your demeanor, *and* **I too know this.**

⟹ 您憂傷不樂，在神色中流露出來，這我也知道。

you were pained and unhappy; this was revealed in your demeanor, and I also know this.

十.五　　君 豈 私 臣 哉 ?

　　　　　　\adv　v　o/ part
　　　　s　　　　p

※ ⋯豈⋯哉 ?

疑問副詞 "豈" 和語氣詞 "哉" 合用，構成一個反問句，表示強烈的感歎語氣。白話可譯成 "⋯難道[是]⋯嗎 ? " 或 "⋯哪裡[是]⋯呢 ? "

When the interrogative adverb "豈" (how...?; could it be...?) is used in conjunction with the modal particle "哉" to form a rhetorical question, the whole sentence carries an additional emphatic exclamatory tone. The paradigm "豈⋯哉 ? " can be translated into spoken Chinese as "難道[是]⋯嗎 ? " or "哪裡 [是]⋯呢 ? " and into English as "How [is]...?" or "How could it be...?"

您難道偏袒臣嗎 ?

How could it be that you favor me?

⟶ 您難道是偏袒我嗎 ?

How *could* anyone say *that* you show favor *to* me?

⟹ 您哪裡是偏袒我呢 ?

How was this showing favor to me?

311

十.六　　天 生 仁人 之 心，[此][乃] 其 固然 也。
np (ex-p. s)　　　\[l.v.]　　p(n)/　part
　　　　　　　　　　[s]　　p

※ 天生仁人之心，其固然也：

根據上文推斷，這句話本來的詞序應該是："
[此][乃]天生仁人之心之固然也"，是個判斷
繁句。全句的謂語是由主語"天生仁人之
心"與謂語"固然"構成的主謂短語。
"天生仁人之心"是由定語"天生仁人"與
中心詞"心"構成的名詞語。語法結構極清楚
，但表達的語氣較平淡。作者要強調"天生仁
人之心"，故把它移出句外，而在它原來的位
置用一"其"字來代替"天生仁人之心"作主
謂短語的主語。文法學家稱這種移出句外的名
詞語為外位語。在本句中它是繁句中主謂短
語的外位主語。

On the basis of the foregoing passage one can infer that the
original word order of this sentence would have been "[此][乃]
天生仁人之心之固然也" (*This is* the "ever-so-ness" of the
humane person's heaven sent heart), which is a **complex
determinative sentence**. The predicate of the whole
determinative sentence is a clausal phrase comprised of the
subject "天生仁人之心" and the predicate "固然". "天生仁
人之心" is a noun phrase comprised of the adjectival modifier "
天生仁人" and the modified noun "心". The structure and
grammar of this sentence are clear, but the tone is rather bland.
The writer wanted to highlight the phrase "天生仁人之心", so
he moved it "outside" the original word order and substituted the
pronoun "其" in its place to serve as the subject of the clausal
phrase. Grammarians refer to noun phrases like this that stand
outside the sentence proper as **extraposed phrases** (外位語).
In this sentence, the **extraposed subject** (外位主語) "天生
仁人之心" is the subject of the clausal phrase in the complex
determinative sentence.

天生來仁人的心腸，它本來如此啊。

Naturally endowed by heaven heart of humane person-- its "ever
so-ness".

312

⟶　[此]　[乃]　天 生 仁 人 之 心 ，　其 固 然 也 。
　　　　[s]　[l.v.]　　　　　　　　　　p(n)

以上 np (ex-p. s)　　　　　s　p　part

[這]　[是]天生來仁人的心腸，[它]本來如此啊。

[This] [is] Heaven endow*ed* humane person's heart, it's innately so.

⟶　此]　[乃]　　天 生 仁 人 之 心[之]　固 然 也 。
　　　　[s]　[l.v.]　　　　　　　　　　p(n)

　　　　　　　　s　　　　　[之]　p　part

[這]　[是]天生來仁人的心腸本來如此啊。

[This] [is] Heaven endow*ed* humane person's heart's innately-so-ness.

⟹　這是天生來仁人的心腸本來如此啊。

The Heaven sent heart of the humane person, it is ever so!

十.七　　此 [乃] 臣 之 所 以 脫 君 也 。"
　　　　　　　　\[l.v.]　　　pn　　/　part
　　　　　　s　　　　　p

　　　　　　s　之　o　prep v　o

這，臣因之使君逃脫的緣故啊。"

This, servant's wherefore escape lord."

⟶這 [就是]我因之而放您逃走的緣故啊。"

This [then is] *the* reason *for* which I cause*d* you *to be able to* escape."

⟹這就是我放您逃走的緣故啊。"

That is why I enabled you to escape."

第三十八課

鄒忌諷齊王納諫

句子分析

一. 鄒忌 修八尺有餘，而 形貌昳麗。

鄒忌高八尺多，而且形貌英俊。

Zōu Jì over six feet tall and look handsome.

⟶ 鄒忌身高八尺多，而且相貌非常英俊。

Zōu Jì *was* over six feet tall and *of* radiant *and* beauteous countenance.

⟹ 鄒忌身高八尺多，而且相貌非常英俊。

Zōu Jì was over six feet tall and of radiant and beauteous countenance.

二. [鄒忌] [於] 朝 服 衣冠 窺 鏡，謂 其 妻 曰：

早上穿衣服戴帽子照鏡子，對他的妻子說：

Morning, put on robe, cap, look in mirror; speak to his wife say:

⟶ [鄒忌] [在]早上穿上衣服戴好帽子照照鏡子，對他的妻子說：

One morning, [Zōu Jì] put on *his* cap *and* gown, look*ed* in *the* mirror *and* spoke to his wife say*ing*:

314

One morning *when* he put on *his* cap *and* gown, *he* look*ed into the* mirror *and* spoke to his wife say*ing*:

====> 他在早上穿上衣服戴好帽子照鏡子，對他的妻子說：

One morning when he put on his cap and gown, he looked into the mirror and spoke to his wife saying:

二.一 "我　孰與城北徐公　美？"
　　　s　　　　　　p

※孰與：　這是由疑問代詞"孰"和連詞"與"構成的極獨特的合成詞，因為它幾乎無法歸入任何詞類。在文言中它專用於比較句的變式結構："A 孰與 B Adj." 中，來比較兩個人的優劣或兩件事的得失。根據它在這種句式中的位置，勉強可算是個"連詞"。

"A 孰與 B Adj." 無法逐字或按序譯成白話，只能根據全句的意思譯成 "A 比起 B 來哪個[更] Adj.?"。

這種**拗句**（詞序異常的句子）之所以出現在文言中，大概是由於古代作者力求句式多變以達到修辭目的的效果。試把這個拗句還原到正常的語序："A與 B 孰 Adj."，逐字譯成白話是："A 跟 B [比／比起來]哪個[更] Adj.?"，意思就清楚得多了。

The phrase "孰與" is a unique **composite word** made up of the interrogative pronoun "孰" (who/which) and the conjunction "與" (and), for which reason it is virtually impossible to classify it under any grammatical category. In classical Chinese, it is used as a variant form of the comparative sentence: "A與 B 孰 Adj.". This phrase is used to compare the relative quality of two persons or the relative preferability of two things or two courses of action. By virtue of its position in this type of sentence, it could perforce be construed as a special "conjunction."

The construction "A 孰與 B Adj." can not be translated into spoken Chinese character by character or according to its original word order; it can only be translated on the basis of the meaning of the entire sentence into the paradigm "A 比起 B 來哪個[更] Adj.?"

315

This sort of **awkward sentence**(拗句 **ào jù**)-- a sentence with an unconventional word order -- very likely came into classical Chinese as a result of ancient writers' enthusiasm for using variations in sentence patterns in order to achieve greater rhetorical effects. If this awkward sentence were put into a more conventional classical Chinese sentence order, it would be: "A 與 B 孰 Adj."; translated character by character into spoken Chinese it means: "A 跟 B [比／起起來]哪個 [更] Adj.?" (A and B [when compared] which one [more] Adj.?) This rearrangement of the word order makes the sense of the sentence pattern much clearer.

※句型變換 ： SENTENCE PATTERN TRANSFORMATION

這個句子可還原成正常的語序 ：

The elements of this sentence can be reconstituted in their conventional grammatical order:

"我與城北徐公　孰　美"
　　　　　　　　\s　　p(adj)/
　　s　　　　　　　　p

"我跟城北徐先生哪個好看 ？"

"I and city north Master Xú, which good-looking?"

⟶ "我跟城北的徐先生比哪一個更好看 ？"

"Comparing myself and Master Xú of *the* north *part of the* city, which one *is* better looking?"

"*Between* myself and Master Xú *in the* north *of the* city, *who is the* better looking?"

⟹ "我跟城北的徐先生比哪一個更好看 ？"

"Between myself and Master Xú in the north of the city, who is the better looking?"

三． 其妻 曰 ： "　　　。　"
　　　　　　\v　　　o/
　　s　　　　p

他的妻子說 ：

His wife said:

三 .— "君 美 甚 ， 徐公 何 能 及 君 也 ？"
　　　　\adj comp/　　　　　\adv aux v o/　part
　　　　s　　p　　　　s　　　　p

"您美得很，徐先生哪能趕上您呢？"

"My lord beauteous exceedingly;　Master Xú, how can come up my lord?

——→ "您好看極了，徐先生哪兒能比得上您呢？"

"You *are* exceedingly good-looking;　how *could* Master Xú *be as* **good-looking *as*** you?"

===⟹ "您好看極了，徐先生哪兒能比得上您呢？"

"You are exceedingly good-looking;　how could Master Xú be as good-looking as you?"

四 . 城北徐公 ， [乃] 齊國之美麗者 也 。
　　　　　　　\l.v.l　　pn　/　part
　　　s　　　　　　p

城北徐先生齊國的美麗的人啊 。

City north Matser Xú - Qí state's beauteous one.

——→ 城北的徐先生 [是] 齊國的美麗的男人啊 。

Master Xú *in the* north *of the* city [is] *one of the* good-looking men *of the* state *of* Qí.

===⟹ 城北的徐先生是齊國的美男子 。

Master Xú in the north of the city was a good-looking man of the state of Qí.

五． 忌 不 自 信 ﹏[美 於 徐公]，而 復 問 其 妾 曰："   "

鄒忌自己不信，就又問他的妾說：

Jì not himself believe, and second time ask his concubine, say:

⟶ 鄒忌不相信自己[比徐先生美]，就又問他的妾說：

Zōu Jì himself *did* not believe *himself* [*to be* better looking than Master Xú], and so next ask*ed* his concubine, say*ing*:

⟹ 鄒忌不相信自己比徐先生美，就又問他的妾說：

Zōu Jì did not believe himself to be better looking than Master Xú and so next asked his concubine saying:

五．一 "我 孰與徐公 美？"
　　　[s]　　　p

　※句子還原：

"我與徐公 孰 美"
　　s　　　p

"我跟徐先生哪個好看？"

"I and Master Xú, which good-looking?"

⟶ "我跟徐先生比哪一個更好看？"

"Comparing myself and Master Xú, which one *is* better looking?"

"*Between* myself and Master Xú, *who is the* better looking?"

⟹ "我跟徐先生比哪一個更好看？"

"Between myself and Master Xú, who is the better looking?"

六． 妾 旦 : " 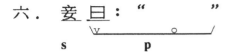 "
　　　　　_v__o__/
　　s　　　　p

妾説 :

The concubine said:

六．一 "徐公 何 能 及 君 也 ?"
　　　　　　\adv aux v o/ part
　　　　s　　　　p

"徐先生 哪能 趕上 您 呢 ?"

"Master Xú, how can come up you?"

——→ "徐先生 哪兒 能 比得上 您 呢 ?"

"How *could* Master Xú *be as* **good-looking** *as* you?"

===⇒ "徐先生 哪兒 能 比得上 您 呢 ?"

"How could Master Xú be as good-looking as you?"

七． [及]旦日， 客 從外 來， [忌]與[之] 坐 談， 問 之 :
　　　\\[prep] o /　　\prep o v/　　\prep[o] v v/　\v o/
　　　　adv　　　　s　　　p　　　[s]　　p1　　　p2

第二天， 客從外來， 跟坐下談話， 問他 :

Following day, guest from without come, sit with/talk to, ask him:

——→ [到] 第二天， 一位客人從外邊來了， [鄒忌] 跟[他]坐下
　　談話， 問他 :

The follow*ing* day, *a* guest arriv*ed* from outside *the area*; [Zōu Jì] s*at* talk*ing*
with [him] *and* ask*ed* him:

319

⟹ 到了第二天，一位客人從外邊來了，鄒忌跟他坐下談話，問他：

The following day, a guest arrived from outside the area; Zōu Jì sat talking with him and asked him:

七．一 "吾與徐公　孰　美？"

                 \s adj/

        [s]   p

"我跟徐先生哪個好看？"

"I and Master Xú, which good-looking?"

⟶ "我跟徐先生比，哪一個更好看？"

"Comparing myself and Master Xú, which one *is* better looking?"

"*Between* Master Xú and myself, *who is the* better looking?"

⟹ "我跟徐先生比，哪一個更好看？"

"Between Master Xú and myself, who is the better looking?"

八． 客 曰："　　　"

             \v⌣⌣⌣o⌣⌣/

      s   p

客人說：

The guest said:

八．一 "徐公　不　若　君之美　也。"

                     s 之 p(a)

          \adv p-l.v.   pn   /   part

        [s]   p

※ 徐公〔之美〕不若君之美也：

這是比較句。用準繫詞"不若"來比較前後
兩項：A（徐公之美）和B（君之美），意思是A
不如B或B勝過A.

320

This is a **Comparative Sentence.** The pseudo linking verb "不若" is used here to compare the two items A and B, with the meaning that A is inferior to B, or B is superior to A.

"徐先生不如您美啊。"

"Master Xú not good-looking like you."

——→ "徐先生不如您美啊。"

"Master Xú *is* not as good-looking *as* you *are*."

===> "徐先生不如您美啊。"

"Master Xú is not as good-looking as you are."

九. [及] 明日, 徐公 來,

第二天, 徐先生來。

Next day, Master Xú come.

——→ [到]第二天的時候, 徐先生來了。

[On] *the* next day, Master Xú *came*.

===> 到第二天的時候, 徐先生來了。

On the next day, Master Xú came.

[忌] 熟 視 之, 自 以為 不如 [徐公];

仔細看他, 自己覺得不如。

Closely regard him; himself think not like.

——→ [鄒忌]仔細地看他, 覺得自己不如[徐先生]。

321

[Zōu Jì] looked *at* him carefully *and* **he thought himself not like** [Master Xú].

Zōu Jì looked *at* him closely and **felt** *he* himself *was* **not as good-looking** *as* [Master Xú].

⟹ 鄒忌仔細地看他，覺得自己不如他。

Zōu Jì looked at him closely and felt he himself was not as good-looking as Master Xú.

窺　鏡　而　自　視，　又　[自　以爲]　弗如　　遠甚。
\v　o　conj　adv　v/　\adv　[adv　v]　adv　p-l.v.　comp/
　　　　p3　　　　　　　　　p4

照鏡子來看自己，又不如遠得很。

Look at mirror to regard himself, again not like far great.

⟶ 照鏡子來看看自己，又自己以爲自己遠遠地不如徐先生。

Look*ing in the* mirror to regard himself, again he thought himself very far *from being* as good-looking *as* Master Xú.

Look*ing* at himself *in the* mirror, again he *felt that* he *was* far inferior *to* Master Xú.

⟹ 照鏡子來看看自己，又覺得自己遠遠比不上他。

Looking at himself in the mirror, again he felt that he was far inferior to Master Xú.

[於]暮　寢　而　思　之，曰："　　　　　"
\adv　v/　conj　\v　o/　\v　　　　　o/
　adv　　　　　p5　　　　p6

晚上睡覺思考它，説：

Evening go to bed and ponder it, say:

⟶ [在]晚上睡覺的時候思考這件事，對自己説：

[In] *the* evening *when he went to* bed, *he* pond*ed the* matter, say*ing* to himself:

⟹ 晚上睡覺的時候思考這件事，對自己說：

In the evening when he went to bed, he thought this over and said to himself:

[妻之]　v　　o
　[s]　　 p
"吾妻之美我者，[乃]　[其]　私　我　也；
　　s　　　　　[l.v.]　　p(n)　　part

"我的妻認爲我美的緣故，偏愛我啊；

"My wife's thinking me good-looking reason, partial to me;

⟶ "我的妻子認爲我美的緣故，[是][她]偏愛我啊；

"*The* reason my wife think*s* I *am* good-looking [is] *that* [she] *is* partial *to* me;

⟹ "我的妻子認爲我美的緣故，是她偏愛我啊；

"The reason my wife thinks I am good-looking is that she is partial to me;

[妾之]　v　　o
　[s]　　 p
妾之美我者，[乃]　[其]　畏　我　也；
　s　　　　　[l.v.]　　p(n)　　part

妾認爲我美的緣故，畏懼我啊；

concubine's thinking me good-looking reason, fearing me;

⟶ 我的妾認爲我美的緣故，[是][她]畏懼我啊；

the reason my concubine think*s* I *am* good-looking [is] *that* [she] fear*s* me;

⟹ 我的妾認爲我美的緣故，是她畏懼我啊；

the reason my concubine thinks I am good-looking is that she fears me;

```
                          [客之]  v   v    o    prep   o
                          [客之]  v _____o_____
                          [s]_____p_____
```

客之美我者，[乃] [其] 欲 有 求 於 我 也。"

　　s　　 [l.v.]　　p(n)　　　 part

客認爲我美的緣故，要向我有要求啊。"

guest's thinking me good-looking reason, wanting to request something from me."

⟶ 客人認爲我美的緣故，[是] [他] 有事要求我啊。"

the reason *the* guest think*s* I *am* good-looking [is] *that* [he] **wants *to* ask me *for* something**."

⟹ 客人認爲我美的緣故，是他有事要求我啊。"

the reason the guest thinks I am good-looking is that he wants to ask me for something."

```
於 是  [忌]  入 朝 見 威 王 曰： " "
\prep o/ [s]  \v o v o/   \v ___o/
  adv       　　p1　　　　 p2
```

在這種情之況下，進入朝廷見威王，説：

Under these circumstances, enter court, see King Wēi, say:

⟶ 在這種想通了的情況之下，[鄒忌] 就進朝廷去見齊威王，説：

Having had this insight, [he] enter*ed the* court, s*aw* King Wēi *of* Qí *and* sa*id*:

⟹ 在這種想通了的情況之下，他就進朝廷去見齊威王，説：

Having had this insight, he entered the court, saw King Wēi of Qí and said:

九、一 "臣 誠 知 [臣] 不 如 徐公美。

```
                    adv l.v.  s    p
             [s]    ──────────p──────
    "臣 誠 知 [臣] 不 如 徐公美。
      \adv  v ──────────────o/
    s         p
```

※徐公美　本來是意思完整的描寫簡句，但此處在 "A(S) 不如 B (n-predicate)" 句型中用作謂語，失掉了獨立性，只能叫**句子形式**。它在整句中的作用與**主謂短語**完全相同。可以說句子形式與主謂短語唯一的區別就在於主語、謂語之間，加或沒加化句子為主謂短語的符號 "之" 字。因此中國有些文法學家乾脆把兩者都叫**句子形式**；但本書中還是根據它們的結構形式，分別叫它們作**句子形式**及**主謂短語**。

"徐公美" is in and of itself a fully comprehensible simple descriptive sentence. Here, however, it functions as the predicate of a sentence constructed on the paradigm "A (s) 不如 B (predicate nominative)". As a grammatical element included in another longer sentence, it loses its independent character, even though it retains the formal characteristics of a simple descriptive sentence (**s-p**). When a complete sentence functions as a grammatical element in another sentence, it can only be referred to as a **"nominal sentence"** (**句子形式**). The only distinction between a **nominal sentence** and a **clausal phrase** (**主謂短語**) is that in a clausal phrase the particle "之" is placed between the subject and the predicate as a grammatical marker that nominalizes the sentence (i.e., indicates its function as a noun phrase in the **embedding sentence**). Consequently, some Chinese grammarians simply refer to both of these constructions as **nominal sentences**; but in this textbook, they are still distinguished as two separate grammatical constructions.

"臣確實知道不如徐先生美。

"Servant truly know not like Master Xú good-looking.

⟶ "我確實知道[自己]不如徐先生美。

"I truly *do* know *that* [I] *am* not as good-looking *as* Master Xú.

⟹ "我確實知道自己不如徐先生美。

"I really do know that I am not as good-looking as Master Xú.

九、二　　　臣之妻　私　臣，
　　　　　　　　 s　　　 p

臣的妻偏愛臣，

Servant's wife partial to servant;

⟶　我的妻子偏愛我，

My wife *is* partial *to* me;

⟹　我的妻子偏愛我，

My wife is partial to me;

　　　臣之妾　畏　臣，
　　　　　 s　　　 p

臣的妾畏臣，

servant's concubine fear servant;

⟶　我的妾畏懼我，

my concubine fear*s* me;

⟹　我的妾畏懼我，

my concubine fears me;

　　　臣之客　欲　有　求　於　臣，
　　　　　 s　　　　　　 p

臣的客要向臣有要求，

servant's guest want ask something of servant:

326

⟶ 我的客人有事要求我，

my guest want*ed to* ask something *of* me:

⟹ 我的客人有事要求我，

my guest wanted to ask something of me:

[　] 皆　以　臣美　於　徐公。
　　　　\adv　v　o/s adj prep　o/
[s]　　　　　　　　p

※ 以　　　　"以"字在本句中用作動詞，意思是"以為"
　　　　　　或"謂"，譯成白話是"認為"或
　　　　　　"說"。見楊樹達《詞詮》，三四八頁。

In this sentence "以" functions as a verb meaning "以為"
(to consider) or "謂" (to say); it can be translated into spoken
Chinese as "認為" or "說" and into English as "to consider" or
"to say". *See Yáng Shùdá, **Cí Quán**, p. 348.*

都說我比徐先生美。

all say servant good-looking compared to Master Xú.

⟶ 他們都說我比徐先生美。

so they all say *that* I *am better* looking than Master Xú.

⟹ 他們都說我比徐先生美。

so they all say that I am better looking than Master Xú.

　　　　　　　[v]　 ○　　　　 [v]　 ○
九、三　 今 齊 [有]地方千里，[有]百二十城。
　　　　adv　s　　　 p1　　　　　　p2

現在齊土地一千里平方，一百二十城。

Now, Qí lands square one thousand *lǐ*, one hundred twenty cities.

327

⟶ 現在齊國[有]國土一千里平方，全國[有]一百二十座城。

Now, *the* state *of* Qí [has] land*s* square *by* one thousand *lǐ on each side*; *the* whole state [has] 120 *walled* cit*ies*.

⟹ 現在齊國有國土一百萬平方里，全國有一百二十座城。

At present, the state of Qí has territory encompassing one million square *lǐ* and the whole state has 120 walled cities.

                          adv v   o

[於]宮婦左右，莫 不 私 王；

  [prep]   o/   s   p

          s   p

宮廷美女左右侍從沒有一個不偏袒大王；

Palace ladies, attendants, not one not partial to king;

⟶ [在]宮廷美女及侍從中沒有一個人不偏袒大王；

[Among] *the* palace lad*ies and* personal attendant*s*, no one *is* not partial *to* you;

⟹ 在宮廷美女及侍從中沒有一個人不偏袒大王；

among the palace ladies and personal attendants, there is not one who is not partial to you;

                          adv v   o

[於]朝廷之臣，莫 不 畏 王；

  [prep]   o/   s   p

          s   p

朝廷的臣子沒有一個不畏懼大王；

servants of royal court, not one not fear king;

———→［在］朝廷的臣子中沒有一個人不畏懼大王；

[among] *the* official*s* of *the* royal court, no one *does* not fear *the* king;

===⇒ 在朝廷的臣子中沒有一個人不畏懼大王；

among the officials of the royal court, there is not one who does not fear you;

$$\underset{\underset{\text{s}}{\underbrace{\text{[prep]}\qquad\text{o}}}}{[於]四境之內}，\underset{\underset{\text{p}}{\underbrace{\underset{\text{s}}{莫}\;\overset{\text{adv}}{不}\;\overset{\text{v}}{有}\;\overset{\text{o}}{求}\;\overset{\text{prep}}{於}\;\overset{\text{o}}{王}}}}{}。$$

四面國境之內，沒有一個人不有求於大王。

inside four borders, not one not have request from king;

———→［在］四面國境之內，沒有一個人不有求於大王。

[within] *the* four borders *of the realm*, not one person *does* not have *a* request of *the* king;

===⇒ 在四面國境之內，沒有一個人不有求於大王。

within the four borders of the realm, there is not one who does not have something to ask of you.

九、四　　$\underset{\underset{\text{indep.elem.}}{\underbrace{\overset{\text{prep}}{由}\;\overset{\text{o}}{此}\;\overset{\text{v}}{觀}\;\overset{\text{o}}{之}}}}{由此觀之}，\underset{\underset{\text{s}}{王之}}{}\overset{之}{}\underset{\underset{\text{p}}{\underbrace{蔽\;\underset{\text{part}}{甚}\;矣}}}{}！"

※由此觀之：

　　"由此觀之"是文言中常見的**固定結構**，其實它是"［臣］由此觀之"的省寫。"此"是指示代詞，指代上文中已說過的情況；"之"是代詞，指代下文將要談到的情況。這個固定結構表示說話人"余"根據上文已說過的情況來

329

察看另一情況，然後對另一情況作出一種論斷。它與下文間隱含有一種 "根據A(前一情況)來推斷B(後一情況)" 的關係。

"由此觀之" (from this view it) is a **fixed construction** frequently encountered in classical Chinese. It is in fact an abbreviated form of the phrase " [臣]由此觀之 " ([I] from this view it). "此" (this) is a demonstrative pronoun that refers here to the situation or circumstances stated in the foregoing text; "之" (it) refers to the situation or circumstances about to be remarked upon in the text immediately following. This **fixed construction** conveys the sense that the implied speaker "臣" is going to use one set of circumstances as the basis for interpreting a second set of circumstances, both of which have been stated, after which he will express a judgement about the second set of circumstances. It serves to introduce the conclusion of an argument by analogy: using the first situation "A/此" as the basis for interpreting the second situation "B/之", one reaches the following conclusion.

"由此觀之" 的 "之"，雖然確有其所指，但為避免重複，翻譯到白話時通常把它虛化，不譯出來。

Although the pronoun "之" does have a specific referent in the phrase "由此觀之", in order to avoid redundance, it is generally left untranslated when this expression is rendered into spoken Chinese. In English, this phrase can be simply translated as "seen in this regard", "seen in this light" or literally translated as "looking at it (i.e., the situation) from this *point of view*", i.e., "looking at [B] in the light of [A],..."

※蔽：

"蒙蔽"，本句中根據上下文，應視為被動，是 "被蒙蔽"、"受蒙蔽" 的意思。參看第八課，句析七·三，"不愛"，第五十頁。

Here the word "蔽" (to delude) should be interpreted in its passive sense (to be deluded) in this contexts. *See also L. 8, sentence analysis 7.3, p. 50.*

從這看它，王蒙蔽厲害啦！"

From this regard it, king deluded great so!"

⟶ 從上述的情形來看王的情形，大王被蒙蔽得太厲害啦！"
Look*ing* at *the king's* situation *in* light *of the* **foregoing remarks,** *the* king's *having* **been** delud*ed is* so very great!"

===⟹ 從這情形來看，大王被蒙蔽得太厲害啦！"

Looking at your situation in this light; you have been severely deluded indeed!"

十　王 曰：" 善！" 乃 下 令：
　　　　＼ v o／　　＼adv v o／
　　　s　　p　　　　　　p

王說：" 好！" 就下令：

King say: "Good!" Then send down order:

⟶ 威王說：" 有道理！" 就下命令：

The king sai*d*: "Agree*d*!" Whereupon *he* issue*d an* order:

⟶ 威王說：" 有道理！" 就下命令：

The king said: "Agreed!" Whereupon he issued an order:

　　　　　　　　aux adv v ___o___ pron
　　　　　　　　___adj. mod_____ pron
十、一 " 群臣吏民　能 面刺寡人之過者，受 上賞；
　　　　‾‾‾‾‾‾‾　　　　　　　　　　　　　　　　＼v o／
　　　　　s　　　　　　s　　　　　　　　　　　p

※定語後置：

　　　" 群臣吏民能面刺寡人之過者"、"[群臣吏
　　　民]上書諫寡人者"、"[群臣吏民]能謗議於
　　　朝市聞寡人之耳者"、是典型的**定語後置**的
　　　名詞語。中心詞是" 群臣吏民"，定語是" 能
　　　面刺寡人之過"、" 上書諫寡人"、" 能謗議
　　　於朝市聞寡人之耳"，後加被飾代詞" 者"複
　　　指那個中心詞" 群臣吏民"。還原成正常的詞
　　　序，應該是" 能面刺寡人之過之群臣吏民"、
　　　" 上書諫寡人之群臣吏民"、" 能謗議於朝市
　　　聞寡人之耳之群臣吏民"；意思雖極清楚，句
　　　構卻顯得笨拙，逐字譯成白話尤其囉嗦、拗口

；原因在於此名詞語不但定語長（"能面刺寡人之過"；"上書諫寡人"；"能謗議於朝市聞[於]寡人之耳"），連中心詞（"群臣吏民"）也相當長。

遇到這種中心詞和定語都長的名詞語，翻譯到白話時，不妨仍照原來定語後置的詞序譯，只要把複指中心詞的"者"（之 "N"）中的 "N" 省略，直接譯成"的"即可。由此三例可見文言名詞語定語後置的結構是有其道理的。

"群臣吏民能面刺寡人之過者"，"[群臣吏民]上書諫寡人者"，"[群臣吏民]能謗議於朝市聞寡人之耳者" are all noun phrases typical of those found in **postpositional adjectival constructions**. In each case, the modified noun phrase is "群臣吏民" and the adjectival modifiers are "能面刺寡人之過"，"上書諫寡人"，and "能謗議於朝市聞寡人之耳". The modified pronoun "者" is attached to the adjectival modifier to reiterate the noun phrase being modified (in this case "群臣吏民"). If these postpositional adjectival modifiers were recast in the conventional sequence of adjectival modifier + noun phrase being modified (**adj+n**), they would be written as follows:
"能面刺寡人之過之群臣吏民"，"上書諫寡人之群臣吏民"，and "能謗議於朝市聞寡人之耳之群臣吏民".
Although the meaning is absolutely clear in this formulation, the construction itself is rather clumsy; literally translated into spoken Chinese, it would appear even more wordy and awkward. This is because in these three noun phrases not only are the adjectival modifiers lengthy ("能面刺寡人之過"，"上書諫寡人"，and "能謗議於朝市聞寡人之耳"), the modified noun phrase ("群臣吏民") is also relatively long.
In such cases where both the adjectival modifier and the noun phrase being modified are comprised of relatively lengthy noun phrases, the whole phrase can be translated into spoken Chinese following the sequence of the original postpositional adjectival construction without any problems; the modified pronoun "者" (之 + "**n**"), which stands for the noun phrase being modified, can be replaced with "的", since the modified noun phrase need not be reiterated. Such lengthy adjectival modifiers are best translated into English as relative clauses (i.e., "who....", "that...."). From these three examples, one can clearly see the reason for employing this type of construction in classical Chinese.

"眾大臣、官吏、民眾能當面指責寡人的過失的，受上等獎賞；

"Court officials, functionaries, common people can face criticize meagre person's faults ones receive top reward;

⟶ "眾大臣、官吏、民眾能當面指出我的過失的，會受到上等的獎賞；

"Those court official*s*, functionar*ies and* common people *who* can criticize my fault*s* to *my* face *shall* receive *the* highest reward;

⟹ "眾大臣、官吏、民眾能當面指出我的過失的，會受到上等的獎賞；

"Those court officials, functionaries and common people who can criticize my faults to my face shall receive the highest reward;

<pre>
            v o v o   pron
              adj. mod   pron
</pre>
十、二 上書諫寡人 者，受 中賞；
        s   p
                      \v o/

上奏章諫正寡人的，受中等獎賞；

present memorial, admonish meagre person ones receive middle reward;

⟶ 上奏章來諫正我的，會受到中等的獎賞；

those who present *a* memorial to admonish me *shall* receive *the* middle reward;

⟹ 上奏章來諫正我的，會受到中等的獎賞；

those who present a memorial to admonish me shall receive the middle reward;

<pre>
         aux v prep o   v [prep]   o   pron
                    adj. mod   pron
</pre>
十、三 能謗議於 朝市聞 [於] 寡人之耳 者，受 下賞。"
        s   p
                                      \v o/

※⋯聞〔於〕寡人之耳：被動句句式之一

這種被動句的句式是："N1(patient or receiver) V
於 N2 (agent or doer)"。介詞"於"引出施事者 N2
(agent or doer)，可譯成白話的"被"。本句中的 N1
是"謗議"，省略了沒說出來；動詞是"聞"
（聽到）；施事者 N2 是"寡人之耳"。全句逐
字譯成白話是"被寡人的耳朵聽到。"

This is also one of the **passive sentences**. The sentence
pattern is: "**N1 V 於 N2**", where **N1** is the receiver or patient
of the verb and **N2** is the doer or agent of the verb. The
preposition "於", which can be rendered as "被" in spoken
Chinese, here introduces **N2**, the **agent**. In this sentence, "**N1**"
is "謗議", (the criticism and discussion) which is understood
and thus omitted; the **verb** is "聞" (to hear or to be heard); N2
is "寡人之耳" (my ears). The whole sentence can be rendered
as "[謗議]被寡人的耳朵聽到" ([their criticisms] were heard
by my ears).

能公開批評議論在朝廷市場聽到我的耳朵的，受下等獎
賞。"

can criticize/discuss in court/marketplace be heard by meagre person's ears
ones receive bottom reward."

⟶ 能在朝廷或市場公開地批評議論被我的耳朵聽到的，會
受到下等的獎賞。"

those who can publicly criticize *and* discuss *my faults in the* court or *in the*
marketplace *and are heard* by my ears *shall* receive *the* lowest reward."

⟶ 能在朝廷或市場公開地批評議論讓我聽到耳中的，會受
到下等的獎賞。"

those who can publicly criticize *and* discuss *my faults in the* court or *in the*
marketplace *and **are heard about*** by me *shall* receive *the* lowest reward."

⟹ 能在朝廷或市場公開地批評議論讓我聽到耳中的，會受
到下等的獎賞。"

those who can publicly criticize and discuss my faults in the court and the
marketplace and are heard about by me shall receive the lowest reward."

十一　令　初　下，群臣　進諫；　　[王宮之] 門庭　　若　　市
　　　　　\adv v/　　　\v o/　　　 [adj.mod.]
　　　　　s　p　　s　p　　　　　　　　　　s　　　p

命令剛下，眾大臣進獻諫言，門前院中像市場。

Order first issued, all court officials present remonstrances, gate/ courtyard
like marketplace.

——→　命令剛下來的時候，眾大臣來進獻諫言，[王宮的]門前跟
　　　院中擠得像市場一樣。

When the order *was* first issue*d*, all *the* court officials present*ed*
remonstrances; *in front of the* [palace] gate*s and in the* [palace] courtyard *it
was* crowd*ed* like *a* marketplace.

══→　命令剛下來的時候，眾大臣來進獻諫言，王宮的門前跟
　　　院中擠得像市場一樣。

When the order was first issued, all the court officials came to present
remonstrances; in front of the palace gates and in the courtyard it was as
crowded as a marketplace.

十二　數月之後，[諫]　時時　而　間　進。
　　　adv　　　　　　\adv conj adv v/
　　　　　[s]　　　　　　　　p

幾月之後，有時偶進獻。

Several months after, time to time occasionally present.

——→　幾個月之後，[諫言]有時偶然被進獻。

Several months after, [remonstrances] *were* occasionally present*ed from* time *to*
time.

——→　幾個月以後，有時偶然有人進獻諫言。

After several month*s had passed*, **people occasionally presented
remonstrances from time to time**.

335

===⇒ 幾個月以後，有時偶然有人進獻諫言。

After several months had passed, people occasionally presented remonstrances from time to time.

十三　期年之後，　［群臣吏民］　雖　欲　言，無　可　進者。
　　　‾‾‾‾‾‾　　　　‾‾‾‾‾‾　　　＼conj aux v　v　　o／
　　　adv　　　　　　　　　＼conj aux v　adv v pron
　　　　　　　　　　　　［s］　　　　　　p

一週年之後，雖然想說沒有可進獻的諫言。

One full year after, even if want speak, not have can present things.

──→　一週年以後，［眾大臣、官吏及民眾］即使想說也沒有
甚麼可以進獻的話了。

After one full year, even if [*the* court official*s*, functionar*ies, and* common people] want*ed to* speak *out, they did* not have anything *to* present.

===⇒　一週年以後，眾大臣、官吏及民眾，就是想說也沒有甚
麼可以進獻的了。

After a full year had passed, even if someone wanted to speak out, there was nothing to present.

十四　燕、趙、韓、魏　聞之，皆　朝　於　齊。
　　　‾‾‾‾‾‾‾‾‾‾‾‾　＼v　o／　＼adv v prep o／
　　　　　s　　　　　　　p1　　　　　　p2

燕、趙、韓、魏聽到它，都到齊來朝。

Yān, Zhào, Hán, Wèi hear it; all pay court to Qí.

──→　燕國、趙國、韓國、魏國聽到這件事，都到齊國來朝見
。

The state*s of* Yān, Zhào, Hán, *and* Wèi hear*d of* this *and* all c*ame to* pay court *to the king of* Qí.

⟹ 燕國、趙國、韓國、魏國聽到這件事，都到齊國來朝見
。

The states of Yān, Zhào, Hán, and Wèi heard of this and all came to pay court to the king of Qí.

十五　此　［乃］所謂戰勝於朝庭。

這說的 "戰勝在朝廷"。

This - that call "win battle at court."

⟶ 這［就是］一般人說的 "在朝廷中戰勝" 的情形。

This [is] *the* situation people call "win*ning the* battle at court."

⟹ 這就是一般人說的 "在朝廷中獲得勝利" 的情形。

This is what is called "gaining the victory at court."

第三十九課

魏節乳母

句子分析

一. 魏節乳母者，[乃]魏公子之乳母也。

魏節乳母，魏公子的奶媽。

Wèi upright wet nurse -- Wèi prince's wet nurse.

⟶ 魏國節烈的乳母，[是]魏國公子的奶媽。

The upright wet nurse *of* Wèi [*was*] *the* wet nurse *of a* prince *of* Wèi.

⟹ 魏國節烈的乳母，是魏國公子的奶媽。

The upright wet nurse of Wèi was the wet nurse of a prince of Wèi.

二. 秦攻魏，破之，殺魏王瑕，誅諸公子，而一公子不得。

秦攻魏，攻破它，殺魏王瑕，殺死眾多公子，可是一個
公子不能得到。

Qín attack Wèi, defeat it, kill Wèi king Xiá, execute princes; but one prince
not get.

⟶ 秦國攻打魏國，把魏國打敗了，殺了魏王瑕，也殺死了眾
多公子，可是還有一位公子捉不到。

The state *of* Qín attack*ed the* state *of* Wèi *and* defeat*ed* it; *the army of* Qín
kill*ed the* king *of* Wèi, Xiá, and execut*ed the* prince*s of* Wèi; but one prince
was not captur*ed*.

338

⟹ 秦國攻打魏國，把魏國打敗了，殺了魏王瑕，也殺死了眾多公子，可是還有一位公子捉不到。

The state of Qín attacked the state of Wèi and defeated it; the army of Qín killed the king of Wèi, Xiá, and executed the princes of Wèi, but one prince was not captured.

三． [秦王] 令 [於] 魏國 ， 曰 ： "＿"
            ＼ v [prep] o   v   o ／
     [s]   p

命令魏國 ， 說 ：

Order Wèi state say:

⟶ [秦王] [在] 魏國下了一道命令 ， 說 ：

[*The* king *of* Qín] issue*d* an order *to the people of the* state *of* Wèi, *which* said:

⟹ 秦王在魏國下了一道命令 ， 說 ：

The king of Qín issued an order to the people of the state of Wèi, which said:

三．一 "得公子者 [寡人] 賜 [之] 金千鎰 ，
       ext.po. o   ＼ v [o]   o ／
              [s]   p

匿之者 [其] 罪 至 夷 。"
         ＼ s   v   o ／
    s   p

"得到公子的人，賞賜黃金一千鎰；藏他的人，刑罰到全家被殺死。"

"Get-prince-one, reward gold thousand ingots; hide-him one, punish to extermination."

⟶ "捉到公子的人， [我] 賞賜 [他] 一千鎰黃金；藏匿公子的人， [他的] 刑罰重到全家被殺死的地步。"

339

"Whosoever capture*s the* prince, [meagre person/I] *shall* award [him] one thousand ingot*s of* gold; whosoever hide*s* him *shall suffer* severe punishment *to the* extent *of the* extermination *of his* entire clan."

===> "捉到公子的人，我賞賜他一千鎰黄金；藏匿公子
的人，他的刑罰重到全家被殺死的地步。"

"Whosoever captures the prince shall be awarded one thousand ingots of gold; whosoever hides him shall suffer severe punishment to the extent of the extermination of his entire clan."

四． 節乳母 與 公子 俱 逃。
　　　　　　＼prep o　adv v／
　　　s　　　　　　p

節乳母跟公子一起逃亡。

Upright wet nurse with prince together flee.

——→ 節乳母跟公子一起逃亡。

The upright wet nurse *fled* together with *the* prince.

===> 節乳母跟公子一起逃亡。

The upright wet nurse fled together with the prince.

五． 魏之故臣 見 乳母 而 識 之， 曰："乳母 無 恙 乎？"
　　　　　　＼v　o／conj＼v　o／　　　＼v　　　　o　　／
　　s　　　　　p1　　　　　p2　　　　　　　　p3

魏的舊臣看見乳母就認識她，說："乳母平安無事嗎？"

Wèi's former minister see wet nurse and recognize her, say: "Wet nurse have no afflictions?"

——→ 魏國的一個舊臣看見乳母就認出她來了，說："乳母平安
無事嗎？"

A former minister *of the* state *of* Wèi s*aw the* wet nurse and recogniz*ed* her, sa*id: "Is the* wet nurse safe and sound?"

⟹ 魏國的一個舊臣看見乳母就認出她來了，說："乳母平安無事嗎？"

A former minister of the state of Wèi saw the wet nurse and recognized her, said: "Are you safe and sound?"

六．乳母曰："嗟乎！吾奈公子何？"

*N1(S)奈N2(O)何？：

"N1(S)對N2(O)怎麼辦？" "N1(S)把N2(O)怎麼辦？"

"What shall N1 do about N2?" This is a desperate expression, meaning that N1 doesn't know what to do about N2, and there seems no way out.

乳母說："唉！我對公子怎麼辦？"

Wet nurse say: "Alas! I what-to-do about prince ?"

⟶ 乳母說："唉！我把公子怎麼辦呢？"

The wet nurse sa*id*: "Alas! What *shall* I do *about the* prince?"

⟹ 乳母說："唉！我把公子怎麼辦呢？"

The wet nurse said: "Alas! What shall I do about the prince?"

七．故臣曰："今公子安在？

舊臣說："現在公子在何處？

Former minister say: "Now prince where is at?

⟶ 那個舊臣説：“現在公子在哪兒啊？

The former minister sa*id*: "Where *is the* prince *at* now?

⟹ 那個舊臣説：“現在公子在哪兒啊？

The former minister said: "Where is the prince now?

七.一　吾聞秦令曰：'　　　　　'

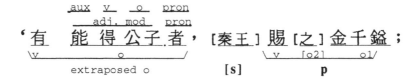

'有　能　得公子者，[秦王]賜[之]金千鎰；

我聽秦下令説：'有能得公子的人，賜黃金一千鎰；

I hear Qín order say: 'Have can get prince one, award gold thousand ingots;

⟶ 我聽到秦國下命令説：'要是有能捉到公子的人，[秦王]賜給[他]黃金一千鎰；

I *have* hear*d that the* state *of* Qín issue*d an* order say*ing*: 'Whosoever *is* able *to* capture *the* prince, [*the* king *of* Qín] *shall* award [him] one thousand ingot*s of* gold;

⟹ 我聽到秦國下命令説：'要是有能捉到公子的人，秦王賜給他一千鎰黃金；

I have heard that the state of Qín issued an order saying: 'whosoever is able to capture the prince shall be awarded one thousand ingots of gold;

七.二　匿之者[其₁]罪至夷。'

藏匿他的人，刑罰到全家被殺死。'

hide prince one punish to extermination.'

⟶ 藏匿公子的人，[他的]刑罰重到全家被殺死的地步。'

whosoever hides *the* prince, [his] punishment *shall be* severe *to the* extent *of the* extermination *of the* entire clan.

⟹ 藏匿公子的人，他的刑罰重到全家被殺死的地步。'

whosoever hides him shall be severely punished to the extent of exterminating the entire clan.

七.三 乳母倘 言之，則 可以 得 千金；
 　　　conj ＼ v o／ conj ＼aux v o／
 s　　　　　p1　　　　　　　　p2

乳母倘若說它，就可以得到一千鎰黃金；

Wet nurse suppose say it, then can thereby get thousand ingots of gold;

⟶ 乳母倘若把公子藏匿的地方說出來，就可以得到一千鎰黃金；

Suppose you **tell where the prince *is* hid***den*, then *you* can get one thousand ingot*s of* gold;

If you reveal *the* whereabouts of *the* prince, then *you* can get one thousand ingot*s of* gold;

⟹ 乳母如果把公子藏匿的地方說出來，就可以得到一千鎰黃金；

If you reveal the whereabouts of the prince, then you can get one thousand ingots of gold;

343

七.四　[汝] 知 而 不 言，則 [爾]昆弟 無 類 矣。"
　　　　　 ＼ v conj adv v／ conj 　　＼ v o／ part
　　　　　[s]　　　 p　　　　　 s　　 p

知道卻不說出來，那麼兄弟就沒有遺留下的族類了
。"

know yet not say, then elder-younger brothers, not-have kinsfolk left
certainly."

——→ [你]知道卻不說出來，那麼在[你的]兄弟中就沒有
遺留下的同族了。"

[you] know yet *do* not say, then *among* [your] elder *and* younger
brothers *there* ceratinly *will* not *be* any kinsfolk *left alive*."

——→ [你]知道卻不說出來，那麼[你的]兄弟就會都被殺
光了。"

if [you] know yet *do* not say, then [your] **brothers *will* ceratinly
all *be* slaughter*ed*.**"

══⇒ 你知道卻不說出來，那麼你的兄弟就會都被殺光了
。"

if you know yet do not say, then your brothers will certainly all be
slaughtered."

　　　　　　　　　　　　　adv　v ＿＿＿o＿＿＿
　　　　　　　interi　s＿＿＿＿＿＿ p ＿＿＿
八．乳母 曰：" 旴！吾 不 知 公子之處 。"
　　 s　　 ＼ v　　　　　 p

乳母說："唉！我不知公子的地方。"

Wet nurse say: "Alas! I not know prince's place."

——→ 乳母說："唉！我不知道公子藏匿的地方。"

The wet nurse sa*id*: "Alas! I *do* not know *the* hid*ing* place of *the* prince."

344

⟹ 乳母说："唉！我不知道公子藏匿的地方。"

The wet nurse said: "Alas! I do not know where the prince is hiding."

九． 故臣曰："＿＿＿＿"
　　 s　　　v　　o
　　　　　　　p

我 聞 公子 與 乳母 俱 逃
　　　s prep o adv v
v　　　　　o
s　　　　p

舊臣说："我聽公子跟乳母一起逃。"

Former minister say: "I hear prince with wet nurse together flee."

⟶ 舊臣说："我聽说公子跟您一起逃亡的。"

The former minister sa*id*: "I *have* hear*d that the* prince fle*d* together with you."

⟹ 舊臣说："我聽说公子跟您一起逃亡的。"

The former minister said: "I have heard that the prince fled together with you."

　　　　　　　conj v o　adv adv adv aux　v
　　　　　s　　　　p1　　　　　　p2
十． 母曰："吾 雖 知之，亦 終 不 可 以 言。"
　　 s　v　　　　　　o
　　　　　　　p

乳母说："我即使知道它，也到底不可以说。"

Wet nurse say: "Even I know it, as well to the end not able to say."

⟶ 乳母说："我就是知道公子藏匿的地方，也到底不可以说出來。"

The wet nurse sa*id*: "Even if I *did* know *the* place *where the* prince *is* hid*ing*, I *still could* not ever speak of *it*."

The wet nurse sa*id*: "Even if I *did* know where *the* prince *is* hid*ing*, I still *could* never speak of it."

⟹ 乳母説："我就是知道公子藏在哪儿，也到底不可以説出来。"

The wet nurse said: "Even if I did know, I still could never speak of it."

十一. 故臣曰："　　"
　　　　 s　　ᵛ　　ᵒ
　　　　　　　 p

舊臣説：

Former minister say:

⟶ 舊臣説：

The former minister sa*id*:

⟹ 舊臣説：

The former minister said:

十一.一　"今 魏國 已 破亡，[王]族 已 滅，
　　　　　 adv　　adv ᵛ　　　　　adv ᵛ
　　　　　　 s　　　 p　　　　 s　　 p

子 匿 之 尚 誰 為 乎？"
ᵛ ᵒ adv ᵒ prep / part
　 s　　　　 p

※魏國已破亡，族已滅：

本句中"破亡"跟"滅"原都是外動詞，但動詞後沒有承接的賓語，它們在句中的意思就變成了受動。（王力，中國文法學初探，頁五十三）。

In this sentence the verbs "破亡" (to destroy) and "滅" (to exterminate) are transitive in nature. But when they are not followed by an object, they automatically become passive in syntactic sense.(*See Wáng Lì, Zhōngguó Yǔfǎxué Chūtàn, p.53*)

346

※誰為：

賓語 "誰" 是疑問代詞，按文言語法的規律，
必須得倒放在介詞 "為" 字之前。

When the interrogative pronoun "誰" (who; whom) functions
as the object in a prepositional phrase, according to the rules of
classical Chinese grammar, it must be transposed in front of the
preposition (in this case the preposition "為" (for)). Thus, "誰
為" (whom for) means "for whom?"

※子匿之尚誰為乎？：

此句正常的詞序應為 "子尚誰為匿之乎？"
作者把介詞語移到動詞語之後，來強調故臣
重利輕義的語氣。故臣認為：既然魏王全家已
死，你藏匿小公子還為誰呢？做這件事對自己
有害無益，因而不值得做。

The conventional word order of this sentence would be "子尚
誰為匿之乎？" (You still whom for hide him?). The writer
moved the prepositional phrase after the verbal phrase
"匿之" in order to highlight the word "誰" (whom) and thereby
accentuate the venal tone of the question. As this former official
saw it, the entire royal clan of Wèi had already been put to death:
for whose sake was she still hiding the princeling? To do this
was simply to invite disaster and consequently not worth doing.

"現在魏國已經破亡，魏王的家族已經被消滅，你
藏匿公子還爲誰呢？"

"Now Wèi state already destroyed, royal clan already exterminated;
you hide him still whom for?"

⟶ "現在魏國已經被打破滅亡了，[魏王的]家族已經
被消滅了，你藏匿公子還爲了誰呢？"

"Now *the* state *of* Wèi *has* already ***been*** destroy*ed, and the* royal clan
has already ***been*** exterminat*ed;* for who*m are* you still hid*ing the*
prince?"

⟹ "現在魏國已經被打破滅亡了，魏王的家族已經被
消滅了，你藏匿公子還爲了誰呢？"

"Now the state of Wèi has already been destroyed, and the royal clan
has already been exterminated; for whom are you still hiding the
prince?"

十二.　　　母 吁 而 言曰："＿"
　　　　　＼v/adv conj v v　 o／
　　　　　　s　　　　　　p

乳母嘆氣說：

Wet nurse sighing say:

——→ 乳母嘆著氣說：

The wet nurse sa*id* with *a* sigh:

⟹ 乳母嘆著氣說：

The wet nurse said with a sigh:

十　　　　　　v o conj v o part
二.一　　"夫 見 利 而 反 上 者 ， 逆 也；
　　　　part　　　s　　　　＼pn/ part
　　　　　　　　s　　　　　　p

"看見利益就背叛主上，叛逆；

"Yea, see profit and turn against superior, treason;

——→ "看見利益就背叛主上是叛逆的行為；

"*To* see advantage and turn against ruler is treason;

⟹ "看見利益就背叛主上的行為是叛逆的行為；

"To see some advantage and turn against one's ruler is treason;

十　　　v o conj v o pron
二.二　　畏 死 而 棄 義 者， 亂 也。
　　　　　　s　　　　　＼pn/ part
　　　　　　　s　　　　　　p

畏懼死就廢棄正義，昏亂。

fear death and abandon righteousness -- folly.

⟶ 畏懼死亡就廢棄正義是昏亂的行為。

to fear death *and* abandon *what is* fitting *and* proper is folly.

⟹ 畏懼死亡就廢棄正義是昏亂的行為。

to abandon what is right and proper for fear of death is folly.

十二.三 今 持逆亂 而 以[之] 求利，吾 不 為 [之] 也。
adv \v o/ conj \prep [o] v o/ s \adv v [o]/ part
_____p_____/ _____p_____/ **p**
_____ex. p.- o_____/

現在拿逆亂用來謀求利益，我不幹啊。

Now hold onto treason/folly and with seek profit, I not do.

⟶ 現在要憑藉逆亂的行為用它來謀求利益，這我絕對不幹啊。

To commit treason *and* folly now and seek thereby *to* profit -- that I absolutely *will* not do.

⟹ 現在要憑藉逆亂的行為來謀求利益，這我絕對不幹啊。

To commit treason and folly now and seek to profit thereby -- that I absolutely will not do.

十二.四 且 夫 為人養子者，務生之，非 為殺之也，
conj dem. \adv v o/ adv prep\v o/ part
               o
        s   **p1**   **p2**

而且那些為人養孩子的人，盡力使孩子活著，不是為殺死他啊，

Moreover, those for person raise child ones, work live it, not for kill it.

⟶ 而且那些為別人照顧孩子的人，盡力使孩子活著
，並不是為了把他殺死啊，

Moreover, those *who* raise another's child do their utmost *to* keep *the* child alive, not *to* kill it.

⟹ 而且那些為別人照顧孩子的人，盡力使孩子活著，
並不是為了把他殺死啊，

Moreover, those who raise another's child do their utmost to keep the child alive, not to kill it.

十
二.五　豈可 以 利賞而畏誅之故，廢正義 而 行逆節 哉！

怎麼可以因為貪圖賞賜跟怕誅殺的緣故，廢棄正義
去做違背節操呢？

How can for covet reward and fear death reason, abandon right/proper and go against moral integrity?

⟶ 怎麼可以因為貪圖賞賜跟怕被誅殺的緣故，廢棄正
義去做違背節操的事呢？

How can *one* abandon *what is* fit*ting and* proper and turn against *what is* righteous because *one* covet*s* reward*s and* fear*s* death?

⟹ 怎麼可以因為貪圖賞賜跟怕被誅殺的緣故，廢棄正
義去做違背節操的事呢？

How can one abandon what is fitting and proper and turn against what is righteous because one covets rewards and fears death?

十
二.六　妾 不能 生 而 令公子 擒 也。"

350

妾不能活著讓公子捉去啊。"

concubine not can living let prince catch."

⟶ 我絕對不能自己活著讓公子被人捉去啊。"

I absolutely cannot *go on* liv*ing* myself *and* let *the* prince *be* capture*d*."

⟹ 我絕對不能自己活著讓公子被人捉去啊。"

I absolutely cannot let the prince be captured while I still live."

十三.　[乳母] 遂 抱 公子 逃 於 深澤之中。

　　　　　　＼adv　v　o　　v　prep　　　o　　／
　　　　　　　　　　　　　　　p
[s]

就抱著公子逃到深窪地裡去。

Thereupon cradle princeling, flee to deep fens' interior.

⟶ 於是 [她] 就抱著公子逃到一片窪地的深處去。

Whereupon [she] cradl*ed* *the little* prince *in her arms and* fle*d* deep into *the* fen*s*.

⟹ 於是她就抱著公子逃到一片窪地的深處去。

Whereupon, cradling the little prince in her arms, she fled deep into the fens.

十四.　故臣 以 [之] 告 秦軍。

　　　　　　＼prep [o]　v　　o／
　　　s　　　　　　　　p

舊臣把報告秦軍。

Former official of report to Qín army.

⟶ 舊臣把 [這件事] 報告給秦國的軍隊。

The former official *of* [it/this matter] repor*ted* to *the* Qín army.

====> 舊臣把這件事報告給秦國的軍隊。

The former official reported this matter to the Qín army.

十
五.　　秦軍 追 見 [之]，爭 射 之。
　　　　　＼ v　v　[o]　　 adv　v　o／
　　　　s　　　　　　p

　　　　　　＊爭射之

　　　　　　　　　　本句用白話翻譯應譯成"爭著射他們"其中
　　　　　　　　　　"爭著"是副詞，"射"是主要動詞。"爭著
　　　　　　　　　　射"是描寫怎樣地射。但在譯成英文時，比較
　　　　　　　　　　自然的說法是 competed to be the first to shoot them, 相
　　　　　　　　　　當於白話的"爭先去射他們。"主要動詞落在
　　　　　　　　　　"爭"上，而"射"成了"爭"的對象。兩者
　　　　　　　　　　的意思雖然相近，重點卻不同了。像這類中英
　　　　　　　　　　兩種語言表達方式的差異，值得注意。

　　　　　　　　　　This predicate can be translated into spoken Chinese as "爭著
　　　　　　　　　　射他們", in which "爭著" is an adverb and "射" is the main
　　　　　　　　　　verb, meaning "shot them in a competitive manner". But when it
　　　　　　　　　　is translated into English, the most common rendition will be
　　　　　　　　　　"competed to be the first to shoot them" where "competed to be
　　　　　　　　　　the first" becomes the main verb, and "to shoot them" is then
　　　　　　　　　　secondary. Though the meaning of these two sentences are very
　　　　　　　　　　close to each other, the emphasis is quite different. This kind of
　　　　　　　　　　discrepency between Chinese and English is very interesting and
　　　　　　　　　　worth noting.

　　　　秦軍追見，爭著射他們。

Qín army pursue, see, compete shoot them.

——> 秦國的軍隊追上去看見他們，爭著用箭射他們。

The Qín army pursue*d* them; *and upon* see*ing* them, *the soldiers* compete*d to
be first to* shoot them.

The Qín army pursue*d* them *and upon* see*ing* them, *the* soldiers compete*d to*
loose *the first* arrow.

====> 秦國的軍隊追上去看見他們，爭著用箭射他們。

352

The Qín army pursued them and upon seeing them, the soldiers competed to loose the first arrow.

十六.　乳母 以 身 為 公子 蔽，矢著身者 數十，
　　　　　　　　＼prep o prep o v／　　　　
　　　　　　s　　　　　p　　　　　　　　s　　　p

　　　　　[乳母] 與 公子 俱 死。
　　　　　　　　＼prep o adv v／
　　　　　　[s]　　　　p

乳母用身體爲公子遮蔽，射在她身上的箭有好幾十枝，跟公子一起死。

Wet nurse, with body for princeling cover, arrows pierce body ones count tens, with princeling together die.

———→　乳母用自己的身體替公子遮蔽著，射在她身上的箭有好幾十枝，[她]跟公子一起死了。

The wet nurse, us*ing her* own body *to* cover *the little* prince, *was* pierce*d by* score*s of* arrow*s and* die*d* together with *the* prince.

═══→　乳母用自己的身體替公子遮擋著，射在她身上的箭有好幾十枝，她跟公子一起死了。

The wet nurse, covering the little prince with her own body, was pierced by scores of arrows and died together with him.

　　　　　　　　　　　　s v o v o
　　　　　　　　　　　　她之＿＿＿p＿＿
十七.　秦王 聞 之，貴 其守忠死義，
　　　　　　＼v p／　＼v　　　o　／
　　s　　　p1　　　　p2

乃 以 卿禮 葬 之，祠[之] 以 太牢。
＼adv prep o v o／　＼v [o] prep o／
　　　p3　　　　　　　　p4

秦王聽到它，敬重乳母保持忠心爲道義犧牲，就用卿的禮儀來埋葬她，用豬牛羊三牲來祭祀。

353

Qín king hear it; esteem wet nurse preserving loyalty dying righteous, so with minister's rites inter her, sacrifice with Great Offering.

——→ 秦王聽到這件事，敬重乳母保持忠心爲道義而犧牲，就
用埋葬卿的禮儀來埋葬她，用豬牛羊三牲來祭祀 [她]。

When the king *of* Qín heard *of* this, *he* esteem*ed the wet nurse for* preserv*ing* her loyalty *by* dy*ing for a* righteous cause *and* so *had* her inter*red* with *the* ceremonial appropriate for *a* great minister *of* state *and* sacrifice*d to* [her spirit] with *the* Great Offering *of* pigs, cattle, *and* sheep.

===⇒ 秦王聽到這件事，敬重乳母保持忠心爲道義而犧牲，就
用埋葬卿的禮儀來埋葬她，用豬牛羊三牲來祭祀她。

When the king of Qín heard of this, he esteemed the wet nurse for preserving her loyalty by dying for a righteous cause and so had her interred with the ceremonial appropriate for a great minister of state and sacrificed to her spirit with the Great Offering.

十
八. [秦王] 寵 其兄 爲 五大夫，賜 [之] 金百鎰。

恩賜她的哥哥做五大夫，賞給黃金一百鎰。

Favor her elder brother, make Grandee of Five, gift gold hundred ingots.

——→[秦王]還封她的哥哥做五大夫，並賜給 [他]一百鎰黃金。

[*The* king *of* Qín] also favor*ed* her elder brother, appoint*ing* him *a* Grandee of Five, *and* bestow*ed on* [him] one hundred ingot*s of* gold.

===⇒ 秦王還封她的哥哥做五大夫，並賜給他一百鎰黃金。

He favored her elder brother, appointing him a Grandee of the Fifth Order, and bestowed on him one hundred ingots of gold.

第四十課

子產不毀鄉校

句子分析

一、　鄭人　游　于　鄉校，　以　論　執政。
　　　　＼v　prep　o／　＼conj　v　o／
　　　s　　　　p　　　　　　　　p

※以：　"以" 字作連詞用時，它在句中的作用與
　　　　"而" 字相同，所連前一小句是行動，後一
　　　　小句是目的。

When it is used as a conjunction, the word "以" functions
like the conjunction "而"; the clause preceding it states an
action and the clause following states the purpose of that action.
It can be translated into English as "to" or "in order to".

鄭人遊玩在鄉校，來評論執掌政權。

Zhèng people saunter to local schools to comment on conducting government.

⟶鄭國人到鄉校去遊玩，來評論執掌政權的人。

The people *of the* state *of* Zhèng saunter*ed into the* local school*s to* comment
on the conduct of government official*s*.

⟹鄭國人到鄉校去遊玩，來評論執掌政權的人。

The people of the state of Zhèng sauntered into the local schools to comment
on the conduct of government officials.

　　　　　　　　　　　　　v　o　　pron l.v.
　　　　　　　　　　　　　　s　　　　　p
二、然明　謂　子産　曰："毀　鄉校，何　如？"
　　　＼v　o　　v　o／
　　s　　　　p

355

然明告訴子產說：“毀掉鄉校，怎麼樣？”

Ránmíng address Zǐchǎn, say: " Destroy local schools; what like?"

——→鄭國的大夫然明對子產說：“把鄉校毀掉，怎麼樣？”

A grand master of *the* state *of* Zhèng Ránmíng sp*oke* to Zǐchǎn say*ing*:
" Destroy *the* local school*s*; how about *that*?"

===>鄭國的大夫然明對子產說：“把鄉校毀掉，怎麼樣？

Ránmíng, a grand master of the state of Zhèng, said to Zǐchǎn: " How about destroying the local schools?"

三、子產 曰： “ 何 為 ［毀 鄉校］？”

※何為：　　為什麼？“何”字是疑問代詞，作賓語用時倒置在動詞或介詞之前。

"What for?" The word "何" is an interrogative pronoun;
when an interrogative pronoun is used as an object, it is placed
in front of the verb or preposition that governs it.

子產說：“爲什麼？

Zǐchǎn say: "What for?

——→ 子產說：“爲什麼［毀掉鄉校］呢？

Zǐchǎn sa*id*: "Why [destroy *the* local school*s*] ?

===> 子產說：“爲什麼把鄉校毀掉呢？

Zǐchǎn said: "Why do that?

三、一　夫人 朝夕 退 而 游焉，以 議 執政之善否。

人民時常回來在那儿遊玩，来議論執掌政權的人善或不
善。

Consider: people frequently come back and saunter there to discuss
conducting goverment being good or not.

———→人民時常工作完了回來到鄉校那儿去遊玩，来議論執掌政
權的人實行的政策妥善不妥善。

Now, *upon* return*ing* from work, people frequently saunter to *the* local school*s* to
discuss *whether the* policies implement*ed by those* conduct*ing the* government
are good *or* not.

====>人民時常工作完了回來到鄉校那儿去遊玩，來議論執掌
政權的人實行的政策妥不妥善。

Now, upon returning from work, people frequently saunter to the local
schools to discuss whether the policies of those governing are appropriate or
not.

三、二　　　其所善者，吾　則 行 之；
　　　　extraposed o　　 \conj v　o/
　　　　　　　　　　　　　　s　　　p

※ 善：　　　本來是形容詞，在這裡是意動用法：以為善。
The word "善" is an adjective which is used here in a putative
sense (i.e., "to think or consider....good")

※其所善者：

這個名詞語原是動詞"行"的賓語，因為要強
調，把它移到句子前面，另外用一個代詞"之
"字放在原來的地位。一般語法學家稱之為"
外位賓語"。

"That which they deem good" is a noun phrase and the object
of the verb "practice"; however, it is moved to the beginning of
the sentence for emphasis, and the pronoun "it" stands in its
place. This word order also serves to highlight or emphasize
the rhetorical importance of the phrase in the sentence.
Grammarians generally call such noun phrases
"extraposed objects".

他們認爲好的那些政令，我就實行；

357

Their think good ones, I then implement them;

⟶ 他們認爲妥善的那些政令，我就實行；

Those polic*ies* they deem appropriate I *will* carry out;

⟹ 他們認爲妥善的那些政令，我就實行；

Those policies they deem appropriate I will carry out;

三、三　　　　其所惡者，吾 則 改 之。
　　　　　　　　o　　　 s ＼conj v　o／
　　　　　　　　　　　　　　　　p

他們認爲不好的那些政令，我就更改。

their think bad ones, I then change them.

⟶ 他們認爲不妥善的那些政令，我就更改。

those polic*ies* they deem inappropriate I *will* alter.

⟹ 他們認爲不妥善的那些政令，我就更改。

those policies they deem inappropriate I will alter.

三、四　　　　是 吾 師 也，若之何 毀 之？
　　　　　　　s　p　 part ＼adv　　 v　o／
　　　　　　　　　　　　　　　　　p

﹡是：　　　　"是"字在此兼指鄉校及鄭人的議論而言

"This" or "it" refers to both the local schools and the critical opinions of the people of Zhèng.

這－我的老師啊，爲什麼毀掉它？

This -- my teacher, why destroy it?

⟶ 鄉校中人民的議論是我的老師，怎麼可以把鄉校毀掉呢？

The critical opinions *of the* people expressed at *the* Local School*s* are my teacher*s*. How can *the* local school*s* *be* destroyed?

====> 鄉校中人民的議論是我的老師，怎麼可以把鄉校毀掉呢？

They are my teachers: how can the local schools be destroyed?

三、五　　　我　聞　忠　〔於〕善　以　損　怨，

※忠善：　　這兩個字本來都是形容詞，現在用作動詞；意思是"盡忠於行善"

"忠" (conscientious) and "善" (good) both usually function as adjectives, but here they are used as verbs meaning "to devote oneself to [something]" and "to do good"; hence, "to devote oneself to doing good [deeds]".

我聽說盡心行善來減少怨恨；

I hear be dedicated to good to diminish ill-will;

——> 我聽說盡心竭力實行妥善的政策來減少人民的怨恨；

I *have* hear*d of being* utterly dedicate*d to* implement*ing* good administrative policies in order to lessen *the* people's ill-will;

I *have* hear*d that one should be* utterly dedicate*d to* implement*ing* good policies in order to lessen *the* people's ill-will;

====> 我聽說盡心竭力實行妥善的政策來減少人民的怨恨；

I have heard that one should be utterly dedicated to implementing good policies in order to lessen the people's ill-will;

三、六　　　不　聞　作　威　以　防　怨。

沒聽說表現威力來防堵怨恨。

not hear display awe to block ill-will.

───→ 卻沒聽說作令人畏懼的事來防堵人民的怨恨。

yet *I have* not hear*d of* do*ing* thing*s to* intimidate *the* people in order to stop up their ill-will.

───→ 卻沒聽說採取嚴厲的措施來防堵人民的怨恨。

yet *I have* not heard *that an administration should* **take harsh measures** *to* stop up their ill-will.

═══> 卻沒聽說採取嚴厲的措施來防堵人民的怨恨。

yet I have not heard that an administration should take harsh measures to stop up their ill-will.

三、七　　　[毀　鄉校]　豈　不　遽　止　[議]　？
　　　　　　　\[v　　 ol]/　\adv　adv　adv　v　[ol]/
　　　　　　　　　s　　　　　　　　p

難道不能很快制止？

How not can at once stop?

───→ [毀掉鄉校]難道不能很快地制止住[人民的議論]？

Would not [*the* destruction *of the* local schools] quickly stop [*the* people's discussion]?

═══> 毀掉鄉校難道不能很快地把人民的議論制止住？

Wouldn't the destruction of the local schools quickly stop the people's discussion?

三、八　　　然　[防][口]　猶　防　川：
　　　　　　 conj \[v]　[ol]　l.v. \v　　o/
　　　　　　　　　　[s]　　　　　　p

　　　※防口：　這兩個字是根據文意補進去的。《國語·周語
　　　　　　　　上》有"防民之口，甚於防川"的話，可為明
　　　　　　　　證。

360

The two characters "防口" have been added to the text because the copula "猶" implies a comparison with a nominal construction preceding it. From the context it is clear that this is the comparison intended. The line "防民之口，甚於防川" (Blocking up people's mouths is worse than blocking up the rivers.) in *GuóYǔ zhōuyǔ shàng* can be used to verify that this is the intended comparison.

"防口"逐字譯成白話是"堵住[人民的] 嘴"，實際的意思是"防止[人民的]議論"。

Literally translated character by character into spoken Chinese, "防口"means"堵住[人民的]嘴" (to block up [the people's] mouths); the implied sense is"制止[人民的]議論" (to prevent [the people's] criticism/to stop [the people *from voicing*] critical opinions).

然而好像是防堵河流一樣：

Even so, like dam running water:

——→ 然而[制止人民的議論]好像是防堵河流一樣：

Even so, [stop*ping the* people *from* voic*ing* critical opinion*s*] is like dam*ming* up run*ning* water:

===⟹ 然而這好像是防堵河流一樣：

Even so, it is like damming up running water:

三、九　　　[川] [於] [其]大決所犯，傷人必多，
　　　　　　　＼[prep]　　　○　　　／　　＼adv adj／
　　　　　　　　　＼　　　　　adv　　　　　　v　o　comp／
　　　　　[s]　　　　　　　　　　　　　p

吾 不 克 救 也；
＼adv aux v／ part
s　　　p

大潰決侵犯的地方，傷害人一定多，我不能救止；

great breach that which ravage, injure people certainly many; I not can save;

——→ [河水][在]大規模衝破堤坊時淹沒的地方，傷害人一定傷害得很多，我不能拯救；

361

[In] the area inundate*d when the* [river water] breach*es the* dikes *on a* large scale, *it will* surely injure many people; I cannot save *them.*

===> 河水在大規模衝破堤坊時淹沒的地方，傷害人一定傷害得很多，我不能拯救；

In the area inundated when the river water breaches the dikes on a large scale, surely many people will be injured, and I cannot save them;

三、十　[防 川]不 如 小 決 [於堤] 使 [之] 道，

不如開小口使流出，

not like breach a little, cause to channel,

——→ [防堵河流]不如[在堤防那兒]開個小口使[河水]流出，

[*to* dam up run*ning* water] *is* not as *good as* open*ing a* small breach [in *the* dike] *to* cause [*the* river water] *to* channel out,

it *is* preferable *to* open a small breach [in *the* dike] *and* channel [*the* water] out,

===> 防堵河流不如在堤防那兒開個小口使河水流出去，

it is preferable to open a small breach in the dike and channel the water out,

三、十一 〔防 議〕不 如 吾 聞 而 藥 之 也。"

※藥之：　　"藥"是名詞的意動用法，"藥之"意思是"以之為藥。"

The noun "藥"(medicinal herbs; medication) is used here in a putative sense; that is, "consider it to be a medicine." or "take it (the criticism) as [if it were] medicine."

不如我聽它然後把它當藥。"

not like I hear it and take it as medicine."

⟶ [防止民議]不如我聽取他們的議論然後把它當作良藥來改
善政策啊。"

[preventing discussion by the people] is not as good as listening to their critical opinions and then using them as medicine to improve the government."

and it is preferable to listen to their criticism and then use it as a medicine (remedy) to improve the government."

====⟹ 防止民議不如我聽取他們的議論然後把它當作良藥來改
善政策啊。"

and it is preferable to listen to their criticism and then use it as a medicine (remedy) to improve the government."

四、 然明曰: " " "

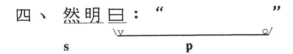

四、一 " 蔑 也 今而後 知 吾子之信 可事 也,

然明說: " 蔑啊,從今後知道您確實值得事奉啊,

Ránmíng say: "Miè today and after know my good sir truly worthy of being served.

⟶ 然明說: " 我從今以後才知道您確實讓人敬佩,讓人願意
追隨啊,

Ránmíng said: "From this day on, I now know you truly *can* **gain people's respect** *and* **make them will**ing **to follow you**.

Ránmíng sa*id*: "From this day on, I now know you truly deserve people's respect *and* following.

====⟹ 然明說: " 我從今以後才知道您確實值得追隨啊,

363

Ránmíng said: "From this day on, I now know you truly deserve people's respect and following.

四、一　　　小人　實　　不才。
　　　　　　　　s＼adv　adj/
　　　　　　　　　　　p

小人實在沒有才能。

Small person really have no ability.

⟶　我的確見事不明。

I *am* really lack*ing in* perspicuity.

⟹我的確看事看得不透徹。

I am really short-sighted.

四、二　　　若　[君]　果　行　此，其鄭國　實賴　之，
　　　　　　conj　[s]＼adv　v　o/　　s＼adv　v　o/
　　　　　　　　　　　　　p　　　　　　　　p

假若果真實行這個，我們的鄭國實在依靠它，

If come to pass implement this, our Zhèng state actually rely on it,

⟶假若[您]果真實行這種重視民意的政策，我們的鄭國實在
　依靠它，

If [you] in fact implement this **policy *of* tak*ing the* people's opinions *seriously***, our state *of* Zhèng *will in* practice rely *on* it,

⟹假若您果真實行這種重視民意的政策，我們的鄭國實在
　依靠它，

If in the end you implement this, actually our whole state of Zhèng will rely on it,

四、三　　豈　唯　二三臣　　〔賴　之〕？"
　　　　　adv adv
　　　　　　　　　s
　　　　　　　　　　　　　　　　　　　\〔v〕　〔o〕/
　　　　　　　　　　　　　　　　　　　　　〔p〕

那裡只二三臣？"

how only two, three officials?"

——→那裡只是我們幾個臣子〔依靠它〕呢？"

how *could it be* only *a* few *of* us court official*s who will* [rely *on* it]?"

===⇒那裡只是我們幾個臣子呢？"

how could it be only a few of us court officials?"

五、　仲尼　聞　是　語　也，　曰："　　　　　　　"
　　　　　　　\v　adj　o/　part　　\v　　　　o/
　　　　s　　　　　p　　　　　　　　　　p

仲尼聽到這話，說：

Zhòngní hear this word, say:

仲尼聽到這些話，說：

Zhòngní hear*d* these word*s and* sa*id*:

仲尼聽到這些話，說：

Zhòngní heard these words *and* said:

五、一　　　"以　是　觀　之，
　　　　　　　prep　o　v　　o

※以是觀之：

　　　　"是"是指示代詞，意思是"這個"，指上述
　　子產與然明談論治國之道這件事。"之"是代
　　詞，指子產。但此處的之字，通常虛化不譯。
　　參看第三十八課，句析九‧四，三二九頁。

365

"是" is a demonstrative pronoun meaning "這個" in spoken Chinese and "this" in English. Here "this" refers to Zǐchǎn and Ránmíng's discussion of the way to rule a state; the pronoun "之" refers to Zǐchǎn here, but in such constructions, "之" is generally not expressed when the phrase is translated into spoken Chinese. In English, the phrase can be conventionally translated as "Viewed in this light" (where the pronoun "之" is not expressed) or more precisely as "Viewing **him** in this light" or "Viewing **him** in light of this *situation*" (*See L. 38, sentence analysis 9.4, p. 329*).

"從這看他,

"From this view him,

——→ "根據這件事情來看,

"*On the* basis *of* this incident view*ing* him,

"Consider*ing* him *in* light *of* this incident,

══⇒ "根據這件事情來看,

"Considering him in light of this incident,

人 謂 子產 不 仁, 吾 不 信 也。"

人 說 子產 不 仁, 我 不 信 啊。"

People say Zǐchǎn not caring: I not believe."

——→人們說子產不仁愛(不愛人民),我絕對不信。"

When people say *that* Zǐchǎn *is* not caring, I *do* not believe at all."

When people say *that* Zǐchǎn *did* not love *the* people, I *do* not believe *it* at all."

══⇒人們說子產不愛人民,我絕對不相信。"

When people say that Zǐchǎn did not love the people, I do not believe it at all."

文法名詞
Grammatical Terminology

詞 類	在 句 中 的 功 用
Parts of speech	Functions in a sentence

1. 名詞 noun ----------------------------------> 主語 subject
　　　　　　　　　　　　　　　　　　　　　　賓語 object
　　　　　　　　　　　　　　　　　　　　　　表語 determinator
　　　　　　　　　　　　　　　　　　　　　　　　(predicate nominative)

   A. 名詞　noun

      魚　fish

      牆　wall

   B. 名詞語　noun phrase

      a. 名詞＋名詞

        鄭相　the Prime Minister of Zhèng

      b. 形容詞＋名詞

        富人　a wealthy man

      c. 代詞＋名詞

        其子　his son

      d. 動詞＋被飾代詞

        耕者　tiller

      e. 名詞語＋名詞

        鄰人之父　the old man next door

2. 代名詞 pronoun ----------------------------> 主語 subject
　　　　　　　　　　　　　　　　　　　　　　賓語 object
　　　　　　　　　　　　　　　　　　　　　　定語 adjectival modifier

367

A. 一般代名詞 genenal pronoun (always in the objective case)

之 him; her; it; them

B. 人稱代名詞 personal pronouns

吾、余;爾;汝;彼;之 I; you; he; him; her

C. 被飾代名詞 a pronoun that must be preceded by a modifier

美者 *the beautiful* one

D. 疑問代名詞 interrogative pronouns

誰;何 who; what

E. 指示代名詞 demonstrative pronoun

其人;其地 that *person* ; that *place*

F. 指示詞兼代名詞 demonstrative & pronoun

a. 代名詞 pronoun

所種 = 種的東西 that *which [they] planted*

b. 指示詞 demonstrative

所契者 = 刻的那個地方 the *place where he cut [the notch]*

所嫁婦人 = 嫁出去的那個女人 that *woman whom you married off*

3. 動詞 verb ------------------------------------>謂語 predicate

A. 動詞 verb

受;失 accept; lose

B. 助動詞 auxiliary verb

可;敢 can; dare

C. 繫詞 copula; linking verb

乃;為 be

D. 準繫詞 pseudo copula; pseudo l.v.

如;若;譬;猶;似 seem; be like

E. 動詞語 verbal phrase

  a. 動詞＋賓語 verb + object

    折頸 broke *the neck*

  b. 動詞＋補語 verb + complement

    捕得 chased *and caught*

  c. 副詞＋動詞 adverb + verb

    芒芒然歸 came home *exhausted*

  d. 助動詞＋動詞＋賓語 aux.+ verb + object

    能更鳴 can change *the sound of [your] cry*

4. 形容詞 adjectives ------------------------> 謂語 predicate
                              定語 adjectival modifier

    智；美；賢 wise; pretty; worthy

    強；富；貧 powerful; rich; poor

5. 副詞 adverb -----------------------------------> 狀語 adverbial modifier

    復；甚；皆 again; very; all

6. 介詞 preposition -------------------------------> 關係語 connective

  A. 介詞 preposition

    於；以；為；與；自 at; by; for; with; from

  B.介詞語 prepositional phrase ------------------> 狀語 adverbial modifier

    以故 for *this reason*

    於塗 in *the mud*

    與君 with *the ruler*

    為之 for *it*

自舟　from *the boat*

7. 連詞 conjunction --------------------------> 關係語 connective

　　　而；則　and/but; then

8. 時間詞 time word ------------------------> 狀語 adverbial modifier

　　　今；昔　presently; formerly

9. 處所詞 place word ---------------------> 狀語 adverbial modifier
　　　　　　　　　　　　　　　　　　　　補語 complement
　　　　　　　　　　　　　　　　　　　　　(postverbial modifier)

　　　田；市　field; market

10. 方向詞 directional word --------------> 狀語 adverbial modifier
　　　　　　　　　　　　　　　　　　　　補語 complement
　　　　　　　　　　　　　　　　　　　　　(postverbial modifier)

　　　東；南；西；北　east; south; west; north

　　　上；下；左；右　above; below; left; right

11. 量詞 measure word ------------------------> 定語 adjectival modifier

　　　張；本；尺　sheet [of paper]; volume [of book] ; foot [of length]

12. 疑問詞 question word --------------------> 定語 adjectival modifier
　　　　　　　　　　　　　　　　　　　　狀語 adverbial modifier

　　　何；安；焉　what/why; where/how

13. 感嘆詞 interjection -------------------> 表感嘆 express an exclamation

嘻；哉　ha!; indeed!

14. 助詞 particle ----------------------------> 表語氣 express a tone

也；矣；焉；耳

乎；哉；與；耶（邪）

15. 主謂短語 clausal phrase ----------------> 主語 subject
　　　　　　　　　　　　　　　　　　　　　　　 賓語 object
　　　　　　　　　　　　　　　　　　　　　　　 不獨立分句
　　　　　　　　　　　　　　　　　　　　　　　 dependent clause

主謂短語：

在句子的主語和謂語之間加一 " 之 " 字就變成主謂短語。

主謂短語通常用作：

Put a " 之 " character between the subject and the predicate of a sentence, then the sentence becomes a **clausal phrase** " 主謂短語 ", which is generally used within a larger sentence, functioning as:

1. 包孕句中的主語或賓語

the subject or object in **an embedding sentence** (i.e., **a complex sentence with a noun clause in its subject or object position.**),

2. 等立複合句中的半獨立分句

a simi-dependent clause in **a coordinate compound sentence** (i.e., **a compound sentence**), or

3. 主從複合句中的不獨立分句

a dependent clause in **a subordinate compound sentence** (i.e., **a complex sentence containing an adverbial clause**).

句子結構

Sentence Structure

1. 基本句式

1. 一個句子基本上由主語、謂語兩部分組成。

   A sentence is basically composed of two parts: the **subject** and the **predicate**.

2. 謂語：動詞／動詞語、形容詞／形容詞語、或名詞／名詞語

   A predicate can be **verbal, adjectival, or nominal**.

   A. 以動詞／動詞語為謂語的句子是**敘述句**。

   A sentence that has a verbal predicate is a **narrative sentence**.

   S   P (V - O)

   如： 梟　　逢鳩。

   For example: An owl met a ringdove.

   B. 以形容詞／形容詞語為謂語的句子是**描寫句**。

   A sentence that has an adjective predicate is a **descriptive sentence**.

   S   P (Adjective)

   如：　君　美甚。

   For example: You are exceedingly good-looking.

   C. 以名詞／名詞語為謂語的句子是**判斷句**。

   A sentence that has a nominative predicate is a **determinative sentence**.

   S   P (L.V. - N)

   如：城北徐公　齊國之美麗者也。

   For example: Master Xú in the north of the city was a good-looking man of the state of Qí.

2. 句子成分 components of a sentence

主語　**Subject**

謂語　**Predicate**

賓語　Object

表語　Determinator

定語　Adjectival Modifier

狀語　Adverbial Modifier

補語　Complement/postverbial modifier

3. 詞序：Word order in a sentence:

1. 動詞用在賓語之前，構成動詞語。

　　　守株　to watch the tree stump

　　　嗜魚　to relish fish

2. 狀語用在動詞及形容詞之前，構成動詞語或形容詞語。

An adverbial modifier always precedes a verb or an adjective to form a verbal phrase or an adjectival phrase.

　　a. 動詞語　verbal phrases

　　　復得　to get again

　　　固辭　to decline steadfastly

　　b. 形容詞語　adjectival phrases

　　　大臭　very stinky

　　　不明　not bright enough

3. 補語用在動詞及形容詞之後，構成動補結構或形補結構。

A complement always follows a verb or an adjective to form a verb-complement or an adjective-complement construction.

　　a. 動補結構　verb-complement construction

　　　捕得　to catch and hold

　　　哭不自禁　unable to stop from crying

373

b. 形補結構 adjective-complement construction

美甚 exceedingly good-looking

深不可測 deep beyond fathoming

4. 定語用在名詞之前，構成名詞語。

An adjectival modifier always precedes a noun to form a noun phrase.

富人 a rich man

耕者 a tiller

CPSIA information can be obtained
at www.ICGtesting.com
Printed in the USA
JSHW011544040720
6453JS00021B/76